T0212514

Communications in Computer and Information Science   713

Commenced Publication in 2007
Founding and Former Series Editors:
Alfredo Cuzzocrea, Dominik Ślęzak, and Xiaokang Yang

More information about this series at http://www.springer.com/series/7899

Constantine Stephanidis (Ed.)

HCI International 2017 – Posters' Extended Abstracts

19th International Conference, HCI International 2017
Vancouver, BC, Canada, July 9–14, 2017
Proceedings, Part I

 Springer

Editor
Constantine Stephanidis
Foundation for Research & Technology –
Hellas (FORTH)
University of Crete
Heraklion, Crete
Greece

ISSN 1865-0929   ISSN 1865-0937   (electronic)
Communications in Computer and Information Science
ISBN 978-3-319-58749-3   ISBN 978-3-319-58750-9   (eBook)
DOI 10.1007/978-3-319-58750-9

Library of Congress Control Number: 2017940246

Printed on acid-free paper

This Springer imprint is published by Springer Nature
The registered company is Springer International Publishing AG
The registered company address is: Gewerbestrasse 11, 6330 Cham, Switzerland

Foreword

The 19th International Conference on Human–Computer Interaction, HCI International 2017, was held in Vancouver, Canada, during July 9–14, 2017. The event incorporated the 15 conferences/thematic areas listed on the following page.

A total of 4,340 individuals from academia, research institutes, industry, and governmental agencies from 70 countries submitted contributions, and 1,228 papers have been included in the proceedings. These papers address the latest research and development efforts and highlight the human aspects of design and use of computing systems. The papers thoroughly cover the entire field of human–computer interaction, addressing major advances in knowledge and effective use of computers in a variety of application areas. The volumes constituting the full set of the conference proceedings are listed on the following pages.

I would like to thank the program board chairs and the members of the program boards of all thematic areas and affiliated conferences for their contribution to the highest scientific quality and the overall success of the HCI International 2017 conference.

This conference would not have been possible without the continuous and unwavering support and advice of the founder, Conference General Chair Emeritus and Conference Scientific Advisor Prof. Gavriel Salvendy. For his outstanding efforts, I would like to express my appreciation to the communications chair and editor of *HCI International News*, Dr. Abbas Moallem.

April 2017   Constantine Stephanidis

HCI International 2017 Thematic Areas
and Affiliated Conferences

Thematic areas:

- Human–Computer Interaction (HCI 2017)
- Human Interface and the Management of Information (HIMI 2017)

Affiliated conferences:

- 17th International Conference on Engineering Psychology and Cognitive Ergonomics (EPCE 2017)
- 11th International Conference on Universal Access in Human–Computer Interaction (UAHCI 2017)
- 9th International Conference on Virtual, Augmented and Mixed Reality (VAMR 2017)
- 9th International Conference on Cross-Cultural Design (CCD 2017)
- 9th International Conference on Social Computing and Social Media (SCSM 2017)
- 11th International Conference on Augmented Cognition (AC 2017)
- 8th International Conference on Digital Human Modeling and Applications in Health, Safety, Ergonomics and Risk Management (DHM 2017)
- 6th International Conference on Design, User Experience and Usability (DUXU 2017)
- 5th International Conference on Distributed, Ambient and Pervasive Interactions (DAPI 2017)
- 5th International Conference on Human Aspects of Information Security, Privacy and Trust (HAS 2017)
- 4th International Conference on HCI in Business, Government and Organizations (HCIBGO 2017)
- 4th International Conference on Learning and Collaboration Technologies (LCT 2017)
- Third International Conference on Human Aspects of IT for the Aged Population (ITAP 2017)

Conference Proceedings Volumes Full List

HCI International 2017 Conference

The full list with the Program Board Chairs and the members of the Program Boards of all thematic areas and affiliated conferences is available online at:

http://www.hci.international/board-members-2017.php

HCI International 2018

The 20th International Conference on Human–Computer Interaction, HCI International 2018, will be held jointly with the affiliated conferences in Las Vegas, NV, USA, at Caesars Palace, July 15–20, 2018. It will cover a broad spectrum of themes related to human–computer interaction, including theoretical issues, methods, tools, processes, and case studies in HCI design, as well as novel interaction techniques, interfaces, and applications. The proceedings will be published by Springer. More information is available on the conference website: http://2018.hci.international/.

General Chair
Prof. Constantine Stephanidis
University of Crete and ICS-FORTH
Heraklion, Crete, Greece
E-mail: general_chair@hcii2018.org

http://2018.hci.international/

Contents – Part I

Perception, Cognition and Emotion in HCI

Data Analysis and Data Mining in Social Media and Communication

Ergonomics and Models in Work and Training Support

Contents – Part II

Learning, Games and Gamification

Health, Well-Being and Comfort

Visual Design and Visualization

Social Issues and Security in HCI

Design and Evaluation Methods, Tools and Practices

Developing and Evaluating a Thai Website Accessibility Checker

Kewalin Angkananon[1], Mike Wald[2(✉)], and Piyabud Ploadaksorn[1]

[1] Suratthani Rajabhat University, Surat Thani, Thailand
k.angkananon@gmail.com
[2] University of Southampton, Southampton, UK
mw@ecs.soton.ac.uk

Abstract. This research addresses the lack of a method to help with the evaluation of the accessibility of Thai websites and web applications by developing and evaluating an online tool with developers, experts and disabled users. The results suggest it is reliable and valid. Future work will extend the evaluation criteria for mobile accessibility.

Keywords: Web accessibility · Check · Thailand

1 Introduction

The motivation for this research is the lack of a method to help users, managers and developers with the evaluation of the accessibility of Thai websites and web applications. The National Statistics Office (NSO) estimated the number of disabled people in Thailand as over 1 million in 1996[1] and a majority of these could benefit from accessible websites: a report commissioned by Microsoft in 2003 estimated that 62% of people in the US of working age could benefit from accessible technologies[2]. Research in 2006 reported that ninety seven percent of websites in Argentina, Australia, Brazil, Canada, Chile, China, France, Germany, India, Japan, Kenya, Mexico, Morocco, Russia, Singapore, South Africa, Spain, United Arab Emirates, United Kingdom and United States of America did not provide even minimum levels of accessibility[3] and while there are no published figures for Thai websites it is very unlikely that they are more accessible as many of the countries tested have web accessibility legislation. Another benefit for making websites accessible to disabled people is that they are then also more likely to be usable on mobile devices.[4]

---

[1] http://siteresources.worldbank.org/DISABILITY/Resources/Regions/East-Asia-Pacific/JICA_Thailand.1.pdf.
[2] https://www.microsoft.com/enable/research/phase1.aspx.
[3] http://news.bbc.co.uk/1/hi/technology/6210068.stm.
[4] http://www.thedrum.com/news/2014/03/04/91-sme-websites-are-not-accessible-mobile-according-basekit-survey.

© Springer International Publishing AG 2017
C. Stephanidis (Ed.): HCII Posters 2017, Part I, CCIS 713, pp. 3–10, 2017.
DOI: 10.1007/978-3-319-58750-9_1

2   Literature Review

Tim Berners-Lee, W3C Director and inventor of the World Wide Web stated "The power of the Web is in its universality. Access by everyone regardless of disability is an essential aspect."[5] The Web was therefore invented to be used by everyone, irrespective of their ability, technology used, or culture and has the potential to remove barriers for people with disabilities, but only if websites are designed accessibly. Access to information through the Web is a basic human right according to The UN Convention on the Rights of Persons with Disabilities.[6] Making the web accessible can help elderly people and those in poorer countries as well as people with disabilities in many aspects of their lives including education, employment, health care and social lives. Accessible websites can provide social, technical, financial, and legal benefits for companies, government and education [1].

Corporation benefits include:

- financial gains and cost savings due to increased potential market share, search engine optimization (SEO), and usability[7].
- reducing risk of legal action, high legal expenses, and negative image[8].
- public relations demonstrating corporate social responsibility (CSR)
- an inclusive workplace that supports employees with disabilities
- increased productivity supporting and retaining older experienced employees

Government ministry or agency benefits include:

- laws and policies requiring public services available to all
- provision of information and services that are accessible to all citizens
- savings from improved server performance and decreased site maintenance
- enabling people with disabilities and older users to interact with them online

An educational institution benefits from:

- students, faculty, or staff with disabilities
- students with different learning styles, older computer equipment, or low bandwidth Internet connections
- increasing percentage of older employees with age-related impairments
- legal or policy requirements

When web pages are not designed accessibly, many people cannot use the Web. For example, people who cannot use a mouse need keyboard access and people who are blind need alternative text for images and this affects many people as they get older. There are estimated to be about two million people in Thailand, the majority in rural areas with 65 per cent unemployed and over 50 per cent working in agriculture and fishing and although there are anti-discrimination laws and guidance for disability

---

[5] http://www.w3.org/standards/webdesign/accessibility.

[6] http://www.un.org/disabilities/default.asp?navid=12&pid=150.

[7] http://www.w3.org/WAI/bcase/tesco-case-study.

[8] http://www.w3.org/WAI/bcase/socog-case-study.

development practice there are no specific laws or regulations for website accessibility.[9] There has been a great deal of international research on the accessibility of websites resulting in the web accessibility guidelines[10] which have been adopted in some countries.[11] However these guidelines were developed for English and simply translating them would not address all the localisation issues of Thai Language and context. Web2Access [2] was developed with the view that check-lists and tests for usability and accessibility are not an ideal way to address the issue of how easy it may be to use on-line learning materials or software in general, and that a more holistic approach is needed.[12] The Web 2.0 Services checks were developed based on the work of W3C[13], Web Accessibility Group University of Washington[14] and WebAIM[15]. A variety of tools were used for evaluation: AIS Web Accessibility Toolbar[16] for Internet Explorer and Web Accessibility Toolbar[17] - for checking web site accessibility: document structure, colours, HTML, CSS, links, images, Mozilla Firefox with WebAIM WAVE toolbar[18], Web Developer Toolbar[19], Accessibar Project toolbar[20], Illinois Firefox Accessibility Extension[21], WebbIE text-only browser[22], Zoom features in major browsers, Colour Contrast Analyser[23], VisCheck[24], Thunder[25] or NVDA[26] screen reader. Documentation included Testing Forms[27], and Criteria for Tests[28]. The Web 2.0 Service Tests included[29]:

1. Accessible Login, Signup and Other Forms: covering all aspects of registering with a service or site, then returning to sign-in and finally to work with forms.
2. Image ALT Attribute: so that a screen reader user can hear about the image.

---

[9] http://www.ilo.org/wcmsp5/groups/public/—ed_emp/—ifp_skills/documents/publication/wcms_112307.pdf.

[10] http://www.w3.org/WAI/intro/wcag.php.

[11] http://www.powermapper.com/blog/government-accessibility-standards/.

[12] http://opus.bath.ac.uk/12111/.

[13] http://www.w3.org/WAI/intro/wcag.php.

[14] http://www.washington.edu/accessibility/web.htm.

[15] http://www.webaim.org.

[16] http://www.visionaustralia.org/info.aspx?page=614.

[17] http://www.paciellogroup.com/resources/wat-ie-about.html.

[18] http://wave.webaim.org.

[19] https://addons.mozilla.org/en-US/firefox/addon/60.

[20] http://accessibar.mozdev.org/.

[21] http://firefox.cita.uiuc.edu/.

[22] http://www.webbie.org.uk/.

[23] http://www.paciellogroup.com/resources/contrast-analyser.html.

[24] http://www.vischeck.com/.

[25] http://www.screenreader.net/.

[26] http://www.nvda-project.org/.

[27] http://www.web2access.org.uk/media/Test_Form.doc.

[28] http://www.web2access.org.uk/media/Criteria_for_Tests.doc.

[29] http://www.web2access.org.uk/test.

3. Link Target Definitions: which need to be understandable when used without a surrounding sentence or button.
4. Frame Titles and Layout: if the frames do not have a title the screen reader user may not know where they are in the page or which piece of content to read next.
5. Removal of Stylesheet: as it is important to check how a site looks with and without style sheets.
6. Audio/Video Features: for those who have sensory disabilities such as deafness or a hearing additional text transcripts, captioning, and sign language can be very helpful.
7. Video/animations - audio descriptions: for those who have visual impairments offering alternatives for animations or videos where there are long scenes with no descriptive dialogue is essential.
8. Appropriate use of Tables: the order of content within the table and the use of row and column headers is important.
9. Tab Orderings Correct and Logical: when you cannot use the mouse the order in which the main navigational elements and links appear in a webpage is very important.
10. Page Functionality with Keyboard: after log-in.
11. Accessibility of Text Editors: many of the sites that allow users to contribute text, images and other multimedia also provide an editor that allows users to change the look and feel of their text as they would in a wordprocesser application.
12. Appropriate Feedback with Forms: once a user has submitted text or an answer to a question or multiple choice items it is important that correct feedback is received to prevent confusion.
13. Contrast and Colour Check: for everyone to have an enjoyable experience when reading web sites content should have good levels of colour contrast and no distracting elements.
14. Page Integrity when Zooming: allowing text and images to be enlarged through a zoom feature or text-resize.
15. Text size, style, blinking elements and Readability: avoiding items that flash or blink at a rate that can cause seizures and small text and serif fonts and complex language that can make text harder to read for some people.

3 Research Methodology

There is no official translation of the Web Accessibility Guidelines into Thai and no research into whether the guidelines require any localisation for the Thai language and culture. An interactive Thai website WebThai2Access was therefore developed to help manually test any Thai Web 2.0 site using a checklist based on Web Content Accessibility Guidelines (WCAG 2.0). In addition it explains the tools which can be used for the evaluation. It has been designed to be easier to use and score as the checklists for Web2access are all developed from the WCAG 2.0 guidelines and have been summarised and compressed into 15 criteria. The scoring has 4 levels corresponding to the WCAG 2.0 conformance levels, where 0% would be fail condition, 33% would be equivalent to an A, 67% would be equivalent to an AA, and 100% would be equivalent to AAA. The phases of the research were:

Phase 1: A literature review was conducted to identify where Thai accessibility guidelines differ from English guidelines and tools to evaluate Thai Websites. The results of this activity helped identify changes to web accessibility guidelines for Thai tools that could be used to evaluate Thai websites.

Phase 2: The guidelines, tests, tools and documentation were localized into Thai for the Thai Language and Culture to develop Thai guidelines, tests, tools and documentation. An expert review was conducted and validation pilot study of the tests and guidelines and tools and documentation involving accessibility experts to validate the Thai guidelines, tests and tools and documentation.

Phase 3: Based on the results of the expert validation and review a Thai version of Web2Access was built and tested. A user evaluation pilot study of WebThai2Access was carried out and based on the results the experimental design was finalized and a user evaluation of WebThai2Access conducted with 30 developers and groups of 30 Visually Impaired, Elderly and Hearing Impaired users.

Phase 4: The results were analysed for how well developers could evaluate Thai websites to predict how disabled users will use the websites.

4 Results and Analysis

Based on research [3] criteria 15's text size, style, blinking elements and readability, was changed from sans-serif fonts to serif and 14–16px instead of 10–12px to suit Thai websites. Three experts followed instructions to evaluate the website http://www.tab.or. th by using a screen reader program such as NVDA, JAWS or Voiceover and also a speech Thai synthesizer program (Tatip, VAJA) by inserting an Outcome (%) which they believe to be appropriate in the 'Evaluation' box and in addition to this, answer all the questions in the 'Technique' box. An Example for the 1st test is as follows:

1. Login, signup, and other forms accessible, such as contact us, feedback form and help form.

Check the process for the signup form, if there is access to the website or not, check how accessible the forms are, and if they can be accessed through the use of a keyboard and screen reader (NVDA, JAWS, and Voiceover) and check if the labelling has a meaningful name which can be understood by the users.

References: (W3C WCAG 2.0 2.1, W3C WCAG 2.0 2.4, CAPTCHAW3C WCAG 2.0 1.1 and W3C WCAG 2.0 3.3).

Target Audiences: Those with blind and severe visual impairment.

Technique

1.1 Check if it is possible to access any forms through the use of tab key and screen readers (NVDA, JAWS, Voiceover).

1.2 Once you have access to a form, check if the label is given a meaningful name by using WAVE look at "Features" and "Form Label".

1.3 Check if it is possible to access the input aspect of the form through a logical order through the use of tab key and screen reader. If the inputted information is incorrect, such as type wrong password, then check to see if the screen reader reads the error message or not.

1.4 Check CAPTCHA (W3C WCAG 1.1.1) if there is an option to change the captcha i.e. the option to change from text to sound or from image to sound or text. Check if these are able to be changed through the use of keyboard or not and also check if the screen reader is able to read the changes.

1.5 Check if there are time limits (W3C WCAG 2.2.1) in the form.

1.6 Check sending the form whilst pressing the button to send the form, to see if the screen reader reads the send button.

1.7 Check if it possible to exit the form through the use of a keyboard and screen reader.

One of 4 ratings are possible:

- 0%: Unable to access the form and CAPTCHA through the use of keyboard and screen reader. Unable to access the form in time, and there is no label.
- 33%: Hard to access the CAPTCHA, the majority of the forms can be accessed by the use of a keyboard and the screen reader program can read the some of the form. There are a few labels used, the form has a time limit.
- 67%: The majority of the form can be access through the use of keyboard and screen reader, however there are some errors i.e. does not read the label or feedback and label identified by screen reader is not the same as displayed on the website. There is no time limit and there is an option for an alternative CAPTCHA.
- 100%: Forms can be accessed easily through the use of keyboard and screen reader, clear labels, no CAPTCHA, and there is no time limit.

The WebThai2Access website has tabs in the navigation linked to the following pages:

- products reviewed and approved by the system administrator
- list of disabilities with descriptions and associated tests
- list and short description of the 15 evaluation criteria. Selecting each criteria displays a page with further details
- Entered review information reviewer's name, email, platform and website. If the website that they want to evaluate is not already listed as having been reviewed they will be required to add website name, URL and short description

Six developers were asked to use the WebThai2Access system at http://138.68.21.192/ and answer questions using a 5 point Likert scale and the average scores are as follows:

1. The content in the main page is easy to understand: 4.67
2. The links from the main page to the products page are all functioning: 5.00
3. All the links in the products page are functional: 5.00
4. The calculations for the products is correct: 4.33
5. The contents for the disability page is easy to understand: 4.33
6. All the links in the disabilities are functioning: 4.67
7. The user is able to enter their name and email in the evaluation form: 5.00
8. The user is able to select the platforms option: 5.00

9. The user can select a website which has been evaluated: 4.3
10. The user can add the name and details of a website which has not already been evaluated: 4.50
11. The system will warn the user if they do not enter the all the required details: 4.33

The average rating of 4.64 showed participants found WebThai2Access very usable. The participants suggested having more text space by increasing the character limit to more than 255, having multiple text boxes corresponding to the techniques and changing the word 'test' to 'testing' in the disability tab since when translated into Thai it is confusing for the user. The WebThai2Access prototype was modified based on the evaluation results and feedback and the 30 developers evaluated it, with an average score of 99%. Twelve criteria were rated 100% whereas criteria 8, 12, 15 were rated 98%, 95% and 99% respectively. The 30 Thai web developers also evaluated 3 websites (www.pantip.com, www.YouTube.com, http://tabgroup.tab.or.th) and the results were compared with how well 30 visually impaired, 30 hearing impaired and 30 elderly Thai People were able to carry out tasks related to their disabilities using the same 3 websites. This comparison was used to determine how well evaluations using WebThai2Access predicts the accessibility of websites for disabled users. The 30 visually impaired users' ages ranged from 13–23 with an average age of 19. Nineteen were blind since birth and 7 became blind later on and 4 had severe visual impairment. Twenty-nine used Jaws and 1 used NVDA screen reader. Ten had 5 years screen reader experience and 20 had 1–2 years' experience and all used the Windows operating system versions 7, 8 or 10. Eighteen used the Google Chrome browser, 9 used Internet Explorer and 3 used Firefox. All 30 hearing impaired users had been deaf since birth and were aged between 12 and 50 with an average age of 20. Twenty-five used a computer and 5 used mobile devices. The 30 elderly users' ages ranged from 60–89, with an average age of 64.5. Twenty-four had 1–2 years experience using websites, 2 had 3years experience while 4 had more than 3years experience. Fourteen used a tablet, 7 used a smartphone and 9 used a computer. The 30 developers all had experience of HTML and developing websites and were trained to use a screen reader for the experiment and WebThai2acess. Analysis of the results suggested that using the test criteria was reliable for evaluating websites as for the 15 criteria the average 95% upper and lower confidence limits of the developer scores were plus or minus 10% for both www.pantip.com and www.YouTube.com websites and plus or minus 3% for http:// tabgroup.tab.or.th and they did not overlap the rating levels of 33% or 67%. Analysis of the results for the disabled users suggested that using the test criteria was reliable for evaluating websites as for the 15 criteria the average 95% upper and lower confidence limits were plus or minus 0% for the visually impaired, plus or minus 2% for the elderly and plus or minus 5% for the hearing impaired and they did not overlap the rating levels of 33% or 67%. Comparing the average scores of the developers and experts the average difference was 18% (ignoring the direction of the difference) and 2% when the sign of the difference was considered. The mode ratings were the same for the developers and experts for 11 criteria on YouTube, 9 criteria on Pantip and 13 on tabgroup and for all websites for criteria 3, 5, 7, 8, 13, 14. Comparing the scores of the 3 groups of 30 elderly, blind and hearing impaired users with those of the developers showed that the average difference for the blind users was 26% and for the elderly was

17% and for the hearing impaired was 8% (ignoring the direction of the difference) and −1%, −17%, −7% when the sign of the difference was considered. The greatest difference between developers and blind users were 54%, 52%, −58% respectively for criteria 1, 2, (www.pantip.com) and 4 (http://tabgroup.tab.or.th). Looking at the mode values there was agreement between the developers and the blind users apart from criteria 1, 2, 4 where the mode ratings for blind users were 33%, 0%, 100% and for the developers were 100%, 67%, 33% respectively. The expert ratings were the same as the mode ratings by the blind users for all criteria suggesting that the experts were better that the developers at predicting how the blind users would perform. This might be because the developers were not experienced at using a screen reader. The greatest difference between developers and elderly users were −23% and −32% respectively for criteria 12, and 13 (www.pantip.com) and the only difference in the mode ratings were for criteria 13 where the elderly mode was 100% and the developer mode was 67%. The expert rating for criteria 13 was also 67% suggesting that the experts were not better than the developers at predicting how the elderly users would perform on criteria 13. The average differences between developers and the hearing impaired people were −12%, −12%, 2% for criteria 1, 12, 15 respectively and the mode ratings were the same, suggesting the developers predicted the hearing impaired people's performance quite well.

5   Conclusion and Future Work

The results showed that WebThai2Access was very accessible and could be used reliably by developers and their evaluations predicted the accessibility of websites for disabled users reasonably well. Future work will investigate how to improve these predictions and also develop criteria and techniques for evaluating accessibility on mobile devices.

Acknowledgement. This research was funded by National Research Council of Thailand.

References

1. Henry, S., Arch, A. (eds.): Developing a Web Accessibility Business Case for Your Organization (2012). http://www.w3.org/WAI/bcase/. Accessed 18 Mar 2017
2. Wald, M., Draffan, E.A., Newman, R., Skuse, S., Phethean, C.: Access toolkit for education. In: Miesenberger, K., Karshmer, A., Penaz, P., Zagler, W. (eds.) ICCHP 2012. LNCS, vol. 7382, pp. 51–58. Springer, Heidelberg (2012). doi:10.1007/978-3-642-31522-0_8
3. Kamollimsakul, S., Petrie, H., Power, C.: Web accessibility for older readers: effects of font type and font size on skim reading webpages in Thai. In: Miesenberger, K., Fels, D., Archambault, D., Peňáz, P., Zagler, W. (eds.) ICCHP 2014. LNCS, vol. 8547, pp. 332–339. Springer, Cham (2014). doi:10.1007/978-3-319-08596-8_52

Usability Tool to Support the Development Process of e-Commerce Website

T.P. Anjos[✉] and L.A. Gontijo

Federal University of Santa Catarina, Florianópolis, Santa Catarina, Brazil
anjos.thaiana@gmail.com

Abstract. Inappropriate usability features in virtual stores can be verified by the high dropout rate of the shopping cart, the increase in maintenance costs and the low conversion rate on the site [1, 2]. Some factors and characteristics, such as inadequate site navigation, the difficulty of finding the shopping cart, the lack of detailed information about the product, a long and confusing checkout process, and few or only image of the product indicates usability problems in e-commerce website [3, 4]. The quality of this type of site can be considerably improved when usability is integrated into the development process of e-commerce site. This work aims to propose a tool to assist and support the development process of e-commerce site focused on usability. This research is characterized, as regards its nature, as a qualitative-quantitative research and, in terms of its objectives, as an "exploratory" research, since it provides greater knowledge of the problem in order to make it more explicit. The creation of the tool will help development teams to create efficient, effective and satisfactory e-commerce sites from the specification of usability requirements, usability metrics and usability evaluation methods.

Keywords: Usability · e-Commerce · Requirement · Metric · Evaluation method

1 Introduction

Electronic commerce is the buying and selling of products or services through electronic media, such as Internet and other computer networks [5]. An online store is an advanced website that gives the ability to buy products over the Internet. Online shops are one of the forms of electronic commerce and work mostly in the business-to-consumer (B2C) business model; so products offered by companies are directed to individual customers. This form is becoming each year more and more popular due to convenience and the lower cost of sales and also allows one to quickly compare prices from various suppliers [6].

An online store is currently one of the most popular forms of doing business on the Internet. Its effectiveness is dependent upon many external factors such as brand recognition, the volume offered and level of the offered prices. However, the popularity and willingness to use the selected store by Internet users is also affected to a large extent on internal factors of ease of use of the this store. These factors include consideration of various aspects of the discipline known as usability [6]. Usability can be

© Springer International Publishing AG 2017
C. Stephanidis (Ed.): HCII Posters 2017, Part I, CCIS 713, pp. 11–18, 2017.
DOI: 10.1007/978-3-319-58750-9_2

defined as "the degree to which a product or system can be used by specified users to achieve specified goals with effectiveness, efficiency and satisfaction in a specified context of use" [7].

In this paper we present a tool to assist and to support the development process of e-commerce website focused on usability. The creation of the tool will help development teams to create efficient, effective and satisfactory e-commerce websites from the identification of usability requirements, usability metrics and usability evaluation methods. The identification of requirements is the basis for the software development process and it is recommended that teams devote time and effort to the correct lifting of the same. The metrics are fundamental to obtain indicators regarding the use of the site, being possible to analyze and identify possible usability problems. Usability evaluation methods can be used throughout the development process, from idea, design, simulation, test prototype or final software, and it is critical to assess whether the site is effective, efficient and user-friendly.

Presently, no tools exist that would enable e-commerce teams to develop theirs e-commerce websites without engaging usability engineers [8]. It was identified more than 100 articles that shows tools to help teams in applying usability heuristics, recommendations and metrics, but none shows requirements, metrics and evaluation methods combined.

2 Background and Related Work

What constitutes a good website has been traditionally explained by relating it to user and usability. In other words, a successful and preferable web site generally refers to one with high usability, which is user-friendly and user-centered in interface and functional aspects. Nielsen [3] stated that usability is associated with learnability, efficiency, memorability, errors and satisfaction.

The literature currently offers several definitions of Usability:

1. The capability of the software product to be understood learned, used and attractive to the user, when used under specified conditions [9].
2. The extent to which a product can be used by specified users to achieve specified goals with effectiveness, efficiency and satisfaction in a specified context of use [10].

We briefly introduce three topics, which are the basis of our research; first we explain what is usability requirement and show some that can be used in e-commerce websites. Next, we reference usability metrics and show some examples. Finally, we explain what usability evaluation method is and show examples that can be used in e-commerce websites.

2.1 Usability Requirements

Several studies suggested guidelines and requirements to help design a better web site. Their focuses mainly lie in usability, although a few guidelines include aesthetic aspects [7]. The quality of e-commerce websites can be improved by abiding such web design guidelines, increasing the high level of usability.

Numerous authors have proposed ergonomic principles, recommendations and heuristics, which constitute a set of ergonomic qualities that interfaces should have [11–13]. The literature currently offers several examples of usability requirements [3, 4, 8]: interface elements (e.g. menus) should be easy to understand; the system should be easy to learn; actions which cannot be undone should ask for confirmation; error messages should explain how to recover from the error; the interface actions and elements should be consistent; the screen layout and colour should be appealing; the homepage of e-commerce websites should display numerous product offerings rather than just displaying one or two products; the 'Add to Cart' button should be obvious, bright, and prominent in comparison to other features on product page such as wish-lists, view product, email to friend, or check out buttons.

The purpose is to establish usability requirements which can be tested later in the development process.

2.2 Usability Metrics

It is necessary to measure those requirements using metrics. "A metric relates a defined measurement approach and a measurement scale. A metric is expressed in units, and can be defined for more than one attribute" [12]. A metric is a way of measuring or evaluating a particular phenomenon or thing. In the usability field, there is a set of specific metrics, like task success, user satisfaction, and errors, among others. Usability metrics can help reveal patterns that are hard or even impossible to see [13].

Some authors have proposed usability metrics, which constitute a set of indicators to use in evaluations [8, 12, 14–16]. Gabriel [8] developed a set metrics measures usability of Business-to-Consumer (B2C) e-commerce sites. The metrics consist of multiple usability indexes. Each of these indexes assesses usability of a particular aspect of the site. The developed usability indexes measure usability of: Navigational support (UI navig); Product search mechanism (UI srch); Product listings (UI pl); Product comparison mechanism (UI cmp); Product information presentation and product selection aspects of a site (UI pips); and others.

These metrics should be used during the development process and collected using a questionnaire or other usability evaluation method.

2.3 Usability Evaluation Methods

It is necessary to evaluate how much websites made by considering the web design guidelines actually satisfy users. For this, many researchers have traditionally emphasized usability: usability of a website is measured taking into account users' perspectives, and thus it can be continuously improved for the benefit of target users through an iterative cycle of development. Over time, methods and techniques to measure usability – usability evaluation methods – have been developed. The goal of the usability evaluation methods is to make a website more usable and preferable by finding what needs to be changed or developed in the website as much as is possible in terms of time and cost.

The usability evaluation methods are classified by two criteria: analytic methods or empirical methods; and expert evaluation, model evaluation, user evaluation, or evaluation location [7]. The literature currently offers several examples of usability evaluation methods [3, 4, 7, 14, 16, 17]: Heuristic evaluation, Focus group, Usability testing, Questionnaire, Scenarios, Card Sorting, Surveys, Interview, and others. Usability evaluation methods focuses on how well users can learn and use a website to achieve their goals [15]. It also refers to how satisfied users are with that process. To gather this information, those and other methods can be used to gather feedback from users about an existing website or plans related to a new website.

3   Methodology

This research is characterized, as regards its nature, as a qualitative-quantitative research and, in terms of its objectives, as an "exploratory" research, since it provides greater knowledge of the problem in order to make it more explicit. Initial interviews were conducted to identify the barriers and difficulties that team members have during the e-commerce websites development process in relation to the usability application. The interviews were composed of three questions and were attended by six team members, one project manager, two interface designers, two programmers and one tester. The professionals interviewed were, on average, 33 years, 2 to 10 years of experience in general website development and different levels of experience in the development of e-commerce websites. After that, usability requirements, usability metrics and usability evaluation methods were identified to be used during the development process of e-commerce websites.

Next steps of this work will be connecting all the requirements, metrics and evaluation methods to each other. From the association between usability requirements and metrics, it will be possible to obtain indicators to ensure that the requirements are being accomplished. The connection between the usability requirements and the metrics aims to facilitate the identification of the indicators; however, only with this relation is not possible to build more effective, efficient and pleasant e-commerce websites for different types of users. To ensure that the requirements are indeed accomplished, it will be necessary to collect usability metrics, from empirical or non-empirical evaluations, and analyze them to identify possible usability issues that users may face in interaction. By doing so, it will be possible to build the tool being necessary to make tests and to validate the previous results.

4   Results and Analysis

4.1   Questionnaire

Initial interviews were conducted to identify the barriers and difficulties that team members have during the e-commerce websites development process in relation to the usability application. The interviews were composed of three questions. The professionals interviewed were men and women who have, on average, 33 years, two to ten years of experience in general website development and different levels of experience in the development of e-commerce websites. Six professionals were interviewed (four men and two women) and they belonged to development teams: one as project manager, two as interface designers, two as programmers and one as tester. Among the professionals, five were graduated in Information Technology field and one was in college.

Based on the premise that there are usability recommendations and tools that evaluate usability, available on websites, books, articles and other researches, it is intended to identify why these teams do not use the material available about usability, or if it is used, what are the most common difficulties during the process. The first question was: **"What is(are) the reason(s)/barrier(s) that makes you (or your team) do not use or use in the wrong way or only partially the usability recommendations? Why?"**. From this initial questioning, the greatest barriers for the use of usability are:

- Time: some interviewees said that sometimes it is not possible to design using usability principles because the website must be developed quickly in the required time, and there is no time left to include the usability.
- Requirements: some interviewees said that the requirements do not cover usability, so, who plans, design or implements does not use it in the website what is not in the requirements passed to them.
- Knowledge: some interviewees reported that have some knowledge about usability but recognize that they need to read and to learn more about usability in e-commerce websites and update themselves on usability recommendations. Some interviewees said that the reason of lack of knowledge is the lack of time to study. Two interviewees said that use finished template and just modify some interfaces elements; however, they did not consider many usability elements for do it.

The second question were due to identify what is(are) the more difficulty phase(s) of development process to apply the usability and why. The question was: **"What is(are) the phase(s) of development process of e-commerce websites that you have more difficulty to apply the usability principles? Why?"**. To help the interviewees answer the question without hesitation, the generic phases, proposed by Sommerville [18], presents on software development (Specification, Design, Implementation, Validation and Evolution) were presented.

It was verified that the teams members have difficulties during the development of e-commerce websites and the phases that most require the application of usability principles are: Specification and Design. During the Specification, the principles are used to help the team to define the requirements, content, behavior and the virtual store's functions. During the Design, principles are used to define layout, architecture, graphic design, content sketching, navigation flow and others common structures of store. All interviewees commented that if in these first two phases (Specification and Design) the usability principles were incorporated into the development of the e-commerce website, the following phases would be simpler to apply usability.

One person commented *"Early phases [Specification and Design] is more important to think more about usability. In those phases is that the team will define how the interface should be. The usability requirements should be very thorough, as this will impact everything that happens next [in the next phases]"*. Another interviewee commented, *"If in those phases [during the Specification and Design phases] everything is correct about usability, I'll code as they designed. If designed with usability, I'll code with usability. That's simple!"*. Another interviewee commented, *"I test the website according to the specifications and requirements defined. If the usability is not defined there, I will not test it on the website"*.

The third question was based on the purpose of this word. Interviewees were asked about the utility of the proposed tool. The question was: **"If there were a tool focused on usability that could assist and support team members during the process of developing e-commerce sites, would it be useful? Would you use it? Why?"**. All interviewees reported that if there were a tool focused on usability it would be useful and used to diminish potential risks involved in the Specification and Design phases. However, some interviewees noted that this tool should be easy to use. "The tool would fall from the sky for us, but it has to be easy and practical, otherwise it will give more work," said one interviewee.

4.2   Identification of Usability Requirements, Usability Metrics and Usability Evaluation Methods

A systematic review was conducted to identify usability requirements, metrics and evaluation methods. According to Biolchini et al. [19], a systematic review is a method that allows identifying and evaluating all the research carried out around a certain topic. The protocol, proposed by Biolchini et al. [19], served as the basis for this work and researches were carried out in three different databases: EBSCO, Scopus and ProQuest. All five stages of the protocol were followed: (1) Propose research questions; (2) Make the selection of the sources and define the research strategies; (3) Define the criteria for inclusion and exclusion of researches; (4) Collect the results and review all selected articles; and (5) Answer the research questions.

Table 1 shows the number of researches identified in each database.

Table 1. Number of researches identified in each database.

Description of terms searched	ProQuest	EBSCO	Scopus	Total
Usability requirements for e-commerce websites	26	13	1	40
Usability metrics for e-commerce websites	59	27	4	90
Usability evaluation methods for e-commerce websites	25	4	0	29

After reading the papers, it was identified 160 usability requirements, 78 usability metrics and 10 usability evaluation methods.

4.3   The First View Tool

The tool is under construction. Its purpose is to relate all the requirements, metrics and evaluation methods identified with the phases of the development process. Figure 1 shows one requirement and the relations among metrics and evaluation methods.

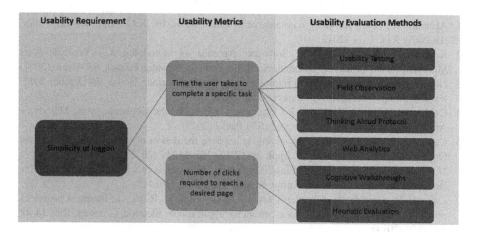

Fig. 1. Relation between usability requirements, metrics and usability evaluation methods.

It will be necessary some steps to finish the tool:

1. To connect all the requirements, metrics and evaluation methods to each other;
2. To relate all the requirements, metrics and evaluation methods to the development process's phases. The tool will propose a list of the requirements, metrics and evaluation methods that can be used in each phase of the process, giving professionals a more focused view of each phase individually;
3. To make tests with real users to validate the previous results.
4. To implement the tool using some programming language.

5   Conclusion and Discussion

The present work aimed to propose a tool to assist and support the process of e-commerce website development with a focus on usability. The purpose of the proposed tool is to integrate usability into the process of developing e-commerce sites, supporting and assisting development teams during all phases of this process.

In the first place, this work considers that the user's tool is a member of development teams, being able to exercise countless positions, such as developer, tester, software architect, systems analyst, among others. The research is based on the creation of the tool, which relates requirements, metrics and usability assessment methods, to be used by the defined audience.

Acknowledgments. The authors wish to thank National Council for Scientific and Technological Development (CNPq) for making this research possible and financed.

References

1. Alshehri, M., et al.: Adopting e-commerce to user's needs. Int. J. Comput. Sci. Eng. Surv. (IJCSES) **3**(1), 1–11 (2012)
2. Kosciancski, A.: Qualidade de Software: Aprenda as Metodologias e Técnicas Mais Modernas Para o Desenvolvimento de Software, 2nd edn. Novatec Editora, São Paulo (2007)
3. Nielsen, J.: Ecommerce usability improvements. Nielsen Norman Group, 24 October 2011. www.nngroup.com/articles/ecommerce-improvements/
4. Cybis, W., Betiol, A.H., Faust, R.: Ergonomia e Usabilidade: Conhecimentos, Métodos e Aplicações, 3rd edn. Editora Novatec, São Paulo (2015)
5. Carmona, C.J., et al.: Web usage mining to improve the design of an e-commerce website: OrOliveSur.com. J. Expert Syst. Appl. **39**(12), 11243–11249 (2012)
6. Nowakowski, M.: Application of usability test for the analysis of a search system in online stores. Stud. Proc. Pol. Assoc. Know. Manag. **72**, 39–49 (2014)
7. Distante, D., Garrido, A., Camelier-Carvajal, J., Giandini, R., Rossi, G.: Business processes refactoring to improve usability in e-commerce applications. Electron. Commer. Res. **14**(4), 497–529 (2014)
8. Gabriel, I.J.: Usability metrics for measuring usability of business-to-consumer (B2C) e-commerce sites. In: Proceedings of the 6th Annual ISOneWorld Conference, Las Vegas, NV, 11–13 April 2007, pp. 74.1–74.19 (2007)
9. ISO/IEC 9126-1:2001: Software Engineering—Product Quality—Part 1: Quality Model, June 2001
10. ISO 9241-11:1998: Ergonomic Requirements for Office Work with Visual Display Terminals (VDTs) – Part 11: Guidance on Usability, March 1998
11. Bastien, C., Scapin, D.: RT-0156 – Ergonomic criteria for the evaluation of human-computer interfaces (1993). http://www.inria.fr/rrrt/rt-0156.html
12. Shneiderman, B., Plaisant, C.: Designing the User Interface: Strategies for Effective Human-Computer Interaction, 4th edn. Addison-Wesley Publishing Company, Boston (2004)
13. Nielsen, J.: Usability Engineering. Morgan Kaufman, San Francisco (1994)
14. Bertoa, M.F., Vallecillo, A.: Usability metrics for software components. In: Proceedings of the 8th ECOOP Workshop on Quantitative Approaches in Object-Oriented Software Engineering (QAOOSE 2004) (2004)
15. Tullis, T., Albert, B.: Measuring the User Experience: Collecting, Analyzing and Presenting Usability Metrics. Morgan Kaufmann, Burlington (2008)
16. Rogers, Y., Sharp, H., Preece, J.: Design de interação: além da interação humano-computador, 3rd edn. Bookman, Porto Alegre (2013). 585 p.
17. Usability.GOV. Usability Evaluation Basics. https://www.usability.gov/what-and-why/usability-evaluation.html. Accessed Feb 2017
18. Sommerville, I.: Software Engineering, 9th edn. Addison-Wesley, Boston (2010)
19. Biolchini, J., Mian, P.G., Natalli, A.C.C., Travassos, G.H.: Systematic Review in Software Engineering. Technical report RT-ES 679/05, COPPE/UFRJ (2005)

Assessing Personality Differences in Human-Technology Interaction: An Overview of Key Self-report Scales to Predict Successful Interaction

Christiane Attig[1(✉)], Daniel Wessel[2], and Thomas Franke[2]

[1] Department of Psychology, Cognitive and Engineering Psychology,
Chemnitz University of Technology, Chemnitz, Germany
`christiane.attig@psychologie.tu-chemnitz.de`
[2] Institute for Multimedia and Interactive Systems,
Engineering Psychology and Cognitive Ergonomics,
Universität zu Lübeck, Lübeck, Germany
`{wessel,franke}@imis.uni-luebeck.de`

Abstract. For a comprehensive understanding of user diversity, a reliable and valid assessment of stable user characteristics is essential. In the field of human-technology interaction, a plethora of personality-related constructs linked to the experience of and interaction with technical systems has been discussed. A key question for researchers in the field is thus: Which are the key personality concepts and scales for characterizing inter-individual differences in user technology interaction? Based on a literature review and citation analysis, a structured overview of frequently used technology-related personality constructs and corresponding self-report scales is provided. Changes in the popularity and content of scales and concepts that occured over time as well as overlap between constructs and scales are discussed to facilitate scale selection.

Keywords: Human-technology interaction · Human-computer interaction · Personality assessment

1 Introduction

We are living in a world that is increasingly pervaded by technology. The first personal computers from the late 1970s and early 1980s were limited in their fields of application (e.g., word processing, programming, gaming). Today, computers are used for an enormous breadth of tasks in professional and private activities, from designing, learning, knowledge sharing, to leisure activities, social networking or videoconferencing. With the increasing number of these functions, users have more degrees of freedom regarding use of devices. Computers, especially mobile devices like tablets, have also tapped into user groups who would rarely use personal computers (e.g., seniors, small children), resulting in a higher user diversity. At the same time, the speed of technological innovation is steadily increasing. Thus, users need to learn to cope with new technology at a faster pace, and understanding how to optimally utilize

© Springer International Publishing AG 2017
C. Stephanidis (Ed.): HCII Posters 2017, Part I, CCIS 713, pp. 19–29, 2017.
DOI: 10.1007/978-3-319-58750-9_3

current technology becomes more and more relevant. Consequently, people do not only differ in their technology usage but also in their success with utilizing new technology. Hence, it becomes increasingly important to take the individual fit between persons and technical systems in the focus of engineering psychology research.

Within human factors and engineering psychology, theory and research are typically focused on what users have in common in terms of experience and behavior [52]. That is, there has been a lack of addressing stable inter-individual psychological differences of human operators. However, in recent years, the call for a more comprehensive integration of personality differences and theories into human factors research has grown (e.g., [41, 52, 53]). Personality traits that reflect inter-individual differences in human-technology interaction are increasingly specified in recent models, for instance within research on technology acceptance and technology interaction (e.g., [1, 7, 51]), or regarding motivational aspects of human-technology interaction (e.g., [53]). A more comprehensive examination of such personality differences is essential for a deepened understanding of user diversity regarding experience and preferences in human-technology interaction [52]. Moreover, certain personality facets constitute resources for a successful interaction with technology. Knowledge about how to cultivate and use these resources can increase users' fit to technology.

Even though personality is hardly addressed in textbooks on engineering psychology (e.g., [55]), investigating inter-individual differences in the field of human-technology interaction is not new [4, 18]. A plethora of personality-related constructs linked to the subjective experience of – and interaction with – technical systems have been discussed. Unfortunately, many of these concepts are interconnected and overlapping, which is reflected by similarities in assessment scales.

A key question for researchers in the field is thus: Which are the key personality dimensions for characterizing inter-individual differences in successful user technology interaction?

2   Background

A single prevailing definition of personality has not been established so far [45] and definitions vary with different theoretical perspectives (e.g., psychodynamic view, cognitive view; [11]). When talking about personality, we refer to the inter-individually differing set of relatively stable attributes that affect one's behavior, cognitions and emotions [3]. Among these attributes are classic personality traits (e.g., the Big Five personality dimensions, see below), cognitive patterns (e.g., attitudes, beliefs), motivational patterns (e.g., interests), and affective patterns (e.g., domain-specific anxiety).

The goal of investigating personality differences in human-technology interaction can be achieved on different levels. First, personality can be broadly assessed by using one of the established Big Five questionnaires (e.g., [16]). Personality is then measured on the five fundamental dimensions openness to experience, conscientiousness, extraversion, agreeableness and neuroticism [33]. While some connections between Big 5 dimensions and technology use [7], acceptance [51], and human-computer interaction (HCI; [28]) have been found, the effect sizes are usually small to medium-sized. These factors are likely too broad to accurately predict specific differ-ence in human-technology interaction.

Second, personality variables that are closely related to Big Five sub-facets (e.g., need for cognition [9], which is connected to openness to experience) as well as other psychological characteristics that are seen as influencing behavior trans-situationally (e.g., self-efficacy; [5]) have been examined regarding human-technology interaction. For instance, locus of control [44] has been identified as a significant predictor for the intention to use internet banking [1], and the stress experienced during first-time interaction with limited range of electric vehicles [20].

Third, a large variety of technology-related personality constructs have been pro-posed to characterize differences in human-technology interaction. These constructs are understood as relatively stable personality traits that are situation-specific, that is, characterize an individual's experience and behavior while interacting with technology. Unfortunately, these constructs and the corresponding scales are often overlapping and interconnected, making it difficult for researchers and practitioners to choose the right construct and scale. For instance, regarding human-technology and human-computer interaction the following constructs are discussed: computer attitudes, computer anx-iety, computer self-efficacy, control beliefs regarding technology usage, playfulness, personal innovativeness, affinity to technology, technology commitment, technology readiness, computer-related motivations, and geekism (see Table 2). Out of this rich-ness of constructs reflecting individual differences in human-technology interaction, an important task of engineering psychology research is to structure the prevailing con-cepts and to provide an overview regarding assessment scales.

As a first step in this research agenda, we aim to answer the following research questions: (Q1) Which technology-related personality constructs and corresponding scales are frequently applied in human factors/ergonomics research?, and (Q2) Which technology-related personality constructs and scales have been proposed and applied in recent years?

3   Method

To identify key scales that characterize inter-individual differences in human-technology interaction, the following procedure was used. In the first step (*S1-identification*), relevant scales were identified using literature search. In the second step (*S2-selection*), the number of relevant scales was narrowed down according to citation frequencies in major human factors/ergonomics and HCI journals in selected time periods (see below).

In the identification step (S1) a literature search in Google Scholar for technology-related personality scales using the search string ("human-technology interaction" OR "human computer-interaction") AND "personal-ity" AND ("questionnaire" OR "scale") AND "reliability"[1] was

---

[1] Parentheses inserted for better legibility. Google Scholar does not utilize parentheses for generating search results.

Table 1. Selected academic journals and conference proceedings. 2015 Impact factors according to journal citation reports (http://admin-apps.webofknowledge.com/JCR/JCR).

Title	IF	5-year IF
Selected academic journals		
Human-Computer Interaction	3.70	4.03
Computers in Human Behavior	2.88	3.72
Applied Ergonomics	1.71	2.11
International Journal of Human-Computer Studies	1.48	2.10
Ergonomics	1.45	1.72
Human Factors	1.37	1.77
International Journal of Human-Computer Interaction	1.26	1.46
Behaviour & Information Technology	1.21	1.49
Interacting with Computers	0.89	1.64
Selected conference proceedings		
CHI (Conference on Human Factors in Computing Systems)		
HCI International		

conducted. Google Scholar was chosen as a database due to its large breadth of covered academic sources. Further, we examined five review articles discussing relevant scales [21, 29, 30, 40, 48]. Moreover, iterative forward and backward search processes revealed additional scales. Within this first step 59 relevant scales were identified.[2]

In the selection step (S2), we looked for the identified scales in nine key journals and two key conference proceedings from the field of human factors/ergonomics and HCI (see Table 1). We selected (1) scales that were cited more than ten times in the mentioned journals/proceedings, (2) scales that were developed within the last ten years and were cited at least five times, and (3) selected scales published within the last five years (i.e., without citation criterion). With selection criterion (1) we detected established, frequently used scales over a longer time period. Because of fundamental technology changes since the emergence of first technology-related personality scales, we were also particularly interested in current developments, both somewhat established (2) and novel (3).

4   Results and Discussion

4.1   (Q1) Established Personality Constructs and Corresponding Scales

Selected scales, journals and citation figures are depicted in Table 2.

With respect to (Q1) the most frequently applied constructs were computer attitude (nine scales), computer anxiety (eight scales) and computer self-efficacy (three scales).

---

[2] Note that this number does not claim to be exhaustive as a distinctive search term for this research question does not exist and many different scholars and research groups developed different scales. Thus, obtaining a comprehensive picture of all developed scales in the field is a hardly achievable task.

Table 2. Selected scales and citation counts overall (Co) and within the last five years (C5)

Authors	Scale names and abbreviations	Co	C5
Scales with ten or more citations in key journals and conference proceedings			
Loyd and Gressard [31]	Computer Attitude Scale (CAS-L)	90	4
Nickell and Pinto [36]	Computer Attitude Scale (CAS-N)	56	6
Kay [26]	Computer Attitude Measure (CAM)	39	0
Popovich et al. [39]	Attitudes-Toward-Computer Usage Scale (ATCUS)	31	1
Dambrot et al. [17]	Computer Attitude Scale (CATT)	30	2
Zoltan-Ford and Chapanis [57]	Attitudes about Computers (AAC)	26	0
Reece and Gable [42]	Attitudes Toward Computers (ATC-R)	11	0
Francis [19]	Attitudes Toward Computers (ATC-F)	10	0
Shaft et al. [49]	Attitudes Toward Computers Instrument (ATCI)	10	3
Heinssen et al. [22]	Computer Anxiety Rating Scale (CARS-H)	87	17
Rosen et al. [43]	Computer Anxiety Rating Scale (CARS-R)	65	2
Barbeite and Weiss [6]	New Computer Anxiety and Self-efficacy Scales	29	17
Simonson et al. [50]	Computer Anxiety Index (CAIN)	20	2
Marcoulides [32]	Computer Anxiety Scale (CAS-M)	16	4
Cohen and Waugh [14]	Computer Anxiety Scale (CAS-C)	14	1
Campbell and Dobson [10]	Computer Anxiety Scale – Short Form (CAS-SF)	10	1
Charlton and Birkett [12]	Computer Apathy and Anxiety Scale (CAAS)	10	5
Compeau and Higgins [15]	Computer Self-Efficacy Measure (CSEM)	180	93
Murphy et al. [34]	Computer Self-Efficacy Scale (CSE)	45	9
Webster and Martocchio [54]	Computer Playfulness Scale (CPS)	70	23
Argawal and Prasad [2]	Personal Innovativeness in Information Technologies (PIIT)	57	38
Parasuraman [37]	Technology Readiness Index (TRI)	17	13
Scales developed in the last ten years and cited at least five times			
Beier [8]	Control Beliefs while Dealing with Technology (KUT)	8	
Karrer et al. [25]	Affinity for Technology Questionnaire (TA-EG)	8	
Schulenberg and Melton [47]	Computer Aversion, Attitudes, and Familiarity Index (CAAFI)	7	
Joyce and Kirakowski [24]	General Internet Attitude Scale (GIAS)	6	
Selected scales from the last five years without citation criteria			
Neyer et al. [35]	Technology Commitment (TB)	1	
Kim and Glassman [27]	Internet Self-Efficacy Scale (ISS)	3	
Yildirim and Correira [56]	Nomophobia Questionnaire (NMP-Q)	3	
Senkbeil and Ihme [48]	Short Scale for Computer-Related Motivations in Adults (FECAF)	0	
Schmettow and Drees [46]	Gex (Geekism, explicit)	0	

Further, one scale for each of the following constructs, computer playfulness, personal innovativeness, and technology readiness was found.

Computer attitudes are usually regarded as a multidimensional construct reflecting users' positive or and negative feelings towards computers [21, 29]. However, scales differ in their definition of attitudes making them difficult to compare [21]. Out of the computer attitude measures, the CAS-L [31] was the most frequently cited scale (90 citations overall). This scale consists of 30 items on three subscales, namely computer liking, computer confidence, and computer anxiety. Interestingly, none of the computer attitude scales was cited more than ten times within the last five years, leaving the impression that computer attitudes (or at least the corresponding scales) play an increasingly smaller role in HCI research.

Computer anxiety can be viewed as a situation-specific form of anxiety characterized by feelings of fear and apprehension when interacting with or thinking of computers [13]. The most frequently used scale to assess computer anxiety is the CARS-H [22], which was cited 87 times overall and 17 times within the last five years. The CARS-H assesses computer anxiety with 20 items, of which 11 reflect anxiety-related cognitive, behavioral and affective responses to computers and 9 items reflect positive attitudes towards computers. This scale correlates highly with the CAS-L, which reveals conceptual overlaps [22]. The New Computer Anxiety and Self-Efficacy Scales [6], which were published 17 years later, were cited 17 times within the last five years. All other established computer anxiety scales were cited five times or less in the last five years.

Computer self-efficacy is defined as the "judgment of one's capability to use a computer" ([15], p. 192) and is based on the more general psychological concept of self-efficacy [5]. Computer self-efficacy is negatively correlated with computer anxiety and positively with ease of use [23], thus, it represents a personal resource for coping with computer demands. By far the most cited scale for assessing computer self-efficacy is the CSEM [15], which was cited 180 times overall and 93 times within the last five years, indicating a constant relevance.

Another construct that can be viewed as a personal resource regarding coping with technology is computer playfulness, which reflects the cognitive spontaneity, curiosity and tendency to explore with respect to computer interactions [54]. The 22-item CPS [54] was cited 70 times overall, of which 23 citations occurred within the last five years.

Closely connected to computer playfulness is personal innovativeness in information technologies. This construct is defined as the "willingness of an individual to try out any new information technology" ([2], p. 206) and can be measured with the 4-item PIIT scale. The scale was cited 57 times since its publication, of which 38 citations appeared within the last five years.

Also, dealing with users' tendency to react to technological innovations is the construct technology readiness, "people's propensity to embrace and use new technologies for accomplishing goals in home life and at work" ([37], p. 308). The 36-item TRI uses four sub-scales (optimism, innovativeness, discomfort, insecurity) to describe this tendency and is more thoroughly than the short PIIT scale. The TRI and the shortened and revised TRI 2.0 [38] were cited 17 times overall and 13 times within the last five years.

4.2   (Q2) Recently Discussed Personality Constructs and Corresponding Scales

Selected recent developments (also depicted in Table 2) represent novel scales we view as particularly promising to predict successful human-technology interaction.

Control beliefs while dealing with technology is based on the more general construct of control beliefs [44], which describes an individual's belief about the relationship between their behavior and the behavioral outcome. The corresponding scale, the 24-item KUT [8], assesses control beliefs on three dimensions: internality (behavioral outcomes depend on factors within the person), technical externality (behavioral outcomes depend on factors within the technical device) and fatalistic externality (behavioral outcomes depend on coincidence). A unidimensional 8-item short form is also available [8].

According to [25], affinity to technology consists of four sub-facets, namely enthusiasm for technology, competence in dealing with technology, positive and negative attitudes towards technology. These facets are measured by the 19-item TA-EG. A similar multidimensional approach is followed with the TB [35], which measures technology commitment on three subscales: technology acceptance, technology competence (i.e., self-efficacy), and technology control beliefs. Another multi-dimensional measure, albeit restricted to computer use, is the CAAFI [47]. This 30-item questionnaire assesses computer familiarity, attitudes towards computers and computer aversion (i.e., discomfort and fear).

Two recent scales deal with internet usage: an internet attitude scale [24] and an internet self-efficacy scale [27]. The 21-item GIAS measures internet attitudes on four dimensions: internet affect, internet exhilaration, social benefit of the internet, and internet detriment [24]. With the 25-item ISS, internet self-efficacy is measured in five dimensions according to five groups of internet activities: self-efficacy regarding information search, communication, information organization, information differentiation, and information generation [27].

The NMP-Q assesses nomophobia, defined as the fear of having no mobile phone contact [56]. The 20-item questionnaire measures nomophobia on four dimensions reflecting different perceived consequences of being out of mobile phone contact: not being able to communicate, losing connectedness, not being able to access information, and giving up convenience.

Computer-related motivations are seen as relatively stable and situation-independent dispositions that determine the purposes of an individual's computer use [48]. The 14-item FECAF measures computer-related motivations on six subscales subsumed under two factors: utilitarian motivation (usage of computers as a learning tool, for information search and for higher efficiency of everyday tasks), and hedonistic motivation (usage of computers for entertainment, escapism, and social communication).

Finally, the construct of geekism reflects the "need to explore, to understand and to tinker with computing devices" ([46], p. 235). While users low in geekism use technology solely as a tool, users high in geekism are intrinsically motivated to use and think about technological devices and explore them. A recently developed self-report measure to assess geekism is the 15-item Gex [46].

5   Conclusion

Our overview of constructs and scales emphasizes the aforementioned problem that constructs – as well as the corresponding scales – are conceptually overlapping. For instance, the CAS-L [31] is supposed to measure computer attitude but comprises subscales assessing computer anxiety and computer confidence (i.e., self-efficacy). On the other hand, the CARS-H [22], a scale for assessing for computer anxiety, contains items regarding positive attitudes towards the computer. Hence, the differentiation between scales and constructs is unclear.

The finding that the established computer attitude scales are rarely cited anymore gives rise to the assumption that measuring HCI on the attitude level might no longer be relevant (see also [21]). In fact, computers have become ubiquitous while the classic attitude scales [17, 19, 26, 31, 36, 39, 42, 57] were developed at times when the digital society was in its infancy. Moreover, a shift from computer anxiety and technophobia to nomophobia, the fear to be *without* a digital device, is occurring. In contrast to the 80s and 90s, when the aforementioned scales were developed, computers can hardly be avoided today. Thus, the need for new scales emerges.

A limitation of our research that has to be kept in mind when interpreting the results is the heuristic solution of inferring actual scale usage from citation counts. First, a cited scale does not automatically mean that the scale was actually employed by the citing source. Thus, based on our data, the absolute usage frequencies might be overestimated. Second, due to the selection of journals and conference proceedings, the absolute usage frequencies might also be underestimated. However, the relative citation frequencies should remain mostly constant.

The next step in the research agenda to structure personality constructs and scales regarding human-technology interaction is to clarify interrelationships between concepts. Thereby, personality facets unique to certain scales – as well as blind spots – should be revealed. This knowledge will further facilitate scale selection and stimulate future scale construction.

References

1. Abu-Shanab, E., Pearson, J.M., Setterstrom, A.J.: Internet banking and customers' acceptance in Jordan: the unified model's perspective. Commun. Assoc. Inform. Syst. **26**, 493–524 (2010)
2. Argawal, R., Prasad, J.: A conceptual and operational definition of personal innovativeness in the domain of information technology. Inform. Syst. Res. **9**, 204–215 (1998). doi:10.1287/isre.9.2.204
3. Ashton, M.C.: Individual Differences and Personality. Elsevier, Amsterdam (2013)
4. Aykin, N.M., Aykin, T.: Individual differences in human-computer interaction: a survey. Comput. Ind. Eng. **20**, 373–379 (1991). doi:10.1016/0360-8352(91)90009-U
5. Bandura, A.: Self-efficacy: Toward a unifying theory of behavioral change. Psychol. Rev. **84**, 191–215 (1977). doi:10.1037/0033-295X.84.2.191
6. Barbeite, F.G., Weiss, E.M.: Computer self-efficacy and anxiety scales for an internet sample: testing measurement equivalence of existing measures and development of new scales. Comput. Hum. Behav. **20**, 1–15 (2004). doi:10.1016/S0747-5632(03)00049-9

7. Barnett, T., Pearson, A.W., Pearson, R., Kellermanns, F.W.: Five-factor model personality traits as predictors of perceived and actual usage of technology. Eur. J. Inform. Syst. **24**, 374–390 (2015). doi:10.1057/ejis.2014.10

8. Beier, G.: Kontrollüberzeugungen im Umgang mit Technik [Control beliefs in dealing with technology]. Rep. Psychol. **9**, 684–693 (1999)

9. Cacioppo, J.T., Petty, R.E.: The need for cognition. J. Pers. Soc. Psychol. **42**, 116–131 (1982). doi:10.1037/0022-3514.42.1.116

10. Campbell, N.J., Dobson, J.E.: An inventory of student computer anxiety. Elem. Sch. Guidance Couns. **22**, 149–156 (1987)

11. Carducci, B.J.: The Psychology of Personality. Wiley Blackwell, Chichester (2009)

12. Charlton, J.P., Birkett, P.E.: The development and validation of the computer apathy and anxiety scale. J. Educ. Comput. Res. **13**, 41–59 (1995). doi:10.2190/5UPE-80NP-W9WN-BE6W

13. Chua, S.L., Chen, D., Wong, A.F.L.: Computer anxiety and its correlates: a meta-analysis. Comput. Hum. Behav. **15**, 609–623 (1999). doi:10.1016/S0747-5632(99)00039-4

14. Cohen, B.A., Waugh, G.W.: Assessing computer anxiety. Psychol. Rep. **65**, 735–738 (1989). doi:10.2466/pr0.1989.65.3.735

15. Compeau, D.R., Higgings, C.A.: Computer self-efficacy: development of a measure and initial test. MIS Q. **19**, 189–211 (1995). doi:10.2307/249688

16. Costa, P.T., McCrae, R.R.: Revised NEO Personality Inventory (NEO PI-R) and NEO Five-Factor Inventory (NEO-FFI): Professional Manual. Psychological Assessment Resources, Odessa (1992)

17. Dambrot, F.H., Watkins-Malek, M.A., Silling, S.M., Marshall, R.S., Garver, J.A.: Correlates of sex differences in attitudes toward and involvement with computers. J. Vocat. Behav. **27**, 71–86 (1985). doi:10.1016/0001-8791(85)90053-3

18. Dillon, A., Watson, C.: User analysis in HCI – the historical lessons from individual differences research. Int. J. Hum.-Comput. Stud. **45**, 619–637 (1996). doi:10.1006/ijhc.1996.0071

19. Francis, L.J.: Measuring attitude toward computers among undergraduate college students: the affective domain. Comput. Educ. **20**, 251–255 (1993). doi:10.1016/0360-1315(93)90024-D

20. Franke, T., Rauh, N., Krems, J.F.: Individual differences in BEV drivers' range stress during first encounter of a critical range situation. Appl. Ergon. **57**, 28–35 (2016). doi:10.1016/j.apergo.2015.09.010

21. Garland, K.J., Noyes, J.M.: Computer attitude scales: how relevant today? Comput. Hum. Behav. **24**, 563–575 (2008). doi:10.1016/j.chb.2007.02.005

22. Heinssen, R.K., Glass, C.R., Knight, L.A.: Assessing computer anxiety: development and validation of the computer anxiety rating scale. Comput. Hum. Behav. **3**, 49–59 (1987). doi:10.1016/0747-5632(87)90010-0

23. Igbaria, M., Iivari, J.: The effects of self-efficacy on computer usage. Omega-Int. J. Manag. Sci. **23**, 587–605 (1995). doi:10.1016/0305-0483(95)00035-6

24. Joyce, M., Kirakowski, J.: Measuring attitudes towards the internet: the general internet attitude scale. Int. J. Hum.-Comput. Inter. **31**, 506–517 (2015). doi:10.1080/10447318.2015.1064657

25. Karrer, K., Glaser, C., Clemens, C., Bruder, C.: Technikaffinität erfassen – der Fragebogen TA-EG [Measuring affinity to technology – the questionnaire TA-EG]. In: Lichtenstein, A., Stößel, C., Clemens, C. (eds.) Der Mensch im Mittelpunkt technischer Systeme. 8. Berliner Werkstatt Mensch-Maschine-Systeme 7. bis 9. Oktober 2009 VDI, Düsseldorf, pp. 196–201 (2009)

26. Kay, R.H.: An exploration of theoretical and practical foundations for assessing attitudes toward computers: the computer attitude measure (CAM). Comput. Hum. Behav. **9**, 371–386 (1993). doi:10.1016/0747-5632(93)90029-R

27. Kim, Y., Glassman, M.: Beyond search and communication: development and validation of the Internet Self-efficacy Scale (ISS). Comput. Hum. Behav. **29**, 1421–1429 (2013). doi:10.1016/j.chb.2013.01.018

28. Kuurstra, J.: Individual differences in human-computer interaction: a review of empirical studies. Master's thesis, University of Twente (2015)

29. LaLomia, M.J., Sidowski, J.B.: Measurements of computer attitudes: a review. Int. J. Hum.-Comput. Inter. **3**, 171–197 (1991). doi:10.1080/10447319109526003

30. LaLomia, M.J., Sidowski, J.B.: Measurements of computer anxiety: a review. Int. J. Hum.-Comput. Inter. **5**, 239–266 (1993). doi:10.1080/10447319309526067

31. Loyd, B.H., Gressard, C.: Reliability and factorial validity of computer attitude scales. Educ. Psychol. Measur. **44**, 501–505 (1984). doi:10.1177/0013164484442033

32. Marcoulides, G.A.: Measuring computer anxiety: the computer anxiety scale. Educ. Psychol. Measur. **49**, 733–739 (1989). doi:10.1177/001316448904900328

33. McCrae, R.R., John, O.P.: An introduction to the five-factor model and its applications. J. Pers. **60**, 175–215 (1992). doi:10.1111/j.1467-6494.1992.tb00970.x

34. Murphy, C.A., Coover, D., Owen, S.V.: Development and validation of the computer self-efficacy scale. Educ. Psychol. Measur. **49**, 893–899 (1989). doi:10.1177/001316448904900412

35. Neyer, F.J., Felber, J., Gebhardt, C.: Entwicklung und Validierung einer Kurzskala zur Erfassung von Technikbereitschaft [Development and validation of a brief measure of technology commitment]. Diagnostica **58**, 87–99 (2012). doi:10.1026/0012-1924/a000067

36. Nickell, G.S., Pinto, J.N.: The computer attitude scale. Comput. Hum. Behav. **2**, 301–306 (1986). doi:10.1016/0747-5632(86)90010-5

37. Parasuraman, A.: Technology readiness index (TRI). J. Serv. Res.-US **2**, 307–320 (2000). doi:10.1177/109467050024001

38. Parasuraman, A., Colby, C.L.: An updated and streamlined technology readiness index: TRI 2.0. J. Serv. Res.-US **18**, 59–74 (2015). doi:10.1177/1094670514539730

39. Popovich, P.M., Hyde, K.R., Zakrajsek, T., Blumer, C.: The development of the attitudes toward computer usage scale. Educ. Psychol. Measur. **47**, 267–269 (1987). doi:10.1177/0013164487471035

40. Powell, A.L.: Computer anxiety: comparison of research from the 1990s and 2000s. Comput. Hum. Behav. **29**, 2337–2381 (2013). doi:10.1016/j.chb.2013.05.012

41. Pozzi, S., Bagnara, S.: Individuation and diversity: the need for idiographic HCI. Theor. Issues Ergon. Sci. **14**, 1–21 (2013). doi:10.1080/1464536X.2011.562564

42. Reece, M.J., Gable, R.K.: The development and validation of a measure of general attitudes toward computers. Educ. Psychol. Measur. **42**, 913–916 (1982). doi:10.1177/001316448204200327

43. Rosen, L.D., Sears, D.C., Weil, M.M.: Computerphobia. Behav. Res. Meth. Ins. C. **19**, 167–179 (1987). doi:10.3758/BF03203781

44. Rotter, J.B.: Generalized expectancies for internal versus external control of reinforcement. Psychol. Monogr.-Gen. Appl. **80**, 1–28 (1966). doi:10.1037/h0092976

45. Saucier, G.: Measures of the personality factors found recurrently in human lexicons. In: Boyle, G.J., Matthews, G., Saklofske, D.H. (eds.) The SAGE Handbook of Personality Theory and Assessment. Personality Measurement and Testing, vol. 2, pp. 29–54. Sage Publications, London (2008)

46. Schmettow, M., Drees, M.: What drives the geeks? Linking computerbenthusiasm to achievement goals. In: Proceedings of HCI 2014, Southport, UK, pp. 234–239. BCS Learning and Development Ltd., Swindon (2014)
47. Schulenberg, S.E., Melton, A.M.A.: The computer aversion, attitudes, and familiarity index (CAAFI): a validity study. Comput. Hum. Behav. **24**, 2620–2638 (2008). doi:10.1016/j.chb. 2008.03.002
48. Senkbeil, M., Ihme, J.M.: Entwicklung und Validierung eines Kurzfragebogens zur Erfassung computerbezogener Anreizfaktoren bei Erwachsenen [Development and Validation of a Short Scale for Computer-Related Motivations in Adults]. Diagnostica (2016). doi:10.1026/0012-1924/a000170
49. Shaft, T.M., Sharfman, M.P., Wu, W.W.: Reliability assessment of the attitude towards computers instrument (ATCI). Comput. Hum. Behav. **20**, 661–689 (2004). doi:10.1016/j. chb.2003.10.021
50. Simonson, M.R., Maurer, M., Montag-Torardi, M., Whitaker, M.: Development of a standardized test of computer literacy and a computer anxiety index. J. Educ. Comput. Res. **3**, 231–247 (1987). doi:10.2190/7CHY-5CM0-4D00-6JCG
51. Svendsen, G.B., Johnsen, J.K., Almås-Sørensen, L., Vittersø, J.: Personality and technology acceptance: the influence of personality factors on the core constructs of the technology acceptance model. Behav. Inform. Technol. **32**, 323–334 (2013). doi:10.1080/0144929X. 2011.553740
52. Szalma, J.L.: Individual differences in human-technology interaction: incorporating variation in human characteristics into human factors and ergonomics research and design. Theor. Issues Ergon. Sci. **10**, 381–397 (2009). doi:10.1080/14639220902893613
53. Szalma, J.L.: On the application of motivation theory to human factors/ergonomics: motivational design principles for human-technology interaction. Hum. Factors **56**, 1453–1471 (2014). doi:10.1177/0018720814553471
54. Webster, J., Martocchio, J.T.: Microcomputer playfulness: development of a measure with workplace implications. MIS Q. **16**, 201–226 (1992). doi:10.2307/249576
55. Wickens, C.D., Hollands, J., Banbury, S., Parasuraman, R.: Engineering Psychology and Human Performance. Pearson, London (2013)
56. Yildirim, C., Correira, A.: Exploring the dimensions of nomophobia: development and validation of a self-reported questionnaire. Comput. Hum. Behav. **49**, 130–137 (2015). doi:10.1016/j.chb.2015.02.059
57. Zoltan-Ford, E., Chapanis, A.: What do professional persons think about computers? In: Anderson, J.G., Jay, S.J. (eds.) Use and Impact of Computers in Clinical Medicine, pp. 51–67. Springer, New York (1987). doi:10.1007/978-1-4613-8674-2_5

Exploring the Building Blocks of Personas for Children with Autism Spectrum Disorders

Ayşe Naciye Çelebi Yılmaz[(⊠)]

Politecnico di Milano, DEIB, Milan, Italy
aysenaciye.celebi@polimi.it

Abstract. There are limited studies in abstract representation of children with severe Autism Spectrum Disorders (ASD). User abstraction is a useful technique in interaction design to anticipate user. Children with ASD are usually defined by diagnosis of ASD. However, it is important to recognize these children beyond these diagnoses. We believe creating personas for children with ASD makes them more familiar, intimate and easier to empathize their characteristics and abilities. Our research focuses on personas as a tool for user abstraction to help developing playful smart technologies including multimedia content and connected tangible object which aim at improving learning skills of children with ASD. The purpose of this paper is to explore the building blocks of Personas for children with ASD and, eventually, to form a foundation document for Personas based on literature review and field studies. Theoretical findings cover Personas literature. On the other hand, empirical findings feed foundation document by considering particularly our target user in target context. Our Personas foundation document integrates theoretical and empirical findings will help us to design Personas and contextual scenarios systematically and rigorously in the future.

Keywords: Personas · Persona creation · Children with ASD · Autism

1 Introduction

There are limited studies in abstract representation of children with severe Autism Spectrum Disorders (ASD). User abstraction is a useful technique in interaction design to anticipate user. Children with ASD are usually defined by diagnosis of ASD; deficits in communication and social behavior, stereotyped behavior, and restricted interests and activities [12]. We believe creating personas for children with ASD makes them more familiar, intimate and easier to empathize their characteristics and abilities instead of recognizing them with a set of diagnosis. Persona creation also forms a common platform for communicating these children with designers, developers and therapists.

Interactive technologies are promising to improve skills of children with ASD [3, 7]. Therefore, usability and accessibility is required to build successful interactions. Our research focuses on personas as a tool for user abstraction to help developing playful smart technologies including multimedia content and connected tangible object which aim at improving learning skills of children with ASD.

© Springer International Publishing AG 2017
C. Stephanidis (Ed.): HCII Posters 2017, Part I, CCIS 713, pp. 30–36, 2017.
DOI: 10.1007/978-3-319-58750-9_4

The purpose of this paper is to explore the building blocks of Personas for children with ASD and, eventually, to form a foundation document. We present a foundation document based on literature review and our field studies. Theoretical findings cover Personas literature. On the other hand, empirical findings have helped us to feed the foundation document by considering particularly our target user in target context. We have observed children with ASD while playing with playful interactive technologies that we have developed. We have collected qualitative data to identify what type of characteristics and behaviors should be considered when composing Personas. Our Personas foundation document integrates theoretical and empirical findings which will help us to design Personas and contextual scenarios systematically and rigorously in the future.

The following section will be a brief introduction in Personas. The third section will explore the content of a foundation paper for creating Personas of children with ASD. We will reflect our theoretical findings in the first part and we will discuss our empirical findings in the second part. In the following section, we will define the content of the categories for our foundation document. Last section will discuss the concluding remarks.

2 Personas

Personas are introduced to interaction design literature by Alan Cooper in 1999 in his famous book "The Inmates are Running the Asylum: Why High Tech Products Drive us Crazy and How to Restore the Sanity" [5]. Personas are powerful and useful tools to represent abstract users. They are fictional characters based on characteristics, needs, and behavior patterns of actual users [10]. They are usually based on user studies to communicate actual attributes of actual users [4, 9, 11]. Furthermore, user studies help to create unbiased personas, especially child-based personas where designers tend to attribute their own memories, experiences and characteristics to abstract a child [6].

There are limited Persona studies in accessible design, for children with ASD to be more precise. When designing for people with limited capabilities in terms of realizing physical and mental activities, creating Personas becomes more useful not only to facilitate developing empathy and anticipation but also to facilitate sharing a common platform amongst designers, developers, caregivers and families [7, 10].

3 Developing the Foundation Paper

3.1 Theoretical Findings

Personas have been studied and created since Cooper [5] has introduced the term in interaction design. These studies mostly targeted users without disabilities, or limited physical and/or mental functions. Furthermore, there are limited studies in persona creation for children with ASD. Therefore, we have investigated Personas for accessible design purposes. Our theoretical findings explored elderly-based personas, child-based personas and personas for children with ASD in order to acquire knowledge to create a relevant and complete categories for foundation document.

Including images and demographic information of the fictional character is mostly a shared category no matter whom the user group is. *Photos*, once Persona is written, are useful to communicate and anticipate the described fictional character [9]. *Demographic information* usually includes name, age and gender of a Persona.

For a typical user, Pruitt and Grudin [9] have defined an umbrella term *Overview* to provide information on user's family, business and such information. Antle [1] has also defined a generic name for this content; *Descriptive attributes* where family structure and school of the child is written. In accessibility, rather than an umbrella term, this content is better to be called as information on *Educational credentials* [7] and *Medical history* [7, 10]. We believe these categories would provide a better understanding of children with ASD since both health and education are important chronic facts about them.

User's *Daily routines* and *Activity types* are important to understand a typical day and preferences of a child with ASD [6, 7, 9, 10]. It is also useful to consider contextual routines namely *Playtimes* and *Playing venues* as decribed by Moser et al. [8]. Even though computer literacy has only been identified by Leal et al. [7] and Pruitt and Grudin [9], we believe it is important to describe user's *Computer skills, knowledge, and abilities* when completing a Persona.

Antle [1, 2] uses a generic term *Experiential goals* where contextual task-oriented technology goals are identified based on a project. Here, we would like to focus on projects similar to ours. da Costa et al. [6] has conducted a user study to design a political educational game for children and Moser et al. [8] has explored children's gaming behaviors and requirements; all for the sake of creating child-based Personas. Therefore, they have precisely identified their contextual goals and behavior patterns; *Gamer style* and *Game preferences* including game genres and game features [6, 8].

So far, generic and technology-wise categories for Personas were elaborated. Ultimately, we need to elaborate exclusive abilities and behavior of children with ASD in order to adapt the content of Personas for our target user. *Developmental abilities*, suggested by Antle [1] are the theoretical understanding of children's abilities for Persona creation. According to Leal et al. [7], these abilities embody the characteristics of *Receptive-expression language*, *Social interaction level* and *Communication and adaptive behavior* (Fig. 1).

Some Personas use *Quotes* from user studies to highlight a sayings of a user. Since children with ASD have problems in expressing themselves verbally, we suggest the use of short videos to represent them in a more expressive way. These videos should give hints on user's mental model to make the empathy easier. We believe using short videos will be useful to achieve what Persona creation aims which is to communicate the fictional user to all stakeholders and abstract the user as representative as possible.

3.2 Empirical Findings

Personas should rely on the information collected on actual users in order to represent an accurate abstraction [4, 9, 11]. They should also include relevant content with the context. Here, we try to find categories for our foundation document through

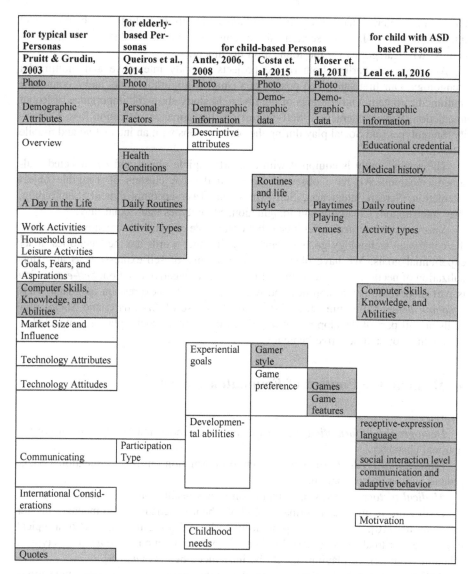

for typical user Personas	for elderly-based Personas	for child-based Personas			for child with ASD based Personas
Pruitt & Grudin, 2003	Queiros et al., 2014	Antle, 2006, 2008	Costa et. al, 2015	Moser et. al, 2011	Leal et. al, 2016
Photo	Photo	Photo	Photo	Photo	
Demographic Attributes	Personal Factors	Demographic information	Demographic data	Demographic data	Demographic information
Overview		Descriptive attributes			Educational credential
	Health Conditions				Medical history
A Day in the Life	Daily Routines		Routines and life style	Playtimes	Daily routine
Work Activities	Activity Types			Playing venues	Activity types
Household and Leisure Activities					
Goals, Fears, and Aspirations					
Computer Skills, Knowledge, and Abilities					Computer Skills, Knowledge, and Abilities
Market Size and Influence					
Technology Attributes		Experiential goals	Gamer style		
Technology Attitudes			Game preference	Games	
				Game features	
		Developmental abilities			receptive-expression language
Communicating	Participation Type				social interaction level
					communication and adaptive behavior
International Considerations					
					Motivation
		Childhood needs			
Quotes					

Fig. 1. Content of foundation paper for Personas. Blue boxes indicate selected theoretical categories for our Personas foundation document. (Color figure online)

qualitative data we have collected. We have conducted two field studies for two different projects. Both of the projects provide interactive and multimodal playing opportunities for children with Intellectual Development Disorder (IDD) to improve learning and social skills at a therapeutic center as aimed in our Personas context.

We have recorded these play sessions for video analysis to observe children's behavior and reaction to interactive technologies. Our analysis was based on the variables formed by observable signals which are developed by the therapists of this therapeutic center. After our analysis, we have come up with clusters of behavior and interaction types. In this section, these clusters will be evaluated to arrive at context-wise categories for the foundation document.

As mentioned earlier, both of the projects embody interactive and multimodal technology. Our first study Teo possesses a smart configurable robot and a connected multimedia content. Our findings of the first field study show the importance of Robot interaction, Screen interaction, Self-expression, Performance, Attention loss, Creativity, Stereotypes and Social play during the play sessions with an interactive and mobile robot [3].

The second study is equipped with a smart tangible object and a connected multimedia content. We have observed signals under the clusters of Tangible object interaction, Screen interaction, Self-expression, Task accomplishment, Scaffolding, Play interruption, Creativity and Imagination, Stereotypes and Social play.

Smart object interaction, let it be robot or tangible object, and screen interaction are the contextual technology goals of our study, in other words are the categories under experiential goals. We have observed the capability of self-expression as an externalization of needs and manifestation of positive and negative emotion. *Self-expression* is part of developmental abilities and related to receptive-expression language. *Task accomplishment* skills, presence of *attention loss*, use of *Creativity*, and *Social play* skills are all part of developmental abilities. Furthermore, social play is connected to communication and adaptive behavior.

4 Defining the Content of Foundation Paper

Overview

Demographic information includes name, age, gender and family structure of the fictional character.

Educational credential is the descriptive information on user's educational background and ongoing program.

Medical history involves information on user's health conditions chronically.

Daily routine provides information on how the user schedules and manages his/her everyday life [10]. The aim is to present the tasks and obligations as part of a typical day of the user to all stakeholders. Furthermore, information on *playtime*, user's typical schedule (routine) for playing, should be introduced here as well [8].

Activity types are the implementation of activities of choice. These tasks and actions are to understand what the user does besides his/her routines. *Playing venues* should fit here to tell the playgrounds the child prefers to play.

Computer skills, knowledge, and abilities show the computer literacy to understand user's capability in using computer.

Experiential Goals

Smart object interaction shows the relation child builds with the object in terms of communication and manipulation [3]. The aim is to define the child's interest in the object taking his/her actions (e.g. approaching, exploring, touching, etc.) and design attributes (e.g. attracting color, shape, size, etc.) of the object into consideration.

Screen interaction shows the relation child builds with the multimedia content. Screen interaction is important to understand child's preferences in receiving an information, demand or feedback via user interface (e.g. text, image, video, audio).

Gamer style is to understand the user's attitude and behavior when playing a game and the character he gets into as a gamer [6].

Game preference includes the user's preferences in genre of games and game features [6, 8].

Developmental Abilities

Receptive-expression language involves the input (receiving) and the output (expressing) language skills or preferences of the user. Receptive language (input) of a child is to understand the preferred tools for comprehension (e.g. visual or oral material, the structure of these material, etc.) [7]. Expression language (outoupt) of a child shows the preferred tools for self-expression (e.g. verbally or non-verbally including writing, drawing, eye or physical contact, the structure of this language, etc.) [3, 7].

Social interaction level shows the events that influence child's social interaction skills [7].

Communication and, adaptive behavior includes child's attitude towards other people and behavior in the classroom [7]. Social play skills are important aspect of this content too. Therefore, decentralization (turntaking) and cooperative learning skills should be elaborated here.

Task accomplishment elucidates child's achievement of any given tasks in order to understand if the child needs scaffolding or any additional instruction [3].

Attention loss is to understand what triggers distraction for that particular Persona.

Creativity: involves child's imagination skills and originality in making up plays.

Illustrative Elements

Photo use is necessary to communicate Persona pictorially. Pruitt and Grudin [9] suggests the use of photos of local people rather than stock images.

Quotes from the user enriches a Persona with his/her own words.

Short video enhances a Persona by showing how the user performs his/her actions.

5 Concluding Remarks

This framework outlines the important and relevant content particularly addressed to children with ASD in the context of interactive technology. The benefit of this work is to create a common platform for Personas not only used by all stakeholders but also built by them too. With the help of Personas in this application domain, remote and customized interactive therapy sessions can be implemented which would reduce costs and increase effectiveness of sessions which disregards user diversity today.

Based on our foundation document which integrates theoretical and empirical findings, we will design Personas and contextual scenarios systematically and rigorously in the future. Short term follow-up study will be the design of Personas for children with ASD. Long term study will be to design playful interactive technologies tailor-made for user diversity.

Acknowledgment. The author warmly expresses her deep gratitude for Prof. Franca Garzotto and the children, therapists, and managers from L'Abilita centre.

References

1. Antle, A.N.: Child-user abstractions. In: CHI 2006 Extended Abstracts on Human Factors in Computing Systems, pp. 478–483. ACM, April 2006
2. Antle, A.N.: Child-based personas: need, ability and experience. Cogn. Technol. Work **10** (2), 155–166 (2008)
3. Bonarini, A., Garzotto, F., Gelsomini, M., Romero, M., Clasadonte, F., Yilmaz Celebi, A.N.: A huggable, mobile robot for developmental disorder interventions in a multi-modal interaction space. In: 2016 25th IEEE International Symposium on Robot and Human Interactive Communication (RO-MAN), pp. 823–830. IEEE, August 2016
4. Chang, Y.N., Lim, Y.K., Stolterman, E.: Personas: from theory to practices. In: Proceedings of the 5th Nordic Conference on Human-Computer Interaction: Building Bridges, pp. 439–442. ACM, October 2008
5. Cooper, A.: The Inmates are Running the Asylum: Why High-Tech Products Drive us Crazy and How to Restore the Sanity. Sams, Indianapolis (2004)
6. da Costa, A.C., Rebelo, F., Teles, J., Noriega, P.: Child-persona: how to bring them to Reality? Procedia Manuf. **3**, 6520–6527 (2015)
7. Leal, A., Teixeira, A., Silva, S.: On the creation of a persona to support the development of technologies for children with autism spectrum disorder. In: Antona, M., Stephanidis, C. (eds.) UAHCI 2016. LNCS, vol. 9739, pp. 213–223. Springer, Cham (2016). doi:10.1007/978-3-319-40238-3_21
8. Moser, C., Fuchsberger, V., Tscheligi, M.: Using probes to create child personas for games. In: Proceedings of the 8th International Conference on Advances in Computer Entertainment Technology, p. 39. ACM, November 2011
9. Pruitt, J., Grudin, J.: Personas: practice and theory. In: Proceedings of the 2003 Conference on Designing for User Experiences, pp. 1–15. ACM, June 2003
10. Queirós, A., Cerqueira, M., Martins, A.I., Silva, A.G., Alvarelhão, J., Teixeira, A., Rocha, N. P.: ICF inspired personas to improve development for usability and accessibility in ambient assisted living. Procedia Comput. Sci. **27**, 409–418 (2014)
11. Sinha, R.: Persona development for information-rich domains. In: CHI 2003 Extended Abstracts on Human Factors in Computing Systems, pp. 830–831. ACM, April 2003
12. World Health Organization: Autism spectrum disorders [Fact sheet] (2016). http://www.who.int/mediacentre/factsheets/autism-spectrum-disorders/en/

Mass Customized Knowledge Management: A Project for Adequate and Dynamic Knowledge Transfer for Small and Medium Enterprises

Michael Becker[1]([✉]), Stephan Klingner[1], Julia Friedrich[1],
Frederik Kramer[2], Martin Schneider[3], and Klaus-Peter Fähnrich[1]

[1] University of Leipzig, Leipzig, Germany
{becker,klingner,jfriedrich,
faehnrich}@informatik.uni-leipzig.de
[2] initOS GmbH, Magdeburg, Germany
frederik.kramer@initos.com
[3] Agri Con GmbH, Jahna, Germany
martin.schneider@agricon.de

Abstract. Knowledge is one of the most important resources today and, thus, companies in general and SMEs in particular need effective and efficient knowledge management solutions. In this paper, activities in the project MACKMA, which aims at implementing a knowledge management system tailored to the needs of SMEs, are introduced. Central findings include methods for establishing the product-service-portfolio of a company, a metamodel for knowledge artifacts and an accompanying incentive system for increasing knowledge management system usage.

Keywords: Knowledge management · Knowledge artifacts · Incentive systems · Knowledge customization

1 Introduction

Today's economic environment is characterized by increasing competition resulting from heterogeneous customer demands. Companies need to provide individual offers that are tailored to the specific requirements of customers. In particular in the domain of services, customer knowledge is a vital quality factor [1]. In addition, modern products and services produce a plethora of data (e.g. due to using sensors) which requires companies to manage, analyze and interpret these data. Working with data is a knowledge-intensive task and, thus, a greater need for knowledge management has to be stated. This results in several challenges, especially for small and medium enterprises (SME). On the one hand, SME usually lack financial resources to implement complex knowledge management solutions. On the other hand, knowledge in SME is often bound to a specific person and needs to be explicated. Though the challenges of SMEs concerning knowledge management are well-known, to date there is no solution satisfying the specific requirements of SMEs [2, 3].

© Springer International Publishing AG 2017
C. Stephanidis (Ed.): HCII Posters 2017, Part I, CCIS 713, pp. 37–43, 2017.
DOI: 10.1007/978-3-319-58750-9_5

Fig. 1. Different representations of knowledge

For effective and efficient use of existing knowledge, companies need to provide their employees with suitable methods and tools for both, knowledge acquisition and knowledge application. In doing so, two dimensions must be taken into account. First, the formalization degree of knowledge has a great impact on the possibility to apply knowledge automatically. Second, the representation of knowledge depends on a specific context which is defined by the information demand and the background knowledge of a user. Figure 1 depicts an example of two different knowledge representations. On the left-hand side of the figure, the characteristics of an agricultural area are presented in a graphical way. On the right-hand side, the same information is presented using a table. While the table allows for quick sorting and filtering, the graphical representation gives a detailed view of the structure of the area.

As the example in Fig. 1 shows, it is not sufficient to view knowledge as a monolithic block. Rather, it is necessary to divide knowledge into flexible knowledge fragments that can be presented (i.e. combined and mixed) according to user demands.

The project MACKMA[1] aims to overcome the mentioned challenges by developing a flexible knowledge management system (KMS) tailored to the specific needs of SME. The remainder of this paper is structured according to the activities that were performed during the project. First, the structural framework for the system was set by establishing a company portfolio consisting of offered products and services (Sect. 2). Second, a metamodel for knowledge artifacts was established (Sect. 3). Based on this metamodel it is possible to implement a KMS. To overcome existing challenges concerning the usage of a KMS (e.g. time and resource constraints in daily work), incentive schemes for using the system were analyzed (Sect. 4). In addition, SME representatives are currently asked to describe their understanding of knowledge. The results of these surveys influence knowledge content and representation and are, therefore, an important aspect of future research (Sect. 5).

2 Product and Service Portfolio

SMEs, in particular, are characterized by organically grown product and service portfolios. Therefore, a KMS must be adapted to individual requirements in these companies with respect to a lack of formalization and rather vague definition of

---

[1] http://mackma-project.eu.

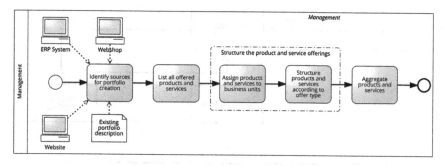

Fig. 2. Process for establishing a company portfolio

responsibilities [4]. To identify the individual situation of a company, it is, on the one hand, necessary to formalize the company structure. On the other hand, the specific portfolio of a company needs to be structured. Using the items of the portfolio, it is possible to assign knowledge artifacts.

For establishing the company structure, a twofold approach is used. First, existing documentation is taken into account, e.g. employee contracts and descriptions of activities. Based on these documents, the formal structure of the company can be identified. However, as stated above, SMEs often have organically grown structures and, thus, analyzing formal documentation is not sufficient. To represent the organizational structure thoroughly, it is necessary to survey employees focusing on their daily work and interactions with other employees. This allows for revealing the embodied company structure.

To represent the entire product and service offering of a company, it is necessary to define its portfolio. The portfolio is used as a starting point for identifying and collecting knowledge artifacts. The general process for establishing a portfolio is presented in Fig. 2.

As a first step, it is necessary to identify possible sources for supporting portfolio creation. These sources are existing collections of products and offers, e.g. the company website, contract templates, or ERP systems. In addition, questioning responsible employees are fruitful resources. In the second step, an unsorted and unstructured list of offered products and services is established. As a third step, the list is structured according to business areas of the company and according to offering types, e.g. hardware, software, and services. In the final step, single items are aggregated into item groups.

3 Metamodel of Knowledge Artifacts

The specification of the product and service portfolio of a company forms the foundation for defining knowledge artifacts. Knowledge artifacts link the portfolio view with the activities of employees. For being able to describe the knowledge artifacts in a structured way, a metamodel was established and is partially presented in Fig. 3. Defining the knowledge metamodel and, thus, specifying the structure of knowledge artifacts, is an important prerequisite for integrating different knowledge sources [5].

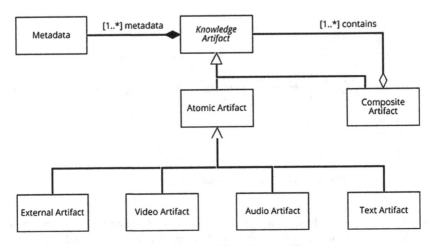

Fig. 3. Metamodel of knowledge artifacts

The metamodel covers three application areas. First, it is possible to define hierarchical knowledge artifacts. Second, responsibilities are assigned to knowledge artifacts to define roles. Third, to capture activities, a processual dimension is included. In this paper, we focus on the hierarchic structure. The interested reader is referred to [6] for further information.

To enable hierarchic structuring of knowledge artifacts, the two entities *atomic artifact* and *composite artifact* are defined. An atomic artifact is a single piece of information and represents knowledge using a textual description, an image, audio data, or video data. Using these different types of artifacts, it is possible to define knowledge artifacts for a specific usage context. For example, video artifacts are suitable for users of desktop applications. Contrary, smartphone users cannot access video artifacts due to bandwidth limitations. Therefore, they are provided with text artifacts. In addition to these types, there exists an entity *external artifact* to foster integration of existing systems (e.g. corporate wikis or issue trackers) into the KMS. External artifacts are of special importance because a large amount of knowledge is distributed over different applications and needs to be integrated redundant free.

Composite artifacts consist of existing knowledge artifacts and enable knowledge reuse. For example, a video and a text artifact might be combined into a composite artifact to increase understandability of the represented information. According to the metamodel specification in Fig. 3, it is also possible to reuse composite artifacts.

To enable a more detailed description of knowledge artifacts, metadata are used. Relevant metadata for knowledge artifacts were identified using a threefold approach consisting of performing a literature review, surveying practitioners, and analyzing existing metadata standards. For consolidation purposes, the list of metadata was aggregated, i.e. redundant metadata were eliminated and synonyms were identified. As a result, 70 different metadata could be identified. To increase comprehensibility,

Table 1. Metadata of knowledge artifacts

Metadata class	Metadata
Lifecycle	Creation date, modification date, creator, contributor, interactions, subscribers
Structure	Categorization, links, tags, identifier, references
Security, Quality	Access privileges, approval process, flaws
Content	Assessment, language, comments, audience, description, format, title, type
Recipient	Affected people, compulsory access

metadata were structured into the groups *lifecycle, structure, security/quality, content,* and *recipient*. An excerpt of the identified metadata is presented in Table 1[2].

4 Fostering SME Knowledge Management

A big challenge in providing a KMS for SMEs results from time and resource constraints. Contrary to large enterprises, SMEs often do not have the financial resources that are necessary to invest in an ample KMS. In addition, SMEs need flexible strategies and systems that support the implementation of KMS. In particular, knowledge management activities in SMEs must not require additional expenditure of time and long training periods [7].

Motivating employees for using a KMS in their daily work is a critical success factor. Incentive systems are an approach to increase the motivation. As Fig. 4 depicts, an incentive system is the combination of single incentives and has impact on the motivation of employees. For establishing an incentive system, it is first necessary to define incentive goals. The incentives that form the incentive system are means to achieve these goals. To identify the influence of incentives, it is important to assess the performance changes using indicators.

Within the MACKMA project, KMS usage is supported by an integrated incentive system based on the connections shown in Fig. 4. Therefore, different approaches concerning incentives were analyzed resulting in the morphological box presented in Table 2. Using the elements of the table, it is possible to define an individual incentive system as a combination of incentive goal, recipient, instrument, reward system, and indicator. For example, increasing the usage quantity is bound to an individual employee's motivation which can be addressed by using bonus payments with a sudden reward. Success of this system is measured by quantitative indicators.

---

[2] The thorough list of metadata is accessible via https://www.informatik.uni-leipzig.de/ifi/fileadmin/ServiceEngineering/files/hcii/WAMetadaten.pdf.

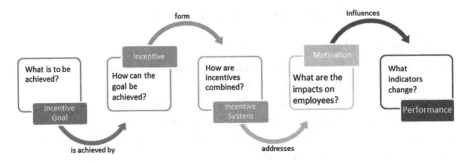

Fig. 4. Components and links of an incentive system

Table 2. Morphological box for incentive systems

Goal	Increase Knowledge Quality			Increase Knowledge Quantity		Increase Usage Quantity
Recipient	Individual			Group		
Instrument	Quiz	Usage Statistics	Peer Recognition	Bonus Payment	Compensatory Time Off	...
Reward System	Sudden Reward	Rolling Reward	Random Reward	Fixed Action Reward	Social Treasure	...
Indicator	Qualitative Indicators			Quantitative Indicators		

Incentive systems for KMS generally can be geared towards increasing the quality of the content, increasing the quantity of the content, or increasing the usage frequency. In addition, achieving the incentive goal might be bound to an individual employee or to a group, i.e. a team of employees.

The incentive system is established by defining the instruments which should be used and by the way the incentives are given to the users. For usage in an IT-based system like the KMS, several instruments are feasible. For example, a quiz is an educational game that increases usage by using gamification approaches [8]. In addition, well-known instruments like bonus payments or non-cash benefits can be used.

5   Conclusion and Outlook

In this paper, insights about the MACKMA project were outlined. The presented steps are necessary preconditions for developing and implementing a KMS tailored to the specific needs of SMEs. Using the product and service portfolio of a company, it is possible to structure existing knowledge using the metamodel. The structure lays the foundation for the KMS content.

To get further insights about specific SME challenges regarding knowledge management, a qualitative survey of SME representatives concerning their understanding of the terms *knowledge, knowledge artifact, knowledge management*, and *knowledge management system* is currently conducted. Though no final results of this survey exist, it can be stated that there exists a wide interpretation spectrum for the different terms. Regarding the term *knowledge management system*, a majority of respondents puts a strong emphasis on methods and tools for supporting knowledge distribution. According to the results, it is also necessary to provide domain-specific knowledge.

The design and implementation of the KMS is influenced by the results of the survey. On the one hand, including an incentive system can help in supporting KMS usage. On the other hand, knowledge distribution requires a unified knowledge description which can be achieved using the metamodel and metadata. Using the metamodel, it is possible to define knowledge artifacts which can be combined according to specific requirements of a company.

Future work will include two aspects. First, a KMS platform will be implemented based on the theoretical findings. The KMS integrates the metamodel and supports the process for defining the product and service portfolio of a company, e.g. by using existing ERP data. The introduction of the KMS will be accompanied by a knowledge management method tailored on the specific needs of SMEs. Second, the customization of knowledge artifacts will be targeted. This is possible by defining influencing factors like the environment which affect possible types and arrangement of knowledge artifacts. For example, the experience of an employee has great impact on the amount of knowledge that is necessary for performing an activity.

References

1. Ojasalo, K.: Customer influence on service productivity. SAM Adv. Manag. J. (07497075) **68**(3), 14–19 (2003)
2. Kramer, F., Wirth, M., Jamous, N., Klingner, S., Becker, M., Friedrich, J., Schneider, M.: Computer-supported knowledge management in SME – a combined qualitative analysis. In: HICSS (2017)
3. Vanini, U., Hauschildt, J.: Wissensmanagement in KMU - Erfahrungen und Implikationen aus dem Praxistest eines Wissensmanagement-Audits in schleswig-holsteinischen Unternehmen. Wissensmanagement **14**(5), 24–26 (2012)
4. Staiger, M.: Wissensmanagement in kleinen und mittelständischen Unternehmen: Systematische Gestaltung einer wissensorientierten Organisationsstruktur und -kultur. Rainer Hampp Verlag, Mering (2008)
5. Stojanovic, L., Stojanovic, N., Handschuh, S.: Evolution of the metadata in the ontology-based knowledge management systems. In: German Workshop on Experience Management (2002)
6. MACKMA Project: MACKMA Architektur, March 2017. https://www.informatik.uni-leipzig.de/ifi/fileadmin/ServiceEngineering/files/hcii/MACKMAArchitektur.pdf
7. Kramer, F., Klingner, S., Becker, M., Friedrich, J., Schneider, M.: The state of SME knowledge management – a multiple case study analysis. In: AMCIS 2016 Proceedings (2016)
8. Mekler, E.D., Brühlmann, F., Tuch, A.N., Opwis, K.: Towards understanding the effects of individual gamification elements on intrinsic motivation and performance. Comput. Hum. Behav. **71**, 525–534 (2017). http://doi.org/10.1016/j.chb.2015.08.048. ISSN: 0747-5632

Design for Inclusion. From Teaching Experiences to Social Changes

Giuseppe Di Bucchianico[⊠]

University of Chieti-Pescara, 65127 Pescara, Italy
`pepetto@unich.it`

Abstract. Aging, disability, multi-ethnicity and multiculturalism, deurbanization, migration: these are some of the most important socio-demographic phenomena that characterize today's society, and which presumably will increase in intensity in the coming decades, especially in Europe. Design for inclusion, through its different approaches, appears immediately as a formidable tool to give a design response to these phenomena, which represent the challenges with which all the social and cultural economic actors will have to confront in the next future. Starting from a short description of the different approaches of design for inclusion, which have developed in recent years for designing environments, products, services and systems that encourage all individuals in the comfortable and self-enjoyment of every aspect of everyday life, this text focuses on the necessity to form consciences and sensitivities related to human diversity and to the value that it brings with it. This starting from the main actors of the design process, ie by designers, but not limited to them, but by involving the largest possible number of active participants in the so-called "value chain". Through the description of some initiatives and teaching experiences, developed in universities, the chapter aims to highlight what the training time can be significant and challenging to increase the sensitivity of the young designers on the issues of human diversity and social inclusion.

Keywords: Design for inclusion · Socio-demographic phenomena · Design teaching experiences

1 The Scenaristic Dimension of Current Social Changes

The scenario of the contemporary world requires new visions and new attitudes, also cultural, to address the current socio-demographic phenomena. Design for inclusion, through its various approaches, offers effective tools with which to address these challenges positively.

1.1 The Social Scenario of Contemporary Life

Contemporary society is changing in character and expectations, with increasing rapidity dynamics. Aging, Disability, multi-ethnicity and multiculturalism, deurbanization, migration flows: these are in fact some of the most important socio-demographic phenomena that characterize today's society, and which presumably will

C. Stephanidis (Ed.): HCII Posters 2017, Part I, CCIS 713, pp. 44–49, 2017.
DOI: 10.1007/978-3-319-58750-9_6

increase in intensity in the coming decades, especially in Europe, where the economic crisis of the past years has contributed to exasperate their negative effects, highlighting tensions and conflicts between peoples, cultures and territories.

With regard to aging, just in Europe, the percentage of the population over 65 has increased by almost 4% in only twenty years[1], with the prediction that in 2060 about 30% of Europe's population will be over 65. Even the growth of "oldest old" (over 80) is particularly significant, quadrupling from 1990 to 2060, reaching 12% of the total population. It is, however, people are often still widely active and so they may have a participatory role and support to social development, from the domestic dimension to that of local communities.

If, with the increase of elderly people in the global demographic picture, also disabilities and sensory, cognitive and physical limitations increase in percentage terms, these add up to those people who have forms of permanent disability: due to medical advances and improved hygienic conditions, in fact, the life expectancy of people with chronic diseases has increased, and this together with a heightened social and cultural awareness to issues of disability, who has put in light requirements and expectations of people with disabilities for a better quality of life and social relationships. This occurred as early as the US movement "barrier free" of the fifties[2], which launched in the Western world a change in public policy process.

In parallel to the qualitative change in the overall demographic picture, in recent decades we are witnessing around the world also to an overall increase of the phenomena related to the mobility of individuals: it is related both to migration of populations who, for various reasons (economic, political, etc.) move between continents, nations, territories, and to the individual scale, leading to the advancement of transportation systems. And if in some ways migration, if properly managed, can probably be for some areas the only possibility of replacement of their working population (and therefore to address the economic difficulties due to the aging of the local population or to the emigration of young generations to richer areas[3]), these phenomena also have an immediate effect on increasing of human diversity (social, ethnic, cultural), immediately putting new issues and challenges to deal with.

1.2   Inclusion and Design for Inclusion

The multigenerational, multi-ethnic and multicultural dimension of contemporary society makes it necessary to reflect on possible ways in which generations, different

---

[1] From 13.7% in 1990 to 17.4% in 2010. Source: European Commission, Third Demography Report, April 2011.

[2] Created to respond especially to the demands in those years of the many people affected by polio, by the war invalids and later by Vietnam veterans, the movement called for more opportunities in education and work rather than an institutionalized health care.

[3] According to a study condicted from AGE Platform Europe, the old-age dependency ratio - the number of elderly people as a share of those of working age - varies significantly between regions. It is highest at 70% in Chemnitz - a region of the former East Germany experiencing significant emigration - and lowest at 15% in inner London, a highly attractive area for young people and workers.

ethnic groups and cultures can meet for a positive share and aware of intercultural conditions, making the relationship between different cultures a tool of coexistence, of wealth and fruitfulness[4].

The way in which different social groups can relate in a positive manner between them are basically two: integration and inclusion, with significant conceptual differences between them.

Social inclusion can be defined as the situation where, in reference to a series of multidimensional aspects (culture, traditions, psychological and physical conditions, etc.), Individuals manage to live according to their original values and traditions and cultures, while improving their own conditions and in mutual respect of other traditions and cultures which they are called to compare with: in this sense the differences between individuals and between the different identities of the groups are socially acceptable, and indeed represent the real wealth of community to which individuals belong.

The term *social integration* means, however, something deeper, that is the inclusion of different identities (cultural, behavioral, etc.). In one unified and uniform framework, within which is not however present any discrimination. Integration is therefore understood as the process by which a social system acquires structural and functional unit, compared to which all are called to conform, acquiring rules and conventions.

In this sense, if social inclusion appears as the first step of an evolutionary process, actually it enhances diversities in the best way and therefore it is more promising in terms of innovation, also from a design point of view.

It follows that design for social inclusion can have clear positive economic and social effects, both in terms of opportunities and visibility for individuals, and especially of collective well-being for the entire economic, social and cultural local systems. Design for inclusion, in fact, is a powerful tool to give a design response to major contemporary socio-demographic phenomena previously mentioned, which represent challenges with which all economic, social and cultural actors will have to compare in the coming decades.

The design for inclusion approaches, however, are numerous, even if related to a common principle and goal, which can be summarized as: "human diversity is a value and every person has the right to receive dignified treatment". Among the main approaches are Universal Design, Inclusive Design and Design for All.

Universal Design (UD). First one to be developed, it not only focuses on people with disabilities, but defines the user extensively, suggesting to make all products and spaces accessible and usable by the greatest extent possible of people. Born in the USA, the didascalic reduction of design validation to seven principles, simple and schematic to be applied and therefore rapidly spreading around the world, it tends not to take into account the individual's complexity and the diversity and variability of mankind.

Inclusive Design (ID). It develops especially in countries of British influence, and poses no dogmatic design principles, but defines a real careful approach to human

---

[4] Consider in this regard, the UNESCO Universal Declaration on Cultural Diversity (Paris, November 2, 2001).

diversity, based on the idea that no criterion, principle or guideline can be absolute but must always deal with the multiplicity of users, contexts and goals. Inclusive Design, in fact, considering the wide range of skills, languages, cultures, genders, ages and all other possible forms of differences among individuals, bases its approach on three "dimensions": to recognize the diversity and uniqueness of individuals, to consider the inclusiveness of the tools and design methodologies, to evaluate the breadth of the impact in terms of benefits.

Design for All (DfA). It aims to improve the quality of life of individuals through the enhancement of their specificity and diversity: a holistic approach to processes and methods of the environments, equipments and services project, accessible "in an autonomous manner" from people with different needs and abilities. It does so mainly through the design development process, which itself is inclusive, participatory and at the same time effective educational, dissemination and social awareness tool, also referred to the same principles of DfA, which was succinctly defined as the "design for human diversity, social inclusion and equality" (EIDD, Stockholm declaration, 2004).

2 The Didactic Dimension of Design for Inclusion

Through new educational experiences included in university courses, aimed at enhancing human diversity and multidisciplinary approach also in addressing simple and seemingly mature project issues, it is possible to start a process of social inclusion, starting from those who will be directly responsible of it in the decades to follow.

2.1 Culture, Behavior and Shared Social Conscience

The first step for inclusion, as complex as necessary, is what needs to be done on the cultural and thus the behavioral level, considering the same "culture" primarily as a cognitive structuring system of experience, individual and collective.

For this purpose it is important, indeed essential, to act on the sensitivity of individuals and their awareness that human diversity is a value and not a problem of contemporary society.

Among them, the designers play a very central role in any planning process. But they are not the only ones to hold this responsibility: it is equally important to involve the largest possible number of active participants to the so-called "value chain" in this action of "conscious awareness" referred to the positive usual meaning of human diversity. This in the idea that to achieve truly "inclusive" projects are not sufficient skill and experience of the designer and the project can not be reduced to simple comparison between client, designer and experienced employees. The best design solution can and must instead come from a widespread social consciousness of participation, including through initiatives to promote "design process" and the dissemination of its results, involving in different ways other social, economic and particularly political "decision makers".

2.2   Some Didactic Experiences

The training time is particularly significant and stimulating to increase the sensitivity of young designers on the themes of human diversity and social inclusion.

In particular, in the Department of Architecture of the University of Chieti-Pescara in recent years some educational experiences aimed at stimulating awareness of young designers on the issues of human diversity and design for inclusion were carried out (in particular concerning the Design for All approach). In particular, among the many possible application areas in relation to which to conduct educational workshops, recently were investigated the productive sectors of equipment and tools of preparation and consumption of food ("Tutti a Tavola!"), and the domestic activities of gardening ("Green for All").

"Tutti a Tavola!". Recently had a particularly successful a teaching project entitled "Tutti a tavola!" ("The dinner is ready ... for All!"). A group of about 70 students of the fourth year of Architecture have addressed the issue of preparation and consuption of food and drink products, through the design of equipment and tools that had to respect the production constraint of being made of ceramic. The most interesting aspect of the experience relates to the diffusion and dissemination of the initiative, which has been able to directly involve different local stakeholders, including government agencies, companies and craftsmen. In fact, a selection of twenty projects have been developed to obtain ceramic prototypes (See Fig. 1). A series of public events organized during the various stages of implementation of the prototypes also allowed to convey awareness on issues of DfA. Finally, the prototypes formed the basis of a collection for a traveling exhibition which has also been presented in the course of some events related to Expo Milano 2015 [1].

Fig. 1. Some moments of the prototype production during public events

"Green for All". A second educational experience, entitled "Green for All", dealt with the issue (in the rapid spread) of home gardening, considered both as a response to the growing awareness of environmental issues, both as a therapy tool (orthicultural therapy) and rehabilitation of specific psychopathology neurological through the care and management of green (growing of flowers, vegetables and other plants). By extending these benefits also to the categories of users not strictly related to disability, and verifying the possible applications in relation to even unconventional contexts, the design workshop urged the students to cope with the design for all issue related to gardening, primarily domestic. With the production constraint of terracotta, the projects were intended to encourage the cultivation of ornamental plants or household spices even in unusual contexts of use (in the kitchen, in the bathroom, in the living room, but also by bike, on the desk or on the bedside table, in the bedroom or in a clinic for long stays). The comparison of the students even with specialists from different fields (technical designer of gardens, etc.) has enabled them to verify the importance of developing multidisciplinary teams (see Fig. 2).

Fig. 2. A design concepts from the didactic lab "Green for All": "height adjustable pot"

3   Conclusions

The experiences synthetically reported in these pages highlight how the training time can be particularly significant and stimulating to increase the sensitivity of young designers on the themes of human diversity and social inclusion.

At the same time educational experiences described also demonstrate how the approach of design for inclusion can be a useful tool to foster innovation, simply by defining design concept referring to productive sectors already consolidated and mature.

Reference

1. Di Bucchianico, G.: Food for All. Sala Editori, Pescara (2015)

Usability Methods and Evaluation Criteria for Published Clinical Guidelines on the Web: A Systematic Literature Review

Soudabeh Khodambashi[(✉)] and Øystein Nytrø

Norwegian University of Science and Technology, Trondheim, Norway
{Soudabeh,Nytroe}@ntnu.no

Abstract. The usability evaluation of published clinical guidelines (GL) on the web is an important analytical tool. This evaluation helps to determine how presentation affects GL use; it identifies the user's needs and assesses whether the user's perceived success rate in finding an answer is reliable or not. Such information is of great value since an inaccurate perceived success rate could lead to potentially critical consequences. This paper explores literature focusing on the usability evaluation of GL web-sites. We examine the evaluation goal, criteria and methods that researchers considered in GL website evaluation. We found that although many researchers have concentrated on the evaluation of clinical decision support systems and their usability; a problem subsists. Evaluation of the usability of published GLs on the Web and the understanding of the users' interaction is in its infancy. Building GL websites is not substantially different than building a highly functional website with high usability in general. However, there are particular factors such as clinicians' time constraints and information overload that need to be considered in the design of a GL website and its evaluation.

Keywords: Clinical guidelines · Guideline website · Evaluation · Usability

1 Introduction

Clinical guidelines (GLs) are widely used. According to the National Guidelines Clearinghouse, more than 320 organizations have been involved in the development of GLs by 2016, including CGLs authoring organizations, academic research groups, and commercial publishers. There is no real length restriction for GLs and they are produced in a variety of digital and print formats. They can be as short as a single page or as long as a booklet of more than 15 pages. Presenting the GL content in PDF format reduces the chance of finding a relevant answer quickly [1]. To increase accessibility, some GL authoring organizations publish their documents on the Web.

Studies on the accessibility of GLs have revealed that clinicians need to find answers to their questions within 2 min [2]. It is therefore highly important that relevant, accurate information is available as quickly and easily as possible and well within this time limit. However, publishing GLs on the Web may not necessarily make them easier to use, as a poor design can make a system difficult to learn and complicated to use and leads to negative consequences [3]. Furthermore finding the right information

C. Stephanidis (Ed.): HCII Posters 2017, Part I, CCIS 713, pp. 50–56, 2017.
DOI: 10.1007/978-3-319-58750-9_7

in a GL and comparing GLs of interest can be challenging for users, especially as the number of electronically available GLs increases. Therefore, a usability evaluation of published GLs on the Web is necessary to investigate how presentation affects GL use. In this paper we systematically reviewed the literature to summarize the existing publications on usability evaluation of published GLs on the Web considering evaluation criteria, metrics and evaluation methods.

2 Materials and Methods

To retrieve and extract data from relevant studies, we performed a systematic literature review using PubMed and Google Scholar databases. The selection process is presented in Fig. 1. The last search was conducted in March 2017. In order to find more relevant literature, we used a backward snowballing method. Note that our literature search did not include clinical decision support system and their usability evaluation. We employed a Thematic analysis method [4] to identify the evaluation themes presented in Table 1: (1) Usability, (2) Using iconic language, (3) Searching, and (4) Patients guidelines.

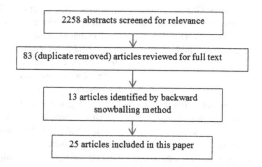

Fig. 1. Selection process of retrieved articles

3 Results

Table 1. Identified articles, their evaluation criteria and methods

Ref.	Evaluation goal/criteria	Method
Theme 1: Usability		
[5]	Evaluation of GL presentation in XML, PDF, and PDA	Evaluation of the satisfaction of GL general users, GL developers and GL reviewers by asking questions
[6]	Evaluating website quality to identify factors affecting health care workers' adoption of GL website: accuracy, completeness, readability,	Semi-structured interviews, the inter-views were based on the PRECEDE (predisposing,

(continued)

Table 1. (*continued*)

Ref.	Evaluation goal/criteria	Method
	design, provided references, disclosures, usability, findability, relevance	reinforcing, and enabling causes in educational diagnosis and evaluation) model
[7]	User experiences of GLs on mobile through the concept of webflow: navigation, learning, focused attention, challenges, orientation	Data from users (who installed the mobile app) was collected through the online questionnaire
[8]	How do GL features influence their use?	Literature search
[9]	Evaluation of acceptability and usefulness	Initial online survey and a more de-tailed follow-up feedback survey emailed to web users
[10]	To assess the effect of differing GL representation formats on the quality of nursing care plans and on the experiences of nurses	Scenario-based and task completion. The GLs were presented in two for-mats: PDF and web based interactive. Participants were asked to 'think-aloud' during task completion and their experiences were recorded, transcribed, and analysed through a cognitive task analysis
[11]	To fine tune the presentation of GL information	Remote collection of both quantitative logging data (browsing) and qualitative use (on user preferences, information) and usability issues from users of GL system
[12]	Case studies on website look and feel	Interviews
[13]	Evaluate how the structure of GLs accompanied with search function impacted finding the right answer, GL usage and efficiency: response accuracy, users' satisfaction and performance	Presenting GLs to the participants (divided in two groups) in two different ways. Survey (questionnaire), scenario based task completion, questionnaire to collect feedback on the GL structure, ease of finding the answer, advantages of the webpage, and their experience with search functionality
[14, 15]	Testing multi-layered presentation format of GLs on their developed prototype: findability, usefulness, usability, understanding, credibility, and desirability	User testing, semi structured interviews (on the overall structure, layout, and components of the format), applying a think-aloud method for exploring important aspects of user experience
[16]	Users' interaction and performance: efficiency, effectiveness, learnability, response accuracy, number of mouse clicks and usage rate for search functions, task completion time, users' objective and perception of task success rate, and learning effect for inexperienced users	Five GL websites were evaluated and compared using an eye-tracker, a preliminary survey, a scenario-based task completion, and a semi-structured interview
[17]	Usability evaluation of five GL websites and users' feedback. Metric: perceived usability	A pretest survey, scenario-based task completion, system usability scale (SUS) questionnaire, observation, and semi-structured interview
[18]	To evaluate the efficacy, acceptability and feasibility of using QR codes to facilitate 'Just in Time' learning of GLs by measuring usage statistics such as page views, unique page views and average time spent on page	Website analytics and semi-structured interviews
[19]	Comparing different methods of GL dissemination: "health professionals' perceived" usability and practice behaviour change of information and communication technologies	Systematic literature survey

Table 1. (*continued*)

Ref.	Evaluation goal/criteria	Method
[14, 20]	To investigate physicians' preferences, perceived usefulness and understanding of a new multi-layered GL presentation format compared to a standard format	View random clinical scenario and GL recommendation in a multi-layered format or standard format to physicians after which they answered multiple-choice questions using clickers

Theme 2: Using iconic language

Ref.	Evaluation goal/criteria	Method
[21]	To assess VCM, if the language is easy to learn, understand and use. Respondents' document length and question type were documented and evaluated	Participants were asked to register VCM training time, to indicate the meaning of VCM icons and sentences, and to answer clinical questions related to randomly generated drug monograph-like documents, supplied in text or VCM format. Compared the correctness of responses and the response times obtained with text and VCM and applied linear regression analysis
[22]	Usability study of an iconic user interface to ease information retrieval of GLs, comparing a Visualization of Concepts (VMC) with a non-VCM inter-face: time taken, users' ability, and perceived usefulness	Scenario-based (two different scenarios for each interface). The ability and time taken to select a relevant re-source were recorded and compared. A usability analysis was performed using SUS
[23]	To evaluate VCM for the consultation of GLs: response times, number of errors, response accuracy, perceived usability	Comparison of response times, response accuracy and the number of recorded errors during task completion using VCM or a textual interface. Users' perceived usability was evaluated with SUS

Theme 3: Searching

Ref.	Evaluation goal/criteria	Method
[24]	Comparing concept-based and context-sensitive GL search in free-text search retrieval performance	Precision and recall of the designed search engines
[25]	Health information-seeking behaviour on the Web: internet use and ascertaining challenges	Literature review on the topic area from 2006 to 2010
[26]	Comparing user experiences and perceived usability on two proto-types: search-based and content-based recommendation ranking of GLs	A survey (pretest questionnaire), scenario-based with given tasks, SUS and interview
[27]	Information searching behaviour of medical students, evaluated the effect of varying levels of task difficulty on search behaviour according to demographic variables. Querying details, search results interaction details, querying versus clicking behaviour and task completion time were evaluated	Participants were attended in an inter-active information retrieval experiment type methodology that was used to study the interactive searching behaviour with structured observation

Theme 4: Patients guidelines

Ref.	Evaluation goal/criteria	Method
[28]	To assess their Portal's functionality, effectiveness and identify any usability problems from perspective of the patients: the quality of the provided information, whether the information they accessed had helped in any decisions they had to make, and the preferred search options	Two focus groups reviewed the usefulness of the Portal, 6 women participated in the pilot usability evaluation, and 13 women participated in the onsite usability evaluation
[29]	User test of a patient version of a SIGN GLs	Using a think-aloud protocol method, all sessions were recorded and transcribed

4 Discussion and Conclusion

According to the results, no gold standard has been considered in the GL website evaluations. We identified that measuring efficiency was the most used criteria in GL evaluation including task completion time, time spent and number of made errors. The second most popular evaluative criteria was perceived usefulness by applying SUS method, followed by presentation format. The number of evaluations focusing on usability and usefulness, however reviewing the articles revealed that it is not clear how they evaluated them. It is necessary for researchers clearly report how they evaluate and measure usefulness and usability. Although searching function is one of the important factors in findability of information on a GL website, not much attention has been paid to it. GL websites should not only be assessed by ease of use, presentation format, layout, and supported digital features with intuitive and simplified navigation, but also it is necessary that efficient search and the format of search results presentation are evaluated. As clinicians' time constraints and information overload are two factors in GLs adoption, evaluation of the search function and its retrieval performance in efficiently identifying relevant GLs is needed (i.e. a trained search function for clinical terms, especially for synonyms, acronyms, and abbreviations).

References

1. Green, M.L., Ciampi, M.A., Ellis, P.J.: Residents' medical information needs in clinic: are they being met? Am. J. Med. **109**, 218–223 (2000)
2. Coumou, H.C., Meijman, F.J.: How do primary care physicians seek answers to clinical questions? A literature review. J. Med. Libr. Assoc. **94**, 55 (2006)
3. Jaspers, M.W.M.: A comparison of usability methods for testing interactive health technologies: Methodological aspects and empirical evidence. Int. J. Med. Inform. **78**, 340–353 (2009)
4. Cruzes, D.S., Dyba, T.: Recommended steps for thematic synthesis in software engineering. In: 2011 International Symposium on Empirical Software Engineering and Measurement (ESEM), pp. 275–284 (2011)
5. Park, M.: Development and evaluation of online evidence based guideline bank system. Stud. Health Technol. Inform. **122**, 105 (2006)
6. Verhoeven, F., Steehouder, M.F., Hendrix, R.M., van Gemert-Pijnen, J.E.: Factors affecting health care workers' adoption of a website with infection control guidelines. Int. J. Med. Inform. **78**, 663–678 (2009)
7. Oinas-Kukkonen, H., Raisanen, T., Leiviska, K., Seppanen, M., Kallio, M.: Physicians' user experiences of mobile pharmacopoeias and evidence-based medical guidelines. Int. J. Healthc. Inf. Syst. Inform. (IJHISI) **4**, 57–68 (2009)
8. Gagliardi, A.R., Brouwers, M.C., Palda, V.A., Lemieux-Charles, L., Grimshaw, J.M.: How can we improve guideline use? A conceptual framework of implementability. Implement. Sci. **6**, 26 (2011)
9. Berk, L., Berk, M., Dodd, S., Kelly, C., Cvetkovski, S., Jorm, A.F.: Evaluation of the acceptability and usefulness of an information website for caregivers of people with bipolar disorder. BMC Med. **11**, 162 (2013)

10. Csima, D.G.: The effect of clinical practice guideline representation on nursing care planning, University of Victoria, Canada (2013)
11. Kushniruk, A., Kaipio, J., Nieminen, M., Hyppönen, H., Lääveri, T., Nohr, C., Kanstrup, A.M., Christiansen, M.B., Kuo, M.-H., Borycki, E.: Human factors in the large: experiences from Denmark, Finland and Canada in moving towards regional and national evaluations of health information system usability: contribution of the IMIA human factors working group. Yearb. Med. Inform. **9**, 67 (2014)
12. Horvath, K.J., Ecklund, A.M., Hunt, S.L., Nelson, T.F., Toomey, T.L.: Developing internet-based health interventions: a guide for public health researchers and practitioners. J. Med. Internet Res. **17**, e28 (2015)
13. Khodambashi, S., Wang, Z., Nytrø, Ø.: Reality versus user's perception in finding answer to clinical questions in published national guidelines on the web: an empirical study. Proced. Comput. Sci. **63**, 268–275 (2015)
14. Kristiansen, A.: Dissemination and adaptation strategies customized for trustworthy practice guidelines using the GRADE framework (2016)
15. Kristiansen, A., Brandt, L., Alonso-Coello, P., Agoritsas, T., Akl, E.A., Conboy, T., Elbarbary, M., Ferwana, M., Medani, W., Murad, M.H.: Development of a novel, multilayered presentation format for clinical practice guidelines. CHEST J. **147**, 754–763 (2015)
16. Khodambashi, S., Gilstad, H., Nytrø, Ø.: Usability evaluation of clinical guidelines on the web using eye-tracker. In: Medical Informatics Europe (MIE 2016) (2016)
17. Khodambashi, S., Nytrø, Ø.: Usability evaluation of published clinical guidelines on the web: a case study. Accepted-under publication (2016)
18. Jamu, J.T., Lowi-Jones, H., Mitchell, C.: Just in time? Using QR codes for multi-professional learning in clinical practice. Nurse Educ. Pract. **19**, 107–112 (2016)
19. De Angelis, G., Davies, B., King, J., McEwan, J., Cavallo, S., Loew, L., Wells, G.A., Brosseau, L.: Information and communication technologies for the dissemination of clinical practice guidelines to health professionals: a systematic review. JMIR Med. Educ. **2** (2016)
20. Brandt, L., Vandvik, P.O., Alonso-Coello, P., Akl, E.A., Thornton, J., Rigau, D., Adams, K., O'Connor, P., Guyatt, G., Kristiansen, A.: Multilayered and digitally structured presentation formats of trustworthy recommendations: a combined survey and randomised trial. BMJ Open **7**, e011569 (2017)
21. Lamy, J.-B., Duclos, C., Bar-Hen, A., Ouvrard, P., Venot, A.: An iconic language for the graphical representation of medical concepts. BMC Med. Inform. Decis. Mak. **8**, 16 (2008)
22. Griffon, N., Kerdelhué, G., Hamek, S., Hassler, S., Boog, C., Lamy, J.-B., Duclos, C., Venot, A., Darmoni, S.J.: Design and usability study of an iconic user interface to ease information retrieval of medical guidelines. J. Am. Med. Inform. Assoc. **21**, e270–e277 (2014)
23. Pereira, S., Hassler, S., Hamek, S., Boog, C., Leroy, N., Beuscart-Zéphir, M.-C., Favre, M., Venot, A., Duclos, C., Lamy, J.-B.: Improving access to clinical practice guidelines with an interactive graphical interface using an iconic language. BMC Med. Inform. Decis. Mak. **14**, 77 (2014)
24. Moskovitch, R., Shahar, Y.: Vaidurya: a multiple-ontology, concept-based, context-sensitive clinical-guideline search engine. J. Biomed. Inform. **42**, 11–21 (2009)
25. Barry, M.M., Domegan, C., Higgins, O., Sixsmith, J.: A literature review on health information seeking behaviour on the web: a health consumer and health professional perspective (2011)
26. Khodambashi, S., Perry, A., Nytrø, Ø.: Comparing user experiences on the search-based and content-based recommendation ranking on stroke clinical guidelines-a case study. Proced. Comput. Sci. **63**, 260–267 (2015)

27. Inthiran, A., Alhashmi, S.M., Ahmed, P.K.: A user study on the information search behaviour of medical students. Malays. J. Libr. Inf. Sci. **20**, 61–77 (2015)

28. McKemmish, S., Manaszewicz, R., Burstein, F., Fisher, J.: Consumer empowerment through metadata-based information quality reporting: the breast cancer knowledge online portal. J. Assoc. Inf. Sci. Technol. **60**, 1792–1807 (2009)

29. Fearns, N., Graham, K., Johnston, G.: Improving the user experience of patient versions of clinical guidelines: user testing of a Scottish Intercollegiate Guideline Network (SIGN) patient version. BMC Health Serv. Res. **16**, 37 (2016)

The Assessment Tool for User Perceived Interactivity from ACG Website Interactivity on Imagination

Juihsiang Lee[✉]

Department of Multimedia Design,
China University of Technology, Taipei, Taiwan, R.O.C.
leockmail@gmail.com

Abstract. The purpose of this study is to examine the relationships between four dimensions of user perceived interactivity: user control, responsiveness, connectedness, social interaction and consumers' perceived imagination composed of reproductive and creative in web interaction environment, finally determining the level of overall satisfaction with ACG website engagements. The process of research aimed at developing a rigorous empirical measurement scale for attitudes toward social media that specifically applies to ACG websites, as suggested by expert interviews. Items covering engagement, satisfaction, and imagination were identified through literature review and expert interviews. Following the suggestion of Churchill (1979), Sethi and King (1994), and relevant literature on scale development, this research followed the process of building the initial pool, interviewing the experts, purifying the items, and assessing the reliability and validity through a pilot test and the formal survey. The final model delete "user control" and retain other three dimensions, "responsiveness", "connectedness", "social interaction" for the construct of perceived interactivity. And the measure scale consisted of 4 items for social interaction, 4 items for responsiveness, 4 items for connectedness, 5 items for engagement, 4 for satisfaction, and 6 for imagination dimensions, respectively. A four-phase method was performed and confirmatory factor analysis was verified.

Keywords: Web interactivity · Perceived interactivity · Imagination

1 Introductory

Social media have managed to bring participants together from all over the world who get in touch online and communicate virtually with each other even if they have never met. Participants provide information on their lives and their selves of their own free will and consent (van Dijck 2013) illustrate the tremendous capabilities existing in social media for connecting and bringing people together, sharing experiences, ideas, information and their lives in general.

Enthusiastic users of ACG (Animation, Comic, Games) have three characteristics arising from their unique behavioral principles described by Kitabayashi (2004): (1) strong orientation toward forming a community, (2) extending their influence with

C. Stephanidis (Ed.): HCII Posters 2017, Part I, CCIS 713, pp. 57–65, 2017.
DOI: 10.1007/978-3-319-58750-9_8

the use of IT, (3) actively creating fan fictions. They are socially inept although but enjoy socializing with others via the Internet (Niu et al. 2012).

One of the advantages of Internet is its potential for interactivity (Kim 2011). Many studies concluded that human creativity may be influenced by the interaction between personal and environmental variables (Shalley et al. 2004). Novel applications of website interactivity are important to attract and retain online users.

Researchers distinguished the features of social media: some sites like Facebook is for the general masses. Other sites, like LinkedIn, are more focused professional networks. Media sharing sites, such as MySpace, YouTube, and Flickr, concentrate on shared videos and photos. Registered users can rate (like/dislike), upload videos, comment on and share them. This phenomenon has given a greater degree of control to social media users in creating and manipulating content not only creating a sense of community (Kietzmann et al. 2011).

And after a slow start in the late 2000s, 2channel, CGSOCIETY, pixiv, ACG artifact work sharing platform have become very popular to artists, because they are easy to create and to maintain. A great deal needs to be learned about why and how users participate and consume information on various online sites.

Exceptional artists and scientists believe that imagination has a profound impact on their creations (Dewey 1910; Trotman 2006). Imagination is different from creativity, but it can be perceived as the vehicle of active creativity (Gaut 2003). Crucial to understanding the future of social media is studying the characteristics that make these sites appealing to people.

This study try to address the factors of ACG website interactivity that influence users' imagination of creativity, and whether the websites engagements and satisfactory would be the mediated factors or not.

2 Literature Review

2.1 Perceived Interactivity

Effective communication with customers is the key to successful business. One of the most important factors for effective communication is known as interactivity. Although the worldwide interconnection of individual networks operated by government, industry, academy and private parties defines the Internet, user communicate online is mediated through the web, using a graphical display without any face-to-face interaction with others. Interactivity is therefore the central to these emerging computer mediated environments.

Cyr et al. (2009) argued that there is no well-established scope and definition for "interactivity" (Johnson et al. 2006; Lee 2005), although the concept is regarded as crucial to successful online marketing (Lee 2005).

This article adopted Srinivasan et al. (2002, p. 42) operationalize interactivity "as the availability and effectiveness of customer support tools on a website, and the degree to which two-way communication with customers is facilitated". Perceived Interactivity will be the individual variable of this research.

Lee identified (1) user control, (2) responsiveness, (3) personalization, and (4) connectedness as important components to interactivity in a mobile commerce setting. Other than these three core constructs, Abdullah and Kamal (2016) pointed out that sociability is a newly emerging component of interactivity. It represents the site's capability to allow users to connect with other people through chat rooms, blogs and social networking tools (Macias 2003).

2.2   Engagement of Social Media

As the usage of information and communication technologies, and most notably social media, has become increasingly widespread, this has also become a research setting in which consumer engagement in particular has become increasingly discussed.

Social media represents a platform that is filled with expressions of social interaction based on activities explicated in this virtual space. Therefore, internet users who participate in social media have been understood to be socially engaged.

Engagement may be viewed as an individual's interaction with media. Hollebeek (2011) viewed engagement as a multidimensional concept that comprises not only behavioral but also cognitive, and emotional aspects. This study adopts Achterberg et al. (2003) defined engagement as an adequate response to social stimuli resulting in participation in social activities and interaction with others. The concept of consumer engagement has been argued to be based on an interactive relationship between consumers, a focal object and the resulting perceived value experience of this interaction (Brodie et al. 2013; Khan 2017). The engagement measured by Khan (2017), builds upon the motives, but also perceives their relationship with user participation in the form of liking, disliking, commenting, uploading, and sharing, and consumption in the form of content reading and viewing.

Engagement will be the mediated variable of the research model, and we will also measure the direct influence by the perceived interactivity.

2.3   Satisfaction

Satisfaction is a post-consumption evaluation based on the comparison between expected value in the pre-consumption stage and perceived post-consumption value after the purchase or after the use of services or products (Oliver 1981; Ravald and Grönroos 1996). Yoo et al. (2010) attempted to extend the relationship between perceived value and satisfaction to an e-commerce context. They examine the relationships between three dimensions of interactivity and consumers' perceived value composed of utilitarian and hedonic values on e-shopping, finally determining the level of overall satisfaction on using interactivity features in e-tailing service.

Satisfaction will be the mediated variable between engagement and imagination of the research model, and we will also find the direct influence by the perceived interactivity.

2.4 Imagination

Imagination enables people to go beyond actual experience and construct alternative possibilities in which a fragmented situation becomes a meaningful whole (Passmore 1985). Imagination is conceptually most-closely related to creativity, generativity, divergent thinking, narrative production, and theory of mind (Crespi et al. 2016). It is one of the most important cognitive capacities, and thus can be perceived as the vehicle of active creativity (Gaut 2003; Heath 2008).

Many scholars have indicated that the activities of human imagination can be classified into two different categories: reproductive imagination and creative imagination (e.g., Betts 1916; Colello 2007).

Reproductive imagination is characterized by the capability to reproduce mental images described by others or images from less accurate recollections of reality. This type of imagination is comprised of four characteristics, namely crystallization, dialectics, effectiveness and transformation (Liang et al. 2012). In contrast, creative imagination emphasizes the attributes of initiation and originality. This type of imagination is composed of six characteristics, namely exploration, concentration, intuition, novelty, productivity and sensibility (Liang et al. 2012).

3 Methodology

Based on the prior literature, a model was proposed and structural equation modeling was conducted using Amos to evaluate the fit of the research model. Structural equation modeling is appropriate for this study, because the proposed relationships can be analyzed simultaneously for their associations.

We used a systematic four-phase process involving a variety of methods to develop and validate the measurement of engagement, satisfaction, imagination, with perceived interactivity in the web environment. This four-phase process is developed based on Churchill (1979) and Sethi and King (1994).

(1) In the first phase, conceptual development and initial item generation, tentative measures were either borrowed or developed from the existing literature.
(2) In the second phase, conceptual refinement and item modification, a list of defined constructs and measures was submitted to a panel of four senior ACG artists, who were recognized as authorities on the subject of ACG graphic and cosplay. We requested the panel members to assign each measure to the construct they believed was appropriate and note whether they thought the construct could be represented by any other measures.
(3) The third phase, survey data collection, 98 university students of sub-cultural group reviewed a preliminary version of the instrument for precision and clearness. Widely applied in numerous fields of knowledge, SEM is a multivariate, statistical technique largely employed for studying relationships between latent variables (or constructs) and observed variables that constitute a model.
(4) In the final phase, data analysis and measurement validation. A pretest was conducted among 121 consumers. During all the stages, the questionnaire was progressively refined, simplified and shortened.

4 Measurement Development Process

(1) In the first phase, conceptual development and initial item generation, tentative measures were either borrowed or developed from the existing literature.

(2) The framework and initial pool of 72 measures resulted from Phase 1 were refined and modified through a sorting procedure and two pilot tests. The sorting procedure was used to qualitatively assess the face validity and the construct validity of the initial items. Four senior ACG enthusiasts with an average of eight years of art creative work experience participated in the sorting procedure. Overall, 54 measures were retained after the sorting procedure.

To further validate the relevance, coverage, and clarity of the measurement items, we conducted two pilot tests. The first pilot test was conducted through one-hour individual interviews with four senior ACG enthusiasts and two IS researchers. In the interview, the participant first filled out a questionnaire regarding the importance and relevance of each item to the creative art sharing website. They were then asked to identify items that appeared to be inappropriate or irrelevant to the creative art sharing website also made suggestions for improving the relevance, coverage, understandability, and clarity of the items. Five items were dropped based on the results of the pilot test. Two items were combined into a single item because of their similarity.

(3) After refining the items, we created an online survey questionnaire using the remaining 48 items. To reveal any potential problems or issues with web-based online survey, a second pilot test was conducted with 98 students form the sub-culture of Japan anima/comic groups who had an average above four platforms experiences in art creative sharing work on the website.

(4) Confirmatory factor analysis with structural equation model was used to test the measures that were resulted from the plot test.

A. The construct of Imagination: The data indicates that 6 observed variables retained whose factor loading were above 0.7, C.R. = 0.947 were above 0.7 (suggested by Hair 1998), AVE = 0.750 were above 0.5 (suggested by Fornell and Larcker 1981), and three items, IMA 2, 3, 8, were delete after confirmatory factor analysis.

B. The construct of Satisfaction: The data indicates that GFI = 0.986 ≥ 0.9, AGFI = 0.932 ≥ 0.9, rmsea = 0.066 < 0.08, 3 observed variables factor loading were above 0.7 only one was lower, and whose C.R. = 0.881 were above 0.7, AVE = 0.653 were above 0.5, all retained after confirmatory factor analysis.

C. The construct of Engagement: There were 15 observed variables in the origin, after CFA only retain EGA 2, 3, 4, 5, 12 whose factor loading were above 0.7, C.R. = 0.907 were above 0.7, AVE = 0.666 were above 0.5, GFI = 0.995 ≥ 0.9, AGFI = 0.985 ≥ 0.9, rmsea = 0.000 ≤ 0.08.

D. The construct of User control: There were 4 observed variables in the origin, but the model fit were not proper even we delete anyone after CFA. Considered the indexes were not proper or significant, this study gives up to retain this construct.

E. The construct of Connectedness: As we delete 2 variables after CFA, then GFI = 0.989 ≧ 0.9, AGFI = 0.943 ≧ 0.9, normed chi-square = 1.068, C. R. = 0.868 were above 0.7, AVE = 0.622 were above 0.5, even there were 6 observed variables in the origin.

F. The construct of Responsiveness: The data indicates that GFI = 0.981 ≧ 0.9, AGFI = 0.905 ≧ 0.9, normed chi-square = 1.879, 4 observed variables factor loading were above 0.7 only one was lower, and whose C.R. = 0.899 were above 0.7, AVE = 0.695 were above 0.5, all retained after confirmatory factor analysis.

G. The construct of Social Interaction: As we delete 2 variables after CFA, then GFI = 0.988 ≧ 0.9, AGFI = 0.942 ≧ 0.9, C.R. = 0.853 were above 0.7, AVE = 0.597 were above 0.5, even there were 6 observed variables in the origin.

5   Results

The final model consisted of 6 items for Imagination, 4 for satisfaction, and 5 for engagement, 3 dimensions for perceived interactivity, 4 for connectedness, 4 for responsiveness, 4 for social interaction dimensions, respectively. All the observed variables See Table 1.

Table 1. The final questionnaire

Constructs	Items	Observed variables
Imagination	IMA1	I am curios to explore the new stuffs or things I might not know, after use this website
	IMA4	I can express an abstract concept instead with concrete image, after use this website
	IMA5	I can reproduce my original idea into new one, after use this website
	IMA6	I produce unique ideas or improve my original idea into new one usually, after use this website
	IMA7	I inspired lots of thinking or ideas, after use this website
	IMA9	I inspired lots of thinking or ideas, after use this website
Satisfaction	SAT1	I was satisfying of the online creative sharing experience overall on this website
	SAT2	I was satisfying for the effective service of the online creative sharing experience overall on this website
	SAT3	I was satisfying for the information searching of the online creative sharing experience overall on this website
	SAT4	I was pleasant of the online creative sharing experience overall on this website

(*continued*)

Table 1. (*continued*)

Constructs	Items	Observed variables
Engagement	EGA2	I am interesting to use this website more frequently to learn how to do things better
	EGA4	I am interesting to use this website more frequently to follow current news or events
	EGA3	I am interesting to use this website more frequently to find what the new things were
	EGA5	I am interesting to use this website more frequently to offer information to others
	EGA12	I am interesting to use this website more frequently to get more fun
Connectedness	CON1	This website offer the "hot collections", help me to know the most popular artifact works
	CON3	This website offer the "rankings", help me to know the evaluate line by the masses
	CON4	This website offer "the drawers you may know", help me easy to search
	CON6	I like this website offer the links help me easy to link in and out
Responsiveness	RES1	I like this website can feedback the users ranking properly
	RES2	I like this website can response users' unique requires, like serials, characters, or labels properly
	RES3	I like this website can help me to receive my regarding user's new work in real time
	RES4	I like this website can offer the latest ACG information from Japan per season
Social interaction	SCI1	I like this website let me what others discussed
	SCI3	I like this website let me express myself free
	SCI5	I like this website let me know who the popular users were
	SCI6	I like this website let me organize my own group

References

Abdullah, J., Kamal, B.M.: A conceptual model of interactive hotel website: the role of perceived website interactivity and customer perceived value toward website revisit intention. Procedia Econ. Financ. **37**, 170–175 (2016)

Achterberg, W., Pot, A.M., Kerkstra, A., Ooms, M., Muller, M., Ribbe, M.: The effect of depression on social engagement in newly admitted Dutch nursing home residents. Gerontologist **43**(2), 213–218 (2003)

Betts, G.H.: Chapter IX: Imagination. The Mind and Its Education (e-Book). D. Appleton and Company, New York (1916)

Brodie, R.J., Ilic, A., Juric, B., Hollebeek, L.: Consumer engagement in a virtual brand community: an exploratory analysis. J. Bus. Res. **66**(1), 105e114 (2013). http://dx.doi.org/10.1016/j.jbusres.2011.07.029

Churchill Jr., G.A.: A paradigm for developing better measures of marketing constructs. J. Mark. Res. **16**(1), 64–73 (1979)

Colello, S.M.G.: Imagination in children's writing: how high can fiction fly? Notandum **10**(14) (2007). http://www.hottopos.com/notand14/silvia.pdf. Accessed 11 Aug 2012

Crespi, B., Leach, E., Dinsdale, N., Mokkonen, M., Hurd, P.: Imagination in human social cognition, autism, and psychotic-affective conditions. Cognition **150**, 181–199 (2016)

Cyr, D., Head, M., Ivanov, A.: Perceived interactivity leading to e-loyalty: development of a model for cognitive-affective user responses. Int. J. Hum. Comput. Stud. **67**, 850–869 (2009)

Dewey, J.: How We Think, p. 7. Dover Publications, Mineola (1910)

Fornell, C.R., Larcker, F.F.: Structural Equation Models with unobservable variables and measurement error. J. Mark. Res. **18**, 39–51 (1981)

Gaut, B.: Creativity and imagination. In: Gaut, B., Livingston, P. (eds.) The Creation of Art, pp. 148–173. Cambridge University Press, Cambridge (2003)

Hair, J.F., Anderson, R.E., Tatham, R.L., Black, W.C.: Multivariate Data Analysis, 5th edn. Macmillan, New York (1998)

Heath, G.: Exploring the imagination to establish frameworks for learning. Stud. Philos. Educ. **27** (2), 115–123 (2008)

Hollebeek, L.D.: Demystifying customer brand engagement: exploring the loyalty nexus. J. Mark. Manag. **27**(7–8), 785–807 (2011)

Johnson, G.J., Bruner, G.C., Kumar, A.: Interactivity and its facets revisited. J. Advert. **35**(4), 35–52 (2006)

Khan, M.L.: Social media engagement: what motivates user participation and consumption on YouTube? Comput. Hum. Behav. **66**, 236–247 (2017)

Kietzmann, J.H., Hermkens, K., McCarthy, I.P., Silvestre, B.S.: Social media? Get serious! Understanding the functional building blocks of social media. Bus. Horiz. **54**, 241–251 (2011)

Kim, S.: Web-interactivity dimensions and shopping experiential value. J. Internet Bus. **9**, 1–25 (2011)

Kitabayashi, K.: The Otaku Group from a Business Perspective: Revaluation of Enthusiastic Customers (PDF). Nomura Research Institute, Tokyo (2004)

Lee, T.: The impact of perceptions of interactivity on customer trust and transaction intentions in mobile commerce. J. Electron. Commer. Res. **6**(3), 165–180 (2005)

Liang, C.: The predictive model of imagination stimulation. J. Technol. Eng. Educ. **46**(2), 50–70 (2013)

Liang, C., Hsu, Y., Chang, C.-C., Lin, L.-J.: In search of an index of imagination for virtual experience designers. Int. J. Technol. Des. Educ. (2012). doi:10.1007/s10798-012-9224-6

Macias, W.: A preliminary structural equation model of comprehension and persuasion of interactive advertising brand web sites. J. Interact. Advertising **3**(2), 36–48 (2003)

Oliver, R.L.: Measurement and evaluation of satisfaction process in retail settings. J. Retail. **57** (3), 25–48 (1981)

Passmore, J.: Recent Philosophers: A Supplement to a Hundred Years of Philosophy. Duckworth, New York (1985)

Niu, H.J., Chiang, Y.S., Tsai, H.T.: An exploratory study of the otaku adolescent consumer. Psychol. Mark. **29**(10), 712–725 (2012). doi:10.1002/mar.20558

Ravald, A., Grönroos, C.: The value concept and relationship marketing. Eur. J. Mark. **30**(2), 19–30 (1996)

Sethi, V., King, W.R.: Development of measures to assess the extent to which an information technology application provides competitive advantage. Manag. Sci. **40**(12), 1601–1627 (1994)

Shalley, C.E., Zhou, J., Oldham, G.R.: The effects of personal and contextual characteristics on creativity: where should we go from here? J. Manag. **30**(6), 933–958 (2004)

Srinivasan, S., Anderson, R., Ponnavolu, K.: Customer loyalty in e-commerce: an exploration of its antecedents and consequences. J. Retail. **78**(1), 41–50 (2002)

Trotman, D.: Evaluating the imaginative: situated practice and the conditions for professional judgment in imaginative education. Int. J. Educ. Arts **7**(3) (2006). http://ijea.asu.edu/v7n3/. Accessed 08 Mar 2013

van Dijck, J.: 'You have one identity': performing the self on Facebook and LinkedIn. Media Cult. Soc. **35**(2), 199–235 (2013)

Yoo, W.S., Lee, Y., Park, J.: The role of interactivity in e-tailing: creating value and increasing satisfaction. J. Retail. Consum. Serv. **17**, 89–96 (2010)

From Spectator to Co-creator for Hybrid Social Space: A New Taxonomy for Participatory Social Interaction and Co-creation

Yun Tae Nam[1(✉)] and Je-ho Oh[2]

[1] Art, Design and Architecture, Monash University,
Melbourne, Australia
yun.nam@monash.edu
[2] GSCT, KAIST, Daejeon, Republic of Korea
anomewho@kaist.ac.kr

Abstract. This study attempts to articulate the taxonomy of contemporary participatory user terms and interactions in participatory design (PD) and HCI research and practice. This research has redeveloped definitions of users based on four levels of users' engagement and social interaction with the artifact (system or design or product or service) – ranging from passive spectators toward active co-creators. This proposed Participatory Co-creator Users Continuum model can be used to support a social context for designing mediated environments with the aim of enhancing participation and social interaction within urban public spaces, where the user is a co-creator involved in meaningful social interaction with others and the world.

Keywords: Third-wave HCI · Urban HCI · Co-design · Participatory design · Social interaction · Hybrid social space · Public space · Shared encounter · Co-creation · Co-creator · Participatory social interaction · Smart city

1 Introduction

Participation and social interaction for designing a mediated environment within public spaces have been engaged with a popular topic of the study in participatory design (PD) and HCI [1–4]. Traditionally, designers and researchers have treated users as passive spectators. The emergence of Co-design; co-creation in PD [5] and Urban HCI [6] with regard to Third-wave HCI [7] has resulted in the user becoming an integral part of the design process. There is also evidence that the use of new communications HCI technology can increase and enhance social interaction such as social media platforms; wikis, Facebook, Twitter, YouTube and Google Docs. Users play an important role of active participation and social interaction in challenges and opportunities for creative innovation. It denotes a paradigm shift from man-machine to socially engaged [8], phenomenologically situated as the Third-paradigm HCI [9]. However, there has been in PD and HCI research and practice numerous broad terms to describe users such as stakeholder, citizen, audience, visitor, actor, user, consumer, customer, people, human,

© Springer International Publishing AG 2017
C. Stephanidis (Ed.): HCII Posters 2017, Part I, CCIS 713, pp. 66–72, 2017.
DOI: 10.1007/978-3-319-58750-9_9

spectator, observer, participant and co-creator. Of course when the designer and researcher use the term in different contexts in relation to their research objectives by their definitions. However it is a problematic to identify what is the factor of transforming the mode of interaction, for instance, from passive spectator to active participant, potentially to co-creator, questions raised whether a system or human factor or social-cultural norm affected or not. We thus propose a new taxonomy of Participatory Co-creator Users Continuum model to better understanding of how people use and interact with the artifact (system or design or product or service) within public spaces, and the aim for facilitating active participation and social interaction through the artifact is to support mediated environments where situated action and meaning-making is valuable in smart city contexts.

2 Participatory Social Interaction by Rule

Social interaction is a set of rules by which people act and react to those around us. [10, 11] Goffman introduced three-layer model of such interaction (occasion, situation and encounter) by observation of human behavior in public spaces [10], the "occasion" is the boarder social construct that defines how we know or should know how to act: for instance, where people gathered, a social-cultural norm operating at a funeral which determined that people behave quietly, whereas, at a concert, participants are allowed to scream. People behave at different "occasions" through learned behavior from previous experience or observation. The environment or society shapes people how to act differently based on social-cultural norms.

The "situation" is the manifestation of the "occasion" and is an environment of potential communication between people. For example, a situation determines how one would talk, react, position oneself in relation to others. A concert is a situation where participants would speak more loudly than normal in order to communicate with a friend nearby. This would be an accepted form of communication because the occasion of the concert created a situation where loud music determined the nature of how people encountered each other.

An "encounter" is the very essential part of social interaction. When two or more people gather and a shared object exits, Goffman argues that such an "encounter" constitutes the norms that shape the interaction [10].

Ludvigsen expanded the user into four different social engagement levels (distributed attention, shared focus, dialogue and collective action) [11] based on the concepts of "occasions", "situations" and "encounters" for public spaces. [10] By considering the impact of HCI technology has on social interactive process such as a dialogue between users and collective experience rather than focus on individuals' experience. Ludvigsen suggests that "dialogue" does not occur in digitally generated environments, basing his argument on online games such as Counter Striker or World of Warcraft. [11] Thus, while his projects utilize HCI technology, they are based in physical spaces such as a library iFloor (2005) [11], where encounters are determined by the rules of the situation, the conventions that are adopted by participants. Dialogue that occurs in an encounter is traditionally understood as a form of actual face to face engagement: in the library, for example, the HCI interface and the media objects aim to encourage dialogue between users determined by the situation of a library, where one looks for books. However, the nature of a social encounter and the dialogue that occurs need not be limited to face to face encounters.

Contemporary Urban HCI technologies are transforming a public space into a social space in unprecedented ways. In fact, the prevalence of HCI is transforming our traditional understanding of the social/economic/cultural/political boundaries of a given space. [12, 13] Ubiquitous computing [14], pervasive computing [15], ambient intelligence [16] and the recent concept of "pervasive connected devices" or "smart devices" often referred to as the internet of Things (IoT) [17]: these have all contributed to arguments for an "anywhere" space [18], a hybrid social space that is transforming the political, social and cultural.

When designers use contemporary HCI projects to transform urban environments into smart cities, they are actively trying to include citizens in the decision-making that is vital to solve social-cultural problems in contemporary society. [19] Urban HCI can be used to promote engagement of users in the public space. However, designing for participation within public space is not an easy task: it needs to address how HCI technologies (and their use as forms of social interaction) are transforming these public spaces and modes of social interaction. In other words, how do designers account for contemporary configurations of social spaces and for new modes of social interaction within them?

3   Proposed Participatory Co-creator Users Continuum Model

We first attempted to redefine certain existing terms such as spectator, user, participant and co-creator, within a potential context of urban public spaces into a hybrid social space facilitated by Urban HCI technology. We then focused on redeveloping the terms (spectator, user, participant and co-creator), utilizing a four-part continuum model of participatory engagement. Following Goffman's three-layer model (occasion, situation and encounter) when the user use or interact with the artifact in urban public spaces. The purpose of redefining these terms is to analyse in detail, the different happenings or "situations" that arise when users interact or "encounters" with others. It also redefines how these different "encounters" or experiences interact with each other. Therefore we propose a new taxonomy of Participatory Co-creator Users Continuum model to describe what types of interaction and engagement can be summarized as the following (Table 1).

The Participatory Co-creator Users Continuum model combines the four key terms above as clear descriptions of human behaviour and interaction in relation to the artifact within urban public spaces. In contemporary urban life users use smart devices, typing on small keyboards on screens to search for information or to message others in every moment of their lives – this phenomenon is called contemporary "participatory culture." [13] Here user's risk remaining passive spectators, lost in the world of their devices and unengaged to the world around them. [20] Our definition of "spectator" is based on this observation of human behavior not only include the passive spectator but also the potential spectator inspired by the concept of flâneurs to redevelop the term

Table 1. Participatory co-creator users continuum model

Re-developed term	Description	Similar term	Mode level
Spectator(s)	• People watch or observer the *situation* such as faced the artifact (system or design or product or service) or individual or group of people	Stakeholder, public, observer, audience, visitor	Passive or potential spectator
User(s)	• People use the artifact for what designed for such as one's needs and requirements such as fixing, feeling pleasure and enjoyment and communicating • People find out problem-solving when they getting used to use the artifact	Consumer, customer, player	User
Participant(s)	• People use the artifact actively to find out what functions are useful for themselves and what can do with the artifact to understand better solutions • People attempt to distribute new knowledge of the better solutions through sharing their experiences and ideas by communicating with others such as wikis, blogs, social media or *actual face-to-face* communication	Participant, actor, prosumer	Active participation or interaction
Co-creator(s)	• People use the artifact together with others to reach a shared goal and co-creation by collaborate, cooperate and collective interaction	Co-designer, co-worker, co-participant	Socially engaged

spectators as digital flâneurs, the contemporary version of the flâneur who walks the city streets while seeking new experiences. [21, 22] That results from design faults which rend the user as proverbial slaves to their machines, subject to external forces such as consumerism and politics. [23] This digital flâneur has the potential with the use of their own digital technology for active users/participants engagement becoming socially engaged co-creators able to influence other spectators/users/participants within hybrid social spaces (Fig. 1).

This Participatory Co-creator Users Continuum model recognizes that it is not just the designer-to-user relationship that is paramount to Urban HCI networked design objects; artifacts, rather it is the user-to-user relationship that is more prominent and that the designer acts more as a facilitator of this relationship with the Third-wave HCI. Based on Ludvigsen's model of social interaction levels [11], the Participatory

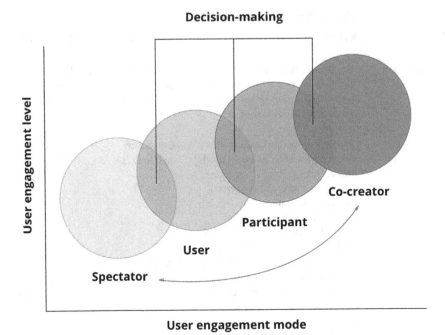

Fig. 1. Participatory co-creator users continuum model as a new social design framework.

Co-creator Users Continuum model recognizes that "users" progress through a continuum of engagement starting out first as "spectators", moving second to "users", then third as "participants" and finally fourth becoming "co-creators". In this model users will then ultimately engage other spectators and thus a closed loop of participatory engagement is formed. This continuum of engagement can be facilitated as a new social design framework that can harness design objects as a means toward participatory social interaction.

4 Conclusions and Further Research

In this approach, the transformation from being passive spectators to being active co-creators is initiated by the decision-making made to participate. This transformation can be made either by the human factor, for instance, actual face to face conversation or other interactions observed by spectator, or the influence of the artifact. We concerned with both the participant influenced by the human factor or the interactive system of the artifact used by users as the transformation factor starts with either of these elements.

This cycle of transformation eventually creates a feedback loop to spectators in public spaces that can influence other potential spectators to become users, then become participants. When spectators becomes participants, they acknowledge a shared goal and analyze themselves in order to determine what the co-creation value should be and what are the participants' needs rather than relying on manufactures to act as agents. The last level of co-creators occurs when participants engage together towards a shared goal overlapped not only with each other's goals but also with the goal of the collective or gathering-at-large. The important thing is the decision-making process that can be manipulated by PD and Urban HCI designers.

The limitation of this approach is that how designers and researchers to identify what factors of social interaction are valuable and useful for the user within the complexity of social contexts of urban public spaces, and what decision-making process should be designed to facilitate the user for the real world. Further research can be extended in the implication of how creative projects can be designed for enhancing participatory social interaction using the conceptual framework of this proposed Participatory Co-creator Users Continuum model.

References

1. Bjögvinsson, E., et al.: Design things and design thinking: contemporary participatory design challenges. Des. Issues **28**(3), 101–116 (2012)
2. Hornecker, E., Buur, J.: Getting a grip on tangible interaction: a framework on physical space and social interaction. In: Proceedings of the SIGCHI Conference on Human Factors in Computing Systems (ACM), pp. 437–446 (2006)
3. O'Hara, K., et al. (eds.): Public and Situated Displays: Social and Interactional Aspects of Shared Display Technologies, vol. 2. Springer Science & Business Media, Heidelberg (2003)
4. Muller, M.J.: Participatory design: the third space in HCI. Hum. Comput. Interact.: Dev. Process **4235**, 165–185 (2003)
5. Sanders, E.B.N., Stappers, P.J.: Co-creation and the new landscapes of design. Co-design **4**(1), 5–18 (2008)
6. Fischer, P.T., Hornecker, E.: Urban HCI: spatial aspects in the design of shared encounters for media facades. In: Proceedings of the SIGCHI Conference on Human Factors in Computing Systems, pp. 307–316. ACM (2012)
7. Bødker, S.: Third-wave HCI, 10 years later—participation and sharing. Interactions **22**(5), 24–31 (2015)
8. Nam, Y.T.: Case study: White Night Melbourne in 2013 and 2014 disruption or contribution toward the socially engaged public (art)? In: Proceedings of the ISEA 2015 Conference: The 21st International Symposium on Electronic Art (2015)
9. Harrison, S., et al.: The three paradigms of HCI. In: Alt. Chi. Session at the SIGCHI Conference on Human Factors in Computing Systems, San Jose, California, USA, pp. 1–18 (2007)
10. Erving, G.: Behavior in Public Places: Notes on the Social Organization of Gatherings. Free Press, New York (1963)
11. Ludvigsen, M.: Designing for Social Interaction. Department of Design, Aarhus School of Architecture, Aarhus (2006)
12. Rheingold, H.: Smart Mobs: The Next Social Revolution. Basic Books, Cambridge (2002)
13. Jenkins, H., et al.: Confronting the Challenges of Participatory Culture: Media Education for the 21st Century. MIT Press, Cambridge (2009)
14. Weiser, M.: The computer for the 21st century. Mob. Comput. Commun. Rev. **3**(3), 3–11 (1999)
15. Nieuwdorp, E.: The pervasive interface. In: Digital Material, p. 199 (2009)

16. Hansmann, U., et al.: Pervasive Computing: The Mobile World. Springer Science & Business Media, Heidelberg (2003)
17. Vermesan, O., et al.: Internet of Things Strategic Research and Innovation Agenda, p. 7. River Publishers Series in Communications, Aalborg (2013)
18. Greenfield, A.: Everyware: The Dawning Age of Ubiquitous Computing. New Riders, Berkeley (2006)
19. Noveck, B.S.: Smart Citizens, Smarter State: The Technologies of Expertise and the Future of Governing. Harvard University Press, Cambridge (2015)
20. Licoppe, C., Heurtin, J.P.: France: preserving the image. In: Perpetual Contact: Mobile Communication, Private Talk, Public Performance, pp. 94–109 (2002)
21. Benjamin, W., Tiedemann, R.: The Arcades Project. Harvard University Press, Cambridge (1999)
22. Baudelaire, C.: The painter of modern life. In: The Painter of Modern Life and Other Essays, translated and edited by Jonathan Mayne. Phaidon Press, Oxford (1964)
23. Robertson, T., Simonsen, J.: Routledge International Handbook of Participatory Design. Routledge, New York (2013)

Understanding Game Design
for the Development of a Game Environment

André Salomão$^{(\boxtimes)}$, Flávio Andaló, and Milton Luiz Horn Vieira

Universidade Federal de Santa Catarina, Florianópolis, Brazil
andresalomao3d@gmail.com

Abstract. In this paper, we will show the importance of understanding game design concepts when creating a game level. In this case, we are using the creation of a game level that has being made as a final project of an undergraduate student, to show the results of this paper. We used three methodologies to help them in this process, coming from these sources: the paper "It's Only a Game", the book "The Art of Game Design: A Book of Lenses", and the paper called "MDA: A Formal Approach to Game Design and Game Research".

Keywords: Game design · Game level · MDA

1 Introduction

The system implemented at the design course for undergraduate students of our university starts with students having multiple classes with a great variety in ideas and approaches with the intention of acquiring knowledge as broad as possible in regard to overall design. After two semesters of introduction, all students move into a more general group of mandatory classes alongside the important part of the course which is the work on projects, where the students start to focus more on practical activities than on learning theories.

The projects are designed to give an introduction of basic concepts and theory behind them and quickly moving into making the student learn and work with the tools used in the market like Autodesk 3Ds Max, Autodesk Motion Builder, Mudbox, Unreal Engine 4 and others and then moving on to actual designing and creating their own projects.

Taking this approach allows the students to become good at learning how to model and texture in those programs, how to operate between them in the required workflow and learn how to work in groups of usually two to four people, and the dynamics behind it.

The consequences behind this is that, even though some of the results became really good projects, some of them were not of great quality or were even left unfinished. So we looked at the reasons behind it, and most of the times, it was the lack of a better knowledge in the theory behind the process of designing and creating a project, which didn't allow the student to execute the project from scratch. One of the problems the students would encounter was getting stuck in some area and not knowing how to proceed accordingly. Another was not taking into account how other areas of the

C. Stephanidis (Ed.): HCII Posters 2017, Part I, CCIS 713, pp. 73–79, 2017.
DOI: 10.1007/978-3-319-58750-9_10

project could influence the decision on its overall design, creating problems late in development that could not be solved easily. The final result was a project which, although not a failure, would not offer the target audience the emotional experience that we were looking for.

The conclusion was that we had great students that knew how to properly use the tools available to them and, eventually when working as a professional, they would be able to follow orders to achieve whatever was asked from them. However, when asked to design projects and ideas, the lack of theory and knowledge in other areas such as, cinematography, communication, creative writing, visual arts, among others, have caused problems to some students. Although we know that it is hard for the under-graduate student to master all these elements, the challenge is to make them understand, because the lack of understanding on how they all work together and influence each other was the problem to be solved to create an emotional experience for the player.

That's the main issue we had with undergraduate students, we still want them to learn how to work on the required tools and the process of how to work in group, but, most important, we needed them to be able to design ideas and projects of their own. To reach the goals proposed in this paper, we needed the students to know how to make proper decisions in the process of developing a game asset while taking into account how all those different areas influence the design and execution of the project. To do this, we looked into theories that we could apply to improve our projects, and the result was an adaptation of different methodologies.

This adaptation was then first applied into a student under graduation final project. The result of this project is being presented and used as an example of this paper and the main reference of a project for future undergraduate students.

2   Methodology

We began our process looking first at MDA: A Formal Approach to Game Design and Game Research [1]. We used this methodology to clarify and reinforce the interactive process of developers, making it easier to decompose the study and design behind games in general by showing the difference in views between the players and devel-opers and how important is the relationship of both, since one change in either side will influence the way the other sees things and affect the overall design of the game. It uses three categories to demonstrate this relationship: Mechanics, Dynamics and Aesthetics, the former being what developers see more clearly and the latter being what the player experience in the game. We can also look at this process through what is referred to as lens. These will give us insights and questions to be answered necessarily in all these areas when designing a game.

So to help us out with this part of the process we used the book The Art of Game Design: a Book of Lenses [2]. The idea behind it was to not only give a checklist of questions that the students should mark, but to improve the "quality" of the questioning made by the students during the development cycle. So instead of keep wondering why something "feels" off, or "doesn't look right" and in the end, going around in circles and taking actions that end up being based on feelings, now they have a clear direction on how and with what to question their work, when trying to solve a problem and to proceed properly.

Alongside the idea of looking through lens, the author also decomposes the game design further than what we've seen before in MDA by separating it in four categories: Mechanics, Technology, Story and Aesthetics. The interaction process between the player and developer is still the same as MDA, but this further breaking down of elements made it easier to visualize things for the undergraduate students. After working with these four elements, we decided that it would be more helpful to add another element that the author called "Theme". This helps the assets being created to be something important because it gives the student a centralized element to their work, since now every choice made must reinforce the main theme of the game and consequently that affects every element being designed in the project.

The importance here was to show to the undergraduate student, when designing a game, that all the elements do not sustain by themselves; they are always being influenced by others and the coherence between all of them is one element that distinguishes a great design from a bad one.

We found out that only these two mixed together wasn't enough. We had a clear way on how to decompose the student's projects and a clear way to question it and have supportive content for the students to look out for, but we still did not have a clear process of workflow to fit in our schedule, to help out the students to organize during a semester.

In order to solve this issue, we took Jim Wallman's article It's Only A Game [3] as a reference for a design cycle with the Formal Loop idea from Jesse Schell [2] so that we could implement it in our process to give the students a pipeline of production. The basic idea of this pipeline was to create a process and loops inside of it, the basic guide line of it worked like this:

- Decide objectives and problems
- Brainstorm it
- Define one idea
- Examine the idea with design elements
- Test the design
- Prototype the idea if approved
- Get feedback and restart the cycle

Using this we gave to the students a cycle of progression while creating feedbacks necessary at each step made, enabling the possibility of showing to the student the results of their own decision, no matter good or bad [3]. This will also allow the process to become dynamic and give the students time to go back and forth to adapt the design choices. This process gives a better support for the choices made by the student mitigating the risk of problems during late progress in the development cycle.

With these ideas mixed together and adapted to your university system, we expect to improve the environment of our classes and increase the chances of a good project being designed and executed by our students.

3   The Project

3.1   Idea Behind the Project

The focus of this project has always been to learn the process behind designing a brand new 3D game level, and the purpose of doing that was to leave it as a reference for future undergraduate students who are considering going into the game industry and want to learn from it. We have learned and documented as much knowledge and theory as possible regarding game design in order to develop this project.

To be able to do so, we knew we would need to theorize a brand new game, inspired by others, sure, and also use it to restrain and set limitations to the level in 3D for the game we were actually creating inside Unreal Engine 4 so that the final product could be a good emotional and fun experience to the players.

3.2   The Project Itself

When this project was at its beginning, the ideas and concepts behind the methodology weren't fully integrated with the entire process. It was something that was incorporated and learned throughout the entire project, which explains why we had so much going back and forth in relation to the idea, and also multiple versions of it until coming up with one to move forward.

In the beginning there were two clear ideas, the first one was the creation of a dungeon for a MMORPG inspired in the likes of World of Warcraft and Final Fantasy XIV. At first this idea came up simply because it was "an amazing idea" or it would "look amazing in Unreal Engine 4" and other very/simple motives. When actually trying to apply the methodology to that idea, it became clear that this project would require a really high complex study behind story, visual and audio design that would influence directly upon the layout and design of the dungeon while also having to take in account the mechanics. In the end, this idea was too complex to be carried out by one person in a period of 4–5 months, at least in the way we were proposing to do it made.

The second idea was the creation of an alternative level for a game called Rocket League. With that idea however, one problems came up: the game was created and is supported by Unreal Engine in version 3. It's outdated since version 4 was released with a complete rewrite with major updates. Since we want our students to use the latest technologies, there were no reason to go back to an old version. Despite this problem, there were still good arguments in favor of that idea as it is a not complex situation story-wise. Another is that the level itself isn't as big as an entire dungeon, the aesthetics behind it is also less problematic because of the natural less complex situation. All of that would make it easier to see and apply the methodology.

So, the first cycle of this idea was an adaptation for a new sport mode which became a beach arena with volley as its game, with a location inspired by the volley arena on the beach of Rio de Janeiro but replacing the players by cars. Here we had the pillars of the methodology, technology would always be Unreal Engine 4 and dictated by that, there would be a simple story behind it, the aesthetics would be more towards a cartoon with reality tendencies, and the mechanics would be set by the rules of volley itself and adapted as feedback given.

We designed the layout of this arena in 2D and went after some feedback and the results were mixed about the idea. But the overall feelings were that it was a gimmick experience for them and with little interest from people to play volley since it's not a popular sport like soccer is, and also that it was still too much like Rocket League as a game and not just an inspiration from it.

So we took the idea back to the drawing board and started to work on it again. And then, we changed it to being undersea, with the possibility to go above sea-level walking through the walls of the arena, which would create a very dynamic level design. This idea was quickly discarded for the risk of not being able to accomplish it in the Unreal Engine 4 for hardware limitation and because the studio of Rocket League announced a similar map was being worked on for the game itself. In the meantime, the sport as a mechanic idea was becoming more of a problem than a solution to our design of an arena level. Most of the times we were put in a situation where soccer would be the only fun experience according to the feedback we were receiving. If we followed that idea, we would just be a recreation of Rocket League in Unreal Engine 4 or could even be interpreted as a pure copy of the game, but with a different aesthetics and with lower budget. So we had to change the fundamentals of our game's the mechanics of our game so that it would create different possibilities to design our assets for the game.

We remembered an alternative game mode from Monster Truck Madness 2. It created a small arena for the players to fight to maintain themselves on the platform centralized in the level which had a ramp and the idea was to survive the longest time on top of it, while trying to push other players away from the platform. The player with highest score would win.

Now we had the aesthetics of an arena from Rocket League with the extra platform added as a mechanic alongside the game mode rules into the things we should account for when creating the assets required for the level. And here is where we realized that the theme had to play a higher role in the project. To centralized the ideas, we had to set in stone that everything from now on had to reinforce the simple theme of "King of The Hill", which was the fight between the players to maintain themselves in the highest position possible during the game.

Now we needed to answer a simple question "What's the best location that will help to increase the experience of the game while reinforcing the now main theme of King of The Hill?"

A beach didn't make sense, a random place in the jungle was kind of pointless and had no purpose in increasing the experience of the player. That's when the story played a role in the creation of the level. After going back and forth with questioning and receiving feedback, we came across the idea of why not make the match between the players some sort of a television event that people are watching inside the game universe?

Now we had decided on all the parameters proposed by [2], as follow:

- Mechanics: Destroy and push people away from the platform using cars in the arena.
- Technology: Unreal Engine 4 would be the limitation of how far we could go.
- Story: The match was a TV show for the universe created.

- Aesthetics: Tendencies close to reality but with a cartoon touch.
- Theme: Fight for the King of the Hill Title.

Once the parameters for our game level were established, we began to brainstorm the new place we would create. So for a television show, it was decided that the best was an isolated place, with viability for cameras and lights everywhere. We didn't want public around the location, given the limitation that this would create upon Unreal Engine 4, taking resources from other places just to have a public, didn't seem worth it. And because the idea was of an exclusive television show, we decided not to have public.

The first idea agreed upon was a game level of an isolated island where you could see silhouette of mountains and cities in the far background and the vast ocean, with cameras around the arena and huge posts of lights source to give the fight more of a spectacular show vibe. It would be a small island, but with heights so players could see the ocean, and in it there was the arena similar to the basic one from Rocket League, but instead of having goals on both sides, it would just be a platform in the middle of it, and spread around the maps, there would be boosters you could gather, just like in Rocket League, to give you a boost in speed making it easier to push/destroy enemy players off the platform. We gave this idea another cycle of feedback and it was received positively and we moved on to prototyping the assets so we could test it out as soon as possible.

So we created the island with the tools Unreal Engine 4, and during this process, we tested it out multiple different layouts for the island, really high heights, very low one close to the waters, shape of the island, we even tested it out a couple of height maps that were originated from islands in the real world. Together with creating the island's level design, we had created a small group of sample placeholder's objects, that were used as a reference for the actual arena inside the said island, so at the same time we could have an idea of how the arena would look like on those islands.

After multiples islands and arena combination were tested, we encountered a fairly problematic situation, every time we tested the prototype, it always gave the player a Rocket League's different mode vibe, instead of a game inspired by it. We went back to looking at the fundamentals applied to the idea to question ourselves why that was happening, and we found out that it was not actual a gameplay mechanic that was giving this experience to the player; it was actually the limits imposed by the arena and its shape and form that were too similar to Rocket League. As a consequence, we had to do something to the arena and adapt the game level to that change in order to change this experience.

First we tried out just removing the arena walls and giving the player free reign on the island, but then the same limitation the walls had, would happen again on the border of the island, to avoid people from falling off. It worked a bit better, but it wasn't ideal to have invisible walls doing this job. Another problem was that the island was created to be a plain field inside the arena, and outside of it, the field was irregular, with ups and downs in the terrain so as not to give the island a plain surface. And when we tried to play with that irregular terrain, a whole new dynamic of gameplay and consequences showed up for us to deal with in order to be able to move on with the island idea.

Second, and what worked best, was actually removing the island of the game, and expanding the actual platform that the players were supposed to fight for, and creating a smaller one in the middle of it, in a slightly higher position. And while testing, we liked the idea of adding the danger of falling off experience to the player. So, in this new level, the player could actually fall off, and the consequences of it are still up to debate because of how balanced the game has to be, but the possibility is now there and now we have a design that doesn't give the player a rocket league feel and experience. The mechanics and aesthetics of the game have changed.

That's why we needed to create cycles of test and later prototypes for feedback, so we could change and adapt as early as possible, since this amount of changing would not be possible if the entire island and arena were already fully modeled and texturized inside Unreal Engine 4. That would have been almost an entire work discarded or even worse, we would have to accept that reality where very few things would be changeable.

With the methodology applied, we were able to move on and produce the game level by following the procedures of modeling, texturing and changing the environment accordantly, making small aesthetics adjustment along the way until the assets and aesthetics were completed and the project itself was able to receive actual gameplay mechanics.

4 Conclusion

This project showcases the reasons why we need to encourage the project to be based on methodologies and studies of game design, otherwise the project would not have developed the way it did, and without it, we would only have developed a good looking arena, with close resemblance to Rocket League, and people might have looked at it and considered it just a good looking game level.

Following this method, we ended up with an arena that is, based upon given theory, ready to be implemented in the rest of the development process of an actual complete game if we wanted to do so.

With this result, we agreed inside the university that this methodology is an improvement upon projects done before this one, and that as the first project being done under this supervision, we still need to learn more to continue improving the quality of the work being done, including this one, it always has some room to improve and grow a little more using this methodology, and that's what we will continue to work with.

References

1. Hunicke, R., LeBlanc, M., Zubek, R.: MDA: a formal approach to game design and game research. In: Game Design and Tuning Workshop at Game Developers Conference 2001–2004
2. Schell, J.: The Art of Game Design a Book of Lenses, 2nd edn. CRC Press Taylor & Francis Group, Boca Raton (2008)
3. Wallman, J.: It's only a game. In: Chestnut Lodge Wargames Group Fourth Annual Conference, October 1995

Communication Model of Web Accessibility

Takayuki Watanabe[✉]

Tokyo Woman's Christian University, 2-6-1 Zenpukuji,
Suginami-ku, Tokyo, Japan
nabe@lab.twcu.ac.jp

Abstract. WCAG 2.0 has played an important role on Web accessibility. Evaluation of Web accessibility is carried out to conform to WCAG 2.0. Authors and evaluators consult specific techniques of WCAG 2.0 to achieve Web accessibility. Web accessibility, however, is not techniques issues but a communication problem.

W3C/WAI has just started a task force to perform preliminary development of a new version of accessibility guidelines. So, now is a good time to reconsider Web accessibility guidelines which focus on communication problems of users.

To have a rationale of requirements for upcoming version of Web accessibility guidelines, the proposed paper tries to draw a holistic view of Web accessibility in terms of communication model, which is derived from semiotics.

This model uses triangle relationship, authors (developers), content, and users, of WAI model. Authors have a message they want to present to users. The message is encoded with Web technologies into content. Multi-modal content is decoded by user agents and assistive technologies to send a message as viewports to users. You must notice that the relation between authors and content is unidirectional. The relation between content and users, however, is bidirectional. Users, who have a goal, interact with content through user agents and assistive technologies in a specific context of use.

Based on this model, the following 4 points are discussed:

(1) It is possible that users interact with content but it is not possible that users interact with authors, which makes communication difficult.
(2) We must pay more attention to users' goal and context when evaluating Web accessibility.
(3) Evaluation guideline which does not focus on WCAG but approach Web accessibility from user side is needed. User-centered evaluation is important.
(4) To compensate a lack of communication between authors and users, an intelligent content is needed.

Keywords: Web · Accessibility · Communication · W3C · WCAG · Evaluation

1 Introduction

WCAG (Web Content Accessibility Guidelines) 1.0 [1] was published in 1999, which had made large impact on Web accessibility. Although WCAG 1.0 was an epoch-making guideline, the one of weak points was that it was written technology-specific.

© Springer International Publishing AG 2017
C. Stephanidis (Ed.): HCII Posters 2017, Part I, CCIS 713, pp. 80–87, 2017.
DOI: 10.1007/978-3-319-58750-9_11

People who use WCAG 1.0 focused not on Web accessibility problems but only focused on specific techniques of HTML. D. Sloan et al. discussed this problem in [2].

W3C/WAI (Web Accessibility Initiative)[1] noticed this problem and published WCAG 2.0 [3] in 2008. As written at the Abstract of WCAG 2.0, it was organized not depending on specific technologies and techniques. However, when authors compose accessible Web content using WCAG 2.0, they still focus on techniques of HTML and CSS because it is easy to use "sufficient techniques" shown in "Techniques for WCAG 2.0" [4]. Accessibility evaluators also focus on specific techniques.

As a development of Web is very fast, techniques may quickly become obsolete. In this paper, I try to incorporate Web accessibility in the communication model, which is derived from semiotics, because Web accessibility is not the issue of techniques but a problem of communication between transmitters and receivers of content.

2 WAI Model

WAI has developed many useful resources to improve Web accessibility. In "Essential Components of Web Accessibility"[2], WAI explains how various components contribute Web accessibility and shows how Web accessibility becomes poor if one component is weak (Fig. 1).

Figure 1 illustrates the WAI model of Web accessibility and has the following characteristics:

- Accessibility starts from developers. Developers develop Content with use of authoring tools and evaluation tools. The content is transmitted to users through user agents and assistive technologies.

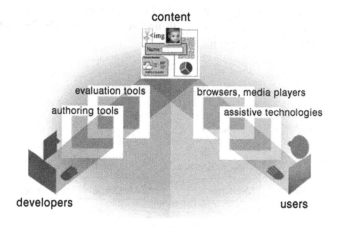

Fig. 1. Essential components of web accessibility

---

[1] https://www.w3.org/WAI/.

[2] https://www.w3.org/WAI/intro/components.php.

- Above relation is series and unidirectional.
- Both the start (developers) and the end (users) of the relation is human. They are connected by content.
- Web accessibility guidelines, ATAG (Authoring Tool Accessibility Guidelines), WCAG, and UAAG (User Agent Accessibility Guidelines), have developed for different components of this model.

3   Communication Model

3.1   Semiotics

Semiotics is basically "the study of signs" ([5], p. 2). Wikipedia defines semiotics as "the study of meaning-making, the study of sign processes and meaningful communication."[3]. As discussed in [6], discussing Web accessibility in terms of semiotics is important. Semiotics extends our knowledge to outside of technology.

3.2   Communication Model

Semiotic approach to communication is important because communication had been deeply studied in terms of semiotic. Communication is considered as transmission in which a transmitter sends a message to a receiver according to the common code. In 1960, structuralist linguist, Jakobson, proposed a model of interpersonal verbal communication ([5], p. 180; [7], p. 353). Ikegami [8] showed the similar communication model (Fig. 2), which are based on semiotics.

Shannon proposed a mathematical theory of communication [9]. Weaver extended it to a communication of human [10]. Essence of all the above model is almost the same. A transmitter has information, the transmitter encodes it into a message according to a code, the message is transmitted through a channel, a receiver decodes the message to extract the information with use of the same code. The whole communication is carried out in a specific context.

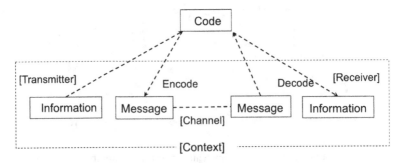

Fig. 2. Communication model (English translation of the Figure at page 39 of [8].)

---

[3] https://en.wikipedia.org/wiki/Semiotics.

As easily noticed, this communication model is somewhat similar to the WAI model (Fig. 1) of Web accessibility.

4 Communication Model of Web Accessibility

Let me combine the WAI model and the communication model to develop a communication model of Web accessibility. Before combing them, two important points, interaction and multi-modality, must be discussed.

4.1 Interaction

Both the WAI model and the communication model is unidirectional. At the WAI model, developers upload content to a server and the content is transmitted to users. In the communication model, a transmitter sends a message and a receiver receives it.

An interaction of humans and computers, however, is bidirectional. For example, Norman's Seven Stages of Action model [11] consists of a stage of execution from an internal human mind to an outer world and a stage of evaluation from an outer world to an internal human mind. This cycle of human interaction to and from an outer world is repeated as many times as possible until the human achieves his/her goal.

WCAG 2.0 has 4 principles. Three of them are Perceivable, Operable, and Understandable, which reflects the above human interaction model and is bidirectional.

4.2 Multi-modal Content

Specifications of Web technologies such as HTML fulfil accessibility requirements. Web content consists of text information as well as non-text information such as images and videos. Non-text information should have alternative text information. Image is only visually perceived by a human. Text can be perceived by human through visual, auditory, and tactile modality.

Therefore, a message is multi-modal in Web communication. As discussed in [12], Web content may have multi-modal information and may be transmitted to users by visually, auditory, or tactile channel.

4.3 Communication Model of Web Accessibility

Regarding above two characteristics of Web communication, I want to propose a communication model of Web accessibility in Fig. 3.

This model uses triangle relationship, authors (developers), content, and users, of WAI model. Authors have a message they want to present to users. The message is encoded with Web technologies into content. Multi-modal content is decoded by user agents and assistive technologies to send a message as viewports to users. You must notice that the relation between authors and content is unidirectional. The relation between content and users, however, is bidirectional. Users, who have a goal, interact with content through user agents and assistive technologies in a specific context of use.

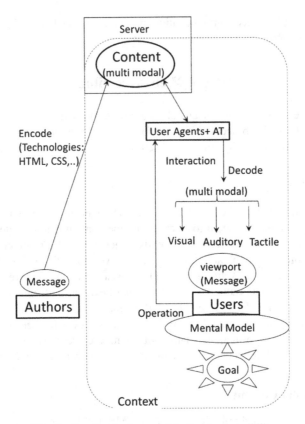

Fig. 3. Communication model of web accessibility

5   Implication of Proposed Model

5.1   Gap Between Authors and Users

One of the important implication of this model is that interaction occurs only between content and users. As the model is separated into the left unidirectional part and the right bidirectional part, users cannot interact with authors. Thus, communication occurs only between content and users, which results in a weak point of Web accessibility because authors cannot modify/adjust the content according to users' needs synchronously.

5.2   Importance of Users' Goal

Web interaction starts from users. Users use Web to fulfill their needs. As D. Norman pointed out in his Seven Stages of Action model, a user has a goal. Thus, identifying user's goal is important.

Usability is defined as "Extent to which a product can be used by specified users to achieve specified goals with effectiveness, efficiency and satisfaction in a specified context of use." in ISO 9241-11 [13]. Considering users with disabilities, usability approaches accessibility. "Achieve specified goals" is important concept of usability and can be applied to accessibility.

WCAG 2.0 has Principles of Perceivable, Understandable, and Operable but does not have the principle of goal-oriented interaction mechanism. We must pay attention to the goal of users as shown in the bottom of users in Fig. 3.

5.3   Importance of Context

Usability definition of ISO 9241-11 mentions "specified context of use." As shown in Fig. 2, context is an important factor in semiotics because meaning of message is determined under context. As discussed in [2], it is also true in Web accessibility. We must pay attention to the context of use when evaluating Web accessibility because accessibility problems occur in a certain context.

5.4   Evaluation of Web Accessibility

It is fine that authors consult specific techniques to compose Web content. It, although, is not fine that evaluation of accessibility is based on techniques. Although the importance of this has been discussed in many papers, the real world still sticks to techniques. Web accessibility is a problem of communication between authors and users, and as illustrated in the proposed model, authors cannot interact with users. Thus, we need an evaluation guideline which focuses on the right part of the model.

WAI has developed Website Accessibility Conformance Evaluation Methodology (WCAG-EM)[4]. As WCAG-EM says "WCAG-EM is an approach for determining how well a website conforms to WCAG.", Web accessibility is determined as a conformance to WCAG at WAI. The proposed communication model, however, claims that Web accessibility should not be measured by the conformance of WCAG because the role of WCAG is the left part of the model but Web accessibility problems occur at the right part.

The current Web accessibility evaluation activity depends too much on WCAG and techniques, which is sufficient or insufficient to conform to WCAG. WAI lists various resource on Web accessibility evaluation at "Accessibility Evaluation Resources"[5]. "Involving Users in Web Accessibility Evaluation"[6] is one of those resources and says:

Web accessibility evaluation often focuses on conformance to accessibility standards such as WCAG. While conformance is important, there are many benefits to evaluating with real people to learn how your website or web tool really works for users and to better understand

---

[4] https://www.w3.org/WAI/eval/conformance.

[5] https://www.w3.org/WAI/eval/Overview.

[6] https://www.w3.org/WAI/eval/users.html.

accessibility issues. Evaluating with users with disabilities and with older users identifies usability issues that are not discovered by conformance evaluation alone.

This is very important point to improve Web accessibility because evaluation of the right part of the model, such as user test, expert review, and heuristic review, can reproduce user problem independently on technology.

5.5   Intelligent Web Content

Human-Computer Interaction is bidirectional interaction between humans and computers. User interface is placed between humans and computers. As for Web, communication only occurs at the right part of the model, content and users. There is a gap between authors and users at the left part.

If content is intelligent enough to fulfill user's need promptly, users can interact with content more easily, which enhances usability and accessibility. AI must play an important role to make content intelligent. Image recognition to extract text and image recognition to describe what the image is are already developed technologies.

Imagine if authors always sit beside users and answer any questions of the content asked by (the disabled) users. Question: "What image is it?" Answer: "This is a drawing of Picasso and …." Question: "How can I purchase this product?" Answer: "I'm investigating. … OK. Click this button." It might greatly improve usability and accessibility. An intelligent content and servers which interact with users gracefully as if there are authors may reduce a lot of accessibility problems.

6   Conclusion

WCAG 2.0 plays an important role on Web accessibility. Evaluation of Web accessibility is carried out to conform to WCAG 2.0 and authors and evaluators consult specific techniques to achieve Web accessibility. Web accessibility, however, is a communication problem. Although researchers and professional evaluators may know the importance of this, other people do not pay attention to it.

W3C has started Silver Task Force[7]. The objective of it is "to perform preliminary development of a new version of Accessibility Guidelines following a research-focused, user-centered design methodology to produce the most effective and flexible outcome." Thus, now is the best time to reconsider Web accessibility holistically.

Inspired from semiotics, the current paper proposes a communication model of Web accessibility to draw holistic view of Web accessibility. The following 4 points are discussed with use of this model:

1. It is possible that users interact with content but it is not possible that users interact with authors, which makes communication difficult.
2. We must pay more attention to users' goal and context when evaluating Web accessibility.

---

[7] https://www.w3.org/WAI/GL/task-forces/silver/.

3. Evaluation guideline which does not focus on WCAG but approach Web accessibility from user side is needed. User-centered evaluation is important.
4. Intelligent content is needed to improve Web accessibility.

References

1. Chisholm, W., Vanderheiden, G., Jacobs, I. (eds.): Web Content Accessibility Guidelines 1.0, May 1999. https://www.w3.org/TR/WCAG10/. Accessed 6 Jan 2017
2. Sloan, D., Heath, A., Hamilton, F.: Contextual web accessibility-maximizing the benefit of accessibility guidelines. In: W4A 2006, pp. 121–131 (2006)
3. Caldwell, B., Cooper, M., Guarino Reid, L., Vanderheiden, G. (eds.): Web Content Accessibility Guidelines (WCAG) 2.0, December 2008. http://www.w3.org/TR/WCAG20/. Accessed 6 January 2017
4. Cooper, M., Kirkpatrick, A., Connor, J. (eds.) Techniques for WCAG 2.0, October 2016. https://www.w3.org/TR/WCAG20-TECHS/. Accessed 6 January 2017
5. Chandler, D.: Semiotics the basics, 2nd edn. Routledge, Abingdon (2007)
6. Laitano, M.: Semiotic contributions to accessible interface design. In: W4A 2015 (2015)
7. Jakobson, R.: Closing statement: linguistics and poetics. In: Sebeok (ed.) (1960)
8. Ikegami, Y.: Invitation to semiotics, Iwanami Sinsyo (1984) (in Japanese)
9. Shannon, C.E.: A mathematical theory of communication, part I. Bell Syst. Tech. J. **27**, 379–423 (1948)
10. Shannon, C.E., Weaver, W.: A Mathematical Model of Communication. University of Illinois Press, Urbana (1949)
11. Norman, D.: The Design of Everyday Things: Revised and Expanded Edition. Basic Books, New York (2013)
12. Obrenovic, Z., Abascal, J., Starcevic, D.: Universal accessibility as a multimodal design issue. Commun. ACM **50**(5), 83–88 (2007)
13. ISO 9241-11:1998. Ergonomic requirements for office work with visual display terminals (VDTs) – Part 11: Guidance on usability

A Study of the Team Management in Design Organizations

Shih-Hsi Yang[1(✉)] and Wen-Tsung Huang[2]

[1] Ph.D. Program in Design, Chung Yuan Christian University,
9F., No. 12, Tianxiang 3rd Street, Taoyuan District,
Taoyuan City 330, Taiwan, R.O.C.
shihhsi.yang@gmail.com
[2] Department of Commercial Design, Chung Yuan Christian University,
Taoyuan City, Taiwan, R.O.C.

Abstract. With the rapid change of technology and the rise of design-driven innovation, creativity is considered as an important role to enterprise's growth. It seems creativity stimulate the economy over the past few decades. However, it is supported by a particular context and condition these days. No matter the creative economy or the flat white economy, it is an outcome of a specific working organization or creative labor relationship. Instead of individual talent, a team could contribute more within organization as a whole. At this point, design manger plays a core role in an organization and design management is seen as the business side of design. Although there is abundant research relating to designer's individual creativity, there have been few studies focus on team management in design organization. The study intends to get into the factors that influence design team and interpret the design management from its attribute and feature in order to organize a communication tendency among the design manager and team members. For further analysis of studies, there is no single effective rule to improve creativity and profession since differences of business environment and leading style among organizations. For design origination, in order to fit into need of team member and client, manager must revise methods in both profession and management part.

Keywords: Creative team · Design management · Design business

1 Creativity and Creative Class

Over the past decade a number of companies have become apparent in their creativity and innovation, the most famous are Apple, Google and Facebook. All of them took a risk and delivered a creative concept into an innovation. They have opened a new appearance of technology and media. Without doubt their success started with a personal talent and creativity. Creativity is usually consider as a product of individual. However, each steps and progress are connected and relied on others in the creative industry. The final result is a incorporating both individual and group's creativity. Unlike mass production always has standard operating procedure, creative workers are expected to have unique and original ideas. That's also why the creativity is valuable.

© Springer International Publishing AG 2017
C. Stephanidis (Ed.): HCII Posters 2017, Part I, CCIS 713, pp. 88–92, 2017.
DOI: 10.1007/978-3-319-58750-9_12

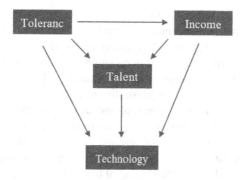

Fig. 1. Structure of 3Ts: technology, talent and tolerance (Source: Florida, p. 153)

Daily routines may not bring creative ideas, but complexity and ambiguity do. They are energy, vitality required for creative workers. Instead of transactional leadership, such as promotion and remuneration, creative workers are willing to bear uncertainty in order to self-fulfilling [1]. Florida claim Creative Class's major work is to create. Comparing with Working Class and Service Class, who execute plans or orders, Creative Class own more autonomy and flexibility. Both creativity and Creative Class are grow in a city that including essential 3 Ts, technology, talent, and tolerance (Fig. 1). With technology, talent people and tolerance, it's easy to stimulate creativity and innovation in a space [2]. The essentials for a creative city could be implied to a creative organization. Tolerance is the willingness to tolerate any career, gender, race, and lifestyle. Tolerance brings diversity and inclusion which are fundamentals for a creative team. Here is the greatest sample of tolerance in the organization, IDEO, a design and innovation consulting firm. Tom Kelley, IDEO partner, also suggested that the Cross-Pollinator connects between unrelated ideas and break fresh ground. In IDEO, the concrete method to implement cross-pollinate is to recruit peopled from different professions fields, such as anthropologist, educator, and so on. The Cross-Pollinator brings in inspiration from the outside world to their team [3]. Many organizations pay attention on creativity and art, and reflect it as a guarantee of profit. Considering the attributes of creative, to manage creative by scientific management is barely possible. For the reason that creative management are considered as a new profession in the creative industry. Mangers plays a central, core role in a creative practice [4].

2 Creative Team and Management

Creative management is a new subject in the industry. Many business and management scholar claimed that creative management is just as same as usual business management. However, many humanities and art academics were encroaching because people ignore "autonomy" in the creative industry [5]. As mentioned earlier, creative works are require diversity and complexity. The most important creative workers' endeavor is the striving for self-fulfilled. In order to achieve the purpose, they accept to take long work hours and the uncertainty of work. To be specific, creative workers would like to work more flexible and fewer limitations, such as flexible work time/hors, casual clothes, work space, and the method to finish the works. Instead of giving orders directly, it goes back to discussion and negotiation. Sometime is argument. With less supervision, more input come from workers themselves [6]. That's why it matters, autonomy brings more diversity and possibility to both creative workers and organizations. These attributes are not accept in the usual business fields, yet it's very common in the creative organizations. Being a creative manager, must to understand these attributes and to make best use of resources within a team.

Multitasking is another characteristic in a creative team. A creative group usually start with only a few people. In the beginning of business, creative workers have to take multi-tasks at the same time. It seems no choice when the team was small. Despite of working hard, having multitasks helps creative workers could think from different angles. By taking multi-tasks and play other roles in the team at a time, creative workers could expanding their empathy and perspectives. It bridges the gap between team members, moreover communicating and articulating inside the team become much easier. The goal is to adapt the changes and to make sure every parts in the team could work together smoothly and effectively. That's the main reason why most creative group keep itself in a small or medium sizes [1]. It's a flatter structure instead of traditional hierarchical structure. Lester et al. [7] point out that the interpretive managerial perspective is seen as a new approach of management. Refer to traditional "hard" management, creative management is more tend to "soft" management [4].

3 Design Team Manager

In this case, a managers plays the role more like a mentor instead of a bureaucratic manager. To manage a group of professionals and creative is not a usual managerial job. According to Ryan's observation in the film industry, a manager works as professional creative/adviser and bureaucratic manager at the same time (see Table 1).

Table 1. Project team positions and conditions (Source: Ryan, p. 133)

Position	Production Relation	Basis Of Authority		Form Of Control
Producer	manager	bureaucratic (executive) charismatic (artistic leadership)	Formatting	managerialism commercialism
Director	contracted artist	bureaucratic (organizational) charismatic (artistic leadership)		managerialism commercialism
leading executant	contracted artist	artistic (commercial reputation)		collaboration commercialism
Supporting executant	professional creative	artistic (professional reputation)		Direction professionalism

Nowadays they are expected to capable of both artistic profession and business acumen. There is no doubt that a creative manger plays a central, core role in a project team [4, 6].

In recent years, more and more people noticed the power of design thinking and design-driven innovation. Design that used to be considered as an appendant's position, namely more colors options for products in the consumerism, but now is viewed as a creative economy. Designer are always expected to bring new, creative, and high quality artworks. To combine artistic idea with business thinking, design should bring good profit for corporation. A motive for designers is self-actualization, the highest need of Maslow's hierarchy of needs. They care about their reputation. Not transactional promotion or remuneration, designers expect to understand the vision and value system of leader or organization [1]. A manager's job is to create a comfortable environment where designers could express intent and play creative, even take risk. A safe space that with "hand-off" culture is much important to designer, for example, Greenhouse in IDEO and Braintrust in Pixar [8]. As a manager, not only have to meet the demand of designers but also need to make commercial guarantee to an organization. Creativity and market are dynamic and unpredictable. Ackoff's 'anticipatory decision-making' is the major responsibility of design manager. It's to plan how design can contribute on and how to realize in the real business world, not only about the design's style or function. That's also one of the reason that why more and people demand to understand design tool, design thinking and design process [9]. In order to make sure that creative teams are always in good condition to have creative, original solutions and ideas. A major responsibility to team manager is to restructure team member to keep diversity. It's not easy for a manager to interference processing of creative, yet a manager could control how to build a team. Different members in a team could stimulate new concepts, break the rules, and help members think in different perspective. In other hand, it could avoid team members always think in the same direction, which may cause small group myths [1]. The manager also needs courage to take risks, accept failure and take other perspectives [10]. The leader sets up a clarity vision, and the manager ensure each steps are in the track, so that the designer can concentrate on deliver good outcomes [9]. The successful management is achieving the best business value outcomes. More and more people consider that creative management as a professional not as usual management.

4 Conclusion

The great piece of work are always come after a creative abrasion among the team members [11]. Team managers are always expected to deal with these abrasion saturations. The glory of a success work may go to the star design leader, yet it must be a team work. Without a clarity leadership and version, designers must wither away. Creative industry is absolutely human-centered field, including both designer and audience. In Taiwan, most design organizations or designers start their business with original equipment manufacturers so that even design manager focus on how to manage project time, cost of project and how to achieve a project. Even the largest design firm in Taiwan, Nova Design, create their own knowledge platform to accumulated project experience and materials, yet not very much on designer or team management [12]. Young designers yearn for a new appearance in Taiwan design industry. To understand and manage the attribute of design industry is an essential. That's all managers' challenge to face on in the new era.

References

1. Bilton, C.: Management and Creativity: From Creative Industries to Creative Management. New World Press, Beijing (2010). (in Chinese)
2. Florida, R.: Cities and the Creative Class. Heliopolis Culture Group, Taipei (2006). (in Chinese)
3. Kelly, T., Littman, J., Peters, T.: The Art of Innovation: Lessons in Creativity from IDEO, America's Leading Design Firm. Locus Publishing Company, Taipei (2002). (in Chinese)
4. Banks, M.: The Politics of Cultural Work. Palgrave Macmillan, New York (2007)
5. Bilton, C.: Management in the cultural industries. In: Oakley, K., O'Connor, J. (eds.) The Routledge Companion to the Cultural Industries, pp. 283–295. Routledge Companions, Abingdon (2015)
6. Ryan, B.: Making Capital from Culture. Walter de Gruyter, New York (1992)
7. Lester, R.K., Piore, M.J., Malek, K.M.: Interpretive management: what general managers can learn from design? Harvard Bus. Rev. **76**, 86–96 (1998)
8. Catmull, E., Wallace, A.: Creativity, INC. Overcoming the Unseen Forces that Stand in the Way of True Inspiration. Yuan-Liou Publishing Company, Taipei (2015). (in Chinese)
9. Best, K.: Design Management: Managing Design Strategy. Process and Implementation. AVA Publishing, Lausanne (2006)
10. Teng, C.L.: Design Management: Organization. Communication and Operation of Product Design. Asia-Pacific Press, Taipei (1999). (in Chines, semantic translation)
11. Hirshbery, J.: The Creative Priority: Putting Innovation to Work in Your Business. Harper Paperbacks, New Your (1999)
12. Chen, W.L.: Design Management Competitiveness Redefined. Yuan-Liou Publishing Company, Taipei (2011). (in Chinese)

Novel Interaction Techniques and Devices

Japanese Sign Language Recognition Based on Three Elements of Sign Using Kinect v2 Sensor

Shohei Awata[✉], Shinji Sako, and Tadashi Kitamura

Graduate School of Engineering, Nagoya Institute of Technology, Aichi, Japan
{awata,sako,kitamura}@mmsp.nitech.ac.jp

Abstract. The visual feature of Japanese sign language is divided into two of manual signals and non-manual signals. Manual signals are represented by the shape and motion of the hands, and convey mainly the meaning of sign language words. In terms of phonology, sign language words consist of three elements: hand's motion, position, and shape. We have developed a recognition system for Japanese sign language (JSL) with abstraction of manual signals based on these three elements. The abstraction of manual signals is performed based on Japanese sign language words dictionary. Features like coordinates of hands and depth images are extracted from manual signals using the depth sensor, Kinect v2. This system recognizes three elements independently and the final result is obtained under the comprehensive judgment from the results of three elements recognition. In this paper, we used two methods for recognition of hand shape, a contour-based method suggested by Keogh and template matching of depth image. The recognition methods of other elements were hidden Markov model for recognition of motion and the normal distribution learned by maximum likelihood estimation for recognition of position, as a same manner of our previous research. Based on our proposal method, we prepared recognition methods of each element and conducted an experiment of 400 sign language words recognition based on a sign language words dictionary.

Keywords: Sign language recognition · Kinect · Hand pose · Contour · Template matching

1 Introduction

In general, sign is represented by combinations of posture or movement of the hands and facial expressions such as eyes or month. These visual features of sign are happened both sequentially and simultaneously. Communication between the hearing people and the deaf can be difficult, because the most of hearing people do not understand sign language. To resolve a communication problem between hearing people and deaf, projects for automatic sign language recognition (ASLR) system is still under way.

One of major problem of current ASLR system is performing small vocabulary. Corresponding to the unknown vocabulary is also important from the view of practical aspect. It is said that the number of JSL vocabulary is over 3,000. In addition, a new

C. Stephanidis (Ed.): HCII Posters 2017, Part I, CCIS 713, pp. 95–102, 2017.
DOI: 10.1007/978-3-319-58750-9_13

sign is introduced to adjust the situation. Obviously, it is inefficient to perform the recognition on individual sign units.

From the point of view, we employ a JSL dictionary and notation system proposed by Kimura et al. [1]. Our system is based on three elements of sign language: hand motion, position, and pose.

This study considers a hand pose recognition using depth image obtained from a single depth camera. We apply the contour-based method proposed by Keogh et al. [2] to hand pose recognition and evaluated by comparison of typical template matching method. The contour-method recognizes a contour by means of classifiers trained from several hand shape contours.

To recognize hand motion and position, we adopted statistical models such as Hidden Markov models (HMMs) and Gaussian mixture models (GMMs). To address the problem of lack of training data, our method utilizes the pseudo motion and hand shape data. We conduct experiments to recognize 400 JSL sign targeted professional sign language interpreters.

2   Overview of the System

An overview of our proposed system is shown in Fig. 1. The features of sign motion are captured by using Microsoft Kinect v2 sensor [3]. At first, time series of hand position is split into moving segment. Second, the three phonological elements are recognized individually by using hand position and hand depth image. Finally, the recognition result is determined by the weighted sum of each score of three elements. The recognition process of the hand pose and other two components employs depth data of the hand region and coordinates of joints, respectively.

We used JSL dictionary proposed by Kimura et al. [1]. In this dictionary, hand poses are classified by several element as shown in Table 1. These elements are also illustrated in Fig. 2. Currently, the vocabulary of this dictionary is approximately 2,600.

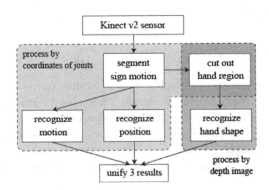

Fig. 1. Flowchart of the entire system.

Table 1. Portion of the database in the dictionary.

Word	SL type	Hand type	Palm direction	Position	Motion
Love	3	B	Down	NS	Circle
Between	4	B	Side	NS	Down
Blue	1	B	Back	Lower face	Back
Red	f	1	Back	Lower face	Right
Baby	4	B	Back	Whole face	Front back

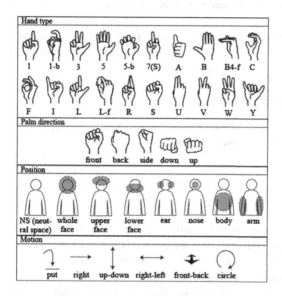

Fig. 2. Elements in sign language dictionary.

3 Hand Pose Recognition

Several study on hand pose recognition using a technique of estimating the finger joints has been proposed [4, 5]. However, these methods still have difficulties when some fingers are invisible due to the complex hand shapes of sign language. From the point of view, we adopt the contour-based technique proposed by Keogh et al. [2] to recognize hand pose. This technique is considered to be robust even when the finger is partially occluded. The details of the method are described below.

3.1 Feature Extraction

Hand shapes can be converted to distance vectors to form one-dimensional sequence. Figure 3 shows the procedure to extract a distance vector from a hand image. At first, the center point of the hand region is determined by distance transform. Distance transform convert one-pixel value of the binary image with the distance between the

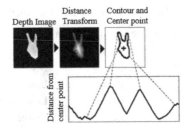

Fig. 3. Feature extraction from an image of hand region

nearest zero value pixel. Next, each distance from the center point to every pixel on the contour is calculated. The distance vector represents a series of these distances.

3.2   Calculation of Distance

A distance D between two distance vectors $P = \{p_0, p_1, \ldots, p_n\}$ and $Q = \{q_1, q_2, \ldots, q_n\}$ is calculated according to the followings.

$$D(P,Q) = \sqrt{\sum_{i=1}^{n}(p_i - q_i)^2} \tag{1}$$

If the length of two distance vectors is different, some normalization process should be required such as dynamic time warping (DTW). To simplify, we adjust length of vector to be same in advance for low computation cost reason.

It can be compared contours by calculating their distances or using classifiers generated from contours. These classifiers are called wedges. Wedges have set of maximum and minimum values at each point. If a contour is located inside a wedge, the distance is zero. The distance D between a wedge W ($U = \{u_o, u_1, \ldots, u_n\}$ means its top, $L = \{l_0, l_1, \ldots, l_n\}$ means its bottom) and a contour $P = \{p_0, p_1, \ldots, p_n\}$ can be calculated by following equation.

$$D(W,P) = \sqrt{\sum_{i=1}^{n}\begin{cases} (p_i - u_i)^2 & (p_i > u_i) \\ (p_i - l_i)^2 & (p_i < l_i) \\ 0 & (otherwise) \end{cases}} \tag{2}$$

3.3   Generate Wedges

Wedges are produced according to the following steps.

1. Extract features from hand images
2. Calculate distances of all contours
3. Combine two contours in ascending order of distances. Wedge is represented by set of maximum and minimum values of merged contours.

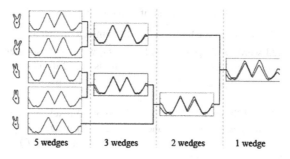

Fig. 4. Making wedges from five contours

Repeat Step 3 until the pre-determined number of wedges. The step of generating wedges is also illustrated in Fig. 4. We prepare various wedges to recognizing each hand type.

4 Sign Movement and Position Recognition

In this paper, HMMs are utilized to recognized hand movement using the feature parameter of hand position provided by the Kinect sensor. 3-dimensional hand position and its speed are used as feature parameter of HMMs. HMMs corresponding to the typical movement of sign are constructed from pseudo-training data. It can be omitted the cost of collecting the sign data. The definition of the hand position is ambiguous in JSL. It is necessary to consider for the hand position recognition. In this paper, the particular position of the hand in sign is modeled by GMMs. 3-dimensional hand position is used as feature parameter of GMMs. GMMs corresponding to the typical position of sign are also trained from pseudo-training data.

5 Experiments

We conduct JSL words recognition experiments by recognizing three elements independently. In order to recognize the hand shape, we used a contour-based method and template matching.

5.1 Experimental Condition

We use 400 JSL words commonly used in the social life for the test data. To recognize this 400 words requires to distinguish 24 hand poses defined by hand types and palm directions. Because hand shapes transform with motions, each hand type is not separated even if the palm direction is different. However, there are a few exceptions to distinguish sign language words which have same motion, position, and hand types, but only palm direction is different.

To simplify the collection of data in our experiments, we used depth images of stationary hand instead of hand images obtained during natural sign motion. Table 2

Table 2. Condition of shape recognition

	Contour-based method	Template matching
Number of test data	223 words × 2 speakers × 2 trials = 892 data	188 words × 2 speakers × 2 trials = 752 data
Image size of test data	120 × 120 pixel	120 × 120 pixel
Image for recognition	120 × 120 pixel 150 images per person, hand type	90 × 90 pixel 12 × 18 images per person and hand type (Rotate by 20°)
Hand type	24 types	

Table 3. Condition of position and motion recognition

Position type	8 types
Features	3-dimensional hand coordinates
Number of training data	6 hand coordinates per a position
Number of GMM mixes	1–6
Motion type	40 types
Features	10 pseudo hand movements per a motion
Number of training data	3-dimensional direction vector + Four-dimensional information on speed
Number of states of HMM	5–18
Number of GMM mixes	1

shows the condition of shape recognition by contour-based method and template matching. The similarity used in template matching is calculated by a method incorporating normalization by luminance. 12 template images were selected from each of the belts when the number of the belt was 12. The target image is the frame with the slowest speed in the sign language movement.

Table 3 shows the condition of position and motion recognition. For the parameters required for position recognition, at each operating position of sign language, draw a circle by hand and use the coordinates of the hand obtained at that time. In the training of HMM, we performed motions that reproduced the movement pattern of dictionary data 10 times and trained the parameters from the obtained feature values.

After recognizing hand shape, position, and motion for the test data, sign language word can be determined by weighted sum of each score of three elements.

5.2   Results

Table 4 shows the results of JSL words recognition experiments. The scores of the three elements are weighted after performing normalization so that the maximum

Table 4. Word recognition rate (%)

	Shape	Position	Motion	Word
Contour-based (Weight)	28.7 (0.1)	78.3 (0.4)	60.0 (0.5)	33.8
Template matching (Weight)	32.7 (0.1)	73.7 (0.7)	51.0 (0.2)	28.1

values are equal. In recognition of hand shape, the recognition rate of template matching was 32.7%, which was better than the contour-based method. Word recognition rate by contour-based method was 33.8%, and word recognition rate by template matching was 28.1%. In either method, the recognition accuracy of the hand shape was the lowest among the recognition of the three elements. One of the main causes of misrecognition is difficulty in recognizing the hand shape during sign language motion using a single camera image. It is assumed that hand shape weight was suppressed to the minimum because hand shape recognition accuracy was low.

6 Conclusion

In this research, we proposed a method to recognize sign language words by constructing recognition models corresponding to hand shapes, hand positions and movements, which are three elements of sign language, based on the notation method of Japanese sign language/Japanese dictionary system. In sign language recognition research, it is difficult to obtain a sign language database currently. As in this research, the method of introducing the sign language academic knowledge and determining the constituent elements of sign language by top down has the advantage that a small number of learning data is enough. Therefore, our method can be said to be suitable for sign language recognition research. Furthermore, by using a sign language word dictionary with a large number of recorded words, we can expect to develop into large vocabulary recognition in the future.

We also conducted sign language word recognition experiments on Japanese sign language words. In this research, pseudo data corresponding to each element of sign language was used as learning data, and recognition was attempted for actual sign language motion. In recognition of hand shape, the recognition rate of template matching was 32.7%, which was better than the contour-based method. Word recognition rate by contour-based method was 33.8%, and rate by template matching was 28.1%.

Improvement of hand shape recognition method and improvement of learning data are future issues.

Acknowledgment. This research was partially supported by JSPS KAKENHI Fostering Joint International Research (15KK0008).

References

1. Kimura, T., Hara, D., Kanda, K., Morimoto, K.: Expansion of the system of JSL-Japanese electronic dictionary: an evaluation for the compound research system. In: Kurosu, M. (ed.) HCD 2011. LNCS, vol. 6776, pp. 407–416. Springer, Heidelberg (2011). doi:10.1007/978-3-642-21753-1_46
2. Keogh, E., Wei, L., Xi, X., Lee, S.-H., Vlachos, M.: LB Keogh supports exact indexing of shapes under rotation invariance with arbitrary representations and distance measures. In: 32nd International Conference on Very Large Data Bases (VLDB2006), pp. 882–893 (2006)
3. Kinect for Windows. http://kinectforwindows.org
4. Liang, H., Yuan, J., Thalmann, D.: Parsing the hand in depth images. IEEE Trans. Multimedia **16**(5), 1241–1253 (2014)
5. Tang, D., Yu, T.-H., Kim, T.-K.: Real-time articulated hand pose estimation using semi-supervised transductive regression forests. In: Proceedings of the 2013 IEEE International Conference on Computer Vision, ICCV 2013, pp. 3224–3231 (2013)

Immersive 3D Environment for Data Centre Monitoring Based on Gesture Based Interaction

Giannis Drossis[1], Chryssi Birliraki[1(✉)], George Margetis[1],
and Constantine Stephanidis[1,2]

[1] Institute of Computer Science,
Foundation for Research and Technology – Hellas (FORTH),
N. Plastira 100, Vassilika Vouton, 70013 Heraklion, Crete, Greece
{drossis,birlirak,gmarget,cs}@ics.forth.gr
[2] Computer Science Department, University of Crete, Heraklion, Crete, Greece

Abstract. Virtual Reality enhances the user experience regarding perception and presence by immersing the users in a virtual world, where vision and hearing are captivated and elided from the real environment. A key factor for such environments is to make the users perceive the virtual world as real and interact with it. User interaction with VR environments can be achieved through a variety of ways, including computer vision techniques. This work presents the potential uses of gestural interaction as a means of navigation in virtual reality environments in a natural manner. In this direction, four alternatives are proposed and utilized in the demanding context of a use case that requires both extensive travelling and view fine-tuning, such as a data centre room monitoring application.

Keywords: Virtual reality · VR · Gestures · Interaction · 3D environment · Data centre · Big data visualization · Gestural navigation · Immersive environment

1 Introduction

Interactive systems increasingly include three dimensional environments as a means of realism, as well as the appropriate interaction techniques to provide natural manipulation of those environments. 3D environments are created to display objects, places, scenes and characters more lifelike and detailed compared to 2D visualizations. Virtual reality technologies (VR) are applied in 3D visualizations in order to enrich user experience and immerse users in the visualized environment [1, 10]. VR is an artificial environment that is created with software and presented to the user in such a way that the user suspends belief and accepts it as a real environment. The most prevalent devices to support VR are head mounted displays including Oculus Rift [4, 12, 15], HTC Vive [8], etc. Another approach for realizing VR environments is the CAVE approach [3] (Cave Automatic Virtual Environment), which, however, is more expensive and difficult to setup, requiring the users to be located in specific positions in the system in order to successfully feel immersed in the VR environment.

© Springer International Publishing AG 2017
C. Stephanidis (Ed.): HCII Posters 2017, Part I, CCIS 713, pp. 103–108, 2017.
DOI: 10.1007/978-3-319-58750-9_14

When using head-mounted displays, immersion is accomplished through stereo-scopic vision and auditory feedback that the devices are capable of. Additionally, while wearing the headset, the users' head movement maps exactly to where the user is looking in the virtual world, allowing scene's investigation just by moving or turning around; however, travelling cannot be accomplished without additional input. In order for users to be able to interact in VR environments, several approaches have been employed facilitating the manipulation, grab or movement of the virtual objects or their view in the virtual world, including not only the wireless controllers that accompany modern VR headsets like Oculus Rift and HTC Vive [8, 12], but also wired gloves [2] and computer vision techniques [6]. The main goal of these approaches is to enable the user to manipulate the VR environment, as well as to navigate, select objects and ultimately explore further visualized data. User interaction modalities that are already used in VR environment include full body kinesthetic interaction [11], hand gestures [9, 14] and tangible interaction [13].

Computer vision based approaches for users' interaction in VR environments are mostly focused on the processing of images acquired by depth sensors such as Kinect [16] and Leap Motion [7]. Each device serves different interaction requirements. The Kinect sensor is more appropriate for interaction from distance and in front of large displays, making use of the whole body and hands [6]. On the other hand, Leap Motion is commonly used in systems which require interaction close to the user and finger-based item selection. Gloves, wands (Wii etc.) and remote controls can also achieve user interaction and navigation both at a distance and close to the user, but require from the user to hold the devices. Computer vision approaches are more unobtrusive and offer a more natural user interaction with the environment since the users just use their bare hands.

This paper discusses the potential of using computer vision approaches for user interaction in VR environments, by providing four different interaction techniques for users' navigation and interaction using their bare hands.

This work proposes the employment of mid-air gestures for head-mounted VR devices, allowing the users to interact with the virtual world in a natural manner without additional equipment. The benefit of gestural interaction is twofold: it allows users to both select elements and travel in space. Item selection is accomplished by pointing towards an item and pinching. In order to move in space, the users can perform a specific hand pose and move it towards the preferred direction and the user's view will fly accordingly in the virtual world. Flying in a virtual environment allows the unobstructed movement in space in 3 dimensions, providing a travelling technique which is applicable to the vast majority of virtual environments.

2 Interaction

The interaction techniques for VR environments presented in this paper are based on the Leap Motion sensor placed in front of an Oculus Rift, which displays a virtual world to the users. This setup allows free user movement in space, enabling them to turn their head towards any direction. Gesture recognition is accomplished with the camera placed in front of the user's head and therefore the user's hands are never occluded by the user's torso, which is a shortcoming for different setups where the depth sensor is placed in a static position. In order to move in space, several alternatives were examined. The users can close their fist and move it towards the preferred direction and the camera will move accordingly.

Four alternatives for navigating using gestural interaction are proposed. The underlying approach relies on the concept of being able to perform a specified hand posture in order to travel in space, whilst not interfering with the ability to point in the virtual environment. In all cases, the gesture is initiated when the user performs a posture and while the posture is tracked, the view of the virtual world moves with regard to the offset vector which is defined by the starting point and the current hand's position.

- **Closed fist** (Fig. 1): the user's hands are closed in order to travel in space. This approach employs the movement metaphor of superman, as they are able to freely look in any direction and travel in virtual space in the direction of the offset vector. The cognitive model used is straightforward, as the users' actions are augmented in a magic way through the common magical belief of the super hero's ability to fly.
- **Open palm** (Fig. 2): the user's hands are open in order to travel in space. This approach is identical to the closed fist technique, however applied with the posture of keeping the hand open with all fingers extended.
- **Open palm-normal vector** (Fig. 3): the gesture is performed while the users keep their hands open, resulting into movement along the axis that is perpendicular to the open palm's plane, both in the front and in the back side of the palm (positive and the negative values). The concept of this gesture is that the users define the direction towards which they want to travel by pointing with the open hand.
- **Open palm with all fingers extended (along palm's normal vector, analyzed)** (Fig. 4): the gesture performed is identical to the open palm-normal vector technique, but analyzes the palm's normal vector with regard to the coordinate system of the users' heads in three axes. The analyzed vector is split in vectors on three axes (x, y and z) and movement is performed along the dominant one, while the movement on the other axes is ignored. As a result, the users are able to move only in one direction at a time (i.e. left-right, up-down and forward-backward), offering increased precision and eliminating accidental movements in other axes, with the drawback of requiring multiple gestures to move in two directions (e.g. front and right).

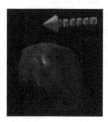 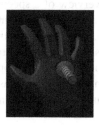  

Fig. 1. Closed fist   **Fig. 2.** Open palm   **Fig. 3.** Open palm-normal vector   **Fig. 4.** Open palm with all fingers extended

The users' hands are rendered in the virtual world in a one to one mapping to the physical world, creating the feeling of a mixed reality environment as the users perceive the hands that appear in their VR view as their own, and thus are confident that they have full control of the system. Furthermore, the movement speed is defined by the length of this vector, allowing the users to increase the travelling speed by moving their hand further away from the starting point.

The proposed approach aids orientation by employing an arrow placed above the user's hands, indicating the applied gesture direction and scaled according to the movement speed (Fig. 5). Even though the feedback of movement in the virtual space might be sufficient in the case of travelling in environments with nearby points of reference, such as the ground, walls or trees, when travelling at a distance from displayed elements, such as flying over a world, in space or in underwater environments, the movement speed and direction may be unclear.

In terms of item selection, directing the pointer finger at an item is used for aiming at an element. The pointing direction is lighted and a circular cursor is placed on the interactive element, if any, to designate the ability to select it (Fig. 6). Selection is accomplished through pinching, following the metaphor of clicking with a mouse.

Fig. 5. Navigation in VR

Fig. 6. Item selection in VR

3   3D Data Centre Environment

In order to experiment with the proposed gestural interaction approaches a Data Centre 3D Visualization application [5] was used as a case study. The application aims at helping data centre experts to get an intuitive overview of a specific data centre room regarding its current condition. Additionally, the application facilitates the inspection of the racks and servers by the users and warns them, in an intuitive manner, about situations that need further investigation, such as an anomaly regarding a particular set of servers that may bring to surface malfunctions or degraded operation. The application was chosen as a case study since it encompasses both extensive travelling when viewing the data centre room from a distance and short movements when examining racks near the room's floor.

The main screen of the Data Centre 3D Visualization application, which comprises a virtual representation of a data centre room and the basic interactive UI components is depicted in Fig. 7. All the room servers are grouped and displayed as 3D racks according to their physical location in space. Each rack may contain at most 40 servers which are displayed as a slice with a specific color, annotating its current condition. The virtual data centre room is constructed as a grid in the 3D space. The environment that encloses the scene is spherical and the servers' grid is placed at the centre, so that users can have a 360° overview.

Upon the selection of a server of a specific rack, the visualization changes and more detailed information per server is displayed. The close – up view (Fig. 8) contains historical data information which is updated while changing the time or upon a server alternation. The historical data is designated through line charts in a spherical view so as the user to be enclosed in a spherical display of information.

Fig. 7. 3D data centre room monitoring   **Fig. 8.** Close up view

4 Conclusion – Future Work

This paper has presented ongoing work regarding the potential uses of gestural interaction as a means of traveling in virtual reality environments in a natural manner. Four alternatives were implemented and utilized in the demanding context of a data centre room monitoring application, which requires both extensive traveling and fine-tuning the view aspect in-between racks. The early users' comments on applying gestural interaction in combination with VR devices were very encouraging, as the approach proved natural, usable and efficient. The next planes steps involve conducting an extensive evaluation, assessing the users' preferences both among the proposed alternate gestural approaches and in comparison to more traditional devices.

Virtual reality can be employed to provide improved user experience in the domain of 3D visualizations. The existing VR headsets will be further enhanced with portable and potentially embedded devices such as Leap motion, providing an environment supporting natural interaction which captivates human senses and offers improved perception of 3D spaces.

Acknowledgements. This research has been partially funded by the European Commission under project LeanBigData (FP7-619606).

References

1. Boas, Y.A.G.V.: Overview of virtual reality technologies. In: Interactive Multimedia Conference 2013 (2013)
2. Bowman, D., Wingrave, C., Campbell, J., Ly, V.: Using pinch gloves (tm) for both natural and abstract interaction techniques in virtual environments. In: Proceedings of HCI International 2001, pp. 629–633 (2001)
3. Cruz-Neira, C., Sandin, D.J., DeFanti, T.A., Kenyon, R.V., Hart, J.C.: The CAVE: audio visual experience automatic virtual environment. Commun. ACM **35**(6), 64–73 (1992)
4. Desai, P.R., Desai, P.N., Ajmera, K.D., Mehta, K.: A review paper on oculus rift-a virtual reality headset (2014). arXiv preprint arXiv:1408.1173
5. Drossis, G., Birliraki, C., Patsiouras, N., Margetis, G., Stephanidis, C.: 3D visualization of large scale data centres. In: Proceedings of the 6th International Conference on Cloud Computing and Services Science - Volume 1: DataDiversityConvergence, pp. 388–395 (2016). ISBN 978-989-758-182-3, doi:10.5220/0005933303880395
6. Drossis, G., Grammenos, D., Adami, I., Stephanidis, C.: 3D visualization and multimodal interaction with temporal information using timelines. In: Kotzé, P., Marsden, G., Lindgaard, G., Wesson, J., Winckler, M. (eds.) INTERACT 2013. LNCS, vol. 8119, pp. 214–231. Springer, Heidelberg (2013). doi:10.1007/978-3-642-40477-1_13
7. Guna, J., Jakus, G., Pogačnik, M., Tomažič, S., Sodnik, J.: An analysis of the precision and reliability of the leap motion sensor and its suitability for static and dynamic tracking. Sensors **14**(2), 3702–3720 (2014)
8. HTC Vive. https://www.vive.com. Accessed 20 Mar 2017
9. Lee, P.W., Wang, H.Y., Tung, Y.C., Lin, J.W., Valstar, A.: TranSection: hand-based interaction for playing a game within a virtual reality game. In: Proceedings of the 33rd Annual ACM Conference Extended Abstracts on Human Factors in Computing Systems, pp. 73–76. ACM, April 2015
10. Lorenz, M., Busch, M., Rentzos, L., Tscheligi, M., Klimant, P., Fröhlich, P.: I'm There! The influence of virtual reality and mixed reality environments combined with two different navigation methods on presence. In: Virtual Reality (VR), 2015 IEEE, pp. 223–224. IEEE, March 2015
11. Nabiyouni, M., Bowman, D.A.: A taxonomy for designing walking-based locomotion techniques for virtual reality. In: Proceedings of the 2016 ACM Companion on Interactive Surfaces and Spaces, pp. 115–121. ACM, November 2016
12. Oculus. https://www.oculus.com. Accessed 20 Mar 17
13. Saar, E.: Touching reality: exploring how to immerse the user in a virtual reality using a touch device, p. 22 (2014). http://hdl.handle.net/2043/17666. Accessed 20 Mar 2017
14. Tecchia, F., Avveduto, G., Brondi, R., Carrozzino, M., Bergamasco, M., Alem, L.: I'm in VR!: using your own hands in a fully immersive MR system. In: Proceedings of the 20th ACM Symposium on Virtual Reality Software and Technology, pp. 73–76. ACM, November 2014
15. Yao, R., Heath, T., Davies, A., Forsyth, T., Mitchell, N., Hoberman, P.: Oculus VR best practices guide. Oculus VR (2014)
16. Zhang, Z.: Microsoft Kinect sensor and its effect. IEEE Multimedia **19**(2), 4–10 (2012)

Interactive Evolutionary Computation Using Multiple Users' Gaze Information

Minatsu Fujisaki[1]([⊠]), Hiroshi Takenouchi[1], and Masataka Tokumaru[2]

[1] Fukuoka Institute of Technology, Fukuoka 811-0295, Japan
f.minatu.2818@gmail.com
[2] Kansai University, Osaka 564-8680, Japan

Abstract. We propose an interactive evolutionary computation (IEC) method that uses the gaze information of multiple users to reduce user evaluation loads. The IEC method employs user sensitivity to evaluate candidate solutions of evolutionary computation. However, IEC has a problem that user evaluation loads of candidate solutions are large. To solve this problem, some researchers have proposed various methods using a simple evaluation of candidate solutions or biological information. Therefore, we use the gaze information of users to evaluate candidate solutions in IEC. By using gaze information, the system can reduce the user evaluation load without the need for users to wear a special measuring device. We created a women's clothing coordination system using IEC with gaze information. We conducted an evaluation experiment to verify the effectiveness of the proposed system. The experimental results show that the proposed system is effective for incorporating users' gaze information into IEC evaluation.

1 Introduction

Interactive evolutionary computation (IEC) is a method that uses human sensibilities to evaluate candidate solutions of evolutionary computation (EC). Therefore, IEC is effective for problems that emphasize human sensitivities [1]. First, the IEC randomly generates an initial population of a predetermined number of individuals. Next, it presents the generated individual to the user, who evaluates it. The user evaluates to the presented individual. Next, the IEC performs an EC based on the user evaluation and presents the newly generated individual again. The IEC repeats these processes until a solution that satisfies the user is obtained.

Because IEC can employ human sensibility, it has been applied in a wide range of fields such as art, engineering, education, and games [1]. Some researchers confirmed the effectiveness of IEC in various fields such as music composition [2] and hearing aid fitting [3]. In addition, some researchers have proposed method in which multiple users evaluate the candidate solutions of IEC [4]. However, IEC has the problem that user evaluation loads of the candidate solutions are large.

© Springer International Publishing AG 2017
C. Stephanidis (Ed.): HCII Posters 2017, Part I, CCIS 713, pp. 109–116, 2017.
DOI: 10.1007/978-3-319-58750-9_15

To solve this problem, some researchers have proposed using human biometric information for the IEC evaluation. Biometric information includes heart rate [5], brain function, and gaze information [6]. However, to acquire heart rate and brain function information, the users must wear a measurement device. This is a user loads. In contrast, gaze information can be measured with a non-contact type measuring device, that does not impose a user loads. Therefore, we measure gaze information using a non-contact type measuring device.

We propose an IEC system that employs multiple user gaze information for evaluating candidate solutions. We aim to reduce the user load using gaze information with a non-contact measuring device. In addition, when multiple users evaluate in IEC, we consider that these evaluations can easily be obtained using gaze information because the system uses the gaze information instead of the evaluation of each user to obtain the final evaluation value.

The system uses women's clothing to make users interested. We performed an evaluation experiment with real users to verify the effectiveness of the proposed system. The results verify the effectiveness of using gaze information to evaluate IEC.

2 Proposed System

2.1 Summary of the Proposed System

In this study, we proposed a female clothing coordination generation system that evaluates solution candidates using the gaze information of multiple users. Figure 1 shows an outline of the proposed system.

First, the system generates an initial population and presents it to the user. The user is presented with two different of clothing coordination. The system evaluates the presented individuals using gaze information. Based on the evaluation, the system performs EC and generates new clothing coordination.

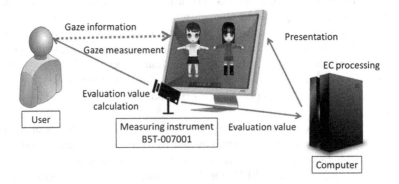

Fig. 1. Outline of the proposed system

The system presents the new individuals to the user, who again evaluates them. The system repeats this process until a solution that satisfies the user is obtained.

In the proposed system, to acquire the user's gaze accurately, the system determines which side of the screen the user is looking at. In addition, to maintain the user's interest, the system retains the relevance of each match. Therefore, we use a winner based paired comparison (WPC) method [7].

We use Human Vision Component B5T-007001 (OMRON, Japan) to acquire gaze information which includes the viewing position and the number of times users looked. We judged the viewing position from the position and angle of the face as well as the angle of gaze.

2.2 Evaluation Method of the Solution Candidate

The proposed system gives one point to the individual that is being observed when gaze information is acquired. The system repeatedly acquires gaze information over a fixed duration. Finally, the system determines the winner from the score.

Next, the system evaluates each individual with a value using the wins and losses. Figure 2 shows the evaluation process for each individual. In advance, the system allocates one point to all individuals generated in the same generation. The system determines the outcome of a match based on the users' gaze information and adds the loser's evaluation value to the winner's. In Fig. 2, first, the system gives each generated individual the one point. Then, A beats B in the first round. Therefore, the system adds the evaluation value of B to the evaluation value of A. The evaluation value of A is then 2 points. If A beats C in the second round, the system adds the evaluation value of C to the evaluation value of A so that it is now 3 points. Assuming D beats A in the third round, the system then adds the evaluation value of A to the evaluation value of D. The evaluation value score of D is hence 4 points. The final evaluation value of A is 3 points, B is 1 point, C is 1 point, and D is 4 points.

Fig. 2. The evaluation process for each individual

2.3 Evaluation Interface

Figure 3 shows the evaluation interface of the proposed system. The user sits in front of the screen and inputs their port number and the baudrate using the keyboard. Next, when the user presses the START button, the system presents two

Fig. 3. Evaluation interface of the system

different women's clothing coordination on the screen. The user looks at his/her preferred clothing coordination of the two options presented. After the clothing coordination is presented for 5 s, the system evaluates each individual from the obtained gaze information. The system presents the clothing coordinates of the next competition based on the evaluation value of the current one. The user continues this operation for five generations. After the final generation is evaluated, the system presents the clothing coordination of the highest evaluation value.

2.4   Coordination Parts

Figure 4 the genetic coding of the clothing coordination. The clothing coordination consists of four parts: hair, tops, bottoms, and shoes [7]. Each part has eight or sixteen designs, which are expressed using 3 or 4 bits. The system can then create 16,384 designs because the gene length is 14 bits.

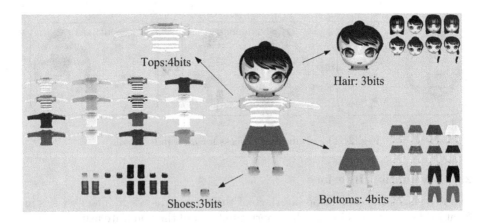

Fig. 4. The genetic coding of the clothing coordination

3   Evaluation

3.1   Experiment Summary

We conducted two verifications using the proposed system. The first verified the effectiveness of using gaze information in the evaluation of IEC for reducing the user load. The second was to evaluate the effectiveness of using gaze information for IEC evaluation that includes multiple users. In this research, we used a system that evaluates with gaze information and a system that performs manual evaluations. In this experiment, we compared the performances of the proposed and conventional systems.

Table 1 shows the parameters in this experiment. When solutions begin to converge, the system generates similar clothing coordination. In such a case, users will become bored and feel a psychological load. Hence, we set the mutation rate to as high as 20%. The proposed system sets the display time to 5 s because the user sees the entire clothing coordination being displayed.

We conducted the following two experiments.

1. A comparison of the user load and satisfaction with the generated clothing coordination in the proposed system versus a conventional system.
2. An investigation of the satisfaction level with the generated clothing coordination when multiple users are targeted.

In Exp.1, 23 university students in their twenties participated. We used two systems: the proposed system and a conventional system. First, each subject used both systems. We randomly determined which system the subject used first. After that, subjects evaluate the satisfaction level of finally generated coordination and the evaluation load in 5 stages evaluation.

Exp.2 consisted of 10 pairs of subjects' consisting of university students in their twenties. We used the proposed system. First, each subject pair used the proposed system together. After that, subjects evaluate the satisfaction level of finally generated coordination in 5 stages evaluation.

Table 1. Parameters in the experiment

Population	8
Gene length	14 bits
Generations	5
Selection method	Roulette selection + Elite preservation
Crossover method	Uniform crossover
Mutation rate	20%
Display time (the proposed system only)	5 s

3.2   Experimental Results

Figure 5 shows the satisfaction results for the final generated clothing coordination in Exp.1. In both systems, the average satisfaction with the generated clothing coordination was about 3.9. To confirm the statistical significance of this result, we performed a sign test but did not confirm a significant difference at a significance level of 5%. Therefore, we conclude that it is possible to generate a satisfactory design to some extent by using gaze information as a method of IEC evaluation.

Figure 6 shows the evaluation loads of the proposed system in Exp.1. The evaluation load average of the proposed system was 1.9, and the evaluation load average of the conventional system was 1.8. To confirm the statistical significance of this result, we performed a sign test but did not confirm a significant difference at a significance level of 5%. Therefore, it seems that there is almost no difference in the evaluation burden of the proposed and conventional systems.

Figure 7 shows the result of satisfaction of with the finally generated coordination in Exp.2. The average satisfaction of the final generated clothing coordination was about 3.75. Although there are some differences in the satisfaction levels of the two users in a pair, it is considered that system can create a clothing

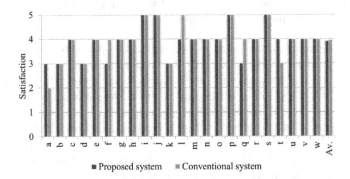

Fig. 5. Satisfaction of the generated coordination

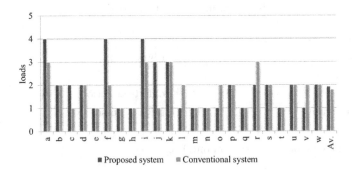

Fig. 6. Evaluation loads of the system

coordination that satisfies the users. Therefore, we confirm that it is possible to generate a satisfactory design to some extent even if the gaze information of two users is used for IEC.

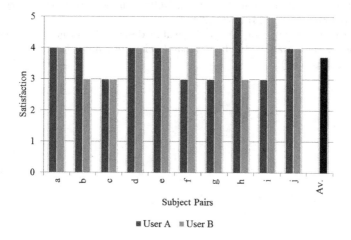

Fig. 7. Satisfaction of the generated coordination

4   Conclusions

We proposed an IEC system employing users gaze information. We verified its effectiveness on real users by using the proposed system. In the experimental results, we confirmed that the proposed system is effective for reducing the user evaluation load. In addition, we confirmed that it is effective to use gaze information in the evaluation of IEC even in the case of multiple people. In future work, we will further verify its effectiveness and consider practical application systems.

References

1. Takagi, H.: Interactive evolutionary computation: fusion of the capabilities of EC optimization and human evaluation. Proc. IEEE **89**(9), 1275–1296 (2001)
2. Tokui, N., Iba, H.: Music composition with interactive evolutionary computation. In: Proceedings of the 3rd International Conference on Generative Art, vol. 17, no. 2, pp. 215–226 (2000)
3. Takagi, H., Ohsaka, M.: Interactive evolutionary computation-based hearing aid fitting. IEEE Trans. Evol. Comput. **11**(3), 414–427 (2007)
4. Sakai, M., Takenouchi, H., Tokumaru, M.: Design support system with votes from multiple people using digital signage. In: 2014 IEEE International Symposium on Independent Computing in IEEE Symposium Series on Computational Intelligence (SSCI) 2014, pp. 25–31 (2014)

5. Fukumoto, M., Nakashima, S., Ogawa, S., Imai, J.I.: Extended interactive evolutionary computation using heart rate variability as fitness value for composing music chord progression. J. Adv. Comput. Intell. Intell. Inform. **15**(9), 1329–1336 (2011)
6. Holnes, T., Zanker, J.: Eye on prize: using overt visual attention to drive fitness for interactive evolutionary computation. In: 2008 Genetic and Evolutionary Computation Conference, pp. 1531–1538 (2008)
7. Takenouchi, H., Tokumaru, M.: Wrist watch design system gased on interactive evolutionary computation. In: 18th Japan Society of Kansai Engineering, vol. P02 (2016). (in Japanese)

Effects of Electrode Configuration on Pattern Recognition Based Finger Movement Classification

Jiayuan He[1], Xiangyang Zhu[2], and Ning Jiang[1(✉)]

[1] Department of Systems Design Engineering,
University of Waterloo, Waterloo, Canada
ning.jiang@uwaterloo.ca
[2] State Key Lab of Mechanical System and Vibration,
Shanghai Jiao Tong University, Shanghai, China

Abstract. Pattern recognition (PR) based myoelectric control could provide intuitive and dexterous control of advanced prostheses. Previous studies showed that the performance of finger movements was not as good as that of wrist movements. As electrode configuration plays an important role in classification performance, this study investigated the effect of the number of electrodes and their locations on finger movement classification. An electrode selection algorithm, sequential forward searching (SFS), was applied on the high density (HD) electrode grid with 192 monopolar electrodes. With the time domain (TD) feature and linear discriminant analysis (LDA), it was found that the error rate was dramatically decreased with the number of electrodes increasing from one to ten. Under the optimized electrode configuration, the error rate could be lower than 10% with 8 electrodes, and 5% with 18 electrodes. The importance of the electrodes was measured and the results showed that the effective site for classification was mainly located around the flexor digitorum superficialis and extensor digitorum communis. This study provides the guideline for optimal placement of electrodes in finger movement recognition, and potentially provide sufficient controllability of advance prostheses with individually articulated fingers.

Keywords: Surface electromyogram · Pattern recognition · Finger movement · Prostheses · High density

1 Introduction

Surface electromyogram (sEMG) signals are electrical manifestation of muscle activity, and contains neural information about the neural signals controlling the muscles [1, 2]. This property has been exploited in many application, including myoelectric prosthesis control, where the sEMG signals collected from the remnant forearm muscles are used to control the prostheses to help the amputees restore their limb functions [3]. Conventional control scheme is based on the amplitude of sEMG signals from one pair of antagonistic muscles [4]. With this scheme, only one degree of freedom (DOF) could be activated at a time. If other DOF is desired, co-contracting the muscle group is

© Springer International Publishing AG 2017
C. Stephanidis (Ed.): HCII Posters 2017, Part I, CCIS 713, pp. 117–122, 2017.
DOI: 10.1007/978-3-319-58750-9_16

needed to switch the mode. As such, this control scheme is obtrusive to the users and resulted in a high device abandonment rate [5].

Another control scheme of myoelectric prostheses is based on pattern recognition (PR) algorithms, which could provide intuitive and dexterous control of multi-function powered prostheses by creating the mapping from the user's movements to analogous prostheses functions [4, 6]. It usually adopts four to six electrodes attached around the circumference of the forearm. The major two parts of PR-based control scheme is feature extraction and classification, which extracted the property of sEMG signals and mapped the signal to the movement, respectively. The state-of-the-art algorithm is time domain (TD) feature combined with linear discriminant analysis (LDA) [7].

Previous myoelectric control studies mostly focused on wrist movements and simple grasp gestures, such as wrist flexion, wrist extension, pronation, supination, hand close and hand open [2, 8]. With only four to six electrodes attached around the forearm, the classification accuracy of these movements could reach 95% [9]. However, with the same settings, the control performance of finger movements is not as good as that of wrist movements [10]. As one of the most flexible parts of human body, finger movements are involved in most activities of our daily lives. In this study, we investigated the effect of electrode configuration on PR-based finger movement classification. High density (HD) electrode grids were used to obtain the sEMG signals of the forearm muscles. An efficient electrode selection algorithm, sequential forward searching (SFS), was applied on the signals to test the effects of the number of electrodes and their locations on classification accuracy of finger movement. The outcome would be beneficial for the socket design of the advanced prostheses.

2 Methods

2.1 Subjects

Ten healthy subjects participated in the experiments (all male and right handed, aged from 20 to 30 years old). The informed consent was obtained before the experiment and the procedures were in accordance with the Declaration of Helsinki.

2.2 Data Collection and Processing

sEMG signals were recorded using a HD electrode system (EMG USB2+, OT Bioelettronica, Italy) with 192 monopolar electrodes. The electrodes were placed on the forearm, about 3 cm distal to the elbow crease, as shown in Fig. 1. Before electrodes attachment, the skin is cleaned with alcohol pads to remove debris to increase the contact condition between the electrode and skin. The inter-electrode distance is 10 mm. The signals were filtered between 10 and 500 Hz, and digitally sampled at 2048 Hz.

Ten classes of finger movements were investigated in this study, as shown in Fig. 2. The subject was asked to sit on a chair, naturally extended their arms toward the ground. They were instructed to perform the movements with a consistent level of effort. One trial is defined as one repetition of eleven classes (ten finger movements and

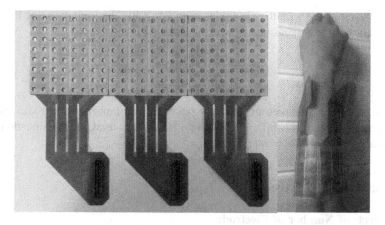

Fig. 1. HD electrode grid and its position on the subject's forearm.

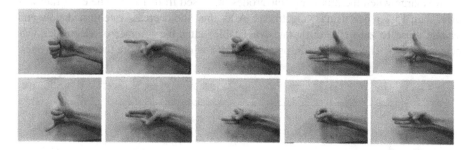

Fig. 2. Ten finger movements investigated in this study

rest), and each lasts 5 s with a 5-s rest between two classes to avoid fatigue. Sixteen trials were completed for each subject, with a 30-s rest between two trials. The entire experiment lasted about 40 min.

The sEMG signals were segmented into 200-ms analysis windows, with 150-ms overlap between two windows. TD feature set (mean absolute value, waveform length, zero crossings, and sign slope changes) [6] was extracted from each analysis window and sent to the LDA classifier.

Sequential forward searching (SFS) is a searching algorithm that selects a subset of electrodes which provides the lowest error rate with the defined number of electrodes [11]. Suppose there are a total of N electrodes, SFS calculates the error rate of one electrode for each electrode, and choose the lowest error rate as its performance of one electrode, denoted as $ER_{n(i)}$, where i is the electrode index, and $n(\cdot)$ represents the number of electrodes (equal to 1 here). Then, SFS calculates the error rate of two electrodes consist of Electrode i and the other from N-1 electrodes, and regards it as the lowest one ($ER_{n(j)}$, where $n(j) = 2$) as the performance of two electrodes. The rest N-2 error rates could be calculated in the same manner. In this study, SFS was used to calculate the error rate with the electrodes from 1 to 130. The importance of Electrode i for classification was measured by weight index (WI)

$$WI_i = \frac{(ER_{n(i)} - ER_{n(j)})}{ER_{n(i)}} \times 100\%$$

where $ER_{n(i)}$ and $ER_{n(j)}$ represents the error rate with the number of electrodes $n(i)$ and $n(j)$ respectively, and $n(j) = n(i) - 1$. When no electrode is used, the classification error is random. So we set $ER_0 = 1/11$.

3   Results and Discussion

3.1   Effects of Number of Electrodes

The relationship between the error rate and the number of electrodes is shown in Fig. 3. The error rate decreased with the increase of the number of electrodes. The decrease rate was large when the number of electrodes increased from 1 to 6. The error rate was lower than 15% when using 6 electrodes. After that, the decrease rate turned slow and became close to zero (the error rate was stable) after the number of electrodes was increased to 25. The error rate dropped below 4% when using more than 25 electrodes.

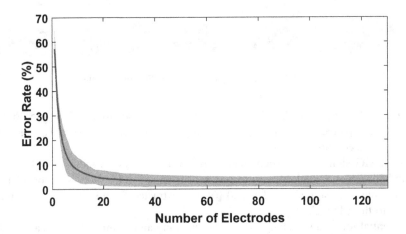

Fig. 3. Error rate of eleven movements classified with different number of the electrodes. The red line is the average value across ten subjects. The grey area represents the standard deviation. (Color figure online)

3.2   WI Distribution

The importance of the electrode in classification is measured by WI value, and their distribution is displayed in Fig. 4. The WI values of most sites were low, and high

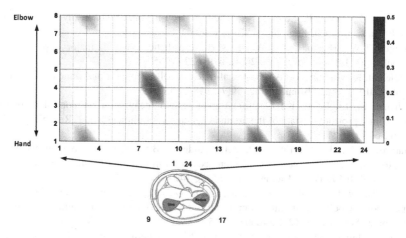

Fig. 4. Weight Index (WI) distribution of the HD electrode grid on the forearm. The vertical and horizontal axis are row and column number of the grid, respectively. The number on the section view is the column number of the grid, which corresponding to the horizontal axis.

plays an important role in finger movement classification. The most important site for finger movement classification is located around the flexor digitorum superficialis and extensor digitorum communis, which coincide with the physiological structure of the human body.

4   Conclusion

The classification of finger movements was influenced by the number of electrodes and their locations. The effect of the number of electrodes decreased with the increase of the number of electrodes, and the error rate became stable after 25 electrodes. The effective electrode location is around the flexor digitorum superficialis and extensor digitorum communis.

Acknowledgement. We thank all volunteers for their participation in the study. This work is supported by the University Starter Grant of the University of Waterloo (No. 203859), the National Natural Science Foundation of China (Grant No. 51620105002, 51375296).

References

1. Dosen, S., Muller, K.-R., Farina, D.: Myoelectric control of artificial limbs—is there a need to change focus? [In the Spotlight]. IEEE Sig. Process. Mag. **29**(5), 150–152 (2012)
2. Parker, P., Englehart, K., Hudgins, B.: Myoelectric signal processing for control of powered limb prostheses. J. Electromyogr. Kinesiol. **16**(6), 541–548 (2006)
3. He, J., Zhang, D., Sheng, X., Li, S., Zhu, X.: Invariant surface EMG feature against varying contraction level for myoelectric control based on muscle coordination. IEEE J. Biomed. Health Inform. **2194**, 1–9 (2014)

4. Hudgins, B., Parker, P., Scott, R.N.: A new strategy for multifunction myoelectric control. IEEE Trans. Biomed. Eng. **40**(1), 82–94 (1993)
5. Wright, T.W., Hagen, A.D., Wood, M.B.: Prosthetic usage in major upper extremity amputations. J. Hand Surg. Am. **20**(4), 619–622 (1995)
6. Englehart, K., Hudgins, B.: A robust, real-time control scheme for multifunction myoelectric control. IEEE Trans. Biomed. Eng. **50**(7), 848–854 (2003)
7. Scheme, E., Englehart, K.: Electromyogram pattern recognition for control of powered upper-limb prostheses: state of the art and challenges for clinical use. J. Rehabil. Res. Dev. **48**(6), 643 (2011)
8. Hargrove, L.J., Li, G., Englehart, K.B., Hudgins, B.S.: Principal components analysis preprocessing for improved classification accuracies in pattern-recognition-based myoelectric control. IEEE Trans. Biomed. Eng. **56**(5), 1407–1414 (2009)
9. He, J., Zhang, D., Jiang, N., Sheng, X., Farina, D., Zhu, X.: User adaptation in long-term, open-loop myoelectric training: implications for EMG pattern recognition in prosthesis control. J. Neural Eng. **12**(4), 46005 (2015)
10. Li, G., Schultz, A.E., Kuiken, T.A.: Quantifying pattern recognition-based myoelectric control of multifunctional transradial prostheses. IEEE Trans. Neural Syst. Rehabil. Eng. **18** (2), 185–192 (2010)
11. Huang, H., Zhou, P., Li, G., Kuiken, T.A.: An analysis of EMG electrode configuration for targeted muscle reinnervation based neural machine interface. IEEE Trans. Neural Syst. Rehabil. Eng. **16**(1), 37–45 (2008)

Prompting – A Feature of General Relevance in HCI-Supported Task Workflows

Thomas Herrmann and Jan Nierhoff[⊠]

Ruhr-Universität, Bochum, Germany
{thomas.herrmann, jan.nierhoff}@rub.de

Abstract. A prompt is a message that is delivered to somebody in a selected situation as an appeal to do something which is possible, but not necessary. To design prompts, we propose the principles of being optional, comprehensible, actionable, purposeful, just in time, unobtrusive, controllable by the user and user specific. The three last-named principles are especially relevant in systems where user acceptance is a critical factor of success. A continuous survey in which that is the case is presented as a case study.

Keywords: Prompting · Unobtrusiveness · Self-determination · Workflow

1 Introduction – Prompting Design Principles

Prompting or prompting systems are used in various domains and for various tasks to support human-computer interaction. However, the need to deliver prompts is not systematically taken into account by design guidelines or heuristics for interactive systems (cf. [1]). This paper argues on the basis of literature and empirical work that it is reasonable to acknowledge prompting as a feature which should be generally considered when interactive systems are designed to support a workflow of several tasks. This is especially relevant in the case of supporting collaboration.

So far, prompting has been used in various domains such as:

- Supporting people suffering from dementia, for example to help them finding their way, to complete a sequence of planned actions etc. [2].
- Computer supported collaborative learning (CSCL) to scaffold students' efforts of knowledge acquiring and construction [3]. CSCL-research aims on providing those prompts within HCI which help students to conduct important steps in the process of learning.
- In the context of persuasive computing to support people in changing their behavior; for example with respect to eating habits, healthy lifestyles, energy saving etc. [4].
- Creativity support and brainstorming to inspire people to overcome cognitive inertia and to find new ways of combining their ideas [5]. To promote people to think about experiences being made and to answer questions in a frequent way. This helps them and others to better understand their conditions of life and work on the basis of long term surveys [6].

© Springer International Publishing AG 2017
C. Stephanidis (Ed.): HCII Posters 2017, Part I, CCIS 713, pp. 123–129, 2017.
DOI: 10.1007/978-3-319-58750-9_17

- To trigger people to start reflecting their behavior and experiences they have collected during work. Triggering reflection pursues the purpose to learn on the basis of existing experience how work in the future can be improved [7].

Prompting is relevant in the context of workflows or repetitive tasks where reminders are needed which help people to comply with their own intentions and plans, or with conventions on which they have agreed upon in the course of collaborating with others. Prompts can help to establish a certain rhythm of action, or to overcome linear thinking and to seek for creative solutions. Prompts are a combination of helping to comply with certain conventions as well as to go beyond them. Prompting can be seen as a part of scaffolding [3] which mostly consists of a guidance through a procedure which combines several mandatory and optional activities.

As a general definition we propose that a prompt is a message that is delivered to somebody in a selected situation as an appeal to do something which is possible but not necessary. From this definition, additional literature [3, 8–10] and research conducted in the case study (see below) we derive the following principles for prompting:

- Optional – and not mandatory. Following the prompt should imply a benefit; not following the prompt must be possible without negative impact.
- Comprehensible – the call to action that is delivered by the prompt should be easily understandable by the user.
- Actionable – the prompt should provide the means to directly execute the call to action.
- Purposeful – the reason why it is significant or advantageous to follow the prompt should be obvious and the values which are addressed by the prompt must be understandable.
- Just in time – prompts should be provided at the moment they are relevant.
- Unobtrusive – the prompt should appear only in appropriate situations in which users don't feel bothered and/or should be presented in an unobtrusive way. Prompts may vanish if they are continuously ignored by the user.
- User control – users should be granted control about prompting characteristics.
- User specificity – the prompt should differ with respect to different characteristics of users.

These principles concern both the technical level of how and when the prompt is presented to a user, as well as the level of the prompt's content.

The main problem with prompts is that they have to be a result of deliberate articulation work [11]. It is challenging to phrase prompts so that they are appropriate for many different users for a longer time period. For example, if users are prompted by questions to give feedback about their situation, these questions might have to be adapted after a while because of changing conditions in the environment. Furthermore, for different questions it is reasonable to repeat them with different frequencies in a certain time period. In many cases, prompting has to be realized as a collaborative endeavor. Prompts are delivered and phrased by individuals for other individuals. This collaborative action can be complemented by phases of automatic prompting where the prompts are delivered according to a pre-specified plan. Prompting is an adequate means to support collaboration since it goes beyond awareness on the one hand and automated workflows on the other hand. Awareness of others does not necessarily propose an appropriate action as prompts do. Automatic workflows are in many cases too prescriptive while prompts offer guidance by offering options for action. Thus, prompting is a beneficial design concept in the middle of the spectrum between awareness and automated workflows.

2   Case Study: Prompting Employees to Give Feedback About the Perceived Working Climate

This case study describes the project 'KreativBarometer' [12] that pursued the goal of monitoring the creativity climate within companies at higher rates than conventional climate assessment tools. To achieve sampling rates of 1 to 3 weeks, employees have to answer short questions repeatedly about how they perceived their recent working life; e.g. "Currently, I feel accepted and understood by my peers". To minimize situational influences on the results, the employees were asked to answer single or small sets of question items from time to time and not in one coherent session (like a conventional survey would do).

To support the continuous data collection several prompting mechanisms were implemented (on different client platforms) and tested:

- E-mails were used to prompt users of a browser based survey client. Participants could choose to get prompts two times a week, once a week or every two weeks. Additionally, an e-mail warning three days before survey related deadlines was available. Due to privacy issues the e-mail addresses were not linked to users' accounts, which prevented a more sophisticated prompting.
- Desktop notifications were used to prompt users of a Java-based client for Windows PCs. Users could choose if a balloon tip (see Fig. 1) acted as a prompt or if a question was displayed directly. Notifications (optionally) appeared if
  - participation fell short of a specified quota of items per time,
  - a survey deadline was less than a configurable amount of days away and the user had not answered all due items,
  - and/or the user did not interact with the computer for a configurable amount of minutes. This approach tried to seize potential task switches of the user.

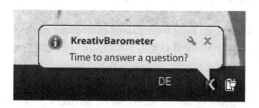

Fig. 1. Windows desktop notification (balloon tip) as a prompt to answer a survey question

Fig. 2. Android system notification; (A) view questions, (B) reduce current participation rate, (C) configure contextual features

- Android system notifications were used to prompt users of a mobile phone client. The mobile client was connected to an improved version of the server system that does not work with survey deadlines. By contrast, it determines when a question is due, based on the time since it has last been answered, its specific repetition rate, the user's current willingness to participate, and contextual information [13]. The prompts on mobile phones (see Fig. 2) allowed users to access questions that are due (Fig. 2A), give feedback about the current participation rate (Fig. 2B), configure the contextual awareness features (Fig. 2C) or dismiss the prompt (in this case no new notifications would appear for at least 5 h).

- Custom prompts in the form of calendar reminders were proactively created by users of the browser client. These allowed a higher control about the prompting rhythm than the e-mail reminders that were offered to them.

Experiments in 41 Teams from 10 test sites were conducted utilizing the browser and desktop clients. We collected over 68000 answers from 465 users. Mixed method evaluations showed that acceptance is the critical factor of success for a continuous survey [13]. As the prompts to answer questions are the main touchpoint between participants and system, they are a major source for potential acceptance problems. In our experience from the experiments, the acceptance towards the system benefits from giving users control about prompting characteristics and making prompts user specific and unobtrusive. These insights caused us to add said aspects to the set of prompting principles.

The following list sums up how we realized prompting in the latest iteration of the continuous survey system (Android client, see Fig. 2) in regard to the aforementioned principles:

- Optional – Prompts can be ignored or dismissed anytime. The survey system is designed to handle heterogeneous amounts of answers from different users. Low participation rates are not penalized. Nonetheless, the system promotes projected participation rates by creating awareness about subpar answering behavior.

- Comprehensible – The prompts feature simple minimalistic phrases, which caused no misunderstandings within the experiments.
- Actionable – The prompts contain direct links to the different actions, which allowed users to access questions that are due (Fig. 2A, give feedback about the current participation rate (Fig. 2B, configure the contextual awareness features (Fig. 2C or dismiss the prompt.
- Purposeful – The system allows for item-specific repetition rates. Prompts that deal with topics of low dynamics are less often presented to the user. Giving weekly feedback about the tools you can access for example may seem unreasonable, if the tool setup changes only every few months. Earlier prototypes that did not feature item-specific repetition rates were criticized by users because they had the feeling of having to give unnecessary answers.
- Just in time – As the survey system grants users control about their participation and thus giving an answer can always be declined, there is no 'right time' to answer a question. Nonetheless, the system implements a relevancy concept that determines when which questions are available to the user at all. Determining these points of time is based on the time since a question has last been answered, its specific repetition rate, the user's current willingness to participate, and contextual information. While there are prompts available that remind users if they did not participate for a certain amount of time, a user is never prompted if no question is available.
- Unobtrusive – The prompts instrumentalize standard notification mechanisms of the android platform and avoid any features that may increase the awareness, like sound or striking colors. With this approach, users know how to handle the prompts and the risk of appearing as an additional source of distraction is reduced. The survey system, which orchestrates the timing of the prompts, aims at reducing annoyance that may be created by the prompts, by implementing context awareness features. These features use contextual information (e.g. time, place or calendar data) to detect favorable and unfavorable situations to send a prompt to the user. The experiments showed that prompts that disrupt the participants' workflow decrease the acceptance towards the whole survey system. Hence, prompts should be no disturbance. As following the prompt is not mandatory, there is no need to do everything to get the user's attention. The risk of losing acceptance by annoying the user with an obtrusive prompt in a critical situation is higher than the price of having a prompt vanish unnoticed.
- User control – Users can give feedback about their current willingness to participate and, by this, configure the prompts in regard to frequency and amount. The experiments showed that user acceptance benefits from granting users self-determination. Rules and restrictions, on the other hand, create the feeling of being patronized, which decreases acceptance.
- User specificity – The wording of the questions is cooperatively negotiated and teams have the possibility to add team-specific items to the questionnaire. Prior to using the tool, the questions were presented to and discussed with the participants. Based on this, the questions were paraphrased to comply to group specific terminologies and jargon. These workshops were also used to collaboratively create team-specific questions. This measures received positive feedback from the

participants; adapting the wording increased identification and comprehensibility and the team-specific questions were often the center of attention when the survey results were put to use.

3 Conclusion

While the case-study examined prompting users to answer questions in the context of a continuous creativity survey, the gained insights can be applied to a more abstract problem statement. A survey system can be divided into two main components: answering items and consuming the fed back results. Giving answers can be interpreted as the compulsory task that is needed to earn the results as a reward. The initial situation is a user who is motivated to participate in a service. The participation requires the users to repeatedly perform (short) actions over a longer period of time. The number of times the user interacts with the system to carry out such an action exceeds the amount of other use cases (e.g. checking the survey results); this makes the prompting of a user to perform an action the main touchpoint between user and system. In general, the user conceives no direct benefit from accomplishing these actions, but gets long-term rewards by using the service. Because of the lack of an immediate reward and the fact that executing the required actions may feel like an obligation, it can happen that the user creates too little input to the service or stops interacting with it at all. Acting upon a prompt to perform the (short) action is beneficial, but not mandatory. Table 1 gives examples of usage scenarios that feature a similar challenge pattern and thus potentially benefit from the principles of making prompts unobtrusive and user specific, while putting the user in control of prompting characteristics.

Table 1. Examples of services that feature the examined challenge pattern

Service	(Short) action that is prompted for	Long-term reward
Continuous survey	Answering item	Improvement of working climate
Reflective learning	Documenting own behavior	Learning about own experiences
Mobile learning	Receiving info/testing knowledge	Improvement of knowledge
Health	Documenting current condition	Stay healthy

These newly proposed principles are critical factors of success to preserve user acceptance. They should be added to the list of principles that can be derived from the definition of prompting and literature. Principles that support the maintaining of acceptance are especially relevant for systems in which the benefit of following a prompt is not directly obvious at the same moment when the user's reaction is required. The benefit is usually created in collaborative constellations where individual contributions support others or the whole group, for example when feedback about the team climate is individually solicited and collaboratively discussed.

References

1. Heuristic Evaluation Articles and Training | Nielsen Norman Group. https://www.nngroup.com/topic/heuristic-evaluation/
2. Carmien, S., Dawe, M., Fischer, G., Gorman, A., Kintsch, A., Sullivan Jr., J.F.: Socio-technical environments supporting people with cognitive disabilities using public transportation. ACM Trans. Comput.-Hum. Interact. TOCHI **12**, 233–262 (2005)
3. Thillmann, H., Künsting, J., Wirth, J., Leutner, D.: Is it merely a question of "what" to prompt or also "when" to prompt? The role of point of presentation time of prompts in self-regulated learning. Z. Für Pädagog. Psychol. **23**, 105–115 (2009)
4. Intille, S.S.: A new research challenge: persuasive technology to motivate healthy aging. IEEE Trans. Inf Technol. Biomed. **8**, 235–237 (2004)
5. Santanen, E.L., Briggs, R.O., Vreede, G.-J.D.: Causal relationships in creative problem solving: comparing facilitation interventions for ideation. J. Manag. Inf. Syst. **20**, 167–198 (2004)
6. Nierhoff, J., Herrmann, T.: Data elicitation for continuous awareness of team climate characteristics to improve organizations' creativity. In: Proceedings of 50th Hawaii International Conference on System Sciences (2017)
7. Prilla, M., Degeling, M., Herrmann, T.: Collaborative reflection at work: supporting informal learning at a healthcare workplace. In: Proceedings of 17th ACM international Conference on Supporting Group Work, pp. 55–64. ACM (2012)
8. McCrickard, D.S., Chewar, C.M., Somervell, J.P., Ndiwalana, A.: A model for notification systems evaluation - assessing user goals for multitasking activity. ACM Trans. Comput.-Hum. Interact. **10**, 312–338 (2003)
9. Byrne, M.D.: Preventing postcompletion errors: how much cue is enough? In: Proceedings of Cognitive Science Society (2008)
10. Herrmann, Thomas, Nolte, Alexander: The integration of collaborative process modeling and electronic brainstorming in co-located meetings. In: Kolfschoten, Gwendolyn, Herrmann, Thomas, Lukosch, Stephan (eds.) CRIWG 2010. LNCS, vol. 6257, pp. 145–160. Springer, Heidelberg (2010). doi:10.1007/978-3-642-15714-1_12
11. Schmidt, K., Bannon, L.: Taking CSCW seriously. Comput. Support. Coop. Work CSCW **1**, 7–40 (1992)
12. Herrmann, T., Carell, A., Nierhoff, J.: Creativity barometer: an approach for continuing micro surveys to explore the dynamics of organization's creativity climates. In: Proceedings of 8th ACM conference on Creativity and cognition, pp. 345–346 (2011)
13. Nierhoff, J.: Cognitive context awareness - a concept for self-determined repetitive data collection within surveys (2016). http://hss-opus.ub.ruhr-uni-bochum.de/opus4/frontdoor/index/index/year/2016/docId/4628

Interaction with Three Dimensional Objects on Diverse Input and Output Devices: A Survey

Adrian Heinrich Hoppe[1]([✉]), Florian van de Camp[2], and Rainer Stiefelhagen[1]

[1] Karlsruhe Institute of Technology (KIT), Karlsruhe, Germany
{adrian.hoppe,rainer.stiefelhagen}@kit.edu
[2] Fraunhofer IOSB, Karlsruhe, Germany
florian.vandecamp@iosb.fraunhofer.de

Abstract. With the emerging technologies of Virtual and Augmented Reality (VR/AR) and the increasing performance of mobile and desktop devices the amount of 3D-based applications rapidly increases. This 3D content demands for an efficient and well suited 3D interaction. Currently there are many manipulation techniques for different input and output devices, like mouse, touchscreen, gestures, 2D-based monitors or 3D-based head mounted displays (HMDs), but there is no general overview covering all interaction techniques. This paper delivers an extensive overview of different approaches and classifies these according to input device, functionality (translation, rotation, scaling, with discrete mode or modeless interaction, uni- or bi-manual). If available, evaluation results or comparisons to other techniques are presented. Each technique is then rated under the aspects of speed, beginner-friendliness and mental and physical demand.

For desktop environments a mouse interaction combined with a 3D widget works well. A six degree of freedom (DOF) device can be more precise but needs additional learning. Virtual environments benefit from a direct manipulation technique which yields a high immersion. On a touch screen, techniques with a fixed amount as well as methods with a variable amount of interacting fingers can be efficient. The contribution of this poster is an overall guide beyond the above mentioned methods which helps to choose a technique suitable for a specific system.

1 Introduction

Manipulation of three dimensional (3D) data includes rotation, translation and scaling (RTS) tasks. Positioning of a virtual object can be subdivided into an initial selection, a coarse, large movement and a final, precise movement [19]. The efficiency and adequacy of a manipulation technique depends strongly on the task [39]. It is influenced by factors like distance from user to object, size of the object, needed amount of RTS and density of objects. Furthermore the input and output devices influence the choice of a possible interaction technique. Therefore this paper aims to give an overview of manipulation techniques grouped by the

© Springer International Publishing AG 2017
C. Stephanidis (Ed.): HCII Posters 2017, Part I, CCIS 713, pp. 130–139, 2017.
DOI: 10.1007/978-3-319-58750-9_18

according input modality. In Sect. 2 some general information for 3D manipulation is established. Section 3 introduces several interaction techniques. Available evaluation results are presented in Sect. 4 and further discussed in Sect. 5. Finally a conclusion is drawn in Sect. 6.

2 Related Work

When interacting with an object it is not advantageous to allow the user to manipulate all DOF of the object at the same time. Users prefer a constrained interaction namely a 2D translation on a plane, a 1D rotation around an axis and an uniform 3D scaling [8]. Rotation is preferred as a 1D task because users cannot deconstruct an orientation into distinct rotations around several axes [59]. Rotation is also a more complex task than translation, as Ware [52] shows it takes about 50% more time. Martinet et al. [31] show that a separated translation and rotation increase the efficiency of users.

The introduction of constraints in a 3D interaction can increase precision and speed if they fit the task [47]. Besides this, a 3D or stereo display helps position and orient objects in a virtual environment (VE) and users perform better than with a classical 2D representation [52].

3 Manipulation Techniques

This section covers different techniques for RTS interaction grouped by the input modality. It covers approaches using a classical 2DOF mouse, an extended mouse with more than 2DOF, a full 6DOF device, a gesture and touch interaction.

3.1 2DOF Mouse Interaction

A possibility to control an object's placement is the use of different sliders which control the dimensions of the movement [8]. However, a mouse interaction with virtual objects often utilizes 3D widgets [9,45]. Typically a partition in different modes for RTS and constraints for 1D or 2D manipulations are presented to the user. Virtual Sphere Methods [8,21,46] let the user rotate an object by clicking & dragging a fictitious sphere that encapsulates the object. Schmidt et al. [45] do not switch between different interaction modes with buttons or shortcuts but rather use sketching gestures to derive manipulation modes accordingly. Techniques like Snapping [9], the Triad Mouse [35] or Snap-Dragging [5,6] place reference points or cursors on objects in the VE which allow the user to perform several transformations on the object. Tail-Dragging [50] links the object to an virtual rope which can be used to drag an object around the VE while simultaneously performing translation and rotation.

3.2 2+DOF Mouse Interaction

Several works exist that increase the DOF of the classical mouse by one or two dimensions in order to perform more complex tasks. Zeleznik et al. [56] take two mice which are controlled by both hands of the user. They split the functionality according to the theory of the dominant and non-dominant hand from Guiard [13]. A bi-manual asymmetric interaction results in an increased performance [3,23]. Another approach is to increase the dimensions of a single mouse as with the Two-Ball Mouse [30], the Rockin'Mouse [4], the Yawing Mouse [2] or the Turntable [12]. These let the user rotate or tilt the mouse for additional input.

3.3   6DOF Mouse Interaction

6DOF controllers consist of isotonic, free moving devices and isometric or elastic, (almost) fixed devices [59]. An isotonic mouse like the VideoMouse [24], the ToolStone [42] or the Bat [53] uses a tracking method that allows the detection of the position and orientation of the device in 6D. Examples for isometric and elastic devices are the SpaceMouse [1] or the Elastic General-purpose Grip (EGG) [60] respectively. The controller for these type of devices moves only a small amount. It measures input based on exerted forces or deviation from a zero position. Isotonic devices benefit from controlling the position of a virtual object directly (zero order control), whereas isometric and elastic devices should control the velocity of the object (first order control) [57]. An isotonic device with first order control and a isometric or elastic device with zero order control result in a significantly slower object manipulation. There is no significant difference between a isometric or elastic device control, except for a slight advantage for elastic controllers in the first 20 min of usage [58]. 6DOF devices may also introduce force feedback to the user with the use of a mechanical arm (e.g. Geomagic Touch X [11] or Haption Virtuose 6D [20]).

3.4   Gesture Interaction

Gesture interaction can utilize a hand and finger tracking or use a physical controller like an isotonic 6DOF mouse in combination with physical buttons on the controller. Using gestures rather than mapping the movement of the hand directly to the virtual object as in Sect. 3.3 allows for different interactions, but also introduces some problems. In the Grab and Twirl technique [10] and a technique from Schlattmann and Klein [43] the user frames a virtual object with both of his hands. The object is hereby grabbed and can be moved in the VE. In addition to that, the Grab and Scale [10] method lets the user set an axis and the amount of rotation with the dominant hand. Jerky Release [44] lets the user grab an object with an implicit grab gesture. The object is manipulated if the user moves his hand steady and controlled. The object is released if he makes some fast or jerky movements. Modeless RTS including constraints can be achieved using two isotonic controllers [16] or the users hands [48].

Focusing on Virtual Reality (VR), new object manipulation techniques need to be introduced because classical mouse or keyboard inputs may not be available or suitable. An object can be manipulated relative to the origin of an object's coordinate system or the users hands [33]. Moving an object relative to its own center results in a direct manipulation. This is intuitive, fast, precise and utilizes proprioception [7,19,34]. Relative movement with respect to the users hand feels more like manipulating the object on the end of a rod and is more prone to tracking noise or a shaking hand. To remove the restriction of a limited interaction range for a direct manipulation, the techniques Go-Go [40], Fast Go-Go and Stretch Go-Go [19] can be used. With this techniques the arm extension of the user is mapped to an disproportionately high movement of the virtual hand. Scaled-World Grab [34] scales the users size in the world to allow him to reach distant objects, whereas Extender Grab moves the object without positioning it in the users hands, but scales the objects translation depending on the initial distance to the user. Other manipulation techniques are Worlds in Miniature (WIM) [33,49], Hand-Held Widgets [34], Voodoo Dolls [37], a hybrid technique by de Haan et al. [15] which combines direct and ray-casting interaction or several projection techniques by Pierce et al. [38].

3.5 Touch Interaction

There are several techniques for a touch screen interaction like Sticky Tools [18], a fluid-based Manipulation by Kruger et al. [27], Screen-Space [41], Depth-Separated Screen-Space (DS3) [31], a Two-Finger interaction by Liu et al. [29], Pie Rotate and Turn & Roll [22], Z-technique and multi-touch viewport technique [32] and rizzo [51]. Hancock et al. [17] show that with one, two or three finger input in a 5DOF manipulation task it is easier and faster to use more fingers for interacting. Mobile devices contain a touch screen and also a gyroscope which can be combined to form device orientation dependent interaction as in [14,55].

4   Evaluation

Chen et al. [8] compare slider-based rotation with the virtual sphere method and find that virtual sphere is faster and better rated by users (also [26,36]). They compare the virtual sphere with a isometric trackball and find no significant differences in neither time nor accuracy. Several works compare a classical mouse with a 2+DOF mouse interaction and find that the mouse with more DOF is about 10–30% faster [2,4]. Still, the given tasks seem to fit the DOF of the input devices exactly and it is questionable if these devices perform as well given a 6DOF task. Comparing isotonic 6DOF mice interaction with a virtual sphere interaction shows that the 6DOF devices are significantly faster (35%) in a rotation task, with equal or slightly better precision and a higher user rating [25]. Ware and Rose [54] show that when using an isotonic device, an object rotation should be done with the object in the same position as the hand of the user. A comparison of an isotonic 6DOF mouse and an isotonic tracked hand with and without an explicit grabbing posture shows that the explicit grabbing is significantly slower and more imprecise [44]. Still, all techniques are accurate. A further analysis gives a similar result, but also shows that a bi-manual method can also be fast at precise movements [43]. High standard deviations for all methods show that the experience of the user with the devices is an important factor for the interaction. Above all an isometric device needs more time to get used to. Zhai et al. [61] compare an isotonic input from a tracked device and a glove. The main difference of the two techniques is the limited movement range of the hand. Since the tracked device could be manipulated with the fingers it did not have that limitation and as a result is about 20% faster. In another experiment Zhai and Milgram [60] compare an isotonic and an elastic control. The isotonic interaction is significantly faster, but the elastic interaction allows for a more controlled object manipulation (discrepancy from the shortest manipulation path). Both devices show a strong learning effect. As of [57,58], there is no significant difference between an isometric and an elastic device concerning speed or user preference.

Comparisons of the touch screen input techniques Sticky Tools, Screen-Space and DS3 show that users have significantly more problems completing a task with Screen-Space while using twice as many touch events [31]. DS3 is about 35% faster in the given experiment. Liu et al. [29] compare these three techniques to their own Two-Finger method, but also consider different screen sizes in their experiment (5 and 11 in.). The Two-Finger method and Sticky Tools are the fastest techniques on all display sizes. Screen-Space performs better on a smaller screen, but is still slow at complex tasks. The technique DS3 is the slowest at executing a simple task and using a 5 in. screen.

5   Discussion

Using a classical mouse with a virtual Sphere technique is common, but inferior to a 6DOF device [59]. 2+DOF devices can be faster than a mouse, but suffer from the fact that other muscle groups are used to compare the other dimensions. On one hand, an isotonic 6DOF interaction is intuitive, but has a limited workspace and therefore needs a clutching method. Also fatigue can be a problem, but does not need to be, because the user might rest his arm on a table and perform movements with his wrist [53]. On the other hand, an isometric or elastic device needs little effort to control and allows for more coordination. However these devices need more time to learn. Zhai and Milgrim [60] conclude that a more direct controller, like an isotonic device or a touch screen, should be used for short tasks and less direct tools, like an isometric/elastic device, should be used for long interactions. Table 1 gives an overview of all mentioned manipulation techniques and their rating, based on the evaluation results.

Table 1. Overview: interaction techniques classified by domain and rated based on evaluation results. Rating from −− (worst) to o (neutral) to ++ (best). Abbreviations: dm = discrete modes, ml = modeless, uni. = uni-manual, bi-m. = bi-manual, R = rotation, T = translation, S = scaling, Beginner = beginner-friendliness, Mental = mental demand, Physical = physical demand

Technique			Functionality		Rating			
Class	Name		Mode	Handedness	Speed	Beginner	Mental	Physical
2DOF Mouse	6 Sliders [8]		ml	uni-m. RTS	−−	+	−	++
	3D Widgets, Virtual Sphere [8,9,21,46]		dm	uni-m. RTS	+	++	+	++
	Widget sketching [45]		dm	uni-m. RTS	o	−	o	++
	Reference points [5,6,9,35]		dm	uni-m. RTS	−−	o	o	++
	Tail-Dragging [50]		ml	uni-m. RT	−−	+	−	++
2+DOF Mouse	Two Mice [56]		dm	bi-m. RTS	o	o	o	+
	Rotating/Tilting Mouse [4,30]		ml	uni-m. RT	+	++	+	+
	Turntable [12]		ml	uni-m. R	+	++	++	+
6DOF Mouse	Isotonic [24,42,53]		ml	uni-m. RT	+	++	++	−
	Isometric [1]		ml	uni-m. RT	++	o	+	++
	Elastic [60]		ml	uni-m. RT	++	+	+	+
Gesture	Object framing [10,10,43]		ml	bi-m. RT	o	++	++	−−
	Implicit Grab [44]		ml	uni-m. RT	+	+	+	−
	Two-handed [16,48]		ml	bi-m	o	o	+	−−
	Direct manipulation [33]		ml	uni-m. RT	o	++	++	−
	Arm extension [19,34,40]		ml	uni-m. RT	+	+	++	−
	Hand-Held [33,34,37,49]		ml	bi-m. RTS	+	+	+	o
	2D projection [38]		ml	uni/bi-m. T	.	++	+	−
Touch	Sticky Tools [18]		ml	bi-m. R, uni-m. T	+	+	++	o
	Fluid-based [27]		ml	uni-m. RT	−−	+	+	o
	Screen-Space [41]		ml	bi-m. R, uni-m. T	−−	+	+	o
	DS3 [31]		ml	bi-m. RT	o	+	++	o
	Two-Finger [29]		ml	uni-m. RT	+	+	++	o
	With gyro [14,55]		ml	uni/bi-m. RT(S)	−	+	+	−

6   Conclusion

In a 3D object manipulation task the best technique depends on the input and output devices and the application domain. Firstly, desktop environments can combine a mouse interaction with a widget based manipulation like the virtual sphere. This works well and since a mouse is always available it is easy to integrate this type of control. Many different solutions try to extend the 2D mouse with one or two more axes, but these additional dimensions only benefit in specific systems that utilize exactly these axes. A 6DOF manipulation, that is translation and rotation, favors from the introduction of a 6DOF mouse. Scaling might be achieved with a mode switch.

Secondly, in a mobile context or on a larger touch screen techniques like Sticky Fingers or the Two-Finger approach by Liu et al. allow efficient and fast interactions. The orientation sensors of a smart phone can also be used to achieve a different interaction style like in [28].

Thirdly, VR and AR may not or do not want to use traditional input methods, but can rely on hand or controller input. This enables the user to interact directly and naturally with objects in the virtual environment (VE) by using a zero order control [19]. Techniques like Go-Go, Scaled-World Grab and Extender Grab or Worlds in Miniature extend on this direct metaphor.

References

1. 3Dconnexion: SpaceMouse (2017). http://www.3dconnexion.de/products/spacemouse.html. Accessed 24 Mar 2017
2. Almeida, R., Cubaud, P.: Supporting 3D window manipulation with a yawing mouse. In: Proceedings of the 4th Nordic Conference on Human-Computer Interaction: Changing Roles, pp. 477–480. ACM (2006)
3. Balakrishnan, R., Kurtenbach, G.: Exploring bimanual camera control and object manipulation in 3D graphics interfaces. In: Proceedings of the SIGCHI Conference on Human Factors in Computing Systems, pp. 56–62. ACM (1999)
4. Balakrishnan, R., et al.: The Rockin'Mouse: integral 3D manipulation on a plane. In: Proceedings of the ACM SIGCHI Conference on Human Factors in Computing Systems. ACM, pp. 311–318 (1997)
5. Bier, E.A.: Snap-dragging in three dimensions. ACM SIGGRAPH Comput. Graph. **24**(2), 193–204 (1990)
6. Bier, E.A.: Skitters and jacks: interactive 3D positioning tools. In: Proceedings of the 1986 Workshop on Interactive 3D Graphics, pp. 183–196. ACM (1987)
7. Bowman, D.A., et al.: An introduction to 3-D user interface design. Presence: Teleop. Virt. Environ. **10**(1), 96–108 (2001)
8. Chen, M., Mountford, J.S., Sellen, A.: A study in interactive 3-D rotation using 2-D control devices. ACM SIGGRAPH Comput. Graph. **22**(4), 121–129 (1988)
9. Conner, B.D., et al.: Three-dimensional widgets. In: Proceedings of the 1992 Symposium on Interactive 3D Graphics, pp. 183–188. ACM (1992)
10. Cutler, L.D., Fröhlich, B., Hanrahan, P.: Two-handed direct manipulation on the responsive workbench. In: Proceedings of the 1997 Symposium on Interactive 3D Graphics, pp. 107–114. ACM (1997)

11. Geomagic: Touch X Haptic Device (2017). http://www.geomagic.com/en/products/phantom-desktop/overview. Accessed 24 Mar 2017
12. Gribnau, M.W., Verstijnen, I.M., Hennessey, J.M.: Three dimensional object orientation using the non-dominant hand. In: Proceedings of the Fourth International Conference on Design and Decision Support Systems in Architecture and Urban Planning. Citeseer (1998)
13. Guiard, Y.: Asymmetric division of labor in human skilled bimanual action: the kinematic chain as a model. J. Mot. Behav. **19**(4), 486–517 (1987)
14. Ha, T., Woo, W.: ARWand: Phone-based 3D object manipulation in augmented reality environment. In: 2011 International Symposium on Ubiquitous Virtual Reality (ISUVR), pp. 44–47. IEEE (2011)
15. de Haan, G., et al.: Hybrid interfaces in VEs: intent and interaction. In: EGVE, pp. 109–118 (2006)
16. Han, S., et al.: Remote interaction for 3D manipulation. In: CHI 2010 Extended Abstracts on Human Factors in Computing Systems, pp. 4225–4230. ACM (2010)
17. Hancock, M., Carpendale, S., Cockburn, A.: Shallow-depth 3D interaction: design and evaluation of one-, two- and three-touch techniques. In: Proceedings of the SIGCHI Conference on Human Factors in Computing Systems, pp. 1147–1156. ACM (2007)
18. Hancock, M., Ten Cate, T., Carpendale, S.: Sticky tools: full 6DOF force-based interaction for multi-touch tables. In: Proceedings of the ACM International Conference on Interactive Tabletops and Surfaces, pp. 133–140. ACM (2009)
19. Hannema, D.: Interaction in virtual reality. In: Interaction in Virtual Reality (2001)
20. Haption: Virtuose 6D (2017). http://www.haption.com/site/index.php/en/products-menu-en/hardware-menu-en/virtuose-6d-menu-en. Accessed 24 Mar 2017
21. Henriksen, K., Sporring, J., Hornbæk, K.: Virtual trackballs revisited. IEEE Trans. Vis. Comput. Graph. **10**(2), 206–216 (2004)
22. Herrlich, M., Walther-Franks, B., Malaka, R.: Integrated rotation and translation for 3D manipulation on multi-touch interactive surfaces. In: Dickmann, L., Volkmann, G., Malaka, R., Boll, S., Krüger, A., Olivier, P. (eds.) SG 2011. LNCS, vol. 6815, pp. 146–154. Springer, Heidelberg (2011). doi:10.1007/978-3-642-22571-0_16
23. Hinckley, K., et al.: Cooperative bimanual action. In: Proceedings of the ACM SIGCHI Conference on Human Factors in Computing Systems, pp. 27–34. ACM (1997)
24. Hinckley, K., et al.: The videomouse: a camera-based multi-degree-offreedom input device. In: Proceedings of the 12th Annual ACM Symposium on User Interface Software and Technology, pp. 103–112. ACM (1999)
25. Hinckley, K., et al.: Usability analysis of 3D rotation techniques. In: Proceedings of the 10th Annual ACM Symposium on User Interface Software and Technology, pp. 1–10. ACM (1997)
26. Jacob, I., Oliver, J.: Evaluation of techniques for specifying 3D rotations with a 2D input device. In: BCS HCI, pp. 63–76 (1995)
27. Kruger, R., et al.: Fluid integration of rotation and translation. In: Proceedings of the SIGCHI Conference on Human Factors in Computing Systems, pp. 601–610. ACM (2005)
28. Liang, H.N., et al.: User-defined surface+motion gestures for 3D manipulation of objects at a distance through a mobile device. In: Proceedings of the 10th Asia Pacific Conference on Computer Human Interaction, pp. 299–308. ACM (2012)
29. Liu, J., et al.: Two-finger gestures for 6DOF manipulation of 3D objects. Comput. Graph. Forum **31**(7), 2047–2055 (2012). Wiley Online Library

30. MacKenzie, I.S., Soukoreff, R.W., Pal, C.: A two-ball mouse affords three degrees of freedom. In: CHI 1997 Extended Abstracts on Human Factors in Computing Systems, pp. 303–304. ACM (1997)

31. Martinet, A., Casiez, G., Grisoni, L.: Integrality and separability of multitouch interaction techniques in 3D manipulation tasks. IEEE Trans. Vis. Comput. Graph. **18**(3), 369–380 (2012)

32. Martinet, A., Casiez, G., Grisoni L.: The design and evaluation of 3D positioning techniques for multi-touch displays. In: 2010 IEEE Symposium on 3D User Interfaces (3DUI), pp. 115–118. IEEE (2010)

33. Mine, M.: Working in a Virtual World: Interaction Techniques Used in the Chapel Hill Immersive Modeling Program. University of North Carolina, Chapel Hill (1996)

34. Mine, M.R., Brooks Jr., F.P., Sequin, C.H.: Moving objects in space: exploiting proprioception in virtual-environment interaction. In: Proceedings of the 24th Annual Conference on Computer Graphics and Interactive Techniques, pp. 19–26. ACM Press/Addison-Wesley Publishing Co. (1997)

35. Nielson, G.M., Olsen Jr., D.R.: Direct manipulation techniques for 3D objects using 2D locator devices. In: Proceedings of the 1986 Workshop on Interactive 3D Graphics, pp. 175–182. ACM (1987)

36. Partala, T.: Controlling a single 3D object: viewpoint metaphors, speed and subjective satisfaction. In: INTERACT, vol. 99, pp. 486–493 (1999)

37. Pierce, J.S., Stearns, B.C., Pausch, R.: Voodoo dolls: seamless interaction at multiple scales in virtual environments. In: Proceedings of the 1999 Symposium on Interactive 3D Graphics, pp. 141–145. ACM (1999)

38. Pierce, J.S., et al.: Image plane interaction techniques in 3D immersive environments. In: Proceedings of the 1997 Symposium on Interactive 3D Graphics, pp. 39-ff. ACM (1997)

39. Poupyrev, I.: 3D Manipulation Techniques (2000). http://citeseerx.ist.psu.edu/viewdoc/download?doi=10.1.1.126.2857&rep=rep1&type=pdf. Accessed 24 Mar 2017

40. Poupyrev, I., et al.: The go-go interaction technique: non-linear mapping for direct manipulation in VR. In: Proceedings of the 9th Annual ACM Symposium on User Interface Software and Technology, pp. 79–80. ACM (1996)

41. Reisman, J.L., Davidson, P.L., Han, J.Y.: A screen-space formulation for 2D and 3D direct manipulation. In: Proceedings of the 22nd Annual ACM Symposium on User Interface Software and Technology, pp. 69–78. ACM (2009)

42. Rekimoto, J., Sciammarella, E.: Toolstone: effective use of the physical manipulation vocabularies of input devices. In: Proceedings of the 13th Annual ACM Symposium on User Interface Software and Technology, pp. 109–117. ACM (2000)

43. Schlattmann, M., Klein, R.: Effcient bimanual symmetric 3D manipulation for markerless hand-tracking. In: Virtual Reality International Conference (VRIC), vol. 2, pp. 1–10 (2009)

44. Schlattmann, M., et al.: 3D interaction techniques for 6 DOF markerless hand-tracking. In: The International Conference on Computer Graphics, Visualization and Computer Vision (WSCG 2009), Plzen, Czech Republic (2009)

45. Schmidt, R., Singh, K., Balakrishnan, R.: Sketching and composing widgets for 3D manipulation. Comput. Graph. Forum **27**(2), 301–310 (2008). Wiley Online Library

46. Shoemake, K.: ARCBALL: a user interface for specifying three-dimensional orientation using a mouse. In: Graphics Interface, vol. 92, pp. 151–156 (1992)

47. Smith, G., et al.: 3D scene manipulation with 2D devices and constraints. In: Graphics Interface, vol. 1, pp. 135–142 (2001)
48. Song, P., et al.: A handle bar metaphor for virtual object manipulation with mid-air interaction. In: Proceedings of the SIGCHI Conference on Human Factors in Computing Systems, pp. 1297–1306. ACM (2012)
49. Stoakley, R., Conway, M.J., Pausch, R.: Virtual reality on a WIM: interactive worlds in miniature. In: Proceedings of the SIGCHI Conference on Human Factors in Computing Systems, pp. 265–272. ACM Press/Addison-Wesley Publishing Co. (1995)
50. Venolia, D.: Facile 3D direct manipulation. In: Proceedings of the INTERACT 1993 and CHI 1993 Conference on Human Factors in Computing Systems, pp. 31–36. ACM (1993)
51. Vlaming, L., et al.: Integrating 2D mouse emulation with 3D manipulation for visualizations on a multi-touch table. In: ACM International Conference on Interactive Tabletops and Surfaces, pp. 221–230. ACM (2010)
52. Ware, C.: Using hand position for virtual object placement. Vis. Comput. 6(5), 245–253 (1990)
53. Ware, C., Jessome, D.R.: Using the bat: a six-dimensional mouse for object placement. IEEE Comput. Graph. Appl. 8(6), 65–70 (1988)
54. Ware, C., Rose, J.: Rotating virtual objects with real handles. ACM Trans. Comput.-Hum. Interac. (TOCHI) 6(2), 162–180 (1999)
55. Yoon, D., et al.: Mobiature: 3D model manipulation technique for large displays using mobile devices. In: 2011 IEEE International Conference on Consumer Electronics (ICCE), pp. 495–496. IEEE (2011)
56. Zeleznik, R.C., Forsberg, A.S., Strauss, P.S.: Two pointer input for 3D interaction. In: Proceedings of the 1997 Symposium on Interactive 3D Graphics, pp. 115–120. ACM (1997)
57. Zhai, S.: Human performance in six degree of freedom input control. Ph.D. thesis, University of Toronto (1995)
58. Zhai, S.: Investigation of feel for 6DOF inputs: isometric and elastic rate control for manipulation in 3D environments. In: Proceedings of the Human Factors and Ergonomics Society Annual Meeting, vol. 37, no. 4, pp. 323–327. SAGE Publications, Los Angeles (1993)
59. Zhai, S.: User performance in relation to 3D input device design. ACM SIGGRAPH Comput. Graph. 32(4), 50–54 (1998)
60. Zhai, S., Milgram, P.: Quantifying coordination in multiple DOF movement and its application to evaluating 6 DOF input devices. In: Proceedings of the SIGCHI conference on Human Factors in Computing Systems, pp. 320–327. ACM Press/Addison-Wesley Publishing Co. (1998)
61. Zhai, S., Milgram, P., Buxton, W.: The influence of muscle groups on performance of multiple degree-of-freedom input. In: Proceedings of the SIGCHI Conference on Human Factors in Computing Systems, pp. 308–315. ACM (1996)

Use of Vibration for Touch Pen to Provide the Feel of Writing on Paper

Makio Ishihara[1(✉)], Ayaka Imato[1], and Yukio Ishihara[2]

[1] Fukuoka Institute of Technology, 3-30-1 Wajiro-higashi,
Higashi-ku, Fukuoka 811-0295, Japan
m-ishihara@fit.ac.jp
[2] Shimane University, 1060, Nishikawatsu-cho,
Matsue, Shimane 690-8504, Japan
iyukio@ipc.shimane-u.ac.jp

Abstract. This poster discusses pen-on-paper experience on a mobile platform for learning a writing system. A writing system is a set of letters such as the English alphabet and the Japanese Hiragana. Each letter is made from a number of strokes and these strokes are written in a specific order or stroke order. For learning a writing system on a mobile platform, this poster focuses on the problem with lack of feeling writing on real paper and builds a vibrotactile feedback pen called a vib-touch pen using a common touch pen and a common vibration speaker to give users pen-on-paper experience. An experiment in pen-on-paper experience is conducted and the result shows that a vib-touch pen gives users more pen-on-paper experience than the other two conditions of a normal touch pen and touch with their own finger.

Keywords: Vibrotactile feedback · Pen-on-paper experience · Touch screens · A writing system · Computer-aided education · Interface design

1 Introduction

Learning a writing system is one of main topics in primary education. A writing system consists of a number of letters. The English alphabet for example consists of 26 letters. Each letter is made from a number of strokes. These strokes are written in a specific order (stroke order). Figure 1 shows the stroke order of letter 'A'. Stroke order helps people balance letters and improve their readability.

In Japan, one of problems with learning a writing system is that kids are not good at keeping motivation for learning because Japanese writing systems, especially Kanji, are complicated. To motivate kids to learn, this poster focuses on a mobile platform because it has multiple means to draw their attention such as sounds, graphics and touch input. A mobile platform however poses another problem with lack of feeling writing on real paper or pen-on-paper experience. Wang et al. [1] built an EV-Pen. An EV-Pen is a vibrotactile feedback pen using electrovibration to give users real pen-on-paper experience. The EV-Pen consists

© Springer International Publishing AG 2017
C. Stephanidis (Ed.): HCII Posters 2017, Part I, CCIS 713, pp. 140–144, 2017.
DOI: 10.1007/978-3-319-58750-9_19

Fig. 1. Stroke order of 'A'.

Fig. 2. Look of a vib-touch pen.

of an ITO transparent electrode sheet applied to a glass plate coated with a layer of silica insulation. While the traditional vibrotactile feedback pens employ mechanical actuators, which may shake the whole pen and disturb movement of the pen tip, the EV-Pen does not rely on mechanical actuators but it requires a high voltage DC supply unit to inject alternating current, whose amplitude is 200 V, to the pen. It is not suitable for mobile platforms because of the need for massive batteries. This poster builds a provisional vibrotactile feedback pen equipped with an common vibration speaker to give users the feel of writing on paper. Our approach relays on neither mechanical actuators nor heavy batteries.

As regards learning a writing system, guiding strokes is an importance aspect. Yamaoka and Kakehi [2] built a traction force feedback pen. Four mechanical actuators are attached on the pen tip and they generate asymmetric acceleration to create a force in the predefined direction. This pen is used to assist users in drawing figures and guide directions. However mechanical actuators may shake the whole pen as mentioned above so that their approach is applicable to creating a virtual traction force but pen-on-paper experience. To guide strokes, this poster attempts to alter the tone played on a vibration speaker to create a virtual traction force.

2   A Vib-Touch Pen

Figure 2 shows our provisional vibrotactile feedback pen called a vib-touch pen. It consists of an ordinary touch pen of Elecom P-TPALBK and a vibration speaker of Vibroy CSP-VI01. The touch pen is about 125 mm long and 8.4 mm wide. The diameter of the pen tip is about 7 mm. It weighs 10 g. The vibration speaker is a semi-sphere in shape and it is 36 mm in diameter and weighs 50 g.

The flat part of the vibration speaker transmits vibration to the attached object. The vibration speaker is attached on the lower part of the touch pen, that is about 30 mm from the pen tip, so that the user perceives vibration at the tip of the pen. To give pen-on-paper experience and create a virtual traction force, the vibration is altered and displayed depending on position of touch with the pen tip on a touch screen.

3   Prototype of Learning a Writing System

Figure 3 shows a schematic diagram of our prototype system. Our prototype consists of a host computer, a touch screen and a vib-touch pen. A vib-touch pen is connected to the host computer. The touch screen detects the position of touch with the pen tip and sends it to the host computer and then the host computer injects vibration to the vib-touch pen.

Figure 4 illustrates timing and frequency of vibration with an example of the first stroke of Japanese Hiragana 'あ'. Every single stroke consists of a sequence of multiple vibration spots represented by gray dots and each vibration spot has a different frequency. The order of frequencies assigned on vibration spots is in a Solfege scale order such as Do, Re and Mi to create a virtual traction force by gradually decreasing friction between the touch screen and the pen tip. As the user places the pen tip on a vibration spot, the corresponding frequency is played so that he/she would perceive pen-on-paper experience. The frequency becomes gradually high while the user moves the pen tip along a stroke correctly so that he/she would perceive a virtual traction force.

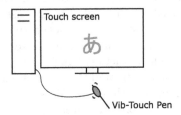

Fig. 3. Prototype of learning a writing system.

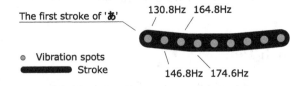

Fig. 4. The timing to display vibration and its frequency.

4   Experiment and Results

Figure 5 shows a series of screenshots of an experiment application in pen-on-paper experience. A single letter of Japanese Hiragana appears on the application window and vibration is displayed as each stroke is drawn by the user in correct order. The figure also shows progress of drawing strokes. The left screenshot shows a scene of drawing the first stroke and the right one does a scene of drawing the third stroke.

In our experiment, three experimental conditions are taken into consideration: vib-touch pen, normal touch pen and touch. The first condition of vib-touch pen is that the subject uses a vib-touch pen to draw strokes and the second one is that he/she uses a normal touch pen without vibration to do. The last one is that the subject draws strokes by touch with his/her own finger. There were twenty subjects with the ages of 21–24. Each subject was asked to draw strokes under each pair among three conditions, resulting in three pairs of conditions: vib-touch pen vs normal touch pen, vib-touch pen vs touch, normal touch pen vs touch. After evaluating each pair of conditions, the subject was asked to fill in a questionnaire about which condition would give more pen-on-paper experience with a 5-point scale shown in Fig. 6.

Table 1 shows the result of the Scheffee's paired comparison test and Fig. 7 shows the psychological scale of pen-on-paper experience. From the result, there is a significant impact between vib-touch pen and the other two conditions on pen-on-paper experience $[q(3,19) = 6.3305, p < .01, Y(0.01) = 0.9092)]$.

Fig. 5. Screenshots of the experiment application.

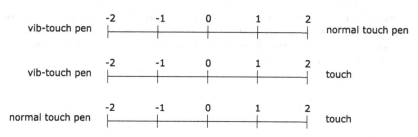

Fig. 6. A questionnaire sheet.

Table 1. Result of the Scheffee's paired comparison test.

Factor	Sum of squares	df	Mean square	F	Sig.
Main effect	44.1333	2	22.0667	17.8285	0.4370×10^{-4}
Main effect × Individuals	64.5333	38	1.6982	1.3721	0.2329
Interaction	0.8167	1	0.8167	0.6598	0.4267
Error	23.5167	19	1.2377	-	-
Total	133	60	-	-	-

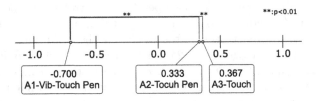

Fig. 7. Psychological scale obtained from the Scheffee's paired comparison test.

5   Conclusions

This poster built a vibrotactile feedback pen called a vib-touch pen using a common touch pen and a common vibration speaker to give users pen-on-paper experience and create a virtual traction force, and conducted an experiment in pen-on-paper experience. The result showed that a vib-touch pen gives users more pen-on-paper experience than the other two conditions of a normal touch pen and touch with their own finger.

In future work, we are going to conduct a further experiment in virtual traction force and evaluate it.

References

1. Wang, Q., Ren, X., Sun, X.: EV-pen: an electrovibration haptic feedback pen for touchscreens. In: SIGGRAPH ASIA 2016 Emerging Technologies (SA 2016). ACM, New York (2016)
2. Yamaoka, J., Kakehi, Y.: A pen-based device for sketching with multi-directional traction forces. In: Proceedings of the Adjunct Publication of the 27th Annual ACM Symposium on User Interface Software and Technology (UIST 2014 Adjunct), pp. 43–44. ACM, New York (2014)

Enhancement of ANN-Based Offline Hand Written Character Recognition Using Gradient and Geometric Feature Extraction Techniques

Y.A. Joarder[(⊠)], Paresh Chandra Barman, and Md Zahidul Islam

Department of Information and Communication Engineering,
Islamic University, Kushtia, Bangladesh
yajoarder@gmail.com, pcb@ice.iu.ac.bd,
zahidimage@gmail.com

Abstract. Offline handwritten character recognition has been one of the foremost difficult analysis areas within the field of image processing and pattern recognition in the recent years. Handwritten character recognition is a terribly problematic analysis space, because writing styles might vary from one user to another. The main goal of this research is to recognize the characters from a given scanned document or an image file where Multilayered Feed Forward network with Back propagation algorithm including two feature extraction techniques have been implemented at the same system. We have considered parameters like number of Hidden Layer, size of Hidden Layer and Epochs and applied some basic algorithms for segmentation of characters and normalization of characters and thrown light on Gradient and Geometry based feature extraction techniques for feature extraction respectively, because Feature Extraction is an integral part of any recognition system as well as improves recognition rate and misclassification. We have described step by step procedure of character recognition using ANN and calculated the number of hidden layer as well.

Keywords: Artificial Neural Network · Hidden layers · Epochs · Back propagation · Offline handwritten character · Feature extraction · Recognition rate · Classification

1 Introduction

The purpose of this research is to take handwritten English characters as input, process the character, train the neural network algorithm, to recognize the pattern and modify the character to a beautified version of the input as well as explain the mechanism of ANN including the calculation of number of hidden layer; by finding the number of hidden layer, it is easy to understand the complexity of the system. Though this work is restricted to English characters solely, this research is aimed toward developing software which can be useful in recognizing characters of English language. It can be additional developed to recognize the characters of various languages later. It engulfs the idea of neural network. One of the first suggests by which computers are dowered with human-like skills is through the utilization of a neural network. Neural networks

© Springer International Publishing AG 2017
C. Stephanidis (Ed.): HCII Posters 2017, Part I, CCIS 713, pp. 145–151, 2017.
DOI: 10.1007/978-3-319-58750-9_20

are notably helpful for resolution issues that cannot be expressed as a series of steps, like recognizing patterns, classifying them into groups, series prediction and data mining. A neural network trained for classification is intended to take input samples and classify them into groups. These groups could also be fuzzy, while not clearly outlined boundaries. This project engages detecting free handwritten characters.

2 Related Work

Today Neural Networks are mostly used for Pattern Recognition. Optical character recognition (OCR) is widespread use of Neural Network. Different Models of Neural Network have been applied on the test set on each to find the accuracy of the respective Neural Network [1]. However, handwritten character and optical character are different format; optical character recognition is easy for recognition, because of its pattern which easy to recognition. On the contrary, handwritten character recognition is difficult because the large range of writing style from one person to another [2]. Feature extraction which improves recognition rate and misclassification is an integral part of any recognition system [2, 3]. The aim of feature extraction is to describe the pattern by means of minimum number of features that are effective in discriminating pattern classes. The gradient measures the magnitude and direction of the greatest change in intensity in a small neighborhood of each pixel where gradient refers to both the gradient magnitude and direct ion). Gradients are computed by means of the Sobel operator. Due to its logical simplicity, ease of use and high recognition rate, Gradient Features should be used for recognition purposes [3]. Recognition of Handwritten text has numerous applications which include, reading aid for blind and conversion of any hand written document into structural text form. To recognize handwritten characters by projecting them on different sized grids by using Mat lab Neural Network toolbox is the best way. The first step is image acquisition which acquires the scanned image followed by noise filtering, smoothing and normalization of scanned image, rendering image suitable for segmentation where image is decomposed into sub images. Character extraction and edge detection algorithm have been used for training the neural network to classify and recognize the handwritten characters [4]. This paper explores the existing ring based method (W.I. Reber 1987), the new sector based method and the combination of these, termed the Fusion method for the recognition of handwritten English capital letters. The variability associated with the characters is accounted for by way of considering a fixed number of concentric rings in the case of the ring based approach and a fixed number of sectors in the case of the sector approach. Structural features such as end points, junction points and the number of branches are used for the pre-classification of characters, the local features such as normalized vector lengths and angles derived from either ring or sector approaches are used in the training using the reference characters and subsequent recognition of the test characters. The recognition rates obtained are encouraging [5]. A geometry based technique for feature extraction is applicable to segmentation-based word recognition systems. It extracts the geometric features of the character contour. These features are based on the basic line types that form the character skeleton. The system gives a feature vector as its output. The feature vectors so generated from a training set were then used to train a pattern recognition engine based on Neural Networks so that the system can be benchmarked [6]. In computer vision research, object detection based on image processing is the task of identifying a designated object on a static image or a sequence of video frames. Projects based on such research works have been widely adapted to various industrial and social applications. The field to which those applications apply includes but not limited to, security surveillance, intelligent transportation system, automated manufacturing, and quality control and supply chain management. The popular computer vision methods have been extensively studied in various research papers and their significance to computer vision research has been proven by subsequent research works. In general, by categorizing those methods into to gradient-based and edge based feature extraction methods, depending on the low level features they use [7].

3   Proposed Approach

We have used two Feature Extraction techniques in the same system so that the system is more flexible; if any of them out of work for any technical issues, then other one work without any problem. We have used Gradient and Geometry based feature extraction techniques for feature extraction respectively because Feature Extraction is an integral part of any recognition system as well as improves recognition rate and misclassification. The proposed method comprises of 4 phases:

1. Pre-processing
2. Segmentation
3. Feature Extraction
4. Classification and Recognition

3.1   Pre-processing

In image representation one is concerned with the characterization of the number that every pixel represents. The number of pixels per unit area i.e. sampling rate must be massive enough to preserve the helpful in-formation within the image.

3.2   Segmentation

In the segmentation stage, an image of sequence of characters is rotten into sub-images of individual character. The pre-processed input image is divided into isolated characters by distribution variety to every character employing a labeling method. This labeling provides info concerning range of characters within the image. Every individual character is uniformly resized into pixels. In normalization, we want to normalize the size of the characters. There are massive variations within the sizes of every Character hence we need a technique to normalize the size. For normalizing the size we have used Character Extraction Algorithm and Edge Detection Algorithm.

Table 1. Sobel masks for gradient (Source: [3])

1	2	1
0	0	0
-1	-2	-1

-1	0	1
-2	0	2
-1	0	1

Horizontal Component   Vertical Component

3.3   Feature Extraction

There are two Feature Extraction methods have been employed:

1. Feature Extraction Using Gradient Feature
2. Feature Extraction Based on Character Geometry

Feature Extraction Using Gradient Feature
The gradient measures the magnitude and direction of the best modification in intensity in an exceedingly tiny neighborhood of every pixel. (In what follows, "gradient" refers to each the gradient magnitude and direction) Gradients are computed by means that of the Sobel operator. The Sobel templates accustomed compute the horizontal (X) and vertical (Y) parts of the gradient are shown below (Table 1):

Given an input image of size $G_1 \times G_2$, each pixel neighborhood is convolved with these templates to work out these X and Y parts, H_x and H_y, severally. Equations (1) and (2) represent their mathematical representation:

$$H(m, n) = I(m - 1, n + 1) + 2 * I(m, n + 1) + I(m + 1, n + 1) - I(m - 1, n - 1)$$

$$-2 * I(m, n - 1) - I(m + 1, n - 1) \tag{1}$$

$$H(m, n) = I(m - 1, n - 1) + 2 * I(m - 1, n) + I(m - 1, n + 1)y - I(m + 1, n - 1)$$
$$-2 * I(m + 1, n) - I(m + 1, n + 1) \tag{2}$$

Here, (m, n) range over the image rows (G_1) and columns (G_2), respectively. The gradient strength and direction can be computed from the gradient vector [H_x, H_y].

After getting gradient vector of every pixel, the gradient image is decomposed into four orientation planes or eight direction planes.

Feature Extraction Based on Character Geometry
It extracts completely different line sorts that form a selected character. It additionally concentrates on the point options of identical. The feature extraction technique explained was tested employing a Neural Network that was trained with the feature vectors obtained from the system proposed.

Universe of Discourse.
Shortest matrix that matches the whole character skeleton.

Zoning.

After the universe of discourse is chosen, the image is split into windows of equal size, and also the feature is completed on individual windows. The image was zoned into nine equal sized windows. Feature extraction was applied to individual zones, instead of the full image.

Starters.

Starters are those pixels with one neighbor within the character skeleton.

Intersections.

It ought to have over one neighbor.

3.4   Classification and Recognition

In Neural Network, each node perform some straight-forward computation and each affiliation conveys a proof from one node to a unique labelled by selection called the "connection strength" or weight indicating the extent thereto signal is amplified or diminished by the connection. Different selections for weight leads to totally different functions are being evaluated by the network. If in a given network whose weight are initial random and provided that we all know the task to be accomplished by the network, a learning algorithm should be accustomed verify the values of the weight which will reach the required task. Learning algorithm qualifies the computing system to be referred to as Artificial Neural Network (Fig. 1).

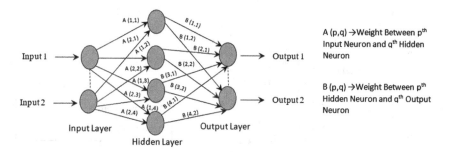

Fig. 1. Neural network

Hidden Layer Calculation

$$T_h = T_s/\{A * (T_i + T_o)\} \tag{3}$$

Here,

T_s = Number of Samples in Training Data Set
T_h = Number of Hidden Layer
T_o = Number of Output Neuron
T_i = Number of Input Neuron
A = Arbitrary Scaling Factor 2-10

Sample Input and Output

The match pattern is obtained to get the associated character, once the network is trained (Fig. 2).

<table>
<tr><td align="center">Sample Input</td><td align="center">Sample Output</td></tr>
</table>

Fig. 2. Desired sample input and output

Test Result Comparison

The given line graph shows the variations of Gradient Feature and Character Geometry Feature Extraction methods on the basis of number of Epochs (Fig. 3).

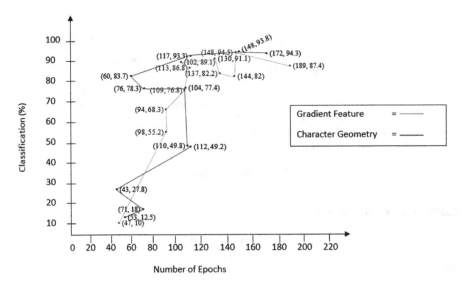

Fig. 3. Test Result comparison on the basis on number of epochs and classification (%)

4 Conclusion

The implementation of the absolutely connected Back propagation network gave affordable results toward recognizing characters. The two strategies specified for feature extraction yield desired and right smart accuracies for recognition. The foremost notable is that the proven fact that it cannot handle major variations in translation, rotation, or scale. Whereas some preprocessing steps is enforced so as to account for these variances, as we did generally they are tough to solve fully.

References

1. Patel, C.I., Patel, R., Patel, P.: Handwritten character recognition using neural networks. Int. J. Sci. Eng. Res. **2**(5), 1–6 (2011)
2. Rani, M., Meena, Y.K.: An efficient feature extraction method for handwritten character recognition. In: Panigrahi, B.K., Suganthan, P.N., Das, S., Satapathy, S.C. (eds.) SEMCCO 2011. LNCS, vol. 7077, pp. 302–309. Springer, Heidelberg (2011). doi:10.1007/978-3-642-27242-4_35
3. Aggarwal, A., Rani, R., Dhir, R.: Handwritten character recognition using gradient features. Int. J. Adv. Res. Comput. Sci. Softw. Eng. **2**(5), 234–240 (2012)
4. Prasad, K., Nigam, D.C., Lakhotiya, A., Umre, D.: Character recognition using Matlab's neural toolbox. Int. J. u- and e- Serv. Sci. Technol. **6**(1), 13–20 (2013)
5. Hanmandlu, M., Murali Mohan, K.R., Kumar, H.: Neural based handwritten character recognition. In: Proceeding of ICDAR 1999, Proceedings of 5th International Conference on Document Analysis and Recognition, p. 241 (1999)
6. Dileep, D.: A Feature Extraction Technique Based on Character Geometry for Character Recognition
7. Wang, S.: A review of gradient-based and edge-based feature extraction methods for object detection. In: 2011 IEEE 11th International Conference on Computer and Information Technology (CIT) (2011)

Shortening Selection Time Using Plural Cursor in Multi-display Environment and Its Preliminary Evaluation

Yuki Mako[✉] and Makio Ishihara

Fukuoka Institute of Technology,
3-30-1 Wajiro-higashi, Higashi-ku, Fukuoka 811-0295, Japan
yuuki-941222@hotmail.co.jp, m-ishihara@fit.ac.jp
http://www.fit.ac.jp/~m-ishihara/Lab/

Abstract. This manuscript proposes a plural cursor to shorten selection time in multi-display environments. A plural cursor is a set of copies of an original mouse cursor, which move in a synchronized manner. Each copy is assigned on a different computer screen. This manuscript conducts an experiment to compare the performance of a normal mouse cursor and a plural cursor in a dual-display environment. The results show that the total path the plural cursor has taken on average was about half the distance of the normal cursor, but their total elapsed time was almost the same. The value of myoelectric spectrum a plural cursor was lower than that of a normal mouse cursor.

Keywords: Plural cursor · Mouse cursor · Multi-display · Fitts's law · Pointing interface

1 Introduction

One of the common pointing devices is a mouse. The mouse is synchronized with the mouse cursor displayed on a computer screen, and moves the cursor to select targets.

When people use a usual mouse cursor in a multi-display environment, they have to move the mouse cursor a long distance, resulting in more time taken to click a target. This is expressed by Fitts's law. According to Fitts's law, the longer the distance from the current position of the cursor to the target, and the smaller the size of the object is, the longer the time elapsed for the selection increases.

Equation (1) shows a formulation of Fitts's law and Fig. 1 shows an illustration of the Fitts's law. T means the time to move the cursor to the target. A and B are constants depending on the input device. D means the distance from the current cursor to the center of the target. W means the size of the target relative to the moving direction of the cursor. In Eq. (1), as W is larger and D is shorter, it is easier to select a target meaning that T is short. According to this

© Springer International Publishing AG 2017
C. Stephanidis (Ed.): HCII Posters 2017, Part I, CCIS 713, pp. 152–157, 2017.
DOI: 10.1007/978-3-319-58750-9_21

rule, in a multi-display environment, the distance D to the target becomes large and the time T elapsed for selecting the target becomes longer.

This manuscript proposes a plural cursol which shortens the distance that people have to move the mouse cursor in a dual-display environment. A plural cursor can be used even when the number of screens is three or more. It is expected that the elapsed time to click on a target will be shorter because this cursor shotens the distance between the cursor and the target. This manuscript also measures and evaluates the myoelectric potential of the arm when using a plural cursor.

$$T = A + B \, \log_2(1 + \frac{D}{W}) \qquad (1)$$

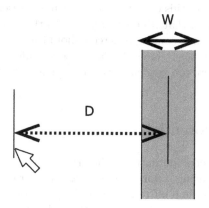

Fig. 1. Fitts's law.

2   Plural Cursor

A plural cursor is a set of copies of an original mouse cursor, which move in a synchronized manner. Each copy is assigned on a different computer screen. If users clicked the mouse, the event is sent to the copy on each screen. Although a new method by hitting the button to switch mouse cursors is conceivable, the number of times the button is hit increases and the elapsed time for switching becomes longer when the number of displays increases. Figure 2 shows the basic idea of a plural cursor in a dual-display. There are copies which move in a synchronized manner at the same coordinates on each screen. The application windows are placed at different positions so that they don't overlap on each screen.

As an advantage, the distance that users have to move the cursor to the target is cut in half because there are two cursors. From this and Eq. (1), it can be predicted that the time T elapsed for moving the cursor becomes shorter.

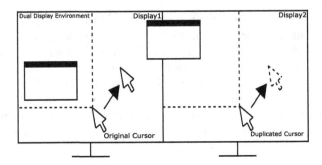

Fig. 2. Basic idea of plural cursor.

Moreover, the operation of this cursor is easy because it resembles a usual mouse cursor. It can also be said that it can be applied to three or more screens. As a disadvantage, a target on a computer screen should not be placed at the same relative position on the other screen because users could click on other targets unexpectedly. Since there are two cursors, the user may feel uncomfortable and may be confused.

3   Myoelectric Potential

We measure the myoelectric potential of the arm in order to evaluate the degrees of a user's stress when using a normal cursor and a plural cursor.

Myoelectric potential is a current flowing between one site and an adjacent site by the generation of an action potential inside and outside of the muscle cell. The action potential is a potential which is always generated by stimulation inside and outside the muscle. It is measured from the flexor carpi ulnaris muscle. This is one of the forearm muscles, and it is used in bending the wrist with a dumbbell or hitting a hammer. Figure 3 (left) shows electromyogram when a fist was clenched and Fig. 3 (right) shows electromyogram when a person is relaxing their hand. The amplitude and the frequency increase when forces are applied to the arm.

4   Experiment and Results

This section conducts an experiment to compare the performance of a normal mouse cursor and a plural cursor in a dual-display environment. It also measures and evaluates the myoelectric potential of the forearm when using them. Five right-handed subjects between the ages of 22 and 23 have experience in using a dual-display. Each subject performs the following task:

Step 1. The subject is explained the procedure of this experiment and the operation method of a plural cursor.

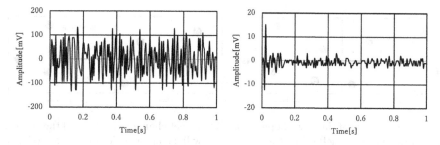

Fig. 3. Electromyogram of flexor carpi ulnaris muscle for one second. Electromyogram when a fist was clenched (left) and electromyogram when a person is relaxing their hand (right).

Step 2. The subject practices it, the experiment starts when he understands the operation method.

Step 3. Five targets are placed on each computer screen and there are 10 targets in total. Figure 4 shows an initial screen of the experiment.

Step 4. One target changes in color and the subject is asked to click on it then the next target will change in color at random. Figure 5 shows an example of the flow of this operation. This procedure is repeated 50 times. The black circles mean objects and the orange one means a target.

Step 5. The subject performs Step 3 to Step 4 using one type of cursor and after a 2 min break, he/she does the same steps with the other type of cursor. The order of the cursors is balanced for each subject, and the placement positions of the 10 targets differs for each subject and for each cursor.

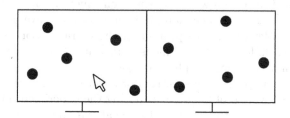

Fig. 4. An initial screen of the experiment.

The acquired data is the distance between targets[px], the path the cursor has actually taken[px], the elapsed time to complete the task[s], the number of miss-click[times] and the myoelectric potential of the dominant arm.

Figure 6 shows the experiment results. The placement position of the targets didn't have much influence on the results because there were no large differences in the total distance between targets. The total path the plural cursor had taken on average was about 47.2% that of the normal mouse cursor, but their total

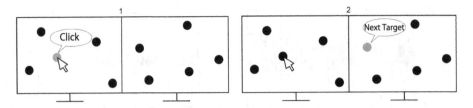

Fig. 5. An example of the flow of operation. One target changes in color and the subject is asked to click on it (left) then the next target will change in color at random (right). (Color figure online)

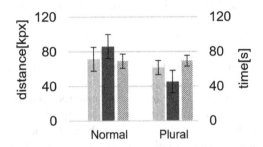

▧ The total distance between targets.
■ The total path the cursor has actually taken.
▨ The total elapsed time to complete the task.

Fig. 6. Experiment results.

elapsed time was almost the same. From this, it is considered that it took time to find the position of the cursor when the screen on which the object was displayed shifted to the other screen. Therefore, it is necessary to have a mechanism to allow the user to always find the position of the plural cursor. As regards the number of miss-click, for the normal mouse cursor it is 2.5 times on average and it is 2.0 times on average for the plural cursor.

Figure 7 shows a myoelectric spectrum of flexor carpi ulnaris muscle, which was obtained from a span of ten seconds during the experiment for each mouse cursor system. From this, the integrated value at the range from 0 Hz to 100 Hz for a normal mouse cursor was 3.34 [mV] while it was 3.01 [mV] for a plural cursor. It is lower than that of a normal mouse cursor by 0.33 [mV]. The integrated value for the flexor carpi ulnaris muscle when holding the fist strongly is 199.95 [mV] and it is 8.30 [mV] when relaxing the arm. The value became smaller when operating the mouse compared to when relaxing the arm. The reason for this may be deviation of the mounting position of the sensor device or depend on the condition of the muscle.

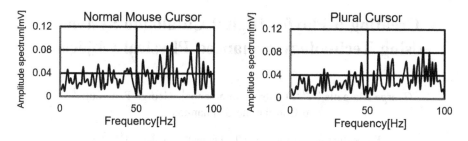

Fig. 7. A myoelectric spectrum.

5 Conclusions

This manuscript proposes a plural cursor to shorten selection time in multi-display environments. We conducted an experiment to compare the performances of a normal mouse cursor and a plural cursor in a dual-display environment. The result shows that the total path the plural cursor had taken on average was about half that of the normal cursor but their total elapsed time was almost the same. From the result of the myoelectric spectra, a plural cursor gave users less stress than a normal mouse cursor.

In the future work, we are going to discover the reason why the total elapsed time for a plural cursor to complete the task wasn't shorter and compare it with other proposed methods. In addition, it is also necessary to measure the myoelectric potential more accurately and analyze muscle fatigue.

Creating a Playful Digital Catalogue System Using Technology-Enhanced Physical Objects

George Margetis[1(✉)], Dimitris Grammenos[1], George Paparoulis[1], and Constantine Stephanidis[1,2]

[1] Foundation for Research and Technology – Hellas (FORTH),
Institute of Computer Science, 70013 Heraklion, Crete, Greece
{gmarget, gramenos, groulis, cs}@ics.forth.gr
[2] Department of Computer Science, University of Crete, Crete, Greece

Abstract. This paper presents a digital catalogue interactive system for promoting cultural heritage and tourism information in public spaces, which employs the notions of playful and tangible interaction. The system features two touch screens, one for displaying high resolution images and one for providing detailed information regarding the presented artifact. Navigation in the contents of the digital catalogue is accomplished through interaction with technology-enhanced physical objects as well as touch gestures. The paper presents how the system has been adapted in terms of content and interaction and physical design to accommodate different types of information and installation contexts, namely an oil mill to present culinary information, a digital museum catalogue, a digital cultural heritage photo album, and a digital nature observatory.

Keywords: Digital catalogue interactive system · Information kiosk · Touch screen · Physical interaction · Playful interaction · Tangible interaction

1 Introduction

The technological world of today has vastly embraced touch interactions, which now prevail in personal devices (smartphones, tablets), household appliances (e.g., refrigerators, cooktops, and washing machines), etc. As a result, touch-enabled interactive systems constitute a popular choice [1] for providing information to visitors of public spaces, such as airports, museums and tourist information points. On the other hand, systems that are designed to be usable but also playful and engaging are expected to offer a higher quality user experience and further entice the audience [2].

Playful interfaces can be characterized as those interfaces that make users feel challenged or engage them in social and physical interaction because they expect it to be fun [3]. In this respect, Tangible User Interfaces (TUIs) [4] have been claimed to make interactive systems more stimulating and enjoyable [5]. Tangible interaction encompasses a broad range of systems and interfaces, which share the following characteristics: tangibility and materiality, physical embodiment of data, embodied interaction and bodily movement as an essential part of interaction, and embeddedness in real space [6].

© Springer International Publishing AG 2017
C. Stephanidis (Ed.): HCII Posters 2017, Part I, CCIS 713, pp. 158–163, 2017.
DOI: 10.1007/978-3-319-58750-9_22

This paper presents a digital catalogue system which supports touch-based interaction and is further augmented with physical object manipulation, building upon the concepts of playful and tangible interaction and combining functionality with playfulness and serendipity. The system allows visitors to browse its content and dwell on details of images, read accompanying texts and follow threads of information.

2 System Design

The system comprises two embedded touch screens and a custom-made technologically-enhanced physical object (such as a traditional oil mill, a ship's wheel, a toy windmill) that acts as an imaginative input device. The two screens are used to provide complementary information and views of a given artifact. The larger screen presents a high resolution photo of the currently selected artifact/image, while the smaller screen mainly aims at providing brief information that depends on the artifact type, a descriptive title and a short text for the artifact presented on the large screen. The large screen supports two types of interaction:

- Hotspots: Each image can include any number of hotspots. If the user touches one of them, the corresponding area is highlighted and a word balloon pops-up with related information. If the user touches any part of the image that does not include a hotspot, then all the available hotspots are highlighted in order to provide feedback about their position.
- Magnification: Users can indicate an area of interest in the image by dragging their finger on the screen and carrying out a circle gesture. Consequently, the selected area is magnified, allowing subsequent iterative zooming to its contents.

Navigation to the items of the collection can take place either through touching the corresponding controls on the smaller touch screen, carrying out a flip gesture on each of the screens, or using the physical object. The interaction speed (e.g. how fast the windmill turns) affects browsing speed and may also trigger music or sound effects.

The system can be customized in terms of the physical object employed, as well as in terms of its external appearance, in order to fit in an optimal way in any given installation context (type of information provided, installation location and atmosphere, etc.). Finally, additional functionality supported includes:

- language selection
- photo capture of the active user
- e-mail communication of selected content, upon user's request
- QR code, which can be scanned by a mobile device (e.g., smartphone, tablet) in order to provided additional related information through a web site.

3 Installations

The system can be used as a powerful promotional tool for commerce, marketing and cultural heritage applications. This section briefly describes how the system has been adapted to four different contexts to present culinary information, a digital collection of museum exhibits, a digital cultural heritage photo album, and a nature observatory.

Fig. 1. (a) Overview of the Oil Mill (b) large screen contents: a high resolution photo of the dish (c) small screen contents: the actual recipe

3.1   An Interactive Oil Mill for Culinary Information

The interactive Oil Mill aims at providing information related to Greek culture and tradition – with a focus on the Cretan diet – combining real traditional artifacts with digital content. Oil Mill (Fig. 1a) incorporates a small-scale stone mill, through which it is possible to browse a digital album offering an introduction to Cretan diet and culinary products. When the metal handle is rotated, real oil flows from one end of the system. The system also comprises lighted glass showcases containing museum replicas of ancient Greek pottery. Users can send information provided by the system (e.g., recipes, information about traditional products) by e-mail.

The two screens of the system have been employed as follows. The larger screen (Fig. 1b) displays a high resolution photo of how the recipe is served, annotated with hotpots that provide additional information regarding individual ingredients. The smaller screen (Fig. 1c) provides the related recipe, so that users can read it and send it to their e-mail accounts. The system has been installed at the Heraklion and Chania airports as a means to promote Cretan gastronomy to the island visitors.

3.2   Panoptes – Displaying a Digital Collection of Museum Exhibits

Panoptes is an interactive system of the permanent interactive exhibition "Macedonia: From fragments to pixels" of the Archaeological Museum of Thessaloniki and presents the gold Macedonian wreaths collection (Fig. 2). These wreaths are among antiquity's most exquisite examples of jewelry, and show a lot about the people who wore them. A children's windmill is located between two touch screens (one larger, one smaller). Blowing on the windmill, the collection of gold wreaths will unfold. By pausing on any image, the large screen presents a high resolution photo of a wreath and the smaller

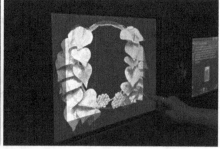

Fig. 2. Panoptes at the Archaeological Museum of Thessaloniki

screen presents relevant textual information for museum visitors. Users can zoom in on any detail of the images presented, or choose from the areas of interest marked on the image that will bring up multimedia windows.

3.3   A Digital Cultural Heritage Photo Album

The digital photo album has been installed at the Heraklion port passenger terminal and aims at informing visitors about the history of locations around the port, such as the dockyards or the fort, buildings dated back to the era when Heraklion was ruled by Venetians (1204–1645 BC). Links with mercantile shipping routes and the settlement of Venetian colonists constituted Heraklion the most important harbor in the Eastern Mediterranean. The large screen of the system displays old photos and maps of harbor locations, while the small screen presents interesting historical information about these

Fig. 3. A user interacting with the digital photo album

locations. Navigation in the album contents is feasible through a ship's wheel placed below the large screen, or through touch gestures on any of the two screens (Fig. 3).

3.4 A Digital Nature Observatory

The digital nature observatory has been installed at the Natural History Museum of Crete, with the aim of presenting landscapes, flora and fauna of Crete protected by the Natura 2000 network[1]. The large screen, which presents high resolution photos, is embedded in a drone-like construction (styled as a sci-fi invention coming from the past) that overlooks the Cretan land and displays diverse sceneries. The smaller touch screen constitutes a kind of "remote control" mechanism, featuring a digital book with multimedia information regarding the photo presented in the large screen. Next to it, resides a ship's wheel which can be used to change the displayed content (Fig. 4).

Fig. 4. The digital nature observatory

4 Conclusions

This paper has presented a digital catalogue interactive system which can act as a public information display and a promotional tool for commerce, marketing and cultural heritage applications. The system employs touch-based interaction, a modality which is widely anticipated in public information systems. Furthermore, building upon the notion of playful interaction, it offers an alternative means for navigating through the digital catalogue contents, using custom-made input devices implemented by using context-related physical objects (e.g., a windmill, a ship's wheel, etc.). For content presentation a two-stratum approach has been adopted using two different screens: one presents a high-resolution image of a digital catalogue artifact, allowing the user to focus on the visual representation, and the other provides detailed information for the presented artifact.

---

[1] Natura 2000 is a network of core breeding and resting sites for rare and threatened species, and some rare natural habitat types which are protected in their own right (http://ec.europa.eu/environment/nature/natura2000/).

Acknowledgments. This work has been supported by the FORTH-ICS RTD Programme "Ambient Intelligence and Smart Environments".

References

1. Müller, J., Alt, F., Michelis, D., Schmidt, A.: Requirements and design space for interactive public displays. In: Proceedings of the 18th ACM International Conference on Multimedia 25 October 2010, pp. 1285–1294. ACM (2010)
2. Kuts, E.: Playful user interfaces: literature review and model for analysis. In: Breaking New Ground: Innovation in Games, Play, Practice and Theory: Proceedings of the 2009 Digital Games Research Association Conference, London, September 2009 (2009)
3. Nijholt, A.: Playful interfaces: introduction and history. In: Nijholt, A. (ed.) Playful User Interfaces. GMSE, pp. 1–21. Springer, Singapore (2014). doi:10.1007/978-981-4560-96-2_1
4. Ishii, H., Ullmer, B.: Tangible bits: towards seamless interfaces between people, bits and atoms. In: Proceedings of the ACM SIGCHI Conference on Human Factors in Computing Systems, ACM, pp. 234–241 (1997)
5. Zuckerman, O., Gal-Oz, A.: To TUI or not to TUI: evaluating performance and preference in tangible vs. graphical user interfaces. Int. J. Hum.-Comput. Stud. **71**(7), 803–820 (2013)
6. Hornecker, E., Buur, J.: Getting a grip on tangible interaction: a framework on physical space and social interaction. In: Proceedings of the SIGCHI Conference on Human Factors in Computing Systems, 22 April 2006, pp. 437–446. ACM (2006)

Automatic Classification of Eye Blinks and Eye Movements for an Input Interface Using Eye Motion

Shogo Matsuno[1]([✉]), Masatoshi Tanaka[2], Keisuke Yoshida[2],
Kota Akehi[1], Naoaki Itakura[1], Tota Mizuno[1], and Kazuyuki Mito[1]

[1] Graduate School of Informatics and Engineering,
The University of Electro-Communications, 1-5-1 Chofugaoka,
Chofu, Tokyo 182-8585, Japan
m1440004@edu.cc.uec.ac.jp
[2] Graduate School of Information Environment, Tokyo Denki University,
2-1200 Muzaigakuendai, Inzai, Chiba 270-1382, Japan

Abstract. The objective of this study is to develop a multi gesture input interface using several eye motions simultaneously. In this study, we proposed a new automatic classification method for eye blinks and eye movements from moving images captured using a web camera installed on an information device. Eye motions were classified using two methods of image analysis. One method is the classification of the moving direction based on optical flow. The other method is the detection of voluntary blinks based on integral value of eye blink waveform recorded by changing the eye opening area. We developed an algorithm to run the two methods simultaneously. We also developed a classification system based on the proposed method and conducted experimental evaluation in which the average classification rate was 79.33%. This indicates that it is possible to distinguish multiple eye movements using a general video camera.

Keywords: Eye gaze · Eye glance · Eye blink · Voluntary blink · Input interface

1 Introduction

Input interfaces that utilize information about the eyes are usually easy to use and intuitive for portable information devices owing to the advanced miniaturization of these devices, including wearable devices and smartphones [1–6]. Currently, the input to almost all such interfaces is by gazing, which requires high precision measuring instruments because this method divides the display area into small-sized sections for analysis [7, 8]. Therefore, it is difficult to use the gazing method for small information devices. On the other hand, some devices use eye blinks or eye motions, which do not depend on the performance of the measurement tools and display size. However, such methods have low operability and convenience because they have few input channels.

The objective of this study is to develop a multi gesture input interface using several eye motions simultaneously, such as eye blinks, eye movements, and simple gazing positions based on our previously proposed input method (eye glance method

© Springer International Publishing AG 2017
C. Stephanidis (Ed.): HCII Posters 2017, Part I, CCIS 713, pp. 164–169, 2017.
DOI: 10.1007/978-3-319-58750-9_23

[9]) that uses the movement of line of sight in oblique directions. The previously proposed input method cannot use different types of gestures. However, if these gestures can be processed simultaneously, complicated inputs such as character inputs can be performed with a simple operation. In this study, we developed a new method to automatically classify eye blinks and eye movements by analyzing moving images.

2 Input Method Using Eye Motions

2.1 Eye Glance Input Method via Image Analysis

Previously, we proposed the eye glance input method as an input method without eye gazing. This method uses four repeated unique eye motions, which are observed at the four corners of a monitor. Figure 1 shows a model of the input eye glances. In the previous system, a web camera was used to detect eye glances via image analysis. This system captures moving images around the user's eyes, and calculates the optical flows. Every eye glance is classified based on a combination of the horizontal and vertical moving vectors during an eye glance motion. Figure 2 shows an example of optical flow waveform of an eye glance to the upper right direction. This waveform is composed of two mountains or valleys resulting from two eye motions. This pair of waveforms is always symmetrical because an eye glance is a round trip eye movement.

Fig. 1. Model of eye glance input

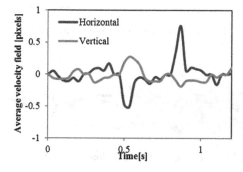

Fig. 2. Example of a waveform during an eye glance to the upper right

2.2 Automatic Detection of Eye Blinks

The proposed method uses not only eye glances but also assumes that an eye blink is the input. Eye blinks can be classified into two types: voluntary and involuntary. Only voluntary blinks are suitable as eye blink input. Voluntary blinks were subsequently detected using the integral value of the eye blink waveform as the feature parameter. Figure 3 shows a model of an eye blink waveform. There are many methods for estimating the feature parameter of eye blinks. In this study, we used a method that utilized a web camera and image analysis as described in Sect. 2.1. Until now, we studied duration and amplitude as features to identify the blink type, with reference to prior research [10]. We define eye-blink duration Dur as the length of time from Ps, the starting point of eyelid closure, to Pe, the end point of the eyelid opening process. In addition, we define Acl, the amplitude of eyelid closure, as the height between Ps and Pm which is the minimum point between Psb, the end point of the eyelid closure process, and Peb, the start point of the eyelid opening process. Similarly, we define Aop, the amplitude of eyelid opening, as the height between Pm and Pe.

Eye blink waveforms are recorded from the temporal change of a pixel value of the eye opening area. The eye opening area was obtained using the binarization technique based on skin color from the captured moving image. Figure 4 shows an example of binarization around the eyes. Voluntary blinks can be determined from the integral value of the waveform because there is a large difference between the integral value of voluntary blinks and that of involuntary blinks.

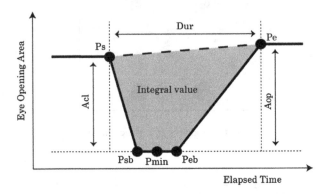

Fig. 3. Model of an eye blink waveform

Fig. 4. Example of binarization around the eyes

3   Experimental Evaluation

3.1   Overview of the Experiment

We conducted experimental tests involving five subjects in order to evaluate the proposed method. The experimental setup comprises a laptop computer (OS: OS X 10.10.5; CPU Intel Core i7 3.3 GHz) and installed web camera (720p Face Time HD camera). The subjects were shown video images of the eye captured using a camera installed on the laptop computer. First, the subjects performed a calibration to determine the threshold classifications for the eye motions. They performed eye motions conforming to when a sign index was displayed at the center of the screen, at each of the four corners, and voluntary blinks in the displayed the screen. After the calibration, the subjects performed 6 trials randomly for each sign. The view angle between the middle indicator and the corner indicators in the experimental image was $15° \times 7°$. Figure 5 shows a screen shot of the experiment.

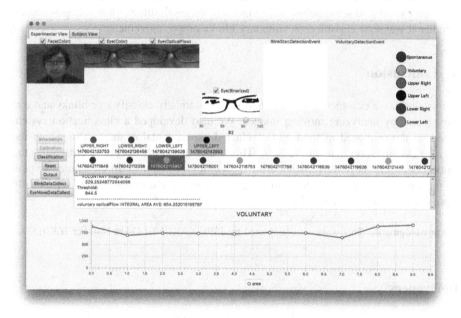

Fig. 5. Indicators for calibration and experiment

3.2   Evaluation of the Proposed Method

Table 1 shows the results of the experimental evaluation conducted with 5 subjects. The results shown in Table 1 indicate that the average accuracy rate for the sum of all indicators on the subjects is 79.33% The results also indicate that generally, the subjects were able to classify all eye motions. The average accuracy rate of the classification in the proposed method was approximately the same as that of our previous eye

Table 1. Results of the experimental evaluation (online)

Subjects	Voluntary (%)	Upper right (%)	Lower right (%)	Lower left (%)	Upper left (%)	Average (%)
A	6/6 (100)	5/6 (83.3)	6/6 (100)	5/6 (83.3)	4/6 (66.6)	26/30(86.67)
B	6/6 (100)	6/6 (100)	5/6 (83.3)	3/6 (50.0)	3/6 (50.0)	23/30(76.67)
C	5/6 (83.3)	4/6 (66.7)	4/6 (66.7)	2/6 (33.3)	2/6 (33.3)	17/30(56.67)
D	6/6 (100)	4/6 (66.7)	4/6 (66.7)	6/6 (100)	5/6 (83.3)	25/30(83.33)
E	6/6 (100)	5/6 (83.3)	6/6 (100)	5/6 (83.3)	6/6 (100)	28/30(93.33)
Average	29/30(96.67)	24/30(80.00)	25/30(83.33)	21/30(70.00)	20/30(66.67)	119/150(79.33)

glance input system. However, in some subjects, the identification rate of some motions was sometimes low. A possible reason is that the movement in a specific direction was small. It is possible that when the movement in a specific direction is small, it cannot be detected because the setting of the threshold value uses the same value in all directions. In addition, there were cases in which the blink waveform and the upper right waveform were similar in some subjects. In this case, the result differs greatly depending on whether it was first classified as voluntary blinks or eye movement.

4   Conclusion

In this study, we designed a new method to automatically classify eye blinks and eye movements by analyzing moving images. We also developed a classification system based on the proposed method and conducted experimental evaluation in which the average classification rate was 79.33%. This shows that it is possible to distinguish the motion of multiple eye movements using a general video camera. In the future, we plan to improve the algorithm in order to improve accuracy, and to develop a user-friendly input interface with user interface.

Acknowledgment. This work was supported by JSPS KAKENHI Grant Number 16K01538.

References

1. Pedrosa, D., Pimentel, M.D.G., Wright, A., Truong, K.N.: Filteryedping: design challenges and user performance of dwell-free eye typing. ACM Trans. Accessible Comput. **6**(1), 1–37 (2015)
2. Sato, H., Abe, K., Ohi, S., Ohyama, M.: Automatic classification between involuntary and two types of voluntary blinks based on an image analysis. In: Proceedings on 17th International Conference on Human-Computer Interaction (HCII), pp. 140–149. (2015)
3. Mollenbach, E., Hansen, J.P., Lillholm, M., Gale, A.G.: Single stroke gaze gestures. In: Proceedings of CHI 2009 Extended Abstracts on Human Factors in Computing Systems, pp. 4555–4560, April 2009
4. MacKenzie, I.S., Ashitani, B.: BlinkWrite: efficient text entry using eye blinks. Univ. Access Inf. Soc. **10**, 69–80 (2011)

5. Kherlopian, A.R., Gerrein, J.P., Yue, M., Kim, K.R., Kim, J.W., Sukumaran, M., Sajda, P.: Electrooculogram based system for computer control using a multiple feature classification model. In: Proceedings of the 28th IEEE EMBS Annual International Conference, pp. 1295–1298, August 2006

6. Mondal, C., Azam, M.K., Ahmad, M., Hasan, S.M.K., Islam, M.R.: Design and implementation of a prototype electrooculography based data acquisition system. In: Proceedings of International Conference on Electrical Engineering and Information Communication technology, pp. 1–6, May 2015

7. Velichkovsky, B., Sprenger, A., Unema, P.: Towards gaze-mediated interaction: Collecting solutions of the "Midas touch problem. In: Proceedings of IFIP TC13 International Conference on Human-Computer Interaction, September, pp. 509–516, July 1997

8. Vrzakova,H., Bednarik, R.: That's not norma(n/l): a detailed analysis of midas touch in gaze-based problem-solving. In: CHI 2013 Extended Abstracts on Human Factors in Computing Systems, pp. 85–90, April 2013

9. Matsuno, S., Akehi, K., Itakura, N., Mizuno, T., Mito, K.: Computer input system using eye glances. In: 17th International Conference on Human-Computer Interaction (HCII), pp. 425–432 (2015)

10. Tanabe, K., Yasui, A.: Changes in blink waveform during addition task. JES Ergon. **46**(2), 180–183 (2010)

A Study on Characteristics of Hand Gesture Pointing Operation Versus Mouse Pointing Operation

A Comparison of Velocity Waves of Operation Time Between Mouse Pointing and Hand Gesture Pointing with Two Kinds of Control-Display Ratio

Shuhei Matsuyama[1][✉] and Mitsuhiko Karashima[2]

[1] Graduate School of Information and Telecommunication Engineering,
Tokai University, Tokyo, Japan
6bjnm011@mail.u-tokai.ac.jp
[2] School of Information and Telecommunication Engineering,
Tokai University, Tokyo, Japan

Abstract. In previous studies, it was clarified that the expanded Fitts' law to the two-dimensional GUI operation was applicable to the operation by the mouse (mouse pointing operation). As for the pointing operation by the hand gesture (gesture pointing operation), it was suggested that it did not necessarily apply to the expanded Fitts' law. This research focused on examining the reason the expanded Fitts' law could not apply to the operation of two-dimensional GUI using hand gestures through two experiments.

Experiment 1 examined the characteristics of the mouse pointing operation and the gesture pointing operation. In Experiment 2 the two kinds of the Control-Display ratio for the gesture pointing operation were prepared because previous studies suggested the cause related to the CD ratio. In both experiments, the participants were required to do the multi directional pointing task. The time between changing the color of the target and putting the cursor on the target was measured as the operation time. The results of the experiments suggested that the velocity waveform of the pointing time of the mouse operation was different from the gesture operation and the difference of the waveform might be influenced by the CD ratio and that the difference in the degree of the application to Fitts' law depended on the difference of the CD ratio.

Keywords: Fitts' law · Two-dimensional GUI · Two-dimensional pointing task · Mouse pointing · Hand gesture · Gesture pointing · Velocity waves · Control-Display ratio

1 Introduction

Conventionally two-dimensional GUI is operated by a finger, a stylus on a touch-screen of a tablet PC, or a mouse on a PC. Recently the operation by using hand gesture in three-dimensional space is proposed as the new method of the operation of

© Springer International Publishing AG 2017
C. Stephanidis (Ed.): HCII Posters 2017, Part I, CCIS 713, pp. 170–176, 2017.
DOI: 10.1007/978-3-319-58750-9_24

two-dimensional GUI. It has some advantages that the user can intuitively operate two-dimensional GUI by using a physical motion, and also operate the GUI from a distance without any device. Fitts' law exists as a model of operation of two-dimensional GUI which is pointing with a mouse.

$$\mathbf{MT} = \mathbf{a} + \mathbf{b} \cdot \mathbf{log_2} \left(\frac{W}{D} + 1 \right)$$

$$\mathbf{ID} = \mathbf{log_2} \left(\frac{W}{D} + 1 \right)$$

In previous studies [1–4], it was clarified that the expanded Fitts' law to the two-dimensional GUI operation was applicable to the time required for the operation by the mouse to move the cursor to the target and click the target on a screen (mouse pointing operation). As for the pointing operation by the hand gesture (gesture pointing operation), it was suggested that the expanded Fitts' law did not necessarily apply to the operation time and that the target size only had a minor influence on the operation time [3]. This research focused on examining the cause the expanded Fitts' law could not apply to the operation of two-dimensional GUI using hand gestures through two experiments.

2 Method

2.1 Participants

Seventeen right–handed university students ranging in age from 20 to 24 who volunteered and were not provided any payment, took part in the experiments. Twelve participants took part in Experiment 1 and five participants took part in Experiment 2. They received a thorough explanation about the method of the experiments and signed the consent form.

2.2 Experiment Tasks

Experiment 1 examined the characteristics of the mouse pointing operation and the gesture pointing operation. Experiment 2 examined the characteristic of the gesture operation by two kinds of the CD (Control-Display) ratio (see Sect. 3.1). The participants were required to do the multi directional pointing task (Fig. 1) which was modified ISO9241-411 Annex B [5] for using hand gesture on the 58-inch large screen. The index of difficulty (ID) has 9 patterns as shown in Table 1 and the method of calculating ID is based on the extended Fitts' Law (two-dimensional model). They were required to place the cursor over the target when it turned red and hold it there for two seconds until the next target turned red.

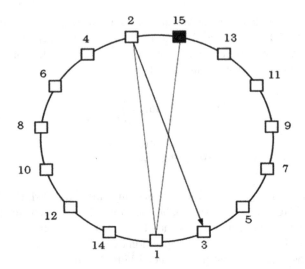

Fig. 1. Experimental tasks

Table 1. Patterns of Index of Difficulty

W(px)	D(px)	ID
48	320	2.939
48	560	3.663
48	800	4.143
36	320	3.306
36	560	4.049
36	800	4.537
24	320	3.841
24	560	4.605
24	800	5.102

2.3   Experiment Environment and Apparatus

For Experiment 1, the gesture pointing operation was done with the large screen (58-inch, 1920px × 1080px). The mouse pointing operation was done with the small screen (21.5-inch, 1920px × 1080px). The visual distance was set to 2 m and 0.7 m respectively. For Experiment 2, the gesture pointing operation was done with a large screen (58-inch, 1920px × 1080px). The visual distance was set to 2 m. In both experiments, the motion capture system used VEANUS 3D, Nobby Tech. Ltd. Also, all the participants required to pick up a reflective material marker by the thumb and index finger of the right hand during the experiment.

The time from changing the color of the target to putting the cursor on the target was measured as the pointing time. For the data obtained, Smirnov-Grubbs test was conducted at a significance level of 0.05 in order to remove the unexpected times values.

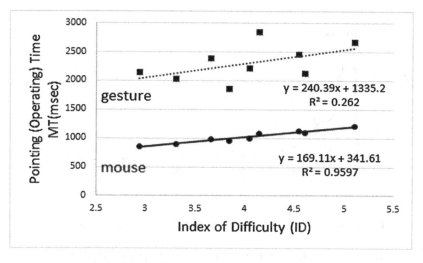

Fig. 2. Relation between the ID and the pointing time

3   Results and Discussions

3.1   Experiment 1

Figure 2 showed that the relation between the ID and the pointing time. The solid line and dotted line showed the results of the simple linear regression analysis.

The regression expression of the mouse pointing operation was

$$MT = 341.61 + 169.11 \times ID \quad R^2 = 0.9579$$

The expression of gesture operation was

$$MT = 1335.5 + 240.39 \times ID \quad R^2 = 0.262$$

The results of the regression analysis revealed that mouse operation applied to Fitts' law and that the gesture operation did not necessarily apply to Fitts' law.

Figure 3 showed that the example of velocity waves of the mouse pointing and the gesture pointing. Both velocity waves of the mouse operation and the gesture operation were convex upward. The waveform of the mouse operation was not monotonously decelerated but there were both the decelerated section and the constant section after the maximum speed was reached. On the other hand, the waveform of the gesture operation monotonically decelerates after the maximum speed was reached. The maximum speed and the appearance time of the maximum speed are different between the mouse operation and the gesture operation. Asahi [6] pointed out that the maximum speed in the mouse operation and its appearance time are influenced by the CD ratio, and that the smaller the CD ratio was, the higher the maximum speed was and the faster the appearance time was. The velocity waveform of the gesture operation in this experiment was very similar to the waveform of the mouse operation with the large CD ratio in the previous research [6]. In addition, the CD ratio of the gesture operation in

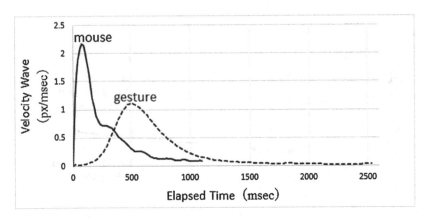

Fig. 3. Velocity waves of the mouse pointing and the gesture pointing

this experiment is larger than the large CD ratio of the previous research. From these relations between the velocity waveform and the CD ratio, it was suggested that the difference of the velocity waveform between the mouse operation and the gesture operation might be influenced by the CD ratio. Therefore, we set two types of CD ratios and conducted Experiment 2 with the gesture operation. One was the conventional CD ratio for the gesture operation (CD ratio = 1), and the other was the CD ratio recommended for the mouse operation (CD ratio = 0.625).

3.2   Experiment 2

Figure 4 showed that relation between the ID and the pointing time. The solid line and dotted line showed the results of the simple linear regression analysis.

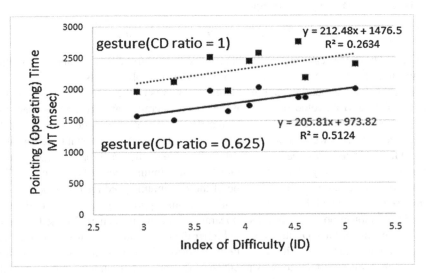

Fig. 4. Relation between the ID and the pointing time

The regression expression of gesture operation with the conventional CD ratio was

$$MT = 1476.5 + 21248 \times ID \quad R^2 = 0.2634$$

The expression of gesture operation with recommended for the mouse CD ratio was

$$MT = 973.82 + 205.81 \times ID \quad R^2 = 0.5124$$

The results of this experiment revealed that the contribution rate of the gesture operation with the recommended CD ratio increased in comparison with the gesture operation with the conventional CD ratio. The results were suggested that the differences in the degree of the appliance to Fitts' law depend on the difference of the CD ratio. However, the gesture operation with the recommended ratio did not satisfyingly apply to Fitts' law in comparison with the mouse operation with the same CD ratio. The small number of the participants might be why the contribution rate was not highly satisfying. In the future, it will be necessary to collect a larger number of the data set and analyze it.

4 Conclusion

This research explored the characteristics of the hand gesture pointing operation through two experiments. In the first experiment (Experiment 1), by comparing the velocity waves of the mouse operation with the gesture operation, we found the difference between them and it was suggested that this difference might be due to the Control-Display ratio. In the second experiment (Experiment 2) it was examined whether the contribution rate of the regression analysis for the pointing time of the gesture operation depended on the CD ratio by two kinds of the CD ratio (CD ratio = 1 as the conventional and CD ratio = 0.625 as the recommended for the mouse operation). The results of the experiment revealed that the contribution rate of the gesture operation with the recommended CD ratio increased in comparison with the conventional CD ratio. However, the gesture operation with the recommended ratio did not satisfyingly apply to Fitts' law in comparison with the mouse operation with the same CD ratio.

In conclusion, the results of the experiments suggested that the velocity waveform of the pointing time of the mouse operation was different from the gesture operation and the difference of the waveform might be influenced by the CD ratio and that the difference in the degree of the application to Fitts' law depended on the difference of the CD ratio. However, the gesture operation with the recommended ratio did not satisfyingly apply to Fitts' law in comparison with the mouse operation with the same CD ratio. In the future, it will be necessary to collect a larger number of the data set and analyze it in order to examine why the contribution rate was not highly satisfying.

References

1. MacKenzie, I.S., William, B.: Extending Fitts' law to two-dimensional tasks. In: Proceedings of the ACM CHI 1992 Conference on Human Factors in Computing Systems, pp. 219–226 (1992). doi:10.1145/142750.142794
2. Burno, R.A., Wu, B., Dohertya, R., Colett, H., Elnaggar, R.: Applying Fitts' law to gesture based computer interactions. Procedia Manufact. **3**, 4342–4349 (2015). doi:10.1016/j.promfg.2015.07.429
3. Moriyama, Y., Nishiguchi, H., Karashima, M.: A study on the characteristics of the operation of two-dimensional GUI by hand gesture–application of Fitts' law to the young subjects' pointing operation. In: Proceedings of the School of Information and Telecommunication Engineering, Tokai University, vol. 8(1), pp. 1–7 (2015). (in Japanese)
4. Murata, A., Iwase, H.: Extending Fitts' law to a three-dimensional pointing task. Hum. Mov. Sci. **20**(6), 791–805 (2001). doi:10.1016/S0167-9457(01)00058-6
5. ISO/TS 9241-411: Ergonomics of Human-system interaction- Part411; Evaluation methods for the design of physical input device (2012)
6. Asahi, M., Takahashi, K., Tsukitani, T., Kitamura, Y., Kishino, F.: An effect of control-display ratio to kinematics features in a pointing task with a mouse. J. Inf. Process. **49**(12), 3879–3889 (2008). (in Japanese)

A Pen Gesture-Based Editing System
for Online Handwritten Objects
on a Pen Computer

Hidetoshi Miyao[(⊠)], Keisuke Nakamura, Shinya Nakazawa,
and Minoru Maruyama

Computer Science and Engineering, Shinshu University, Nagano, Japan
{miyao,maruyama}@cs.shinshu-u.ac.jp

Abstract. In our system, handwritten characters (which include other kinds of objects written in a text line) and figures can be edited by using pre-defined pen gestures on a pen computer, and handwritten characters around the edited objects are automatically aligned. The prototype system has three modes: character writing, figure drawing, and editing modes. In the character writing mode, a user can write any characters along the ruled line in the main window. In the figure drawing mode, any objects can be drawn without limitation. In the editing mode, a user can edit handwritten objects by using the pre-defined pen gestures. Among the processes, the system does not permit an overlap area between characters and figures. In our experiments with objects handwritten by 10 test users, a good result was obtained.

Keywords: Character segmentation · Pen gesture · Online handwritten object

1 Introduction

When a user makes notes of a lecture or an idea, a pen and a sheet of paper are often used since he/she can handwrite objects immediately on the paper and their positions and shapes can be freely decided. However, if the handwritten objects have to be edited, the user must delete the handwritten objects with an eraser and rewrite them appropriately. It is a troublesome task. To solve the problem, objects handwritten on a pen based computer are recognized by pattern recognition techniques and they are treated as coded character set [1, 2]. But the user has to correct misrecognized objects manually and a system cannot deal with objects which are outside the scope of pre-defined recognition targets. Therefore Chen [3] has developed an application software where a user can edit handwritten objects by using pen based gestures and they are automatically aligned with maintenance of each object shape without a recognition process. However, the software has the following drawbacks:

- A user must do many operations to edit an object. For example, 6 and 8 operations are needed for object deletion and object transfer processes, respectively.
- The accuracy of character segmentation process is not high enough. It causes an error in editing processes.

© Springer International Publishing AG 2017
C. Stephanidis (Ed.): HCII Posters 2017, Part I, CCIS 713, pp. 177–184, 2017.
DOI: 10.1007/978-3-319-58750-9_25

- Figures cannot be inserted freely. For example, both a text and a figure don't exist simultaneously in one line of text.

Therefore, we propose a new system to solve the problems.

2 System Overview

Our system has three modes: character writing, figure drawing, and editing modes. The mode can be selected by tapping the appropriate icon in the sub window (See Fig. 1(a)). In the character writing mode, a user can write any characters along the ruled line in the main window. We call the objects written in this mode *character objects*. In the figure drawing mode, any objects can be drawn without limitation. We call the objects written in this mode *figure objects*. In these modes, handwritten objects are represented by one or more strokes. Each stroke is a connected component from pen-down to pen-up and it is represented as a sequence of 2D sampling points obtained by a pen computer device. To distinguish between character objects and figure ones, we prepare a table as shown in Fig. 1(b). The main window is quantized by dividing to equal size blocks, each of which denotes a drawing status. We call the 2D blocks *ID table*. For character objects, blocks overlapped with a bounding box of each stroke are denoted by -1 in the ID table. For figure objects, blocks overlapped with a bounding box of all handwritten strokes for the time from the beginning of figure writing mode to the end, are denoted by a certain positive integer. We assign the value 0 to the other blocks (That is, all the blocks have the value 0 in initial state). Among the processes, the system does not permit an overlap between blocks with different values except for the blocks of the value 0. In the editing mode, a user can edit handwritten objects by using pre-defined pen gestures and character objects around the edited objects are automatically aligned. If the object positions are changed, contents of the ID table are also updated properly.

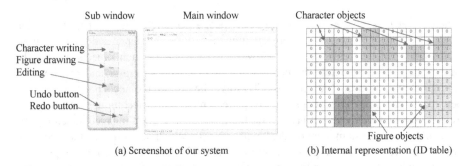

(a) Screenshot of our system   (b) Internal representation (ID table)

Fig. 1. System overview and internal representation for the main window

3 Segmentation of Character Objects

To apply the editing and alignment processes, strokes in character objects must be grouped every character symbol in advance. This segmentation process is applied when the mode is changed from character writing mode to the others or character objects are inserted by using a text input popup dialog box. We assumed that characters hand-written along the ruled line are almost the same size. We propose a segmentation method based on this assumption as follows:

1. If a bounding box of a handwritten stroke overlaps with a bounding box of another stroke, these strokes are merged since they can belong to a same character symbol. In this stage, we call the set of merged strokes character candidate set A.
2. For each candidate of set A, we obtain width and height of bounding box of it. For all candidates of set A, the obtained values are sorted in descending order and the average value of upper half is calculated as an estimate character size α.
3. Candidates of set A are ordered based on the horizontal position of the left side of the bounding box of the character candidate. Let $\{a_1, a_2, \cdots, a_n\}$ be the ordered candidates. In the candidates, it is assumed that neighboring candidates can be concatenated as one character. Thus, we calculate all combination of candidates. That is, combination list $\{a_1\}, \{a_1, a_2\}, \{a_1, a_2, a_3\}, \cdots, \{a_1, a_2, \cdots, a_n\}, \{a_2\}, \{a_2, a_3\}, \{a_2, a_3, \cdots, a_n\}, \{a_3\}, \cdots, \{a_n\}$ is obtained. For the width of bounding box of each combination, if the combination has the closest width to the estimate size α, the candidates which belong to the combination, are merged. The combinations which include the merged candidates, are deleted from the list. This process continues until the combination list is empty. Thus, we obtain the set of merged candidates and we call it character candidate set B.
4. For each candidate of set B, we obtain the width of bounding box of it. For all candidates of set B, the obtained values are sorted in descending order and the average value of upper half is calculated as an estimate character size β.
5. After the stage 3, small size candidates can be remained. Therefore, for each candidate of set B, if the width of it is smaller than the value obtained by rounding down $\beta/2$ to the nearest integer, it is concatenated to either left-hand side candidate or right (If the candidate is concatenated to the left-hand side candidate and β is closer to the width of the bounding box of them than the width of the bounding box produced by the concatenation of the candidate and the right-hand side candidate, the left-hand side candidate is adopted. Otherwise, the right-hand side one is adopted.) Thus, we obtain a new set of merged candidates and we call it character candidate set C.
6. For each candidate of set C, if the bounding box of the candidate overlaps with bounding boxes of other candidates, they are merged. Finally, a set of merged candidates is obtained and we call it *character candidates*. Each character candidate consists of one or more strokes.

4   Editing Functions

In the editing mode, a user can edit handwritten objects by using pre-defined pen gestures. 4 types of pen gestures are prepared and each of them are represented by two stroke gestures as shown in Fig. 2. In the figures, the numbers and the arrowed lines denote stroke order and direction, respectively. The type of gestures is recognized based on the positions of start and end points of each stroke.

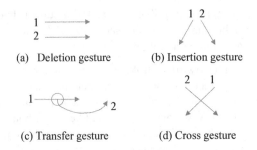

(a) Deletion gesture   (b) Insertion gesture

(c) Transfer gesture   (d) Cross gesture

Fig. 2. Pre-defined pen gestures

4.1   Deletion Process

When two horizontal lines are drawn (see Fig. 2(a)) over a target object, the overlapped strokes with the bounding box of the lines are deleted. In the case of character object deletion, the deleted region is filled with the neighboring handwritten character objects if necessary (see Fig. 3). This character alignment procedure is done based on the information of the precomputed character candidates and the alignment procedure propagate along the ruled lines until an end of character objects or a line feed mark is detected.

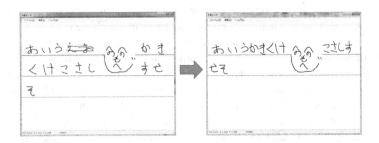

Fig. 3. An example of deletion process

When a cross gesture is drawn (see Fig. 2(d)) over a figure object, an ID number is extracted from the ID table corresponding to the position of the intersection point of the two stroke lines and the strokes with this ID number are removed. In this case, the character alignment procedure is done if necessary.

4.2   Insertion Process

When two lines as shown in Fig. 2(b) are drawn over the target character objects, a dialog box is appeared (see Fig. 4). A user can handwrite characters in the box and they are inserted at a position. The position is the closest point of the divided positions for the character candidates to the center position of the starting points of the two lines in the insertion gesture. The character alignment procedure is also applied if necessary.

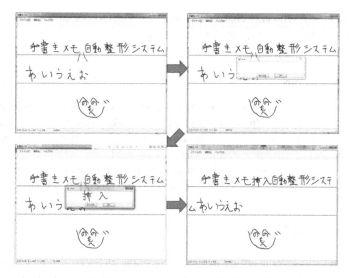

Fig. 4. An example of insertion process

When the insertion gesture (see Fig. 2(b)) is drawn over a figure object, a user can add any strokes to the original figure object. The system gives the added strokes the ID number which is the same as the number assigned to the original figure object.

4.3 Transfer Process

When a horizontal line is drawn over the target objects, the system displays a circle on the line as shown in Fig. 2(c). If a user draws a line from the circle position to the destination, the target objects are moved to the destination (see Fig. 5). The transfer process is done by using the deletion and insertion processes.

If the first stroke of a gesture is drawn over a figure object, the deleted target is all strokes with ID assigned to the figure object. If the target object is moved over character objects, they avoid the transferred object and the character alignment procedure is applied to them. On the other hand, the first stroke is drawn over character objects, the

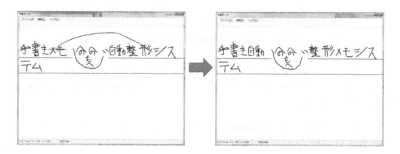

Fig. 5. An example of transfer process

deleted target is selected every character candidates. The target character candidates are moved to the destination by using the method of Sect. 4.2.

4.4   Other Functions

When a cross gesture as shown in Fig. 2(d) is drawn over a character candidate, a line feed mark is inserted before the candidate and the candidate is moved to the head of the next line if necessary. The system displays a red point at the left-side of the candidate. To release the status, the same gesture can also be used.

As shown in Fig. 1(a), the sub window is equipped with the undo and redo buttons. Using the buttons, a user can undo and redo up to the recent 30 actions.

5   Experimental Results

To evaluate the system concerning the accuracy of the character segmentation and the usability of the proposed editing functions, 10 test users used the system.

First, we describe the evaluation of the accuracy for the segmentation of character objects. Each test user wrote the 29 characters three times. They consist of Japanese Hiragana, Katakana, Kanji characters, and alphabets (block letters) shown in Fig. 6(a). As the result of segmentation process, the average accuracy was 76%. For each test user, the lowest accuracy was 40% and the highest was 95%. If the written characters have almost the same size and each gap between characters is large enough, the high accuracy rate was obtained. On the other hand, the rate tends to go down for the opposite situation since it is difficult to estimate a unified size for all characters.

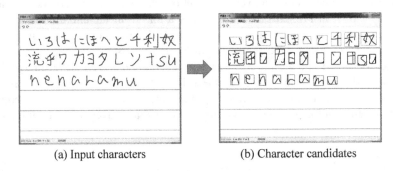

(a) Input characters   (b) Character candidates

Fig. 6. An example of segmentation of character objects

Next, to evaluate the usability of the editing functions, test users responded a questionnaire which consists of the following three evaluation items on a 5-point scale (5 is high and 1 is low):

1. Are the pen gestures easy to memorize?
2. Are the pen gestures easy to draw?
3. Are the edit functions processed as expected?

Table 1. Questionnaire result for three evaluation items

	Type of gestures			
	Deletion	Insertion	Transfer	Cross
Easy to memorize	4.5	4.8	4.4	3.7
Easy to draw	3.9	4.5	4.2	4.3
Processed as expected	3.7	4.8	4.1	4.6

Table 1 shows the result. Thus, for the first evaluation item concerning the cross gesture, the average evaluated value was 3.7. It is relatively low. It is considered that most test users usually drew the two strokes of the cross with opposite order and they were not easy to memorize the gesture. Moreover, the cross gesture has two different functions: Insertion of a line feed mark for a character candidate and deletion for a figure object. Therefore, the test users were confused to use the gesture. For the second evaluation item concerning the deletion gesture, somewhat low value 3.9 was obtained. The cause of this is the misrecognition of gesture types. For the final evaluation item concerning the deletion gesture, the average value 3.7 was obtained. If the two strokes of the deletion gesture are drawn at a short distance, the upper strokes or lower ones for the bounding box of the gesture strokes are remained without user's intent. This is the reason why the evaluation value was relatively low. However, the other evaluation value is more than 4.0 and the proposed edit functions are practical enough. Furthermore, all the pen gesture can be drawn with only two strokes. It is much simpler than the editing method of the existing software [3].

6 Conclusion

We have proposed the new pen gesture-based editing system for online handwritten objects. In the system, to improve the performance of segmentation of character objects, we proposed the method where handwritten strokes are merged properly based on an estimated character size. As the experimental result for 870 characters written by 10 test users, the average accuracy rate 76% was obtained. It is confirmed that the accuracy rate could go up, if sizes of handwritten characters are almost the same and gaps between neighboring characters are large enough.

Next, to simplify the existing editing operations, we proposed the editing methods where we adopted 4 types of pen gestures, each of which consists of only 2 strokes. As the experimental results for the usability evaluation, most test users gave high evaluation marks for all the editing functions.

We also proposed the area management method by using the ID table for the drawing window. As a result, a user can freely transfer a figure object into any text lines while prohibiting existence of overlap regions between character objects and figure ones.

Thus, it is concluded that the system is practical enough for editing of online handwritten objects.

To realize a more user-friendly system, a performance of character segmentation must be improved and the stroke order of writing gestures must be free. In the current system, cursive handwriting cannot be treated properly, so that we plan to solve the problem in future works.

Acknowledgments. This work was supported by JSPS KAKENHI Grant Number JP15K00480.

References

1. Davis, R.: Magic paper: sketch-understanding research. IEEE Comput. **40**(9), 34–41 (2007)
2. Pittman, J.A.: Handwriting recognition: tablet PC text input. IEEE Comput. **40**(9), 49–54 (2007)
3. Chen, Q.: eFinger Notes Pro Version 3.0, App Store. https://itunes.apple.com/US/app/id367256852?mt=8. Accessed 13 Mar 2017

AnywhereTouch: Finger Tracking Method on Arbitrary Surface Using Nailed-Mounted IMU for Mobile HMD

Ju Young Oh[1,2], Jun Lee[3], Joong Ho Lee[2], and Ji Hyung Park[2(✉)]

[1] HCI and Robotics, University of Science and Technology,
Gajeong-ro, Yuseong-gu, Daejeon, Korea
dhwndud407@gmail.com
[2] Center for Robotics Research, Korea Institute of Science and Technology,
5, Hwarang-ro 14-gil, Seongbuk-gu, Seoul, Korea
yapl53@naver.com, jhpark@kist.re.kr
[3] Division of Computer Information and Engineering, Hoseo University,
Hoseo-ro79 gil, 20, Baebang-eup, Asan-si, Chungcheongnam-do, Korea
junlee@hoseo.edu

Abstract. Owing to the development of mobile head mounted display (HMD)s, a mobile input device is becoming necessary in order to manipulate virtual objects which are displayed in an HMD anytime and anywhere. There have been many research studies using ray-casting technique for 3D interactions using an HMD. However, traditional ray-casting-based interactions have limitations of usability due to additional cumbersome input devices along with their limited recognition area. In this paper, we propose the AnywhereTouch, a finger tracking method using nailed-mounted inertial measurement unit (IMU) to allow a user to easily manipulate a virtual object on arbitrary surfaces. The AnywhereTouch activates recognizing process for touch input events when a user's finger touches on an arbitrary surface. It calculates the initial angle of rotation between a finger and the arbitrary surface. Then the AnywhereTouch tracks the position of a fingertip using inverse kinematics models with the angle detected by the IMU. The AnywhereTouch also recognizes tap and release gestures through analyzing changes of acceleration and angular velocity. We expect the AnywhereTouch to provide effective manipulation for the adoption of anywhere touching gesture recognition in the mobile HMD.

Keywords: Nailed-mounted device · Touch gesture · Social acceptable gesture · Virtual reality · Augmented reality

1 Introduction

A head-mounted display (HMD) is a display device, worn on the user's head and displays virtual objects for a user who wants to experience virtual reality (VR) and augmented reality (AR). In the past, it was necessary to connect a high-performance desktop to display virtual objects on the HMD, but recently, the mobile HMD, which can display virtual objects through its connection with a high-performance smartphone or built-in high-performance chip on the HMD itself, has appeared and allows the user

© Springer International Publishing AG 2017
C. Stephanidis (Ed.): HCII Posters 2017, Part I, CCIS 713, pp. 185–191, 2017.
DOI: 10.1007/978-3-319-58750-9_26

to see virtual objects with no limit of time and space. However, in order for a user to interaction with virtual objects displayed on the mobile HMD, a portable input device is needed to manipulate those objects. Especially, to select the target virtual object, the input device can control the ray-casting which is one of the easily and fast selection method in VR or AR [1].

Conventional input devices such as a mouse, a keyboard, and a wand are not suitable for a mobile environment because a user needs to carry these devices. Therefore, the input device embedded in the HMD itself is proposed. Oculus Rift [2] and Gear VR [3] use an IMU sensor to track the orientation of a user's head. The device allows user to move the cursor at the center of the screen on the HMD by rotating his/her head, but when the user wants to move the cursor quickly or frequently, it can cause the dizziness to the user. FaceTouch [4] proposed touch interaction by touch pad attached on the HMD, and Hololens [5] proposed a method of recognizing the user's hand gesture by a camera attached on the HMD. When a user uses these methods in order to interact with virtual objects for a long time, his/her arm fatigue increases because the user must raise his/her hand. In addition, using these methods in a public space, he/she feels uncomfortable because these methods increase attention from others.

Therefore, in order to recognize socially acceptable gesture in a public place, the input device should be independent of the HMD [6] and be easily carried by attached on the user's body. There have been much research on social acceptable devices and gestures. Belt [7] proposed a touch interface using the belt with multiple touch sensors. Although the menu can be easily manipulated depending on the position of the belt, there are limitations in selecting and manipulating virtual objects in 3D. FingerPad [8] and uTrack [9] proposed a method of tracking the finger position using a magnet attached to a finger and a sensor tracking magnetic field changes attached another finger. But these method is cumbersome to use because two sensors need to be attached. LightRing [10] uses a ring type device for tracking fingertip movements on the surface. However, this method is difficult to track the fingertip when the finger is unfolded and needs to add another sensor for the selection.

In this paper, we propose the AnywhereTouch, a finger tracking method using nailed-mounted inertial measurement unit (IMU) to allow a user to easily manipulate a virtual object on arbitrary surfaces. If a finger touches an arbitrary surface, AnywhereTouch calculates the normal vector of the touched surface and the angle between the surface and the finger with the defined finger gesture. Next, the finger movement on the arbitrary surface is tracked based on the inverse kinematics model and the quaternion measured from the IMU. And the finger tap gestures are recognized by analyzing the three-axis acceleration and the three-axis angular velocity from the attached IMU sensor. The virtual object can be selected by controlling the ray-casting based on the finger movement and finger tap gestures.

2   Method

2.1   Hardware

Figure 1-A shows the nailed-mounted 9-axis IMU. The 9-axis IMU can sense the 3-axis acceleration, angular velocity, and magnetic field. And orientation of the IMU is

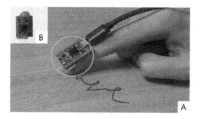

Fig. 1. (A) An example of AnywhereTouch with a nailed-mounted IMU on the surface. (B) IMU is attached on the middle of the nail to prevent the sensor from touching the surface.

calculated from the 9-axis IMU data [11]. Bending the fingers on the arbitrary surface causes the nail to touch the surface, so the IMU is attached to the middle of the nail as shown in Fig. 1-B.

2.2 Calibration

When an index finger touches an arbitrary surface, AnywhereTouch calculates the slope of the arbitrary surface, the angle between the surface and the finger. After the index finger is unfolded and the wrist is fixed as shown in Fig. 2–(A), the wrist rotates from side to side to calculate the slope of an arbitrary surface. Figure 2–(B) illustrates how to create the arc in unit sphere using the rotation angle from the IMU when the wrist moves side to side. The normal vector of the contacted surface is calculated based on points A, B, and C of the created arc from Eq. (1). Both ends of the arc are A and B, and C is the point on the arc that is closest to the center point of A and B. $\vec{n}$ is a normal vector of the arbitrary surface touched by the index finger. The slope of the surface is calculated based on $\vec{n}$ and $\vec{z}$ from Eq. (2). $\vec{z}$ is a unit normal vector of the x-y plane in the global coordinate system, and q_{plane} is a unit quaternion representing the rotation angle of the contact surface. θ_{init} is the angle between the surface and the index finger and is calculated from Eq. (3). $\overrightarrow{CO}$ is the direction of the finger from point C on the arc to the origin point.

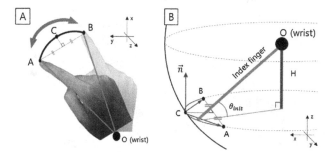

Fig. 2. (A) The movement of the index finger side to side for calibration. (B) Illustration of calibration.

$$\vec{n} = \overrightarrow{CA} \times \overrightarrow{CB} \tag{1}$$

$$q_{plane} = (\vec{v}, w)(\vec{v} = \vec{n} \times \vec{z}, w = 1 + \vec{n} \cdot \vec{z}) \tag{2}$$

$$\theta_{init} = 90 - acos(\frac{\overrightarrow{CO} \cdot \vec{n}}{\left\| \overrightarrow{CO} \cdot \vec{n} \right\|}) \tag{3}$$

2.3 Tracking the Finger Movement

The anatomical model of the index finger and the quaternions measured by the IMU is used to track the movement of the fingers. The index finger' joints consist of metacarpophalangeal joint (MCP) joint, proximal interphalangeal (PIP) joint, and distal interphalangeal (DIP) joint, which has 2 degrees of freedom (DOF), 1DOF, and 1DOF, respectively [12]. The side to side movement of the index finger is tracked by MCP joint's z-axis rotation angle and the bent index finger is tracked by MCP joint, PIP joint, and DIP joint's y-axis rotation angle. However, when the index finger moves from side to side, it is difficult to move the index finger because the range of MCP joint's z-axis rotation angle is very small. Thus, as shown in Fig. 2-A, the side to side movement of the index finger includes the side to side movement of the wrist. The side to side movement of the index finger can be tracked by the z-axis rotation angle from the IMU.

If an external force is not applied to the fingertip, anatomically PIP's y-axis rotation angle has $3/2*\theta$ when the DIP's y-axis rotation angle is θ [12]. And because the index finger is bent on the surface as shown Fig. 3-A, each joint of the index finger can be expressed as α, which is the y-axis rotation angle from the IMU, and θ, which is the angle of DIP as shown Fig. 3-B. θ is calculated from Eq. 5. H is the height from the surface to the hand and is calculated using the θ_{init}. Equation 5 means H isn't changed when the index finger is bent. 39.8, 22.4, 15.8 are the average lengths (mm) of the proximal phalanx, intermediate phalanx, and distal phalanx, respectively [13].

$$f(\theta) = H - \left(15.8 \cdot \sin(a) + 22.4 \cdot \sin(a - \theta) + 39.8 \cdot \sin\left(a - \frac{5}{2}\theta\right)\right) = 0 \tag{4}$$

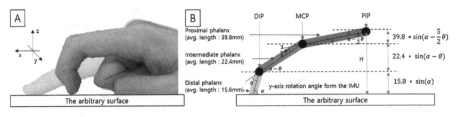

Fig. 3. (A) The bent index finger on the arbitrary surface. (B) Illustration of tracking the bent index finger based on IMU's rotation angle and anatomical model of index finger.

2.4   Recognizing the Finger Tap Gestures

In this paper, we defined two finger tap gestures, which are 'tap' and 'double tap' as shown Table 1. The 3-axis acceleration and angular velocity from the IMU are used to recognize the finger tap gestures. The acceleration from the IMU includes the gravitational acceleration. The linear acceleration removed the gravitational acceleration can be calculated form Eq. (5). q_{IMU} is the quaternion from the IMU and $\vec{G}$ is the gravitational acceleration. Table 1 shows the angular velocity and the linear acceleration during the finger tap gestures. When a user performs 'tap', y-axis of the angular velocity generates a negative trough after a positive crest, and z-axis of the linear acceleration generates a positive crest after a negative trough. Similarly, when a user performs 'double tap', the signal of linear acceleration and angular velocitygestures and the signal of acceleration generated in 'tap' gesture is repeated twice.

$$\overrightarrow{a_{cali}} = q_{IMU} \cdot \overrightarrow{a_{IMU}} - \vec{G} \tag{5}$$

Table 1. Defined the finger tap gestures and the signal of acceleration and angular velocity of each defined finger gesture

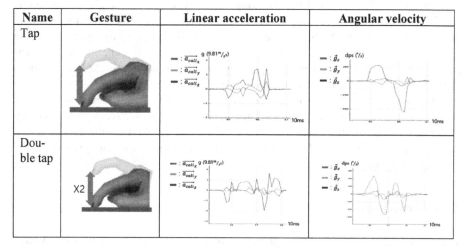

3   Experiments and Results

Accuracy evaluations of the proposed method were conducted about tracking the index finger movements and recognizing the finger tap gestures. To measure the accuracy of tracking the index finger movements, we display the circle, the square, and the triangle pictures to participants and participants drew along the displayed images using their index finger. And to measure the accuracy of recognizing the finger tap gestures, participants were instructed to finger tap gestures on the rectangle divided 9 areas. After each experiment, we interview each participant.

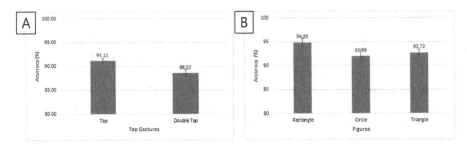

Fig. 4. Results of the evaluations (A) Accuracy of recognizing the finger tap gestures. (B) Accuracy of tracking the finger movements.

10 participants is selected to participate in the experiments. We explained how to use the proposed method for 5 min. After then, we proceeded to experiment. The experiment was conducted on a desktop PC with Intel i5 4690 CPU, 8 GB RAM, and nVidia GTX 960 graphic card. And we used 'MyARHS+' to attach the the 9-axis IMU to index fingernail.

Figure 4 shows results of the accuracy. The average accuracy of the index finger movements is 93.19%. In detail, tracking accuracy of the rectangle movement is 94.85% (standard deviation (stdev): 2.66, standard error (se): 0.84), tracking accuracy of the circle movement 91.99% (stdev: 4.29, se: 1.36), and tracking accuracy of the triangle movement is 92.72% (stdev: 2.07, se: 0.65). After the experiment, 3 participants gave feedback that moving to a diagonal or curved line using the proposed method is a little bit harder than the straight line.

The average accuracy of the finger tap gesture is 89.81%. In detail, recognition accuracy of the 'tap' gesture is 91.11% (stdev: 1.67, se: 0.56), and recognition accuracy of the 'double tap' gesture is 88.52% (stdev: 2.42, se: 0.80). After the experiment, 7 participants gave feedback that it was difficult to perform finger tap gestures in the lower part of 9 divided areas.

4 Conclusion

The conclusion to be drawn here is that we proposed AnywhereTouch which can track the finger movements and recognize the finger tap gestures on the arbitrary surface using nailed-mounted IMU. The experimental results have convincingly demonstrated the accuracy of the proposed method. The proposed method has great potential in various applications of VR or AR with socially acceptable interaction in public space. In the future work, we will research how to easily manipulate virtual objects displayed on HMD in a public space based on the proposed method.

Acknowledgement. This work was supported by the Global Frontier R&D Program on <Human-centered Interaction for Coexistence> funded by the National Research Foundation of Korea grant funded by the Korean Government (MSIP) (NRF-M1AXA003- 2011-0031380).

References

1. Bowman, D.A., Johnson, D.B., Hodges, L.F.: Testbed evaluation of virtual environment interaction techniques. Presence: Teleoperators Vir. Env. **10**(1), 75–95 (2001). doi:10.1162/105474601750182333. MIT Press, Cambridge
2. Oculus Rift. https://www.oculus.com/
3. Samsung Gear VR. http://www.samsung.com/global/galaxy/gear-vr/
4. Gugenheimer, J., Dobbelstein, D., Winkler, C., Haas, G., Rukzio, E.: Facetouch: enabling touch interaction in display fixed UIs for mobile virtual reality. In: 29th Annual Symposium on User Interface Software and Technology, pp 49–60. ACM Press, New York (2016). doi:10.1145/2984511.2984576
5. Microsoft Hololens. https://www.microsoft.com/microsoft-hololens/en-us
6. Hsieh, Y.T., Jylhä, A., Orso, V., Gamberini, L., Jacucci, G.: Designing a willing-to-use-in-public hand gestural interaction technique for smart glasses. In: The 2016 CHI Conference on Human Factors in Computing Systems, pp. 4203–4215. ACM Press, New York (2016). doi:10.1145/2858036.2858436
7. Dobbelstein, D., Hock, P., Rukzio, E.: Belt: an unobtrusive touch input device for head-worn displays. In: the 33rd Annual ACM Conference on Human Factors in Computing Systems, pp. 2135–2138. ACM Press, New York (2015). doi:10.1145/2702123.2702450
8. Chan, L., Liang, R.H., Tsai, M.C., Cheng, K.Y., Su, C.H., Chen, M.Y., Chen, B.Y.: FingerPad: private and subtle interaction using fingertips. In: The 26th Annual ACM Symposium on User Interface Software and Technology, pp. 255–260. ACM Press, New York (2013). doi:10.1145/2501988.2502016
9. Chen, K.Y., Lyons, K., White, S., Patel, S.: uTrack: 3D input using two magnetic sensors. In: the 26th Annual ACM Symposium on User Interface Software and Technology, pp. 237–244. ACM Press, New York (2013). doi:10.1145/2501988.2502035
10. Kienzle, W., Hinckley, K.: LightRing: always-available 2D input on any surface. In: the 27th Annual ACM Symposium on User Interface Software and Technology, pp. 157–160. ACM Press, New York (2014). doi:10.1145/2642918.2647376
11. Madgwick, S.O., Harrison, A.J., Vaidyanatha, R.: Estimation of IMU and MARG orientation using a gradient descent algorithm. In: 2011 IEEE International Conference on Rehabilitation Robotics (ICORR), pp. 1–7. IEEE press, New York (2011). doi:10.1109/ICORR.2011.5975346
12. Lee, J., Kunii, T.L.: Model-based analysis of hand posture. IEEE Comput. Graph. Appl. **15**(5), 77–86 (1995). doi:10.1109/38.403831. IEEE press, New York
13. Alexander, B., Viktor, K.: Proportions of hand segments. Int. J. Morphol. **28**(3), 755–758 (2010). doi:10.4067/S0717-95022010000300015

Vibration Ring Device Which Supports Deaf Students to Learn How to Use Illustrator

SZCAT: Synchronized Click Action Transmitter

Takuya Suzuki[1,2(✉)], Makoto Kobayashi[1], and Yuji Nagashima[2]

[1] Tsukuba University of Technology, Tsukuba City, Ibaraki, Japan
suzukit@a.tsukuba-tech.ac.jp,
koba@cs.k.tsukuba-tech.ac.jp
[2] Kogakuin University, Shinjuku-ku, Tokyo, Japan
nagasima@cc.kogakuin.ac.jp

Abstract. A vibration ring device is developed for the purpose of supporting deaf or hard of hearing students to learn how to use drawing software like an Adobe Illustrator. The device consists of solenoid coils and a controller board based on Arduino. It transmits teacher's mouse click operation to the student's fingers as a vibration. Owing to this device, the student can understand which button was clicked and the operation was a click or a double click or a drag intuitively. Estimation questionnaire was conducted to thirteen deaf or hard of hearing students and twelve of them answered the device was effective to understand teacher's operation and practical for the lecture class.

Keywords: Deaf or hard of hearing student · Solenoid coil and mouse operation

1 Introduction

Our university, Tsukuba University of Technology is a unique one, which is only for visually handicapped or hard of hearing students including blind and deaf students. We have two campuses for each type of impaired students respectively. The campus for the hard of hearing students has well equipped lecture room for them. For example, several beamers which are hanging from the ceiling in front of a whiteboard in the lecture room can be slid in lateral direction and it allows teachers to overlay their handwritings on the whiteboard with outputs by the beamer. Another example is that some tables has whiteboard surface and students and teacher can discuss with writing and drawing on the table directly. Addition to such equipment, most of teachers in the campus can talk with sign language in their classes. We also prepares captioning services for several classes which is conducted by visiting lecturers who does not know sign language.

However, in the class of learning how to use a drawing software like an Adobe Illustrator, there still remains some problems. Teachers frequently shows a model operation to their students using a beamer in a practical lecture class though, they cannot explain their operation with sign language by themselves at the same time. Even though a sign language translator or a captioning service which is effective in usual

C. Stephanidis (Ed.): HCII Posters 2017, Part I, CCIS 713, pp. 192–197, 2017.
DOI: 10.1007/978-3-319-58750-9_27

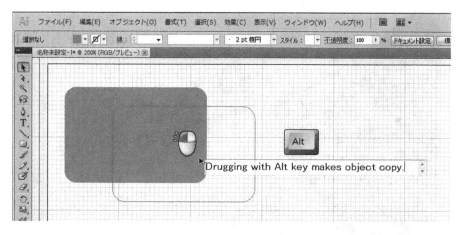

Fig. 1. Appearance of the supporting software for deaf or hard of hearing students. Indication icons and explanation texts appears besides mouse cursor.

conference [1], the translation would be delay and students cannot see both of the translation information and the model operation, because these positions are far from each other. These delay and position difference are critical problems especially in the class of teaching how to use Illustrator, in which combination keys and its timing is quite important for the correct operation.

Therefore, we developed and estimated a supporting software which shows teacher's operation using icons around a mouse cursor in past research project [2]. The appearance of the software is shown in Fig. 1. It shows which mouse button was clicked and what kind of keys was pressed. The mouse icon appears when the teacher clicks the mouse button and it keeps to display until he/she releases the button, hence students can understand that the operation was click or double click or drag. Addition to them, instruction text is displayed under the mouse cursor as well. This software is apparently effective to teach how to use Illustrator and students can acquire techniques of it in shorter period than the way before. On the other hand, few students still has difficulty to understand the timing of clicking and pressing a combination keys, because some deaf or hard of hearing students tend to take much time to read text information and it might cause to miss these icons. We need additional system to teach to such kind of students.

2   System Design and Components

To solve the problem mentioned above, a pair of vibration ring device for an index finger and a middle finger is developed. The overview of the device is shown in Fig. 2. Deaf or hard of hearing student wares this device on his/her dominant hand, and it acquaints the student which mouse button is pressed by the teacher. The ring continues to vibrate until the teacher releases the mouse button, hence the students can understand how long the teacher presses the mouse button. It means they can distinguish the action

Fig. 2. An overview of vibration ring devices and its controller.

is a click or a drag by the vibration pattern. Of course when the teacher makes double click action, the ring vibrates twice and the student can be aware of it. We named the device as Synchronized Click Action Transmitter, SZCAT.

These rings consist of plastic cases and Velcro straps. The size of these cases is 29.5 [mm] (length) by 19.5 [mm] (width) by 17.5 [mm] (height). Inside them, there are small solenoid coils (ROB-11015, SparkFun electronics) respectively. The end of the axis of the coil protrudes 5 [mm] from the case. These solenoids are assigned in parallel to each fingers and the axis knocks the inside wall of the case when an electric power comes. The distance between the end of the axis and the wall of the case effects the feeling of vibration. By the difference of this distance, the vibration on the index finger is smooth and light. On the contrary, the vibration on the middle finger is rough and strong. These difference adds clear information of which button was pressed.

Here, the reason of selecting solenoid coils instead of vibrating motors can be said that a feelings of the solenoid coil is stronger than that of the motor. Moreover, the fact that the solenoid vibration starts and stops immediately and clearly is one of the reason.

A controller unit for these rings is composed of an Arduino Nano and a small circuit with switching transistors. To avoid back electromotive forces by coils, diodes are assigned on the circuit. A software which uses a mouse hook function detects the action that the mouse button is pressed, then, the software sends a message to itself. When the software receives this message, a signal to control Arduino is send via USB port. Finally the switching transistor drives the solenoid coil and it knocks the case, then the student feels the ring is vibrating. The device produces approximately 100 [Hz] vibration by the software on Arduino. As a result, the vibration makes an attention and the students correctly comprehends when the mouse action starts and ends, which side of buttons are pressed.

3 System Estimation by Hard of Hearing Students

3.1 Subject Profile and Procedure

Subjects for the estimation were deaf or hard of hearing students in a department of synthetic design, in our university. They have official certification for disability person in Japan. The total number of estimating students was thirteen. At first, they were required to relearn basic skills of Adobe Illustrator with wearing SZCAT on their index finger and middle finger. All of them already know these skills. After the relearning session with SZCAT, they were requested to answer several questionnaire describes below.

3.2 Estimation Questionnaires

Prepared questionnaires were as follows;

1. If you had stress feeling from SZCAT, Please describe it. Especially about its weight and fitting feelings.
2. How correct SZCAT could transmit teacher's mouse operation timing?
3. What do you think about the difference of vibration between index finger and middle finger?
4. Is SZCAT helpful to transmit teacher's mouse operation to students?
5. Is SZCAT effective in practical lecture class?

Questionnaire from number one to three is required to answer in free-form, number four and five is required to answer in range of scores on a 5-point Likert scale.

3.3 Estimation Results

In the results of questionnaire number one, seven students answered there were no stress from waring SZCAT. Remained six students described some comment about the stress feelings. Four students of the six mentioned that the cables between solenoid cases and the controller unit is cumbersome for operation, and two students of the four mentioned that the weight was little bit heavy. Two students of the first six mentioned that the Velcro tape is obstructive. One student commented that the sound from solenoids on middle finger would be noisy in case he would uses it for a long time. The problem of the cable should be solved in the future though, the fact that half of the estimating students do not care about the ring device surprised to us. Actually some students started to talk in sign language with their hand without putting off SZCAT after the relearning session, then the experimenter scrambled to stop it to avoid to break the device.

About questionnaire number two, all of students answered optimistic. It seemed that they can feel the teacher's mouse action correctly. One student proposed a function of adjusting the frequency of vibrate, another student commented the solenoid motion of the middle finger was little bit strong in negative meanings.

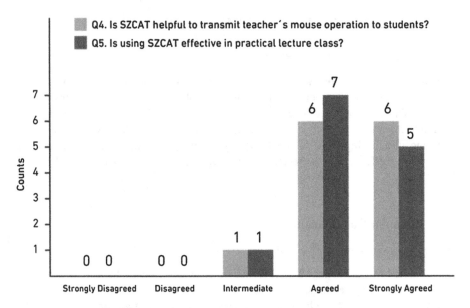

Fig. 3. Results of questionnaire number four and five.

The third questionnaire reveals the difference of vibration is practical and effective. Twelve students answered that they preferred this difference and ten of these twelve commented the condition (vibration on the index finger is smooth and it on the middle finger is rough) is fit for learning. Because the click by the middle finger is not so frequently operations, hence stronger vibration is impressive to learn the timing.

The results of questionnaire number four and five are shown in Fig. 3. About questionnaire number four, six students answered "5-strongly agreed" and another six students answered "4-agreed," last one student answered "3-intermediate." The trend of this result is similar to the answers of questionnaire number five. Five students answered "5-strongly agreed" and another seven students answered "4-agreed," last one student answered "3-intermediate." Totally twelve of thirteen (92%) thought that SZCAT is effective in practical lecture class.

4   Summary

Overall, we can say that the vibration ring device which transmits teacher's mouse button operation during making a model drawing is helpful and effective in the lecture class, since twelve students in the thirteen estimating students made positive reaction to the device. We think that the character of solenoid coil vibration is a kind of reason they preferred to it. The components of "solenoid case" will be available not only for this device but for other notification device which deaf or hard of hearing person use in daily life.

Acknowledgment. This work was supported by JSPS KAKENHI Grant Number 16K01056.

References

1. Damm, C., Ondra, S., Tuzil, J.: Universal access to presentations and lectures using a real-time wireless system distributing speech-to-text reports and mirroring presentation screen to enhance legibility for individuals. Universal Learning Design, pp. 39–48 (2013)
2. Kobayashi, M., Suzuki, T., Wakatsuki, D.: Teaching support software for hearing impaired students who study computer operation. In: Miesenberger, K., Karshmer, A., Penaz, P., Zagler, W. (eds.) ICCHP 2012. LNCS, vol. 7382, pp. 10–17. Springer, Heidelberg (2012). doi:10.1007/978-3-642-31522-0_2

Creating a Gesture-Speech Dataset for Speech-Based Automatic Gesture Generation

Kenta Takeuchi[1]([✉]), Souichirou Kubota[2], Keisuke Suzuki[2], Dai Hasegawa[2], and Hiroshi Sakuta[2]

[1] Graduate School of Aoyama Gakuin University, 5-10-1 Chuo-ku Fuchinobe, Sagamihara-shi, Kanagawa, Japan
`c5616160@aoyama.jp`
[2] Aoyama Gakuin University, 5-10-1 Chuo-ku Fuchinobe, Sagamihara-shi, Kanagawa, Japan

Abstract. In our research, we recorded 298 min (1049 sentences) of speech audio data and the motion capture data of the accompanying gestures from two 25-year-old male participants aiming for future usage in deep learning concerning gesture and speech. The data was recorded in form of an interview, the participant explaining a topic prepared in advance, using a headset microphone and the motion capture software Motivë. The speech audio was stored in mp3, and the motion data was stored in bvh, related as data from the same sentence. We aimed to mainly acquire metaphoric gestures and iconic, as categorized by McNiel. For the categories of the recorded gestures, metaphoric gestures appeared the most, 68.41% of all gestures, followed by 23.73% beat gestures, 4.76% iconic gestures, and 3.11% deictic gestures.

Keywords: Speech · Metaphoric gesture · Iconic gesture · Dataset

1 Introduction

In recent years, virtual characters with a similar body structure with humans, often referred to as virtual humans, have gained much interest. Implementing these virtual humans in a system allows you to make use of non-verbal information, which is frequently used in face-to-face communication to clarify one's intentions or the context of the words spoken [2], in a system-human interaction. Especially, gestures play an important role in aiding comprehension of the content presented. Many researches concerning the extent and actual effects of gestures in interactions have been carried out [3].

In the current state, there are two common ways of making the gestures to be implemented with a virtual human: using the data collected from actual humans using motion capture technology, and creating animation for the virtual human's model manually. However, these ways are considered costly, the former requiring financial costs for actually purchasing a motion capture system, and the latter requiring professional knowledge and experience. In research level, utilizing

© Springer International Publishing AG 2017
C. Stephanidis (Ed.): HCII Posters 2017, Part I, CCIS 713, pp. 198–202, 2017.
DOI: 10.1007/978-3-319-58750-9_28

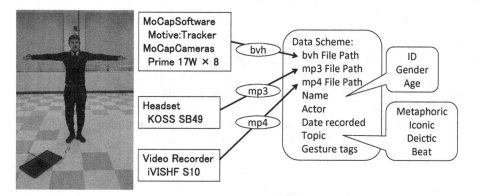

Fig. 1. Recording and data overview

Behavior Markup Language (BML) [5] has also been a popular method, although this too requires expertise for application. Many attempts have been made to automatically generate gestures from text or speech data, but not many have utilized deep learning in doing so. However, there are no datasets with speech and gesture paired that could be used for such learning. Therefore in this paper, we aim to create a dataset of pairs of speech data and motion data of the accompanying gestures that could be used for future deep learning (Fig. 1).

2   Method

In this section, we will describe the details of the data and how it was acquired. A total of 298 min (1049 sentences) of speech audio data with the motion data of the accompanying gestures were recorded. Additionally, video data of the participants was also recorded so the validity of the two data could be checked afterward.

In our recordings, we aimed to mainly acquire metaphoric gestures and iconic gestures, as categorized by McNiel [3]. Metaphoric gestures are gestures in which an abstract meaning is visually expressed as if it had a physical form, such as showing an empty palm as to indicate one is 'presenting an idea'. Iconic gestures are used to illustrate physical, concrete items or acts, like expressing how large an object is or rapidly moving one's hand up and down to indicate the action of chopping something. These gestures aid listeners in comprehending the structure and events or objects depicted in the speech, and have many potential uses in explanation, learning, and teaching [4]. Deictic gestures, used to indicate real/imaginary objects, people, directions, etc. around the speaker, were considered inappropriate for usage in deep learning aiming to learn the association between speech and gesture, heavily depending on the speaker's surrounding environment rather than the actual context of the speech. Also, beat gestures, used for emphasis and expressing the rhythm of conversations, have little relation to the actual context of speech and were not considered to be viable to be used in the learning.

2.1 Devices

Motion data was acquired using the software Motive:Tracker by SPICE Inc., along with a motion capture suit with 49 markers and 8 OptiTrack Prime 17 W cameras, placed in an 850×850 m area. The recorded motion data was exported to bvh format, in which motion data is described as the hierarchy and initial pose of the skeleton and time sequence data of each joint's rotation angle.

Speech data was acquired using a headset, as to not hinder the subject's movement. The recorded speech data was stored in mp3 format. Video data was acquired using a stationary video camera and stored in mp4 format.

2.2 Participants and Procedure

The participants were 2 male undergraduate students, both at the age of 25.

The data was recorded in form of an interview, where the participant explains a topic prepared and thought about beforehand. Several other methods were attempted, but these methods were considered unsuited for the recording.

First, when having the participant read a transcript out loud, valid gestures did not appear. This is thought to be because the speaker has to have a concrete enough image about the context of what they were talking about for gestures to naturally appear during speaking.

Second, when having the participant make a presentation using a slide show, deictic gestures appeared with too much frequency, since the speaker tended to point at his presentation slide while explaining.

Third, when having the read a transcript of easy context such as fairy tales, and instructing the participant to concentrate on using plausible gestures while speaking, the participant often used gestures too frequently, and gestures that were too exaggerated. Putting too much emphasis on doing gestures led the gesture usage to be unnatural, and having such gestures in the dataset would have a negative effect on the learning.

Recording took place in a comfortably large quiet room, where only the subject of the motion/speech data and the person operating the recording devices were allowed to enter so that the recorded speech contains as less static as possible. One participant was to wear the headset and motion capture suit and make sure there are no problems with the positions and number of markers. Then, the participant was to take a T-pose so the recorder can make sure that the motion tracking was calibrated correctly. After checking, the recorder starts recording. Before proceeding to speak, the participant claps his hands once so that portion could be used to sync the speech, motion, and video data. When finished, the participant goes into a T-pose once again.

2.3 Creating the Dataset

The recorded motion, speech, and video data were split per sentence and saved to a server through a simple Ruby on Rails web program. The paths to the bvh motion data, mp3 speech data, mp4 video data, along with meta information

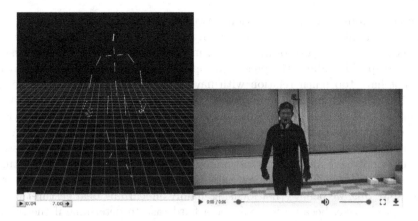

Fig. 2. Viewing bvh and video data

concerning them such as the information of the actor, date recorded, the topic which the sentence belongs to, and tags concerning which type of gesture and how much of each type appeared during the sentence, were stored in a MySQL database on the server. The motion, speech, and video data could be previewed when uploading, and played back after saving, as shown in Fig. 2. Also, the data could be played simultaneously with any combination, to verify that the data were synced properly.

3 Results

The categories of the recorded gestures were as shown in Table 1, metaphoric gestures appearing the most, 68.41% of all gestures. Beat gestures were next most common, appearing 23.73% of all gestures. Iconic and Deictic gestures appeared very scarcely, both being under 5% of the gestures recorded.

Table 1. Number and ratio of gesture appearance

	Number (ratio) of gestures	Number (ratio) of sentences
Iconic	202 (4.76%)	127 (12.11%)
Metaphoric	2906 (68.41%)	901 (85.89%)
Deictic	132 (3.11%)	96 (9.15%)
Beat	1008 (23.73%)	346 (32.98%)
Total	4248 (100%)	1049 (100%)

4 Discussion and Conclusions

We aimed to create a dataset of speech data and motion data of the gestures accompanying the spoken content that could be used for incorporating deep learning methods to learn the relation between speech and gesture. We were able to keep the number of deictic gestures seen to a very small limit. This is because the method of our data recording did not involve having to rely on any physical objects in speaking about the presented topic. As long as the spoken topic itself does not have too much relation with having to indicate objects or places, it should be able to suppress the number of deictic gestures to a fair extent. Also, it is not surprising that beat gestures also appeared frequently, as it is known to be a common type of gesture in communication, appearing unconsciously even in situations where the speaker cannot see the listener [1]. Although the gesture itself does not have any semantic meaning, researches state that beat gestures can have a positive effect on the semantic processing of the accompanying words [6]. Despite this, we believe that focusing mainly on learning beat gestures would not be productive, because it would be a hard task to determine if the results are appropriate, since judging if the short-baton like movements are correct for the accompanying content in viewpoints other than timing would be too vague of a judgment. If there is a need to include beat gestures in learning gestures, one must take into account the prosodic features and/or pitch of the speech data, because points of emphasis and the rhythm of the speech usually cannot be determined by the context of the speech alone. Reducing the number of beat gestures remains as an issue.

5   Future Work

As future work, we aim to increase the number of data in the dataset if possible, and use it to train a Recurrent Neural Network to learn the association between speech features and gestures, as they are both sequential data, so that the result can be used to automatically generate appropriate gestures for the input speech. We plan on using Mel-Frequency Cepstrum Coefficients (MFCC), often used in speech recognition, to vectorize the speech data to act as input data, and use the time sequential joint rotation data of motion bvh data as label data.

References

1. Alibali, M.W., Heath, D.C., Myers, H.J.: Effects of visibility between speaker and listener on gesture production: some gestures are meant to be seen. J. Mem. Lang. **44**(2), 169–188 (2001)
2. Knapp, M.L., Hall, J.A., Horgan, T.G.: Nonverbal Communication in Human Interaction. Cengage Learning, Boston (2013)
3. McNeill, D.: Hand and Mind: What Gestures Reveal About Thought. University of Chicago Press, Chicago (1992)
4. Roth, W.M.: Gestures: their role in teaching and learning. Rev. Educ. Res. **71**(3), 365–392 (2001)
5. Vilhjálmsson, H., et al.: The behavior markup language: recent developments and challenges. In: Pelachaud, C., Martin, J.-C., André, E., Chollet, G., Karpouzis, K., Pelé, D. (eds.) IVA 2007. LNCS (LNAI), vol. 4722, pp. 99–111. Springer, Heidelberg (2007). doi:10.1007/978-3-540-74997-4_10
6. Wang, L., Chu, M.: The role of beat gesture and pitch accent in semantic processing: an ERP study. Neuropsychologia **51**(13), 2847–2855 (2013)

Psychophisiological Measuring and Monitoring

Driver's Modeling with System Identification Algorithm to Aim Reducing Drowsiness

Hirotoshi Asano[1(✉)], Kiwamu Goto[1], and Tota Mizuno[2]

[1] Kagawa University, Hayashi, Takamatsu, Kagawa 2217-20, Japan
asano@eng.kagawa-u.ac.jp
[2] The University of Electro-Communications,
1-5-1 Chofugaoka, Chofu, Tokyo, Japan

Abstract. The purpose of this study is to develop a biological model between skin temperature change and cooling stimulation to prevent drivers from becoming drowsiness. The traffic accident by an operation mistake or aimless operation has occurred. A factor of these accidents has a driver's nap. In recent years, many researchers have studied eagerly this theme. The purpose of their studies is to detect a driver's drowsiness. On the other hand, the aim of our study is to contribute to development of technology for safe drive assistance to maintain a driver's arousal levels. This technology may give a technical innovation in the relevant area. In general, a change in blood volume in nasal part depends on the vasoconstrictive effect of the sympathetic nervous system along with changes in physiological and psychological conditions. The nasal skin temperature changes depending on the blood flow, thus, the temperature reflects the physiological state. The temperature also decreases as the blood flow in the nasal area decreases during sympathetic hyperactivity. The temperature increases as the blood flow in the nasal area increases due to sympathetic suppression. Previous studies have showed a relationship between nasal skin temperature reflecting autonomic nervous system activity and arousal level. The experiment was conducted to gather data for constructing a biological model of a driver and the relationship between cooling stimulation and nasal skin temperature was modeled with system identification. And the usefulness of models was examined with time response simulation and nyquist diagram. In summary, it is possible to construct biological model based on relationship between thermal stimulation and nasal skin temperature by using ARX, ARMAX and BJ of low order.

Keywords: Nasal skin temperature · Autonomic nervous system activity · Driver's drowsiness · System identification · Biological model

1 Introduction

So far, we have studied safety driving support technology to reduce driver's drowsiness based on nasal skin temperature reflecting sympathetic nerve activity [1, 2]. Approximately 30% of the total traffic accidents in Japan are inattentive accidents such as mucking [3]. One of the factors is thought to be transient drowsiness. Therefore, it is a social problem to reduce accidents caused by dozing driving. In general, the

© Springer International Publishing AG 2017
C. Stephanidis (Ed.): HCII Posters 2017, Part I, CCIS 713, pp. 205–209, 2017.
DOI: 10.1007/978-3-319-58750-9_29

sympathetic nerve accelerates and the arterio-venous anastomoses shrinks when the driver concentrates on his driving. The skin temperature becomes lower than the temperature at rest. Also, the sympathetic nerve suppresses and the arterio-venous anastomoses returns to previous size when the driver feels drowsy. Then, the nasal skin temperature rises. Based on this physiological mechanism, our system had given cooling stimulations to keep the driver's nasal skin temperature at the lowest value. The current system operates by switching biological models at regular intervals using Box - Jenkins method. The biological signal is a nonlinear time-varying system. Therefore, periodic switching of the biological model is effective. However, if biological signal characteristics change immediately after switching biological models, it is difficult to properly control them. Also, the current biological model is a high order number. Therefore, stability cannot be guaranteed.

Therefore, the purpose of this study is to examine the possibility of adaptive biological modeling which sequentially updates the identification algorithm. The voltage to the thermoelectric element and the nasal skin temperature are measured for driver in the experiment regarding this study. Based on these data, biological models are constructed in which the applied voltage is an input signal and the nasal skin temperature is an output signal. Then, the models are evaluated by time series analysis and frequency analysis.

2   System Identification

The experiment is examined whether four modeling methods are effective for constructing biological model. The four models are Auto Regressie eXogeneous (ARX), Auto Regressie Moving Average eXogeneous (hereafter, ARMAX), Output Error (OE), Box and Jenkins (BJ) model. ARX, ARMAX, OE, and BJ model are polynomial models. The parameters of these equations are shown in Table 1. The parameters are determined based on the least squares method.

Table 1.   Models of system identification.

Model	$G(q)$	$H(q)$
ARX	$B(q)/A(q)$	$1/A(q)$
ARMAX	$B(q)/A(q)$	$C(q)/A(q)$
OE	$B(q)/F(q)$	1
BJ	$B(q)/F(q)$	$C(q)/D(q)$

3   Experimental Method

The experimental system is shown in Fig. 1. A subject wears a thermistor (503 ET - 3 H 87 U, SEMITEC) at nose and an electrode (LT - USB 1, Gram Corporation) for measurement of nasal skin temperature and a thermoelectric element (TEC 1 - 12706) in neck. Afferent fibers from peripheral temperature receptors are transmitted to the center of the brain by the spinal nerve. Therefore, the cervix is selected at the place to stimulate. The skin temperature of subject's neck is controlled by the thermoelectric

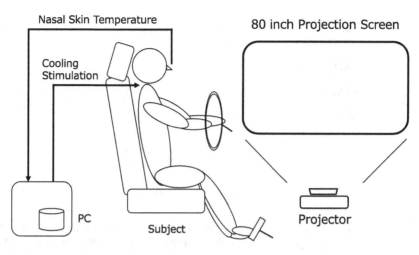

Fig. 1. Experimental system. The nasal skin temperature is measured while subject is driving on driving simulation. The measurement time is 1800 s.

element based on the nasal skin temperature change acquired from the thermistor. When a voltage signal is applied to a component of a thermoelectric element, the nasal skin temperature changes according to a cooling stimulation. The measurement time is 1800 s. A biological model is updated by sequentially performing system identification with these data. These models are evaluated using time series analysis and frequency analysis. In the time series analysis, the models are evaluated by the fitting rate of the estimated value and the measured value. The formula the fitting rate is shown in (1). In frequency analysis, the models are evaluated using the Nyquist diagram.

$$\text{Fit}(\%) = \left(1 - \frac{\sqrt{\sum_{k=1}^{N} [\hat{Y}(k) - Y(k)]^2}}{\sqrt{\sum_{k=1}^{N} [y(k) - \bar{y}]^2}} \right) \times 100 \tag{1}$$

4   Result and Consideration

The estimation results of the model in the time series analysis are shown in Figs. 1 and 2. The estimated output value of the model is expressed as ye and the true value as y. In the case of ARX model and the ARMAX model, the approximate value of the true value y are estimated except for the start several seconds. The fitting rate of the ARX model was 94.46% on average. The fitting rate of the ARMAX model was 96.07% on average. On the other hand, when the OE model and the BJ model are applied, there is a difference between the true value y and the estimated value. The fitting rate was −2.63% on average for the OE model and 78.13% on average for the BJ model. The biological signal about human is a nonlinear time-varying signal. The ARX model and the ARMAX model is a linear model. The data suggest that these models are

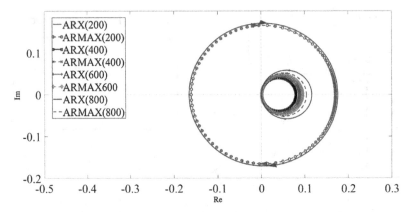

Fig. 2. An example of Nyquist diagram on driving. The Nyquist diagram of all models is on the right side of the real part of −1 and a circle is drawn around the origin at the time point of 200 s.

compatible with the sequential switching method. On the other hand, the OE model and the Bj model are nonlinear models. It can be considered effective if modeling is performed with a certain time width. However, there is a high possibility of becoming a high-order model that cannot ensure stability. The results of the Nyquist diagram in the ARX model and the ARMAX model are shown in Fig. 2. The Nyquist diagram shows results at 400, 800, and 1600 s. The Nyquist diagram of all models is on the right side of the real part of −1. That is, it can be seen that the controlled object is stable. At the time point of 200 s, a circle is drawn around the origin. This indicates that there is a dead time. In other words, it takes time to stimulate and react. The above results show that sequential update is effective for lower order. Therefore, these data suggests that the system contributes more stably than the conventional system. In addition, the point that the skin temperature changes gradually is considered to be one of the factors that the low order model functions effectively (Table 2).

Table 2. Fitting rate of each subject.

No	ARX	ARMAX	OE	BJ
No1	94.43	94.41	−3.23	59.89
No2	99.52	97.74	−5.55	99.77
No3	99.76	99.8	−2.19	61.68
No4	93.13	93.18	−2.22	93.19
No5	95.46	95.24	0.02	76.15
Average	96.46	96.074	−2.634	78.136

5   Conclusion

In this study, the effectiveness of the low order biological model based on the identification algorithm was examined. As a result, we showed that it is possible to construct biological models by sequential updating of system identification.

References

1. Goto, K., Asano, H., Kajiwara, Y., Bando, S., Mizuno, T., Nozawa, A.: Comparison of cool and warm thermal stimulations to reduce driver's drowsiness. IEEJ Trans. Electron. Inf. Syst. **136**(12), 1815–1820 (2016)
2. Kajiwara, Y., Asano, H., Bando, S., Nomura, S., Mizuno, T., Ogose, S., Nozawa, A.: Driver's drowsiness inhibition by subcutaneous stimulation based on SNS activity. Artif. Life Robot. **20**(4), 341–346 (2015)
3. Cabinet Office.: Traffic Safety White Paper (2016)

Wearables and User Interface Design: Impacts on Belief in Free Will

D.A. Baker[(⊠)]

Missouri University of Science and Technology, Rolla, MO, USA
bakerden@mst.edu

Abstract. This research investigates the social implications of sensor driven self-quantification technologies designed to direct user behaviors. These self-sensoring prescriptive applications (SSPA's), often referred to as "wearables," have a strong presence in healthcare as a means to monitor and improve health, modify behavior, and reduce medical costs. However, the commercial sector is quickly adopting SSPA's to monitor and/or modify consumer behaviors as well [1–3]. Interestingly, the direct impact biosensor data have on user decision making, attitude formation, and behavior has not been well researched. SSPA's offer an opportunity for users to monitor the "self" in terms of quantitative, objective, biological terms that may be beyond the user's control. Research suggests some states of the body (e.g. chronic pain, hunger) can affect underlying beliefs in free will (BFW), finding that the less control a person has over those physical states, the weaker their BFW [4]. It is not known, however, whether reminders about physical states of the body, such as heart rate monitors used during exercise, may also serve to reduce BFW. This is an important gap in knowledge when considering that reduced BFW can have numerous negative impacts on individual behavior [5–7]. This preliminary work examined the impact of such technologies on underlying BFW. Participants who monitored their heart rate during a short walk using a wearable heart rate and activity tracker had lower BFW than participants who merely look at the device's various tracking features and participants in the control condition.

Keywords: Belief in free will · Wearable · Activity tracker · Self-quantification · Self-sensoring

1 Introduction

Self-sensoring prescriptive applications (SSPA's), often referred to as "wearables," have a strong presence in healthcare as a means to monitor and improve health, modify behavior, and reduce medical costs. However, the commercial sector is quickly adopting SSPA's to monitor and/or modify consumer behaviors as well [1–3]. Interestingly, the direct impact biosensor data have on user decision making, attitude formation, and behavior has not been well researched. Social scientists and a number of regulatory bodies have begun to tackle questions about how to manage the reliability and value of these devices [8–11], however even if SSPA were designed with benevolence and transparency, omnipresent and robust monitoring of the physiological self may still have numerous unintended consequences. One of these is the activation of

© Springer International Publishing AG 2017
C. Stephanidis (Ed.): HCII Posters 2017, Part I, CCIS 713, pp. 210–217, 2017.
DOI: 10.1007/978-3-319-58750-9_30

certain beliefs related to free will and determinism which have been shown to have numerous negative impacts on individual behavior.

Definitions of free will vary, but generally tend to refer to an individual's belief in their ability to make deliberate choices and the belief that they are responsible for those choices [12, 13]. The following section highlights experimental research as evidence of the possible social impacts of altering individual beliefs through priming and draws attention to how SSPA's may contribute to altering these beliefs.

Early research related to BFW and deterministic world views demonstrated that attributing learning outcomes to innate qualities of intellect rather than learned behaviors (such as hard work) had a negative impact on personal effort and motivation [5]. However, [6] examined whether the effects of priming such deterministic[1] beliefs could lead to overt negative moral behaviors. In their study, participants were asked to read a series of statements that either supported a belief in free will, refuted such a belief, or were neutral in nature. Participants then completed a set of problems in reading, math, logic, and reasoning and were told they would receive $1 per correct answer. In some conditions of the experiment participants were presented with an opportunity to cheat by grading their own answers. Results showed that participants who read the deterministic statements and were given an opportunity to cheat took home more money than all other participants.

While research has demonstrated that BFW can influence behavior and perception, to understand how this is related to SSPA's it is important to understand what environmental cues may reduce or enhance this belief. The studies mentioned above employed written prompts, but other researchers have demonstrated that less explicit cues play a role as well. For example, [15] found that BFW is related in a number of ways to an individual's perceived ability to make choices. They found that participants who had been asked to recall past choices during a specific time period had stronger beliefs in free will relative to participants asked only to recall specific actions they had taken during a similar time period. In the same study they found that asking participants to make simple choices (in this case, choosing between different pen types) also increased BFW relative to participants who were asked instead to perform a series of simple actions.

Consumer SSPA's monitor and process a user's sensor data and implicitly or explicitly direct their actions based on this data. Research suggests that how these directives are presented to the users could impact that user's BFW. Directives presented as a choice between two or more actions would be less likely to reduce the user's BFW than directives presented as a single command. For example, an SSPA that informs a user his potassium is low could suggest the user take one of three actions (e.g. eat a banana, drink a glass of fat free milk, or take a supplement) rather than just one.

Even more relevant to the discussion of free will and SSPA is research conducted by [4] regarding physical states of the body and belief in free will. The perception of conscious control over one's bodily actions could be considered a form of "evidence"

---

[1] [6] did not specifically define the relationship between "free will" and "determinism," but the two terms are treated similarly to antonyms in the paper, such that a prime characterized as "anti-free-will" was also characterized as "deterministic." Some philosophers argue that this is not necessarily the case [12, 16].

to strengthen belief in free will [14], but what happens when control of the body's actions seems difficult or impossible? [4] first compared the strengths of belief in free will between individuals with medical conditions that cause physical symptoms beyond conscious control (epilepsy and panic disorders) and individuals who did not have these medical conditions. They found that participants who had epilepsy and participants who had a panic disorder had weaker beliefs in free will than participants who had neither condition. In a follow up study they found that more temporary states of the body can also affect BFW. Participants were first asked about their BFW and were subsequently asked about the intensity of some of their physical needs at that moment, including urination, sexual desire, fatigue, thirst, and hunger. They found that participants who had reported more intense needs for urination, sexual desire, or fatigue had expressed weaker beliefs in free will. For hunger, they found that this was also the case for individuals who were not currently dieting[2]. [4] interpret their broader findings as evidence that physical states can influence BFW. They also extrapolated that the less control a person has over those physical states, the weaker their BFW.

[4] does not specify whether they believe physical states impact BFW because the physical sensations create an unconscious awareness of those states (i.e. the stronger the sensation the weaker the belief) or whether reminding a person about their physical state in the past may have a similar effect even in the absence of sensations. In their second study, [4] asked participants about physical states that are typically associated with sensations that the participants could have been experiencing at the time (e.g. hunger pains, fullness of bladder). However, in their first study it is not known whether participants who identified as having a current or past diagnosis of epilepsy or a panic disorders had been experiencing physical sensations at the time they completed the online study or if, instead, the effect was a result of those participants having been reminded about these physical states by being asked to identify as having that particular diagnosis in order to participate. Due to the disruptive nature of seizure disorders and panic disorders, intuitively it seems reasonable to believe that most participants would not have been experiencing major symptoms at the time they completed the study. What this suggests is that reminding participants about physical states that are beyond a person's control may also weaken BFW. This is particularly relevant to the discussion of the social impacts of SSPA's, because they are specifically designed to unmask the hidden nature of our internal states. Being reminded (whether through physical sensations or environmental cues) that our free will must sometimes be trumped by our physical needs is an integral part of the human experience and, since most people maintain a belief in free will [12, 13], the weakening effects are likely transitory as these reminders come and go. But ubiquitous SSPA's offer an unprecedented opportunity to remind users of the countless physiological states of the body that change without willful intent. In this light, SSPA's may serve to continually depress belief in free will, even those that are genuinely meant to improve general wellness. To investigate this potential risk, this study tests the hypothesis that participants using a

---

[2] For individuals who were dieting, more intense hunger was correlated with stronger belief in free will. The researchers suggested this is because these participants were more likely to be actively engaging in control over hunger which is an expression of free will [4].

wearable activity tracker to monitor heart rate for a short period of time will have reduced BFW relative to participants who explore the menu's of the device, and to participants in the control condition.

2 Method

Sixty-nine Missouri University of Science and Technology students participated in the study. The research was framed to potential volunteers as a short usability study for a wearable activity tracker and modest compensation was offered. The final sample size included 69 participants with a mean age of 20.49, mean of 2.5 years of secondary education, 67% were male, 81% identified as white, 7% identified as Black/African American, 7% identified as Hispanic, and 5% identified as Other.

The wearable technology used for the study was the Garmin vívoactive® HR which tracks a number of activity types, including step count and heart rate [18]. To measure Belief in Free Will (BFW), participants completed the twenty-seven item Free Will and Determinism Plus scale (FAD+; [17]) that measure layperson's beliefs not only in free will but also related constructs of scientific determinism, fatalistic determinism, and unpredictability. The items (e.g., "People are always at fault for their bad behavior.") were rated using a 5 point Likert scale from 1 (strongly disagree) to 5 (strongly agree).

The study used a between-subjects design with two groups plus a control condition where the independent variable was the task performed with the wearable device (Task) and the primary dependent measure was BFW.

Participants were randomly assigned to one of three Task conditions: Heart Rate, Usability, and Control. In the Heart Rate condition, participants were asked to don the wearable device on their wrist for about 30 s and then asked to read their heart rate as reported by the watch. They were then asked to make a prediction about what their heart rate might be if they were to walk at a moderate pace down the corridor of the building in which the lab was located. Finally, participants in this condition walked the corridor while wearing the device and were asked to retake their heart rate when finished. In the Usability task, participants were asked to sit and complete a short list of activities with the watch. The activities (e.g. identify what types of exercises you can track with the device, identify what information you can track about the body) were designed to ensure the user viewed the main functions of the device, without actually taking their heart rate, and spent the same amount of time interacting with the device as participants in the Heart Rate condition. In both the Heart Rate condition and the Usability condition, after the task was completed, participants were asked to complete a survey which was described to the them as containing questions about the watch and questions completely unrelated to the watch.

The first set of questions presented was the FAD + scale [17]. This was followed by a series of questions about design aspects of the device (e.g. look and feel, brightness of screen, ease of use, etc.), but these were primarily meant as cover to confirm the participants' beliefs that the study was about usability of an activity tracker. The survey also asked participants if they currently own a wearable activity tracker, whether they have a chronic health condition that requires daily management, to what degree they currently felt hungry, tired, in pain, in control of thoughts and feelings, and the need to use the bathroom. Demographic questions were included at the end of the survey. Participants in the Heart Rate condition were also asked how accurately they were able to predict what their heart rate would be after walking the corridor. In the Control condition participants completed the same task and survey as those in the Usability condition, however they completed the FAD + scale [17] prior to interacting with the device. Upon completion participants were compensated and debriefed.

3   Results and Analysis

A factor analysis using maximum likelihood extraction, promax rotation, and four fixed loadings indicated that of the 7-item subscale measuring layperson's Belief in Free Will (BFW) (included in the 27-item FAD + scale [17]) only 6 items loaded ($\alpha = .76$). These 6 items were converted to factor scores for each participant and used in further analysis as a measure of BFW, however means scores of these 6 items are included for readability.

An Analysis of Variance (ANOVA) on BFW indicated significant variation across the three conditions, $F(2, 67) = 7.73$, $p = .001$, $\eta_p = .197$. Since all contrast were of interest and sample sizes were nearly equal across all conditions, Scheffé post hoc criterion for significance were conducted. Participants in the Heart Rate ($M = 3.49$, $SD = .68$) condition had significantly lower scores on the BFW scale than the Control condition ($M = 3.79$, $SD = .63$, $p = .001$) but not the Usability condition ($M = 4.09$, $SD = .52$) and BFW scores did not significantly differ between the Usability condition and the Control condition.

To better understand these findings a number of other analyses were conducted. First, to determine if reduced BFW in the Heart Rate condition could be explained by how accurate participants perceived themselves to be about predicting their heart rate, a correlational analysis was conducted using the BFW factor scores and Perceived-Accuracy rating (measured using a Likert scale from 1(completely inaccurate) to 5 (completely accurate)), however there was no significant correlation between the two variables (p = .731).

To address the possibility that physical states of the body at the time participants completed the study could explain any changes in BFW [4], an ANOVA was conducted on the BFW factor scores for the five questions asking participants to rate the degree to which they currently felt hungry, the need to use the bathroom, pain, tiredness, and in control of their thoughts and feelings. Only the question about feeling in control of thoughts and feelings varied by condition, $F(4, 65) = 3.96$, $p = .006$. However, when an ANOVA on BFW and the Task variable was conducted using this new variable as a covariate, it did not change the significance of effect of Task variable ($p = .002$).

Other potential covariate including gender, perceived socio-economic status, age, and education were found to have no impact on BFW, nor did current ownership of a wearable activity monitor, or perceptions about the perceived usefulness of wearable activity monitors (all p's > .05). The presence of a chronic health condition requiring daily management did not have an impact on BFW, however only 17% of respondents responded yes to this question so further investigation with a larger sample size is needed.

3.1   Discussion and Conclusion

These preliminary results suggest that monitoring heart rate with a wearable activity tracker could, at least in the short term, lower BFW. However, it is worth noting that participants in the Usability condition were not told to complete their list of activities in a particular order so they, in fact had a slightly higher degree of choice than participants in the Heart Rate condition. [15] found that allowing participants to make simple choices (such as choosing between different pen types) increased BFW relative to participants who were asked instead to perform a series of simple actions. It is possible that participants asked to complete the Heart Rate task merely felt less choice than participants asked to complete the Usability task. This could explain why BFW scores were lower in the Heart Rate condition than the Usability condition, but it would not necessarily explain why the Usability condition did not have lower BFW scores than the Control condition.

Cutting edge wearables aim to employ sensor data to monitor states of the body that users may have even less control over than heart rate, particularly in the short term, such as vitamin deficiencies and cholesterol. In these cases, an ongoing state of awareness of factors beyond one's control may act to reduce BFW which could lead to negative affect and a decrease in prosocial behaviors. Planned future research will examine the duration of the effect that heart rate monitoring has on reducing BFW scores and whether this reduction also leads to negative consequences found in past research. Finally, examination of how the design of SSPA user interface impacts this potential risk factors should be explored.

For SSPA's (and too many other forms of technological innovation) the approach to considering these broader social implications is often to bring products to market, see what sticks around, and evaluate outcomes post-adoption. It is not immediately clear whose should be held accountability for these social implications. Although engineers are centrally located in reflecting on and responding to the ethical implications of SSPA design and deployment, it is critical that regulatory bodies, such as the US Food and Drug Administration and the US Federal Trade Commission, place a higher emphasis on the risks of SSPA, one that goes far beyond the current focus on privacy, data security, and to some degree, sensor reliability.

The economic success of consumer SSPA's relies on convincing users that their physiological states should not only be monitored, but also controlled. SSPA's that promise this affordance will no doubt be appealing to a consumer base driven to evaluate, understand, and compare the "self" relative to others and socially constructed notions of normality. It is this affordance and this drive that could lead to unprecedented ubiquity of SSPAs, making it that much more critical to get ahead of potential negative impacts of such technologies before technological inertia takes hold.

On a final note, it will be tiresome to some and critical to others to point out that the research and arguments presented here, though critical of SSPAs, do not, in fact, constitute a luddite call to ban SSPA's. Rather, it constitutes a call to acknowledge that there may be social behavioral risk associated with SSPA design that are not considered in existing ethical analysis and regulatory processes. And to underscore that the promises of user empowerment and personalized wellness stemming from advocates of self-quantification rest not merely in the expansions of the variety and details of

self-sensor data made available to users, but in the design and deployment of the
SSPA's that use these data to influence user behavior and define the self.

References

1. Swan, M.: Health 2050: the realization of personalized medicine through crowdsourcing, the
   quantified self, and the participatory biocitizen. J. Per. Med. **2**(3), 93–118 (2012). doi:10.
   3390/jpm2030093
2. Swan, M.: The quantified self: fundamental disruption in big data science and biological
   discovery. Big Data **1**(2), 85–99 (2013). doi:10.1089/big.2012.0002
3. Bolluyt, J.: Wearable tech devices: Can they really change your mood? CheatSheet.com,
   29 June 2015. http://www.cheatsheet.com/technology/can-wearable-devices-improve-your-
   focus-or-your-mood.html/?a=viewall
4. Ent, M.R., Baumeister, R.F.: Embodied free will beliefs: some effects of physical states on
   metaphysical opinions. Conscious. Cogn. **27**(1), 147–154 (2014). doi:10.1016/j.concog.
   2014.05.001
5. Mueller, C.M., Dweck, C.S.: Praise for intelligence can undermine children's motivation and
   performance. J. Pers. Soc. Psychol. **75**(1), 33–52 (1998). doi:10.1037/0022-3514.75.1.33
6. Vohs, K.D., Schooler, W.: The value of believing in free will: encouraging a belief in
   determinism increases cheating. Psychol. Sci. **19**(1), 49–54 (2008). doi:10.1111/j.1467-
   9280.2008.02045.x
7. MacKenzie, M.J., Vohs, K.D., Baumeister, R.F.: You didn't have to do that: belief in free
   will promotes gratitude. Pers. Soc. Psychol. Bull. **40**(11), 1423–1434 (2014). https://doi.org/
   10.1177/0010088048102200214
8. Baker, D.A.: Self "sensor" ship: an interdisciplinary investigation of the persuasiveness,
   social implications, and ethical design of self-sensing prescriptive applications. Doctoral
   dissertation, Arizona State University (2016)
9. US Food and Drug Administration. General wellness: Policy for low risk devices draft
   guidance for industry and Food and Drug Administration staff. U.S. Department of Health
   and Human Services Food (2015)
10. US Federal Trade Commission: Prepared statement of the federal trade commission on
    opportunities and challenges in advancing health information technology. Washington, DC.
    (2016)
11. Boulos, M.N.K., Brewer, A.C., Karimkhani, C., Buller, D.B., Dellavalle, R.P.: Mobile
    medical and health apps: state of the art, concerns, regulatory control and certification.
    Online J. Public Health Inform. **5**(3), 1–23 (2014). doi:10.5210/ojphi.v5i3.4814
12. Nahmias, E., Morris, S., Nadelhoffer, T., Turner, J.: Surveying freedom: folk intuitions about
    free will and moral responsibility. Philos. Psychol. **18**(5), 561–584 (2005). doi:10.1080/
    09515080500264180
13. Monroe, A.E., Malle, B.F.: From uncaused will to conscious choice: the need to study, not
    speculate about people's folk concept of free will. Rev. Philos. Psychol. **1**, 211–224 (2010)
14. Wegner, D.M., Wheatley, T.: Apparent mental causation: sources of the experience of will.
    Am. Psychol. **54**(7), 480–492 (1999)
15. Feldman, G., Baumeister, R.F., Wong, K.F.E.: Free will is about choosing: the link between
    choice and the belief in free will. J. Exp. Soc. Psychol. **55**, 239–245 (2014). doi:10.1016/j.
    jesp.2014.07.012

16. Campbell, J.K.: A compatibilist theory of alternative possibilities. Philos. Stud. **88**(3), 319–330 (1997). doi:10.1023/A:1004280421383
17. Paulhus, D.L., Carey, J.M.: The FAD-Plus: measuring lay beliefs regarding free will and related constructs. J. Pers. Assess. 93(1), 96–104 (2011) https://doi.org/10.1080/00223891.2010.528483
18. Garmin vivoactive HR. Activity Tracking. www.garmin.com, https://buy.garmin.com/en-US/US/cIntoSports-c571-p1.html. Accessed 22 Mar 2017

Stress Measurement and Inducement in Experiments with Low Cost Flight Simulator for Testing of General Aviation Pilots

Ondřej Bruna$^{(\boxtimes)}$, Tomáš Levora, and Jan Holub

Faculty of Electrical Engineering, Department of Measurement, Czech Technical University in Prague, Technická 2, 16627 Praha 6, Czech Republic
{brunaond,levortom,holubjan}@fel.cvut.cz

Abstract. Full flight simulators are mainly a domain of airliner pilots. Such simulators with moving platform are high fidelity devices, which can reliably replicate real flight experience. Unfortunately the cost of a flight hour and maintenance is rather high and therefore not suitable for training of pilots of ultra-light aircraft. Yet there are accidents which might have been prevented with extended flight hours and additional training, like emergency landings, dealing with spiral spin, engine outage. Low cost simulators can be a viable solution for additional training and practice. This poster is based on data taken from stress inducing experiment. Poster presents analysis of physiological measurements taken from pilots interacting with a low cost 6DOF flight simulator of ultra-light aircraft with the goal to assess presence of stress and identify its generating factors. Proper identification and classification of these factors may help to generate such state during training and testing. The goal is to evaluate physiologically measurable response. The experiment attempts to generate stress with engine outage observing ECG and respiration signals.

Keywords: Simulation · Human factors

1 Introduction

The current work discusses the influence of external stimuli in form of in flight engine failure to physiological state. Measurements are reflecting situation awareness and workload [4]. It is assumed, that experiencing engine failure causes mental and physical load. Pilot has to maintain airplane airborne for as long as possible, select most convenient landing site, eventually communicate the situation. All these tasks are well managed by a well trained pilot, but in case of a ultra–light aircraft or the light sport aircraft, the training is not so extensive and the pilots do not receive many flight hours. Cost of an aircraft flight hour is greater than cost of low end stimulator. Simulators have different fidelity classes based on their interior, available systems, motion capabilities, and latencies. Full flight simulators (FFS) of type D (type 7) are the most advanced simulators allowing IFR training and testing. Although the FFS are well established there

© Springer International Publishing AG 2017
C. Stephanidis (Ed.): HCII Posters 2017, Part I, CCIS 713, pp. 218–223, 2017.
DOI: 10.1007/978-3-319-58750-9_31

are experiments with using new ways of simulation such as the dynamic seat by Sparko et al. [5]. FFS still remain the main simulation and training device, but it seems likely to see more attempts to leverage virtual reality and other ways of simulation to provide credible simulating environment. Assessing simulator credibility in terms of HW was analysed by Ekk in [1]. This paper aims to evaluate the credibility of flight experience.

The difference of FFS to a real cockpit is very small. Training in this simulator has demands as flying a real airplane. Unfortunately for general aviation pilots, there are no FFS, since there are too many types of aircraft with different equipment. Therefore the interest is to create a low cost simulator which would emulate glass cockpit and motion platform with 6DOF to simulate the movement. The interior does not reflect a specific type of aircraft and uses generally accessible control parts. Focus is to recreate an emergency situation with engine outage and observe, whether the pilots will in any way react to the situation. The more it is possible to induce stress or startle in pilots, the more credibility can training on such simulator have and be used as a part of preparation of pilots for a fraction of price.

It could improve general readiness to deal with complex situations such as loss of control in flight, which is according to National transportation Safety Board (NTSB) the most critical reason of accidents in general aviation. European Aviation Safety Agency (EASA) states in the Annual Safety Review 2016, that Aircraft upset in flight is responsible for 47% of fatal accidents. NTSB calls for extensive training of pilots of such situations and European Union is attempting to deal with the problem in similar way.

2   Methodology

Group of 20 pilots was selected for a simulated flight. The group was diverse with different flight hours (200 in average) and age (30 in average). For each pilot two different flights were planned. For the first flight pilots were seated in the simulator and flew a simple navigation flight, where they were asked to approach a city and then fly around it. The second flight they were asked the same, but during the flight engine failure happened and the pilot was forced to emergency landing.

During both flights pilot's ECG and respiration was collected for evaluation. These physiological values were used extensively to evaluate stress and workload as stated in [2] The goal is to assess whether there is any change in pilots physiology while experiencing engine failure compared to normal flight.

Following parameters were extracted from ECG signal: SDNN, Standard deviation of RR intervals in one segment of flight; SDANN, Standard deviation of average RR intervals in 10-s intervals in a segment; RMSSD, Squared root of average of squared difference of two consecutive RR intervals; SDSD, Standard deviation of two consecutive RR intervals; LFHF, ratio Power ration of high frequency and low frequency band of HRV.

Respiration recording was processed to provide following parameters: RF1, Average power in frequency spectrum band 0 to 0.5 Hz; RF2, Average power in frequency spectrum band 0.5 to 1 Hz; RF3, Average power in frequency spectrum band 1 to 1.5 Hz; RF4, Average power in frequency spectrum band 1.5 to 2 Hz; FPVS, Average amplitude of minimum and maximum pairs in one breath cycle; SDPVS, Standard deviation of amplitude of single breath cycles; ABF, Average of breathing frequency; SDBF, Standard deviation of breathing frequency.

Analysis of variance was then carried out to evaluate significant parameters on level $\alpha = 0.05$. Flights were divided into four parts reflecting situation during the flight. In the flight with engine failure, the first segment was flight before the failing incident, second segment is 60 s starting with engine failure followed by third segment glide. Fourth segment is approach and landing. Since in normal flight there are no significant points in time as the engine outage, the flight is simply separated into four equal parts to allow distinguishing the beginning, cruise, and final part. The normal flight was flown first and pilots were given time to get acquainted with the simulator.

3   Results

From all used parameters only four were found significant: standard deviation of RR intervals (SDNN), average power in frequency spectrum band 0 to 0.5 Hz (RF1), average power in frequency spectrum band 1 to 1.5 Hz (RF3), average breathing frequency (ABF). Each Figure is showing comparison of flight without engine failure denoted as flight 1, and the flight with engine failure as flight 2.

SDNN has significantly different means with respect to phase $p = 0.018$, to flight $p = 0.0175$ and with phase against flight interaction $p = 0.0433$ which is near to evaluated level of significance.

RF1 with interaction phase against flight of $p = 0.018$ is also below the desired $\alpha = 0.05$. The significant differences are noted to be in the phase 4 of flight with engine failure and in the phase 1 of the free flight. Unfortunately the absolute value of the power level of RF1 is too low to be considered important for the assessment of actual effect of the stimuli.

With parameter RF3 the phase against flight interaction results in $p = 0.0056$. The phase and flight significance is $p < 0.001$. It appears as the phase 1 where the flight starts is the calm region and after the pilots takes over the plane and must focus on its control, the power increases with the effort to control the plane.

Average breathing frequency is significantly different in the fourth phase of failure flight ($p = 0.0011$) and in the second and fourth phase of training flight. It is not significant in flights and interaction.

4   Conclusions

The expectation was to observe more apparent changes in ECG, which was used successfully to evaluate stress and workload in previous experiment according to [2]. The only significant parameter was SDNN in Fig. 1. It exhibited large deviation at the beginning of the first flight which seems to be related to unfamiliarity

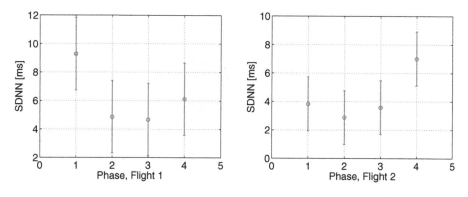

Fig. 1. Standard deviation of RR intervals.

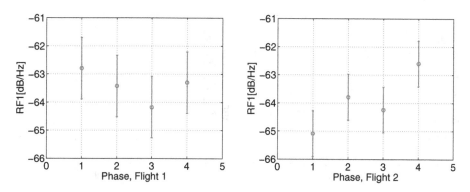

Fig. 2. Average power in frequency spectrum band 0 to 0.5 Hz.

with the simulator and environment. Once the pilots gets familiar the deviation decreases. In case of second flight the increase happens during the fourth phase, which is related to approach and landing. In this phase it would be expected to observe elevated heartbeat and increased breathing frequency. Unfortunately no significant changes in heart rate variability were measured.

Average breathing frequency did change its level during both flights as seen on Fig. 4. During the first flight the ABF remained elevated after the first segment around 26 breaths per minute. It would suggest increased effort and workload to maintain the trajectory. It could also be caused by getting used to new environment. The second flight started with breath lower, at around 21 breaths per minute and afterwards gradually elevated to 27 breaths per minute.

Average power in frequency spectrum in band from $1\,Hz$ to $1.5\,Hz$ on Fig. 3 shows similar trend.

As Fig. 2 suggests, the RF1 parameter is excluded, since the absolute change is considered too small, though significant. On the other hand RF3 exhibited.

It seems that approach and landing impose more workload to pilot, but at the moment of failure there does not seem to be directly visible change in

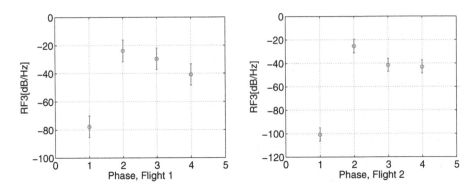

Fig. 3. Average power in frequency spectrum band 1 to 1.5 Hz.

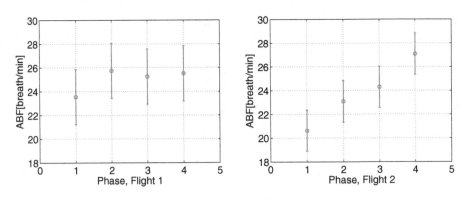

Fig. 4. Average breathing frequency.

physiology. There is a significant change between the first and following phases showing, that pilot needs to concentrate and put effort into flying even low cost simulator, which is expected. The approach and landing appear to have more stimulating effect on pilot than engine failure. The approach and landing most likely requires pilot to focus on where to land the airplane and how to manage the landing properly in emergency situation. Some pilots for example did n manage to land in nearby airfield, but were forced to land to terrain. This will be considered for further evaluation of the data.

For future evaluation of workload it will be considered to use other ways, such as control stick movements. Unfortunately there is no keyboard to be directly used as for keyboard dynamics evaluation [3], other control interfaces of glass cockpit are possible to be used instead. Also considering better data segmentation might help to improve the results.

Acknowledgments. This work was supported by the Grant Agency of the Czech Technical University in Prague, grant No. SGS17/100/OHK3/1T/13.

References

1. Eek, M., Hällqvist, R., Gavel, H., Ölvander, J.: A concept for credibility assessment of aircraft system simulators. J. Aerosp. Inf. Syst. **13**(6), 219–233 (2016). http://dx.doi.org/10.2514/1.I010391
2. Karthikeyan, P., Murugappan, M., Yaacob, S.: A review on stress inducement stimuli for assessing human stress using physiological signals. In: 2011 IEEE 7th International Colloquium on Signal Processing and its Applications, pp. 420–425, March 2011
3. Ott, T., Wu, P., Paullada, A., Mayer, D., Gottlieb, J., Wall, P.: ATHENA – a zero-intrusion no contact method for workload detection using linguistics, keyboard dynamics, and computer vision. In: Stephanidis, C. (ed.) HCI 2016. CCIS, vol. 617, pp. 226–231. Springer, Cham (2016). doi:10.1007/978-3-319-40548-3_38
4. Schulte, A., Donath, D., Honecker, F.: Human-system interaction analysis for military pilot activity and mental workload determination. In: 2015 IEEE International Conference on Systems, Man, and Cybernetics, pp. 1375–1380. IEEE, October 2015. http://ieeexplore.ieee.org/lpdocs/epic03/wrapper.htm?arnumber=7379376
5. Sparko, A.L., Bürki-Cohen, J., Go, T.H.: Transfer of training from a full-flight simulator vs. a high level flight training device with a dynamic seat. In: Proceedings of the AIAA Modeling and Simulation Technologies Conference and Exhibit, vol. 8218, pp. 1–28, August 2007

A Portable and User Friendly REM Sleep Detection System Based on Differential Movement of Eyeball Using Optical Sensors

Chi Yeon Hwang[1], Geun do Park[1], Hyang Jun Jeong[1], In Gyu Park[1],
Yun Joong Kim[3], Hyeo-Il Ma[2], and Unjoo Lee[1(✉)]

[1] Department of Electrical Engineering, Hallym University, 1 Hallymdaehak-gil,
Chuncheon, Gangwon-do, Republic of Korea
ejlee@hallym.ac.kr
[2] Department of Neurology, Hallym University Sacred Heart Hospital,
Hallym University College of Medicine, Hallym University, Chuncheon,
Republic of Korea
[3] Department of Neurology, Hallym University Sacred Heart Hospital,
Hallym University College of Medicine, Anyang, Republic of Korea

Abstract. The REM (Rapid Eye Movement) sleep as one of the five stages of sleep is the restorative part of the sleep cycle. During REM sleep, eyes move quickly in different directions and most dreams occur. Why people need REM sleep, why we dream, and what purpose our dreams serve are not known exactly. RBD (REM Behavior Disorder), a parasomnia, involves abnormal behavior during REM sleep phase, such as loss of muscle atonia. RBD is most often associated with elderly and in those with neurodegenerative disorders such as Parkinson's disease, multiple system atrophy and Lewy body dementia. A portable and user friendly REM sleep detecting system is proposed based on differential shift of the eyeball localization using infrared optical sensor in this study. The system consists of an optical source/detector, current regulator, differential amplification, data acquisition, feature extraction, and classification parts, where a 730 nm light emitting diode and two photo detectors were used in the optical source/detector part, and wavelet transformation was applied in the feature extraction and the classification parts. In the feature extraction part, sleep time series data obtained from the data acquisition part was resampled to a sampling frequency of 256 Hz and then filtered with a 1st order 0.16 Hz high pass filter to remove dc offset and a 2nd order 60 Hz band limit filter. Finally, the filtered data was transformed using Matlab dwt function to detect periods of REM sleep. The performance of this REM sleep detecting system was evaluated with overnight recordings of 5 subjects. The results showed sensitivity of 85% and specificity of 92%, suggesting that this system can be a very practically efficient in automatic detection of REM sleep stages in a mobile environment.

Keywords: REM sleep · Eyeball localization · Optic sensor · Wavelet transformation

© Springer International Publishing AG 2017
C. Stephanidis (Ed.): HCII Posters 2017, Part I, CCIS 713, pp. 224–228, 2017.
DOI: 10.1007/978-3-319-58750-9_32

1   Introduction

REM (Rapid Eye Movement) sleep as one of the five stages of sleep is the restorative part of the sleep cycle. During REM sleep, eyes move quickly in different directions and most dreams occur. Why people need REM sleep, why we dream, and what purposes our dreams serve are not known exactly. RBD (REM Behavior Disorder), a parasomnia, involves abnormal behavior during REM sleep phase, such as loss of muscle atonia. RBD is most often associated with elderly and in those with neurodegenerative disorders such as Parkinson's disease, multiple system atrophy and Lewy body dementia.

There are many devices for monitoring sleep stages by measuring heart rate, respiration, motion, chest movement on breathe, sound of body movement on bed, body temperature, galvanic skin response, etcs using a thin sensor pad under the mattress, bedside sonar, sound sensor clipped onto pillow, or biosensors on wrist [1–5]. However, RBD detection is still accomplished on heavy expensive devices such as polysomnography and/or videographical analysis.

This study suggests a portable REM sleep detecting system based on the localization of eyeball using optical sensors.

2   Method

Figure 1 shows a diagram of the portable REM sleep detecting system in which the principle of the localization of eyeball using optical sensors is represented. Optical sensors used in the system consist of two infrared detectors and one infrared led source in the middle of the detectors. The localization of the eyeball is estimated by the difference of the reflected portion of the light emitted to the surface of the eyelid between the two detectors while eyeball moves.

Figure 2 shows the circuit diagram of the portable REM sleep detecting system. The system consists of an optical source/detector, current regulator, differential amplification, data acquisition, feature extraction, and classification parts, where a 730 nm light emitting diode and two photo detectors were used in the optical source/detector part.

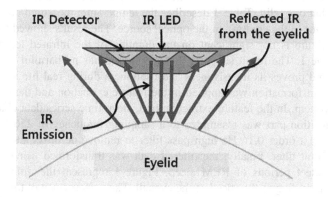

Fig. 1. A schematic diagram of the principle of the localization of eyeball using optical sensors.

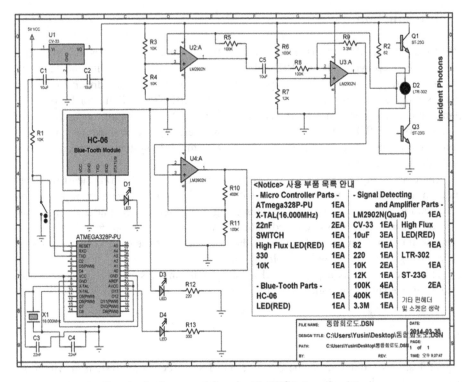

Fig. 2. The circuit diagram of the portable REM sleep detecting system.

3   Results and Discussions

A simulation study was carried out by the human eyeball model constructed using 3D printer based on the design verified through rendering. Figure 3 shows the design and the constructed human eyeball model.

The invasiveness of the system to human was tested for various durations of the emitting of the optical source. The test was accomplished to the arm with the similar skin type to that of eyelid. Table 1 describes the temperature measured on the skin for various durations of the emitting of the optical source. The results showed the variation of the temperature is not significant on the duration of the infrared led emitting as shown in Table 1. The result suggests that the system has no harmful side effect on human skin and proves its invasiveness and usefulness during real life sleep hours.

Wavelet transformation was applied in the feature extraction and the classification parts of the system. In the feature extraction part, sleep time series data obtained from the data acquisition part was resampled to a sampling frequency of 256 Hz and then filtered with a 1st order 0.16 Hz high pass filter to remove dc offset and a 2nd order 60 Hz band limit filter. Finally, the filtered data was transformed using Matlab dwt function to detect periods of REM sleep. Figure 4 represent the difference of the spectrogram according to the speed of the eyeball. The performance of this REM sleep detecting system was evaluated with overnight recordings of 5 subjects. The results

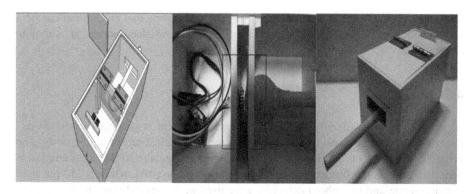

Fig. 3. A human eyeball model constructed using 3D printer based on the design verified through rendering.

Table 1. The temperature measured on the skin for various durations of the emitting of the optical source.

Duration (hrs)	1	2	3	4	5	6	7	8
Temperature (°C)	34.5	33.8	33.9	34.1	33.8	34.2	34.5	34.2

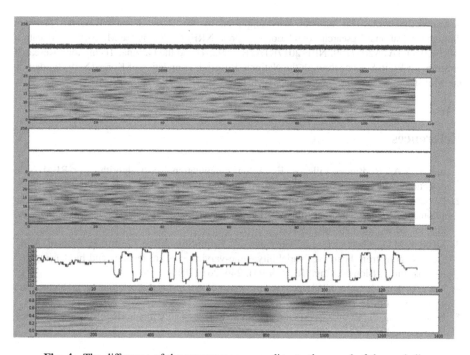

Fig. 4. The difference of the spectrogram according to the speed of the eyeball.

showed sensitivity of 85% and specificity of 92%, suggesting that this system can be a very practically efficient in automatic detection of REM sleep stages in a mobile environment.

4 Conclusions

A portable and user friendly REM sleep detecting system is proposed based on differential shift of the eyeball localization using infrared optical sensor in this study. The system consists of an optical source/detector, current regulator, differential amplification, data acquisition, feature extraction, and classification parts, where a 730 nm light emitting diode and two photo detectors were used in the optical source/detector part, and wavelet transformation was applied in the feature extraction and the classification parts. In the feature extraction part, sleep time series data obtained from the data acquisition part was resampled to a sampling frequency of 256 Hz and then filtered with a 1st order 0.16 Hz high pass filter to remove dc offset and a 2nd order 60 Hz band limit filter. Finally, the filtered data was transformed using Matlab dwt function to detect periods of REM sleep. The performance of this REM sleep detecting system was evaluated with overnight recordings of 5 subjects. The results showed sensitivity of 85% and specificity of 92%, suggesting that this system can be a very practically efficient in automatic detection of REM sleep stages in a mobile environment.

Acknowledgement. This research was supported by the Basic Science Research Program through the National Research Foundation of Korea (NRF) funded by the Ministry of Education (NRF-2014R1A1A2057199, NRF-2017R1A2B1009234) and the Original Technology Research Program for Brain Science through the National Research Foundation of Korea (NRF) funded by the Ministry of Education, Science and Technology (NRF-2016M3C7A1947307).

References

1. Imtiaz, S.A., Rodrigues-Villegas, E.: A low computational cost algorithm for REM sleep detection using single channel EEG. Ann. Biomed. Eng. **42**(11), 2344–2359 (2014)
2. Herscovici, S., Pe'er, A., Papyan, S., Lavie, P.: Detecting REM sleep from the finger: an automatic REM sleep algorithm based on peripheral arterial tone (PAT) and actigraphy. Physiol. Meas. **28**, 129–140 (2007)
3. Mendez, M.O., Matteucci, M., Castronovo, V., Ferini-Strambi, L., Cerutti, S., Bianchi, A.M.: Sleep staging from heart rate variability: time-varying spectral features and hidden markov models. Int. J. Biomed. Eng. Tech. **3**(3/4), 246–263 (2010)
4. Nam, Y., Kim, Y., Lee, J.: Sleep monitoring based on a tri-axial accelerometer and a pressure sensor. Sensors **16**, 750 (2016)
5. Hao, T., Xing, G., Zhou, G.: iSLeep: unobtrusive sleep quality monitoring using smartphones. In: SenSys 2013, Rome, Italy, 11–15 November (2013)

Psychophysiological and Intraoperative AEPs and SEPs Monitoring for Perception, Attention and Cognition

Sergey Lytaev[1,2(✉)], Mikhail Aleksandrov[2], and Aleksei Ulitin[2]

[1] Saint Petersburg State Pediatric Medical University, Saint Petersburg, Russia
slytaev@gmail.com
[2] Federal Almazov North-West Medical Research Centre,
Saint Petersburg, Russia
mdoktor@yandex.ru

Abstract. Auditory and somatosensory evoked potentials (AEPs and SEPs) in 14 patients with pathological processes of the brainstem and in 24 healthy subjects were recorded. The procedure of submission of relevant and deviant signals was used for stimulation and registration of evoked potentials. Key evoked potentials changes are as follows. Low amplitude of AEP in patients during a simple rhythmic stimulation generalized was registered. Mainly increasing of the middle latency AEP amplitude during activation of attention was observed. Amplitude increasing of the SEP late components in the central and frontal brain areas normally accompanied by a similar topomaps marked earlier (N30) waves. When pathology increased the amplitude of the field moved to the parietal and occipital cortex.

Keywords: Auditory evoked potentials · Somatosensory evoked potentials · Perception · Selective attention · Corticofugal modulation

1 Introduction

"Excitation process drawn up and sent by braking" – wrote about 100 years ago physiologist Ukhtomskii [12]. In the psychophysiology language such the organization of excitatory processes is the basis of selective attention. Modern views on the possible structural providing of selective attention mechanisms are formed largely due to the results of the registration of fast auditory and somatosensory evoked potentials (EPs). For example, there is information about the effects of efferent nerve centers of the cerebral cortex on the initial (brainstem) signal processing stages. A long time it was thought that the early (fast) waves of the EPs reflect only the transfer for specific sensory information. Now facts about the modulation of endogenous have been received. In other words, fast components have a connection with the processes of sensory perception, selective attention and consciousness [1, 3, 10]. It should be noted that similar results from the registration of EP in the pathology both in neurosurgery and in psychiatry were obtained [4, 7, 8].

© Springer International Publishing AG 2017
C. Stephanidis (Ed.): HCII Posters 2017, Part I, CCIS 713, pp. 229–236, 2017.
DOI: 10.1007/978-3-319-58750-9_33

Modern intraoperative monitoring (IOM) of the sensory EPs aims to address three practical problems. Firstly, IOM assists in accurate localization of the pathological process area, secondly, minimizes the random access and (or) transcranial operational corridors for neuronavigation procedures, and, thirdly, it serves for increase the accuracy of registration processes at the physical and molecular levels. From the physiological points of view IOM allows objectively evaluating the function of the nervous system in real time [2].

According to brainstem auditory EPs (BAEPs) in three-dimensional brain space can be calculated wave generators and separate as a result their influence on the pathological lesions. For these goals there are evoked potentials mapping, method of dipole localization (MDL) and method for constructing a three-dimensional Lissajous trajectory (3-DLT).

The aim of this study was to analyze the fast, middle and late components of the auditory and somatosensory evoked potentials in the performance of the psychophysiological tests and evaluation of fast AEP and SEP waves on the results of monitoring neurosurgical operations.

2   Methods

Evoked potentials in the psychophysiological test in 24 healthy subjects (right-handed men aged 20–22 years) and patients with brainstem pathology (before operation, 14 patients aged from 38 to 56 years) in 19 monopolar points were recorded. Data for IOM EPs only for patients on 4 monopolar points were analyzed. At the AEPs recording technique to highlight the relevant background deviant signals having different frequency tone was used. Deviant stimuli for SEPs registration incentives electric current to 40 V above the individual absolute threshold supplied from the electrical stimulator in the projection of the right median nerve were applied. The target (relevant) electrocutaneous signals applied to the area of the right hand were used. Discriminant analysis ($F > 4.0$) and MDL algorithm were applied.

3   Results

Statistical analysis of the AEPs spatiotemporal characteristics compared to healthy subjects is as follows. In a simple rhythmic auditory stimulation significant relief N18 amplitude in parietal ($F = 4.1$ and $F = 6.6$) and a central cortex (sites Cz, $F = 11.0$ and C4, $F = 4.3$), as well as reduction of N40 amplitude in P3 ($F = 4.9$) and C4 ($F = 4.4$) points were registered (Table 1). Relevant stimulation in these cases does not cause significant differences.

Rhythmic auditory stimulation has little effect on the N90 component. N145 wave amplitude increases in left parietal site ($F = 4.6$), and the peak latency (PL) in the vertex ($F = 4.4$). The perception of the target signal is accompanied by a generalized increase of an amplitude and latency N90 (Table 1). At N145 amplitude component in almost all points of registration is recovered, but remains elevated PL in C3 ($F = 5.0$) and C4 ($F = 6.3$).

Table 1. The amplitude-time characteristics (A, uV/T, ms) of the N40 and N90 components AEPs during auditory stimulation with the target signals in patients when compared with the control group

Para-sites meters	N40			N90	
	Control	Pathology	Control	Pathology	
T	P4	40.4 ± 9.6	42.3 ± 9.5	83.8 ± 10.0	98.0 ± 14.0*
A		2.7 ± 0.4	1.7 ± 1.1	2.1 ± 0.7	2.5 ± 1.7
T	P3	42.6 ± 8.2	44.0 ± 8.8	81.8 ± 8.1	95.0 ± 13.6*
A		2.5 ± 0.5	0.9 ± 0.2*	1.5 ± 1.2	2.7 ± 1.1
T	Cz	41.0 ± 7.7	43.6 ± 9.0	84.0 ± 6.3	93.6 ± 11.5*
A		2.1 ± 0.7	1.6 ± 1.0	1.3 ± 0.6	3.4 ± 1.6*
T	F4	43.0 ± 7.1	41.3 ± 4.3	87.4 ± 5.5	95.3 ± 9.2*
A		2.3 ± 1.1	1.3 ± 1.0	1.7 ± 1.0	4.6 ± 1.1*
T	F3	43.0 ± 7.0	41.0 ± 2.4	88.0 ± 3.7	94.3 ± 13.4
A		2.2 ± 0.4	1.9 ± 1.2	1.3 ± 0.3	3.9 ± 1.6**

Notes. F-statistic value by compared to the control: $^*F > 4.0$; $^{**}F > 10.0$; in other, the differences are insignificant $F < 4.0$.

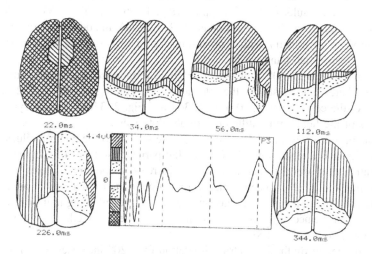

Fig. 1. SEP topomaps in healthy subject in a rhythmic electrical stimulation, ms.

Consider the most typical example of SEP mapping in healthy subjects in both tests (Figs. 1 and 2). With a simple rhythmic electrical stimulation wave P22 of topomap is accompanied by a uniform activation of the entire brain surface (Fig. 1, 22 ms).

In contrast, for the situation with the separation of a useful signal, a less symmetrical pattern is characteristic (Fig. 2, 24 ms). The N30 topomaps in both tests are characterized by the symmetry of excitation of the neocortex with a difference in quantitative values (Fig. 1, 34 ms; Fig. 2, 38 ms). For N60 in almost all parts of the

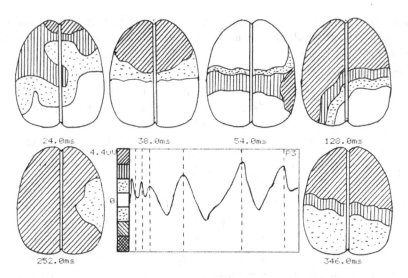

Fig. 2. SEP topomaps in healthy subject in the attention activation, ms.

brain reduction of the amplitude is typical in carrying out the task for attention, as is confirmed by the results of brain mapping (Fig. 1, 56 ms; Fig. 2, 54 ms). The following topomaps are similar to each other (112, 128 ms). In addition, here for the first time there is an asymmetry with a predominance of excitation in the hemisphere, a contralateral stimulated hand.

Marking the wave N200 is characterized by a pronounced map with activation of both hemispheres in the test with the selection of a useful signal (Fig. 2, 252 ms). The topomaps of the component N350 (Fig. 1, 344 ms, Fig. 2, 346 ms) show symmetrical excitations of the field with a difference in absolute values.

The amplitudes N30 and P40 of the SEPs are similar to the control values. At the same time there is a reduction in N30 in the left parietal site (F = 4.5). In the test with the allocation of a useful signal, a significant increase in the amplitude of the N30 in both occipital sites (Table 2) and a marked reduction in the frontal regions are recorded as compared to the first test in patients. In addition, PL lengthening in the occipital and parietal areas of the neocortex is observed. In parallel, there is a reduction PL P40 in the right occipital cortex (F = 4.8).

In conditions of rhythmic electric stimulation PL N200 increases (F > 4.0) only in the parietal cortex. This fact is also characteristic in the attention task, where also an increase in the amplitude of N200 in the occipital sites (F > 4.0) (Table 2) is also observed. The temporal characteristics of N350 differ little from the control ones in different tests (F < 4.0), however, in the second test there is a significant (F > 4.0) relief of the N350 amplitude in the parietal cortex of both hemispheres and in the right frontal cortex.

Table 2. The amplitude-time characteristics (A, uV / T, ms) of the N30 and N200 components SEPs during electrical stimulation with the target signals in patients when compared with the control group

Para-sites	meters	N30		N200	
		Control	Pathology	Control	Pathology
T	O2	35.4 ± 4.4	39.5 ± 2.6*	206.4 ± 26.4	232.0 ± 36.5
A		1.0 ± 0.6	3.9 ± 1.6*	2.3 ± 1.5	3.3 ± 2.7 *
T	O1	35.4 ± 3.6	35.0 ± 3.7	206.1 ± 23.7	237.0 ± 31.0*
A		1.5 ± 1.1	3.9 ± 1.8*	1.9 ± 1.4	3.8 ± 1.4*
T	Pz	33.8 ± 3.6	38.5 ± 5.9*	211.8 ± 29.0	243.3 ± 26.7*
A		1.0 ± 0.2	2.0 ± 1.7	1.9 ± 1.1	2.6 ± 1.3
T	F4	34.0 ± 2.9	38.0 ± 6.9	211.5 ± 28.4	231.6 ± 16.5
A		1.0 ± 0.3	1.7 ± 0.5*	2.2 ± 1.6	2.5 ± 0.9*
T	F3	35.2 ± 4.2	37.3 ± 7.3	215.1 ± 29.3	225.6 ± 20.2
A		1.5 ± 0.5	1.3 ± 1.1*	2.2	2.7 ± 0.6

Notes. See Table 1.

4   Discussion

There are quite contradictory information about middle latency AEPs (10–60 ms), their source and localization. These waves can reflect the activity of the first relay neurons of the auditory way or refer to the responses of the primary auditory cortex. There are data that AEPs with PL 12–37 ms from the Hirschlian gyrus of both temporal lobes were recorded. The same components may indicate the inclusion of subcortical delay mechanisms [2–5].

Our data from registering middle latency AEPs (MLAEPs) in the time interval 15–40 ms under the action of the target signals in healthy subjects showed a significant increase in the amplitude of these waves (F > 4.0) in the parietal, left temporal and frontal areas of the neocortex. This fact testifies about intensification of consciousness in the form of a mechanism of reverse influence of these parts of the brain cortex to brainstem structures that generate MLAEPs in conditions of activation of attention. Brainstem pathology increases the involvement of parietal cortex in providing feedback afferent mechanisms. This is confirmed by hyperactivation N18 amplitude with predominance in the parietal cortex and the central fields.

The solution of back tasks in order to establish the functional significance of brainstem and subcortical structures in the literature data are controversial. Our IOM data recorded from the midbrain structures show the presence of negative waves in the time sequence following the brainstem auditory EPs. AEPs near-field sequentially recorded at the level of the brain stem and from scalp. These results confirm the importance of brainstem formations in generation MLAEPs. It can be assumed about the localization of the generator of these waves on the brainstem-thalamic level, where cortex is given function of regulator for "volley" of the deep-generated potentials.

If the changes in the components of the MLAEPs in the time interval of 15–35 ms in the control group were reliable, the amplitude-time parameters of N40 and P60 did not practically differ in both tests. These facts were regarded either from the point of the identity of the mechanisms that ensure the transformation of auditory signals of varying complexity, or the absence of influence of overlying formations on this interval of time on the attention processes. N40 wave in brain pathology is generalized reduced with rhythmic stimulation. However, the amplitude of the next component (P60) under these conditions increases with brain damage mainly in the vertex. In the control group, a noticeable reduction of the N90 AEP can be observed under the conditions of presentation of the target task in all brain areas. In contrast, brainstem pathology, regardless of the nature and location of the lesion, is accompanied by a generalized increase in the N90 amplitude.

The mechanism considered in many respects explains the results obtained by us, where the amplitude of the N90 AEP in normal much higher with simple rhythmic stimulation. Obviously, under such conditions the summation of the allocated signal is more adequate. On the contrary, when the target signal is allocated with brainstem pathology, the amplification of the N90 amplitude is recorded. Thus, for the auditory system there is evidence of a possible selective corticofugal modulation already at the level of the switching brainstem neurons [3, 5].

Researchers of the somatosensory systems [11, 13] are less single-valued to correlate the early SEP components, reflecting the activity of the lemniscus pathways at the level of the brainstem before the switching nuclei of the thalamus, with the target test by subjects performing.

Usually the early somatosensory complex P25–30/N35–40 is considered as the first specific sensory indicator recorded at the thalamo-cortical level. The source of the first of these components (P22 in this work) is considered the switching nuclei of the ventral-basal thalamus complex [2]. Wave N35–40 (N30 in our study) reflects the specific sensory activity resulting from the arrival of afferentation to the primary projection zone along oligosynaptic pathways from the relay thalamus nuclei. The psychophysiological significance of these waves was previously commonly associated with modulation by the physical characteristics of the signal. This is convincingly confirmed by the results of studies with an increase in the intensity of the stimuli. Recently, there have been reports indicating the cognitive role of early waves of SEPs [6, 10, 11]. In particular, it is considered that the components P30 and P40 reflect the activation of information selection mechanisms.

In this research the test with a relevant signal in healthy persons drew attention to the reduction of early SEP waves (P22 and N30) in the frontal and parietal points of the brain, as well as reducing N70 amplitude in frontal sites and in the vertex. It seems to us these facts can be explained from two perspectives. Firstly, by adjusting the peripheral switch to receiving certain information. And, secondly, due to the descending influences from frontal brain to the ascending afferentation. The presence of the descending influences at all levels of the somatosensory systems is currently not in doubt. According to our data brainstem volume processes are accompanied by increased amplitude of the N30 SEP in the occipital departments in the activation of attention. This indicates about the inclusion of adaptive mechanisms with the movement in the occipital cortex.

AEPs and SEPs at the epoch of 150–300 ms are caused both by nonspecific afferent flows from the side of the reticular formation and thalamic nuclei, and from the mediobasal areas of the limbic cortex, the temporal and frontal lobes, and reflect the decision-making processes [3]. As a rule, the integration center at this time interval moves to the frontal cortex, which plays a key role in managing the processes of attention [1, 9, 13]. In addition, healthy subjects showed similarity in the relationship between excitable areas of the neocortex when labeling SEP waves with 38 ms and 346 ms, suggesting some identity of the processes occurring. Simple rhythmic electric stimulation on these time intervals is also characterized by similar topomaps (34 and 344 ms). These facts can probably be viewed from the position of the mechanisms of the redistribution of attention resources in the CNS with simple stimulation to the early (brainstem) stages of signal processing, and in more complicated ones, to later ones. This situation can also be traced in brainstem pathology where there is an increase in amplitude at these time intervals – N30 and N200 in the occipital cortex of both hemispheres, and N350 – in the parietal cortex.

5 Conclusion

During rhythmic sound stimulation for brainstem pathology generalized reduction and disappearance of MLAEPs and N90 wave of AEP are recorded. Activation of attention is accompanied by an increase in the amplitude of N40 and N90. In both tests PL of the late components is extended. For auditory system there is evidence of a possible selective corticofugal modulation at the level of the switching brainstem neurons.

The increase amplitude N200 and N350 in the central and frontal sites in healthy subjects in both tests is accompanied by similar topomaps with the labeling of early (N30) SEP waves, which is considered from the position of the mechanisms of redistribution of attention resources in the CNS with simple stimulation to the early (brainstem), and at more complex – to later processing. With brainstem pathology the activation of attention strengthens this position, but regions of increased amplitude move to the parietal and mainly to the occipital cortex of both hemispheres.

References

1. Jones, S.J., Vaz Pato, M., Spraque, L., et al.: Auditory evoked potentials to spectro-temporal modulation of complex tones in normal subjects and patients with severe brain injury. Brain 123(5), 1007–1016 (2000)
2. Khil'ko, V.A., Lytaev, S.A., Ostreiko, L.M.: Clinical physiological significance of intraoperative evoked potentials monitoring. Hum. Physiol. 28(5), 617–624 (2002)
3. Lytaev, S.: Brain topography of perception of target and non-target acoustic signals. In: Tolstoy, A., Teng, Y.-C., Shang, E.C. (eds.) Theoretical and Computational Acoustics 2003, 291–297. World Scientific, New Jersey, London, Singapore, Beijing (2004)
4. Lytaev, S., Belskaya, K.: Integration and disintegration of auditory images perception. In: Schmorrow, Dylan D., Fidopiastis, Cali M. (eds.) AC 2015. LNCS (LNAI), vol. 9183, pp. 470–480. Springer, Cham (2015). doi:10.1007/978-3-319-20816-9_45
5. Lytaev, S., Aleksandrov, M., Surovitskaj, Y., Lytaev, M.: EEG markers for recognition auditory images in norm and psychopathology. J. Int. Psychophysiol. 108, 80 (2016)

6. Miwa, H., Nohara, C., Hotta, M., Shimo, Y., Amemiya, K.: Somatosensory-evoked blink response: investigation of the physiological mechanism. Brain **121**, 281–291 (1998)

7. Patterson, J.V., Sandman, C.A., Jin, Y., Kemp, A.S., Potkin, S.G., Bunney Jr., W.E.: Gating of a novel brain potential is associated with perceptual anomalies in bipolar disorder. Bipolar Disord. **15**, 314–325 (2013)

8. Pojda-Wilczek, D.: Visual-evoked potentials in patients with brain circulatory problems. Int. J. Neurosci. **125**(4), 264–269 (2015)

9. Razavi, B., O'Neill, W.E., Paige, G.D.: auditory spatial perception dynamically realigns with changing eye position. J. Neurosci. **27**(38), 10249–10258 (2007)

10. Tinazzi, M., Fiaschi, A., Rosso, T., et al.: Neuroplastic changes related to pain occur at multiple levels of the human somatosensory system: a somatosensory-evoked potentials study in patients with cervical radicular pain. J. Neurosci. **20**(24), 9277–9283 (2000)

11. Touge, T., Gonzalez, D., Wu, J., et al.: The interaction between somatosensory and auditory cognitive processing assessed with event-related potentials. J. Clin. Neurophysiol. **25**(2), 90–97 (2008)

12. Ukhtomskii, A.A.: The Doctrine of Parabiosis. Publ. Com. Acad., Moscow (1927)

13. Waberski, T.D., Gobbele, R., Darvas, F., et al.: Spatiotemporal imaging of electrical activity related to attention to somatosensory stimulation. NeuroImage **17**(3), 1347–1357 (2002)

Development of Device for Measurement of Skin Potential by Grasping of the Device

Tota Mizuno[1(✉)], Shogo Matsuno[1], Kota Akehi[1], Kazuyuki Mito[1],
Naoaki Itakura[1], and Hirotoshi Asano[2]

[1] The University of Electro-Communications, 1-5-1 Chofugaoka,
Chofu, Tokyo 182-8585, Japan
mizuno@uec.ac.jp
[2] Kagawa University, 2217-20 Hayashi-cho,
Takamatsu, Kagawa 761-0396, Japan

Abstract. In this study, we developed a device for measuring skin potential activity requiring the subject to only grasp the interface. There is an extant method for measuring skin potential activity, which is an indicator for evaluating Mental Work-Load (MWL). It exploits the fact that when a human being experiences mental stress, such as tension or excitement, emotional sweating appears at skin sites such as the palm and sole; concomitantly, the skin potential at these sites varies. At present, skin potential activity of the hand is measured by electrodes attached to the whole arm. Alternatively, if a method can be developed to measure skin potential activity (and in turn emotional sweating) by an electrode placed on the palm only, it would be feasible to develop a novel portable burden-evaluation interface that can measure the MWL with the subject holding the interface. In this study, a prototype portable load-evaluation interface was investigated for its capacity to measure skin potential activity while the interface is held in the subject's hand. This interface, wherein an electrode is attached to the device, rather than directly to the hand, can measure the parameters with the subject gripping the device. Moreover, by attaching the electrode laterally rather than longitudinally to the device, a touch by the subject, at any point on the sides of the device, enables measurement. The electrodes used in this study were tin foil tapes. In the experiment, subjects held the interface while it measured their MWL. However, the amplitude of skin potential activity (which reflects the strength of the stimulus administered on the subjects) obtained by the proposed method was lower than that obtained by the conventional method. Nonetheless, because sweat response due to stimulation could be quantified with the proposed method, the study demonstrated the possibility of load measurements considering only the palm.

Keywords: Skin potential activity · Autonomic nerve activity · Gripping device

C. Stephanidis (Ed.): HCII Posters 2017, Part I, CCIS 713, pp. 237–242, 2017.
DOI: 10.1007/978-3-319-58750-9_34

1   Introduction

Recently, Mental Work-Load (MWL), owing to the use of mobile phones and tablet PCs, has become a major social problem. Although an appropriate level of MWL positively affects human health, long-term excessive MWL can cause fatigue, which adversely affects concentration and thus leads to human errors and consequent health hazards. Evaluation of MWL of workers is critical for preventing and reducing such effects. Autonomic nerve activity is closely related to physical and physiological stress; its measurement or estimation using biological information can serve as the foundation for methods of objectively assessing bodily activity and physical and physiological stress in humans [2]. A method is available for measuring the skin potential activity, which serves an index for evaluating MWL. When humans experience mental burden such as tension or excitement, emotional perspiration appears at skin sites such as the palm and sole [3]. Skin potential varies according to this emotional state. The extant methods measure skin potential activity considering the entire arm, as illustrated in Fig. 1. The probe electrode, reference electrode, and earth electrode are attached to the palm, forearm refraction portion, and forearm portion, respectively. As this method measures the parameters by attaching electrodes, it is suitable for continued evaluation of MWL. However, as it necessitates pasting the electrodes over the whole arm, it is not suitable for providing instantaneous feedback if the subject requires it. If skin potential activity (and consequently emotional sweating) can be measured with an electrode placed only on the palm and by the subject gripping the device, development of a portable load-evaluation interface for measuring MWL is feasible. Therefore, in this study, we developed the prototype of a portable MWL evaluation interface and investigated whether skin potential activity can be evaluated with an electrode of this device kept in contact with the palm.

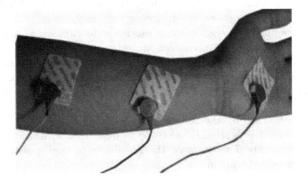

Fig. 1. Conventional method of attachment

2   Emotional Sweating

Emotional sweating is a reaction to mental excitement. This reaction is rapid and involves the cortical premotor cortex, limbic system, hypothalamus, etc. It is evaluated by physiological indexes such as perspiration amount and skin potential activity (SPA). SPA is categorized into: SPR (Skin Potential Reflex), which is an alternating current (AC) component, and SPL (Skin Potential Level), which is a direct current (DC) component. SPL is a reaction of arousal degree. SPR responds with mental arithmetic and thinking. The amplitude reflects the strength of the stimulus [1].

3   Developed Device

It has been confirmed in previous studies that the amount of perspiration differs at each part of the hand such as fingers and mother-child spheres. Instead of pasting the electrode on the body, we conceived a device that enabled measurement by it being grasped. Figure 2 illustrates the proposed device. Considering the nature of the actual application, a mobile terminal case was utilized. In addition, as illustrated in Fig. 2, by attaching the electrode to the side of the case rather than vertically, measurement was possible by touching any point on the side surface of the case. Electrodes were prepared using tin foil tape. The probe, reference, and ground electrodes were attached to the side of the measurement case. When gripping the case, the finger and palm were required to touch the case at the electrodes. Consequently, we created two devices: (1) one in which the electrodes were distributed and pasted over both sides faces of the case; and (2) one in which all the electrodes were pasted over one side face of the case.

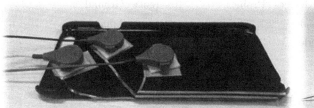

Fig. 2. The proposed device

In the case of (1), wherein electrodes are attached to both sides, there is a possibility of measurement of the skin potential activity from the difference in the amount of perspiration at the contacting parts. However, in the case of (2), wherein the electrode is attached to one side, as the positions of all the electrodes are close to each other, the amounts of perspiration recorded by them are highly similar. Consequently, there is a possibility that large skin potential activity may not be measurable. Therefore, we examined whether skin potential activity can be measured by varying the widths and positions of the electrodes.

4 Verification Experiment

4.1 Protocol

Subjects took rest for approximately 3 min before the experiment started. Then, the subjects closed their eyes, and as a stressor, pain was stimulated on the forearm by striking three times with a rubber hammer. To ensure uniform intensity of stimulation, we unified the quality of rubber, length to extend (15 cm), width to hook (5 cm). The subjects were five healthy male university students in their twenties. For comparison of the proposed devices, measurement was carried out simultaneously using a skin potential meter (Nishizawa Electric Co., Ltd. SPN-01). The skin electrometer was attached to the subjects' left hand by the conventional attachment method. On the subjects' right hand, the proposed devices were placed and grasped by the subject and measurements were taken. The width and position of the electrodes are presented in Fig. 3 and Table 1.

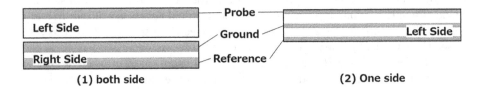

Fig. 3. Position of electrodes

Table 1. Width and position of electrode

Proposed devices	Probe	Reference	Ground
(1) Both side	1, 2 and 3 mm	1 mm	1 mm
(2) One side	3 and 6 mm	3 mm	3 mm

4.2 Evaluation Method

Emotional sweating by pain sensory stimulation is evaluated by skin potential. "Spr" signify the skin potential value measured by the extant research method, and Nspr is that by the proposed device. The proposed method is evaluated using the ratio of the amplitudes of Spr and Nspr.

4.3 Experimental Results and Discussion

(1) Electrodes Attached to both Sides: Figure 4 (a) illustrates the waveform when the width of the search electrode on Subject 1 is 3 mm, and Fig. 4 (b) illustrates the waveform when the width is doubled to 6 mm. In the figure, the time at which the stimulus is provided is set as 0 s. The reaction to the stimulus in the case of both Nspr and Spr occurred approximately 2 s after stimulation. The fact that the reactions appeared simultaneously in the two methods indicates that the proposed device has the capacity to measure mental sweating. However, the proposed method recorded lower amplitude than the conventional method. The amplitude ratio is presented in Table 2. Although there are individual differences, for three of the subjects, amplification was increased when the area of the probe electrode was doubled. Moreover, the amplitude reversed for all the subjects. The probable cause for this is that the amount of perspiration was larger on the palm than on the finger.

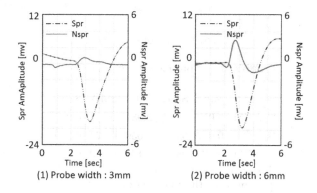

Fig. 4. Results of case (1)

Table 2. Amplitude ratio of case (1)

	Sub1	Sub2	Sub3	Sub4	Sub5
(A)/CM	0.19	0.65	0.59	0.12	0.41
(B)/CM	0.45	0.34	0.84	0.64	1.11

CM: Conventional method
(A): 3 mm (Width of electrode)
(B): 6 mm (Width of electrode)

(2) Electrodes Attached to One Side: The results are illustrated in Fig. 5.
    For this device, in the case of both Nspr and Spr, the reaction occurred approximately 2 s after stimulation. This demonstrated that the proposed device is capable of measuring emotional sweating. The amplitude ratio is presented in Table 3. From Table 3, it can be observed that the amplitude measured using this method is marginal when compared to that by the conventional method. This marginal difference in impedance is attributed to the close proximity of the measurement site. However, it was demonstrated that the amplitude increased as the width of the search electrode was widened. An increase in the width of the search electrode led to a decrease in the impedance. As a result, the potential fluctuation on the search electrode side becomes marginal. Thus, potential fluctuation on the reference electrode side is considered to be emphasized.

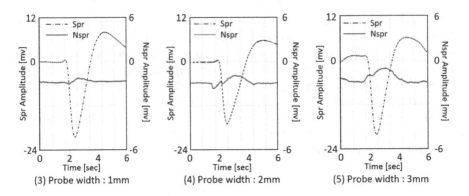

(3) Probe width : 1mm   (4) Probe width : 2mm   (5) Probe width : 3mm

Fig. 5. Results of case (2)

Table 3. Amplitude ratio of case (2)

	Sub1	Sub2	Sub3	Sub4	Sub5
(C)/CM	0.017	0.027	0.037	0.101	0.227
(D)/CM	0.047	0.022	0.059	0.178	0.270
(E)/CM	0.073	0.069	0.134	0.590	0.324

CM: Conventional method
(C): 1 mm (Width of electrode)
(D): 2 mm (Width of electrode)
(E): 3 mm (Width of electrode)

5   Conclusion

In this study, we developed two prototype portable MWL evaluation interfaces and investigated the effectiveness of measuring skin potential activity using hand contact with the electrode. Fluctuations in the waveform were observed in both the devices, one of which had electrodes attached on both sides of the device and the other had electrodes attached to one side of the device. Moreover, the feasibility of burden measurement in the palm area was demonstrated.

References

1. Miyata, H., Fujisawa, K., Kakigi, S., Yamazaki, K.: New physiological psychology, vol. 1998/05, pp. 210–220
2. Mizuno, T., Nomura, S., Nozawa, A., Asano, H., Ide, H.: Evaluation of the effect of intermittent mental work-load by nasal skin temperature. IEICE Trans. Inf. Syst. **J93–D**(4), 535–543 (2010)
3. Matsuno, S., Terasaki, T., Aizawa, S., Mizuno, T., Mito, K., Itakura, N.: Physiological and psychological evaluation by skin potential activity measurement using steering wheel while driving. In: Stephanidis, C. (ed.) HCI 2016. CCIS, vol. 618, pp. 177–181. Springer, Cham (2016). doi:10.1007/978-3-319-40542-1_28

Evaluating NeuroSky's Single-Channel EEG Sensor for Drowsiness Detection

Kishan Patel[1], Harit Shah[1], Malcolm Dcosta[2], and Dvijesh Shastri[1(✉)]

[1] Department of Computer Science and Engineering Technology,
University of Houston-Downtown, Houston, TX, USA
{patelk,shahha,shastrid}@uhd.edu
[2] Department of Mathematics and Computer Science, Elizabeth City State
University, Elizabeth City, NC, USA
mtdcosta@ecsu.edu

Abstract. NeuroSky's single-channel EEG sensor has drawn researchers' interest because the sensor offers higher usability at a significantly lower cost. The sensor is minimally obtrusive, measuring the brainwaves from a single location on the head. This is an excellent feature from a usability standpoint. Yet, the sensor needs to be evaluated for specific applications. This paper presents preliminary assessment of the sensor in detecting drowsiness. A simulated driving task was used as a testbed. A total of 14 participants participated in the study. The results reveal no statistically significant difference in brain activities between the drowsy and the attentive states, indicating that the brainwaves used in the analysis are unable to distinguish the two driving states.

Keywords: Driver's distraction · Brain-computer interface · Brainwaves · Single channel EEG Sensor · NeuroSky

1 Introduction

Traditionally, electroencephalography (EEG) sensors are multichannel (with as many as 256 channels in some cases), use wet electrodes, and transmit data through a set of wires [24]. Although the sensors precisely record brain activities with proper preparation, their usage is largely limited to the clinical and laboratory setups primarily because the sensors demand longer preparation time and offer lower usability.

Recent development of the single-channel, dry-electrode EEG sensor technology has drawn researchers' interest because the technology features higher usability at a significantly lower cost, offering possibility of conducting studies in informal environments such as schools and homes, and while mobile. One such widely used sensor is MindWave Mobile from NeuroSky which we used in this study [18]. iBrain Device from NeuroVigil is another single-channel EEG sensor [19]. However, it was not available for purchase during the time of our experimentation. Other commercial offerings are specific to certain applications

© Springer International Publishing AG 2017
C. Stephanidis (Ed.): HCII Posters 2017, Part I, CCIS 713, pp. 243–250, 2017.
DOI: 10.1007/978-3-319-58750-9_35

including Zeo's sensor for sleep monitoring, EmBand Headset from EmSense for neuromarketing [8], and a seven-channel EEG sensor from Muse for meditation exercise [17]. Emotiv's EPOC+ is another off-the-shelf low-cost device, which records brainwaves from 14 channels [12]. We did not use the sensor in our study because the 14 channel configuration is not minimally obtrusive and hence, may bring discomfort to some drivers, especially when it is required to wear for a longer period.

The use of the NeuroSky sensor has been increasing for Human-Computer Interaction (HCI) and Brain-Computer Interface (BCI) research. Marchesi and Ricco proposed an e-learning system that customizes educational experience according to the attention and meditation signals captured via the NeuroSky sensor [16]. Al-Barrak and Kanjo used the same signals to distinguish relaxing outdoor places from boisterous places [3]. Yoh et al. developed a Brain-Computer Interface (BCI) game, called NueroWander, which uses the sensor's attention and meditation signals as game controllers [29]. Blondet et al. used the sensor in a prototype system for detecting the user's mental states in real-time [5]. Hal et al. proposed a real-time stage 1 sleep detection system that uses the sensor [26].

In this research we investigated the applicability of the sensor in detecting drowsiness. Specifically, we wanted to examine whether the NeuroSky's Mind-Wave sensor can differentiate machine operator's attentive state from his/her drowsy state. If it can, then the sensor can be a viable low cost solution to multiple applications where an operator's drowsiness can potentially be harmful. A case in point is security guards who are required to monotonously monitor security video feeds. Other cases are operating airplanes or driving vehicles in which drowsiness can cost lives.

We used simulated driving as a testbed because it is a cost effective setup for a feasibility study such as this one. Driver's drowsiness can be detected in several ways. One approach focuses on monitoring of vehicle behaviors via lane and steering tracking [4,14]. This approach offers good practicality in sense that there is no need of attaching any sensors to the driver's body. However, this approach performs suboptimal in bad weather and for poor lane markings, and requires additional hardware attachments to the vehicle. Machine vision is another approach that is routinely explored for monitoring driver's face and eyes [15,20,27]. Yet, most vision-based methods are not very successful in handling real-life challenges such as monitoring in the low light environments, under facial occlusion, and for drivers with eyeglasses.

Multiple studies reported usefulness of EEG in drowsy driving detection. Most studies, however, used multichannel EEG sensors which limit their practicality [2,11,13]. Recently, Sarno et al. used Emotiv EPOC+ (14 channel sensor) for the detection of driver's fatigue [21]. A six-channel EEG-based drowsy detection system was demonstrated by Tsai et al. [25]. They placed the six electrodes approximately at the Fp1, Fp2, T5, T6, O1 and O2 locations (see Fig. 1), and reported 90% accuracy rate in drowsy state detection and 80% accuracy rate in attentive state detection. SmartCap is a commercially available EEG-based system for driver fatigue detection that uses only a few electrodes [23]. These systems demonstrate that reduction in the number of electrodes improves EEG's usability. In the current study, we focused our attention on a single-channel EEG sensor for drowsiness detection.

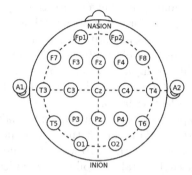

Fig. 1. EEG Electrode locations of International 10–20 system. The letter codes F, T, C, P and O stand for frontal, temporal, central, parietal, and occipital lobes, respectively. The letter codes A, and Fp identify the earlobes, and frontal polar sites respectively [28].

2   Experimental Design

2.1   Driving Simulator

We used simulated driving as a testbed. Specifically, we simulated monotonous driving through a pc-based software tool, City Car Driving v1.3 [9]. The simulator allowed us to stage a late evening highway driving scenario with medium to low traffic. To control the simulator, we used Logitech's G-27 controllers which included a steering wheel, and gas and brake pedals. The controllers' force feedback mechanism gives the feeling of actual driving.

2.2   Single-Channel EEG Sensor

We used a MindWave headset from NeuroSky to collect neuronal activities [18]. The headset consists of a single dry electrode which is attached to the driver's forehead at the Fp1 position and a ground electrode which is attached to an earlobe (see Fig. 1). The sensor samples neuronal activities with a frequency up to 512 Hz and outputs EEG power of brainwaves (delta, theta, alpha, beta, and gamma) at 1 Hz frequency. It also outputs proprietary eSense meters for attention and meditation. The sensor transmits the data wirelessly via a Bluetooth connection.

2.3   Experiment

The experiment has been approved by the Institute's Review Board. A group of seven participants (5 males and 2 females) volunteered for a 30 min driving session and another group of seven participants (5 males and 2 females) volunteered for a 60 min driving session. Their ages ranged from 18 to 40 years. After completing the consent form, the participants explored the driving simulator for about 10 min to acquaint themselves with the experimental setup. Next, they performed the driving task for either 30 min (short session) or 60 min (long session). The two driving sessions facilitated thorough evaluation of the sensor. Specifically, the initial study was conducted for 30 min driving only, but after observing indistinguishable brainwave patterns between the two driving states, we expanded the experiment for 60 min driving period to make sure that the driving period is not the affecting factor.

The lighting in the experiment room was dimed to make the driving environment conducive to drowsiness. Throughout the driving period, the participants' faces were recorded via a Logitech HD C270 webcam. The videos were later used to identify drowsy instances. In total, we collected 14 videos (14 participants × 1 recording per participant) and 14 sets of EEG signals (14 participants × 1 set per participant) during the experiment.

3   Data Analysis

3.1   Face Videos

The face videos were used to mark drowsy instances. Specifically, each 10 s driving period was annotated as *Drowsy Driving* if any facial clues of drossiness were observed including frequent eye blinking, heavy eyelids, rubbing eyes, constant yawning, and struggling to hold the head up. Otherwise, the period was annotated as *Attentive Driving*. The drowsy indictors were chosen based on Summala et al. research on detecting driver's drowsiness from video images [22]. The annotations were done independently by the two coders and then synthesized into a single binary signal of driving state per participant.

3.2   EEG Data

EEG data is typically divided into bands of frequency, including delta, theta, alpha, beta and gamma bands. Each band represents certain mental states. Specifically, the delta band (1–3 Hz) represents deep dreamless sleep, the theta band (4–7 Hz) represents sleepy mental state, the alpha band (8–12 Hz) represents relaxed mental state, and the beta band (13–30 Hz) represents active thinking.

Eoh et al. reported several EEG studies that showed a close correlation between the EEG power of the alpha and theta waves and drowsy driving [13]. Specifically, one study in their report showed that the EEG power of the alpha and theta waves was increased as the alertness level of the driver decreased [13]. Another study showed a decrease in the relative energy parameter (alpha+theta)/beta with drowsiness [11]. Craig et al. reported that the alpha and theta waves are most typically associated with fatigue or drowsiness

[10]. Therefore, in our analysis we decided to include the theta and alpha waves, and the (alpha+theta) and the (alpha+theta)/beta parameters. We also used the proprietary attention and mediation signals. In total, we utilized 6 signals from each participant's EEG data.

The EEG signals were averaged for a 10 s epoch, having 180 samples (6 samples per minute × 30 min) for each 30 min driving session and 360 samples

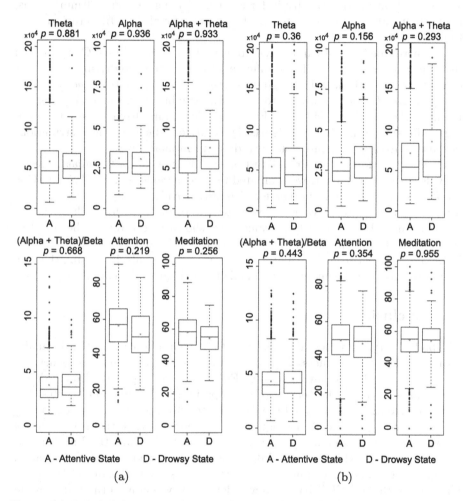

Fig. 2. (a) Boxplot diagrams represent analysis of the EEG signals for the 30 min driving sessions. The ∗ symbols in the box-plots indicate the mean values of the distributions. $n = 1027$ (about 90% of the samples) for Attentive State (A). $n = 127$ (about 10% of the samples) for Drowsy State (D). (b) Boxplot diagrams represent analysis of the EEG signals for the 60 min driving sessions. The ∗ symbols in the box-plots indicate the mean values of the distributions. $n = 2215$ (about 90% of the samples) for Attentive State (A). $n = 253$ (about 10% of the samples) for Drowsy State (D). (Color figure online)

for each 60 min driving session. Although the 10 s period was heuristically chosen, the previous studies used similar sized periods [6, 13, 22].

4   Experimental Results

We observed an average drowsy driving period of 3 min for the short driving sessions (30 min) and about 6 min for the long driving sessions (60 min). Thus, the participants experienced episodes of drowsiness for about 10% of their driving time.

We performed statistical analysis to examine whether the EEG signals can reveal any statistically significant difference between the two driving states. For each of the six EEG signals, we grouped the signal values into *Drowsy Driving* and *Attentive Driving* according to the binary driving state signal. The distributions of the signals are shown in Fig. 2a for the 30 min driving sessions and in Fig. 2b for the 60 min driving sessions. Qualitatively speaking, the distributions of the two driving states are not much different in most cases.

Next, we performed a paired-T test on each pair of the EEG signals. Specifically, for every participant, we computed two mean values per EEG signal: One for *Drowsy Driving* and another for *Attentive Driving*. Finally, we performed a paired-T test on these values. These steps were repeated for each of the six EEG signals. The test results (p values) are shown at the top of the boxplots (see Fig. 2). The results reveal no statistically significant difference ($p > 0.05$) in EEG energy between the driving states for all the signals, indicating that the brainwaves used in the analysis are unable to distinguish the two driving states.

5   Conclusion

The preliminary assessment demonstrates that the brainwaves used in the analysis fail to detect drowsiness. The primary reason of the failure, we believe, is the location of the measurement site (Fp1 location). Typically, drowsy detection studies focus on the central (C) and parietal (P) measurement sites. For instance, Brown et al. analyzed the C3, C4, Pz, P3, and P4 sites for identifying drowsy driving periods [7]. Broughton et al. reported that theta activities of drowsiness were maximum at the Cz and Fz sites [6]. Thus, the Fp1 location alone was never used in the past drowsiness detection studies. The Fp1 location is typically examined in conjunction with the other sites. For instance, Tsai et al. for their six-channel EEG-based drowsy detection system used the Fp1 location in conjunction with the Fp2, T5, T6, O1 and O2 locations [25]. Similarly, Eoh et al. explored the Fp1 location along with the Fp2, T3, T4, P3, P4, O1, and O2 locations [13].

The other possible reason for the failure in detecting drowsiness could be the EEG data processing approach that we employed. We used only the mean values (per ever 10 s) of the EEG signals. A recent study by Abdel-Rahman et. al extracted multiple statistical features (max, min, mean, and standard deviation) and a frequency-based feature (power spectral density) from the MindWave's

EEG signals [1]. They reported 98.5% accuracy for the awake state and 96% accuracy for the sleepy state classifications.

Our future work includes exploration of other single-measurement sites, in particular the Cz and Fz sites as they are reported to be relevant for theta activities of drowsiness. We will also extract from our existing EEG signals the features reported in [1] and reevaluate the sensor.

Acknowledgments. This material is based upon work supported in part by the National Science Foundation (NSF) under Grant No. # CNS-1042341 and the College of Sciences and Technology Dean's Discretionary fund.

References

1. Abdel-Rahman, A., Seddik, A.F., Shawky, D.M.: An affordable approach for detecting drivers' drowsiness using EEG signal analysis. In: 2015 International Conference on Advances in Computing, Communications and Informatics (ICACCI), pp. 1326–1332. IEEE (2015)
2. Akerstedt, T., Kecklund, G., Knutsson, A.: Manifest sleepiness and the spectral content of the eeg during shift work. Sleep **14**(3), 221–225 (1991)
3. Al-Barrak, L., Kanjo, E.: Neuroplace: making sense of a place. In: Proceedings of the 4th Augmented Human International Conference, pp. 186–189. ACM (2013)
4. Barickman, F.S., Stoltzfus, D.L.: A simple CCD based lane tracking system. Technical report, SAE Technical Paper (1999)
5. Blondet, M.V.R., Badarinath, A., Khanna, C., Jin, Z.: A wearable real-time BCI system based on mobile cloud computing. In: 2013 6th International IEEE/EMBS Conference on Neural Engineering (NER), pp. 739–742. IEEE (2013)
6. Broughton, R., Hasan, J.: Quantitative topographic electroencephalographic mapping during drowsiness and sleep onset. J. Clin. Neurophysiol. **12**(4), 372-hyhen (1995)
7. Brown, T., Johnson, R., Milavetz, G.: Identifying periods of drowsy driving using EEG. Ann. Adv. Automot. Med. **57**, 99 (2013)
8. Chi, Y.M., Jung, T.P., Cauwenberghs, G.: Dry-contact and noncontact biopotential electrodes: methodological review. IEEE Rev. Biomed. Eng. **3**, 106–119 (2010)
9. CityCarDriving: City car driving simulator v1.3. http://citycardriving.com/
10. Craig, A., Tran, Y., Wijesuriya, N., Nguyen, H.: Regional brain wave activity changes associated with fatigue. Psychophysiology **49**(4), 574–582 (2012)
11. De Waard, D., Brookhuis, K.A.: Assessing driver status: a demonstration experiment on the road. Accid. Anal. Prev. **23**(4), 297–307 (1991)
12. Emotiv: Epoc+. https://www.emotiv.com/epoc/
13. Eoh, H.J., Chung, M.K., Kim, S.H.: Electroencephalographic study of drowsiness in simulated driving with sleep deprivation. Int. J. Ind. Ergon. **35**(4), 307–320 (2005)
14. Friedrichs, F., Yang, B.: Drowsiness monitoring by steering and lane data based features under real driving conditions. In: 2010 18th European Signal Processing Conference, pp. 209–213. IEEE (2010)
15. Ji, Q., Yang, X.: Real-time eye, gaze, and face pose tracking for monitoring driver vigilance. Real-Time Imaging **8**(5), 357–377 (2002)

16. Marchesi, M., Riccò, B.: BRAVO: a brain virtual operator for education exploiting brain-computer interfaces. In: CHI 2013 Extended Abstracts on Human Factors in Computing Systems, pp. 3091–3094. ACM (2013)
17. Muse: The brain sensing headband. http://www.choosemuse.com/
18. NeuroSky: Mindwave mobile. http://store.neurosky.com/pages/mindwave
19. NeuroVigil: ibrain device. http://www.neurovigil.com
20. Patil, R.M., Gajare, A.M., Agrawal, D.G.: Drowsy driver detection system. Glob. J. Eng. Appl. Sci. **2**(1), 1 (2012)
21. Sarno, R., Nugraha, B.T., Munawar, M.N.: Real time fatigue-driver detection from electroencephalography using emotiv EPOC+. Int. Rev. Comput. Softw. (IRE-COS) **11**(3), 214–223 (2016)
22. Summala, H., Hakkanen, H., Mikkola, T., Sinkkonen, J.: Task effects on fatigue symptoms in overnight driving. Ergonomics **42**(6), 798–806 (1999)
23. Tadayon, R., McDaniel, T., Goldberg, M., Robles-Franco, P.M., Zia, J., Laff, M., Geng, M., Panchanathan, S.: Interactive motor learning with the autonomous training assistant: a case study. In: Kurosu, M. (ed.) HCI 2015. LNCS, vol. 9170, pp. 495–506. Springer, Cham (2015). doi:10.1007/978-3-319-20916-6_46
24. Troy M, L., Joseph T, G., Daniel P, F.: How many electrodes are really needed for EEG-based mobile brain imaging? J. Behav. Brain Sci. (2012)
25. Tsai, P.Y., Hu, W., Kuo, T.B., Shyu, L.Y.: A portable device for real time drowsiness detection using novel active dry electrode system. In: Annual International Conference of the IEEE Engineering in Medicine and Biology Society, EMBC 2009, pp. 3775–3778. IEEE (2009)
26. Van Hal, B., Rhodes, S., Dunne, B., Bossemeyer, R.: Low-cost EEG-based sleep detection. In: 2014 36th Annual International Conference of the IEEE Engineering in Medicine and Biology Society (EMBC), pp. 4571–4574. IEEE (2014)
27. Vural, E., Cetin, M., Ercil, A., Littlewort, G., Bartlett, M., Movellan, J.: Drowsy driver detection through facial movement analysis. In: Lew, M., Sebe, N., Huang, T.S., Bakker, E.M. (eds.) HCI 2007. LNCS, vol. 4796, pp. 6–18. Springer, Heidelberg (2007). doi:10.1007/978-3-540-75773-3_2
28. Wikipedia: 10–20 system (EEG) (2001). https://en.wikipedia.org/wiki/10-20_system_(EEG)
29. Yoh, M.S., Kwon, J., Kim, S.: Neurowander: a BCI game in the form of interactive fairy tale. In: Proceedings of the 12th ACM International Conference Adjunct Papers on Ubiquitous Computing-Adjunct, pp. 389–390. ACM (2010)

Neurophysiological Indices of Human Social Interactions Between Humans and Robots

S.J. Smith[1], B.T. Stone[1], T. Ranatunga[2], K. Nel[3], T.Z. Ramsoy[4], and C. Berka[1(✉)]

[1] Research Advanced Brain Monitoring Inc., Carlsbad, CA, USA
[2] Fellow Robots, San Jose, CA, USA
[3] Lowe's Innovation Lab., Mooresville, NC, USA
[4] Neurons Inc., Holbaek, Denmark

Abstract. Technology continues to advance at exponential rates and we are exposed to a multitude of electronic interfaces in almost every aspect of our lives. In order to achieve seamless integration of both, human and technology, we must examine the objective and subjective responses to such interactions. The goal of this study was to examine neurophysiological responses to movement, communication, and usability with a robot assistant, in comparison to human assistant, in a real-world setting. OSHbot (robot assistants designed by Fellow Robots) were utilized as mobile store clerks to identify and locate merchandise in order to assist customers in finding items within a hardware store. By acquiring neurophysiological measures (electroencephalogram; EEG and electrocardiogram; ECG) of human perception and interaction with robots, we found evidence of Mirror Neuron System (MNS) elicitation and motor imagery processing, which is consistent with other studies examining human-robot interactions. Multiple analyses were conducted to assess differences between human-human interaction and human-robot interaction. Several EEG metrics were identified that were distinguishable based on interaction type; among these was the change observed across the Mu bandwidth (8–13 Hz). The variance in this EEG correlate has been related to empathetic state change. In order to explore differences in the interactions related to gender and age additional analyses were conducted to compare the effects of human-human interaction versus human-robot interaction with data stratified by gender and age. This analysis yielded significant differences across these categories between human-human interaction and human-robot interaction within EEG metrics. These preliminary data show promise for future research in the field of human-robot relations in contributing to the design and implementation of machines that not only deliver basic services but also create a social connection with humans.

Keywords: HCI · HRI · Social interaction · Robots · Mu · EEG · Eye tracking

1 Introduction

Social interactions and relationships involve far more than facial recognition and conversation; rather, exchanges between humans draw upon many aspects of communication including language form and content [1], interrelation synchrony in

© Springer International Publishing AG 2017
C. Stephanidis (Ed.): HCII Posters 2017, Part I, CCIS 713, pp. 251–262, 2017.
DOI: 10.1007/978-3-319-58750-9_36

gestures, postures, and tones [2–4], and social perspectives of trust [5]. Humans receive both conscious and unconscious cues during social interaction. We are able to automatically align on many different levels and adapt to various external factors during these interactions [6]. Taken together, auditory and visual perceptions greatly impact human emotional responses when placed in a social setting. However, little is understood about the biological underpinnings that modulate the behaviors exhibited during an interaction. Increasingly, technology is playing a significant role in this largely unknown space of mechanisms governing intrapersonal connections. Technology is being integrated into nearly every aspect of daily life; with capabilities of watching, assessing, and even learning from our actions. Furthermore, advancements in technology are increasing at a rapid pace. According to the Nielsen Q1 Total Audience Report for 2016, computers, cell phones, tablets, and touch screen devices consume upwards of 11 h of the average person's day, which is an entire hour more than reported in 2015 [7]. While some science fiction writers offer a darker view of a future where malevolent machines dominate, predictions have been made that one day humans and technology will seamlessly live in synchrony [8]. By examining cognitive and emotional effects of human-technology interactions, researchers are implementing ways to modify these advancements for more cohesive integrations between humans and technology, specifically examining human relationships with computers and robots [9]. In bridging this gap, it is important to consider the impact of physical appearances, movements, and social interaction perceptions which can vary dramatically across cultures, generations, and genders [6]. As autonomous machinery is nearing integration in many fields, such as medicine, the application of cortical responses is of utmost importance. Robots, as well as other technological agents, are currently limited in their capacity for autonomy. It is proposed that an influx of dependence on autonomous machine agents, not only for health care, but for companionship and assistance with daily functioning, will occur within the next century so it is important to anticipate and plan for adaptations to the new social environment.

Human Robot Interaction (HRI) and the goal of seamlessly integrating robots to live in harmony with humans is under exploration, with robots designed to reflect human appearance, mannerisms, and motions [6]. The resulting technological challenges include improving our understanding of human-human social interactions as well as human-machine interactions. An examination of our own social interaction can be used as a calibration technique for understanding perception and objective responses to technologies like autonomous robots [10]. Advanced Brain Monitoring, Inc. (ABM), located in Carlsbad, California is a neurophysiologic research company, which, in collaboration with Lowe's Innovation Lab (LIL), Neurons Inc., and Fellow Robots has completed three phases of a Human-Robot Interaction study. Our initial intent for the study design was to explore how humans may respond to different personalities in robot assistants to understand at what level humans experience an eerie–or uncomfortable feeling when interacting with robots, known as the "Uncanny Valley" [11]. We concluded that it would be most beneficial to use somewhat extreme examples from the human-likeness spectrum; one personality that was not human like, and one that exhibited human friendliness, humor, and empathy. A collaborative project between Fellow Robots, a robotics company based out of Silicon Valley, CA, and LIL, had previously created an assistive retail robot named OSHbot. Although OSHbot has no physical resemblance to a human, it was used in the current study to interact with human participants because of its programmability and ease of use. However, noting this, many studies have shown that there are cortical response trends to non-visual components of interaction, which is why this method was employed for this study [12]. OSHbot is also equipped with 2 large touch screen interfaces that a human can use to interact with OSHbot; providing one more level of normality in the sense of communication.

In conjunction with using ABM's B-Alert® X10 wireless sensor headset for EEG and ECG recording, our study incorporated focal attention assessment using the Tobii mobile eye-tracker during several tasks performed by participants with human and robot assistance in an Orchard Supply Hardware store in San Jose, CA. Neurons Inc., an applied neuroscience company based in Holbaek, Denmark, that focuses on neurological responses from consumer-based studies for marketing research. EEG and eye-tracking were integrated to characterize participants focal attention and assess the neural signatures associated with key events and interactions [13]. Data were analyzed by events to explore the neural responses to each of the multiple instances of recorded human-human and human-robot interactions.

In exploring neurophysiological correlates of social interactions, previous work has shown that slow theta (3–5 Hz) suppression has been linked to the "uncanny valley" response of humans towards androids and robots [14]. Furthermore, mu suppression (calculated from log ratios of power spectral densities (PSDs) across central sites C3, Cz, and C4 from 8 to 13 Hz bins of the participant's experimental and baseline tasks) has been shown to be linked to the activation of the brain's mirror neurons and empathy responses in human-to-human interactions [15–17]. Additionally, midline theta (calculated by summarizing PSDs from 3 to 7 Hz bins across sites Fz, Cz, Pz, and POz) activity has been shown to be associated with encoding into, and retrieval from, long term memory, visual stimuli matching, long term episodic memories, sustained or concentrated attention, visual working memory, positive emotions, and decreased levels of anxiety [17–19]. These neurophysiological and behavioral indices associated with human-robot interactions can uncover aspects of social experiences to help shape the design and function of future robots.

2 Methods

2.1 Participants

A total of N = 34 participants comprised of 47% male with an age range of 34–55 were tested. Participants were recruited by LIL through a partnered external firm database, whereby regular Orchard Supply Hardware (OSH) shoppers, upon meeting pre-screening criteria (available upon request), were asked to participate in a study to assess and better understand how they reacted to, and interacted with, products offered in the store. The robot interaction was not disclosed to the participants prior to the study to allow for unbiased demeanor towards the tasks and the robot (OSHbot; see Fig. 1A). Participants were compensated for their participation with a $100 gift certificate to OSH.

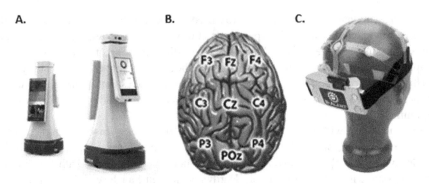

Fig. 1. Study equipment: (A) OSHbot; (B) EEG recording sites; (C) B-Alert® X10 headset

2.2   Equipment

Psychophysiology. EEG and ECG were acquired simultaneously and in synchrony throughout the study tasks, using the B-Alert® X10 wireless sensor headset (Advanced Brain Monitoring, Inc., Carlsbad, CA). This system has 9 referential EEG channels located according to the International 10–20 system at Fz, F3, F4, Cz, C3, C4, POz, P3, and P4 and an auxiliary channel for ECG (Fig. 1B/C). Linked reference electrodes were located behind each ear on the mastoid bone. Impedances were recorded below 40 kΩ for all sites before recording began. ECG electrodes were placed on the right and left clavicles. Data were sampled at 256 Hz with a high pass at 0.1 Hz and a fifth order, low pass filter at 100 Hz, obtained digitally with A/D converters. Data were transmitted wirelessly via Bluetooth to the computer, where acquisition software then stored the psychophysiological data. The ABM's proprietary acquisition software also included artifact decontamination algorithms for eye blink, muscle movement, and environmental/electrical interference such as spikes and saturations.

Tobii Pro 2 Eye Tracking Glasses. Tobii's Pro Glasses 2 is equipped with two cameras for each eye that use a proprietary 3D eye model, full-HD scene camera for wide field view for accuracy and precision with minimized gaze data loss. The embedded accelerometer and gyroscope sensors allowed for differentiation between head and eye movements which eliminated the impact of head movements on eye tracking data. Eyes were tracked using corneal reflection of dark pupils with a 50 Hz sampling rate. After the eye tracking glasses were situated on the participant, they were calibrated using the eye tracking software and further calibration was automated throughout duration of use.

OSHbot. Fellow Robots, in previous collaboration with LIL, created an assistive robot enabled with the capacity of helping consumers in real-life OSH stores. It uses 2 LiDARs, a device that uses a combination of "light" and "radar" which also stands for Light Detection and Ranging (1x 3D LiDAR and 1x 2D LiDAR), and 2 IR-based 3D depth sensors to maneuver around the store, and simultaneously localize its position (SLAM) so that it safely avoids obstacles/people. OSHbot is programmed with the specific store information so that navigation and product information are accurate when it assists shoppers. Participants were able to interact with OSHbot via 2 touch screen interfaces, a microphone and speakers (see Fig. 1A).

2.3 Procedure

Benchmark Testing. ABM's B-Alert® X-10 EEG headset (See Fig. 1C) was applied and participants completed the ABM benchmark neurocognitive tasks: 3-Choice Vigilance Task (3CVT), Verbal Psycho-Vigilance Task (VPVT), and Auditory Psycho-Vigilance Task (APVT), to individualize the model to support classification and quantification of engagement and workload. The three-choice active vigilance task (3CVT) is a 5-min long task that requires participants to discriminate one target (70% occurrence) from two non-target (30% occurrence) geometric shapes. Each stimulus was presented for a duration of 200 ms. Participants were instructed to respond as quickly as possible to each stimulus by selecting the left arrow for target stimuli and the right arrow for non-target stimuli. A training period was provided prior to the beginning of the task in order to minimize practice effects. The VPVT and APVT tasks are passive vigilance tasks that lasted 5 min each. The VPVT repeatedly presented a 10-cm circular target image for a duration of 200 ms. The target image was presented every 2 s in the center of the computer monitor, requiring the participant to respond to image onset by pressing the spacebar. The APVT consisted of an auditory tone that was played every 2 s, requiring the participant to respond to auditory onset by pressing the spacebar. The Tobii mobile eye-tracker was then applied, and calibrated to use in tandem with the EEG headset to assess focal responses to the robot interaction during the in-store tasks.

In-Store Tasks. Participants were randomly selected into two groups: Group 1 interacted with OSHbot which responded with the participants in a neutral, factual, and robotic tone; Group 2 interacted with OSHbot which represented some human characteristics- humorous, social, and empathetic (a script of these programmed speeches is available upon request). The participants were instructed to follow the printed instruction cards that were given to them once they reached the designated starting area. They were asked not to read the consequential task until the technician instructed them to do so. Each participant was given the same scenario and tasks for in-store shopping and, depending upon the task, they were to ask either a robot or human for assistance. The scenario: participants were told that they were working on a kitchen remodel, specifically painting, and they would be shopping for items that would help them complete their remodel. The shopping list is as follows: (1) paint; (2) sponge for textural paint application; (3) screwdriver; and (4) vent covers. A game of bean bag toss was used as a distractor task between task 3 and 4 in order to obtain repeated measures of human-robot interaction in a short time frame, without asking the participant to return a second time [20]. The participant was lead to a different area of the store to play the game. Throughout the tasks, OSHbot was programmed to speak from a script specific to the group participants were assigned. OSHbot was pre-programmed before each in-store data acquisition to follow the same script outline, but depending on the group and participant information, presentation differed.

Unbeknownst to all participants, OSHbot was programmed with details about the person that we intended to elicit an unexpected response. We intended for the participants to experience something outside their perception of what a robot could do/know, specifically, knowing somewhat personal things about the participant (e.g. how frequently they shop at OSH, if they own/rent a house/apartment, their latest renovation project, future projects, and the number of people in their households). These participant-specific details were recorded prior to the in-store tasks during the pre-test questionnaire, or upon arrival.

Analysis and Statistics. All analyses were conducted using the B-Alert® LabX software. Data quality check and decontamination algorithms were used to identify and remove epochs contaminated by electromyography (EMG), signal excursions, or other environmental noise. Once the signals were decontaminated, the EEG data was converted from the time domain to the frequency domain. The absolute and relative power spectral densities (PSDs) were calculated for each 1 s epoch (1–60 Hz bins) for standard EEG bandwidths (delta, theta, alpha, sigma, beta, gamma, and high gamma). PSDs were summarized over the frontal, central, parietal, anterior, temporal, and left/right (asymmetric) brain region. Participant data was excluded due to poor data quality because of the intrinsic EMG signals caused by walking within each task ($N = 6$), unlogged events within trials ($N = 4$), and inability to process data ($N = 2$). The resulting analyses encompass the remaining $N = 22$ participants' data.

3 Results

3.1 Interaction Type

To investigate how interaction type effects psychophysiological indices, several one-way ANOVAs were conducted with Tukey adjustments made for multiple comparisons with the goal of establishing how a human interacting with another human differed at a biological level from a human interacting with a robot agent. We revealed that there was greater suppression of slow wave (3–5 Hz) theta, as calculated from subtracting the antilog epoch-by-epoch PSD Bandwidth value of the OSHbot task from the averaged antilog PSD Bandwidth value of the APVT task, in the frontal, midline, and parietal regions during human-human interactions: $F(1, 21) = 9.80$, $p = 0.003$; $F(1, 21) = 9.49$, $p = 0.004$; and $F(1, 21) = 7.89$, $p = 0.008$ respectively. Specifically, slow wave theta activity was lower when a human interacted with another human, as opposed to interaction with a robot. This agrees with recent work that has shown humans experiencing heightened frontal theta activity upon observation of a robot [14].

This may indicate that theta activity is indicative of bridging the gap(s) of common semantics and visual recall between conversing with a robot than with a human. Another ANOVA indicated that the mu bandwidth (8 to 13 Hz EEG power recorded over the sensorimotor region) was higher for human-human relations (M = 3.40, SD = 0.52) than in human to robot (M = 3.09, SD = 0.31); $F(1, 21) = 5.76$, $p = 0.02$. These data are reported in Table 1 and graphically represented in Fig. 2. As mu suppression has not been shown to change much based on agent type upon observation [14], our results showing increased mu activity while meeting with another human

Table 1. One way ANOVA – interaction type

Metric	Correlate	Condition	x̄ (Hz)	σ² (Hz)	F	df	P
PSD Bandwidth	Frontal slow theta (3–5 Hz); Sup	H	0.83	0.42	9.80	1, 22	0.003
		R	0.50	0.24			
	Midline slow theta (3–5 Hz); Sup	H	0.87	0.41	9.49	1, 22	0.004
		R	0.55	0.24			
	Parietal slow theta (3–5 Hz); Sup	H	0.98	0.43	7.89	1, 22	0.008
		R	0.65	0.33			
	Mu alpha (8–13 Hz)	H	3.40	0.52	5.76	1, 22	0.021
		R	3.09	0.31			

Sup = Suppression; x̄ = mean; σ² = standard deviation H = Human interaction with Human; R = Human interaction with Robot

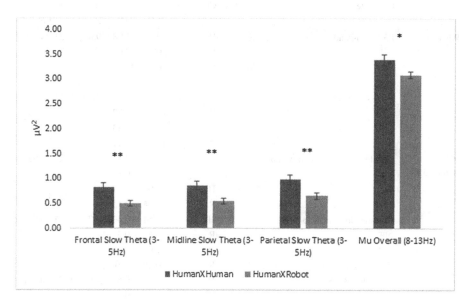

Fig. 2. ANOVA results of Interaction type (*p < 0.05; **p < 0.01); Error bars represent the standard error from mean (SEM).

could suggest a sensory-motor mechanism reflecting preparation for engagement with a like-being. Prior work has linked this EEG correlate to empathetic state change, active concentration, as well as motor imagery and visual activation [17, 21]. These findings prompted an exploration of how such metrics may vary as a function of age and gender.

3.2 Gender Differences

Additional analyses were conducted to assess how neurophysiological metrics varied across gender identity (Females - N = 12; Males - N = 10) based on interaction type.

Several unbalanced 2-way ANOVAs were conducted with Tukey adjustments made for multiple comparisons. No PSD bandwidth, nor ECG, differences amongst gender groups were found, however, upon further exploration of the metrics, significant variances in EEG wavelets were revealed. EEG PSD bandwidths are composed of frequency subbands which use statistical coefficients called wavelets [22, 23]. With this, we unveiled statistically significant wavelets comprised of the theta and gamma frequencies within the Parietal region: $F(1, 21) = 9.04$, $p = 0.019$ and $F(1, 21) = 4.70$, $p = 0.037$, respectively. This could mean that throughout the tasks, an increase in mental task load occurred, especially when participants anticipated decision making from the other interacting agent, as found in other studies [24, 25]. Previous studies reported increases in theta activity may indicate an activation of the superior temporal

Table 2. Two way ANOVA – indentity type X interaction

Metric	Correlate	Identity	Condition	$\bar{x}$ (Hz)	σ^2 (Hz)	Interaction F	df	P
Wavelets	P3 θ-sub-band	F	H	79.52	31.98	9.04	1, 21	0.019
			R	30.12	7.65			
		M	H	36.38	24.79			
			R	23.09	9.68			
	P4 γ-sub-band	F	H	37.75	16.08	4.70	1, 21	0.037
			R	14.59	7.32			
		M	H	15.77	8.33			
			R	11.03	4.11			
PSD Bandwidths	Cz Slow theta (3–5 Hz); Sup	1	H	0.65	0.35	4.57	1, 21	0.039
			R	0.66	0.33			
		2	H	1.04	0.35			
			R	0.64	0.15			
	Midline slow theta (3–5 Hz); Sup	1	H	0.54	0.40	4.78	1, 21	0.035
			R	0.50	0.27			
		2	H	1.06	0.36			
			R	0.66	0.16			
	Cz alpha (8–13 Hz)	1	H	3.83	0.59	4.97	1, 21	0.032
			R	3.04	0.35			
		2	H	3.49	0.25			
			R	3.16	0.20			
	Mu alpha (8–13 Hz)	1	H	2.79	0.65	6.30	1, 21	0.017
			R	3.03	0.36			
		2	H	3.52	0.29			
			R	3.20	0.21			
	Hemispheric frontal Alpha (8-13 Hz)	1	H	3.17	0.61	4.60	1, 21	0.039
			R	3.34	0.40			
		2	H	3.65	0.30			
			R	3.32	0.21			

θ = 4–8 Hz; γ = 32–64 Hz; Sup = Suppression; $\bar{x}$ = Mean; σ^2 = Standard Deviation
F = Female; M = Male; 1 = Age < 40; 2 = Age > 40;
H = Human × Human Interaction; R = Human × Robot Interaction

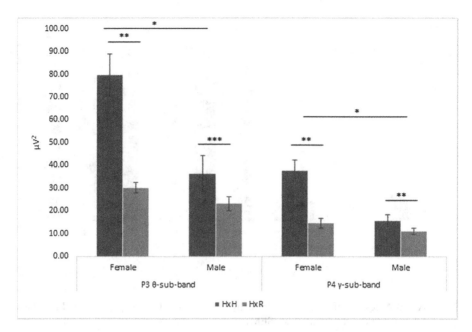

Fig. 3. ANOVA results of Interaction type by Gender (∗p < 0.05; ∗∗p < 0.01; ∗∗∗p < 0.001); Error bars represent the standard error from mean (SEM)

sulcus (STS), which has been linked to observation of biological kinematics and social cognitive tasks [26, 27]. Our findings are consistent with other reports in that comparing brain activity between organic and inorganic motion or interaction results in stronger STS activation [26]. These data are shown in Table 2 and represented in Fig. 3.

3.3 Age Differences

Like the gender analyses, further statistics were conducted to examine age-related differences in human-human and human-robot interaction using two brackets: below age 45 (n = 12) and over age 45 (n = 10). This analysis yielded significant differences in greater Cz and midline slow theta suppression within the older cohort between human-human interaction and human-robot interaction: $F(1, 21) = 4.57, p = 0.039$ and $F(1, 21) = 4.78, p = 0.035$, respectively. This suggests that theta cortical responses may be age-mediated and that perhaps younger individuals may find it easier discerning visual and social context between varying interactions. This seems plausible in the sense that those who are younger have likely been exposed to this high level of technological integration for longer, and at critical developmental periods, than those from older generations–making the interaction with a robot less of a cognitive demanding task. Furthermore, through this analysis, we also exposed differences in Cz, mu, and hemispheric (F3–F4) frontal alpha. Namely, we observed higher Cz alpha for the younger cohort; $F(1, 21) = 4.97, p = 0.032$, and higher mu and hemispheric frontal

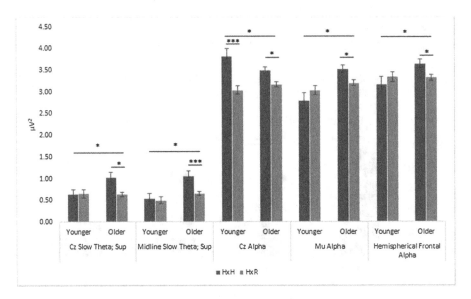

Fig. 4. ANOVA results of Interaction Type by Age (∗p < 0.05; ∗∗∗p < 0.001); Error bars represent the standard error from mean (SEM)

alpha for the older cohort; $F(1, 21) = 6.30$, $p = 0.017$ and $F(1, 21) = 4.60$, $p = 0.039$ respectively. These data are presented in Table 2 and represented in Fig. 4. General findings suggest that theta activity may indicate differentiation and recognition of movement and appearance between biological and non-biological agents as well as semantic and memory related aspects thereof. Previous studies found greater theta activity of robot observation when compared to android and human observation [14]. We suspect that both cohorts experienced an increase in processing load during their interactions with OSHbot when compared to human-human interactions because interacting with the robot was intrinsically more difficult than interacting with a more biological agent. Yet, when comparing the younger to older cohort, the latter had more theta suppression, suggesting they may have found the interaction more challenging than those that most likely had more exposure to similar technologies. Recent HCI research has found that ease of usability may be causing an increase in reluctance from older adults towards using and adapting to new technologies [28]. A natural decline in physical, perceptual, and cognitive ability could also affect an older cohort's performance when interacting with technology and interpretation of device use [28]. We suspect that the observed differences across these cohorts may be reflective of the reluctance to interact with OSHbot due to a lack of familiarity with robots (Fig. 4).

4 Conclusions

These neurophysiological indices associated with human-human interactions and human-robot interactions across gender and age could be tapping into aspects of social experiences which may potentially help shape the physical design and automation of future robots. We decided to focus our analysis efforts on results showing higher levels of frontal slow theta, and overall mu activity between different age cohorts and genders because these significant findings were similar to the results of previous studies with human-robot and human social interactions and could help substantiate current research used to better autonomous technologies. We conclude from this dataset that social interactions between humans and robots do indeed result in different temporal changes in neural responses, which can be attributed to the gender and age of the individual. Furthermore, we suggest these observed changes highlight important aspects of human emotion and cognition during social interactions with humans and robots during a real-world shopping experience.

Future analyses of this data are planned in hopes of revealing further, unique aspects of robots and human social encounters. As we see that gender and age greatly impact neurophysiology during these interactions, we also propose that an expansion of this study be conducted whereby the appearance and vocal features of the robot are varied to more closely align with different gender and age groups. This future work has the propensity to establish how individuals perceive a robot when the autonomous machine is programmed to elicit a greater sense of familiarity and comfort within an interaction. In incorporating an analysis of EEG data in conjunction with eye-tracking data, we also hope to view specific metrics in real time providing an opportunity for adaptation of the robot behaviors based on the neural responses of the human during an encounter. Thus, assistive agents will be more capable of characterizing features of social meetings that can create a more seamless relationship between humans and machine.

5 Funding

The work presented herein was supported by DARPA Contract No. W31P4Q-12-C-0200 issued by U.S. Army Contracting Command. The views expressed are those of the author and do not reflect the official policy or position of the DoD or the U.S. Government.

Acknowledgements. We would like to extend a heartfelt thank you to our collaborators, Fellow Robots, Neurons Inc., Lowe's Innovation Lab, as well as the participants in this study, and the OSH store assistants.

References

1. Maynard, D.W., Peräkylä, A.: Language and social interaction. In: Delamater, J. (ed.) Handbook of Social Psychology, pp. 233–257. Springer, New York (2006)
2. Kendon, A.: Movement coordination in social interaction: some examples described. Acta Psychol. **32**, 101–125 (1970)
3. Girges, C., et al.: Event-related alpha suppression in response to facial motion. PLoS ONE **9**(2), e89382 (2014)
4. Chartrand, T.L., Bargh, J.A.: The chameleon effect: the perception–behavior link and social interaction. J. Pers. Soc. Psychol. **76**(6), 893 (1999)

5. Molm, L.D., Takahashi, N., Peterson, G.: Risk and trust in social exchange: an experimental test of a classical proposition. Am. J. Sociol. **105**(5), 1396–1427 (2000)
6. Hari, R., et al.: Centrality of social interaction in human brain function. Neuron **88**(1), 181–193 (2015)
7. Nielsen, The Total Audience Report: Q1 2015. (2015)
8. Erdt, T., Moravec, H.: Mind Children. The Future of Robot and Human Intelligence. Harvard University Press, Cambridge (1989). JSTOR
9. Woods, D.D., et al.: Envisioning human robot coordination in future operations. IEEE Trans. Syst. Man Cybern. Part C (Appli. Rev.) **34**(2), 210–218 (2004)
10. Breazeal, C.: Social interactions in HRI: the robot view. IEEE Trans. Syst. Man Cybern. Part C (Appl. Rev.) **34**(2), 181–186 (2004)
11. Geller, T.: Overcoming the uncanny valley. IEEE Comput. Graph. Appl. **28**(4), 11–17 (2008)
12. Tracy, K., Haspel, K.: Language and social interaction: its institutional identity, intellectual landscape, and discipline-shifting agenda. J. Commun. **54**(4), 788–816 (2004)
13. AH Do, P.W., King, C.E., Abiri, A., Nenadic, Z.: Brain-computer interface controlled functional electrical stimulation system for ankle movement. J. Neuroengineering Rehabil. **8**(1), 49
14. Urgen, B.A., et al.: EEG theta and Mu oscillations during perception of human and robot actions. Front. Neurorobotics **7**, 19 (2013)
15. Oberman, L.M., Pineda, J.A., Ramachandran, V.S.: The human mirror neuron system: a link between action observation and social skills. Soc. Cogn. Affect. Neurosci. **2**(1), 62–66 (2007)
16. Singh, F., Pineda, J., Cadenhead, K.S.: Association of impaired EEG mu wave suppression, negative symptoms and social functioning in biological motion processing in first episode of psychosis. Schizophr. Res. **130**(1), 182–186 (2011)
17. Correa, K.A., et al.: Characterizing donation behavior from psychophysiological indices of narrative experience. Front. Neurosci. **9**, 1–20 (2015)
18. Inanaga, K.: Frontal midline theta rhythm and mental activity. Psychiatry Clin. Neurosci. **52**(6), 555–566 (1998)
19. Aftanas, L., Golocheikine, S.: Human anterior and frontal midline theta and lower alpha reflect emotionally positive state and internalized attention: high-resolution EEG investigation of meditation. Neurosci. Lett. **310**(1), 57–60 (2001)
20. Trask, P.C., Sigmon, S.T.: Ruminating and distracting: the effects of sequential tasks on depressed mood. Cogn. Ther. Res. **23**(3), 231–246 (1999)
21. Ubeda, A., et al.: Classification method for BCIs based on the correlation of EEG maps. Neurocomputing **114**, 98–106 (2013)
22. Subasi, A.: Automatic recognition of alertness level from EEG by using neural network and wavelet coefficients. Expert Syst. Appl. **28**(4), 701–711 (2005)
23. Subasi, A.: EEG signal classification using wavelet feature extraction and a mixture of expert model. Expert Syst. Appl. **32**(4), 1084–1093 (2007)
24. Smith, M.E., et al.: Monitoring task loading with multivariate EEG measures during complex forms of human-computer interaction. Hum. Factors J. Hum. Factors Ergon. Soc. **43**(3), 366–380 (2001)
25. Dumas, G., et al.: Inter-brain synchronization during social interaction. PLoS ONE **5**(8), e12166 (2010)
26. Rutherford, M., Kuhlmeier, V.A.: Social Perception: Detection and Interpretation of Animacy, Agency, and Intention. MIT Press, Cambridge (2013)
27. Furl, N., et al.: Cross-frequency power coupling between hierarchically organized face-selective areas. Cerebral Cortex, p. bht097 (2013)
28. Leung, R., McGrenere, J., Graf, P.: Age-related differences in the initial usability of mobile device icons. Behav. Inf. Technol. **30**(5), 629–642 (2011)

Study on the Influence of Drivers' Physiological Characteristics of Urban Bus Stop

Fengyuan Wang, Xiaoting Chen[✉], Gang Sun, and Xing Liang

Qingdao University of Technology, Qingdao 266520, China
122290913@qq.com

Abstract. Bus driver is the only operator of bus, and bus stop is a driving stage in which bus differs from other social vehicles. In this paper, bus driver's physiological characteristics in the process of bus stop-and-go were studied which were analyzed by theoretical analysis, comparison and significant difference analysis to obtain the changes of drivers' physiological and psychological characteristics and to provide the guide basis for drivers' fatigue and driving safety analysis. The real vehicle test was designed and put into effect, and the bus drivers' physical data were obtained by using physiological tester. Then the comparison analysis of bus drivers' physiological data such as BSA and HRV between the real vehicle test and the natural state was carried out. The results showed that there were significant differences in the changes of BSA and HRV between the real vehicle test and the natural state. When the driver was under natural state the characterization parameters of BSA were merely fluctuating with time. The stable value of ECG, dz/dt and GSC was around 0.35 V, 0.3 Ω and 0.018 V respectively and changed very little. The characterization parameters of HRV changed little. Heart rate stabilized at 70 beats/min and breathing rate stabilized at 17.5 times/min; when the vehicle decelerated into station, driver's ECG declined from 0.4 V to 0.25 V, and dz/dt increased from 0 Ω to 3.5 Ω, at the same time, heart rate rose to 98 beats/min, which had significantly fluctuations comparing with the natural state; when the vehicle stopped, driver's ECG of the driver increased from 0.3 V to 0.5 V, the dz/dt declined from 0.5 Ω to 0.35 Ω, and the respiration rate also reduced to 14.7 times/min, which had significantly fluctuations comparing with the natural state; When the vehicle accelerated to bus stop, the dz/dt increased from 0.3 Ω to 0.41 Ω. The change threshold of GSC was 0.09 V, which was much higher than the stable value under natural state, and then GSC decreased to 0.17 V.

The experimental consequences indicated that the driver would be more sensitive in the process of bus stop-and-go than in the natural state, due to the external environment (platform setting, traffic flow, etc.) influences. The changes of electrical conductivity of the skin were caused by psychological changes; In addition, with the stimulus increased, HR and RSA were increased, on the contrary, the Resp Rate decreased. At the same time, the paired samples T-test method was used to test the mean value, the maximum value and the root mean square of the parameters of the driver's physiological characteristics under the natural state and real vehicle test of the import and export conditions. The results showed that there were significant differences in the physiological characteristics, with the exception of the minimum of dz/dt.

© Springer International Publishing AG 2017
C. Stephanidis (Ed.): HCII Posters 2017, Part I, CCIS 713, pp. 263–272, 2017.
DOI: 10.1007/978-3-319-58750-9_37

It could be seen from the experiment that reasonable station environment settings were conducive to improving drivers' physiological state, reducing the driving fatigue and providing a safer driving.

Keywords: Urban bus · Traffic environment · Station environment setting · Bus driver · Physiological characteristics

1 Introduction

With the development of urbanization and motorization, the role of urban public transport in the transportation system has been continuously improved, and the safety of travel has become very important. According to statistics, 90% to 95% traffic accidents due to the driver factors [1]. As the only manipulator in the process of driving, bus driver has always been concerned about the physiological, psychological and driving behavior [2].

Collet [3] tested the psychological workload of bus driver, and tested their electric index by the degree of the bus automation system. The results showed that as the workload was reduced, the workload of the driver was reduced; Southeast University Tang Dengke found the road alignment and road traffic physiological psychological needs of the inherent relationship and law through road driving test. According to the change of heart rate in different driving conditions, the vehicle speed model was established by combining the relationship between vehicle speed and heart rate, and the corresponding recommended speed limit was obtained [4]. According to Li Xiansheng, the driver's behavior mechanism was established according to the theory of human behavior error analysis of the driving behavior of the various physiological states of the driver, and the driver's physiological state caused by a variety of driving behavior errors [5]. At present, the study of driver physiology at home and abroad mostly focused on the relationship between road alignment, highway linearity and driver physiology, and the research on the physiology of bus drivers was less.

This paper analyzed the physiological data of bus drivers by theoretical analysis and statistical analysis, and compared the physiological characteristics of drivers under natural state and real vehicle test. The psychological characteristics changing laws in different driving stages were made into analysis and comparisons, which could help to improve the driver's physiological state, reduce driving fatigue, improve driving safety.

2 General Design of Bus Driver Test

2.1 The Composition of the Test Platform

The real vehicle test platform included the test vehicle and the test instrument, as shown in Fig. 1. The physiological characteristic data BSA and HRV of the bus driver were collected by using the BioLAB channel physiological recorder from Mind Ware Company, USA, as shown in Fig. 2.

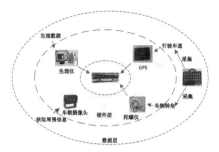

Fig. 1. Real vehicle experiment platform

Fig. 2. Driver factors in data acquisition systems BioLAB

2.2 The Selection of Test Personnel

The 15 road vehicles with high accident rate were selected as test vehicles. The test was supported by Qingdao Zhenqing Bus Co., Ltd., which provided 25 bus drivers with different ages and driving ages. The information of the tested persons was shown in Table 1.

Table 1. Basic information of all subjects

Tester	Age		Driving age		Accumulated mileage	
	Range	27–40	Range	0.5–15	Range	10–105
25 professional bus driver	Mean	31.04	Mean	5.68	Mean	39.76
	Standard deviation	3.57	Standard deviation	3.79	Standard deviation	26.52

2.3 The Actual Vehicle Test Process

According to the test purpose and precautions, the test was designed in good process. The time recording and staff division work should be done to ensure the accuracy of data collection. Test flow chart is shown in Fig. 3.

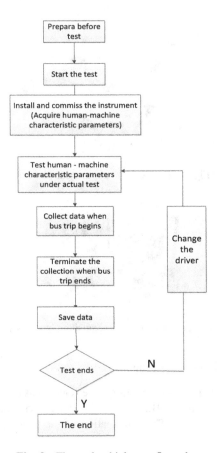

Fig. 3. The real vehicle test flow chart

3   Driver Physiological Characteristics of Data Analysis

The basic signals (BSA), heart rate variability (HRV), cardiac impedance (IMP), skin electrical activity (GSC), and EMG could be made into analysis by the BioLAB. In this paper, we focused on basic signal (BSA) and heart rate variability (HRV).

3.1   BSA Analysis

There were four channels in BSA analysis, including ECG, impedance Z0, derivative dz/dt and skin electrical GSC. In this paper, the changes of BSA physiological characteristics of driver in natural state and real vehicle test were analyzed respectively, and then the difference of BSA in different working conditions was found.

(1)   Driver's BSA basic laws in natural state
Figure 4(a)–(d) showed the physiological data of drivers entering and leaving harbor stations in natural state. The test time was 30 s. In the figure, the horizontal

axis represented time and the vertical axis represented amplitude. It could be seen that ECG, impedance Z0, derivative dz/dt and skin electricity GSC were in a stable state, with no significant fluctuations.

(2) Driver's BSA basic laws in real vehicle test

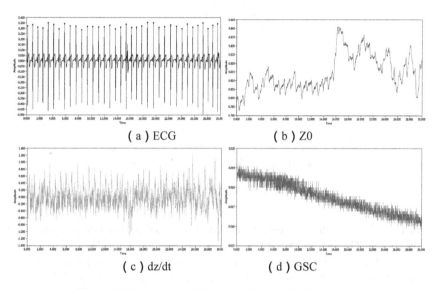

(a) ECG   (b) Z0

(c) dz/dt   (d) GSC

Fig. 4. The bus driver BSA data under standard conditions

The physiological data under the actual road environment were shown in Fig. 5. In Fig. 5(a), at 1530 s, 1544 s, 1557 s, the driver's ECG amplitude fluctuation significantly increased. According to the actual vehicle test records, this three time points corresponded to slowing down, stopping and accelerating outbound stages. It could be seen from Fig. 5(b) and (c) that Z0 fluctuated obviously at 1530 s, 1537 s, 1544 s, and dz/dt also showed three large amplitudes. Indicating that in these three time points, the driver accepted the external stimulus, and would take some controlling. Figure 5(d) showed driver's skin test results, corresponding to the driver turning the steering wheel size. It could be seen that in 1537 s, GSC curve decreased significantly, indicating that the driver turned the steering wheel into the station; in 1557 s, GSC curve increased significantly, indicating that the driver began to turn the steering wheel outbound.

(3) Comparison of driver's BSA basic laws between the natural state and real vehicle test.

When the driver drove in the natural state, the characterization parameters of BSA were only fluctuating with time, and the stable values of ECG, dz/dt and GSC were around 0.35 V, 0.3 Ω and 0.018 V respectively. The ECG of driver decreased from 0.4 V to 0.25 V, the dz/dt derivative increased from 0 Ω to 3.5 Ω, and the fluctuation of the vehicle was significantly enhanced compared with that

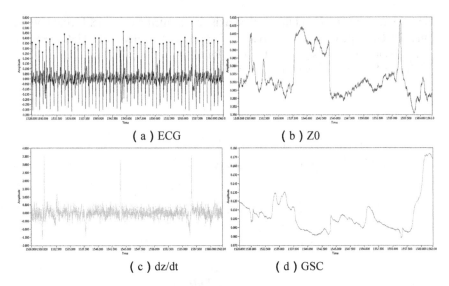

(a) ECG   (b) Z0

(c) dz/dt   (d) GSC

Fig. 5. Real vehicle test driver BSA data

of the vehicle in the real vehicle test condition. During the braking process, the driver's ECG increased from 0.3 V to 0.5 V, and the dz/dt derivative decreased from 0.5 Ω to 0.35 Ω, which was significantly different from the steady state value in natural state. During the acceleration of the vehicle, the dz/dt arose to 0.41 Ω and the starting point for GSC changes was 0.09 V, which was much higher than that in natural state, and then GSC dropped to 0.17 V with significant fluctuations.

Test results indicated that the driver would be more sensitive under real vehicle conditions than that in the natural state. There were significant increasing by the psychological changes in skin electrical conductivity changes, which resulting in the driver's ECG, dz/dt and GSC fluctuations.

The mean, maximum, minimum, and root mean square values of the 22 test drivers' BSA data were discussed in this paper.

(1) Comparison of ECG distribution laws
     In order to obtain the distribution laws of driver's physiological data in the process of entering and leaving the bus station, the data were analyzed according to the theory of mathematical statistics, and the result was described by box diagram. As shown in Fig. 6, there was no significant difference between the mean and RMS of ECG data, and the maximum and minimum in real vehicle test data were higher than that in natural state.

(2) Comparison of Z0 distribution laws
     As shown in Fig. 7, the Z0 means, maximum, minimum, and RMS data in the natural state were 0.4 higher than those in real vehicle test, which indicated that physiological indicators of cardiac impedance Z0 was subjected to interference and stimulation in natural state with small values.

(3) Comparison of dz/dt distribution laws

As shown in Fig. 8, there was no significant difference between the mean and RMS of dz/dt data, and the maximum and minimum values in real vehicle state were higher than that in natural state.

(4) Comparison of GSC distribution laws

As shown in Fig. 9, there was no significant difference between the mean and RMS of GSC data. The maximum and minimum values of the actual vehicle test data in real vehicle state were higher than that in natural state.

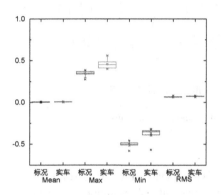

Fig. 6. ECG comparative distribution

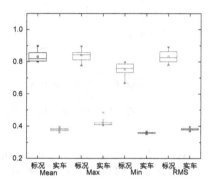

Fig. 7. Z0 comparative distribution

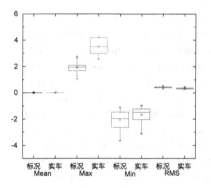

Fig. 8. dz/dt comparative distribution

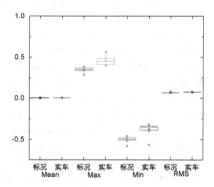

Fig. 9. GSC comparative distribution

3.2 HRV Basic Law Analysis

The HRV analysis window showed six graphs: ECG, heartbeat interval, cardiac cycle time series, heart rate power spectrum, respiratory time series and respiratory power spectrum. In this paper, the changes of the physiological characteristics of the driver's HRV in natural state and in real vehicle test were analyzed respectively, and then the differences were analyzed under different working conditions.

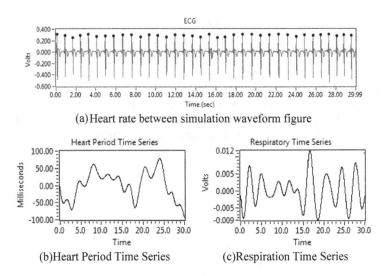

(a) Heart rate between simulation waveform figure

(b) Heart Period Time Series   (c) Respiration Time Series

Fig. 10. The bus driver HRV data standard conditions

(1) Driver's HRV basic laws in natural state
The HRV data of bus driver in natural state was shown in Fig. 10(a)–(c). It could be seen that the heartbeat frequency, heartbeat interval and respiratory rate were in a steady state without significant fluctuation in natural state.

(2) Driver's HRV basic laws in real vehicle state
The physical data of bus drivers in real vehicle test were shown in Fig. 11. From Fig. 11(a) the heartbeat between the analog waveform, it could be seen that in the 374 s, 387 s, 401 s, the driver's heart rate fluctuations significantly increased. According to bus records, this three time points corresponded to the slowdown stopping, braking and accelerating outbound stages. From Fig. 11(b) and (c), it could be seen that in the same points, intermittent intervals and breathing signals were significant fluctuations in the signal, indicating that the driver accepted the external stimuli and would take some actions at this time. The above analysis showed that when driver was in the inbound and outbound process under real vehicle test, they due to the stimulation of the external environment, and then, the physiological characteristics of HRV data would have a greater volatility.

(3) Comparison of driver's HRV basic law in natural state and real vehicle state
When the driver drove in natural state, the characterization parameters of HRV remained constant with time, and the stable value of heartbeat fluctuation frequency was 7 times in 5 s. In real vehicle test, during the process of vehicle deceleration, the heart rate increased from 0.2 to 0.4 times and the respiratory rate increased from 0.01 to 0.021 times, up and down fluctuations than the natural state significantly enhanced; in braking process, the driver's heartbeat frequency fluctuations decreased from 0.35 times to 0.15 times, and respiratory rate decreased from 0.025 times to 0.011 times, which was significantly different

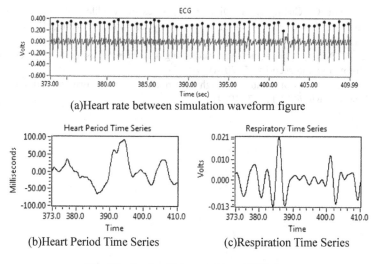

(a)Heart rate between simulation waveform figure

(b)Heart Period Time Series

(c)Respiration Time Series

Fig. 11. Real vehicle test driver HRV data

from those in natural state; in acceleration process, the heartbeat interval decreased to −50, which was much lower than the stable fluctuations value in natural state. The results showed that when the driver was in real vehicle test, their alertness would be significantly increased than in natural state, and the heart rate, respiratory rate and other physiological characteristics would fluctuate significantly.

4   Conclusion

By comparing the BSA and HRV physiological characteristics of bus drivers in natural state and real vehicle test, it could be concluded that the characterization parameters of BSA and HRV varied with little fluctuation when drivers drove in natural state; in real vehicle test, due to the external environment (platform set form, traffic flow and other traffic conditions), the driver's alertness would increased significantly than in natural state, and the physiological characteristics of BSA and HRV of driver were obviously fluctuated during deceleration, braking and acceleration.

References

1. Treat, J.R.: A study of precrash factors involved in traffic accidents. HSRI Res. Rev. **10**(6), 1–35 (1980)
2. Kim, S.Y., Choi, H.C., Won, W.J., Oh, S.Y.: Driving environment assessment using fusion of in- and out-of vision systems. Int. J. Autom. Technol. **10**(1), 103–113 (2009)

3. Collet, C., Petit, C., Champely, S., Dittmar, A.: Assessing workload through physiological measurements in bus drivers using an automated system during docking. Hum. Factors **4**, 539–548 (2003)
4. Jin, L., Li, K., Niu, Q.: A new method for detecting driver fatigue using steering performance: traffic information and security, **5** (2014)
5. Solomn, D.: Accidents on main rural highways related to speed, drivers, and vehicle. Bur. Public Roads Wash. **6**(3), 11–17 (1964)

A Functional Near-Infrared Spectroscopy Study of Auditory Working Memory Load

Shih-Min Wu, Hsien-Ming Ding, and Yi-Li Tseng[(⊠)]

Department of Electrical Engineering, Fu Jen Catholic University,
New Taipei City, Taiwan
yltseng@mail.fju.edu.tw

Abstract. Brain correlates of cognitive performance have received considerable attention in the area of augmented cognition. Studies focused on the correlation between brain activations and cognitive load have laid their focus on connections integrated by frontal region. Most of the studies have manipulated visual or verbal cognitive load, though the effect of auditory memory load in cognitive performance is still unknown. In this study, functional near-infrared spectroscopy (fNIRS) of twelve subjects were measured when they were performing a paradigm of auditory working memory task. For the auditory n-back task, there are three experimental conditions, including two *n*-back task conditions of memorizing the stimuli with different memory load, and a condition of passive listening to the stimuli. The stimuli are sound combinations of major, minor, and dissonant chords. Hemodynamic responses from frontal brain regions were recorded using a wireless fNIRS device. Brain activations from ventrolateral and orbital prefrontal cortex are measured with signals filtered and baseline wandering removed. The fNIRS signals are then standardized with statistical test and group analysis carried out. The results revealed that there are significantly stronger hemodynamic responses in bilateral ventrolateral prefrontal cortex when subjects were attending to the auditory working memory task with high load. This study demonstrated the possibility of incorporating fNIRS as an index to evaluate cognitive performance regarding its benefit on the flexibility for portable applications than other neuroimaging techniques. The performance in cognitive function could therefore be quantitatively measured with the proposed method.

Keywords: Functional near-infrared spectroscopy (fNIRS) · Auditory working memory · Memory load

1 Introduction

In the past few years, functional near-infrared spectroscopy (fNIRS) is proved to be a flexible and convenient device to record brain hemodynamic response during the performance of cognitive tasks such as learning, memory, and motor reactions [1–3]. In several studies of memory function, the hemodynamic responses recorded by a fNIRS system from prefrontal cortex is claimed to be highly correlated with gray-matter functional magnetic resonance imaging (fMRI) activities during a working memory task [4]. Ogawa et al. have found that there is correlation between working memory

© Springer International Publishing AG 2017
C. Stephanidis (Ed.): HCII Posters 2017, Part I, CCIS 713, pp. 273–277, 2017.
DOI: 10.1007/978-3-319-58750-9_38

performance and the neural activations measured using an fNIRS system. Subjects with better working memory performance have higher levels of oxyhemoglobin activations [5]. Consistent with the previous findings in fMRI, activations in lateral prefrontal cortex (LPFC) recorded from fNIRS systems are also proved to be associated with working memory in adults and even preschool children. The activations in the bilateral LPFC is depend on the memory-load [6]. These evidences suggest that fNIRS is useful and convenient for measuring the cognitive load and working memory performance [5].

Studies focused on the relationship between the brain activations and cognitive load have laid their focus on connections integrated by frontal region [7, 8]. Most of the studies have manipulated visual or verbal cognitive load, though the effect of auditory memory load in cognitive performance is still unknown. In this study, hemodynamic responses recorded from a fNIRS system of twelve subjects were measured when they were performing a paradigm of auditory n-back working memory task [9]. Brain activations from ventrolateral and orbital prefrontal cortex are measured with signals filtered and baseline wandering removed. This study demonstrated the possibility of incorporating fNIRS as an index to evaluate cognitive performance regarding its benefit on the flexibility for portable applications than other neuroimaging techniques.

2   Materials and Methods

2.1   NIRS Experiment and Preprocessing

The fNIRS signals are recorded using a wireless and portable system, BRAIN-NIRS Hb13 (ASTEM Co. Ltd., Japan), as shown in Fig. 1A. The concentration of oxygenated hemoglobin (oxy-Hb) and deoxygenated hemoglobin (deoxy-Hb) are recorded from four locations of the scalp. The center of the probe is placed in the frontal area (Fpz), and four sensors were set on Fp1, Fp2, F7, and F8 according to the international

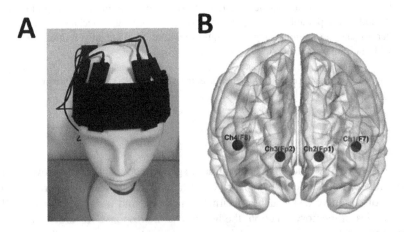

Fig. 1. The four locations of fNIRS sensors on the subject's scalp (A). These electrodes are corresponded to F7, F8, Fp1, and Fp2 in the 10–20 system, which are localized over left and right ventrolateral prefrontal cortex (VLPFC) and orbital prefrontal cortex (OPFC).

10–20 system for electroencephalography, as illustrated in Fig. 1B [10]. These four positions are corresponded to the left/right dorsal and ventral prefrontal cortex (DLPFC and VLPFC), respectively, based on an anatomical cranio-cerebral correlation study [11, 12]. The concentration change of oxy-Hb is used for further analysis since it is more sensitive to the changes of cerebral blood flow.

Twelve subjects were recruited in the experiment with their fNIRS data recorded in a shielded room. The raw data are band-pass filtered (0.01–0.1 Hz) to attenuate the high frequency noise, respiration, and cardiac cycle effects [13–15]. The data recorded from each subject are checked for any potential saturation when light intensity at the detector was higher than the device limit. The signals are then standardized with baseline-wandering removed. Group analysis and statistical test are then carried out to compare different conditions of working memory load.

2.2   Auditory N-Back Working Memory Task

The subjects are requested to participate in a paradigm of auditory n-back working memory task [9]. The memory load are manipulated in this auditory task with different type of emotional stimuli. There are three conditions with distinct memory load during chord listening: 1-back (1B), 2-back (2B), and a task of passive listening (PL) to the stimuli. Each music stimulation is composed of four sound combinations of one of the major, minor, or dissonant chords. A random combination of task conditions (PL, 1B or 2B) and chord categories (major, minor or dissonant) is designed as a stimulation in each trial. Each participant are requested to attend a 2-session experiment with a 2-min rest with each session consists of 18 blocks. Twenty trials were presented in a block with each trial constructed of a sound lasting 1000 ms, followed by a 1500-ms silence before the next trial. Participants were instructed to press the left button in the n-back task when they recognized the chord matching that of the last n trials.

3   Results and Discussions

The behavior results in the auditory n-back task revealed that the average correctness of the 1-back task is $85.6 \pm 7.1\%$, which is 17.8% larger than that of the 2-back task ($67.8 \pm 7.5\%$). As illustrated in Fig. 2, the hemodynamic responses recorded by the fNIRS system are standardized to z-score. Stronger activations were observed from channel 1 and 4, which are localized over VLPFC. Activations are more pronounced in higher working memory load. In left VLPFC (channel 1), significant difference ($p = 0.01$) was found between PL and 1B. The difference is more pronounced in right VLPFC with significance between PL and 1B ($p = 0.006$), and also PL and 2B ($p = 0.004$). The results revealed that there are significantly stronger hemodynamic responses in bilateral VLPFC when subjects were attending to the auditory working memory task with higher memory load. The findings in this study showed consistent results with previous studies in visual working memory study [6]. The cognitive performance could therefore be quantitatively and consistently measured.

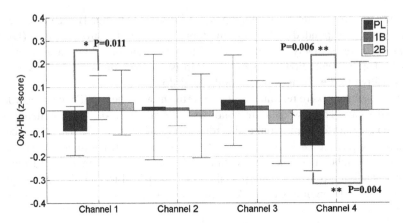

Fig. 2. Hemodynamic responses recorded by the fNIRS system when subjects were attending to *n*-back auditory working memory tasks including three conditions: passive listening (PL), one-back (1B), and two-back (2B). Stronger activations were observed from channel 1 and 4, which are localized over ventrolateral prefrontal cortex. Activations were more pronounced in higher working memory load.

4   Conclusions

This study demonstrated the flexibility of incorporating fNIRS as an index to evaluate cognitive performance. In addition, fNIRS can potentially be applied to functional mapping in childhood or patients with mental disorder [6]. Since it imposes fewer constraints on behavior than fMRI, fNIRS appears to be more practical than fMRI for investigating cognitive neuroscience on the primate cortex [16]. In addition to the studies of brain functions, fNIRS may also be a useful tool to the development of brain-computer interface [17–19] or the validation of drugs for mental diseases that can cause reduction in lateral prefrontal activities accompanied by improved cognitive performance [20].

Acknowledgment. This work was supported by grant 105-2221-E-030-001- from the Ministry of Science and Technology, Taiwan.

References

1. Noah, J.A., Ono, Y., et al.: fMRI validation of fNIRS measurements during a naturalistic task. JoVE - J. Visualized Exp. (2015). doi:10.3791/52116
2. Shimada, S., Hiraki, K.: Infant's brain responses to live and televised action. NeuroImage **32**(2), 930–939 (2006)
3. Shimada, S., Oki, K.: Modulation of motor area activity during observation of unnatural body movements. Brain Cogn. **80**(1), 1–6 (2012)
4. Sato, H., Yahata, N., et al.: A NIRS–fMRI investigation of prefrontal cortex activity during a working memory task. NeuroImage **83**, 158–173 (2013)

5. Ogawa, Y., Kotani, K., Jimbo, Y.: Relationship between working memory performance and neural activation measured using near-infrared spectroscopy. Brain Behav. **4**(4), 544–551 (2014)
6. Tsujimoto, S., Yamamoto, T., et al.: Prefrontal cortical activation associated with working memory in adults and preschool children: an event-related optical topography study. Cereb. Cortex **14**(7), 703–712 (2004)
7. Kane, M.J., Engle, R.W.: The role of prefrontal cortex in working-memory capacity, executive attention, and general fluid intelligence: an individual-differences perspective. Psychon. Bull. Rev. **9**(4), 637–671 (2002)
8. Ma, L., Steinberg, J.L., et al.: Working memory load modulation of parieto-frontal connections: evidence from dynamic causal modeling. Hum. Brain Mapp. **33**(8), 1850–1867 (2012)
9. Pallesen, K.J., Brattico, E., et al.: Cognitive control in auditory working memory is enhanced in musicians. PLoS ONE **5**(6), e11120 (2010)
10. Jasper, H.H.: The ten twenty electrode system of the international federation. Electroencephalogr. Clin. Neurophysiol. **10**, 371–375 (1958)
11. Okamoto, M., Dan, H., et al.: Three-dimensional probabilistic anatomical cranio-cerebral correlation via the international 10–20 system oriented for transcranial functional brain mapping. Neuroimage **21**(1), 99–111 (2004)
12. Sanefuji, M., Takada, Y., et al.: Strategy in short-term memory for pictures in childhood: a near-infrared spectroscopy study. Neuroimage **54**(3), 2394–2400 (2011)
13. Izzetoglu, M., Izzetoglu, K., et al.: Functional near-infrared neuroimaging. IEEE Trans. Neural Syst. Rehabil. Eng. **13**(2), 153–159 (2005)
14. Ayaz, H., Izzetoglu, M., et al.: Sliding-window motion artifact rejection for functional near-infrared spectroscopy. In: Annual International Conference of the IEEE Engineering in Medicine and Biology Society (EMBC) (2010)
15. McKendrick, R., Ayaz, H., et al.: Enhancing dual-task performance with verbal and spatial working memory training: continuous monitoring of cerebral hemodynamics with NIRS. NeuroImage **85**(3), 1014–1026 (2014)
16. Fuster, J., Guiou, M., et al.: Near-infrared spectroscopy (NIRS) in cognitive neuroscience of the primate brain. Neuroimage **26**(1), 215–220 (2005)
17. Coyle, S., Ward, T., et al.: On the suitability of near-infrared (NIR) systems for next-generation brain–computer interfaces. Physiol. Meas. **25**(4), 815 (2004)
18. Fazli, S., Mehnert, J., et al.: Enhanced performance by a hybrid NIRS–EEG brain computer interface. Neuroimage **59**(1), 519–529 (2012)
19. Kaiser, V., Bauernfeind, G., et al.: Cortical effects of user training in a motor imagery based brain–computer interface measured by fNIRS and EEG. Neuroimage **85**, 432–444 (2014)
20. Ramasubbu, R., Singh, H., et al.: Methylphenidate-mediated reduction in prefrontal hemodynamic responses to working memory task: a functional near-infrared spectroscopy study. Hum. Psychopharmacol. Clin. Exp. **27**(6), 615–621 (2012)

Perception, Cognition and Emotion in HCI

Analysis of Paradoxical Phenomenon Caused by Presenting Thermal Stimulation on Three Spots

Keisuke Arai[✉], Satoshi Hashiguchi, Fumihisa Shibata,
and Asako Kimura

Ritsumeikan University, 1-1-1 Noji-Higashi, Kusatsu, Shiga 525-8577, Japan
arai@rm.is.ritsumei.ac.jp

Abstract. Thermal referral (TR) and thermal grill illusion (TGI), known as illusions of thermal sensation, have been well studied. In a previous study, an experiment using two thermal-tactile stimulations to the forearm revealed that these illusions simultaneously occurred. In this experiment result, a few subjects perceived a hot stimulation as a cold sensation and/or a cold stimulation as a hot sensation. This paradoxical phenomenon of thermal sensation, which is not discussed specifically in the previous study, could be a fatal problem in the case presenting thermal stimulation on multiple spots intentionally. Therefore, we decided to analyze this paradoxical phenomenon. In this paper, we confirmed that this phenomenon occurs when we present thermal stimulation on two spots and three spots. In comparing the results of thermal stimulation on two spots and three spots, the occurred probability increased on three spots.

Keywords: Thermal sensation · Thermal referral · Thermal grill illusion

1 Introduction

Thermal referral (TR) and thermal grill illusion (TGI) are known as illusions of thermal sensation. TR is a phenomenon in which thermal sensation changes when thermal stimulation is presented to one location and tactile stimulation is presented to another [1–3]. TGI refers to paradoxical sensations of heat and pain resulting from the simultaneous application of interlaced hot and cold stimuli [4, 5].

In a previous study, an experiment using two thermal-tactile stimulations to the forearm revealed that these illusions simultaneously occurred [6]. From the result of this study, we noticed that a few subjects perceived a hot stimulation as a cold sensation and/or a cold stimulation as a hot sensation. This paradoxical phenomenon of thermal sensation, which is not discussed specifically in the previous study, could be a fatal problem in the case presenting thermal stimulation on multiple spots intentionally. Therefore, we decided to analyze this paradoxical phenomenon of thermal sensation.

As a first step (experiment 1), we verified that this phenomenon occurred by presenting thermal stimulation on two spots in a manner similar to the previous study. In the next step (experiment 2), we investigated whether this phenomenon occurred

C. Stephanidis (Ed.): HCII Posters 2017, Part I, CCIS 713, pp. 281–286, 2017.
DOI: 10.1007/978-3-319-58750-9_39

when we expanded the stimulation from two spots to three spots. Also, we compared the results of experiments in cases of thermal stimulation on two spots and three spots.

2   Thermal Stimulations

In our experiments, hot and cold stimulations are presented by using Peltier devices (size: 40 × 40 mm) and temperature controller sets (VPE-20-5 V, VICS Ltd., Fig. 1). Considering the stability of the temperature stimulation, we sat the devices on a table and asked subjects to put the inside of their forearms on them. Three devices were set 100 mm apart in a row on the table. Each device had contact with the wrist, the center, and the elbow spot of the forearm (Fig. 2). Also, two pillows were prepared for each subject's wrist and elbow to hold and stabilize his or her forearm.

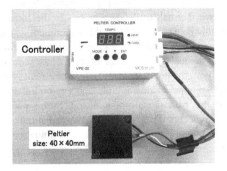

Fig. 1. Device for presenting thermal

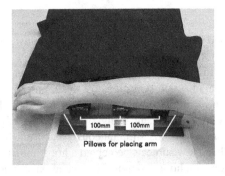

Fig. 2. Experimental scene

Thermal stimulation becomes painful when the temperature is too low or too high (the cold stimulation: 10 °C, the hot stimulation: 45 °C) [7]. We selected 11 °C and 44 °C as the cold and hot stimulations to avoid pain. The experiments were conducted in a room with a constant temperature of 25 °C.

3 Experiment 1: Presenting Thermal Stimulation on Two Spots

3.1 Objective

In the previous study, a few subjects perceived a hot stimulation as a cold sensation and/or a cold stimulation as a hot sensation when a hot stimulation and a cold stimulation were presented simultaneously to two spots on the forearm. In experiment 1, we reevaluated this phenomenon.

3.2 Condition

In experiment 1, the hot and cold stimulations were presented to two of the three spots and a null stimulation, which was neither hot nor cold, was presented on the remaining spot of the forearm. This null stimulation was set to 32 °C because the indifferent temperature (when humans do not feel hot or cold sensations) is known to be between 30 °C and 36 °C. In our preliminary experiment presenting this null stimulation on three spots (the wrist, the center, and the elbow), we confirmed that none of 10 subjects feel hot and/or cold.

The center of subject's right forearm was placed on the Peltier device as shown in Fig. 2. At the same time, the remaining two devices had contact with the wrist and the elbow of the forearm. After a 20-second interval of placing his forearm on the devices, the subject was asked to describe the sensation he perceived (hot, null, or cold) at each of the three spots. We also asked whether the subject felt pain at any of the spots. A series of the 12 combinations (Table 1) was presented in random order. The subjects included 10 males in their 20 s to their 30 s.

Table 1. Answer rate of temperature and pain sensations in each pattern when thermal stimulation is presented on two spots (subjects = 10)

	Pattern	Hot	Null	Cold	Pain	Pattern	Hot	Null	Cold	Pain	Pattern	Hot	Null	Cold	Pain	Pattern	Hot	Null	Cold	Pain
Wrist	H	80%	20%	0%	10%	C	10%	0%	90%	10%	H	80%	20%	0%	0%	C	0%	0%	100%	10%
Center	H	70%	30%	0%	10%	C	0%	20%	80%	20%	C	30%	10%	60%	30%	H	60%	30%	10%	0%
Elbow	N	70%	30%	0%	0%	N	0%	80%	20%	0%	N	20%	50%	30%	0%	N	90%	10%	0%	0%
Wrist	H	70%	30%	0%	0%	C	0%	0%	100%	0%	H	70%	20%	10%	0%	C	0%	0%	100%	10%
Center	N	70%	30%	0%	0%	N	0%	20%	80%	0%	N	20%	40%	40%	20%	N	20%	80%	0%	0%
Elbow	H	90%	10%	0%	10%	C	0%	10%	90%	0%	C	0%	20%	80%	10%	H	100%	0%	0%	0%
Wrist	N	40%	60%	0%	0%	N	0%	80%	20%	0%	N	70%	30%	0%	0%	N	20%	40%	40%	0%
Center	H	70%	30%	0%	10%	C	0%	20%	80%	0%	H	40%	30%	30%	10%	C	10%	30%	60%	20%
Elbow	H	90%	10%	0%	10%	C	0%	0%	100%	0%	C	10%	0%	90%	10%	H	70%	10%	20%	10%

※Patterns in the table indicate that the stimulation was presented on the wrist, the center, and the elbow spot in order from the top
※H, N, C indicate the type of presentation stimulation (H: Hot stimulation, N: Null stimulation, C: Cold stimulation)

3.3 Procedure

The experimental procedures were as follows:

(1) Measure the center position of the forearm.

(2) Set the temperature and wait until the temperature is stabilized.
(3) Put the subject's forearm on the devices and wait for 20 s.
(4) Determine the subject's sensation on each of the three spots.
(5) Provide sufficient intervals (more than 2 min) to eliminate the effects of temperature change on the skin.
(6) Steps (2) to (5) are repeated 12 times.

If the subject wanted to redo procedure (4), then we provided a sufficient interval and repeated the same trial.

3.4   Result and Discussion

The results are shown in Table 1. The letters "H", "N", and "C" in the table indicate the presented hot, null, and cold stimulations, respectively. These characters are described in the order of the wrist, the center, and the elbow. The values in Table 1 show the answer rate of the temperature and pain sensations perceived at each spot. The dotted values are the correct answers, and the double underlined values indicate the opposite answers.

(i) When only the hot or the cold stimulation was presented, the subjects correctly answered the presented stimulation.

In the patterns (HHN, HNH, NHH, CCN, CNC, NCC) that present the same thermal stimulations (e.g., hot and hot/cold and cold), the subjects perceived the presented thermal stimulation accurately. However, the null stimulations were substantially affected by the neighboring thermal stimulation (TR phenomenon).

(ii) When both hot and cold stimulations were presented, a few subjects gave opposite answers.

In the patterns (HCN, HNC, NHC, CHN, CNH, NCH) that present the opposite thermal stimulation, especially in the patterns (HCN, NHC, CHN, NCH), the answer rate that correctly perceived the presented thermal stimulation became lower than the result of (i). A few subjects commented that "I could not feel some of the hot/cold spots" or "Perceived the temperature reversely to the presented stimulation." Particularly in the center spot of HCN and NHC, the occurrence of the paradoxical phenomenon of thermal sensation was 30%. Most of the null stimulations were under the influence of the neighboring stimulation (TR phenomenon).

(iii) A few subjects perceived pain sensation on the center spot.

From the results of this experiment, we confirmed that the influence of the TR phenomenon made the null stimulation inaccurate. Furthermore, the thermal stimulation was not necessarily perceived accurately, and even paradoxical perception could occur.

4 Experiment 2: Presenting Thermal Stimulation on Three Spots

4.1 Objective

In experiment 2, we evaluated the incidence of paradoxical phenomenon of thermal sensation when thermal stimulation was presented on three spots on the forearm.

4.2 Condition and Procedure

In experiment 2, the hot or cold thermal stimulation was presented on three spots. The null stimulation was not used. Eight combinations of hot and cold stimulations on the three spots (Table 2) were presented to the subjects in random order. Other experimental conditions and procedures were the same as those in experiment 1.

Table 2. Answer rate of temperature and pain sensations in each pattern when thermal stimulation is presented on three spots (subjects = 10)

Answer/Pattern		Hot	Null	Cold	Pain		Hot	Null	Cold	Pain		Hot	Null	Cold	Pain		Hot	Null	Cold	Pain
Wrist	H	90%	10%	0%	0%	H	80%	10%	10%	10%	C	0%	10%	90%	0%	H	60%	10%	30%	0%
Center	H	100%	0%	0%	20%	H	70%	0%	30%	0%	C	30%	10%	60%	10%	C	40%	10%	50%	40%
Elbow	H	100%	0%	0%	0%	C	30%	0%	70%	0%	H	80%	10%	10%	10%	H	90%	0%	10%	0%
Wrist	C	10%	10%	80%	0%	C	0%	0%	100%	0%	H	60%	40%	0%	10%	C	10%	10%	80%	10%
Center	C	0%	20%	80%	0%	H	70%	10%	20%	30%	C	30%	10%	60%	40%	H	60%	0%	40%	20%
Elbow	C	0%	0%	100%	10%	H	90%	0%	10%	0%	C	20%	0%	80%	0%	C	50%	0%	50%	10%

※Patterns in the table indicate that the stimulation was presented on the wrist, the center, and the elbow spot in order from the top
※H C indicate the type of presentation stimulation (H: Hot stimulation C: Cold stimulation)

4.3 Result and Discussion

The results are shown in Table 2.

(i) When only the hot or the cold stimulation was presented, the subjects correctly answered the presented stimulation.

Similar to the result of experiment 1 (i), in the patterns (HHH, CCC) that present the same thermal stimulations, the subjects perceived the presented thermal stimulation accurately.

(ii) When two identical thermal stimulations were aligned side by side, a few subjects perceived the presented stimulation reversely.

Similar to the result of experiment 1 (ii), in the patterns (HHC, CHH, HCC, CCH), which present two of the same thermal stimulations side by side, the answer rate that correctly perceived the presented thermal stimulation was lower than the result of (i).

(iii) When the hot and cold stimulations were aligned alternately, half of the subjects reversely perceived the presented stimulation.

In the patterns (HCH, CHC) that present the thermal stimulations alternately, the incidence of paradoxical phenomenon of thermal sensation increased more than the result of experiment 1 (ii) and the result of experiment 2 (i) and (ii); 40% in the center spot of HCH and CHC, and 50% in the elbow spot of CHC.

(iv) Some subjects perceived pain sensation at the center spot.

Particularly, in the patterns (CHH, HCC, HCH) that aligned the hot and cold stimulations side by side, more subjects perceived pain sensation than the result of experiment 1 (iii).

From these results, we found that the paradoxical phenomenon of thermal sensation also occurred in experiment 2. In addition, we found that increasing the number of spots of thermal stimulation increased the incidence of paradoxical phenomenon of thermal sensation and TGI.

5 Conclusions and Future Work

In experiment 1, we confirmed that paradoxical phenomenon really occurs when we present thermal stimulation on two spots. In experiment 2, we evaluated the incidence of paradoxical phenomenon of thermal sensation when thermal stimulation is presented on three spots on the forearm. As a result, this phenomenon occurred in the patterns that alternately present thermal stimulation with a probability of 50%. In comparing the results of two spots and three spots, the incidence increased on three spots.

In the future, we want to investigate why this paradoxical phenomenon of thermal sensation occurs by changing some parameters, such as presentation temperature and positions, to determine how we can avoid this.

References

1. Green, B.G.: Localization of thermal sensation: an illusion and synthetic heat. Percept. Psychophys. **22**(4), 331–337 (1977)
2. Green, B.G.: Thermo-tactile interactions: effects of touch on thermal localization. In: Kenshalo, D.R. (ed.) Sensory Functions of the Skin of Humans, pp. 223–240. Springer, Heidelberg (1979)
3. Ho, H.N., Watanabe, J., Ando, H., Kashino, M.: Somatotopic or spatiotopic? Frame of reference for localizing thermal sensations under thermo-tactile interactions. Atten. Percept. Psychophys. **72**(6), 1666–1675 (2010)
4. Green, B.G.: Synthetic heat at mild temperatures. Somatosens. Mot. Res. **19**(2), 130–138 (2002)
5. Bach, P., Becker, S., Kleinböhl, D., Hölzl, R.: The thermal grill illusion and what is painful about it. Neurosci. Lett. **505**(1), 31–35 (2011)
6. Watanabe, R., Okazaki, R., Kajimoto, H.: Mutual referral of thermal sensation between two thermal-tactile stimuli. In: IEEE Haptics Symposium, pp. 299–302 (2014)
7. Kumamoto, E., Fujita, T.: Regulation of nociceptive information transmitting to the spinal dorsal horn from periphery: the modulation of synaptic transmission and nerve conduction. Pain Res. **26**(4), 197–214 (2011)

Gaze Behavior and Emotion of Crane Operators for Different Visual Support System

Jouh Yeong Chew[✉], Koichi Ohtomi, and Hiromasa Suzuki

Department of Precision Engineering, University of Tokyo, Tokyo, Japan
{jychew,koichi.ohtomi}@delight.t.u-tokyo.ac.jp,
suzuki@den.t.u-tokyo.ac.jp

Abstract. This study described a method of using glance behavior as design indices of In-Vehicle Visual Support (IVVS) system. The method was implemented to evaluate information content of the IVVS to facilitate operation of a mobile crane, which was challenging due to depth perception and load oscillation. The results suggested information content was well-discriminated using gaze behavior, which indicated its feasibility as design indices. Most importantly, emotional response was well-defined using gaze behavior. By not requiring self-evaluation of emotional response after the experimental procedure, design of IVVS could be evaluated by observing gaze behavior simultaneously during the experiment. In addition, elements of bias and social masking could be minimized because gaze response is sub-conscious.

Keywords: Gaze behavior · In-Vehicle Visual Support system · Crane operation · Operator psychology and distraction · Dynamic Area-of-Interests

1 Introduction

The main challenges of crane operation are load oscillation [1–3] and depth perception, where it is difficult for operators to estimate the radial distance of the load from obstacles in the environment. In-Vehicle Visual Support (IVVS) systems are able to provide information to facilitate human-machine interaction and to make crane operation easy. Implementation of IVVS in other applications such as driving, have been beneficial [4, 5]. The objective of this study is to evaluate the impact of IVVS design on crane operator's emotion (Kansei) and gaze response, and to find the correlation between them. This correlation enables estimation of Kansei from gaze behavior which is important because sub-conscious gaze is less affected by bias and influence of cultural difference and social masking [6, 7].

Previous studies have discussed about improving design of crane cabins [8–10]. However, these studies mainly focused on anthropometric assessment. To our best knowledge, specific design of IVVS for crane cabin was not evaluated by previous studies. Nonetheless, IVVS design was not a new area of study and has been proven to be important to enhance human-machine interaction. Its implementation has been discussed for fighter cockpit [11] and driving [12]. In both cases, gaze response was used for evaluation. Despite this, it was noteworthy that these implementations did not consider estimation of subjective emotion based on sub-conscious gaze behavior. This

© Springer International Publishing AG 2017
C. Stephanidis (Ed.): HCII Posters 2017, Part I, CCIS 713, pp. 287–292, 2017.
DOI: 10.1007/978-3-319-58750-9_40

novelty is beneficial to reduce reliance on subjective user response. In essence, it allows simultaneous evaluation of IVVS design without having to carry out post-operation analysis such as self-evaluation tests and analysis of gaze data.

In this study, a model was established using multiple linear regression to estimate emotion using gaze behavior. This model was useful to reduce reliance on self-evaluation response such as questionnaires and interviews. Different information contents of IVVS were evaluated using the crane simulator. Gaze behavior was measured simultaneously during the experiment and the 3D perspective projection was used for autonomous mapping of gaze fixations to dynamic Area-of-Interests (AOIs), and these transitions were analyzed using the first order Markov model [13].

2 Materials and Methods

2.1 Participants

There were fifteen participants who were novices, and each of them performed the same task for eight trials, which were randomly distributed across four different positions to evaluate spatial consistency of gaze behavior with respect to same information content. At each position, two types of information content were tested. This study focused on novices because crane operation was particularly challenging for them. Gaze behavior was measured simultaneously during the experiment and Kansei response was observed after each trial using the Semantic Differential (SD) method with seven-level Likert scale. There were five pairs of Kansei adjectives – "Tense-Relax", "Difficult-Easy", "Disappointment-Satisfaction", "Unclear-Clear", and "Inconvenience-Convenience", and they were commonly understood by a group of five participants during the pre-test.

2.2 Crane Simulator System

The dynamics model of the crane was built on the Simulation X software based on the Modelica modelling language. Figure 1a shows the experimental setup of the system, where Fig. 1b and c shows the Tobii Pro X3-120 eye tracker and the operation levers, respectively. The simulator was designed to mimic the actual crane operation environment as much as possible. First, an 80-in. screen was used as the display to show the operator's view. Objects such as the load and the cabin's frame were scaled according to the operator's view in a real crane. Secondly, the seat and operation levers were built according to real crane. In this case, the same seat and operation levers were used.

Figure 2a and b shows the operator's view of a real crane and that of the simulator. Similarity between the real and virtual environment could be observed from the scale of the objects in the environment. This is vital to provide similar user experience to minimize the gap between the lab and real environment. There were two types of design – the conventional (Fig. 2c) and the revised version (Fig. 2d) with the view of an overhead camera, herein referred to as "NoTV" and "TV", respectively. The latter provided bird's eye view of the environment to address the issue on depth perception.

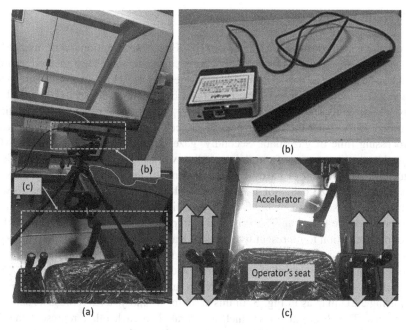

Fig. 1. (a) The experimental setup of the crane simulator system, (b) Tobii Pro X3-120, and (c) operator's seat and operation levers of simulator system mimicking setup of the real crane.

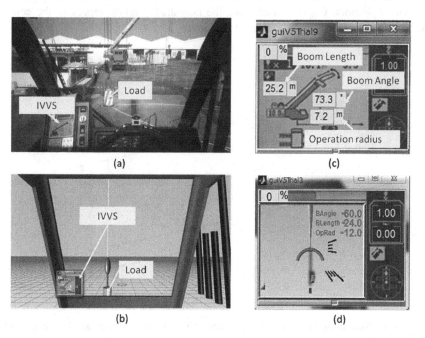

Fig. 2. (a) The IVVS of real crane, (b) the IVVS of simulator, (c) the conventional IVVS – "NoTV", and (d) the revised IVVS with camera view from the top end of the boom – "TV".

3 Results

Gaze behavior analysis was done in two steps. First, gaze fixations were mapped to dynamic AOIs using the 3D perspective projection method. This method enabled autonomous mapping of gaze fixations onto discrete AOIs, which was better than most of the existing methods provided by makers of eye-tracking devices. Their methods usually required dynamic AOIs to be moved frame-by-frame, which was time-consuming. Thus, using the 3D perspective projection method significantly improved the processing time of gaze data. Secondly, gaze transitions between dynamic AOIs were analyzed using metrics from the preceding work [13]. These metrics provided a reasonable representation of gaze behavior in terms of uniformity and randomness.

As the result, gaze behavior was represented using six metrics, and the forward sequential feature selection method was used to identify the subset which best minimized the objective function. The Principal Component Analysis (PCA) was used for feature transformation to represent five pairs of Kansei adjectives as smaller number of components. This simplified the multivariate SD results for regression analysis.

Correlation between subset of gaze metrics and the first principal component (PC1) of Kansei was evaluated using the multiple linear regression. The results were represented using a 2D map as in Fig. 3. In this case, the x- and y- axes represents subset of gaze metrics. The diagonal lines which are parallel to each other represent the first principal component of Kansei adjectives. The preferred IVVS design is visualized by plotting the average of each trial (n = 15) on the contour. The shaded labels represent IVVS with the view of an overhead camera (Fig. 2d), which was consistently preferred by novice operators. On the other hand, the non-shaded labels represent the conventional IVVS (Fig. 2c), which was least preferred.

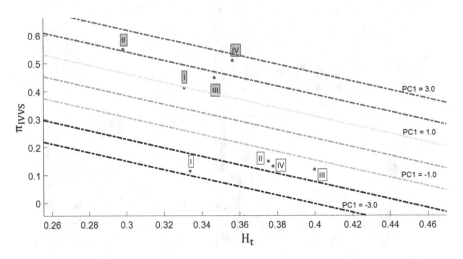

Fig. 3. Visualization of the correlation between subset of gaze metrics and the first principal component of Kansei using a 2D map.

4 Summary and Conclusions

The results indicated cases of TV and NoTV was successfully discriminated from each other, where TV obtained higher PC1 score compared to NoTV, which consistently scored lower (Fig. 4). In other words, different information content of IVVS were well-discriminated using Kansei adjectives. The addition of the view from an overhead camera to show the surrounding environment of the load has successfully addressed the issue on depth perception. This was reasonable and within expectation. Most importantly, this distinction between different information content was also reflected by gaze behavior (Fig. 4), where statistical significant difference was also observed by every gaze metrics.

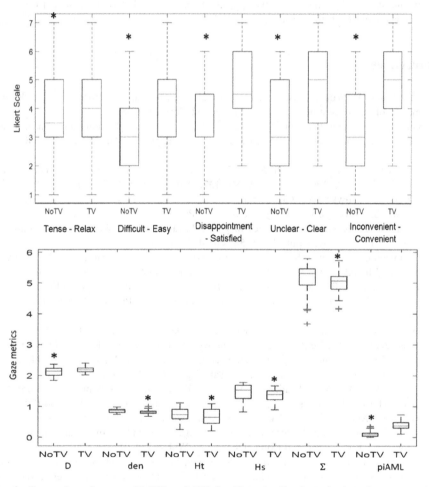

Fig. 4. Comparison between NoTV and TV for Kansei adjectives (top) and gaze metrics (bottom). Paired t-test was carried out and statistical significant difference (p < 0.05) was indicated using asterisk on the smaller counterpart. Statistical significant difference were observed from five pairs of Kansei adjectives and six gaze metrics.

Preliminary results (Fig. 3) of the estimation model showed clear distinction between different IVVS information content, which suggested the feasibility of using gaze behavior to estimate Kansei of crane operators. This finding is significant because design of IVVS could be evaluated by observing gaze behavior simultaneously during the experiment and self-evaluation of emotional response after the experiment is not necessary. In addition, elements of bias and social masking could be minimized. It was noteworthy the methods for autonomous gaze mapping and Kansei estimation were general solutions which could be implemented on different case studies.

Acknowledgements. Special thanks to Tadano Ltd for providing facilities to study behavior of crane operators and for taking part in the experiment, and to Mr. Hiroyuki Katayama for building the dynamics model of crane for the simulator. The experiment protocol was approved by New Energy and Industrial Technology Development Organization (NEDO) of Japan, and we would like to thank them for their assistance.

References

1. Maczynski, A., Wojciech, S.: Dynamics of a mobile crane and optimization of the slewing motion of its upper structure. Nonlinear Dyn. **32**, 259–290 (2003)
2. Ouyang, H., Zhang, G., Mei, L., Deng, X., Wang, D.: Load vibration reduction in rotary cranes using robust two-degree-of-freedom control approach. Adv. Mech. Eng. **8**, 1–11 (2016)
3. Vazquez, C., Fridman, L., Collado, J., Castillo, I.: Second-order sliding mode control of a perturbed-crane. J. Dyn. Syst. – T ASME **137**, 081010-1–081010-7 (2015)
4. Birrell, S.A., Fowkes, M.: Glance behaviors when using an in-vehicle smart driving aid: a real-world, on-road driving study. Transp. Res. Part F **22**, 113–125 (2014)
5. Ahlstrom, C., Kircher, K.: Changes in glance behavior when using a visual eco-driving system – a field study. Appl. Ergon. **58**, 414–423 (2017)
6. Drummond, P.D., Quah, S.H.: The effect of expressing anger on cardiovascular reactivity and facial blood flow in Chinese and Caucasians. Psychophysiology **38**, 190–196 (2001)
7. Jang, E.H., Park, B.J., Park, M.S., Kim, S.H., Sohn, J.H.: Analysis of physiological signals for recognition of boredom, pain, and surprise emotions. J. Physiol. Anthropol. **34**, 1–12 (2015)
8. White, T.G.: Ergonomic survey of mobile cranes. Appl. Ergon. **4**, 96–104 (1973)
9. Spasojevic, B.V.K., Veljkovic, Z.A., Golubovic, T., Brkic, A.D.J., Kosic, S.I.: Workspace design for crane cabins applying a combined traditional approach and the Taguchi method for design of experiments. Int. J. Occup. Saf. Ergon. **22**, 228–240 (2016)
10. Zunjic, A., Brkic, V.S., Klarin, M., Brkic, A., Krstic, D.: Anthropometric assessment of crane cabins and recommendations for design: a case study. Work **52**, 185–194 (2015)
11. Wang, H., Xue, C., Liu, Q.: The eye movement experiment and the usability evaluation of the fighter cockpit digital interface. In: Proceedings of the 2nd International Conference on Information Engineering and Computer Science, Wuhan (2010)
12. Poitschke, T., Laquai, F., Stamboliev, S., Rigoll, G.: Gaze-based interaction on multiple displays in an automotive environment. In: International Conference on Systems, Man, and Cybernetics, Alaska (2011)
13. Chew, J.Y., Ohtomi, K., Suzuki, H.: Skill metrics for mobile crane operators based on gaze fixation pattern. In: Advances in Human Aspects of Transportation: Advances in Intelligent Systems and Computing, Florida (2016).

A Study on the Differences Among M3D, S3D and HMD for Students with Different Degrees of Spatial Ability in Design Education

Po-Ying Chu[✉], Li-Chieh Chen, Hsiao-Wen Kung, and Shih-Jen Su

Department of Industrial Design, Tatung University, Taipei, Taiwan
{juby,lcchen}@ttu.edu.tw, blue.star7987@gmail.com,
joe28281285@gmail.com

Abstract. In the curriculum of product design education, some teaching materials for demonstrating and discussing case studies are always presented in images with monocular depth cues. However, using this approach to train students with different spatial abilities is a great challenge. It was reported that stereoscopic 3D (S3D) displays were helpful for the performance of depth-related tasks. Some research groups had tried to use stereoscopic visualization for teaching Descriptive Geometry, and some research reported that the effect of stereoscopic displays on science learning was related to the spatial ability of the viewer. In product design education, identifying proportion and manipulating proportional relationships were important practices of form-giving training. Whether the correctness of proportion judgement would be influenced by different displays remained an open question. Therefore, this study aimed to explore the performances of students with different background across three display modes, i.e. M3D, S3D, and head-mounted display (HMD). In the experiments, physical chairs and the corresponding digital models with different proportions were used as the stimuli. The participants were asked to identify the correct digital models of chairs. The results indicated that HMD approach could facilitate the reflection and adaptation of dimensions and proportions, compensating the differences of spatial abilities, and therefore enhancing the learning effects significantly.

Keywords: Design education · Spatial ability · Stereoscopic 3D · Head-mounted display

1 Introduction

In the field of design education, students learn how to estimate proportion and to manipulate proportional relationships of an object is a very important training. However, using conventional 2D displays with monocular depth cues, namely the so-called monocular 3D (M3D) images, to train students with different spatial abilities is a great challenge. Although, some literature has indicated that stereoscopic 3D (S3D) displays are helpful for depth-related tasks, whether S3D is helpful for proportion estimation is an open question. Therefore, the objective of this research is to study whether using

© Springer International Publishing AG 2017
C. Stephanidis (Ed.): HCII Posters 2017, Part I, CCIS 713, pp. 293–299, 2017.
DOI: 10.1007/978-3-319-58750-9_41

S3D for design department students could assist them in improving their ability to interpret the proportions of product shapes.

In our daily life, the display technique has been developed from monocular 3D (M3D) to stereoscopic 3D (S3D) technology with binocular depth cues. With the S3D technology, the system could display not only colorful and high-resolution images, but also process the depth of space. Furthermore, head-mounted display (HMD) with virtual reality (VR) even makes it easier to immerse the viewer in the proposed reality environment. Stereoscopic 3D displays have been used by some research groups to present learning contents for medical, geological research, entertainment, games and education. This project hopes to explore the benefits of research on the students with different spatial abilities for design education through S3D or HMD devices.

2 Literature Review

Stereoscopic images were used not only in audiovisual entertainment and the game industry, but also in medicine, geology, education, and other research fields. Unlike a monocular 3D (M3D) display, an S3D display increased the composite of visual depth cues. Existing S3D display technologies comprised two types, i.e., stereoscopic with glasses and autostereoscopic without glasses [1, 2]. In addition, the head mounted Virtual Reality system offered an alternative stereoscopic display without wearing glasses [3]. Although these systems differed in the technologies of facilitating depth perception [4], overall, stereoscopic 3D displays were helpful for the performance of depth-related tasks. For example, the comprehension, memorization, and recall of 3D scenes and objects could be enhanced [5, 6]. The estimation of depth was more accurate compared to M3D display [7]. In the processes of product design education, the teaching materials and sample cases for demonstration, explanation, and discussion were always presented using images with monocular depth cues [8]. The depth cues of these graphics were identified based on the relative attributes of objects and heavily relied on the experiences and complicated cognition processes of the observers. For freshman and sophomore students of universities, their capabilities of drawing, observation, and spatial imagination are still under construction, design educators need to consider the impact of stereoscopic technologies on traditional design education [9], and try to reduce the gap between communication methods and learning performances [10, 11].

3 Experiment

The stimuli of experiments were drawn from five masterpiece chairs that students in the Department of Industrial Design were familiar with (Fig. 1). The digital models of these chairs were then imported into Unity 3D to construct the experimental system (Fig. 2).

At the beginning of experiments, participants were asked to observe the physical chairs and tried to memorize the proportions of each chair (Fig. 3). After the stage of

Fig. 1. Five masterpiece chairs

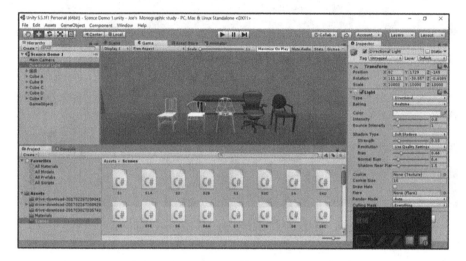

Fig. 2. 3D digital models in the Unity 3D system

Fig. 3. Participants observing the physical chairs

observations, these physical chairs were removed before the digital models of chairs were displayed on the screen, so that no physical chairs were available for reference.

Each computer experiment started with displaying a 3D digital chair with correct proportion. The model rotated with respect to the vertical axis to enhance the

Fig. 4. A 3D digital chair with correct proportion and rotating animation

Fig. 5. Four digital chairs, with one in correct proportion and three in different proportion

Fig. 6. M3D, S3D, and HMD experiment conditions

impression of the masterpiece (Fig. 4). Then four digital chairs, with one in correct proportion and three with the adjustment of width, height, and depth, were put together (Fig. 5). The participants were asked to identify the correct chair within designated time.

There were three experiment conditions, i.e., M3D, S3D, and HMD (Fig. 6). An LG Cinema 3D TV was used for M3D and S3D. While in in S3D, the display mode was switched to stereoscopic and viewed with polarized 3D glasses. An HTC VIVE was used for HMD. The experiments were conducted in a room with illumination controls.

4   Results and Discussions

Ten students, 6 female and 4 male, were invited to participate in the experiments. Among them, five students majored in industrial design, and five students were from other departments. Each participant was asked to identify the correct digital models of five masterpiece chairs, with three deformation rates (20%, 10%, and 5%) in three viewing conditions. The scores were counted based on the correctness of judgement for each task. The results were shown in Table 1.

Table 1. Descriptive statistics for computer-based test with different deformation rates

Deformation rate			20%		10%		5%	
Conditions	Groups	N	Mean	SD	Mean	SD	Mean	SD
M3D	Design	5	4.0	0.71	3.2	1.10	1.6	1.14
	Non-design	5	3.4	1.82	1.6	1.52	1.2	0.84
S3D	Design	5	3.6	1.52	3.6	1.67	2.2	0.84
	Non-design	5	3.8	0.84	2.0	0.71	1.0	1.22
HMD	Design	5	3.8	1.10	3.2	1.48	2.6	0.55
	Non-design	5	2.6	0.55	2.8	0.84	2.0	0.71

The results indicated that the scores decreased with the increase of task difficulty levels. However, the HMD condition yielded less performance drops in both user groups compared to M3D and S3D conditions. HMD was more helpful for proportion judgements.

In M3D and S3D conditions, the performance drops from 20% to 5% deformation rates were consistent. The threshold for students from design department was the deformation changes from 10% to 5%. The threshold for students from other departments was the changes from 20% to 10%. However, in the HMD condition, the performance drop from 20% to 5% was less than the performance drops of M3D and S3D conditions (Fig. 7).

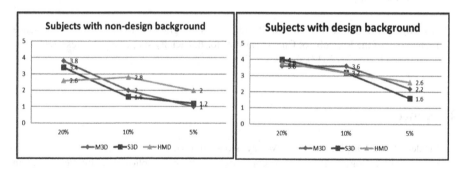

Fig. 7. The performance line charts for participants with design and non-design background

In the M3D condition, the performance gaps between two student groups increased as the level of difficulty increased (Fig. 8). However, in the HMD condition, the gaps between two student groups did not increase significantly. This result indicated that 3D displays with disparity depth cue, a binocular depth cue, could compensate the performance gaps for students with different education background and different spatial abilities.

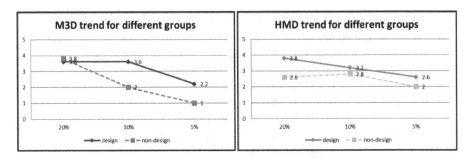

Fig. 8. The performance line charts for M3D and HMD

5 Conclusion

The result of experiment indicated that the advance of technologies could provide with new solutions for traditional design education. Compared to traditional M3D teaching methods with two-dimensional displays, S3D or HMD teaching methods offer the experiences of the third dimension, i.e. perceived depth. This approach could facilitate the reflection and adaptation of dimensions and proportions, compensating the differences of spatial abilities, and therefore enhancing the learning effects significantly. Although the outcome of preliminary experiment had revealed the opportunities, the number of participants was limited. In the future, more participants will be invited to consolidate the results.

Acknowledgement. The authors would like to express our gratitude to the Ministry of Science and Technology of the Republic of China (Taiwan) for financially supporting this research under Grant No. MOST 105-2410-H-036-007.

References

1. Lueder, E.: 3D Displays, 1st edn. Willey, Hoboken (2012)
2. Howard, I.P., Rogers, B.J.: Stereoscopic techniques and applications. In: Perceiving in Depth: Volume 2 Stereoscopic Vision. Published to Oxford Scholarship Online (2012)
3. Masia, B., Wetzstein, G., Didyk, P., Gutierrez, D.: A survey on computational displays: pushing the boundaries of optics, computation, and perception. Comput. Gr. **37**(8), 1012–1038 (2013)
4. Reichelt, S., Häussler, R., Fütterer, G., Leister, N.: Depth cues in human visual perception and their realization in 3D displays. In: Javidi, B., Son, J.Y. (eds.) Proceedings of SPIE, Three Dimensional Imaging, Visualization, and Display 2010, vol. 7690, p. 76900B (2010). doi:10.1117/12.850094
5. Patterson, C., Cristino, F., Hayward, W.G., Leek, C.: Stereo information benefits view generalization in object recognition. In: The 12th Annual Meeting of the Vision Sciences Society (VSS 2012), Naples, FL, pp. 11–16 May 2012 (2012). J. Vis. **12**(9), Article no. 1044
6. McIntire, J.P., Havig, P.R., Geiselman, E.E.: Stereoscopic 3D displays and human performance: a comprehensive review. Displays **35**(1), 18–26 (2014)

7. Price, A., Lee, H.S.: The effect of two-dimensional and stereoscopic presentation on middle school students' performance of spatial cognition tasks. J. Sci. Educ. Technol. **19**(1), 90–103 (2010)
8. Martín, S., Rubio, R.: Parallax cues in the design of graphics used in technical education to illustrate complex spatial problems. Comput. Educ. **53**(2), 493–503 (2009)
9. Danzer, M.: Establishing a new digital/virtual product development process in design education. In: 2011 IDA Congress Education Conference, pp. 22–27 (2011)
10. Mukai, A., Yamagishi, Y., Hirayama, M.J., Tsuruoka, T., Yamamoto, T.: Effects of stereoscopic 3D contents on the process of learning to build a handmade PC. Knowl. Manag. E-Learn.: Int. J. **3**(3), 491–505 (2011)
11. Guedes, K.B., Guimarães, M., Méxas, J.G. (2012). Virtual reality using stereoscopic vision for teaching/learning of descriptive geometry. In: eLmL 2012: The Fourth International Conference on Mobile, Hybrid, and On-line Learning, pp. 24–30 (2012)

Mirrored Perception Cognition Action Model in an Interactive Surgery Assist System

Jiachun Du$^{(\boxtimes)}$, Thomas van Rooij, and Jean-Bernard Martens

Department of Industrial Design, Eindhoven University of Technology,
Postbus 513, 5600 MB Eindhoven, The Netherlands
{J.Du,T.J.A.v.Rooij}@student.tue.nl,
J.B.O.S.Martens@tue.nl

Abstract. Interaction systems with complex sensors are often required to operate in a social context, and hence need to respect social rules of engagement. We propose that reasoning about such systems, and designing them, can be supported by the mirrored-perception-cognition-action model that we introduce in this paper. We illustrate the model and the associated design approach for the specific case of a surgery assist system containing both a graphical and a tangible user interface. Tests were performed to establish how successful users were in making sense of this sensing system.

Keywords: Complex sensors · Social interaction · Tangible user interface · Leap motion · MPCA model

1 Introduction

Ubiquitous computing is a vision on how technological systems can integrate into our daily life in a socially acceptable way. Such systems need to be able to collect information about identity, position, activity, etc. of the users that are present and of events that occur within the environment. They use complex sensors such as cameras with their accompanying image analysis software (e.g., Real Sense from Intel [10]) or tracking sensors (e.g. Leap Motion hand tracking [7]). However, complex sensors tend to be hard to understand by users as they demonstrate intelligent (or at least interactive) behaviour in aspects that they are trained for, but limited or no understanding in other aspects.

In this paper the Mirrored-Perception-Cognition-Action (MPCA) is proposed as a model that can assist designers when reasoning about complex sensing systems. MPCA emphasizes that all interactions between the user and the (digital) system need to pass through a shared physical environment. Rules of social behavior play a role in this interaction, while the designer also needs to take into account the asymmetry in abilities of the user and the system.

The proposed framework has been adopted in the design of a surgery assist system named TPSurgery (Fig. 1). This system allows a surgeon operating in a sterile environment to control both a patient information system and the surgery lighting in a touch-free manner. The MPCA framework has not only been used in the design of the system, but also as a reference framework when analyzing the feedback from a pilot user test.

© Springer International Publishing AG 2017
C. Stephanidis (Ed.): HCII Posters 2017, Part I, CCIS 713, pp. 300–306, 2017.
DOI: 10.1007/978-3-319-58750-9_42

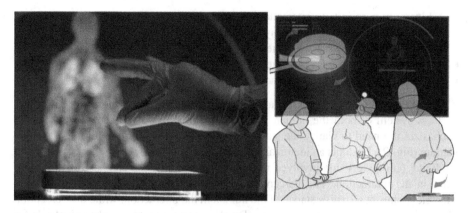

Fig. 1. An overview of TPSurgery

2 Background

Perception Cognition Action (PCA) is a widespread model for describing the information processing within the human brain. It considers three main steps: a human perceives his environment through diverse senses (hearing, vision, touch, smell), interprets these perceptions, combining them with past experiences stored in memory, and plans possible actions, after which such actions are executed using his motor system [8]. This model is clear and simple and has for instance been adopted in robotics [3, 5], human-computer interaction [1] and neuroscience [4].

Several models of interaction have been developed based on this PCA model. For instance, ACT-R [1] is a theory for "simulating and understanding human cognition". The EPIC [6] architecture models "human multimodal and multiple-task performance" and includes "peripheral sensory-motor processors surrounding a production-rule cognitive processor to construct precise computational models for a variety of human-computer interaction situations". Ullmer and Iishi [11] in turn have presented MCRpd as a conceptual framework for tangible user interaction. They promote a system perspective that simultaneously considers the physical and the digital side of the interface.

These models provide insight into how a cognitive process is embedded in human-machine interaction. However, they do not show how information is passing back-and-forth between a user and a system, and how the human and technical system need to be matched to each other at every stage in the interaction.

3 MPCA Framework in Design

Designers are expected to integrate complex sensors in the user context in a way that these sensors can attain optimal performance. They also need to organize the feed-forward and feedback information such that the occurrence and effect of accidents in the interaction are minimized. Bellotti et al. [2] provide an interesting set of questions to consider when assessing the social behavior of such sensing systems:

- **Address:** how to initiate interaction with a system
- **Attention:** establishing that the system is attending
- **Action:** expressing what the system needs to do
- **Alignment:** monitoring system actions
- **Accident:** recovering from interaction errors or misunderstandings

These steps already indicate that an interaction involves one or more loops in which the PCA system of both the human and the system are involved. The MPCA model emphasizes the need to clarify the status of both systems at any time through a single diagram (Fig. 2). It adopts an identical structure for both the cognitive (human) side and the digital (computer) side involved in the interaction, but also emphasizes the asymmetry in the interaction. The Perception (Senses) - Cognition (Reasoning) - Action (Motoric) points at an active stance of the human in the interaction, while the Perception (Control) – Cognition (Model) – Action (Display) points at a more subservient role for the system. Another aspect that the model emphasizes is that both partners in the interaction can only understand each other's intentions when they are expressed in changes in the physical environment that they can both perceive and interpret.

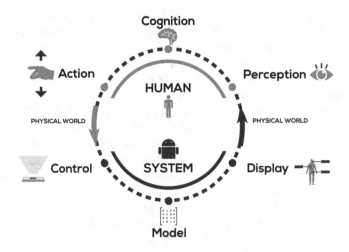

Fig. 2. Mirrored Perception Cognition Action (MPCA) model.

The MPCA loop starts with the perception of the user. The user senses the system and tries to understand the options offered by the system, which is the cognition stage. After that the user formulates a goal and tries to express it by interacting with the system in the action stage. This leads to some changes in the physical world that the system can sense and interpret in the control stage. Adaptations to the model maintained by the system are executed accordingly. These changes in the model are reflected through feedback with actuators in the display stage. The physical world undergoes some changes that the user can observe for the next loop.

This MPCA model emphasizes that the system does not only need to provide feedback about the actions that it has performed itself, but also feed-forward that can help the user understand better what actions he can perform in response [12].

The MPCA model is intended to help the designer in making explicit the issues that need to be considered in each stage of the interaction:

- What a system can do and how it communicates its abilities (assist the user perspective)?
- Sensors: how the system is controlled, i.e., how does it sense what is expected of it? (input variables)
- Actuators: what are adequate ways for the system to display its response? (output variables)
- Transformations: how does the system use the incoming variables (+memory) to extract meaningful information? (mapping from variables to information)
- Which information needs to be maintained in order to demonstrate intelligent behavior (i.e., behavior that does not only depend on the input variables, but also on past events)? (memory)

We illustrate how to apply the MPCA model in an interaction design with the leap motion sensor.

4   Designing with a Complex Sensor

An existing surgery assist system [9] was redesigned using the MPCA model. The redesigned system will be called TPSurgery. It is an interactive surgery assist system that supports browsing patient information and adjusting the lighting within the surgery room. Because of the sterile environment, all interactions need to be accomplished without touching. The system is controlled by hand gestures that are sensed by the leap motion, while the feedback and feed-forward are accomplished through a combination of a tangible user interface (TUI) and a graphical user interface (GUI).

The context is described in the following sentences: Once the surgery begins, the system is powered on and is waiting for interaction. The surgeon holds his/her hand in a position that can be detected in order to activate the system. He/she uses the system to adjust the surgery light. He/she stops adjusting and starts performing surgery. When he/she needs patient information, he/she re-activates the system and switches it to information browsing mode. After browsing patient information, he/she stops looking at the display and continues with the surgery. When the surgery ends, the system is switched off.

Different stages in the interaction for which an MPCA model need to be considered are the following:

- When the system is on, it provides feed-forward information in both the GUI and by means of LEDs blinking in the TUI to inform the user to start interaction through hand gestures (perception) (Fig. 3-a). For simplifying the interaction, only single-hand gestures are allowed. Warning is provided in both the GUI and the TUI when detecting two hands.

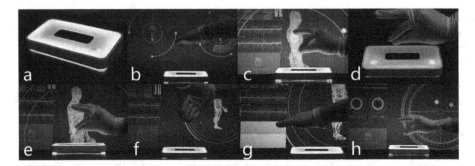

Fig. 3. Workflow of TPSurgery. From left-top to bottom-right is: (a) TPSurgery starts working, (b) setting default hand, (c) browsing patient information with pinch gesture, (d) out of detection warning, (e) not reacting to wrong gestures, (f) rolling hand to recover from error, (g) switching between different modes, (h) controlling surgery light with pinch gesture.

- If the user considers his/her left hand as the 'default hand' (cognition), he/she will put his/her left hand above the leap motion and holds it still for a little while (action). The sensor can detect the hand and identify it as a left hand (control). The system stores that the left hand is the default hand and keeps track of the time that the hand was held still (modeling). The GUI provides feedback for both parameters once the time that the hand is detected exceeds a set threshold (display). On the TUI, the LED with the left hand shape is turned on, informing the user that the left hand has been detected as the preferred hand and that the system is ready to accept input from it. Note that forcing the user to hold his hand still above the leap motion for a little while before starting to interact with it has a very positive influence on the performance of the sensor to correctly interpret hand gestures (Fig. 3-b).

- In the 'infomapping' stage displaying patient information, a blue dot on the screen indicates that the system is attending to the hand and is tracking hand gestures. The LEDs on the TUI indicate the detection range of the leap motion. If the hand starts crossing one of the borders of the detection range, the LEDs on this border turn from blue to red, urging the user to adjust the position of his hand (Fig. 3-d). When the 'infomapping' stage is inactivate, the human body displayed on the GUI is white to inform the user that the system is not accepting hand gestures (Fig. 3-e).

- The user can use a pinch gesture to interact with the GUI display (action). The system decides whether the pinch is intended or not by comparing the pinch strength, which is derived from how well the thumb and forefinger form a closed loop, to a preset threshold (control & modeling). If the user action is interpreted as intentional, the color of the displayed human body will change to blue (display). This informs the user that the system is attending to him (perception & cognition) (Fig. 3-c).

- The user can move his/her default hand to change the position and orientation of the displayed human body. In order to prevent that the system responds to unintended movements, the user has to keep pinching. So from the point of view of the user, the action to be performed is 'pinch and move'. If the user unintentionally moves the display to an unwanted orientation, he can extend his hand and hold it for a little while, which will return the display to its original orientation (Fig. 3-f).

- If the user wants to change the lighting, he/she needs to move his/her hand to the location of the button 'switch' (Fig. 3-g). Then he/she has to hold his/her hand on that button for a few seconds to switch the mode for avoiding unintended action. During this time the button will turn blue to tell the user it is paying attention to his hand gesture (Fig. 3-h). The gestures used for positioning the surgery light are similar to the gestures used to control the displayed human body, so that the user is not expected to learn two separate sets of gestures.

This above description clarifies how design decisions for the prototype have been influenced by the MPCA framework. A small user test was also performed with the protoype. Most users thought the system made sense in telling the detection range while trying to establish interaction by means of having their hand being recognized. The feed-forward and feedback offered through both the graphical user interface and tangible user interface were mostly deemed appropriate. In short, they could quickly made sense of the sensing system. Some subjects were however confused by the context of the application, which was however not the primary topic of the reported study.

5 Discussion and Future Work

This paper proposes the MPCA model as a useful framework when designing inter-action systems with complex sensors. An example of how to design an interaction system with the help this model was explained in some detail. User tests were per-formed in order to establish whether or not users were able to make sense of the sensing system. Results showed that users praised the GUI and TUI feed-forwards and feedbacks.

More design examples and user tests are obviously required to more firmly establish that this MPCA model is indeed useful for designers and leads to designs of complex sensor systems that users can understand and appreciate. The model is therefore actively promoted in a design courses at our department. This paper describes one of the student project outcomes from this design course.

References

1. Anderson, J.R., Matessa, M., Lebiere, C.: ACT-R: a theory of higher level cognition and its relation to visual attention. Hum.-Comput. Interact. **12**(4), 439–462 (1997). http://doi.org/10.1207/s15327051hci1204_5
2. Bellotti, V., Back, M., Edwards, W.K., Grinter, R.E., Henderson, A., Lopes, C.: Making sense of sensing systems: five questions for designers and researchers. In: Proceedings of the SIGCHI Conference on Human Factors in Computing Systems, pp. 415–422. ACM (2002). http://dl.acm.org/citation.cfm?id=503450
3. Cassimatis, N.L., Trafton, J.G., Bugajska, M.D., Schultz, A.C.: Integrating cognition, perception and action through mental simulation in robots. Robot. Auton. Syst. **49**(1), 13–23 (2004)

4. Gottlieb, J.: From thought to action: the parietal cortex as a bridge between perception, action, and cognition. Neuron **53**(1), 9–16 (2007)
5. Haazebroek, P., Van Dantzig, S., Hommel, B.: A computational model of perception and action for cognitive robotics. Cogn. Process. **12**(4), 355–365 (2011)
6. Kieras, D.E., Meyer, D.E.: An overview of the EPIC architecture for cognition and performance with application to human-computer interaction. Hum.-Comput. Interact. **12**(4), 391–438 (1997)
7. Motion, L.: Leap Motion (n.d.). https://www.leapmotion.com/. Accessed 16 Sept 2016
8. Neisser, U.: Cognitive Psychology. Appleton-Century-Crofts. [aAc], New York (1967). Nelson, K.: Self and social functions: individual autobiographical memory and collective narrative. Memory **11**(2), 12536 (2003)
9. Bizzotto, N., Costanzo, A., Bizzotto, L.: Leap motion gesture control with OsiriX in the operating room to control imaging: first experiences during live surgery. Surg. Innov. **1**, 2 (2014)
10. Overview of Intel® RealSense™ SDK | Intel® Software (n.d.). https://software.intel.com/en-us/intel-realsense-sdk. Accessed 16 Sept 2016
11. Ullmer, B., Ishii, H.: Emerging frameworks for tangible user interfaces. IBM Syst. J. **39**(3), 915–931 (2000)
12. Van Den Hoven, E., Frens, J., Aliakseyeu, D., Martens, J.-B., Overbeeke, K., Peters, P.: Design research & tangible interaction. In: Proceedings of the 1st International Conference on Tangible and Embedded Interaction, pp. 109–115. ACM (2007). http://dl.acm.org/citation.cfm?id=1226993

Research on Human Acceptability of Household Environment Temperature Fluctuation

Huimin Hu[1], Rui Wang[1(✉)], Chaoyi Zhao[1], Hong Luo[1], Aixian Li[1],
Li Ding[2], and Yifen Qiu[3]

[1] Ergonomics Laboratory, China National Institute of Standardization,
Beijing, China
{huhm,wangrui,zhaochy,luohong,liax}@cnis.gov.cn
[2] Key Laboratory for Biomechanics and Mechanobiology of Ministry
of Education, School of Biological Science and Medical Engineering,
Beihang University, Beijing, China
dingl971316@buaa.edu.cn
[3] Laboratory for Man-Machine-Environment Engineering,
School of Aeronautic Science and Engineering,
Beihang University, Beijing, China
qiuyifen@buaa.edu.cn

Abstract. In this paper, temperature fluctuation in the room which was tested in which environment is built by the domestic air conditioner Different air conditioning set temperature may cause different temperature fluctuation in each position. From the subjective assessment results it can be known that, under the thermal comfort environment condition, the biggest acceptable temperature fluctuation is obtained and is 0.6 °C in summer and 0.8 °C in winter. In summer working condition, temperature fluctuation in each test point is compared with the acceptable temperature fluctuation (0.6 °C) and then the satisfaction rate for each working condition can be obtained. The test results show that the highest satisfaction rate about temperature fluctuation is 94% when the indoor air temperature is about 26 °C. Air temperature higher or lower than 26 °C will reduce the satisfaction rate about temperature fluctuation. Working condition in the winter, using the same method, the satisfaction rate about temperature fluctuation for each working condition can be obtained, it is higher than the summer, it can reach to 90% in every working condition. It is because that tester wears a lot of clothes in winter, the clothes can reduce the body's sensitivity to the environment temperature changes. Test results are matched well with subjective assessment. The research in this article can provide basis for thermal comfort evaluation of typical residential air conditioning room and also can guide the design of air condition system in order to ensure the thermal comfort of the room.

Keywords: Household environment · Thermal comfort · Temperature fluctuation · Satisfaction rate

C. Stephanidis (Ed.): HCII Posters 2017, Part I, CCIS 713, pp. 307–315, 2017.
DOI: 10.1007/978-3-319-58750-9_43

1 Introduction

According to statistics, more than 80% of the time in a person's life is spent indoors, and indoor environment quality such as sound, light, heat environment and indoor air quality have significant impact on people's physical and mental health, comfort and work efficiency [1]. As shown by physiological studies, when a person is in thermal comfort conditions, his thought, observation ability and operational skills, etc. are at the best state [2]. There are two kinds of methods to evaluate the thermal comfort: subjective assessment and objective assessment [3]. Subjective assessment about thermal comfort can be obtained by subjective evaluation questionnaire and the result is usually discrete [4]. Temperature fluctuation is a very important parameter in thermal comfort evaluation index. Temperature fluctuation means the range of changes in the indoor temperature with a specified period of time after the indoor temperature reaches the state of thermal stability. With significant temperature fluctuations, the human body will feel hot and cold, affecting the body's thermal comfort sensation. In order to study the range of comfort environment parameters, subjective assessment and objective assessment are combined and used in this article.

In this paper, the thermal environment laboratory was used to test the temperature fluctuations of indoor environment caused by ordinary household air conditioner at temperatures set differently. In addition, the subjects' subjective evaluation method was adopted to determine the acceptable temperature fluctuation within the typical residential air conditioned room under the thermal comfort conditions in winter and summer.

2 Test Equipment and Method for Household Environment Temperature Fluctuation

2.1 Artificial Environment Laboratory

The artificial environment room used in the thermal comfort experiment of residential air-conditioned room was 4.20 m long, 3.8 m wide and 2.5 m high with the wall structure fully consisting of insulation storage boards. Room windows were 1.6 m long, 1.4 m wide and 1 m from the ground. The air conditioner in laboratory was installed at the height of 2.2 m. The temperature and other parameters of the external environment of laboratory were controlled by the environmental control unit, so as to simulate the climates in winter and summer. The temperature measurement points in laboratory were arranged according to the $5 \times 5 \times 5$ temperature measurement point layout method, and the room layout diagram and the temperature measurement point distribution are shown in Fig. 1(a) below. According to people's daily major postures of indoor activities, room temperature measurement points of this experiment room were determined to be arranged with five measurement points in the vertical direction of, as shown in Fig. 1(b). The temperature measurement points are located at the four walls and ceiling in the room, the air outlet and return air inlet of air conditioner and the outdoor wall. In order to test radiation temperature in the room, a black ball thermometer was placed inside and outside the air conditioning sector respectively and a hygrograph was placed above the black ball to record the humidity.

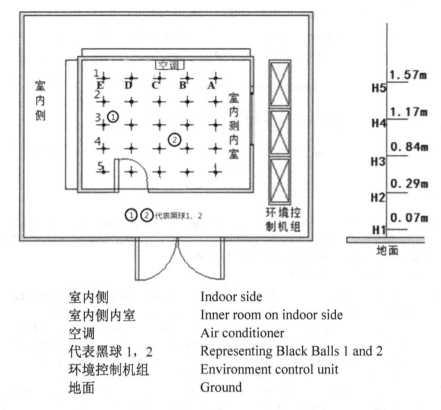

室内侧	Indoor side
室内侧内室	Inner room on indoor side
空调	Air conditioner
代表黑球 1，2	Representing Black Balls 1 and 2
环境控制机组	Environment control unit
地面	Ground

Fig. 1. Diagram of thermal comfort test room

The model air conditioner used in this evaluation was a variable frequency air conditioner, which could automatically provide the cooling (heating) capacity required based on the room environment temperature; when the indoor temperature reaches the expected value, the air conditioner operated at a constant speed to accurately maintain the temperature and achieved "non-stop operation" so as to ensure the stability of ambient temperature. There was, however, a range of changes in its cooling (heating) capacity, so the indoor temperature also had a range of changes, i.e. the temperature fluctuation. Although there are definitions of scope set out in the internal standard specifications of some enterprises in respect of the exact temperature fluctuation acceptable by human body, there is no specific description about their basis and source, so there is no uniform definition now. This research is aimed at determining the temperature fluctuation acceptable by human body based on the human thermal sensation experiment and the related theoretical calculations.

2.2 Selecting and Test of Subjects

This research was performed on the basis of residential air conditioner, so the region, age, gender, BMI and other differences should be taken into account when the subjects

Table 1. Information of subjects selected

Category of subjects		Number (person)
The senior (55–70)	Male	3
	Female	3
The middle-aged (33–35)	Male	3
	Female	3
Young people (16–35)	Male	3
	Female	3
Children (7–15)	Male	3
	Female	3

were selected, and they should have the mentality to provide positive cooperation, certain basic knowledge of thermal comfort, healthy body and serious attitude. The specific information of subjects are listed in Table 1.

Specific experimental steps:

(1) The indoor temperature and humidity were adjusted to achieve the expected values and remained stable. The specific steps are as follows: the environmental control system outdoors was started; the temperature and humidity were adjusted to the expected value and remained stable, with the temperature fluctuation within the scope of ± 0.2 °C; the temperature difference of two black balls indoors was no more than 0.2 °C with humidity fluctuation value of $\pm 3\%$.

(2) The subjects wore winter/summer test clothes. The summer clothes included underwear, short sleeve, shorts and shoes, with the total thermal resistance of 0.26col; the winter clothes included underwear, three-layered cotton pajamas, socks and shoes, with total thermal resistance of 0.9clo.

(3) The subjects entered the experiment room to experience the environment comfort, and they were allowed to walk or stand at any position in the room to feel the temperature, humidity and wind speed. Subjects experienced for 10 min, and the completed the subjective questionnaire after the end of experience.

(4) Subjective questionnaires were collected and the temperature and humidity of the next experiment were adjusted. The subjects returned to the transition room for a break. After the new experiment temperature and humidity were stabilized (about 40 min), the subjects entered the experiment room for experience again. Considering the long duration of one experiment, if one subject experienced multiple temperatures at the same time, the total experiment duration would be too long, causing subjects' negative emotions such as agitation. Therefore, each subject experienced only 3 or 4 temperatures.

Test picture is shown in Fig. 2.

Fig. 2. Test picture

3   Test Results of Indoor Temperature Fluctuation

In the natural environment, the temperature will not have significant change in a relatively short period of time (such as 1 h). In the artificially created environment, such as the use of air conditioner, heating radiator or fan as environment creating equipment, it is also hoped that they could be simulated in the work and such effect could be achieved. In the actual operation of the air conditioning equipment, however, the temperature will have in significant fluctuations in a relatively short period of time because of the mechanical cycle problems (such as fan blade swing problem of vertical air conditioner). This temperature fluctuation may cause discomfort in the human body, and it will also result in discomfort of being sometimes hot and sometimes cold. The temperature distribution in the test room is shown in Fig. 3,

In order to evaluate the temperature fluctuation acceptable by human body, the temperature fluctuation experiment was performed in the summer operating conditions. The maximum acceptable temperature fluctuation at different environment temperatures was determined through the subjective evaluation of subjects. In this experiment, the temperature fluctuation period was set at 7 min. The temperature fluctuation of air conditioner was observed by subjects at the positions with vertical distances of 2 m and 2.5 m from the outlet of air conditioner. It is found through the experiment that the distance from the air outlet has no significant impact on the acceptable temperature fluctuation range. According to the preliminary research results of our research group, the comfortable temperature range within residential room is 25–28 °C in summer and 22–25 °C in winter [5]. On this basis, the research on the temperature fluctuation acceptable by human body in comfortable environment was performed. Under operating conditions in summer, the experimental results of acceptable temperature

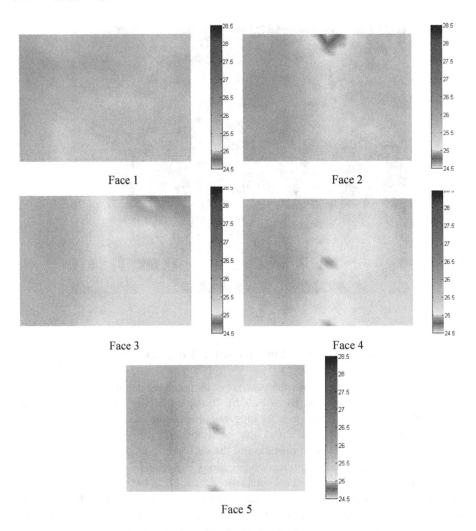

Face 1   Face 2

Face 3   Face 4

Face 5

Fig. 3. Temperature distribution in the test room

fluctuation when the environment temperature changes in the range of 25–28 °C are shown in Fig. 4. Under operating conditions in winter, the experimental results of acceptable temperature fluctuation when the environment temperature changes in the range of 22–25 °C are shown in Fig. 5.

As shown by the experiment results in Fig. 4, there is a small range of changes in temperature fluctuation acceptable by human body with the current environment temperature in the comfortable temperature environment of summer, and the range of temperature fluctuation acceptable by human body is about 0.6 °C; in Fig. 5, however, there is a large range of changes in temperature fluctuation acceptable by human body with the environment temperature in the comfortable temperature environment of winter, and a large range of temperature fluctuation acceptable by human body, which

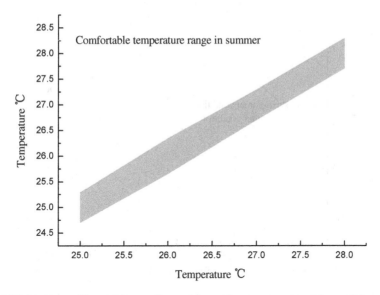

Fig. 4. Acceptable temperature fluctuations under summer operating conditions

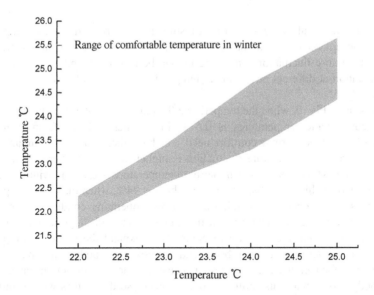

Fig. 5. Acceptable temperature fluctuations under winter operating conditions

is about 1 °C. The range of temperature fluctuation acceptable by human body becomes larger with the rise of environment temperature. The clothes worn in winter are thicker with larger thermal resistance, resulting in decreased sensitivity to temperature of the human body, so the range of temperature fluctuation acceptable by human body in winter is larger than that in summer.

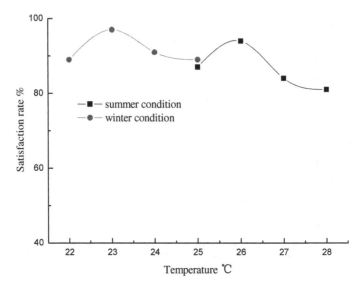

Fig. 6. Human body's acceptability rate of temperature fluctuation at different environment temperature

According to the aforesaid experiment results, it is determined that the temperature fluctuation acceptable by human body is 0.6 °C in summer and 1.0 °C in winter. Based on this temperature fluctuation range, the human body's acceptability of this temperature fluctuation at different environment temperatures was tested, with the test results shown in Fig. 6:

As shown by Fig. 6, when the temperature fluctuation acceptable by human body at different comfortable temperatures is 0.6 °C in summer and 1.0 °C in winter, the majority of people's thermal comfort need can be satisfied and the human body's acceptability rate of temperature fluctuation is higher than 80%. There is the highest satisfaction rate, which is 97%, when the room temperature is 23 °C in winter operating conditions, and the highest satisfaction rate, which is 94%, when the room temperature is 26°C in summer operating conditions. In winter operating conditions, the overall satisfaction rate is still higher than that in summer even with large temperature fluctuation, indicating that the increase in clothes will expand the range of temperature fluctuation acceptable by human body and improve the body's thermal comfort. Wearing too much clothes, however, will cause the decline in action capability of human body and increase discomfort in other aspects, so the clothes worn should also meet the requirements of activities performed by the human body.

4   Conclusion

Through the combination of objective test and subjective evaluation, the range temperature fluctuation acceptable by human body in comfortable indoor thermal environment has been researched, and the range of temperature fluctuation acceptable by human body has been determined in winter and summer operation conditions, respectively, providing a theoretical basis for developing air conditioning control strategy for thermal comfort. The specific conclusions are set out below:

1) From the subjective assessment results it can be known that, under the thermal comfort environment condition, the biggest acceptable temperature fluctuation is obtained and is 0.6 °C in summer and 0.8 °C in winter.

2) The highest satisfaction rate about temperature fluctuation is 94% when the indoor air temperature is about 26 °C in summer; working condition in the winter, the satisfaction rate about temperature fluctuation is higher than the summer, it can reach to 90% in every temperature.

Acknowledgments. This research is supported by "Special funds for the basic R&D undertakings by welfare research institutions" (522016Y-4488, 712016Y-4940 and 242016Y-4700) and General Administration of Quality Supervision, Inspection and Quarantine of the People's Republic of China (AQSIQ) science and technology planning project for 2016, which is Research on Chinese thermal manikin used for evaluating the comfort of indoor thermal environments (2016QK177 and 2015QK237).

References

1. Xiaolin, X., Baizhan, L.: Influence of indoor thermal environment on thermal comfort of human body. J. Chongqing Univ. **4**(28), 102–105 (2005)
2. Li, S., Lian, Z.: Discussions on the application of Fanger's thermal comfortable theory. Shanghai Refrigeration Institute Academic Annual Conference (2007)
3. Holmér, I., Nilsson, H., Bohm, M., et al.: Thermal aspects of vehicle comfort. Appl. Hum. Sci. J. Physiol. Anthropol. **14**(4), 159–165 (1995)
4. Hai, Y., Runbai, W.: Evaluation indices of thermal environment based on thermal manikin. Chin. J. Ergon. **11**(2), 26–28 (2005)
5. Hu, H., Wang, R., Zhao, C., Luo, H., Ding, L., Qiu, Y.: Experimental study on thermal comfort of indoor environment. In: Soares, M., Falcão, C., Ahram, T. (eds.) Advances in Ergonomics Modeling, Usability & Special Populations. AISC, vol. 486. Springer, Cham (2017)

Continuous Affect Rating in Cartesian Space of Pleasure and Arousal Scale by Joystick Without Visual Feedback

Mitsuhiko Karashima[(✉)] and Hiromi Nishiguchi

Tokai University, Tokyo, Japan
mitsuk@tokai-u.jp

Abstract. This research proposed the continuous affect rating method that rated the affective states by joystick in the Cartesian space from two dimensions of pleasure-displeasure and arousal-sleepiness without visual feedback. This research also examined the effectiveness of the proposed method through two experiments.

In Experiment 1 an edited video, which consisted of four video clips, was prepared as the dynamic visual and auditory stimuli. Twelve participants were required to manipulate the joystick in the Cartesian space without any visual feedback so as to make the coordinates (pleasure-displeasure, arousal-sleepiness) correspond to their affective states while watching the edited video. In Experiment 2, the same four video clips as in Experiment 1, were prepared as the dynamic stimuli. Eleven participants were required to manipulate the joystick while watching each clip and also required to describe their current mood after watching each clip with the PANAS.

The results of Experiment 1 revealed that the coordinates obtained by the proposed method changed according to the changes of the dynamic visual and auditory stimuli, and that the coordinates could reflect the changes of the affective states caused by the dynamic stimuli. The results of Experiment 2 revealed that the proposed method could rate the difference of the affective states between the different dynamic stimuli confirmed by the results of the responses of the self-reports. The results also suggested that the coordinates obtained by the proposed method were highly consistent with the response of the self-reports.

Keywords: Continuous affect rating · Joystick · Without visual feedback

1 Introduction

Many methods that self-reported the affective states have been developed with questionnaires [1–5]. The methods with the questionnaires, however, have the common limitation that they cannot provide continuous affect rating with a real time resolution. Some continuous affect rating methods have been developed in order to overcome this limitation [6–10]. Some of them rated the affective states only on one particular dimension [6, 7, 10]. Russell [2, 11–13] demonstrated that affective states could be mapped in the Cartesian space from two bipolar dimensions of pleasure-displeasure

C. Stephanidis (Ed.): HCII Posters 2017, Part I, CCIS 713, pp. 316–323, 2017.
DOI: 10.1007/978-3-319-58750-9_44

and arousal-sleepiness. It meant that one dimensional rating methods could not rate general affective states but a specific affective state (positive-negative [6, 7], pleasure-displeasure [10]). On the other hand, Shubert [8] proposed the continuous affective rating method in two dimensional space of happiness-sadness and aroused-sleepy with multiple visual feedbacks. Nigel et al. [9] also proposed the continuous affective rating method in two dimensional space of positive-negative and arousing-calming with visual feedback. Both of the methods had the visual feedbacks to the participants about the cursor position when they manipulated the device such as the joystick or the mouse. These feedbacks might make it easy for the participants to manipulate the device to the cursor position they wanted and also keep the participants' workload for manipulating the device low. These methods were applied to rating the affective states caused by temporally static stimuli or music. However, the visual feedbacks might interfere with watching the stimuli if the dynamic visual and auditory stimuli such as a movie was used. The continuous affect rating method in two dimensional space of pleasure-displeasure and arousal-sleepiness without visual feedback might be valuable for rating the affective states caused by the dynamic visual and auditory stimuli though it might be difficult for the participants to manipulate the device to the cursor position they wanted.

This research proposed the continuous affect rating method that rated the affective states by joystick in the Cartesian space from two dimensions of pleasure-displeasure and arousal-sleepiness without visual feedback and examined the effectiveness of the proposed method for rating the affective states caused by the dynamic visual and auditory stimuli through two experiments.

2 Proposed Continuous Affect Rating Method

In this session, we describe the construction of our proposed continuous affect rating method. The participants are required to manipulate the joystick in order to rate their affective states in the Cartesian space from two dimensions of pleasure-displeasure and arousal-sleepiness [2]. The joystick is placed at the origin of the pleasure-displeasure (x) axis and the arousal-sleepiness (y) axis written on the desk. In order to express the maximum pleasure state, for example, the participants are required to tilt the joystick to the right as possible and in order to express the maximum arousal state the participants are required to tilt the joystick forward as possible. If the participants release the joystick, it returns the neutral position. The original software records the joystick movements within the virtual square ranging from −100 to 100 in increments of 10 on each axis and the sampling rate is 100 ms. For example, the maximum pleasure state is recorded as 100 on x axis and the maximum arousal state is recorded as 100 on y axis. The neutral position of the joystick is recorded as (0, 0). The relationship between the orthogonal projection of the tilt angle of the joystick to each axis and the recorded coordinate of each axis in the virtual square is the linear relationship. When the participants manipulate the joystick, there is not any visual feedback except in the training mode. In the training mode, the coordinates box on the screen provides the numerical feedback about the coordinates (x, y) in the virtual square which the manipulated joystick expresses.

3 Experiment 1

The aim of the first experiment was to examine whether the coordinates obtained by the proposed method could reflect the changes of the affective states caused by the changes of the dynamic visual and auditory stimuli.

3.1 Method

Participants. Twelve participants (mean age 21.8, *SD* 0.39, 6 females and 6 males) who were voluntary right-handed undergraduate students and were not provided any payment, took part in Experiment 1. They received a thorough explanation about the method of Experiment 1 and signed the consent form.

Apparatus. The original software for the proposed continuous affect rating method was written in Visual Basic 2015 and was made operational on the windows 10. The software controlled the presentation of the dynamic visual and auditory stimuli, the transformation from the tilted angle of the joystick (Defender Joystick Cobra R4 USB 12 buttons) to the coordinates in the virtual square, and the records of the joystick movements. In the training mode, the software provided the coordinates box on the screen as a visual feedback.

An edited video was prepared as the dynamic visual and auditory stimuli. The edited video consisted of four video clips, "M1 Grand Prix", "The Champ", "Juon", "Maldives Beach" in this order. "M1 Grand Prix" ("M1") was the contest for comedy duos and was expected to make Japanese participants delight [14]. The clip was edited to 4 min 14 s. "The Champ" ("Champ") was the famous American movie in 1979 and expected to make the participants sad [15]. The clip was edited to 2 min 52 s. "Juon" was Japanese horror movie in 2003 and was expected to make the participants afraid [16]. The clip was edited to 1 min 26 s. "Maldives Beach" ("Beach") was the background video and was expected to make the participants satisfied [15]. The clip was edited to 40 s.

The training video was also prepared for the training mode. The video consisted of 100 sets of the coordinates (x, y) generated randomly between -100 and 100 in increments of 10. The interval between every two sets was 20 s.

Procedure. At first the participants manipulated the joystick in the training mode in order to be able to manipulate the joystick at will. They were required to manipulate the joystick in order to make the values of the coordinates box correspond to the presented coordinates (x, y) as soon as possible and, after that, also required to make the joystick keep the same position till the next set of the coordinates was presented. After training, the participants were required to manipulate the joystick to correspond to their affective states which were caused by the dynamic visual and auditory stimuli.

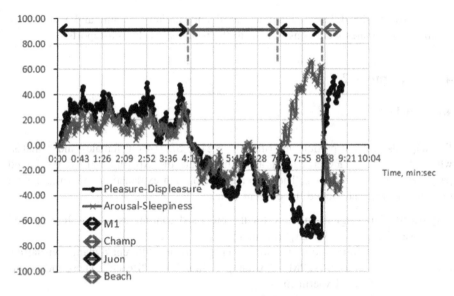

Fig. 1. Averaged time series of the coordinates expressed by the joystick

3.2 Results and Discussions

Unfortunately, the data of one participant (male, 22 years old) could not be recorded correctly. The data of eleven participants were adopted as the results of this experiment. Figure 1 shows eleven participants' averaged time series of the coordinates in the virtual square which the manipulated joystick expressed. The sampling rate of these time series was 1 s by obtaining the average data from every 10 data whose sampling rate was 100 ms.

Both of the coordinates of pleasure-displeasure (x) axis and arousal-sleepiness (y) axis showed the positive intermediate value in "M1" and coordinates almost corresponded to the position of "DELIGHTED" in a circumplex model of affect [11, 12]. Both of the coordinates showed the negative intermediate value in "Champ" where coordinates almost corresponded to the position of "SAD". The coordinate of x axis showed the negative intermediate value and the coordinate of y axis showed the positive intermediate value in "Juon". The coordinates almost corresponded to the position of "AFRAID". The coordinate of x axis showed the positive intermediate value and the coordinate of y axis showed the negative intermediate value in "Beach". The coordinates almost corresponded to the position of "RELAXED". These results revealed that the coordinates obtained by the proposed method changed according to the changes of the dynamic visual and auditory stimuli, and that the coordinates could reflect the changes of the affective states caused by the dynamic stimuli.

However, these results are only the trend by eleven participants' average and it cannot be examined whether the obtained coordinates were consistent with the subjective response. Experiment 2 was held in order to examine statistically whether the proposed continuous affect rating method could rate the difference of the affective states between the different dynamic visual and auditory stimuli and whether the obtained coordinates were consistent with the response of the self-reports.

4   Experiment 2

4.1   Method

Participants. Eleven participants (mean age 21.8, *SD* 0.40, 6 females and 5 males), who participated in Experiment 1 and whose data of Experiment 1 were adopted, participated in Experiment 2. They received a thorough explanation about the method of Experiment 2 and signed the consent form.

Apparatus. The original software for the proposed continuous affect rating method, which was the same as for Experiment 1.

Four different four video clips were prepared as the different dynamic visual and auditory stimuli as follows; "M1", "Champ", "Juon", and "Beach". These video clips were the same as for Experiment 1.

Positive and Negative Affect Schedule (PANAS) Japanese version [17] was prepared as the self-reports of the current mood immediately after watching the clip. The PANAS Japanese version consists of two scales: Positive Affect (PA) and Negative Affect (NA), each with 8 items. The response format provided six alternatives from "1. Not at all" to "6. Extremely". PA score and NA score were respectively obtained by adding the scores on each 8 items.

Procedure. Experiment 2 consisted of four sessions composed of four different video clips. In each session, the participants were required to manipulate the joystick to correspond to their affective states which were caused by a video clip. After watching through the clip, the participants were required to describe their current mood with the PANAS Japanese version. The order of the sessions was the same for all the participants as follows: "M1", "Champ", "Juon", and "Beach".

4.2   Results and Discussions

Affective States Ratings by the PANAS. The results of one way repeated measures ANOVA revealed that the averaged scores were significantly different between four different clips (PA score $F(3,30) = 25.84$, $p < 0.01$, NA score $F(3,30) = 55.70$, $p < 0.01$). The results of the multiple comparison by Bonferroni revealed that the averaged scores between any two clips has the significant difference in one at least of the PA and NA scores as shown in Table 1. These results of the responses of the self-reports of the current mood confirmed that the four different clips caused the different affective states immediately after watching the clips each other.

Affective States Ratings by the Proposed Method. The results of one way repeated measures ANOVA revealed that the averaged coordinates were significantly different between four different clips (Pleasure-Displeasure $F(3,30) = 17.86$, $p < 0.01$,

Table 1. The results of multiple comparison by Bonfferoni for the averaged PA and NA scores

PA					NA			
	M1	Champ	Juon	Beach		M1	Champ	Juon	Beach
M1		>*	>*	>*	M1		<*	<*	n.s.
Champ			n.s.	n.s.	Champ			<*	>*
Juon				n.s.	Juon				>*
Beach					Beach				

* p<0.05 n.s. p>0.05

Arousal-Sleepiness F(3,30) = 23.15, p < 0.01). The results of the multiple comparison by Bonferroni revealed that the averaged coordinates between any two clips has the significant difference in one at least of the coordinates as shown in Table 2. From these results the proposed continuous affect rating method could rate the difference of the affective states between the four different clips confirmed by the results of the responses of the self-reports.

Table 2. The results of multiple comparison by Bonfferoni for the averaged coordinates

Peasure-Displeasure			(x)		Arousal-Sleepiness			(y)
	M1	Champ	Juon	Beach		M1	Champ	Juon	Beach
M1		>*	>*	n.s.	M1		n.s.	n.s.	>*
Champ			n.s.	<*	Champ			<*	>*
Juon				<*	Juon				>*
Beach					Beach				

* p<0.05 n.s. p>0.05

Relationship of Affective States Ratings Between by PANAS and by the Proposed Method. As mentioned above, the proposed continuous affect rating method could rate the difference of the affective states between the four different clips, which was confirmed by the results of the PANAS scores. However, the relationship between the coordinates obtained by the proposed method and the PANAS scores was not examined directly because the dimensional space, pleasure-displeasure and arousal-sleepiness, for rating by the proposed method was different from the dimensional space, positive affect and negative affect, for the PANAS scores. As the dimensional space labeled positive affect and negative affect could be produced by 45° rotating the dimensional space, pleasure-displeasure and arousal-sleepiness [18], the new averaged coordinates (PA', NA') were produced by rotating the obtained averaged coordinates (x, y) of each clip and each participant by −45°. And the correlation coefficients between the new averaged coordinates and the PANAS scores of each clip and each participant were calculated.

Table 3. The correlations between the new (averaged, peak) coordinates and the PANAS scores

Averaged				Peak		
	PA'	NA'			PA'$_{peak}$	NA'$_{peak}$
PA	0.468**	-		PA	0.729**	-
NA	-	0.803**		NA	-	0.791**
		** p<0.01				** p<0.01

Table 3 shows the results of the correlation analysis between the new averaged coordinates and PANAS scores. There were the significant correlations between PA and PA' and between NA and NA'. It suggested that the coordinates obtained by the proposed method were relatively consistent with the response of the self-reports.

Though the correlation between PA and PA' was significant, the correlation coefficient was not so high as shown in Table 3. Fredrickson and Kahneman [7] suggested that the responses of the self-reports after watching the clips correlated more highly to the peak of the continuous affect rating than to the average. So the peak coordinates (x_{peak}, y_{peak}) of each clip and each participant were obtained and the new peak coordinates (PA'_{peak}, NA'_{peak}) were produced by $-45°$ rotations. The results of the correlation analysis between the new peak coordinates and the PANAS scores were shown in Table 3. There were the significant correlations between PA and PA'$_{peak}$ and between NA and NA'$_{peak}$. It suggested that the coordinates obtained by the proposed method were highly consistent with the response of the self-reports.

5 Conclusion

This research proposed the continuous affect rating method that rated the affective states by joystick in the Cartesian space from two dimensions of pleasure-displeasure and arousal-sleepiness without visual feedback. The effectiveness of the proposed method for rating the affective states caused by the dynamic visual and auditory stimuli was examined through two experiments. The results of Experiment 1 revealed that the coordinates obtained by the proposed method changed according to the changes of the dynamic visual and auditory stimuli, and that the coordinates could reflect the changes of the affective states caused by the dynamic stimuli. The results of Experiment 2 revealed that the proposed method could rate the difference of the affective states between the different dynamic stimuli confirmed by the results of the responses of the self-reports. The results also suggested that the coordinates obtained by the proposed method were highly consistent with the response of the self-reports. From these results of the experiments, it seemed that the proposed continuous affect rating method was effective though the proposed method had no visual feedback.

This research could not confirm sufficiently the validity of the time series variation of the coordinates obtained by the proposed method. In the future research, the coherence between the time series of the coordinates by the proposed method and the time series of some physiological data such as heart rate will be tested [6].

References

1. Watson, D., Clark, L.A., Tellegen, A.: Development and validation of brief measures of positive and negative affect: the PANAS scales. J. Pers. Soc. Psychol. **54**(6), 1063–1070 (1988). doi:10.1037/0022-3514.54.6.1063
2. Russell, J.A., Weiss, A., Mendelsohn, G.A.: Affect grid: a single-item scale of pleasure and arousal. J. Pers. Soc. Psychol. **57**(3), 493–502 (1989). doi:10.1037/0022-3514.57.3.493
3. Thayer, R.E.: The Biopsychology of Mood and Arousal. Oxford University, New York (1989)
4. Spielberger, C.D.: Manual for the State-Trait Anger Expression Inventory (STAXI). Psychological Assessment Resources, Odessa (1988)
5. Spielberger, C.D.: State-Trait Anxiety Inventory: Bibliography, 2nd edn. Consulting Psychologists Press, Palo Alto (1989)
6. Gottman, J.M., Levenson, R.W.: A valid procedure for obtaining self-report of affect in marital interaction. J. Consult. Clin. Psychol. **53**(2), 151–160 (1985). doi:10.1037/0022-006X.53.2.151
7. Fredrickson, B.L., Kahneman, D.: Duration neglect in retrospective evaluations of affective episodes. J. Pers. Soc. Psychol. **65**(1), 45–55 (1993). doi:10.1037/0022-3514.65.1.45
8. Schubert, E.: Measuring emotion continuously: validity and reliability of the two-dimensional emotion-space. Aust. J. Psychol. **51**, 154–165 (1999). doi:10.1080/00049539908255353
9. Nagel, F., Kopiez, R., Grewe, O., Altenmuller, E.: EMuJoy: software for continuous measurement of perceived emotions in music. Behav. Res. Methods **39**(2), 290–293 (2007). doi:10.3758/BF03193159
10. Sakurai, Y., Shimizu, R.: Development of the real-time joystick rating method for affect and establishing its validity. Jpn. J. Res. Emot. **16**(1), 87–96 (2008). (in Japanese)
11. Russell, J.A.: A circumplex model of affect. J. Pers. Soc. Psychol. **39**(6), 1161–1178 (1980). doi:10.1037/h0077714
12. Russell, J.A., Lewicka, M.: A cross-cultural study of a circumplex model of affect. J. Pers. Soc. Psychol. **57**(5), 848–856 (1989). doi:10.1037/0022-3514.57.5.848
13. Russell, J.A.: Core affect and the psychological construction of emotion. Psychol. Rev. **110**, 145–172 (2003). doi:10.1037//0033-295X.110.1.145
14. Takada, T., Yukawa, S.: Comparison of emotions elicited by watching films. Tsukuba Psychol. Res. **45**, 49–55 (2013). (in Japanese)
15. Noguchi, M., Sato, W., Yoshikawa, S.: Films as emotion-eliciting stimuli: the ratings by Japanese subjects. Technical report of IEICE, HCS104(745), pp. 1–6 (2005). (in Japanese)
16. Takada, T., Yukawa, S.: Title in Japanese. Jpn. J. Res. Emot. **23**(Suppl.), ps14 (2013). doi:10.4092/jsre.23.supplement_ps14
17. Sato, T., Yasuda, A.: Development of the Japanese version of positive and negative affect schedule (PANAS) scales. Jpn. J. Pers. **9**(2), 138–139 (2001). (in Japanese)
18. Watson, D., Tellegen, A.: Toward a consensual structure of mood. Psychol. Bull. **98**(2), 219–235 (1985). doi:10.1037/0033-2909.98.2.219

Attention Value of Motion Graphics on Digital Signages

Tsubasa Kato and Nahomi Maki[✉]

Kanagawa Institute of Technology,
1030 Shimo-ogino, Atsugi-Shi, Kanagawa 243-0292, Japan
maki@ic.kanagawa-it.ac.jp

Abstract. In recent years, movie advertisements in digital signages have been shown at various places, such as train stations and street corners. Digital signages are installed in busy environments where people come and go. Therefore, people watch advertisements in digital signages in a shorter time than they do on TV commercials at home. Accordingly, movie advertisements shown in digital signages should attract attention the moment people look at them. In this study, we discuss the attention value of colors, which is mainly utilized in still media, and combine this concept with motion graphics elements.

1 Introduction

In recent years, movie advertisements in digital signages have been shown at various places, such as train stations and street corners. Digital signages are installed in busy environments where people come and go. Therefore, people watch advertisements in digital signages in a shorter time than they do on TV commercials at home. Accordingly, movie advertisements shown in digital signages should attract attention the moment people look at them. In this study, we discuss attention value of colors, which is mainly utilized in still media, and combine this concept with elements of motion graphics elements. We propose a method for effectively attracting attention, create original advertisements using the method, and conduct experiments on a digital signage in the Kanagawa Prefecture Office (Fig. 1).

Fig. 1. Digital signage in the Kanagawa Prefecture Office

C. Stephanidis (Ed.): HCII Posters 2017, Part I, CCIS 713, pp. 324–329, 2017.
DOI: 10.1007/978-3-319-58750-9_45

2   Attention Value of Motion Graphics in Digital Signages

2.1   Attention Value of Motion

Human beings have a peripheral visual field used for taking in the first impression and the entire view before gazing at a target and adjusting the focus. In the peripheral visual field, the sight is not sharp and the resolution is low. The ability to recognize the details is inferior, but one can see more than 90% of the view. Through this peripheral visual field, people have excellent ability to sense movement and have a high possibility of instinctively noticing faint movements at the edge of the field of vision (Hayafuku et al.).

The direction of human eyes tends to move naturally. The eyes move from top to bottom naturally because people are used to reading characters and from left to right because of a sense of gravity. The eyes also move naturally from the upper left to the lower right because they are accustomed to reading characters and because of a sense of gravity.

2.2   Psychological Effect of Motion

Sijll [1] argued that movements could make people feel either comfortable or uncomfortable. People generally feel comfortable when seeing movement from left to right. On the contrary, people feel uncomfortable when seeing the movement from right to left (Fig. 2). With regard to diagonal motion, people feel comfortable when seeing the motion from upper left to bottom right and slightly comfortable from upper right to bottom left. By contrast, people feel uncomfortable when seeing the motion from bottom right to upper left and slightly uncomfortable from bottom left to upper right (Fig. 3).

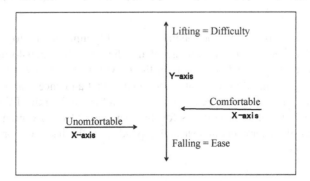

Fig. 2. Comfortable and uncomfortable horizontal motions

2.3   Motion Graphics that Attracts Attention

Based on an investigation of visual attraction and a psychological action to a motion, we explored the direction of motion graphics to be used for a movie advertisement for display in a digital signage. A study showed that human eyes have a natural movement that could be felt as either comfortable or uncomfortable. Moreover, people receive a

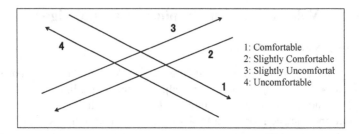

Fig. 3. Comfortable and uncomfortable diagonal motions

strong impression from the movement that makes them feel uneasy. Therefore, using the eye direction that is not natural and an uncomfortable movement in motion graphics can attract attention and make the audience feel uncomfortable. However, making an uncomfortable motion become noticeable from a movie produced only with an unnatural eye movement and uncomfortable motion was difficult. Thus, we combined them with the natural eye movement and comfortable motion to be noticeable.

3   Movie Production for the Experiment

In this study, we created movie advertisements for the Kanagawa Prefecture TV program shown daily from Monday to Friday. We combined the rules and determined which movement would attract attention.

3.1   Motion Graphics Through the Transformable Animation of Figures (Movie 1)

When a motion is sensed in the peripheral visual field, humans tend to try to see it in the center visual field. Taking advantage of this feature, clear transformable motion graphics was used for the balloon shape in the movie. In this study, we produced an advertisement movie that draws visual attraction and that audiences can watch without getting tired by changing the shape of the balloon and expanding the TV program title on the screen. For the motion graphics for the characters of the TV program title, the motion in which the characters appear and expand from the back and line up in front quickly was created.

Fig. 4. Motion graphics process of the TV program title expansion

Fig. 5. Process of the balloon shape transformation

For the transformable animation of shapes, the motion of a polygon's changing vertex position was created.

Figures 4 and 5 illustrate the processes of the motion graphics for a TV program title expansion and balloon shape transformation, respectively.

3.2 Motion Graphics Using Comfortable and Uncomfortable Directions (Movie 2)

In the advertisements, we showed TV programs and applied effective movie transitions between each program to attract attention using the proposed method. We made the audience feel uneasy by introducing complicated, pleasant, and uncomfortable movements and changing up their combinations to attract attention. We hypothesized that repeating comfortable and uncomfortable motions creates the effect of attracting attention. Two kinds of movie transitions were used: a transition that combines a slightly uncomfortable motion that moves from the lower left to the upper right and a comfortable motion that moves from the upper right to the lower right and then to the

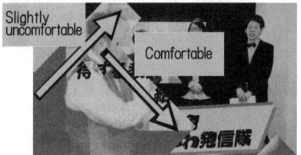

Fig. 6. Example of a movie transition in the experiment

upper left, and a transition that combines an uncomfortable motion that moves from the lower right to the upper left and a slightly comfortable motion that moves from the upper right to the lower left.

Figure 6 shows an example of a movie transition from the cut. The program title is presented to the cut, which shows the introduction sentences.

4   Experiment

We conducted an experiment to determine whether or not the produced Movie1 and Movie2 could attract attention. The movies were displayed on the digital signage in the Kanagawa Institute of Technology, which had a similar environment to the Kanagawa Prefecture Office.

As comparative targets in the broadcasting experiment, the Movie1-A and Movie2-A versions, the effective motions of which had been taken from Movie1 and Movie2, respectively, were prepared. In the broadcasting experiment, Movie1, Movie1-A, Movie2, and Movie2-A were repeatedly broadcast for 1 h for five days.

The result of the five-day experiment showed that while Movie1 was showing, 277 pedestrians walked by the digital signage and 33 (12%) actually watched the movie.

While Movie1-A was showing, 339 pedestrians walked by the digital signage and 35 (10%) actually watched the movie.

While Movie2 was showing, 519 pedestrians walked by the digital signage and 65 (13%) actually watched the movie were 65.

While Movie2-A was showing, 525 pedestrians walked by the digital signage and 48 (9%) actually watched the movie.

The result of the broadcasting experiment is illustrated in Fig. 7.

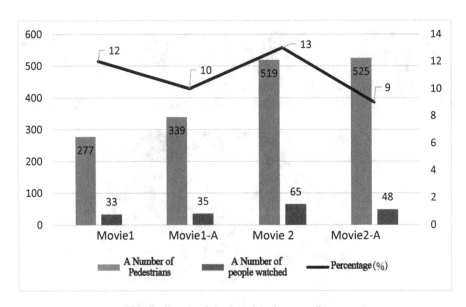

Fig. 7. Result of the broadcasting experiment

Overall, the percentage of people who watched Movie1 and Movie2 was higher than that of those who watched Movie1-A and Movie2-A. Motion graphics was able to successfully attract attention.

5 Conclusion

In this study, two advertisement movies of the Kanagawa Prefecture were created for showing in a digital signage in the Kanagawa Prefecture Office. The result showed that more people could be attracted to watch advertisement movies in digital signages installed in an environment where people come and go by using effective visual attraction.

However, when visual attraction is emphasized too much, decreased visibility becomes a problem. Moreover, understanding the contents of the movie becomes difficult because of excessive use of complicated colors, motions, and shapes. Visual attraction sometimes defeats its own purpose. In future research, the appropriate balance of colors, motions, and shapes should be determined to explore more effective motion graphics for digital signages.

Reference

1. Van Sijll, J.: Cinematic Storytelling, Ubiquitous Learning: Michael Wiese Film Productions (2005)

Towards a Cognitive Agility Index: The Role of Metacognition in Human Computer Interaction

Benjamin J. Knox[1(✉)], Ricardo G. Lugo[2], Øyvind Jøsok[1,3], Kirsi Helkala[1], and Stefan Sütterlin[2,4]

[1] Norwegian Defence Cyber Academy, Lillehammer, Norway
{bknox, ojosok}@cyfor.mil.no, khelkala@mil.no
[2] Department of Psychology, Inland Norway University of Applied Sciences, Oslo, Norway
{Ricardo.Lugo, Stefan.Sutterlin}@inn.no
[3] Child and Youth Participation and Development Research Program, Inland Norway University of Applied Sciences, Lillehammer, Norway
[4] Center for Clinical Neuroscience, Oslo University Hospital, Oslo, Norway

Abstract. Research on human factors in the cyber domain is lacking. Metacognitive awareness and regulation have been shown to be important factors in performance, but research integrating metacognitive strategies in socio-technical systems is lacking. This study aims to investigate metacognition as a potential index of evaluating individual cognitive performance in cyberspace operations. Cyber military cadets were tested during a cyber-exercise to see how metacognitive awareness and regulation influenced performance in the Hybrid Space conceptual framework. Findings suggest that metacognitive strategies could explain Hybrid Space performance outcomes and support the development of a *cognitive agility index* for cyber operators. Future research and training programs for cyber officers should incorporate metacognition as measurement outcomes and in training to help index development and performance.

Keywords: Cognitive agility · Metacognition · Cyber operations · Performance · Hybrid Space

1 Introduction

Introduction of cyber as a domain of operations [1] places enhanced metacognitive demands on individuals as task characteristics require effective coordination between multiple agents and asset types (human, technical and intangible). Human factors in cyber defence are getting increased attention from research communities (see. e.g. [2–5]), however there are currently no available performance measures to evaluate human performance in cyber operations [6, 7]. Consequently no common best practice or guidelines are found in the area of education and training for cyber defence individuals and teams [8–10].

© Springer International Publishing AG 2017
C. Stephanidis (Ed.): HCII Posters 2017, Part I, CCIS 713, pp. 330–338, 2017.
DOI: 10.1007/978-3-319-58750-9_46

1.1 Hybrid Space

This contribution aims to address the issue of performance measurement by utilising the versatility of the Hybrid Space framework (HS) (Fig. 1a; [11]). The HS frames the interconnection between cyber-physical (x-axis) and the strategic-tactical (y-axis) dimensions. The adaptability of the HS framework allowed researchers to visualize the location of a cognitive focus, at a given point-in-time, based upon the subjects' self-report. Understanding the processes and actions required to enhance performance in a hybrid environment may rely on metacognitive skills in human computer interaction and consequently how these skills aid cognitive agility in the HS.

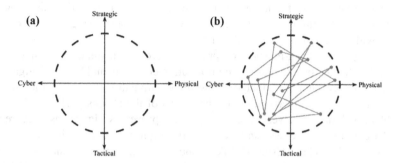

Fig. 1. (a) The Hybrid Space. (b) Exemplary visualization of cognitive agility

1.2 Metacognition

Metacognition refers to 'thinking about thinking' and includes the components knowledge of one's abilities, situational awareness, and behavioral regulation strategies [12]. Individuals with high metacognitive skills have more accurate and confident judgment of their own performance in relation to task demands and are better able to accurately describe their strengths, weaknesses, and their potential to improve. Metacognition is considered as having two dimensions: metacognitive awareness and metacognitive regulation [12].

Metacognitive Awareness and Regulation: Metacognitive awareness refers to what learners know about learning and includes knowledge of one's own cognitive abilities (e.g. 'I have trouble remembering dates in history') and knowledge of the particular tasks (e.g. 'The ideas in this chapter that I'm going to read are complex'). High metacognitive awareness of own cognitive processes (planning, monitoring, evaluations) can facilitate accurate judgment of performance levels [13]. Metacognitive regulation refers to how people monitor their learning and control their cognitive processes while learning, for example, realising that a particular strategy is not efficient in reaching one's goals and being able to change to more efficient strategies. In a cyber operations context this can mean recognising a potential threat in cyberspace as exceeding individual technical abilities and consider activating additional personal or technical resources in the physical domain. Developing a metacognitive understanding of own behavior can be understood as becoming aware that the outcomes of previous actions were taken under immense time pressure to serve short-term goals serving primarily tactical purposes, then re-adjust previous short-term goals to focus on more strategic and long term goals. The ability to be metacognitively aware of own performance without underestimation of own capacities or inappropriate over-confidence is considered a relatively stable personality trait that can be quantified and made subject to training and improvement [11].

1.3 State of Art

While much research is found in the field of metacognition, critical thinking and learning (see [14] for full review), there is a growing interest focusing on metacognitive strategies within the cyber security domain.

The ability of decision-makers and problem-solvers to maintain cyberspace operations can be affected by changes in the information environment [15]. To mitigate this, cognitive constructs should be included into future simulations and modeling of cyber attacks to increase the understanding of the effects of the attacks [15].

Problem solving involves several cognitive processes. Problems that require high-order cognitive processes can be characterized into well-, semi-, ill-, and severely ill-structured problem [16]. Critical thinking and metacognition are needed when semi-, ill-, and severely ill structured problems are solved successfully. In the extended paper of their original study, [17] the authors discuss further the need to develop learning tools that elicit sense-making and metacognitive processes. Empowering novices' sense-making skills and metacognitive processes would accelerate their path to become expert.

The above research can also be applied when attempting to improve human performance in Cyberspace operations. The challenges presented via cyber come in many known and still to be discovered forms. Typically they can vary from well-structured to severely ill-structured.

What is a 'good' performance in cyber tasks is still under discussion [6, 7]. Earlier research shows that measuring performance in cyber security training scenarios requires more than simply 'capture-the-flag' type competitions [18, 19]. Increasingly the importance of developing human abilities to grasp threat complexities, understand and minimize consequences and communication are taken into consideration when performance is evaluated [20].

Good situational awareness is a factor that increases the probability for good performance, though it does not guarantee it, it is a good starting point [21]. This emphasizes the benefit of education and training methods that build on cognitive processes capable of improving human capacities to gain and maintain situation awareness. For example, an experiment that contains four elements for measuring performance that are measured at random times: mission, cyber solution, metrics and game, can support prospects of improved cyber situational awareness [22]. The following two examples are techniques capable of measuring situational awareness in cyber training scenarios.

SAGAT [23] protocol contains several questions on three different situational awareness levels: perception, comprehension, and projection. Answers are compared to the selected variables and the more accurate the answers are the higher-level awareness a person has. The results are provided on each situational awareness level.

QUASA [24] is a quantitative, combined probe and self-evaluation technique, where a person is required to answer 'probe statements' by either agreeing or disagreeing. After agreeing or disagreeing, the subject evaluates to what degree of confidence the prior assessment was made and states which of the other teams (participating the same experiment) will most likely give a correct answer to this probe.

In our study, the HS framework was used as a tool to measure cognitive focus movements, aka. *cognitive agility*, with the aim of relating these movements to metacognitive strategies. Focusing on these strategies during pre-training and educational programmes could support long-term development and application of high order cognitive skills during cyber defence scenarios, resulting in improved performance.

1.4   Hypothesis

Based on these previous findings and our assumptions, we hypothesized that higher metacognitive awareness would be positively associated with more movement in the HS. We further expected stronger metacognitive regulatory skills to be positively related to HS movements.

Focusing on metacognitive strategies as means of evaluating cognitive performance gave us the opportunity to validate the above core assumptions on which the HS is based. We tested how metacognitive strategies, as measured by meta-cognitive awareness and self-regulatory processes influence HS movement.

2   Method

This study operationalized and quantified cyber operators' subjective movements in the HS as a function of metacognitive abilities in individual officers during a cyber defense exercise (CDX).

2.1   Cyber Defense Exercise

Data was collected during the Norwegian Defense Cyber Academy's (NDCA) annual Cyber Defense Exercise (CDX). This is an arena that facilitates the opportunity for fourth year cyber engineer students to train in tactics, techniques and procedures for handling various types of cyber attacks. The exercise contributes to improving appreciation for the human and technical competences necessary to establish, manage and defend a military information infrastructure under simulated operational conditions. The students worked in four teams of 9 or 10 members (of a total of 37 students, 31 participated in the study), took decisions and acted in order to strengthen operational freedom, mission assurance and control in the cyber domain. The four teams participating in the exercise worked independently from each other but not against each other.

Success was given in the form of expert feedback to the decisions and actions taken during the exercise. Intrusions were initiated by an affiliated agency engaged to help the NDCA with their education.

2.2   Measurements and Metrics

The teams were composed of 31 cyber officer cadets (M_{age} = 22.7 years, SD = 0.71) resembling a complete cohort enlisted in the NDCA. The exercise lasted four days and data was collected on the third day.

The HS is mapped on a Cartesian plane visualizing the cyber-physical and tactical-strategic dimensions. Participants were asked to simultaneously mark their cognitive location within the HS [11] (see Fig. 1b) each hour from 08:00 to 20:00. In addition, students noted their current task at each position, to give context to further analysis (Fig. 2).

Hybrid Space Operationalization: Movement in the HS is operationalized through four constructs and represents the dependent variables in the study. Four dependent variables were created:

- HSDT: distance traveled in the Cartesian Plane measured by Euclidian distance
- HSQC: Number of quadrant changes
- HSxM: Movement along the cyber-physical domain (x-axis)
- HSyM: Movement along the strategic-tactical domain (y-axis)

To measure metacognitive awareness, the Metacognitive Awareness Inventory [25] was used. It is a self-report scale comprising of 52 items that includes several subscales assessing knowledge of cognition (declarative knowledge, procedural knowledge, conditional knowledge) and regulation of knowledge (planning, information management strategies, monitoring, debugging strategies and evaluation). Items are assessed on bipolar responses (true/false) and then ratios are computed from the subscales. Sample items include 'I find myself using helpful learning strategies automatically' (procedural knowledge) and 'I ask myself if I have considered all options when solving

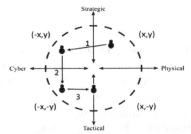

Movement in the Hybrid Space: (1) operator reporting quadrant change (x,y) to (-x,y); (2) operator moving along the y-axis; (3) an operator reporting movement to an axis but not crossing to other quadrant

Fig. 2.   Hybrid space movements

a problem' (comprehension monitoring). The test shows high reliability on all subscales (Cronbach's $\alpha = .90$).

To measure metacognitive regulation, the Self-Regulation Questionnaire [26] was used. The SRQ-63 is a 5-point Likert self-report scale ranging from strongly disagree to strongly agree. The scale has 7 subscales that consist of receiving, evaluating, triggering, searching, formulating, implementing, and assessing. Sample items include; 'I usually keep track of my progress toward my goals' and 'I have sought out advice or information about changing'. The test shows high reliability (test-retest: $r = .94$, $p < .0001$; $\alpha = .91$).

2.3   Statistical Analysis

To test the hypothesis multiple regression analyses on each of the HS dependent variables was performed. Metacognitive awareness and self-regulatory scores were entered as the independent variables and HS operationalizations were entered as the dependent variables. Alpha (α) significance levels are set to .05.

3   Results

To test the hypothesis, four regression analyses were performed where each of the Cognitive Agility Indices were entered as dependent variables and MCAI and SRQ correlates was entered as independent variables. Results are shown in Table 1.

Table 1. Descriptive Statistics ($N = 31$)

Cognitive Agility Indices (CAI)	Mean	SD	Min.	Max.
HSDT	8.32	2.58	3.29	13.39
HSQC	3.00	2.07	0.00	7.00
HSxM	1.27	0.69	0.29	2.78
HSyM	1.27	0.68	0.15	2.84
Metacognitive Awareness Inventory (MCAI)				
Declarative knowledge	1.30	0.18	1.00	1.63
Procedural knowledge	1.41	0.25	1.00	1.75
Conditional knowledge	1.30	0.19	1.00	1.80
Planning	1.55	0.22	1.14	1.86
Comprehension	1.57	0.27	1.14	2.00
Information management	1.29	0.15	1.00	1.60
Debugging	1.16	0.17	1.00	1.40
Evaluation	1.52	0.29	1.00	2.00
Metacognitive self-regulation (total)	*213.00*	*13.86*	*178.00*	*241.00*
Receiving	30.65	3.50	23.00	37.00
Evaluating	30.29	4.73	19.00	39.00
Triggering	30.45	2.95	23.00	37.00
Searching	33.00	3.06	27.00	38.00
Planning	29.52	3.96	21.00	37.00
Implementing	29.32	4.10	18.00	37.00
Assessing	29.77	3.53	23.00	36.00

Hybrid Space distance travelled (HSDT): Metacognitive awareness (debugging $b = -.235$, $t = -1.317$, $p = .199$) and total scores on self-regulation ($b = .293$, $t = 1.644$, $p = .111$) explained 17.8% of the distance moved in the Hybrid space ($F = 3.040$, $p = .032$, $R^2 = .178$, Adjusted $R^2 = .120$).

Quadrant changes (HSQC): Self-regulation predicted quadrant changes ($F = 3.407$, $p = .023$, $R^2 = .345$, Adjusted $R^2 = .243$) but only evaluating ($b = .259$, $t = 1,484$, $p = .075$), triggering $b = .347$, $t = 1.964$, $p = .030$), searching ($b = .198$, $t = 1.122$, $p = .136$) and implementing ($b = -.229$, $t = -1.323$, $p = .099$) were the only factors that contributed in explaining the variance.

Only self-regulation (evaluation $r = .371$, $F = 4.640$, $p = .040$, $R^2 = .138$, Adjusted $R^2 = .108$,) was positively associated with cognitive movements relative to the x-axis.

Neither metacognitive awareness nor self-regulatory processes could explain cognitive movements relative to the y-axis.

4 Discussion

Metacognition could predict movement in the HS, but not for y-axis movements. Y-axis movements may be dependent on fundamental cognition (i.e. rumination, worry, and self-efficacy) that may better explain vertical maneuvering. Metacognitions did have positive relationships to all other HS operationalizations but it was specific processes that could predict changes. Total distance travelled in the Hybrid Space (HSDT) was predicted by metacognitive debugging strategies, defined as a regulation of cognition used to correct comprehension and performance errors, and self-regulation. Evaluative metacognitive regulatory behaviors predicted x-axis movements, and along with triggering behaviors, searching for solutions, and implementing new strategies was associated with more quadrant changes.

This empirical contribution supports implementing the OLB pedagogic model as pathway to improved communication performance in socio-technical cyber-physical environments [27]. Formal teaching programmes designed to build metacognitive competence could facilitate cyber cadets' use of intrinsic cognitive agility, as planned action. By measuring these performance metrics during cyberspace education and training scenarios - as cadets make planned conscious cross-quadrant maneuvers in the HS - the results can be collated into *Cognitive Agility Index*. It is hoped that this work will lead to the first science based performance indicator scale for cyber teams and individuals.

5 Conclusion

This research demonstrate that metacognition - measured as movements in the Hybrid Space framework - can be a useful method of evaluating individual cognitive performance in cyberspace operations.

The findings indicate impulsive cognitive movement due to the sample group acting without conscious thought. This is typical for people who have not undergone formal educational programmes of metacognitive learning. The participants reported movements could be defined as representing an intrinsic cognitive agility index. Given that metacognitive ability is trainable, the results of this experiment clearly indicate techniques to improve performance in a complex environment: such as that presented by the Hybrid Space framework.

Acknowledgements. The authors wish to specify that Benjamin J. Knox and Ricardo Lugo are equal lead authors.

References

1. Cooperative Cyber Defence Centre of Excellence, NATO (2016). https://ccdcoe.org/nato-recognises-cyberspace-domain-operations-warsaw-summit.html
2. Gutzwiller, R.S., Fugate, S., Sawyer, B.D., Hancock, P: The human factors of cyber network defense. In: Proceedings of the Human Factors and Ergonomics Society Annual Meeting, vol. 59, no. 1. SAGE Publications (2015)
3. Knott, B.A., Mancuso, V.F., Bennett, K., Finomore, V., McNeese, M., McKneely, J.A., Beecher, M.: Human factors in cyber warfare: alternative perspectives. In: Proceedings of the Human Factors and Ergonomics Society Annual Meeting, vol. 57, no. 1. SAGE Publications (2013)
4. Mancuso, V.F., Christensen, J.C., Cowley, J., Finomore, V., Gonzalez, C., Knott, B.: Human factors in cyber warfare II emerging perspectives. In: Proceedings of the Human Factors and Ergonomics Society Annual Meeting, vol. 58, no. 1. SAGE Publications (2014)
5. Rajivan, P., Janssen, M.A., Cooke, N.J.: Agent-based model of a cyber security defense analyst team. In: Proceedings of the Human Factors and Ergonomics Society Annual Meeting, vol. 57, no. 1, pp. 314–318. SAGE Publications (2013)
6. Buchler, N., Fitzhugh, S.M., Marusich, L.R., Ungvarsky, D.M., Lebiere, C., Gonzalez, C.: Mission command in the age of network-enabled operations: social network analysis of information sharing and situation awareness. Front. Psychol. 7(937) (2016)
7. Forsythe, C., Silva, A., Stevens-Adams, S., Bradshaw, J.: Human dimension in cyber operations research and development priorities. In: Schmorrow, D.D., Fidopiastis, C.M. (eds.) AC 2013. LNCS (LNAI), vol. 8027, pp. 418–422. Springer, Heidelberg (2013). doi:10.1007/978-3-642-39454-6_44
8. Arnold, T., Harrison, R., Conti, G.: Towards a career path in cyberspace operations for army officers. In: Small Wars Journal (2014)
9. Franke, U., Brynielsson, J.: Cyber situational awareness–a systematic review of the literature. Comput. Secur. 46, 18–31 (2014)
10. NATO Cyber Defence Pledge (2016). http://www.nato.int/cps/en/natohq/official_texts_133177.htm?selectedLocale=en
11. Jøsok, Ø., Knox, Benjamin J., Helkala, K., Lugo, Ricardo G., Sütterlin, S., Ward, P.: Exploring the hybrid space. In: Schmorrow, D.D.D., Fidopiastis, C.M.M. (eds.) AC 2016. LNCS (LNAI), vol. 9744, pp. 178–188. Springer, Cham (2016). doi:10.1007/978-3-319-39952-2_18
12. Metcalfe, J., Shimamura, A.P.: Metacognition: Knowing About Knowing. MIT Press, Cambridge (1994)
13. Keith, N., Freese, M.: Self-regulation in error management training: emotion control and metacognition as mediators of performance effects. J. Appl. Psychol. 90(4), 677 (2005)

14. Abrami, P.C., Bernard, R.M., Borokhovski, E., Waddington, D.I., Wade, C.A., Persson, T.: Strategies for teaching students to think critically: a meta-analysis. Rev. Educ. Res. **85**(2), 275–314 (2015)

15. Haas, M.W., Mills, R.F., Grimaila, M.R.: Aiding understanding of a contested information environment's effect on operations. In: Rothrock, L., Narayanan, S. (eds.) Human-in-the-Loop Simulations, pp. 175–202. Springer, Heidelberg (2011)

16. Smy, V., Cahillane, M., MacLean, P.: Cognitive and metacognitive prompting in ill-structured tasks: the art of asking. In: Proceedings of International Conference on Information, Communication Technologies in Education (2015)

17. Smy, V., Cahillane, M., MacLean, P.: Sensemaking and metacognitive prompting in ill-structured problems. Int. J. Inf. Learn. Technol. **33**(3), 186–199 (2017)

18. Fink, G., Best, D., Manz, D., Popovsky, V., Endicott-Popovsky, B.: Gamification for measuring cyber security situational awareness. In: Schmorrow, D.D., Fidopiastis, C.M. (eds.) AC 2013. LNCS (LNAI), vol. 8027, pp. 656–665. Springer, Heidelberg (2013). doi:10.1007/978-3-642-39454-6_70

19. Bashir, M., Wee, C., Memon, N., Guo, B.: Profiling cybersecurity competition participants: self-efficacy, decision-making and interests predict effectiveness of competitions as a recruitment tool. Comput. Secur. **65**, 153–165 (2017)

20. Cyber 9/12 Student Challenge, CSC (2017). http://www.gcsp.ch/Events/Cyber-9-12-Student-Challenge-2017

21. Endsley, M.R.: Measurement of situation awareness in dynamic systems. Hum. Factors **37**(1), 65–84 (1995)

22. Brynielsson, J., Franke, U., Varga, S.: Cyber situational awareness testing. In: Akhgar, B., Brewster, B. (eds.) Combatting Cybercrime and Cyberterrorism. Advanced Sciences and Technologies for Security Applications, pp. 209–233. Springer, Heidelberg (2016)

23. Endsley, M.R.: Situation awareness global assessment technique (SAGAT). In: Proceedings of the IEEE National Aerospace and Electronics Conference, pp 789–795 (1988)

24. McGuinness, B.: Quantitative analysis of situational awareness (QUASA): applying signal detection theory to true/false probes and self-rating. In: Proceedings of the Command and Control Research and Technology Symposium (2004)

25. Schraw, G., Dennison, R.S.: Assessing metacognitive awareness. Contemp. Educ. Psychol. **19**(4), 460–475 (1994)

26. Aubrey, L.L., Brown, J.M., Miller, W.R.: Psychometric properties of a selfregulation questionnaire (SRQ). Alcohol. Clin. Exp. Res. **18**(2), 420–525 (1994)

27. Knox, B.J., Jøsok, Ø., Helkala, K., Khooshabeh, P., Ødegaard, T., Sütterlin, S.: Socio-technical communication: The Hybrid Space and the OLB-Model for science-based cyber education. Manuscript under revision (2017)

A Practice for the Certification of Minimum Flight Crew Workload

Haiyan Liu$^{(\boxtimes)}$, Xianchao Ma, Yinbo Zhang, Zhefeng Jin,
and Dayong Dong

Shanghai Aircraft Design and Research Institute, Shanghai, China
liuhaiyan@comac.cc

Abstract. Although FAR/CCAR25.1523 addressed the accessibility and ease of operation of necessary controls in addition to individual workload, the methods of evaluating workload are far less straightforward, and usually dominate the determination of the minimum flight crew.

This paper sets a Practice for the certification of minimum flight crew workload. With respect to the construct of "Workload" there are no absolute norms available to test against. Workload has many contributing factors such as the tasks at hand, ease of use of the equipment, working and flight conditions, automation etc. Task load can be predicted, however workload is what is measured (and experienced) in flight. Pilot workload may be evaluated using a number of techniques: Direct comparisons, indirect comparisons and standalone evaluation techniques.

Keywords: Flight deck · Minimum flight crew · Workload · Certification

1 Introduction

This rule has been in place since 1993 and was used to prevent possible workload overload in flight crew due to reduced crew complement from three to two crew members and the advent of advanced flight deck automation. Automation sometimes unexpectedly increases task load. Furthermore the complexities of flight deck automation were also of such nature, that a special new rule was introduced on flight deck error, EASA Certification Specification 25.1302. That rule addresses much more complex issues in comparison with 25.1523 where the focus is on workload and overall ease of operation.

FAR/CCAR 25.1523 Minimum flight crew

The minimum flight crew must be established so that it is sufficient for safe operation, considering

(a) *The workload on individual crew members;*
(b) *The accessibility and ease of operation of necessary controls by the appropriate crew member; and*
(c) *The kind of operation authorised under FAR/CCAR 25.1525. (IFR)*

The criteria (see 5.d. this document) used in making the determinations required by this paragraph are set forth in Appendix D.

© Springer International Publishing AG 2017
C. Stephanidis (Ed.): HCII Posters 2017, Part I, CCIS 713, pp. 339–346, 2017.
DOI: 10.1007/978-3-319-58750-9_47

According to the AC 25.1523-1, The purpose of the evaluations conducted under 25.1523 is to corroborate by demonstration the predicted crew workload submitted by the applicant to substantiate compliance with 25.1523, and to provide an independent and comprehensive assessment of individual crewmember workload in a realistic operating environment. Any problems encountered would probably be resolved by system redesign or procedural changes to redistribute workload more evenly.

2 Certification Approach

With respect to the construct of "Workload" there are no absolute norms available to test against. Workload has many contributing factors such as the tasks at hand, ease of use of the equipment, working and flight conditions, automation etc. Task load can be predicted, however workload is what is measured (and experienced) in flight.

What is used for workload assessments are comparisons of experimental designs with known and/or accepted designs under equivalent test conditions. Such a baseline for heart rate, as an example, could be relaxation, standard computer work, a relaxed flight segment like cruising or flying the same scenario in another well known aircraft.

If there is no existing data or experience to build on. It is envisaged to select a reference aircraft that is already certificated on a similar or equal basis. Selection of the final reference aircraft needs to be agreed at an early stage of the certification process with the authority.

In general, the approach proposed will require pilots to fly the same scenarios in the certificated aircraft and in the aircraft which to be certified. If the crew results on workload and ease of operation are similar, certification can be requested [1].

Personal preferences and habits can play a subjective role in such an evaluation. It is therefore recommended to also use both objective measures such as heart rate to verify any difficulties indicated.

The basic workload function in Appendix D to CCAR/FAR 25.1523 comprise

(1) Flight path control.
(2) Collision avoidance.
(3) Navigation.
(4) Communications.
(5) Operation and monitoring of aircraft engines and systems.
(6) Command decisions.

The basic workload factors in Appendix D to CCAR/FAR 25.1523 comprise:

(1) The accessibility, ease, and simplicity of operation of all necessary flight, power, and equipment controls, including emergency fuel shutoff valves, electrical controls, electronic controls, pressurization system controls, and engine controls.
(2) The accessibility and conspicuity of all necessary instruments and failure warning devices such as fire warning, electrical system malfunction, and other failure or caution indicators. The extent to which such instruments or devices direct the proper corrective action is also considered.

(3) The number, urgency, and complexity of operating procedures with particular consideration given to the specific fuel management schedule imposed by centre of gravity, structural or other considerations of an airworthiness nature, and to the ability of each engine to operate at all times from a single tank or source which is automatically replenished if fuel is also stored in other tanks.

(4) The degree and duration of concentrated mental and physical effort involved in normal operation and in diagnosing and coping with malfunctions and emergencies.

(5) The extent of required monitoring of the fuel, hydraulic, pressurization, electrical, electronic, de-icing, and other systems while en route.

(6) The actions requiring a crewmember to be unavailable at his assigned duty station, including: observation of systems, emergency operation of any control, and emergencies in any compartment.

(7) The degree of automation provided in the aircraft systems to afford (after failures or malfunctions) automatic crossover or isolation of difficulties to minimize the need for flight crew action to guard against loss of hydraulic or electric power to flight controls or to other essential systems.

(8) The communications and navigation workload.

(9) The possibility of increased workload associated with any emergency that may lead to other emergencies.

(10) Incapacitation of a flight crewmember whenever the applicable operating rule requires a minimum flight crew of at least two pilots.

To comply with the requirements of FAR/CCAR 25.1523, AC25.1523-1 clearly states that: *"... The test program should address all workload functions and factors listed in 25.1523 and Appendix D..."*, and also should consider the following circumstances:

(1) On a series of representative routes with a representative mix of navigation aids, airports, instrument approaches and Air Traffic Control (ATC) services.

(2) The routes should be selected to provide the likelihood of encountering types of adverse weather appropriate to the aircraft's intended operation (IMC conditions, night, turbulence, icing, etc.).

(3) The test crew should be assigned to a daily work schedule that is representative of the type of operations for which the airplane was developed. The program should include the duration of the work day and the maximum expected number of departures and arrivals, flights which begin at night, maximum allowable duty times, and minimum rest periods.

(4) With representative dispatch configurations with inoperative equipment from the minimum equipment list (MEL). Combinations of these representative dispatch configurations with probable subsequent simulated malfunctions should form the basis of many of the evaluation scenarios.

(5) The airplane should be operated on routes that would adequately sample high density areas in both IMC and VMC and should also include precision and non-precision approaches, holdings, missed approaches, and diversions to alternate airports.

(6) With an incapacitated demonstrating that workload remains acceptable during the total incapacitation of a crewmember at any point in a given flight. It must be shown that the airplane can be operated safely and landed safely with the remaining crew at a planned or unplanned destination. Incapacitated crewmember tests need not be additive to all other "dispatch plus subsequent failure" scenarios. Incapacitation should be viewed as another example of "subsequent failure" to be included within one or more scenarios beginning with a dispatch configuration which includes selected items from the proposed Minimum Equipment List.

(7) With system failures demonstrating the workload consequences of changes from normal to failed modes of operation. Both primary and secondary systems should be considered and representative combinations of failures should be included.

Crew procedures are designed in such a way to evenly distribute the task load over crew members under normal flight conditions and/or to redistribute tasking under abnormal and emergency conditions. Next to the system design, these procedures determine or influence the actual and predicted task loading of the crew members. Bad procedures produce high workload. Similarly, the flight manual influences the way that crews will operate the airplane. Complex flight manuals will result in less effective and safe operations. It is therefore recommended to review the existing material or amend it (if required) before actual data collection is set in motion.

The minimum flight crew workload scenarios should be addressed including various aircraft configurations based around the requirements of the Minimum Equipment List (MEL).

3 Workload Data Collection

Workload evaluations will be undertaken by both Test Pilots and line pilots currently qualified on the reference aircraft. As in many instances the aircraft will be operated in either a degraded condition, during particularly high workload phases of flight or during emergency situations, undertaking data collection in a simulator is preferred for reasons of safety. These data will, however, be validated from in-flight data collected during later route proving flights.

Workload is a dynamic and varying state during stages of the flight. Task load can be increased by many factors such as ATC requests or a Runway change. Such events need to be monitored and stored on file in order to allow tracking of the event and evaluating the crew responses. As a general backup, video recordings are used that provide an overall flight deck view of both crew members and also separate views on each crewmember showing on-going activities

Workload will be measured at three levels:

Performance

(1) Aircraft performance (deviations from track, altitude, speed, heading)
(2) Control inputs (column & rudder activity, timing of switches, Display pages)
(3) Task completion times of assigned test tasks (chronometer)
(4) Task completion of selected operability tests (initial flight deck evaluation)
(5) Communications (RT external, intercom internal)

Subjective ratings

(1) Workload/Spare mental capacity Bedford scale
(2) ISA estimates of momentary workload, response 1–5 triggered by evaluator call out.
(3) Form to collect Pilot vehicle interface and Workload data (AC 23.1523-1)
(4) Form to collect Pilot comments and feedback in open format. (AC 23.1523-1)

Subjective approaches to the assessment of pilot workload come in two basic types:

(1) uni-dimensional measures of workload, usually based upon modified Cooper-Harperscales (e.g. the Bedford Scale by Ellis and Roscoe, 1982), see Fig. 1.
(2) multi-dimensional measures (e.g. the NASA Task Load Index – TLX; Hart and Staveland 1988). See Fig. 2 [2].

Physiological

(1) Heart rate recordings with accurate R-wave determination, each beat stored.
(2) Respiration to control for effects on heart rate and check speech utterances
(3) Activity recording via motion sensor(s) on wrist of one or both hands (in simulator only)

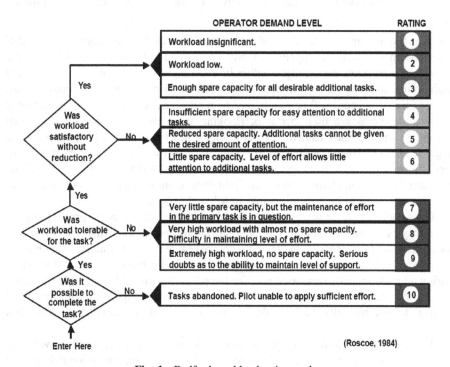

Fig. 1. Bedford workload rating scale

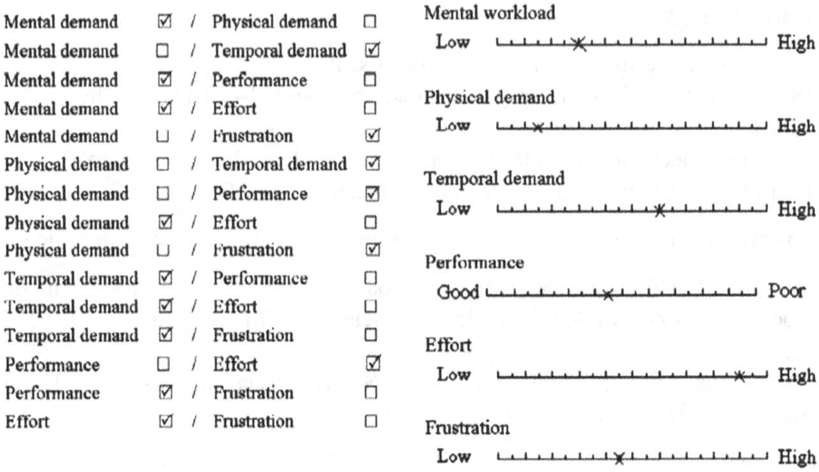

Mental demand	☑	/	Physical demand	☐
Mental demand	☐	/	Temporal demand	☑
Mental demand	☑	/	Performance	☐
Mental demand	☑	/	Effort	☐
Mental demand	☐	/	Frustration	☑
Physical demand	☐	/	Temporal demand	☑
Physical demand	☐	/	Performance	☑
Physical demand	☑	/	Effort	☐
Physical demand	☐	/	Frustration	☑
Temporal demand	☑	/	Performance	☐
Temporal demand	☑	/	Effort	☐
Temporal demand	☑	/	Frustration	☐
Performance	☐	/	Effort	☑
Performance	☑	/	Frustration	☐
Effort	☑	/	Frustration	☐

Mental workload
Low ⊢⊣⊢⊣⊢✳⊣⊢⊣⊢⊣⊢⊣⊢⊣ High

Physical demand
Low ⊢⊣✳⊣⊢⊣⊢⊣⊢⊣⊢⊣⊢⊣⊢⊣ High

Temporal demand
Low ⊢⊣⊢⊣⊢⊣⊢⊣⊢✳⊣⊢⊣⊢⊣ High

Performance
Good ⊢⊣⊢⊣⊢⊣✳⊣⊢⊣⊢⊣⊢⊣ Poor

Effort
Low ⊢⊣⊢⊣⊢⊣⊢⊣⊢⊣⊢⊣✳⊣ High

Frustration
Low ⊢⊣⊢⊣⊢✳⊣⊢⊣⊢⊣⊢⊣⊢⊣ High

Fig. 2. NASA task load index

Data Synchronization

Data will be recorded from and on different storage devices (Hard disks, recorders, data loggers). Means must be provided that allow the time synchronisation of such data.

Data Collection

To undertake the time line analysis of crew activities in each of the workload scenarios described in the scenario appendix it will be necessary to observe and record the activity of both pilots during flight (either in 'real' flight in the aircraft or in simulated flight in the simulator). Data will need to be recorded for pilot behavior in both aircraft.

A video data record will be required of both pilot's activities. It is suggested that at least two cameras are used per pilot (looking from above and behind over both shoulders) and a further camera is used giving a full flight deck view (using a wide angle lens). All cameras will need to be synchronised to a common time base (potentially recording to 1/10 s) and with the output of the flight simulator to coordinate pilot activity with simulator events. The flight deck on most simulators is quite dark, so cameras will need to be able to operate in low light conditions [3].

Conversely, if cameras are used in the aircraft itself during route proving flights, glare may be a major problem. All external (radio) and internal (intercom) communications should be recorded on the audio component associated with the video record.

A trained observer (an experienced pilot) should be present on the flight deck during all trials to make structured notes of the pilot's activities (for example recording any errors made). It is recommended that this observer is equipped with an 'event marker' to electronically mark on the audio/video record and significant events that occur during trials.

In flight (real or simulated) the fundamental rule is never to interfere with the performance of the primary task. As a result only simple, uni-dimensional workload scales can be used in these circumstances. Uni-dimensional scales can be very quick and easy to complete, and because they can often be completed on-task, even in flight it is proposed to supplement the task load analyses with regular subjective workload assessments (a workload 'speedometer').

Verbal subjective workload ratings will be taken from the PF and PNF at regular intervals during a task (for example one minute intervals) using the Bedford scale (this workload scale has been used on previous certification programmes, for example the BAe 146). These ratings will be elicited and recorded by the trained observer (however, they will also be recorded on the audio record as well). An example of the Bedford workload scale is included in the appendix Rating scales.

At the end of each scenario an overall workload assessment will be made using a multidimensional workload scale. The NASA TLX (Hart and Stavelend 1988) requires workload ratings to be made on three explicit dimensions; mental demand (how mentally demanding was the task); physical demand (how physically demanding was the task) and temporal demand (how hurried or rushed was the pace of the task)? In addition to these ratings concerning the sources of workload, three further ratings are also required: performance (how successful were you in accomplishing what you were asked to do; effort (how hard did you have to work to accomplish your level of performance) and frustration (how insecure, discouraged, irritated, stressed, and annoyed were you)? The latter group of ratings represent an interaction of the particpant's performance with the task at hand. The importance of each of these dimensions to the task being undertaken is then rated by making a series of 15 pair wise comparisons (see Appendix Rating scales) the idea being that different sources of workload are more important in different situations. The ratings for each scale are then multiplied by their associated importance weightings derived from the pair wise comparisons and summed to provide an overall workload score. In this way the NASA TLX can also provide a diagnostic workload profile for any particular task [4].

4   Conclusion

In general, the certification approach requires pilots to fly the same scenarios in the certificated aircraft and in the aircraft which to be certified. The test program should address all workload functions and factors listed in FAR/CCAR25.1523 and Appendix D. If the crew results on workload and ease of operation are similar, certification can be requested. It is proposed to demonstrate compliance with the workload requirements required in FAR/CCAR25.1523 using a combination of task load and workload evaluation techniques.

This minimum flight crew certification procedure has been successfully used in some civil aircraft in China.

References

1. Barnes, R.B., Adam, C.F.: Minimum crew certification human factors issues and approaches. In: World Aviation Congress and Exposition (1996)

2. Ruggiero, F.T.: Pilot subjective evaluation of workload during a flight test certification programme (1987)
3. Speyer, J.J., Fort, A.: Certification experience with methods for minimum crew demonstration (1983)
4. Xu, M., Jie, Y.: Research of airworthiness certification oriented scenario. Civil Aircraft Des. Res. (2014)

Investigation of Facial Region Extraction Algorithm Focusing on Temperature Distribution Characteristics of Facial Thermal Images

Tomoyuki Murata[✉], Shogo Matsuno, Kazuyuki Mito,
Naoaki Itakura, and Tota Mizuno

The University of Electro-Communications, Chofu, Tokyo, Japan
m1310136@edu.cc.uec.ac.jp

Abstract. In our previous research, we expanded the range to be analyzed to the entire face. This was because there were regions in the mouth, in addition to the nose, where the temperature fluctuated according to the mental workload (MWL). We evaluated the MWL with high accuracy by this method. However, it has been clarified in previous studies that the edge portion of the face, where there is no angle between the thermography and the object to be photographed, exhibits decreased emissivity measured by reflection or the like, and, as a result, the accuracy of the temperature data decreases. In this study, we aim to automatically extract the target facial region from the thermal image taken by thermography by focusing on the temperature distribution of the facial thermal image, as well as examine the automation of the evaluation. As a result of evaluating whether the analysis range can be automatically extracted from 80 facial images, we succeeded in an automatic extraction that can be analyzed from about 90% of the images.

Keywords: Mental work load · Facial thermal image · Nasal skin temperature · Face detection

1 Introduction

In recent years, the proportion of mental work in everyday life has been increasing owing to the advancement of information technology in society. The load and burden due to mental work is called mental workload (MWL) [1], and it is said that the continuation of excessive MWL has effects such as fatigue, monotonous feelings, decreased attention, mental saturation, etc. Appropriate evaluation and management of the MWL is important for reducing human error and health damage [2–5].

We have evaluated the MWL using nasal skin temperature. Nasal skin temperature is an indicator that reflects autonomic nerve activity well and has demonstrated the capacity for MWL evaluation. However, there were also regions in the mouth, in addition to the nose, where the temperature fluctuated according to the MWL. Therefore, in order to capture the areas other than the nose area where the temperature fluctuates, we expanded the range to be analyzed to the entire face, and have proposed

© Springer International Publishing AG 2017
C. Stephanidis (Ed.): HCII Posters 2017, Part I, CCIS 713, pp. 347–352, 2017.
DOI: 10.1007/978-3-319-58750-9_48

an MWL evaluation method and study [6, 7]. By this method, we can evaluate the MWL with higher precision than in the previous research. On the other hand, it has been clarified in previous studies that at the edge of the face, where there is no angle between the thermography and the object to be photographed, there is decreased emissivity measured by reflection or the like, and, as a result, the accuracy of the temperature data decreases. In extracting facial regions from thermal images by previous methods, it was found that the estimation accuracy was degraded by the manual extraction that included edge areas.

In order to solve this problem we performed face detection using machine learning; however, since there were many occurrences of false detection of clothes and background, the automatic extraction of facial regions was not accomplished. Therefore, in this study, we examined a facial-region extraction algorithm focusing on the temperature distribution characteristics of facial thermal images and aimed at the automatic extraction of the analysis range.

2 Proposed Method

Several methods for automatically detecting a facial region from a general visible light image have been proposed [8]. However, the conventional face detection method cannot be applied to thermal images because thermal images express temperature distribution as color information. Therefore, we propose a unique face detection method. Figure 1 shows the flow of the proposed method, which is as follows:

1. Take a thermal image, including facial region, with thermography.
2. Set the temperature range to extract the region of the facial skin temperature from the background temperature. In this study, we set the threshold as the skin temperature range from 31 to 36 °C because we assume from 18 to 28 °C as the room temperature in the laboratory environment.
3. Scan the thermal image horizontally and vertically to determine the maximum area. The maximum area is defined as the largest thermal area among areas that are determined by multiplying every vertical length by every horizontal length. The length equals the number continuous pixels within the skin temperature range.
4. Create a histogram of the temperature distribution within the maximum area in order to find the most frequent temperature and the maximum temperature.
5. Extract the pixels included in the temperature range w or w' within the maximum area to remove noise, such as hair and background. The temperature range between the most frequent temperature and the maximum temperature is defined as w. The temperature range obtained by subtracting w from the most frequent temperature is defined as w'.
6. Determine the facial region based on the edge of the area extracted in step 5. The facial region includes all of the pixels inside of this edge.
7. Extract a facial thermal image from the original image based on the region obtained in step 6.

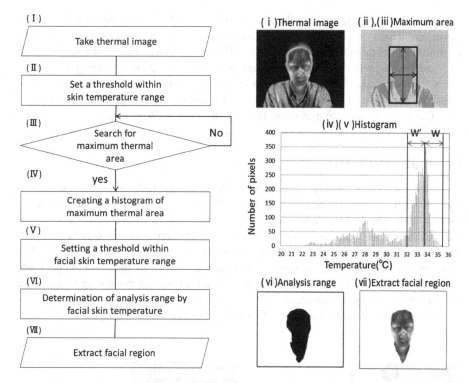

Fig. 1. Outline of algorithm

3   Evaluation Experiment

In order to evaluate the proposed algorithm, we use a facial thermal image. In this research, we aim to evaluate the MWL. Therefore, we evaluate the proposed method by using a series of facial thermal images in which the subject's mental state changes. We take the facial thermal image of the subject before the experiment, every 2 min from the start of the experiment, and finally after the experiment. We use eight thermal images per subject.

3.1   Experimental Protocol

The following experiment was conducted to take facial thermal images of different mental states when a test subject is under an MWL. In our experiment, ten 22-year-old test subjects in good health were tasked with performing mental arithmetic calculations in order to impose an MWL. Specifically, they were asked to solve two-digit number addition problems displayed on a PC. They were given 3 s for each problem, after which the next problem appeared, regardless of whether or not their answer was correct. After the test subjects relaxed for a few minutes in a seated position, the measurement commenced with 3 min of the rest, followed by 10 min of mental arithmetic calculation tasks, and then 3 min of rest. At the end of this 3-min rest, the measurement was stopped. The total length of the experiment was 16 min. In the measurement, infrared thermography (XA 0350 manufactured by View Ohre Imaging Co., Ltd.) was used. The thermal image size for this apparatus was recorded as 320 × 256 pixels, and the sampling period was recorded as 1 s. The facial skin emissivity was 0.98. The apparatus was set at a distance of 0.5 m from the subject's face. The subject was sitting at room temperature kept at 24 ± 1 °C.

3.2   Experiment Results

The results are shown in Fig. 2. We were able to extract facial regions as targets of analysis in 10 subjects. According to Fig. 2(a) and (b), we could extract the facial region clearly. On the other hand, it can be seen from the extraction result of Fig. 2(c) that the cheek and mouth could not be extracted. These are considered to be removed along with the edge because the cheek is low in temperature. In addition, Fig. 2(d) shows that the neck had a temperature distribution similar to the face, and the neck and cloth part were extracted together with the face. As a result of evaluating whether the analysis range can be automatically extracted by using 80 facial thermal images, we succeeded in an automatic extraction that can be analyzed in 77 images.

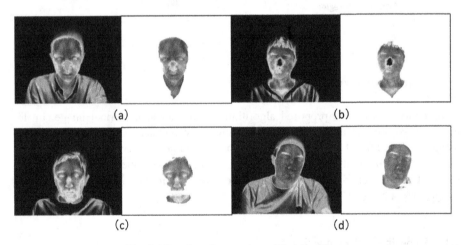

(a)   (b)

(c)   (d)

Fig. 2. Results of extraction of facial region

4   Discussion

The proposed MWL evaluation method requires the temperature of the nose and mouth and the average temperature of the entire face. However, despite testing with the same protocol, the nose and mouth were not extracted with several thermal images. There are several possible reasons for this, which are outlined below:

- In some subjects, there were individual differences in the influence of the MWL resulting from the task, and the differences in the temperature exposed on the face caused by these individual differences prevented the appropriate extraction of the facial region.
- There were individual differences in the areas of the face where the low temperature occurred.
- There is the possibility that the proposed method has a weakness related to the inclination of the face in the horizontal direction.

To investigate the first and second hypotheses, it will be necessary to impose a variety of experiment conditions. The third hypothesis stems from the result of Fig. 2(c). The results show that the proposed method makes it possible to estimate autonomic nerve activity. In our future studies, it will be necessary to automatically correct the direction and tilt of an input image. If the facial region from the thermal image is extracted from an input image whose tilt is corrected, it is possible to extract the facial region with relatively more stability.

5   Conclusion

In this paper, we proposed an algorithm to automatically extract facial regions from thermal images by focusing on the temperature distribution of the thermal image. We succeeded in an automatic extraction that can be analyzed in 77 images out of 80 facial thermal images. As a result, we showed that facial regions can be automatically extracted using the proposed method, and, by using this method, our study is closer to the evaluation of the MWL in real time. However, the extraction of the face from several thermal images did not go well: something prevented the extraction of the cheek and mouth from the thermal image. Therefore, we continue to aim for the stable extraction of the facial region.

In future, in order to estimate the autonomic nerve activity in a real environment, we aim for a stable facial region extraction. For that purpose, we will develop algorithms that can respond to high temperature environments, such as in summer, and the effect of the subject's hair style and clothing. We will examine facial region extraction for facial thermal images taken in various environments.

Acknowledgments. This work was supported by JSPS KAKENHI Grant Number 15H05323.

References

1. Nachreiner, F.: International standard on mental work-load – the ISO 10075 series. Ind. Health **37**(1), 125–133 (1999)
2. Hioki, K., Nozawa, A., Mizuno, T., Ide, H.: Physiological evaluation of mental workload in time pressure. Trans. Inst. Electr. Eng. Jpn C **127**(7), 1000–1006 (2007). Electronics, Information and Systems Society

3. Mulder, G.: Mental effort and mental workload. In: Proceedings of the First International Symposium of Human Engineering for Quality of Life, pp. 25–32 (1992)
4. Mulder, G., Mulder, L.J.M.: Information processing and cardiovascular control. Psychophysiology **18**(4), 392–402 (1981)
5. Vincente, K.J., Thornton, D.C., Moray, N.: Spectral analysis of sinus arrhythmia: a measure of mental effort. Hum. Factors **29**(2), 171–182 (1987)
6. Mizuno, T., Kawazura, S., Matsuno, S., Akehi, K., Asano, H., Itakura, N., Mito, K.: Autonomic nervous activity estimation algorithm with facial skin thermal image. In: The Ninth International Conference on Advances in Computer-Human Interactions, Italy, pp. 262–266, April 2016
7. Matsuno, S., Kosuge, S., Kawazura, S., Asano, H., Itakura, N., Mizuno, T.: Basic study of evaluation that uses the center of gravity of a facial thermal image for the estimation of autonomic nervous activity. In: The Ninth International Conference on Advances in Computer-Human Interactions, Italy, pp. 258–261, April 2016
8. Viola, P., Jones, M.: Rapid object detection using a boosted cascade of simple features. In: Proceedings of the 2001 IEEE Computer Society Conference on Computer Vision and Pattern Recognition, CVPR 2001, vol. 1, pp. 511–518 (2001)

Change in Subjective Evaluation of Weight by the Proteus Effect

Kengo Obana[1]([✉]), Dai Hasegawa[2], and Hiroshi Sakuta[2]

[1] Graduate School of Aoyama Gakuin University, 5-10-1 Chuo-ku Fuchinobe,
Sagamihara-shi, Kanagawa, Japan
c5616146@aoyama.jp
[2] Aoyama Gakuin University, 5-10-1 Chuo-ku Fuchinobe,
Sagamihara-shi, Kanagawa, Japan

Abstract. In virtual environments, it is known that synchronizing the actions of an avatar with the operator causes a change in the operator's self-perception, resulting in a change of behavior. This phenomenon is called the Proteus effect. In the research concerning the Proteus effect, researches on the behavior change have been actively conducted. However, the difference between the self-perception changed by the Proteus Effect and the physical sense in real world has not been sufficiently discussed. Therefore, in this research, we prepared two different kinds of avatars with different appearances, and investigated the influence of the change of self-perception changed for each avatar on the evaluation of physical sensation. As a result, a significant difference in the evaluation of weight between the two conditions was found. It was clarified that the Proteus effect affects the evaluation of physical sensation.

Keywords: Proteus effect · Self-perception · Virtual reality

1 Introduction

1.1 Background

In virtual environments, it is known that synchronizing the actions of an avatar with the operator causes a change in the operator's self-perception, resulting in a change of behavior. This phenomenon is called the Proteus effect [4,5]. It has been clarified that the reason why this change occurs is because the operator infers the attitude and role expected of the avatar from its appearance [1] (e.g. When the operator uses an avatar that is expected to behave attractively, the operator's behavior becomes attractive.). Also it has been clarified that this phenomenon lasts for some extent even after stopping using the avatar [4]. Riva [3] clarified that self-perception can be distorted and malformed when accepting the improper evaluation from others and become locked. So, the Proteus effect is looked forward to a treatment method for such mental diseases.

© Springer International Publishing AG 2017
C. Stephanidis (Ed.): HCII Posters 2017, Part I, CCIS 713, pp. 353–357, 2017.
DOI: 10.1007/978-3-319-58750-9_49

1.2 Related Works

Nicks [1] investigated whether opinions on the cause of sexual assault will change in accordance to how revealingly dressed the used avatar is. The results showed that, more participants using avatars that were less revealingly dressed stated that the cause of sexual assault is the revealing dressing of the victim. Nicks assumed that these opinions were a result of self-defence, as the participants reflected on the avatars as "themselves" and did not want to be subject to sexual assault. Konstantinas [2] used three kinds of avatars, wearing a formal suit, dressed in casual wear, and hands without a body, to investigate how the avatar's appearance affects how the participants play the drum. The results revealed that whether or not the avatar is assumed "suited" for the task has more influence on the change of behavior than simply inferring the avatar's behavior. In addition, due to more sense of body ownership leading to an increase of drumming performance variety, the sense of body ownership found to have a significant effect on the magnitude of the occurring Proteus effect. This body-ownership is a state in which a particular body is perceived as one's own body. It is known that this can transfer to objects other than your body when synchronized with a tactile stimulus. According to these studies, the Proteus Effect affects real people if the motion of the avatar and the motion of the operator are synchronized with movement or tactile information.

1.3 Purpose

Although self-perception can be changed in Proteus Effect, physical sensations such as tactile sense and vision stays the same such as tactile sense and vision does not change (e.g. Even if you use a muscular avatar in virtual space, it doesn't mean you actually gain strength in real space). This, together with a change in the perception of physical sensation due to a change in self-perception may cause an illusion. Therefore, there is a possibility that a physical representation that causes improper self-perception may cause a malformation of physical sensations by treatment actions such as psychological rehabilitation. As a result of changes in the evaluation of physical senses, there may be a possibility of the appearance of new psychological diseases such as objects feeling heavier than they actually are. So, in this research, we aim to investigate the effects of changed self-perception due to the Proteus Effects on the evaluation of physical senses by examining the influence of an avatar's arm thickness on the evaluation of weight in a VR space.

2 Method

In this research, a system as shown in Fig. 1 was constructed. The flow of data is explained below.

We used Leap Motion to track and acquire the avatar operator's hand skeleton information. The skeleton Information is sent to unity to update the avatar's movement. To track other information such as the position of the weight held

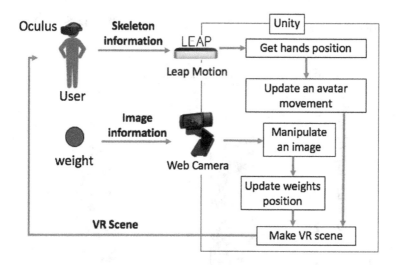

Fig. 1. System overview

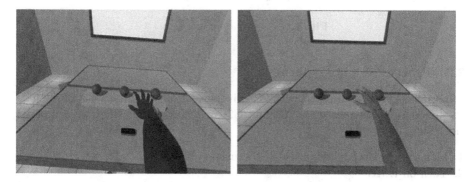

Fig. 2. Avatars in each condition (left: C1, right: C2)

by the operator, we used a web camera. The image information from the web camera is sent to Unity, then image processing is performed to binarize the colors in the image using binary preset thresholds. Based on the processed image data, the movement of the ball is updated in Unity. Finally, the constructed VR space is drawn with oculus (Fig. 2).

2.1 Design

In order to investigate the change in the subjective evaluation of the weight caused by the avatar's arm's appearance, the experiment was conducted under the following C1 and C2 conditions.

C1: Avatar that seems to be strong with a thick arm
C2: Avatar that seems to be weak with a thin arm

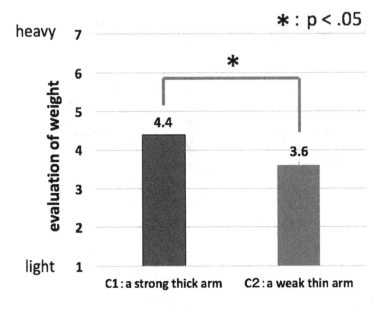

Fig. 3. The evaluation of weight

2.2 Procedure and Hypothesis

Experiments were conducted with 25 university students subjects, according to the following procedure under C1 and C2 conditions. After that, we compared the result.

1. Memorize reference weight in HMD turned off
2. Turn on HMD
3. Synchronize work to make the Proteus effect occur
4. Compare the weight to the reference one
5. Evaluate in 7 steps

We hypothesized that operator will evaluate more heavy than the reference under C1 and more light than the reference under C2.

3   Results and Discussion

An average t-test with a pair of specimens was performed for the difference between the average of the evaluations of C1 and C2. The results are shown in Fig. 3. There was a significant difference in the change in the subjective evaluation of the weight due to the change in thickness of the t avatar's arm.

The change in the evaluations can be explained as follows. First with the HMD turned off, the weight is memorized as body knowledge based on the participant's mental body representation the real space. Next, after turning on the

HMD and performing the synchronization task in the VR space, operators perceived the avatar's arms as their own arm. After that, by evaluating the arm of the avatar that he is manipulating, the Proteus effect occurred, and the participants mental body representation changed (the arm of avatar is evaluated to be more muscular than their actual arm). Nonetheless, the participants evaluated a weight that is the same weight as the previous one in VR space. Finally, operators had an illusion that the weight they have now is heavier than the reference.

4   Conclusions

In this research, we investigated the influence of the change in self-perception by the Proteus effect on subjective evaluation of weight in VR space. In the experiments, participants made an illusion in the perceiving of physical sensation due to a change in self-perception. Therefore, in environments where the Proteus effect occur, there is a possibility that the appearance of the avatar may cause an illusion on the evaluation of physical sensations, so the appearance of the avatar must be selected carefully. Further investigation on how to reduce the duration and magnitude of the illusion of physical sensations is needed.

References

1. Fox, J., Bailenson, J.N., Tricase, L.: The embodiment of sexualized virtual selves: the Proteus effect and experiences of self-objectification via avatars. Comput. Hum. Behav. **29**(3), 930–938 (2013)
2. Kilteni, K., Bergstrom, I., Slater, M.: Drumming in immersive virtual reality: the body shapes the way we play. IEEE Trans. Vis. Comput. Graph. **19**(4), 597–605 (2013)
3. Riva, G.: Neuroscience and eating disorders: the allocentric lock hypothesis. Med. Hypotheses **78**(2), 254–257 (2012)
4. Yee, N., Bailenson, J.: The Proteus effect: the effect of transformed self-representation on behavior. Hum. Commun. Res. **33**(3), 271–290 (2007)
5. Yee, N., Bailenson, J.N., Ducheneaut, N.: The Proteus effect: implications of transformed digital self-representation on online and offline behavior. Commun. Res. **36**, 285–312 (2009)

Making Implicit Knowledge Explicit – Acquisition of Plant Staff's Mental Models as a Basis for Developing a Decision Support System

Dorothea Pantförder$^{(\boxtimes)}$, Julia Schaupp, and Birgit Vogel-Heuser

Institute of Automation and Information Systems,
Technical University of Munich, Munich, Germany
{pantfoerder,j.schaupp,vogel-heuser}@tum.de

Abstract. Monitoring of industrial production plants is a complex task, which requires a hight level of knowledge about the interrelations in the production process in many cases. This knowledge on the one hand, is available as handbooks, process models or process data. On the other hand, the plant's staff has implicit knowledge in the form of mental models. Experienced process engineers and operators have improved these mental models over years of working with the process.

In this paper, a procedure is described, of how implicit knowledge can be made explicit by the acquisition of plant's staff mental models. The aim is to build a cause-effect model for different quality parameters, which can be integrated into a decision support system (DSS), which helps the operator in decision-making.

Keywords: Mental model · Knowledge acquisition · Decision making · Plant manufacturing

1 Introduction

In spite of increasing automation of industrial production plants, there are challenges and task fields as well as unexpectedly occurring problems, which can only be handled by operators and their implicit knowledge about the plant. The operator collected this knowledge over years of experience. Consequently, the investigation, preservation and processing of this valuable knowledge is very important to increase product quality and plant availability. Hence, it would be beneficial to transfer the implicit knowledge into explicit knowledge through several steps [1].

An important component of this procedure is the collection of knowledge. It is realized through the acquisition of mental models, which are subjective, virtual images of how a system works. A distinction between different mental models, e.g. the implemented and presented model, depending on the knowledge and the task fields of the user groups can be made [2]. The mental model of a process engineer, the so-called implemented model, contains the knowledge about the actual functioning of the system and process at a technical level. Depending on his/her task field, the mental model of an

© Springer International Publishing AG 2017
C. Stephanidis (Ed.): HCII Posters 2017, Part I, CCIS 713, pp. 358–365, 2017.
DOI: 10.1007/978-3-319-58750-9_50

operator (the presented model) is how the system can be influenced and should behave in a particular use case during operation. Depending on the system, both kinds of mental models can deviate strongly from each other [2]. In addition, the mental models within one user groups can deviate, due to the level of knowledge or educational levels of the user.

In this paper, an approach to acquire knowledge from the engineering and operating staff of plant manufacturing companies is described to preserve implicit knowledge and to process the empirical knowledge collection for the implementation into a Decision Support System (DSS). The DSS provides services, especially on monitoring and process control. Particularly, for quality control of quality features that are not directly observable within the production process, a DSS could be a valuable tool. As automatically learned models from available quality parameters cannot contain the whole plant behavior, expert knowledge will be added to complete the model [3].

2   Related Work

Implicit knowledge is one of the most valuable as well as most challenging assets of organisations [1, 4]. Specifically, industrial manufacturing plants face challenging task areas and problems, which require the accumulated implicit knowledge of operators. In order to enable the preservation and transfer of such knowledge, and therefore augmenting the plants productivity, it needs to be transformed into explicit knowledge [1].

Rooted in the research field of psychology, mental models are seen as internal reflections of explicit knowledge about the components and structure of a system [5]. Therefore, mental models constitute as appropriate concepts to represent the complexity, subjectivity and abstractness of the interaction between a person's implicit and explicit knowledge [4, 5]. Moreover, they inhere the reflection of "beliefs, values, and assumptions that we personally hold" [6] and are linked assertions which explain how systems work [7]. Hence, an individual depends on subjective mental models which facilitate cognition, problem solving and decision-making by simplifying external reality with a "small scale model" [8].

Butz and Krüger [2] suggest that mental models can depend on different model types, namely conceptual, implemented and presented model. Designing a system or device requires a mental model about how it is supposed to work, making it a conceptual model. The implemented model describes the most detailed model, as it represents a technologist's or process engineer's mental model, which is needed in order to realize the design on a technical level. Finally, the presented model describes an operator's mental model, which is limited to the information needed to use the device or system. The implemented and presented model can be identical or deviate strongly, depending on the system itself and the difference in operators and process engineers level of knowledge and education [2].

While explicit knowledge can be documented, implicit knowledge is stored in mental models [4]. In conclusion, the implemented model can inhere explicit and implicit knowledge and the presented model is based on an individual's, subjective and implicit knowledge.

In the context of this paper, it is important to understand how and why the acquisition of plant staff's mental models is needed in order to detect errors and optimize plant availability. Although the acquisition of technical data is of utter importance for a plant's operation, analysis of implicit knowledge, particularly the process engineer's and operator's mental models, comprises valuable information. For instance, an operator's implicit knowledge of the usage of a new machine is crucial but very difficult to documented [4]. In conclusion, acquiring mental models can contribute to the externalization of implicit knowledge and thus supports operators in decision-making during process control.

2.1 Elicitation of Mental Models

In order to capture the core of mental models, solely elicitation techniques that meet the requirements to gather tacit knowledge are taken into consideration. Card sorting allows extraction of implicit knowledge and concepts about the participant's mental information organization, categories and priorities [9]. The adjacent Software Engineering domain has been utilizing card sorting as an effective method to gather data from experts [10]. Additionally, card sorting has been successfully applied in requirement engineering [11, 12].

Card sorting is an elicitation technique where test subjects arrange the cards according to their subjective structure of the provided information [13]. There are two types of card sorting, open card sorting and closed card sorting. In open card sorting, the participants create their own cards and categorizations, which enables the subject to rank the topics in order of their importance [14, 15]. Contrary to this, in closed card sorting, categories are given by the test conductor. This method is used to gather more in-depth information about the selected topics. In addition to the structured procedure, closed card sorting also facilitates the comparability of results [15]. According to the information mentioned above, closed card sorting is to be conducted after an initial elicitation of topics using open card sorting [16].

While research has been addressing the methods of obtaining data on mental models [11, 17, 18], none of them has particular focus on the field of industrial manufacturing plants. For recording a knowledge base only analyst leading methods are taken into consideration. Amongst analyst leading methods, interviews generally unveil explicit knowledge [17] and processes [19], which emphasized to be eligible for the first step of our concept.

Literature has been indicating that a combination of different data collection methods can be beneficial. Hussain and Ismail [10] and Vásquez et al. [9] suggested that card sorting and interviews supported by protocol analysis might be a suitable method to obtain data on mental models. While card sorting can provide a structure to collect implicit knowledge, interviews provide an adequate framework for explicit knowledge collection in a more detailed fashion.

3   Concept of Plant Staff's Mental Model Acquisition

To acquire plant staff's mental models and make them usable for integration in a DSS, a two-step procedure with several sub steps is chosen (Fig. 1). Firstly, the knowledge of process engineers, the implemented model, has to be collected as process engineers possess the knowledge about the theoretical dependencies and a wider knowledge base regarding the functionalities of the technical process. Secondly, the mental model of the operator, the presented model, has to be acquired, to get more detailed information about controlling a specific plant and its possibilities of influencing the quality of a specific product. Since the DSS is primarily intended to support quality control, quality parameters of a process form a basis for the knowledge acquisition. The aim of this concept is to build a cause-effect model for different quality parameter, which can be integrated into the DSS.

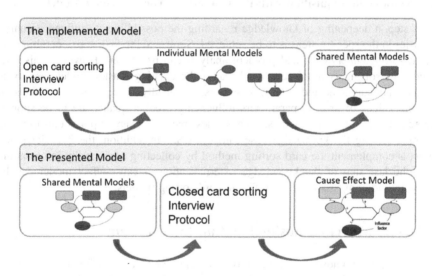

Fig. 1. Procedure of plant staff's knowledge acquisition

3.1   Knowledge Acquisition with Process Engineer – The Implemented Model

As stated in the related work, a combination of card sorting, interview and protocol analysis is a promising choice to acquire mental models. For the collection of a broad knowledge base, open card sorting is suitable. An advantage of this method is that the process engineer is able to emphasize the topics, which are most important in his/her opinion. Only a few labeled cards regarding the quality parameters of the processed product are provided in order to gain more information about the production process. The provided cards represent a guide for the subjects' answers and improve the compatibility and comparability of the results. The task of the subjects is to fill out cards with (1) the part of the plant in which a quality parameter is influenced, (2) the influencing factor and (3) an action recommendation in case of a failure. An interview complements the card sorting method. A large amount of data collected during the card sorting and the interview is desired to build a comprehensive knowledge base. An additional protocol analysis enables a detailed evaluation and thus the collection of all data generated in the interview with the process engineers. The protocol analysis can be realized in the form of photos and audio recordings during the interview.

Subsequent to the knowledge collection, it is beneficial to present the knowledge base in form of master models for each quality parameter from the card sorting model and the acquired protocol data comparing the models of all process engineers. The master model represents the shared mental model, i.e. the specific mental model of one user group. The resulting master models form the basis for the following step, the knowledge acquisition with the operator.

3.2 Knowledge Acquisition with the Operator – The Presented Model

In this step, a deepening of knowledge regarding the possibilities to influence quality properties in the specific areas is to be achieved. Similar to the first step, a combination of card sorting, interviews, and protocol analysis can be chosen. However, this time closed card sorting is more suitable, because the existing master models are to be certified and supplemented by the operators. Especially the causes and effects of changing values of process parameters influencing product quality are to be supplemented in the given master models, because these parameters are important information for implementing the knowledge base into the DSS. In addition, the interviews and protocols complement the card sorting method by collecting additionally information.

In the last step of the knowledge externalization, a cause-effect model can be created by the comparison of the different card sorting models.

4 Mental Model Acquisition Within the Company

The procedure of knowledge acquisition was applied in a manufacturing plant for plastic film production. Quality properties describe the resulting product. During the production, the process is monitored by operators, which are able to influence the quality of the film in the different sub plants, based on the current process data and his/her experience.

For the first step of the described concept, knowledge acquisition with process engineers, experts of the company had chosen eight properties that described the quality of the final product to collect a broad knowledge base for these properties. The knowledge acquisition was conducted with four process engineers with different levels of knowledge. The knowledge acquisition of each process engineer lasted two and a half hours and contained the card sorting method, interviews and the protocol analysis. Outputs of this step were collected as pictures of the card sorting model and audio files of the interviews. The collected knowledge of the different process engineers was compiled into different concept maps and represents the individual implemented models of the technical system. The different concept maps were compared and combined into a master model, containing all information of all acquired concept maps. Similarities, meaning aspects mentioned by more than one process engineer, were combined and highlighted. The completed master model was validated by the process engineers and key aspects for the following steps were selected.

In the second step, the validated and selected master model was modified for the knowledge collection of the operators. This step was conducted with two operators, both operation staff employed in the company and regularly monitoring the respective plant. Due to the limited time of the knowledge acquisition, the properties were prioritized and limited to three core properties. As a template for the closed card sorting, the modified master model of the process engineers were presented to the operators. The operator only described the process without using the card sorting method, so that the outputs of this step were only audio files of the interviews. During the interview, the interview leader repeatedly requested the operator to provide a recommendation for each influencing variable related to the quality parameters. Based on the audio files, the master models were extended and cause-effect models for each quality parameter were created.

5   Results and Discussion of the Knowledge Acquisition

The combination of card sorting, interviews and protocol analysis were well received by all of the process engineers, but the weighting of card sorting and explaining the process differed. All process engineers used the card sorting method to structure their description of the influencing parameters to the quality properties and to assign them to the different sub parts of the manufacturing plant. A consistent semantics in the structuring could not be achieved. However, the method of card sorting was unknown for the subjects and a previous training in the method did not take place. All process engineers have described the processes comprehensively and agreed to audio recording of the interviews. Therefore, it can be assumed that the knowledge acquisition was not a problem, but solely the card sorting method being unknown to them.

In some topics, only few similarities were found when comparing the different interview results of the process engineers. The validation of the master model showed that even though some influencing parameter were only mentioned by one subject and not the others, this was not due to it being incorrect. Instead, many differences in the master models were possibly caused by the wide range of information, collected in a limited time slot in the first step of the elicitation of the mental models.

A similar result could be observed by the operators, with the difference that none of the subjects used the card sorting method. Nevertheless, the operators were also comprehensively describing the processes and explaining their description directly during operation at the demonstrator plant. Thus, it was shown that the combined method of card sorting, interviews and protocol analysis was a suitable choice, because it was possible to create cause-effect models for three quality properties from the resulting data, despite the differing use of the individual methods.

6 Conclusion and Outlook

This article described a two-step concept for the acquisition of manufacturing plant staff's mental models (process engineers and operators) within an industrial manufacturing plant. The aim was to develop a cause-effect model for different quality properties, which can be integrated into a decision support system [3]. For this purpose, a combined method of card sorting, interviews and protocol analysis was chosen. During the knowledge acquisition, card sorting showed to be partly suitable without previous training. Prior to further investigations, these methods should be sufficiently trained to acquire more structured results. Furthermore, for the elicitation of the implemented models with the process engineers, the number of quality properties should be limited, to allow the acquisition of more in-depth knowledge in the available amount of time.

Acknowledgement. The project leading to this application has received funding from the European Union's Horizon 2020 research and innovation programme under grant agreement No. 678867.

References

1. Sutter, J.: Grafische Visualisierungen bei der Stellenübergabe. Ein Werkzeug zur Externalisierung von implizitem Wissen. Springer, Wiesbaden (2016)
2. Butz, A., Krüger, A.: Mensch-Maschine-Interaktion. De Gruyter, Oldenbourg (2014)
3. Vogel-Heuser, B., Karaseva, V., Folmer, J., Kirchen, I.: Operator knowledge inclusion in data-mining approaches for product quality assurance using cause-effect graphs. In: 20th IFAC World Congress, July 2017, accepted paper (2017)
4. Bach, N.: Mentale Modelle als Basis von Implementierungsstrategien. Konzepte für ein erfolgreiches Management. Springer, Wiesbaden (2000)
5. De Kleer, J., Brown, J.S.: Assumptions and ambiguities in mechanistic mental models. In: Gentner, D., Stevens, A.L. (eds.) Mental Models, pp. 155–191. Erlbaum, Hillsdale (1983)
6. Maani, K., Cavana, R.Y.: Systems Thinking, System Dynamics: Managing Change and Complexity. Pearson Education, North Shore City (2007)
7. Groesser, S.N., Schaffernicht, M.: Mental models of dynamic systems: taking stock and looking ahead. In: 28th International System Dynamics Conference, Seoul (2012)
8. Craik, K.J.W.: The Nature of Explanation. Cambridge University, Cambridge (1943)
9. Vásquez-Bravo, D., Sánchez-Segura, M., Medina-Domínguez, F., Amescua, A.: Combining software engineering elicitation technique with the knowledge management lifecycle. Int. J. Knowl. Soc. Res. (IJKSR) 3(1), 1–13 (2012)
10. Hussain, D., Ismail, M.: Requirements engineering. A comparison between traditional requirement elicitation techniques with user story. Linköping University (2011)
11. Maiden, N.A.M., Hare, M.: Problem domain categories in requirements engineering. Int. J. Hum.-Comput. Stud. 49(3), 281–304 (1998)
12. Maiden, N.A.M., Rugg, G.: ACRE: selecting methods for requirements acquisition. Softw. Eng. J. 11(3), 183–192 (1996)
13. Nielsen, J.: Card Sorting to Discover the Users' Model of the Information Space (1995). http://www.useit.com/papers/sun/cardsort.html

14. Barrett, A.R., Edwards, J.S.: Knowledge elicitation and knowledge representation in a large domain with multiple experts. Expert Syst. Appl. **8**(1), 169–176 (1995)
15. Spencer, D.: Card Sorting: Designing Usable Categories. Rosenfeld Media, New York (2009)
16. Tullis, T.S.: Using closed card-sorting to evaluate information architectures. In: Proceedings of Usability Professionals Association, Austin (2007)
17. Gavrilova, T., Andreeva, T.: Knowledge elicitation techniques in a knowledge management context. J. Knowl. Manag. **16**(4), 523–537 (2012)
18. Canonne, C., Aucouturier, J.: Play together, think alike: shared mental models in expert music improvisers. Psychol. Music **44**(3), 544–558 (2015)
19. May, K.A.: Interview techniques in qualitative research: concerns and challenges. In: Morse, J.M. (ed.) Qualitative Nursing Research: A Contemporary Dialogue, pp. 188–201. Sage, Upper Saddle River (1991)

Eye Contact Detection via Deep Neural Networks

Viral Parekh, Ramanathan Subramanian$^{(\boxtimes)}$, and C.V. Jawahar

International Institute of Information Technology, Hyderabad, India
parekh.viral@research.iiit.ac.in, {s.ramanathan,jawahar}@iiit.ac.in

Abstract. With the presence of ubiquitous devices in our daily lives, effectively capturing and managing **user attention** becomes a critical device requirement. While gaze-tracking is typically employed to determine the user's focus of attention, *gaze-lock* detection to sense eye-contact with a device is proposed in [16]. This work proposes eye contact detection using **deep neural networks**, and makes the following contributions: (1) With a convolutional neural network (CNN) architecture, we achieve superior eye-contact detection performance as compared to [16] with *minimal data pre-processing*; our algorithm is furthermore validated on multiple datasets, (2) Gaze-lock detection is improved by combining head pose and eye-gaze information consistent with social attention literature, and (3) We demonstrate gaze-locking on an Android mobile platform via CNN model compression.

Keywords: Eye contact detection · Human-Computer Interaction · Convolutional neural networks

1 Introduction

The importance of **eye-contact** in non-verbal human communication cannot be understated. Right from infanthood, humans use eye-contact as a means for attracting and acknowledging attention, and can effortlessly sense others' eye-gaze direction [5]. In today's ubiquitous computing environment, it becomes critical for devices to effectively attract and manage users' attention for proactive communication and information rendering. Therefore, HCI would greatly benefit from devices that can sense user attention via eye-contact– a phenomenon termed *gaze locking* in [16].

Gaze locking is a sub-problem of *gaze-tracking*, where the objective is to determine where the user is looking. Gaze tracking has been extensively studied by the HCI [11,12], psychology [14,20], medical [7] and the multimedia/computer vision communities [10,19]. Gaze-tracking techniques (with the exception of few such as [8]) have inferred the point-of-gaze using eye-based cues even though social attention literature has identified that other cues such as head orientation contribute significantly to this end [9].

© Springer International Publishing AG 2017
C. Stephanidis (Ed.): HCII Posters 2017, Part I, CCIS 713, pp. 366–374, 2017.
DOI: 10.1007/978-3-319-58750-9_51

This paper proposes gaze-locking using deep convolutional neural networks (CNNs), which have recently become popular for solving visual recognition problems as they obviate the need for hand-crafted features (*e.g.*, expressly modeling head pose). Specifically, our work makes the following research contributions:

(1) Even though the gaze-locking methodology outlined in [16] detects eye-contact from distant faces, it requires an elaborate processing pipeline which includes: eye region rectification for head pose compensation, eye mask extraction, compression of a high-dimensional eye appearance feature vector via dimensionality reduction and a classifier for gaze-lock detection. Differently, we leverage the learning power of CNNs for gaze-locking with minimal data pre-processing. We validate our model on three datasets, and obtain over 90% detection accuracy on the Columbia Gaze (CG) [16] test set. In comparison, [16] reports 92% accuracy on the CG *training set*.

(2) Different from [16] and most gaze-tracking methods, we use facial appearance, which implicitly conveys face pose, in addition to eye appearance. As seen in Fig. 1, face orientation crucially determines if the user is gaze-locked with a (reference) camera or not. The eyes in the left and right images have very similar appearance; however, eye-contact is clearly made only in the right instance when one infers gazing direction as the eye orientation *relative* to head pose. Combining face and eye cues achieves superior gaze locking than either of the two as demonstrated in prior works [17].

(3) CNNs are implemented on CPU/GPU clusters given their huge computation and memory requirements; their implementation on mobile platforms is precluded by the limited by the computation and energy resources in these environments. We demonstrate gaze-locking on an Android mobile platform via CNN compression using ideas from the *dark knowledge* concept [6].

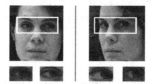

Fig. 1. Left image is ***non-gaze-locked***, while right image is ***gaze-locked***. Their eye crops however look very similar.

2   Methodology

Figure 2 presents our proposed system and the convolutional neural network (CNN) architecture. CNNs *automatically learn* problem-specific features, obviating the need for devising hand-crafted descriptors like HoG [3]. Furthermore, replacing the largely independent *feature extraction* and *feature learning* modules by an end-to-end framework allows for efficient handling of classification errors. System components are described below.

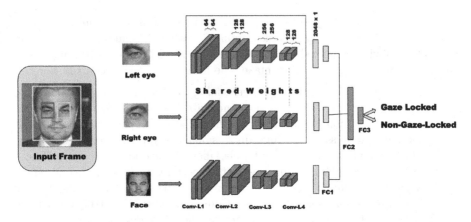

Fig. 2. Overview of our **gaze-lock detector**. Inputs include 64 × 64 *left eye*, *right eye* and *face images*, and the detector outputs a binary label assigned as either *gaze-locked* or *non-gaze-locked*. CNN architecture has **three** parallel networks each comprising **four** convolutional layer blocks (denoted as filter size/number of filters): CONV-L1: 3 × 3/64, CONV-L2: 3 × 3/128, CONV-L3: 3 × 3/256, and CONV-L4: 3 × 3/128, and **three** fully-connected layers denoted as FC1 (of size 2048 inputs × 128 outputs), FC2: 384 × 128 and FC3: 128 × 2. (Color figure online)

2.1 Image Pre-processing

We essentially use the face and eye appearance to detect eye-contact, and pre-processing is limited to extraction of these regions. A state-of-the art facial landmark detector [1] is used to obtain 64 × 64 left and right eye patches. Since face pose serves as an additional cue, a 64 × 64 face patch obtained using the Viola-Jones detector [18] is also fed to the CNN. The red, green and blue channels for each patch are z-normalized prior to input.

2.2 CNN Architecture

Our system comprises three parallel networks (one each for face, left eye and right eye) with a VGGnet [15]-like configuration. CNNs are stacked with *convolutional* (Conv) layers composed of groups of *neurons* (or filters), which automatically compute locally salient features (or activations) from input data. Conv layers are interleaved with *max pooling* layers, which isolate the main activations on small data blocks and allow later layers to work on a 'zoomed out' version of previous outputs facilitating parameter reduction. Convolutions are also usually followed by a non-linear operation (called *rectified linear unit* or ReLU [13]) to make the CNN more expressive and powerful. Finally, in a *fully-connected* (FC) layer, neurons have access to *all* activations from a previous layer as against a Conv layer whose neurons only access local activations.

Each of our three networks have four blocks, with each block including two Conv layers, a ReLU and a max-pooling layer (only Conv layers are shown in Fig. 2). Similar activations are enforced for the left and right eye networks by constraining their neurons to learn identical/shared weights. The *filter size* or spatial extent of activations input to a Conv layer neuron is 3×3 for all blocks, and there are 64, 128, 256 and 128 neurons respectively in the four blocks. A stride length of 1 is used while convolving (computing dot product of) the filter with the input patches. The Conv-L4 outputs are vectorized to a 2048 dimensional vector, which is input to the FC1 layer with 128 outputs. FC1 outputs from the three networks are combined and fed to FC2 followed by FC3, which assigns the input label as either *gaze-locked* or *non-gaze-locked*. The CNN model was implemented on *Torch* [2], and trained over 250 epochs with a batch size of 100. An initial learning rate of 0.001 was reduced by 5.0% after every epoch. To avoid overfitting, a dropout technique was used to randomly remove 40% of the FC layer neurons during training. Interested readers may refer to [15] for further details.

3 Experiments and Results

3.1 Datasets

To expressly address eye-contact detection, authors of [16] compiled the **Columbia Gaze** (CG) dataset which comprises 5880 images of 56 persons viewing over 21 different gaze directions and 5 different head poses. Of these, 280 are *gaze-locked*, while 5600 are *non-gaze-locked*– sample CG images are shown in Fig. 3 (left). The CG dataset is compiled in a controlled environment, and contains little variation in terms of illumination and background. The limited size of the CG dataset makes it unsuitable for training CNNs, and we therefore used two large datasets to train our CNN, namely, (1) **MPIIGaze** [21] comprising 213,659 images compiled from 15 subjects during everyday laptop use. As shown in Fig. 3 (center-top), MPIIGaze images vary with respect to illumination, face size and background. However, only cropped eye images (center-bottom) are publicly available for MPIIGaze; (2) The **Eyediap** dataset [4] (Fig. 3 (right)) contains 19 HD videos with more than 3000 images each captured from 16 participants. We ignore the depth information available for this dataset, and only use the raw video frames for our purpose.

Fig. 3. (left) Sample images from the **CG** dataset. (center-top) Original exemplars and (center-bottom) publicly available eye-only images from **MPIIGaze**. (right) Sample images from **Eyediap**.

3.2   Data Synthesis and Labeling

As only 280 *gaze-locked* images exist in the CG dataset, we generated 2280 *gaze-locked* and 5900 *non-gaze-locked* samples by scaling and randomly perturbing original images as described in [16]. On the contrary, we downsampled the number of images for the MPIIGaze and Eyediap datasets. MPIIGaze comprises images with continuous gaze direction from $0°$ to $-20°$ *pitch* (vertical head rotation) and $-20°$ to $20°$ *yaw* (horizontal rotation). The 3D gaze direction (x, y, z) is converted to 2D angles (θ, ϕ) as $\theta = \arcsin(-y), \phi = \arctan(-x, -z)$. Then, *gaze-locking* implies $(\theta, \phi) = (0, 0)$. This way, we obtained 6892 *gaze-locked* and 12000 *non gaze-locked* images from MPIIGaze. Likewise, Eyediap images show users making eye-contact with various screen regions on a 24″ PC monitor. We labeled images with the target looking straight ahead (around screen center) as *gaze-locked*, and others as *non gaze-locked*. Table 1 presents the training and test sets statistics for the three datasets. We now discuss gaze-locking results with different train and test sets.

Table 1. Training and test set details for the various datasets.

Attribute	CG	MPIIGaze	EYEDIAP
Total images	5880	214076	125000
Synthesized	8180	18892	24575
Training set	7000	15000	19660
Test set	1180	3892	4915

Experiment 1 (Ex1). To begin with, we used only the CG dataset for model training[1]. Specifically, we trained our detector with (a) images of only *one eye*; (b) images from *both eyes*; (c) only *face* images, and (d) *face-plus-eye* images as in Fig. 2.

Experiment 2 (Ex2). Here, we repeated Ex1(a) and (b)[2], but first pretrained the CNN with MPIIGaze and *fine-tuned* the same using CG. Fine-tuning involved modifying only the FC layer weights by re-training with CG images, assuming that the learned Conv-L4 activations were relevant for both MPIIGaze and CG.

Experiment 3 (Ex3). We repeated Ex1(a–d), but pre-trained the CNN with Eyediap followed by fine-tuning on CG.

---

[1] The CNN was trained and validated with a 80:20 split of the training set in all experiments.

[2] Since MPIIGaze does not contain face images, we could not repeat Ex1(c) and (d).

Table 2. Detection performance for Ex1(a)–3(d) and comparison with [16]. Model tested on **CG** in all cases. [16] reports results only on the training set.

	1(a)	1(b)	1(c)	1(d)	2(a)	2(b)	3(a)	3(b)	3(c)	3(d)	Smith *et al.* [16]
Acc (%)	70.8	70.6	68.4	64.4	86.1	90.8	85.5	90.2	88.4	**92.7**	92.00
MCC	0.69	0.72	0.67	0.36	0.74	0.81	0.74	0.80	0.78	**0.83**	0.83

Experiment 4 (Ex4). To examine the effect of our framework on datasets other than CG, we repeated Ex1(a–d) with a CNN trained on CG and fine-tuned with Eyediap.

3.3 Results and Discussion

Gaze-locking results are tabulated in Tables 2 and 3. Detection performance is evaluated in terms of accuracy, and the Mathews correlation coefficent (MCC). MCC is useful while evaluating binary classifier performance on unbalanced datsets, as with our case where the number of *gaze-locked* instances are far less than *non-gaze-locked* ones. In Ex1, accuracy and MCC decrease as more information is input to the CNN (*e.g.*, face = plus-eyes vs eyes/face only), contrary to our expectation. This reduction is attributable to *overfitting* due to the small CG dataset size in comparison to the number of CNN parameters.

However, the benefit of using additional information for gaze-lock detection is evident from Ex2, Ex3 and Ex4 (Ex2 and Ex3 involve pre-training of the CNN model with larger and visually richer datasets). Using *two-eye* information as against *one-eye* in Ex2 improves accuracy and MCC by 4.7 and 7% respectively. Ex3 and Ex4 results are consistent with social attention literature. They confirm that while gaze direction is more critical than head pose for inferring eye contact, combining head and eye orientation cues is optimal for gaze-locking. Our system achieves a best accuracy of 93% and MCC of 0.83 on the CG dataset. Table 2 also compares our results with the state-of-the-art [16]. [16] reports detection results on the *training set*, while our results are achieved on an independent test set. With minimal data pre-processing, our model performs similar to [16] using only eye appearance, and outperforms [16] with face-plus-eye information. Finally, while the results for Ex4 again confirm the insufficiency of the CG dataset for training the CNN, the gaze-locking performance significantly improves on incorporating facial and binocular information.

Table 3. Detection results for Ex4. Model trained on **CG** and fine-tuned/tested on **Eyediap**.

Input	One eye	Both eyes	Face only	Face & eyes
Acc	62.9	65.6	64.5	**66.9**
MCC	0.57	0.58	0.57	**0.61**

3.4   Visualizing CNN Activations

Figure 4 illustrates four neuronal activations learned in the Conv-L1 layer of our
CNN model for the input eye and face images. Conv-L1 activations are informa-
tive as ReLU network activations are dense in the early layers, and progressively
become sparse and localized. As eye gaze direction is given by the pupil orientation, the eye activations capture edges and textures relating to the pupil.
Similarly, the face network activations encode face shape and structural details
for pose inference.

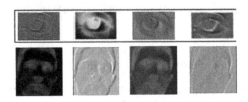

Fig. 4. Exemplar Conv-L1 neuron outputs for input eye (top) and face (bottom)
images.

4   CNN Implementation on Android

While our CNN based gaze-lock detector requires minimal pre-processing, the
end-to-end framework obviates need for heuristics as with the eye mask extraction phase in [16]. Our system achieves 15 fps throughput on an Intel Core
I7 2.6 GHz, 16 GB RAM PC with GeForce GTX 960M GPU. However, CNNs
require large computational and memory resources which precludes their implementation on mobile devices with limited computation and energy capacity.

Fig. 5. Compressed version of our model working on an Android (Quad-core, 2.3 GHz,
3GB RAM) phone. Green rectangle denotes gaze-locking, while red denotes non-gaze-
locking. (Color figure online)

This problem can be circumvented by compressing knowledge in a large,
complex model to train a simpler model with minimal accuracy loss using the

dark-knowledge concept [6]. Figure 5 shows our gaze-lock detector on an Android platform, which has a throughput of 1 fps. A more efficient implementation described in [8] can achieve upto 15 fps throughput.

5   Conclusion

This work exploits the power of deep CNNs to perform passive eye-contact detection with minimal data pre-processing. Combining facial appearance with eye information improves gaze-locking performance. Our system can also run on an Android mobile device with limited throughput. Our end-to-end system with minimal heuristics can be leveraged by today's smart devices for capturing and managing user attention (*e.g.*, a *smart selfie* application), as well as in image/video retrieval (detecting shots where a certain character is facing the camera). Future work involves implementation of a seamless, real-time vision-voice system for assistive applications such as photo-capturing for the blind.

References

1. Baltrusaitis, T., Robinson, P., Morency, L.P.: Constrained local neural fields for robust facial landmark detection in the wild. In: International Conference on Computer Vision Workshops, pp. 354–361 (2013)
2. Collobert, R., Kavukcuoglu, K., Farabet, C.: Torch7: a matlab-like environment for machine learning. In: BigLearn, NIPS Workshop (2011)
3. Dalal, N., Triggs, B.: Histograms of oriented gradients for human detection. In: CVPR, pp. 886–893. IEEE Computer Society, Washington, DC (2005)
4. Funes Mora, K.A., Monay, F., Odobez, J.M.: EYEDIAP: a database for the development and evaluation of gaze estimation algorithms from RGB and RGB-D cameras. In: Eye Tracking Research and Applications, pp. 255–258. ACM, New York (2014)
5. Hains, S.M., Muir, D.W.: Infant sensitivity to adult eye direction. Child Dev. **67**, 1940–1951 (1996)
6. Hinton, G., Vinyals, O., Dean, J.: Distilling the Knowledge in a Neural Network. CoRR, March 2015
7. Holzman, P.S., Proctor, L.R., Levy, D.L., Yasillo, N.J., Meltzer, H.Y., Hurt, S.W.: Eye-tracking dysfunctions in schizophrenic patients and their relatives. Arch. Gen. Psychiatry **31**(2), 143–151 (1974)
8. Krafka, K., Khosla, A., Kellnhofer, P., Kannan, H., Bhandarkar, S., Matusik, W., Torralba, A.: Eye tracking for everyone. In: CVPR (2016)
9. Langton, S.R.: Do the eyes have it? Cues to the direction of social attention. Trends Cogn. Sci. **4**(2), 50–59 (2000)
10. Li, R., Shi, P., Haake, A.R.: Image understanding from experts' eyes by modeling perceptual skill of diagnostic reasoning processes. In: CVPR, pp. 2187–2194 (2013)
11. Majaranta, P., Bulling, A.: Eye tracking and eye-based human–computer interaction. In: Fairclough, S.H., Gilleade, K. (eds.) Advances in Physiological Computing. HIS, pp. 39–65. Springer, London (2014). doi:10.1007/978-1-4471-6392-3_3
12. Morimoto, C.H., Mimica, M.R.: Eye gaze tracking techniques for interactive applications. CVIU **98**(1), 4–24 (2005)

13. Nair, V., Hinton, G.E.: Rectified linear units improve restricted Boltzmann machines. In: ICML, pp. 807–814 (2010)
14. Rayner, K.: Eye movements in reading and information processing: 20 years of research. Psychol. Bull. **124**, 372–422 (1998)
15. Simonyan, K., Zisserman, A.: Very deep convolutional networks for large-scale image recognition. CoRR abs/1409.1556 (2014)
16. Smith, B.A., Yin, Q., Feiner, S.K., Nayar, S.K.: Gaze locking: passive eye contact detection for human-object interaction. In: User Interface Software and Technology, pp. 271–280. ACM (2013)
17. Subramanian, R., Staiano, J., Kalimeri, K., Sebe, N., Pianesi, F.: Putting the pieces together: multimodal analysis of social attention in meetings. In: ACM International Conference on Multimedia, pp. 659–662. ACM (2010)
18. Viola, P., Jones, M.: Rapid object detection using a boosted cascade of simple features. In: CVPR, vol. 1, pp. 1–511. IEEE (2001)
19. Volokitin, A., Gygli, M., Boix, X.: Predicting when saliency maps are accurate and eye fixations consistent. In: CVPR, pp. 544–552 (2016)
20. Vrânceanu, R., Florea, C., Florea, L., Vertan, C.: NLP EAC recognition by component separation in the eye region. In: Wilson, R., Hancock, E., Bors, A., Smith, W. (eds.) CAIP 2013. LNCS, vol. 8048, pp. 225–232. Springer, Heidelberg (2013). doi:10.1007/978-3-642-40246-3_28
21. Zhang, X., Sugano, Y., Fritz, M., Bulling, A.: Appearance-based gaze estimation in the wild. In: CVPR, pp. 4511–4520. IEEE Computer Society (2015)

Let Our Mind Wander: Employing IT-Induced Incubations to Enhance Creativity

Xixian Peng[1(✉)], Xinwei Wang[2], and Hock Hai Teo[1]

[1] Department of Information Systems, National University of Singapore,
Singapore, Singapore
pengx@comp.nus.edu.sg
[2] School of Business, University of Auckland, Auckland, New Zealand

Abstract. Creativity is becoming increasingly important for personal and business success, thus cultivating creativity should be an indispensable goal for education programs at all levels. As learning is increasingly taking place on IT-supported learning systems, these learning systems should explore what functions can be made available to foster creativity. This study tries to investigate this topic from a novel perspective, based on recent psychological findings that engaging in unrelated tasks that exhibit mind wandering can foster creativity. This positive effect emerges because mind wandering triggers successful incubation intervals, during which fixating elements that impair creativity are released and more importantly the default brain network and unconscious associative processing are activated. Specifically, we try to demonstrate that people's creative performance can be improved after an incubation interval with external task (a computer game in this study) introduced by distracting IT features.

Keywords: Creativity · Mind wandering · IT-based interruption · Unconscious thought

1 Introduction

Creativity is the cornerstone of human civilization. The story of human progress is always written by our ability to change existing thinking patterns, break with the present and build something new [1]. With the ever-accelerating information boom, technological advances and cultural evolution, the world is becoming more and more complex. Creativity is thus more important now than ever before because it can enable one to remain flexible when facing advances, opportunities, and changes [2, 3]. In addition, creativity has also become one of the key strategic differentiating factors in organizations' pursuit of creative business solutions and innovative products. These social and business realities dictate that educators should have a better understanding about how to nurture creative potential. Cultivating creativity should be an indispensable goal for education programs at all levels. As learning is increasingly taking place on IT-supported learning systems, these learning systems should also explore what functions can be made available to foster creativity in the learning and thinking process. Prior information systems research has mainly examined the effects of the use

© Springer International Publishing AG 2017
C. Stephanidis (Ed.): HCII Posters 2017, Part I, CCIS 713, pp. 375–382, 2017.
DOI: 10.1007/978-3-319-58750-9_52

of computer systems (e.g. decision support systems) on individuals', groups' and organizations' creativity and how these effects are affected by various internal and external factors (e.g. personal difference, leadership) [4]. However, few studies have investigated how to facilitate creative thinking with distinct IT system design, although it has been highlighted that the effectiveness of computer-mediated creativity depends on how we intelligently design interfaces and skillfully leverage the capabilities of various IT features for enhancing creativity [5]. Hence, this study draws on psychological findings of incubation effect to explore a novel perspective of IT design to facilitate individuals' creative thinking.

Recent psychological literature has indicated that mind wandering can escalate the incubation effect and thus foster human creativity performance [6, 7]. Mind wandering triggers successful incubation intervals, during which the brain can be rested, fixating elements are released, and more importantly the default brain networks and unconscious associative processing are activated. Then, when getting back to the problem after successful incubation, people can generate more creative ideas. We extend these findings to explore whether IT learning and education systems can utilize IT feature to introduce mind wandering for incubation to take place and thus facilitate creative thinking. Specifically, we will experiment with common IT artifact distracting features (e.g. pop-ups) and seek to understand whether appropriate use these features can improve people's creative performance. Based on the theory of incubation, we expect to show that when people are performing creative tasks, their creative performance can be improved after an incubation interval with external tasks (a computer game named whack-the-mole in this study) introduced by distracting IT features, and the level of mind wandering during the incubation mediates the effect.

2   Theoretical Background and Hypothesis Development

The theoretical foundations of this paper are the theories of incubation effect and how mind wandering facilitates this effect. The basic phenomenon of incubation effect is a familiar one: when we are working on a problem and can't solve the task, we leave it aside for some period of time, named the incubation period, and when we return attention to the task we can have some new insight that helps us to solve the problem.

Several causes have been proposed to account for the incubation effect and they mainly can be divided into two views: conscious work and unconscious work [7, 8]. Conscious work holds that it is the absence of conscious thought that drives creativity. Because of absence of conscious thought, incubation helps creative performance by relaxation or reduction of mental fatigue, additional covert problem solving, and facilitating cues from environment [9–11]. More recently, researchers find that absence of conscious thought cannot explain that incubation effects also happen when people are distracted by cognitive demanding tasks [12], thus the unconscious work attracts more attentions recently. This stream suggests that unconscious problem solving processes occur when individuals shift their attention away from the problem to other mental activities. This idea is supported by the unconscious thought theory which systematically differentiates conscious and unconscious thought process and suggests that unconscious processing is more adept at associating and integrating information

Table 1. Two mechanisms of the incubation effect

Conscious work
• **Relaxation or reduction of mental fatigue:** Being well-rested, one can do better the next time one engages in the problem
• **Covert work:** Problems are more easily solved after incubation because they are reflected on during the intervening interval
• **Facilitating cues from environment:** Environmental cues trigger retrieval of previously un-retrieved relevant information
Unconscious work
• **Facilitating remote association:** Unconscious processes facilitate eliciting new knowledge. Compared with conscious thoughts, unconscious thoughts are more associative and divergent that activation spread to previously ignored but relevant items
• **Weakening fixating elements:** Unconscious processes can lead to mental set-shifting that wrong cues or activation of inappropriate solution concepts become less accessible during initial attempts, leading to a fresh, new and unbiased start
• **Problem restructuring:** An individual's mental representation of a problem will be reorganized into more appropriate and stable form after initial unsuccessful attempts by unconscious thoughts. Problem restructuring mostly emerge from switching strategy which can happen unconsciously

than conscious processing is [13]. Three different unconscious processes have been proposed to account for incubation effects: facilitating remote association, weakening fixating elements, and problem restructuring [9, 10, 14–17]. The unconscious and conscious work theories are not necessarily mutually exclusive. That is, both unconscious and conscious work may occur during incubation intervals, and both may contribute to the resolution of creative problems [18] (Table 1).

Previous research also has found that the incubation effect can be facilitated by mind wandering, as it's highly related with unconscious thinking [7]. Mind-wandering is a state of mind that occurs spontaneously, and largely autonomously, whenever an individual is not engaged in a cognitively demanding task. When the mind wanders, people will engage more in unconscious thoughts. Recent neuroimaging studies have found that during mind wandering a network of regions in the frontal and parietal cortex, named as the default of mode network, is activated, which is highly related to complex, evaluative and unconscious forms of information processing [19]. The default network actually has greater volume in the counterpart of the cognitive control network [20]. This is also the reason why unconscious thought can perform better than conscious thought when people are doing complex tasks [21]. Mind wandering increases the activation of the default network, and thus activate ones' unconscious thoughts. In the incubation with mind wandering, people can be more divergent to spread their mental thoughts to previously ignored but relevant items and also their mental representation of the creative problem will be reorganized into more appropriate and stable form after the initial thinking [7].

Nowadays, the high penetration rate of computers and mobile devices exposes people to different kinds of interruption introduced by distracting IT features, such pop-ups. Distracting IT features can interrupt users' concentration on a primary task, driving their cognitive resources to other alternative activities [21]. For example, a notification of email may suddenly jump out, which can attract people's attention from their focus task; video advertisement can easily distract users' attention when they are browsing webpages. These IT-based interruptions can prevent people from focusing on their focal tasks and create a period of incubation. We expect that they can increase performance in creative thinking tasks by triggering the incubation effect. First, according to conscious work theory, with an interruption, people's pressure of mental activity on the creative problem is attenuated. The mental fixation caused by initial thinking of the creative problem is released. With relaxation and less mental fixation, one can do better the next time one engages in the problem [7]. In addition, during the incubation introduced by IT-base interruption, people can also enter into unconscious thinking process [7]. As people are interrupted suddenly, some core elements of creative problem are still stored in their brains. When they turn their cognitive resources to the task induced by IT-based interruption, their unconscious thoughts will continue to work on the creative problem. We also argue that the incubation effect of IT-based interruption with external task on creativity may be more positive over the incubation introduced by taking a same time of rest. Some studies have shown that taking a rest can enhance ones' creativity because an absence of conscious thought on the creative problem can help them relax and recover from fatigue [9]. However, when people take a rest, there is no unconscious thought processing which can further enhance creativity by shifting mental fixation, restructuring the focal problem, and associating new elements.

Some psychological studies have confirmed the effect of distracting incubation on creativity. For example, Baird et al. [6] investigate how mind wandering facilitates incubation effect on participants' unusual uses task (UTT). In this study, participants who have a break to do other task can list more unusual uses for a common house hold item (e.g. a brick can be used as door stop, weapon) than those who either take a same time of rest or no break. Therefore, we hypothesize that:

H1: Incubation introduced by IT-based interruption with external task can lead to better creativity performance than taking a same time of rest or having no break.

H2: The degree of mind wandering mediates the effect of incubation introduced by IT-based interruption on creative performance.

Different types of distracting task could induce various levels of mind wandering. In this study, we propose that when the distracting task is undemanding which needs less cognitive effort, people could have more opportunities to wander their mind during the distracting incubation. The relationship between the degree of cognitive demand of the task and incubation effect has been examined in previous studies [8]. The default mode of network, which responsible for the unconscious thought and mind wandering, competes resources with the control network. Usually, one network is activated, the other is deactivated [7]. When the distracting task demands more cognitive resources, there is less space and resources for people to wander their mind. The incubation effects would be stronger when the incubation period is filled with a low cognitive demand task, because the undemanding distracting task gives more opportunities for people to mind-wandering, and allows the occurrence of some unconscious problem solving processes [6]. Hence, we hypothesize the following:

H3: IT distractions with undemanding tasks can induce stronger incubation effect on creativity than those with demanding tasks.

3 Methodology

We will conduct a lab experiment to test the three hypotheses. Students from an Asian university will be recruited to participate in the study with monetary bonus. In the experiment, we will prepare two idea generation tasks as focal creative tasks, which are adapted from previous study [22]: generating ideas to increase tourism or reduce pollution within a fictitious city. To finish the tasks, participants will be instructed to generate as many useful solutions as they can think of for the given problem. Students from departments related to the two creative problems, such as environment and tourism, will be excluded from our experiment.

Stimuli: There will be four between-subject conditions: two experimental and two control conditions. Participants in the experimental groups will be interrupted by IT distraction (pop-up) with different tasks to create incubation. We will prepare a whacking mole game with two difficult levels as stimuli of IT-based interruption: a mole comes out on screen from one of the five holes randomly, and participants have to force the mole back into its holes by hitting them on the head with a click using mouth. Every mole will stay on the computer screen for 750 ms, and the interval between two moles will be randomly set between 1,000 ms to 3,000 ms. The relatively simple one is a choice reaction version which demands less cognitive effort: participants can click the mole whenever it come out on the screen. The relatively difficult version is a 1 back memory game that demands more cognitive effort: there are five moles with different colors; only when the mole has the same color to the previous one, participants can whack the mole. Studies have shown that the reaction choice task without a working memory induce more mind wandering than 1-back working memory task [23]. In the first control condition, participants will also have a period of incubation that they are asked to take a same time period of rest that they can sit quietly or walk around in the lab. This control condition is to imitate a real life case that students have several minutes of break between two classes. The participants in the second control condition will not receive an incubation break from the creative task.

Procedure: The experiment will be conducted in a computer system developed by the authors. The experiment procedure will follow a pattern of learning-testing that participants will first learn basic knowledge from videos by themselves and then answer relevant objective and subject questions. At the beginning, participants will be randomly assigned to two creative tasks: pollution and tourism. They will be presented with a 15 min long video of the corresponding topic. The videos will describe basic knowledge of pollution/tourism and the situations in a factious city. After watching the videos, participants will be asked to take a test with objective questions about pollution/tourism and the corresponding idea generation task. 16 min will be given to generate as many as useful solutions to the creative problem. The text box for typing the answers will expire after 16 min automatically.

When the participants enter into lab, they will be assigned to one of four between-subjects conditions (incubation with demanding game, incubation with undemanding game, incubation with rest, and no break). These incubations will be triggered by a pop-up window with different tasks after they answer the creative problem for 8 min. The incubation interval will also last 8 min. Immediately following the incubation interval in the demanding game and undemanding game conditions, participants will be directed to fill a commonly used self-report measure of mind wandering, the Dundee Stress State Questionnaire [24], to confirm the manipulation of the difference in mind wandering of the experimental conditions. In order to keep consistent with the incubation conditions, participants in the rest incubation condition will also be asked to complete the same questionnaire.

After the incubation interval (or following the first 8 min of creative problem solving, in the case of the control group of no break), participants will be informed that they can continue to work on the same creative problem. Then, the participants back to the same computer with the same problem. Once completing, participants will be directed to another survey to collect their demographic information (e.g. age, gender) and control variables, including their previous knowledge in the domain of pollution or tourism, general propensity to mind-wander, and emotion.

Data Analysis: Our dependent variable is percentage improvement of post-incubation creativity performance relative to the baseline performance. This is calculated as [(post-incubation creativity performance − baseline creativity performance)/(baseline creativity performance)] * 100. We will measure creative performance from four dimensions: fluency, workability, novelty and relevance. We will calculate their improvement percentage respectively and obtain four dependent variables for each participant. To assess participants' performance, we will invite independent raters to score. In the term of fluency, two independent will be instructed to identify all of the non-redundant ideas proposed in each submission. For the other three creative performance variables, we first will pool all the unique responses to each problem to create two master idea lists. Other two independent variables will be instructed to score each idea. According to the coding scores, we will calculate the baseline and post-incubation performance of all the three dimensions for each participant. To examine our hypotheses, we plan to use multivariate analysis of covariance (MANCOVA) to analyze the data.

4 Conclusion

The current study tries to provide evidence that when individuals are distracted by a computer game which introduces mind wandering, they can have better creative performance in idea generation problem. If the hypotheses are supported, the current study may contribute to previous literature from the following ways. First, by extending psychological findings of the effect of mind wandering on creativity into IS domain, this study makes an important contribution to the growing debate surrounding computer-mediated creativity. Previous studies mainly focus on whether computer systems benefit creativity and how to use them properly to improve innovativeness in workplace. It's also meaningful and important to find ways to utilize IT-related features to improve people's creative ideation. Our study also confirms the importance of flexibly using IT artefacts that these existing common technologies still have significant potentials to enhance human performance. Last, this paper increases our understanding of distracting IT features such as pop-ups, animated banners and floating advertisements. Most previous studies support the negative effects of them. These IT features could distract users' attention and evoke frustration in users, resulting in unintended consequences. This paper provides evidence to support a balanced perspective of using distracting IT features [21].

This study may also have important practical implications if the hypotheses are supported. It provides inspiring cues for the design of educational and online learning software. The population who uses information technologies to support education and learning has exploded in recent years. For instance, there are millions of interesting education applications on Apple store and Google Play for children to use. This paper calls for practitioners' attention to introduce incubation effects into their software design. We believe that incubation with simple computer games inducing mind wandering may contribute more creative thinking rather than incubation of taking a rest. This paper provides a meaningful design juice for educational software designers. Beside to IT based education, we believe our research can also be applied to the design of other systems that support creative problem solving (e.g. electronic brainstorming software).

References

1. Dietrich, A., Kanso, R.: A review of EEG, ERP, and neuroimaging studies of creativity and insight. Psychol. Bull. **136**(5), 822–848 (2010)
2. Hennessey, B.A., Amabile, T.M.: Creativity. Annu. Rev. Psychol. **61**, 569–598 (2010)
3. Runco, M.A.: Creativity. Annu. Rev. Psychol. **55**, 657–687 (2004)
4. Lee, M.R., Chen, T.T.: Digital creativity: research themes and framework. Comput. Hum. Behav. **42**, 12–19 (2015)
5. Javadi, E., Gebauer, J., Mahoney, J.: The impact of user interface design on idea integration in electronic brainstorming: an attention-based view. J. Assoc. Inf. Syst. **14**(1), 1–21 (2013)
6. Baird, B., Smallwood, J., Mrazek, M.D., Kam, J.W., Franklin, M.S., Schooler, J.W.: Inspired by distraction mind wandering facilitates creative incubation. Psychol. Sci. **23**(10), 1117–1122 (2012)
7. Ritter, S.M., Dijksterhuis, A.: Creativity—the unconscious foundations of the incubation period. Front. Hum. Neurosci. **8**(4), 1–10 (2014)
8. Sio, U.N., Ormerod, T.C.: Does incubation enhance problem solving? A meta-analytic review. Psychol. Bull. **135**(1), 94–120 (2009)
9. Yaniv, I., Meyer, D.E.: Activation and metacognition of inaccessible stored information: potential bases for incubation effects in problem solving. J. Exp. Psychol. Learn. Mem. Cogn. **13**(2), 187–205 (1987)
10. Sternberg, R.J.: The Nature of Creativity: Contemporary Psychological Perspectives. Cambridge University Press, Cambridge (1988)
11. Browne, B.A., Cruse, D.F.: The incubation effect: illusion or illumination? Hum. Perform. **1**(3), 177–185 (1988)

12. Dijksterhuis, A., Meurs, T.: Where creativity resides: the generative power of unconscious thought. Conscious. Cogn. **15**(1), 135–146 (2006)
13. Dijksterhuis, A., Bos, M.W., Nordgren, L.F., Van Baaren, R.B.: On making the right choice: the deliberation-without-attention effect. Science **311**(5763), 1005–1007 (2006)
14. Seifert, C.M., Meyer, D.E., Davidson, N., Patalano, A.L., Yaniv, I.: Demystification of cognitive insight: opportunistic assimilation and the prepared-mind hypothesis. In: Sternberg, R., Davidson, J. (eds.) The Nature of Insight, pp. 65–124. MIT Press, Cambridge (1994)
15. Smith, S.M.: The constraining effects of initial ideas. In: Paulus, P.B., Nijstad, B.A. (eds.) Group Creativity: Innovation Through Collaboration, pp. 15–31. Oxford University Press, New York (2003)
16. Smith, S.M., Blankenship, S.E.: Incubation and the persistence of fixation in problem solving. Am. J. Psychol. **1**(104), 61–87 (1991)
17. Smith, S.M., Ward, T.B., Finke, R.A.: The Creative Cognition Approach. MIT Press, Cambridge (1995)
18. Kohn, N., Smith, S.M.: Partly versus completely out of your mind: effects of incubation and distraction on resolving fixation. J. Creat. Behav. **43**(2), 102–118 (2009)
19. Spreng, R.N., Stevens, W.D., Chamberlain, J.P., Gilmore, A.W., Schacter, D.L.: Default network activity, coupled with the frontoparietal control network, supports goal-directed cognition. Neuroimage **53**(1), 303–317 (2010)
20. Kühn, S., Ritter, S.M., Müller, B.C.N., van Baaren, R.B., Brass, M., Dijksterhuis, A.: The importance of the default mode network in creativity—a structural MRI study. J. Creat. Behav. **48**(2), 152–163 (2014)
21. Tan, B., Yi, C., Chan, H.C.: Research note—deliberation without attention: the latent benefits of distracting website features for online purchase decisions. Inf. Syst. Res. **26**(2), 437–455 (2015)
22. Denis, A.R., Minas, R.K., Bhagwatwar, A.P.: Sparking creativity: improving electronic brainstorming with individual cognitive priming. J. Manag. Inf. Syst. **29**(4), 195–215 (2013)
23. Smallwood, J., Nind, L., O'Connor, R.C.: When is your head at? An exploration of the factors associated with the temporal focus of the wandering mind. Conscious. Cogn. **18**(1), 118–125 (2009)
24. Barron, E., Riby, L.M., Greer, J., Smallwood, J.: Absorbed in thought the effect of mind wandering on the processing of relevant and irrelevant events. Psychol. Sci. **22**(5), 596–601 (2011)

Guiding Visual Attention Based on Visual Saliency Map with Projector-Camera System

Hironori Takimoto$^{(\boxtimes)}$, Katsumi Yamamoto, Akihiro Kanagawa,
Mitsuyoshi Kishihara, and Kensuke Okubo

Okayama Prefectural University,
111, Kuboki, Soja, Okayama 719-1197, Japan
takimoto@c.oka-pu.ac.jp

Abstract. Many attention retargeting methods based on a visual saliency model of bottom-up attention for guiding a human's attention to a region of interest (ROI) have recently been proposed. However, conventional attention retargeting methods focus only on modulating an image or a movie that is presented on a display device. In this paper, we propose an attention retargeting method used with a projector-camera system to realize attention retargeting in real space. We focus on the realization of an appearance control method for attention retargeting to the plane of a real space as a first step of our research.

Keywords: Attention retargeting · Visual attention · Saliency map · Projector-camera system

1   Introduction

Human beings typically choose to direct their attention to a region of interest (ROI) on the basis of the information obtained from their peripheral vision [1,2]. In a system that supports the activity of humans, a visual attention retargeting method that naturally guides a human's gaze to an ROI is required for realizing the natural interaction between the system and the human. A user can easily find and access the necessary and important information by guiding his/her gaze so that improvement in the usability of the system can be expected. Therefore, it is commonly believed that guiding a human's gaze to a particular region allows many types of human activities to be effectively facilitated and directed [3].

Humans choose important information from an enormous volume of visual information; this is called "visual attention." The traditional attention retargeting approach that is used in television and movies is to present visual stimuli such as arrows or a bounding box in the peripheral visual field [1]. This traditional approach is more coercive than effective from a viewer's standpoint. A better approach would be to smoothly and effectively direct a human's attention toward an ROI without impeding his/her current visual attention.

Several attention retargeting methods that use visual saliency maps to guide a human's attention to an ROI have recently been proposed, which are divided into

© Springer International Publishing AG 2017
C. Stephanidis (Ed.): HCII Posters 2017, Part I, CCIS 713, pp. 383–390, 2017.
DOI: 10.1007/978-3-319-58750-9_53

two groups: color-based methods and orientation-based methods [4–9]. The color-based methods modify each color component so that the visual saliency inside the ROI increases, whereas that outside the ROI decreases. The advantage of this method is that it generally guides the attention to the ROI while maintaining a high resolution for the non-ROI. Veas et al. [4] proposed a saliency modulation technique that prompts attention shifts and influences the recall of the ROI without a perceptible change to the visual input. Mendez et al. [5] proposed a method for dynamically directing a viewer's gaze by analyzing and modulating the bottom-up salient features. Recently, Takimoto et al. [6] used a novel saliency analysis and color modulation to create modified images in which the ROI is the most salient region in the entire image. The proposed saliency map model that is used during the saliency analysis reduces the computational costs and improves the naturalness of the image by using the L*a*b* color space and a simplified normalization method. On the other hand, the orientation-based methods guide the viewer's attention to a non-blurred region by blurring the colors outside the specified region. Hitomi et al. [7] proposed a saliency map based on a wavelet transform and an image modification method to direct a viewer's gaze to a given region in an image. These methods adaptively modified the visual features based on bottom-up visual attention by reverse engineering a typical visual saliency map model. However, these attention retargeting methods focus only on modulating an image or a movie that is presented on a display device. Therefore, it is difficult to guide a viewer's gaze toward any region in real space.

In this paper, we propose a novel attention retargeting method used with a projector-camera system for realizing attention retargeting in real space. We focus on the realization of an appearance control method for attention retargeting to the plane of a real space as a first step. First, we capture the region where we can control the appearance by using a projector-camera system. Second, a target image that matches the ideal saliency map of the ROI that has the highest saliency is created from the captured image by reverse engineering a visual saliency model for bottom-up attention. Third, we calculate an optimum projection pattern for attention retargeting by using a projector-camera dynamic feedback system.

2   Proposed Method

The aim of this study was to create an effective attention retargeting method in real space that is strictly based on a bottom-up computational model of visual attention by using a projector-camera system. Our method consists of three phases: calibration of the projector-camera system, image modulation for saliency enhancement, and pattern projection. A flowchart of the proposed method is shown in Fig. 1.

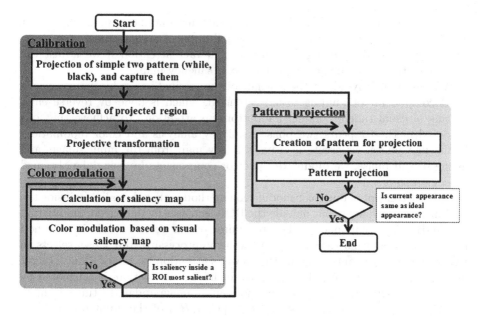

Fig. 1. Flowchart of the proposed method

2.1   Calibration of the Projector-Camera System

It is necessary to estimate the relationship between the projector and the camera in a projector-camera system. We project and capture two simple patterns to determine the correspondence between the projected pattern and each pixel in the captured image.

First, a whole black image and a whole white image are continuously projected and are then captured as images I_B and I_W, respectively. Second, the subtracted image I_S is calculated from both the I_B and I_W images. From the subtracted image I_S, the four corners of the projected region can be easily detected by using a snake model combined with a Hough transform.

Finally, the projected region in the captured image I_B is extracted from the coordinates of the detected four corners. In addition, a projective transformation is applied to the extracted region so that the region has the same size as that of the projected pattern. Henceforth, this transformed image T_B is defined as the actual and original appearance. The term "original" means any pattern that is not projected. The transformed image T_W is created from the captured image I_W in the same way as for T_B.

2.2   Image Modulation

Visual saliency may be defined as an estimation of how likely a given region can attract human visual attention. Itti et al. [10] proposed a computational model of visual saliency based on Koch and Ullman's early vision model [11]. They demonstrated in their study, wherein they measured actual human gazes, that a saliency map matches well with the distribution of actual human attention. Therefore, an ROI with high saliency can attract attention if we adjust the features of the whole image on the basis of a saliency map.

We can indirectly adjust the saliency of the original image by changing each RGB component for guiding visual attention, which is done by reverse engineering a visual saliency model for bottom-up attention. To achieve this, our proposed method repeats two phases: saliency analysis and color modulation. In the first phase, we create a visual saliency map from the input image, and in the second phase, we modulate the color components by using the obtained saliency map.

A basic concept of our color modulation method is that the saliency inside the ROI increases, whereas that outside the ROI decreases by iteratively modulating the RGB color components. The procedures of our color modulation method based on a saliency map are as follows. In the preprocessing step, a user selects an ROI where he/she wants to guide the viewer's attention to. In addition, a target image T, which is the initial image used for image modulation, is calculated by averaging T_B and T_W. Let T^t be the modulated image updated t times from T. Let k_{ij}^t be the color component k_{ij} ($k \in \{R, G, B\}$) of the input image T^t at pixel (i, j).

Step 1: The saliency map SM^t of image T^t is calculated.

Step 2: The intensity coefficient w_{ij}^t and the modification value $Q_{(k,ij)}^t$ are calculated.

Step 3: Each pixel value k_{ij}^t is temporarily modulated by the following equation:

$$k_{ij}^{t+1} = \begin{cases} k_{ij}^{0,B} & k_{ij}^M \le k_{ij}^{0,B} \\ k_{ij}^M & k_{ij}^{0,B} < k_{ij}^M < k_{ij}^{0,W} \\ k_{ij}^{0,W} & \text{otherwise} \end{cases} \tag{1}$$

$$k_{ij}^M = k_{ij}^t + \alpha w_{ij}^t Q_{(k,ij)}^t \tag{2}$$

where α is the weight coefficient used for color modulation and $k_{ij}^{0,B}$ and $k_{ij}^{0,W}$ are the color component of T_B and T_W at pixel (i, j), respectively. Even though the processing time decreases with the increase in the parameter α, the image quality gradually decreases because there is a trade-off between these two. Therefore, this parameter is optimized by a subjective experiment.

Step 4: If the saliency SM^{t+1} inside the ROI is the highest in the modulated image T^{t+1}, image modulation is finished after the following equation is applied; otherwise, k_{ij}^t is set to k_{ij}^{t+1} and the procedure goes back to Step 1.

The intensity coefficient w_{ij}^t, which is the weight of the modulation values of each pixel in the target image T^t, is defined by

$$w_{ij} = \begin{cases} \overline{SM}_{\text{ROI}} & (i, j) \in \text{ROI} \\ -S_{ij} & \text{otherwise} \end{cases} \tag{3}$$

Here,

$$\overline{SM}_{\text{ROI}} = \frac{1}{m} \sum_{(i,j) \in \text{ROI}} SM_{ij} \tag{4}$$

where m is the number of pixels in the ROI.

On the other hand, the modification value $Q^t_{(k,ij)}$ is defined by reverse engineering the saliency map calculation. $Q^t_{(k,ij)}$ reflects how much a feature influences the saliency and is obtained by back-calculating the saliency map. This indicates the influence rate of the saliency for each color component.

By using the proposed image modulation method, we can obtain the modified image T^{Prop}, which is the ideal appearance for attention retargeting.

2.3 Pattern Projection

We calculate a pattern that is projected onto a plane. Here, the projector and camera devices may have nonlinear characteristics such as gamma characteristics. In addition, the pattern light projected from a projector may be attenuated before it arrives at the plane. For these reasons, it is difficult to change the actual appearance to the optimum appearance by projecting a subtracted pattern between the actual appearance T_B and the ideal appearance T^{Prop} onto the actual plane only once.

Therefore, the actual appearance is imitated to look like the ideal appearance T^{Prop} by iteratively calculating the optimum projection pattern on the basis of the projector-camera feedback system. The procedures of the pattern calculation are as follows.

Step 1: The projection pattern P between the actual appearance T_B and the ideal appearance T^{Prop} is calculated.

$$P = T_B \ominus T^{Prop} \tag{5}$$

where $\ominus$ indicates the corresponding pixel-wise subtraction.

Step 2: The current appearance is captured after the subtracted pattern P is projected onto the plane. The captured appearance, which is the actual appearance, is transformed by projective transformation as T^{act}_{cap}.

Step 3: The subtracted pattern D between the captured image T^{act}_{cap} and the ideal appearance T^{Prop} is calculated.

$$D = T^{Prop} \ominus T_{cap} \tag{6}$$

Step 4: If the following conditions are satisfied for D, the iterative projection is finished:

$$\frac{\sum^i \sum^j D_{ij}}{n} < Th \tag{7}$$

where n is the number of pixels in D and Th is the threshold.

On the other hand, if the condition is not satisfied, the projection pattern P is updated by applying the following equation and the procedure returns to Step 2.

$$P = P \oplus D \tag{8}$$

where $\oplus$ indicates the corresponding pixel-wise summation.

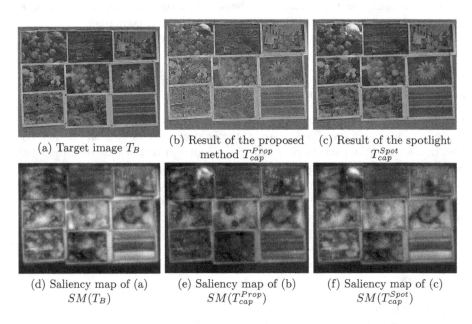

(a) Target image T_B

(b) Result of the proposed method T_{cap}^{Prop}

(c) Result of the spotlight T_{cap}^{Spot}

(d) Saliency map of (a) $SM(T_B)$

(e) Saliency map of (b) $SM(T_{cap}^{Prop})$

(f) Saliency map of (c) $SM(T_{cap}^{Spot})$

Fig. 2. Examples of the target image, result of the proposed method, result of the conventional approach, and their saliency maps

Table 1. Example of the saliency analysis inside/outside the ROI

	Inside the ROI			Outside the ROI		
	SM_{min}^{I}	SM_{max}^{I}	SM_{ave}^{I}	SM_{min}^{O}	SM_{max}^{O}	SM_{ave}^{O}
Target image $SM(T_B)$	0.102	0.758	0.380	0.000	1.000	0.385
Proposed method $SM(T_{cap}^{Prop})$	0.102	**1.000**	**0.555**	0.000	**0.794**	**0.269**
Spotlight $SM(T_{cap}^{Spot})$	0.130	1.000	0.504	0.000	0.806	0.332

3   Experiments

3.1   Experimental Setup

To show the effectiveness of the proposed attention retargeting method, we compared our method to a conventional technique. In the conventional technique, we projected a white pattern only on the ROI. In other words, this approach is like a spotlight.

We employed an EPSON EB-935W projector and a Logicool B910 HD webcam. In this experiment, nine A4-sized pictures were arranged on a gray board. The target image T_{cap} and its saliency map $SM(T_{cap})$ are shown in Fig. 2. In the saliency map, a whitish pixel indicated that the saliency was high. The watermelon in the upper left part of the image was chosen as the ROI.

3.2   Experimental Results and Discussion

Bottom-up attention induced by visual features obtained from a visual stimulus dominantly influences visual attention in the early stages, i.e., immediately after the visual stimulus is presented. Itti et al. [10] proposed a visual saliency computation model based on the early vision model proposed by Koch and Ullman [11]. Using human gaze measurements, they demonstrated that their saliency map matches well with the distribution of actual human attention. Therefore, we evaluated the effectiveness of each method for attention retargeting by using a saliency map.

The result of the proposed method T_{cap}^{Prop}, the result of the conventional method T_{cap}^{Spot}, and their saliency maps are shown in Fig. 2(a) and (d). The detailed results are listed in Table 1. In this table, the average, maximum, and minimum values of the saliency map inside or outside the ROI are shown.

The average value of the proposed method $SM(T_{cap}^{Prop})$ inside the ROI was higher than that of the spotlight $SM(T_{cap}^{Spot})$. In addition, the average of the proposed method $SM(T_{cap}^{Prop})$ outside the ROI was lower than that of the spotlight. Here, the larger the difference was between the saliency inside the ROI and that outside the ROI, the easier it was to direct a viewer's attention to the ROI. The effectiveness of the proposed method for attention retargeting was sufficient compared with that of the conventional approach.

4   Conclusions

In this paper, we proposed a novel attention retargeting method used with a projector-camera system to realize attention retargeting in real space. We focused on an actual appearance control method for attention retargeting to the plane of a real space as a first step. On the basis of the evaluations results, we have confirmed that the proposed method achieved efficient and effective attention retargeting compared with the conventional approach. It is necessary to evaluate the effectiveness of the attention retargeting method by using an eye tracking system as a future work.

This research was partially supported by a Grant-in-Aid for Scientific Research (C) from the Japan Society for the Promotion of Science (grant no. 15K00282).

References

1. Posner, M.: Orienting of attention. Q. J. Exp. Psychol. **32**, 3–25 (1980)
2. Bailey, R., McNamara, A., Sudarsanam, N., Grimm, C.: Subtle gaze direction. ACM TOG **28**(4), 1–14 (2009)
3. Kimura, A., Yonetani, R., Hirayama, T.: Computational models of human visual attention and their implementations: a survey. IEICE Trans. Inf. Syst. **96**(3), 562–578 (2013)
4. Veas, E., Mendez, E., Feiner, S., Schmalstieg, D.: Directing attention and influencing memory with visual saliency modulation. In: Proceedings of the SIGCHI Conference on Human Factors in Computing Systems, pp. 1471–1480 (2011)
5. Mendez, E., Feiner, S., Schmalstieg, D.: Focus and context in mixed reality by modulating first order salient features. In: Taylor, R., Boulanger, P., Krüger, A., Olivier, P. (eds.) SG 2010. LNCS, vol. 6133, pp. 232–243. Springer, Heidelberg (2010). doi:10.1007/978-3-642-13544-6_22
6. Takimoto, H., Kokui, T., Yamauchi, H., Kishihara, M., Okubo, K.: Image modification based on a visual saliency map for guiding visual attention. IEICE Trans. Inf. Syst. **E98–D**(11), 1967–1975 (2015)
7. Hitomi, S., Kokui, T., Takimoto, H., Yamauchi, H., Kishihara, M., Okubo, K.: Guiding visual attention using saliency map based on wavelet transform. In: Proceedings of RISP International Workshop on NCSP 2015, pp. 90–93 (2015)
8. Mateescu, V.A., Bajić, I.V.: Guiding visual attention by manipulating orientation in images. In: Proceedings of 2013 IEEE International Conference on Multimedia and Expo, pp. 1–6 (2013)
9. Su, Z., Takahashi, S.: Real-time enhancement of image and video saliency using semantic depth of field. In: VISAPP 2, pp. 370–375. INSTICC Press (2010)
10. Itti, L., Koch, C., Niebur, E.: A model of saliency based visual attention for rapid scene analysis. IEEE Trans. PAMI **20**(11), 1254–1259 (1998)
11. Koch, C., Ullman, S.: Shifts in selective visual attention: towards the underlying neural circuitry. Hum. Neurobiol. **4**(4), 219–227 (1985)

Detection System of Unsafe Driving Behavior Significant for Cognitive Dysfunction Patients

Tomoji Toriyama[✉], Akira Urashima, and Satoshi Yoshikuni

Toyama Prefectural University, Toyama, Japan
{toriyama, a-urasim}@pu-toyama.ac.jp

Abstract. Cognitive dysfunction patient could have symptoms such as attention disorder, execute function disorder and so on. These symptoms may cause unsafe driving in daily life. The degree of these symptoms can be evaluated by neuropsychological examination, however, the correspondence relationship between these symptoms and unsafe driving is uncertain. Therefore, it is difficult to judge the patient's driving capability with only neuropsychological examination. Though evaluation methods such as driving simulator are also used alongside neuropsychological examination, driving simulator has limitations on reproducibility of the acceleration shift, visual resolution or coverage angle of the display. To solve this problem, we are developing an unsafe driving detection system to be used in a real car, based on an analysis of the cognitive dysfunction patient's behaviors. It requires some small wireless sensors measuring triaxial angular velocity and acceleration to be attached on user's head and steering wheel, and GPS sensor on a car. This experiment which uses a real car was conducted in our designed "private course" in Toyama Driving Education Center Japan. In order to confirm various expected driving actions, the subject, 13 cognitive dysfunction patients and 12 adults without cognitive dysfunction, were equipped with small wireless sensors. As a result of video analysis, two hypotheses can be made about the difference between the cognitive dysfunction patients and adults without cognitive dysfunction. One is the sequence of the "safety checking action" and "lane changing operation" when changing lane, and another is the reacceleration when decelerating on planned slowdown from high speed. According to the result of the sensor data analysis, the significant difference is confirmed on chi-square test same as in video analysis.

Keywords: Cognitive dysfunction · Wearable sensor · Deceleration behavior · Driving Skill

1 Introduction

When a part of the brain is affected by apoplexy, brain tumor or injury to the head, cognitive dysfunction symptoms including attention disorder and execute function disorder may appear. Although these symptoms may improve through medical treatment, it may be dangerous to drive a car in daily life depending on the degree of the symptom. In Japan, under the road traffic law, driving licenses may be suspended or canceled in case of problems with recognition, judgment and operation, identified

© Springer International Publishing AG 2017
C. Stephanidis (Ed.): HCII Posters 2017, Part I, CCIS 713, pp. 391–396, 2017.
DOI: 10.1007/978-3-319-58750-9_54

through aptitude tests. However, there are no standard guidelines to judge the driving ability of the patients with cognitive dysfunction. In some hospitals, neuropsychological examination is used to evaluate the degrees of symptoms and driving simulators are used to measure the reaction time to sudden dangers on the road when pedestrians run out onto the road and avoidance operation such as braking and steering to avoid collision. However, the correspondence relationship between these symptoms and unsafe driving is uncertain and such simulators do not give the sense of acceleration and deceleration to the user, and visual resolution or coverage angle of the display is limited, so there is a certain gap between real and virtual driving. We have been developing the Driving Skill Evaluation System [1] for cognitive dysfunction patients, which acquires the driver's behaviors through the use of wearable and wireless motion sensors and GPS sensor. In this paper, we focus on the difference of deceleration and lane change behavior between cognitive dysfunction patients and adult drivers without cognitive dysfunction. We report the result of analysis on patients' driving data acquired from the experiments by using our system on a designed "private course".

2   Experiment on Designed Driving Cource

The experiments are conducted with subjects equipped with wearable wireless motion sensors using real cars on "private course" in Toyama Driving Education Center Japan. Figure 1 shows the designed "private course" for the experiment with the aim to test our hypotheses. The course includes several kinds of road conditions, such as signalized/nonsignalized, with/without stop sign intersections and lane change point, and roads with several kinds of speed limitation that take 10–15 min to drive. The subjects are 13 cognitive dysfunction patients and 12 adults without cognitive dysfunction. They drive the course with wearable wireless motion sensors in order to generate their motion data. Six video cameras are installed inside and outside of the car in order to record driving behavior in detail. These video cameras record the drivers from forward, side and backward. One video camera is also attached near the driver's foot in order to record pedal action.

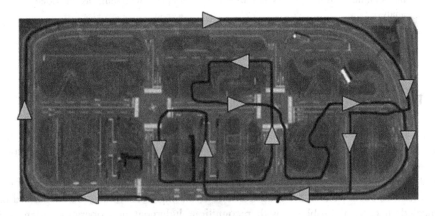

Fig. 1. Designed "private course"

3 Hypotheses from Video Analisis

As a result of the video analysis, two hypotheses can be made about the difference between the cognitive dysfunction patients and adults without cognitive dysfunction. The first hypothesis concerned with the sequence of "safety checking action" and "lane changing operation" when changing lane. We find that many of the cognitive dysfunction patients tend to do their "lane changing operation" earlier than "safety checking action". This sequence is unsafe if the following car is in the progress of overtaking a slower car. Hypothesis 1: Although the steering wheel should be operated after a safety checking, cognitive dysfunction patients sometimes are unable to follow this sequence. Another hypothesis is concerned with the reacceleration when decelerating on planned slowdown from high-speed. We find that many cognitive dysfunction patients tend to reaccelerate when decelerating on planned slowdown from high-speed. Reacceleration on planned slowdown from high speed is unsafe because if the following car expects gradual deceleration and keeps minimum distance between cars, then rear-end collision would occur. Hypothesis 2: decelerating on planned slowdown from high-speed should be gradual but cognitive dysfunction patients sometimes decelerate more than they intend to, and therefore, must reaccelerate again.

4 Unsafe Driving Detection System

Figures 2 and 3 shows wireless wearable motion sensors (Objet sensor [2, 3]) used in our Unsafe Driving Detection System. All sensors can measure triaxial angular velocity and acceleration. We put the sensors on the driver's head and toe, as well as the car's steering wheel and body in order to measure their movements. The black one also has GPS sensor inside.

4.1 Detection of a Reacceleration

In order to detect a reacceleration of the car, we acquire latitude and longitude values per second from GPS sensor. The car speed is calculated from them. To avoid the influence of GPS data error, we set the threshold value. If over threshold speed acceleration occurs when decelerating on planned slowdown, we would determine the car to be reaccelerating.

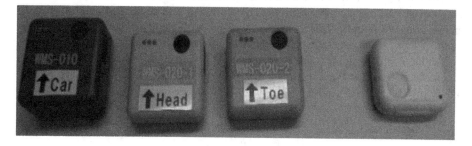

Fig. 2. Wireless wearable motion sensors

Fig. 3. Attached position of sensors

4.2   Detection of a Driving Operation Sequence

We obtain yaw angle (relative angle around the vertical axis from the ground) of the head from sensor data of acceleration and angular velocity by Kalman filter, where constant offset of angular velocity is removed based on the data while the car stops before starting. In order to obtain relative yaw angle from the car body, we subtract yaw angle of a car body from that of the driver's head. However, there still remains irregular offset drift of angular velocity, which affects the estimated yaw angle. To remove the irregular offset, we calculate the reference value from the middle point between the minimal and maximal values of the yaw angle obtained above in a certain period. We obtain a corrected yaw angle (face direction) by subtracting the reference value from the yaw angle. Furthermore, we also obtain rotation angle of the steering wheel from sensor data of acceleration and angular velocity by Kalman filter.

5   Deference Detection by the Sensors

5.1   Detection of Reacceleration When Decelerating on Planned Slowdown from High-Speed

The GPS sensor was leave near the driving course for an hour as a preliminary experiment. Figure 4 shows the GPS sensor error translated to the velocity. This shows errors over 3.5 km/h merely occurred. Therefore, we defined the threshold of reacceleration as over 3.5 km/h. Table 1 shows the number of people who make reacceleration over 3.5 km/h when decelerating on planned slowdown from high-speed.

All the people without cognitive dysfunction gradually decelerated. The significant difference is confirmed on chi-square test from the data in Table 1. $\chi 2(1, N = 24) = 4.042$, $p < .05$.

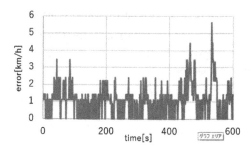

Fig. 4. GPS sensor error

Table 1. Number of people reaccelerate

	Reaccelerate	No reaccelerate	Total
Without cognitive dysfunction	0	12	12
With cognitive dysfunction	5	7	12
Total	5	19	24

5.2 Detection Result of Sequence of the Safety Checking Action and Steering Wheel Operation

Figure 5 shows a safety checking action when changing lane was calculated from the attached sensor data. An evaluator decides the threshold on each subject's face angle, which indicates the starting of "safety checking action", and threshold on each subject's steering wheel indicating the start of "lane changing operation".

The threshold value used to judge the start of "safety checking action" and "lane changing operation" is calculated by averaging these values. Table 2 shows the number of people who make the wrong/good sequence of "safety checking action" and "lane changing operation".

Only 1 person without cognitive dysfunction makes wrong sequence. The significant difference is confirmed on chi-square test from the data in Table 2. $\chi 2(1, N = 25) = 4.033$, $p < .05$.

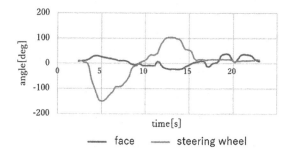

Fig. 5. Face and steering wheel angle when changing lane

Table 2. Number of people who make wrong sequence of operation

	Wrong sequence	Good sequence	Total
Without cognitive dysfunction	1	11	12
With cognitive dysfunction	7	6	13
Total	8	17	25

6   Conclusion

We established two hypotheses from the results derived from the driving experiment video analysis. To confirm these hypotheses, we proposed the method of the car reacceleration judgement and the sequence checking for the element of the unsafe driving detection system. As a result of the experiment, we identified some significant differences between cognitive dysfunction patients and adults without cognitive dysfunction on the action of car reacceleration, and the sequence of "safety checking action" and "lane changing operation".

Acknowledgment. We would like to thank Toyama Driving Education Center and Toyama rehabilitation Hospital for the cooperation in the experiments. This work was supported by JSPS KAKENHI Grant Number 15K01472.

References

1. Toriyama, T., Urashima, A., Nakamura, M., Nomura, T., Ohshima, J., Yoshino, O.: A study of driving skill evaluation system using wearable sensors for cognitive dysfunction. IEICE Technical report, WIT2013-48, vol. 113, no. 272, pp. 29–34, October 2013. (in Japanese)
2. Objet. http://www.sensetech.jp/ATR-SensetechGV.html. (in Japanese)
3. Tada, M., Nayo, F., Ohmura, R., Okada, M., Noma, H., Toriyama, T., Kogure, K.: A method for measuring and analyzing driving behavior using wireless accelerometers. IEICE Trans. Inf. Syst. (Japanese edition) **J91-D**(4), 1115–1129 (2008)

Measurement of Eyeblink Frequency Variation for Cognitive Dysfunction Patients' Safe Driving Skill Evaluation

Akira Urashima$^{(\boxtimes)}$, Yoshiki Otsuki, and Tomoji Toriyama

Toyama Prefectural University, Toyama, Japan
{a-urasim, toriyama}@pu-toyama.ac.jp

Abstract. As cognitive dysfunction can cause unsafe driving, it is necessary to evaluate the driving skills of the cognitive dysfunction patients. We have been studying the safe driving skill evaluation system with wearable sensors, and found some characteristics of the unsafe driving behavior of the cognitive dysfunction patients. In this paper, we focus on the eyeblink frequency that is said to be affected by cognitive processes. We carried out the driving experiment in real traffic condition at Kanazawa, Japan in Oct. 2015. When we extracted the eyeblink frequency from the EOG (electrooculography) data of the experiment, there was a difference between healthy subject and cognitive dysfunction subject in the degree of eyeblink frequency variation in the situation that requires attention. From this results, it is possible that the eyeblink frequency while driving includes useful information for analyzing the driving skill of cognitive dysfunction patients.

Keywords: Cognitive dysfunction patients · Driving skill · Public road · Eyeblink frequency

1 Introduction

Cognitive dysfunction can be caused by organic brain damage from cerebral stroke, traumatic head injury and/or the other kind of cerebral events. Its symptoms such as attention disorder, executive dysfunction and so on may cause unsafe driving. As the symptoms become lighter, some patients will need to drive a car for the necessity of life and social participation.

The attention disorder patients have difficulty to concentrate one's attention and/or to give one's attention for the surroundings, and the executive dysfunction patients have difficulties in planning, flexibility and/or execution in required time. Although the degree of symptom can be evaluated by neuropsychological examination, the effects of these degrees of the symptom to the safe driving behavior are hard to tell. Therefore, the objective evaluation method of the cognitive dysfunction patient's driving skill is necessary.

There is driving simulator for this purposes, but it has lack of the acceleration/ deceleration feedback and limitation of view angle in most cases. Tada et al. developed the automatic evaluation system of driving skill, which uses a real car and wearable sensors and identifies shortcomings in driving skills [1]. However, their subjects ware

© Springer International Publishing AG 2017
C. Stephanidis (Ed.): HCII Posters 2017, Part I, CCIS 713, pp. 397–401, 2017.
DOI: 10.1007/978-3-319-58750-9_55

healthy adults and elderly, and not cognitive dysfunction patients. Therefore, we have studying the safe driving skill evaluation system with wearable sensors for cognitive dysfunction patients. From the experiments on private road in the driving education center, we found the difference in the driving operation sequence at lane change and the deceleration control on the planed slowdown [2–4].

In this paper, we focus on the eyeblink frequency which is said to be affected by recognition process [5]. The eyeblinks while driving is an unconscious behavior, whereas the differences mentioned above relate to conscious behavior. So the eyeblink frequency variation from time to time may indicate the attention from the risk prediction, and become an indicator of safe driving skill. In the following sections, we describe the method of eyeblink frequency measurement, the experiments on the public road and its results.

2 Method of Eyeblink Frequency Measurement

There are several methods to detect eyeblinks such as using wearable camera, using camera installed in the environment and using EOG (Electrooculography). Although the method using EOG has a disadvantage of taking much time and effort to install, it has an advantage that it is not affected by ambient light. In this experiment, we took the method using EOG since the installation can be supported by the assistants of the experiment and the subject can be in direct sunlight while driving.

Figure 1 shows the position of the EOG electrodes attached on the subject. The EOG electrodes are connected to the biometer/logger "Polymate Mini" (Miyuki Giken Co. Ltd.) and the EOG is recorded in it with 200 Hz sampling rate.

The eyeblink frequency can be extracted from the recorded electrical potential of the EOG. The procedure is as follows:

1. Subtract moving median value from Ch.1 of EOG data in order to remove the effects of eye movement. The window length of median is 1 s, which is a sufficiently long time compared to a normal eyeblink.
2. Detect eyeblinks by threshold. In this study, the threshold value is −200 uV. This value was determined from the obtained data.
3. Calculate eyeblink frequency at each moment from the number of eyeblinks in a certain time window. The time window for this calculation is between 5 s before and after.

Fig. 1. Electrodes attached on the subject

3 Experiment and Result

In Oct. 2015, we carried out the driving experiment on the public road at Kanazawa, Japan[1]. The subjects of this experiment were a cognitive dysfunction patient and a healthy adult. The subjects wore the wearable acceleration/gyro sensors on one's head and right foot, and the Electrodes of EOG around the eyes. The acceleration/gyro sensor, GPS receiver and the video cameras was install on the car in order to record the movement of the car, the surroundings and the driver's behavior. The car used in the experiment was the car for driving school and has an additional brake on the floor of the front passenger seat.

The subjects drove on the predetermined course (shown in Fig. 2) under the direction of the driving instructor in the front passenger seat. The course is about 7 km in length and takes about 20 min driving. It includes various road widths, lane numbers and intersection conditions. However, because of the public road, we could not control other cars, pedestrian and signal conditions.

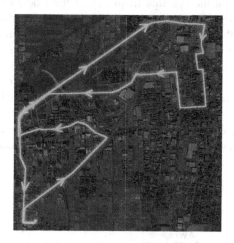

Fig. 2. The course map of the experiment in Kanazawa, Japan.

After the experiment, the eyeblink frequency was extracted from the recorded EOG data and synchronized with the video data and the GPS data. By this synchronization, we can see the frequency variation associated to the specified scene determined by location or by video surveillance.

We chose two scenes that require carefulness for safe driving. One is the scene passing straight at the intersection with low visibility and no signal. The other is the scene changing lanes when other cars were in the vicinity.

Figure 3 shows the eyeblink frequency around the intersection. The left graph in the figure is of the cognitive dysfunction subject and the right graph is of the healthy adult subject. The bi-directional arrow in the graph indicates the region of the

---

[1] This experiment was approved by the ethics committee in Toyama Prefectural University.

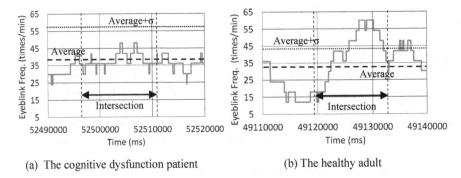

(a) The cognitive dysfunction patient   (b) The healthy adult

Fig. 3. The eyeblink frequency when passing straight at the intersection.

intersection passing. The horizontal dashed lines is the average value of the eyeblink frequency of the whole course for each subject. The dotted line shows the value adding the standard deviation of the eyeblink frequency of the whole course to the average. The eyeblink frequency of the cognitive dysfunction subject did not vary so much while that of the healthy adult subject varied much in the region of the intersection.

Figure 4 shows the eyeblink frequency around the lane changing. The left graph in the figure is of the cognitive dysfunction subject and the right is of the healthy adult subject. The bi-directional arrow in the graph indicate the time region from the start to the end of lane-changing action. The dashed line and the dotted line mean same as above. As in the case of the intersection passing mentioned above, the eyeblink frequency of the cognitive dysfunction subjects did not vary so much while that of the healthy adult subject increased in the region of lane changing and decreased after the lane changing.

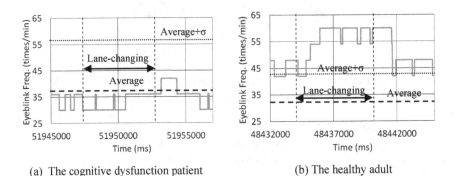

(a) The cognitive dysfunction patient   (b) The healthy adult

Fig. 4. The eyeblink frequency while lane-changing

4   Discussion and Conclusion

In the experiment on the public road, there were differences in the eyeblink frequency variation between the cognitive dysfunction subject and the healthy adult subject in the scenes which requires carefulness for safe driving. This may indicate that the cognitive dysfunction subject was unable to predict the risk in those scene and had difficulties in paying appropriate attention to the surroundings. If so, it may be possible to use the measurement of the eyeblink frequency as one of the indicator of the safe driving skills. Since there are eyeglasses type devices for measuring EOG on the market, the cost of installation can be reduced. However, as there is possibility that it is simply due to the individual differences, so the experiments by more subject and verifications are necessary for the further study.

Acknowledgement. This work was supported by JSPS KAKENHI Grant Number JP15K01472.

References

1. Tada, M., Noma, H., Utsumi, A., Segawa, M., Okada, M., Renge, K.: Elderly driver retraining using automatic evaluation system of safe driving skill. IET Intel. Transport Syst. **8**(3), 266–272 (2014)
2. Nakayama, T., Tone, S., Toriyama, T., Urashima, A., Nakamura, M., Nomura, T., Ohshima, J.-I., Yoshino, O.:Detection of brake pedal and accelerator pedal operation using wearable sensors. In: The Proceedings of the 23rd International Conference on Artificial Reality and Telexistence, pp. 155–156 (2013)
3. Yamamoto, T., Nakamura, M., Urashima, A., Toriyama, T.: A study of deceleration behavior for cognitive dysfunction drivers on public road. J. Adv. Control Autom. Robot. (JACAR) **1** (1), 44–46 (2015). Applied Science and Computer Science Publications
4. Toriyama, T., Yoshikuni S., Urashima, A.: Detection system of unsafe driving significant for cognitive dysfunction patients. In: The Proceedings of HCI International (2017, to appear)
5. Bentivoglio, A.R., Bressman, S.B., Cassetta, E., Carretta, D., Tonali, P., Albanese, A.: Analysis of blink rate patterns in normal subjects. Mov. Disord. **12**(6), 1028–1034 (1997)

Experimental Research on the Armored Crew's Depth Perception

Qianxiang Zhou, Jintao Wu, and Zhongqi Liu[✉]

Key Laboratory for Biomechanics and Mechanobiology of the Ministry of
Education, School of Biological Science and Medical Engineering,
Beihang University, Beijing 100191, China
liuzhongqi@buaa.edu.cn

Abstract. To establish the depth perception database of Chinese armored crews
and provide base information for the selection and training of the related population. The depth perception data of 565 Chinese young males from seven
natural areas were collected. The Participants' age range from 17 to 32. The data
were statistically analyzed and compared with related researches in China and
abroad. Within a certain range, the distance between the variance simulation and
the standard constant stimulation had no significant effect on the depth
description. A significant difference existed among the monocular and binocular.
Depth perception in armored crews of different education and living areas did
not exhibit significant different. Depth perception of armored crews was better
than general population, seamen and drivers. By sampling on a national scale,
the depth perception database is established for Chinese armored crews. This
study provides the basic data for the training and selection of armored crews and
can be also used as reference for cognitive parameters researchers.

Keywords: Armored crews · Parallax angle · Sampling · Depth perception

1 Introduction

Depth perception is a vital index to evaluate human cognitive function, and also an
important basis for selecting and training some professional positions. Kellman et al.
[1] designed the visual cliff experiment and proved that human beings have good
ability of deep perception since birth. Johson [2] proposed that the depth perception
have certain relevance with complex social perception. By experiment Walk and
Gibson [3] proved that the most important factor affecting the depth perception were
binocular disparity and the integration ability of brain. Individual genes, depth perception training and psychological quality were also proved by them to be related to the
depth perception. By virtual scene experiment, Poyade et al. [4] proved that the
influence of the size of the target object on the perception of depth is greater than that
of binocular disparity, and they put forward the position of the target object and
binocular cues will affect depth perception simultaneously. When the binocular parallax is fixed, the closer the target is, the smaller the depth perception error is. By disk
experiment, Tai and Inanici [5] demonstrated that the increase of contrast between the
target and the surrounding environment can enhance the depth perception. Bell et al.

© Springer International Publishing AG 2017
C. Stephanidis (Ed.): HCII Posters 2017, Part I, CCIS 713, pp. 402–407, 2017.
DOI: 10.1007/978-3-319-58750-9_56

[6] showed that human depth perception will slightly weaken at the age of 40 and significantly impaired at the age of 45 due to degradation of retinal metabolic function.

Hao et al. [7] tested the depth perception of 245 seamen and 87 marine students, and proved that the depth perception of seamen was significantly higher than that of ordinary marine students. By measuring the depth perception of basketball players, Yuede [8] proved that depth perception is related to professional training. Testing the depth perception of 248 male truck drivers by depth perception instrument, Weili et al. [9] proved that the depth perception accuracy of drivers in safe group was significantly higher than that of accident group in motion state. Liben et al. [10] experiment showed that the depth perception had certain relevance with traffic accidents.

There is no related research on the depth perception of armored crew till now. This paper will analyze the influence of variance simulation position, monocular or binocular, education and living area on the depth perception of armored crew, hoping to provide reference for the testing and training of armored crew's depth perception.

2 Method

2.1 Participants

The depth perception test covered seven natural regions, the north China, east China, central China, south China, southwest China, northwest China and northeast China and the depth perception data of 565 armored crews were collected. Participants' ages range from 17 to 32, with an average age of 23.3. All participants' vision was normal or normal after corrected and they were not color blinded. During experiment, 150 participants were selected randomly to test depth perception of monocular.

2.2 Apparatus and Test Method

The device in this experiment for testing depth perception was BD-V-104A depth perception tester, which is based on the principle of Haime Hertz's three needles experiment. During the experiment, two needles were fixed as standard simulation and the third needle was mobile as variance stimulation. The participants kept a certain distance to the standard stimulations and adjust the variance stimulation to make all the needles in the same plane.

The parallax angle PA (arc.sec) was used to evaluate depth perception and the calculation formula of PA is as follows:

$$PA = 206265 * b * d / (D * (d + D)) \tag{1}$$

In the formula, b is the distance between two eyes, which is about 65 mm; D is the observation distance, which is 2000 mm, and d is the parallax distance, namely judgment error.

In the experiment, the subjects kept the head static and sit 2000 mm away from observation window where they can see the central part of the variance simulation. The distance between the variance simulation and the standard stimulation was 100 mm,

600 mm, 700 mm, 1200 mm respectively. The subjects Held the handle to adjust the position of the variance simulation and they would stop the adjustment when they think that the variance stimulation and the two standard stimulations are in a horizontal line. Then experimenter recorded the actual distance error and the parallax distance of the variance stimulation and standard stimulation. To eliminate the interference of speed, the variance stimulation moved at same speed. The distance between variance stimu-lation and standard stimulation were recorded in 4 positions respectively.

2.3   Statistical Analysis

After eliminating abnormal values of the samples by triple standard difference method, the effective samples of 405 monocular and 142 binocular were obtained. The influence of position of variance stimulation on depth perception and difference among the monocular and binocular were analyzed. The influence of education and living areas on armored crew's depth perception were also analyzed with the binocular data.

3   Result and Discussion

3.1   The Effect of Initial Position of Variance Stimulation on Depth Perception

The monocular and binocular parallax angle of four points, which were respectively at a distance of 100 mm, 600 mm, 700 mm, and 1200 mm from variance stimulation to standard stimulation, were tested and the descriptive statistic analysis shown the mean value and standard deviation in Table 1. The monocular and binocular parallax angle at different position was analyzed by One-Way ANOVA. The results of binocular data were $F_{(31616)} = 0.004$, the level of significance was $P = 0.996 > 0.05$, and the result of monocular data was $F_{(3564)} = 1.064$, the significance level was $P = 0.496 > 0.05$. Therefore, it could be concluded that the distance between the variance simulation and the standard constant stimulation has no significant effect on the depth description.

By experiment based on the virtual reality technology, Poyade et al. [4] proved that the position of the variance stimulation had influence on depth perception, that the closer the position of the variance stimulation is, the smaller the depth perception error is Zhongxian and Xiuru [11] proved that the distance of 2/4 is the most accurate when judging relative distance between two objects. because of the limitations of the

Table 1. Monocular and binocular parallax angle data of different location

Distance (mm)	Binocular parallax angle (arc•sec)		Monocular parallax angle (arc•sec)	
	Average	Standard deviation	Average	Standard deviation
100	2.53	1.98	10.01	6.43
600	2.47	2.03	9.24	4.81
700	2.42	1.31	10.23	5.03
1200	2.52	2.21	9.63	6.98

experimental conditions that the change of the position of variance stimulation is too small to has a significant effect on the depth perception, The results of this study were different from that of Xiuru Sun. Binocular convergence is the most important factor of distance judgment. The experimental results showed that with the increase of the distance between the variance simulation and the standard constant stimulation, the angle of the convergence was smaller, and the effect of binocular convergence was gradually weakened. However, it still plays an important role in the range of 30 m and subjects' assessment of the distance was still accurate [12]. The observation distance of this experiment was 2 m, under this premise, it is believed that the position of variance stimulation of this research have no significant effect on depth perception.

3.2   Depth Perception Analysis of Monocular and Binocular

Statistical analysis of parallax angle of 405 monocular and 142 binocular subjects was made and means, maximum, minimum value, standard deviation and 3 percentile (5, 50, 95th) that commonly used in cognitive measurement were obtained that are shown in Table 2.

Table 2. Monocular and binocular parallax angle data (arc•sec)

	Average	Standard deviation	Minimum value	Maximum value	P5	P50	P95
Binocular	2.46	1.73	0.00	26.32	0.0	1.67	7.30
Monocular	9.31	6.56	0.33	44.28	0.67	6.36	29.10

Comparison between monocular and binocular parallax angle was done with independent sample T-test. The results shown that a significant difference($p < 0.05$) existed among the monocular and binocular depth perception limens and the results are the same as those of previous studies [13]. The main reason was that binocular parallax plays an more greater role than monocular cue when judging the relative distance.

Compared with the depth perception of general population, seamen and drivers, the parallax angle of armored crews was smaller [7, 9, 13]. The reason for this may be related to the special environment and working properties of the armored crews who must be trained to finish the task and to some extent the level of depth perception was raised.

3.3   Analysis of Binocular Parallax Angle in Different Education and Living Area

The maximum, minimum and mean values of binocular parallax angle in different educational backgrounds and living areas were shown in Tables 3 and 4. One-Way ANOVA was made to analyze the influence of the two factors on binocular parallax angle. The test results of education and living areas were $F(3,6) = 0.541$, $P = 0.654 >$

Table 3. The binocular parallax angle data of different living areas

Living areas	Number of samples	Average (arc•sec)	Maximum value (arc•sec)	Minimum value (arc•sec)
North China	58	2.46	22.23	0.00
East China	81	2.43	26.32	0.27
Central China	99	2.35	21.62	0.35
South China	34	2.32	22.91	0.26
Southwest China	64	2.21	21.32	0.00
Northwest China	35	2.39	23.61	0.33
Northeast China	34	2.29	21.31	0.27

Table 4. The depth description data of different education

Education	Number of samples	Average (arc•sec)	Maximum value (arc•sec)	Minimum value (arc•sec)
Middle school	70	2.23	19.65	0.87
Secondary special school	78	2.67	22.01	1.03
High school	148	2.37	26.03	0.00
Vocational university	89	2.41	25.92	0.15
University	30	2.45	23.98	0.23

0.05 and $F_{(2,6)} = 0.387$, $P = 0.680 > 0.05$. Therefore, it could be concluded that education and living areas have no significant influence on depth perception.

There was no report about influence of education and living areas on depth perception and couldn't find data to compare. However, researchers have proved that depth perception training program could improve one's depth perception [7, 8]. The results showed that training can improve the individual depth perception, excluding the experimental environment factors (brightness, experimental instruments, object size, clues etc.), so it could be concluded indirectly that education level and living areas have no correlation with depth perception.

4   Conclusion

This is the first study on the depth perception of armored crews that sampling in nationwide with large sample. Based on the sampling and statistical analysis of data of seven natural regions, the following conclusions can be drawn: (1) Depth perception of armored crews is better than general population, seamen and drivers. (2) There is significant difference between binocular and monocular depth perception and binocular depth perception is better than that of monocular depth perception. Therefore, the work relate to depth perception need for people concern with normal vision. (3) Within a certain range, the distance between the variance simulation and the standard constant stimulation have no significant effect on the depth description. (4) Depth perception in armored crews of different education and living areas do not exhibit significant different.

References

1. Kellman, P.J., Elizabeth, S., Kenneth, R.: Infant perception of object unity from translatory motion in depth and vertical translation. Child Dev. 72–86 (1986)
2. Johnson, S.P.: Object perception and object knowledge in young infants: a view from studies of visual development. Percept. Dev.: Vis. Audit. Speech Percept. 211–240 (1998)
3. Walk, R.D., Gibson, E.J.: A comparative and analytical study of visual depth perception. Psychol. Monogr.: Gen. Appl. **75**(15), 1–3 (1996)
4. Poyade, M., Reyes-Lecuona, A., Viciana-Abad, R.: Influence of binocular disparity in depth perception mechanisms in virtual environments. In: Macías, J.A., Saltiveri, A.G., Latorre, P.M. (eds.) New Trends on Human-Computer Interaction, pp. 13–22. Springer, London (2009)
5. Tai, N., Inanici, M.: Depth perception as a function of lighting, time, and spatiality. In: 2009 Conference on Illuminating Engineering Society (IES) (2009)
6. Bell, B., Wolf, E., Bernholz, C.D.: Depth perception as a function of age. Int. J. Aging Hum. Dev. **3**(1), 77–81 (1972)
7. Hao, Y., Guofeng, Z., Cundao, H., et al.: Study of seamen distance perception. Chin. J. Naut. Med. Hyperb. Med. **13**(1), 15–17 (2006)
8. Yuede, Z.: Preliminary study of basketball athletes distance perception. Appl. Psychol. **4**, 007 (1988)
9. Weili, G., Cundao, H., Xuhai, G., et al.: Study of truck drive distance perception. Hum. Ergon. **5**(3), 10–13 (1999)
10. Liben, Y., Lingchao, Z., Tao, L., et al.: Evaluation and analysis for depth perception of service vehicle drivers. J. Transp. Inf. Saf. **31**(1), 17–19 (2013)
11. Zhongxian, L., Xiuru, S.: Factors affecting the accuracy of depth perception and distance judgment. J. Psychol. **3**, 005 (1986)
12. Yunqiu, F., Qicheng, J.: The influence of convergence on size-distance judgments. J. Psychol. **4**, 32–35 (1963)
13. Jisheng, Y., Liluo, F., Jisheng, Z.: A measurement of the visual depth among chinese male young people I. J. Psychol. **3**, 006 (1980)

Data Analysis and Data Mining in Social Media and Communication

Instructional Information System for the Introduction of Data Journalism Techniques Based on User Centered Design Methodology

Belén Alazañez-Cortés, Zayra Montserrat Miranda-Aguirre[(✉)],
Jocelyn Lizbeth Molina-Barradas, Erick Monroy-Cuevas,
Rocío Abascal-Mena, Rodrigo Gómez-García,
and Román Esqueda-Atayde

Master in Design, Information and Communication (MADIC),
Universidad Autónoma, Metropolitana, Cuajimalpa, Mexico City, Mexico
belenalazagnez@gmail.com, zayry08@gmail.com,
d9molina@gmail.com, ermoncu@gmail.com,
{mabascal, rgomez}@correo.cua.uam.mx,
resqueda@neuralresearch.com.mx

Abstract. In this paper we analyze how effective the learning of the methodology proposed by Data Journalism could be assimilated by Mexican investigative journalists with the use of a proposed information system. This information system is called "Dataísta" -in Spanish-, which main function is to provide the investigative journalists main concepts and practical skills to integrate the reasoning behind Data Journalism methodology into their own knowledge. By following a process based on User-Centered Design, the main user's needs were identified. Also, prototypes were built and tested in order to know the relevance of the information system proposed. Besides, Dataísta can be used by the journalists to practice the skills they learned using some tools developed to filter, analyze and visualize information.

Keywords: Data Journalism · Information system · User-Centered Design · Learning environment

1 Introduction

During the last few years, the journalism has faced different kind of challenges mainly related with the technological innovations. The addition of Information and Communication Technologies (ICT) in the world has changed the way journalism is practiced being confronted to a big amount of information in real time.

Nowadays the journalists have a huge variety of information sources, there are a lot of data bases published by governments, NGO's reports, even information obtained from social media networks like Twitter or Facebook. It's needed to emphasize that most of the journalists use Open Data to begin their investigations. The Open Data Handbook defines Open Data as *"data that can be freely used, re-used and*

© Springer International Publishing AG 2017
C. Stephanidis (Ed.): HCII Posters 2017, Part I, CCIS 713, pp. 411–419, 2017.
DOI: 10.1007/978-3-319-58750-9_57

redistributed by anyone – subject only, at most, to the requirement to attribute and sharealike" [1]. That means that the Open Data Bases must be available as a whole and preferably by downloading over the Internet; must be provided under terms of re-use and redistribution and that everyone must be able to use, re-use and redistribute without discrimination about fields, endeavor, persons or groups.

The use of several information sources could be a great support for the journalists, however, the truth is that a certain level of specialization is required in order to be able to process all the information obtained from them. In our days, data is no longer used as facts to make more interesting the articles, now they take the main role; stories can be found through data bases. The mix between the traditional way to make journalism and the technological advance gave rise to a new kind of journalism specialization called "Data Journalism".

To have a better understanding of what Data Journalism is, we can use Aron Pilhofer's definition, *"an umbrella term that, encompasses an ever-growing set of tools, techniques and approaches to storytelling. It can include everything from traditional computer-assisted reporting (using data as a "source") to the must cutting edge data visualization and news application and analysis to help inform us all about important issues of the day"* [1]. This definition describes the way journalism meets technology in order to face the digital era. Data Journalism is not replacing the process followed by journalists through decades, it's just a new methodology and possibility that could help journalists to approach other disciplines to produce wider and robust investigations [2].

The transition from traditional journalism to Data Journalism has been given in a slow way. Mostly because the journalists don't have the time, the knowledge or the infrastructure needed to begin with their specialization [3]. According to the Global Investigative Journalism Network, Data Journalism has become relevant mostly because *"governments and business become increasingly flush with information, more and more bigger data is getting available from across the globe"* [3]. Thus, we observe a research opportunity to collaborate in the generation of skills and tools related to Data Journalism.

Our paper is composed as follows: in Sect. 2, where we analyze the state of art of the handbooks, articles and tools that were created to introduce the journalists to the methodology proposed by the Data Journalism. Section 3, presents the contextual study, the explanation of the process and the methodology followed to develop the prototype and the evaluation with the final user: Mexican Journalists. In that last stage is demonstrated the relevance of the proposal and the usability. Section 4 is dedicated to present the prototype, how it works and the evaluation. Finally, we present the future work and the conclusions.

2   State of Art

On 2011, the European Journalism Centre (EJC) circulated a survey in order to identify the training needs for Data Journalism. They found that there was a growing group of journalists interested in further investigation of datasets, unfortunately there are some knowledge gaps that must be filled. It is needed a systematic approach, there is a common misinterpretation of numbers and statistics. Wrongly extrapolating trends, misinterpretation of complex developments and lacking of information are often encountered mistakes in journalistic disclosure. Trainers and institutions in the journalistic field shouldn't skip the basics when working with numbers and statistics. There is a need for diligence and accuracy [4].

As a result of that survey, on 2011 MozFest the first Data Journalism Handbook [5] was born. It is an effort leaded by the European Journalism Centre and the Open Knowledge Foundation with the collaboration of media like Australian Broadcasting Corporation, the BBC, the Chicago Tribune, Deutsche Welle, the New York Times, ProPublica, the Washington Post, the Texas Tribune, Verdens Gang, Wales Online, Zeit Online and many others. In this handbook, the reader can find what does Data Journalism means, how does journalists works with it, and by analyzing some cases, it's explained how to obtain, understand and spread data [6]. Even though, this handbook is useful, most of its contents are focus on how certain Data Journalists solved their investigations by the use of the methodology and some tools. It is not clear the way researchers approach the problem and the thinking behind all the research. Examples are great, but it's crucial to help investigative journalists understand why following Data Journalism methodology would help them to improve their investigations and more important, they need to know how to approach data bases.

By 2013, the Spanish version of the handbook was released by the newspaper "La Nación" from Argentina. It was translated in order to help Spanish speakers to improve their news by the use of "data" [1]. This handbook was the first one about Data Journalism in Spanish, unfortunately, as it was a translation from the original in English, most of the contents were about cases and situations that can't be applied to Latin America. Both versions, can be downloaded for free, also they can be shared and reuse as a base to develop new contents.

It took two more years until a handbook generated by and for the Latin American journalists were available. Edited by Felipe Perry and Miguel Paz, in collaboration with more than 40 journalists, designers and programmers from countries like Chile, Argentina, Brazil, Venezuela, Spain and some others. It is a collection of articles about the actual situation of information access and the challenges that Data Journalism has to face in the region. The "Manual de Periodismo de Datos Iberoaméricano" intends to be a support material to help journalists, media and organizations to reduce the digital gap, mainly cause most of the tools and online tutorials are under a different language -most of them are written in English- [6].

Written by Hidalgo and Torres, journalists who worked at the digital newspaper "Ojo Público" from Peru. "La navaja Suiza del Reportero y el Método de Ojo Público" is a handbook that contains the knowledge and the methodologies that "Ojo Público" had obtained since its foundation. It mainly focusses on suggesting a change in investigative journalists' mentality in relation to the technological advance and the necessity to process huge amounts of data [7].

Also, Crucianelli, with the support of Google and the Knight Center in Texas have made available a Massive Open Online Course (MOOC) for those journalists who wants to learn more about Data Journalism. It was focused on digital tools for the Data Journalism practice. There are also some courses available to learn how to apply the Data Processing at Courseraor YouTube. Unfortunately just a few, like Knight Center's MOOC are fully created thinking on the Spanish speakers' journalists' needs.

The review of all the available material created to learn the Data Journalism process helped us to identify the methodology followed by most of the Data Journalists around the world. It is based on 5 steps: (1) data retrieve, (2) filter or cleaning, (3) analysis, (4) verification of the information and (5) data visualization.

According to Giannina Segnini, this steps could be described as [8]:

1. Data retrieve: it's the first part of the methodology, it could be seen like the easiest part of the process. The truth is that it's getting harder, mainly because there are some public servants that don't understand why journalists ask access to a data base.
2. Filter or cleaning: once the journalists have the data base, it's necessary to review and standardize them according to the investigation. Usually, data can be duplicated, wrong written or with incorrect codes, that's why this part of the process it's the hardest for the journalists. It must be done very cautiously because it is the input for the next steps of the methodology.
3. Analysis: this is the most important step in the Data Journalism process. Here, the journalists have to compare the information obtained from the data base, match it up with others, exchange data to identify tendencies, patterns and atypical behaviors.
4. Verification of the Information: once the journalists obtain the results of their analysis, it's necessary to verify the information. The journalists have to keep in mind that the data bases not always have the absolute truth.
5. Data Visualization: this is the final step of the methodology. Here the journalists have to think how are they going to show up the information to the readers. Nowadays, the journalists need to think as a designer, because a good data visualization could help the readers' to a better understanding.

The survey run by the EJC showed that the journalists has a huge gap of knowledge that must be filled, also that the lack of time, resources and support are the main barriers they face.

As it was described above in this section, there is a lack of contents thought for the Latin American journalists. Most of them are focus on telling success cases or to suggest the importance of having Data Journalism's teams in every redaction, some others assume that the journalists have already some basics knowledge on the use of searching engines, statistics or even programming languages. Journalists must have an information system that provides them the fundamentals of Data Journalism methodology, so they can figure out how to approach Open Data Bases and use them.

In the next section, the contextual study is showed up in order to identify users' needs to propose a prototype that fits to them.

3 Contextual Study

Based on the User-Centered Design method (UCD), a contextual study was applied as a methodology to identify the investigative journalists' needs. Using participative observation, interviews and surveys it was possible to get to know the main characteristics that must be included in a learning environment in order to help investigative journalists to introduce them into Data Journalism Methodology.

UCD method was chosen to help the development of a more accurate information system. In this case, the presence of the user, the investigative journalist, its crucial to identify their needs and have a successful prototype. The contents must be based on their experience, not on our assumptions, because at the end of the day, we want to make their work easier.

To identify the users' main needs, we interviewed a group of Mexican data journalists who are well known in their community. They helped us to identify first the real final user, the investigative journalists. We realized that there was a huge gap of knowledge that doesn't let them to learn in an adequate way, the Data Journalism methodology so they can apply it during their daily investigations. That's the main reason why in Mexico there are so few media with data working groups.

Once the final user was defined, we look for a group of investigative journalists willing to work with us. We apply a survey to know how much they knew about Data Journalism, how many parts of the methodology they have used in their investigations, which were their main problems when they tried to apply it. Also, we asked our users about which topics related to Data Journalism do they want to learn more. Figure 1 shows the steps that the investigative journalists are more interested to learn. We found that most of the topics that they were more interested to learn were related to the difficulties they had when they tried to apply the methodology.

Fig. 1. Investigative journalists knowledge needs.

As seen on the figure above (Fig. 1) the users' needs are related to the Data Journalism methodology, reason why we decided that the contents of the information system are going to be related to the whole methodology and the working process. The information obtained helped us to create more accurate contents.

3.1 Rapid Prototyping

Including all the users' needs we develop a digital prototype that was tested by some of the Data Journalists interviewed at the very beginning.

To develop the prototype, we were inspired by some information systems and also courses related to the learning of Data Processing, mainly for their interfaces and the recommendations given by the group of journalists we interviewed.

Interviewed users had different backgrounds and level of expertise. All of them agreed that the best option was a website to access the Information System, even though, they use their mobile phones for almost all of their activities. They realized that for data management and learning, it's more comfortable to work on a computer. In Figs. 2, 3, 4 and 5 we can see some screens of the prototype. The first one shows the home page. Figures 3, 4 and 5 show the main structure of one of the steps of Data Journalism methodology, showing a tutorial video, a support tool to practice the practical skill reviewed and the external links to try other tools to keep practicing.

During our research, we found out that most of the users don't have the time to read long texts, because of that, it's important to keep the contents fast and easy to process. Tutorial videos are a great way to explain in a few minutes the main and key topics of every step of the methodology.

Our users need to have tools that help them to accomplish specific tasks of their work, unfortunately some of them are expensive, in other language or requires certain level of programming knowledge. So, Dataísta is a support tool, according to journalists needs, that is easy to manage and designed to help them to learn the methodology by practicing.

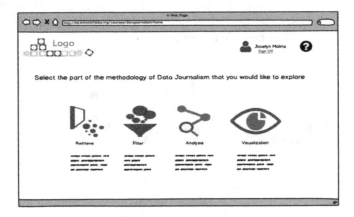

Fig. 2. Dataísta home page

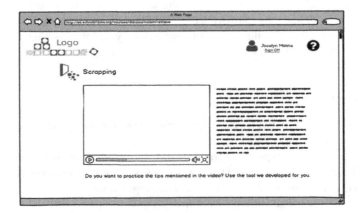

Fig. 3. Scrapping section – tutorial

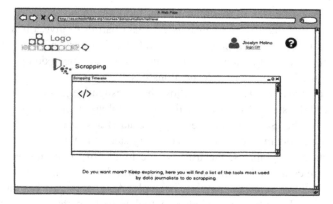

Fig. 4. Scrapping section – support tool

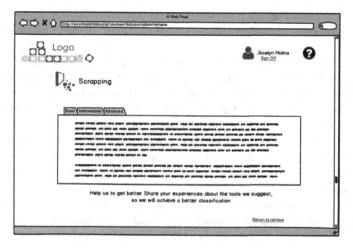

Fig. 5. Scrapping section – external links

During the research, our users claimed to need where to find tools created to help them during every Data Journalism methodology step. That's why we include in the Information System, a classification of tools, in order to provide them suggestions to keep learning.

4   Dataísta: Information System for the Introduction to Data Journalism Methodology

Dataísta is an information system to help the understanding of the steps marked on the Data Journalism methodology. Based on bibliographical review and our users' comments, we identify most of the problems the investigative journalists faced when they try to apply that methodology in their day by day investigations. In our hypothesis we tried to prove that "the lack of theoretical basis and knowledge about Data Processing by the Mexican investigative journalists is the main barrier to give a better use to the Open Data". In this way, the conception of an Information System, based on the users' needs, will allow their training on the Data Journalism methodology application, making easier the built of more investigations based on data.

The main objective of Dataísta is to allow the investigative journalists recognize the activities behind the steps of Data Journalism methodology in order to be able to create investigations by the use of the different Open Data Bases that are available.

The prototype contains basic concepts of every step of the methodology, by the use of the interactive infographics, the user is able to identify how all the parts of the methodology are connected. Some parts, have a tutorial to explain very clearly and fast how to do something, like scrapping for example. Also, each part has their own tool developed by us. The point of including a tool is to help the user to practice the practical skills they just got. Our users are very interested on learning how to use online tools in order to work faster and easier. Finally, at the end of every step, there is a classification of tools, this part is important for the journalist, because they want to keep practicing an improving, so providing them a catalogue of tools makes their work easier.

There is also a forum, where users can write their doubts and interact with other journalists. During our observation, we found out that the Data Journalisms community is really close and committed to help other trough their specialization journey.

The application of the User-Center Design method was very effective to know in a complete way our users, we were able to identify their needs, habits, barriers, levels of knowledge and the way they work and learn. We are certain that applying this kind of methods are key during the development of Web Sites or any kind of digital tool in general, UCD saves a lot of time and resources if you get the time to know exactly what your user wants.

In the future, we are going to test a second version of the prototype with some focus groups. This time we want to evaluate the contents, how much they can learn from *Dataísta*, how well the methodology is explained and how well the tools works. This could provide us information to polish contents or to know if *Dataísta* is ready to be online.

5   Primary Conclusions

We conclude that the investigative journalists have a lack of knowledge which limit them to use the Open Data Bases available. By studying by their own, using books and online tools they can't acquire the basics because an understanding of the process is needed as punctual explanations knowing that Data Journalism is an interdisciplinary work which needs knowledge from other fields. Also, they don't have enough time or the institutional support to begin their specialization.

The development of an information system in Spanish might help to reduce this gaps, until the schools and media realize how important is the investment on this new way to make journalism.

Articles based on data can explain clearly how numbers impact could help the citizens of any nation to change public policies, also can bring new readers to the media's web site or could help to convince media to include a Data Journalism team under their editorial department.

References

1. Open Data Handbook. http://opendatahandbook.org/
2. Manual de Periodismo de Datos. http://interactivos.lanacion.com.ar/manual-data/
3. Zanchelli, M., Crucianelli, S.: Integrando el Periodismo de Datos en las Salas de Redacción. Knight International Center for Journalists, Washington (2013)
4. Global Investigative Journalism Network. Data Journalism. http://gijn.org/resources/data-journalism/
5. Lorenz, M.: Training data driven journalism: mind the gaps. Eur. J. Cent. (2011). http://datadrivenjournalism.net/news_and_analysis/training_data_driven_journalism_mind_the_gaps
6. Pery, F., Paz, M.: Manual de Periodismo de Datos Iberoamericano. Fundación Poderomedia, Santiago (2016)
7. Hidalgo, D., Torres, F.: La navaja suiza del reportero. Consejo de la Prensa Peruana, Perú (2016)
8. Ramirez, F.: Periodismo de Datos, el periodismo de siempre, Diario la Patria (2012)

Implicit Evaluation of User's Expertise in Scientific Domains

Alessandro Bonifacio, Claudio Biancalana, Fabio Gasparetti,
Alessandro Micarelli, and Giuseppe Sansonetti[✉]

Department of Engineering, Roma Tre University,
Via della Vasca Navale 79, 00146 Rome, Italy
ailab@ing.uniroma3.it

Abstract. In this article, we propose a system able to implicitly assess a user's expertise in a particular topic based on her publications (e.g., scientific papers) on it and available through online bibliographic databases. This task is performed through two different approaches, both of them based on a graph-based model. The first approach (content-based) considers the text content, the second one (collaborative) analyzes the relationships in the same content in terms of co-citations. Preliminary experimental results are encouraging and raise several interesting considerations. In particular, they show that the best solution is obtained by integrating the two approaches above, in which each of them allows the system to overcome the limitations of the other one.

Keywords: Expertise retrieval · User profile · Graph model

1 Introduzione

Among the various information that a user profile in adaptive systems may include, there is also her competence in a specific knowledge domain. In this article, we propose a system able to implicitly assess the user's expertise in a particular topic based on her publications (e.g., scientific papers) on it and available through online bibliographic databases, such as $Scopus^1$, $Google\ Scholar^2$, and $ResearchGate^3$. The proposed system takes in input a candidate user u and a specific knowledge area ka and returns a $score(u, ka)$ expressing the level of competence of u in ka. This task is performed through two different approaches, both of them based on a graph-based model. The first approach (content-based) considers the text content, the second one (collaborative) analyzes the relationships in the same content in terms of co-citations. Specifically, the content-based approach retrieves the most relevant documents for a given knowledge area ka, extracts the most significant entities and stores them in a graph database. Then, it performs the same operations on the documents generated by u on ka and

---

¹ https://www.scopus.com.
² https://scholar.google.com.
³ https://www.researchgate.net.

© Springer International Publishing AG 2017
C. Stephanidis (Ed.): HCII Posters 2017, Part I, CCIS 713, pp. 420–427, 2017.
DOI: 10.1007/978-3-319-58750-9_58

builds a second graph. Finally, the similarity between the two graphs is computed in order to estimate $score(u, ka)$. The collaborative approach always involves the collection of documents related to the topic ka, but takes into account only the co-citations among them and, therefore, their authors. The evaluation of $score(u, ka)$ is performed through a version of the well-known *Hyperlink Induced Topic Search (HITS)* algorithm [16], which considers the incoming and outgoing edges among nodes.

2   The Proposed System

Nowadays, the increasing availability of online material has led to the need for adaptive systems for its personalized selection [6,7,10], based on the target user's characteristics. Those systems can take into account the personality [8,17], the context [4,5], as well as the effective nature [11–15] and the temporal dynamics [1,3,9] of users' interests. Some adaptive systems also consider the information on the user's expertise in specific knowledge areas. Such information may be obtained through the so-called *expertise retrieval* systems [2]. Approaches to expertise retrieval can be categorized in two main classes, inherited from the Information Retrieval techniques: the first one based on the information content (*content-based*) and the second one independent of it (*collaborative*). The former ones take advantage of the information extracted from the domain of the individual's knowledge to create a profile of her experiences, where the relevance of her documents to the specific field is evaluated. Differently, in collaborative systems user's expertise is assessed based on the authority inferred by analyzing her social network. Both of these approaches have been implemented within the proposed system.

Content-Based Approach. In Fig. 1 the diagram of the overall content-based approach is depicted. Specifically, the first step consists in extracting a set of

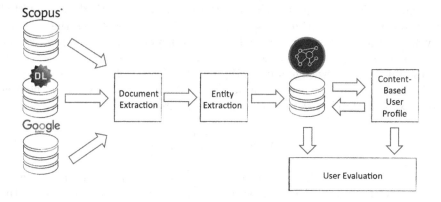

Fig. 1. Content-based approach schema.

documents related to the subject from the knowledge database. A topic anno-tator[4] is used to extract the entities that characterize those documents. Such entities are stored in a graph database along with information about authors, abstract, affiliations, tags, and categories. When a user has to be profiled, the system performs steps similar to the previous ones but only comprising informa-tion regarding her content. Figure 2 illustrates a snapshot of the graph database with regard to the content-based approach. Note the different types of node, such as authors, papers, abstracts, entities, and categories.

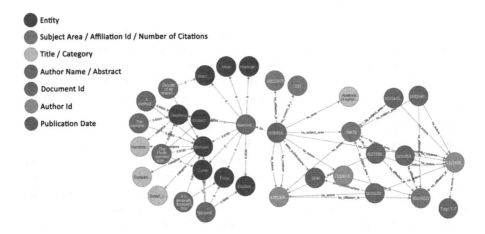

Fig. 2. Snapshot of the graph database in the content-based approach.

Once the domain is defined, different strategies can be applied to evaluate a user's expertise. More specifically, the following four strategies have been imple-mented in the proposed system:

- *Occurrences.* The first method performs the analysis of occurrences by com-paring the keywords extracted from the user's profile with those extracted the stored domain within the graph. The ratio is then between the absolute value of their intersection set and the set of keywords that characterize the domain, as expressed in the Eq. 1, where KW_{ka} identifies the set of keywords describing the knowledge area, KW_u denotes the set of keywords related to the topic used by the user. Such ratio gives a *score*, which expresses the user u's expertise level in that specific knowledge area.

$$score(u, ka) = \frac{|KW_u \cap KW_{ka}|}{|KW_{ka}|} \qquad (1)$$

- *Weighed Occurrences.* The second method is a variant of the first one, in which it is also considered the weight that each identified entity within the

---

[4] https://tagme.d4science.org/tagme/.

domain and the user's profile has associated according to how much that entity is relevant to the topic under examination. Such weight is calculated by estimating the distance, namely, the number of levels between pages and categories, between the Wikipedia page associated with the extracted term and the page related to the domain of interest. The weight is also stored inside the edge that links the tag to its abstract within the graph. The method can be described through the following equation:

$$score_{weight}(u, ka) = \frac{|WeightedKW_u \cap WeightedKW_{ka}|}{|WeightedKW_{ka}|} \qquad (2)$$

– *Log-Entity.* It relies on the comparison through the cosine-similarity metric between the vector representing the candidate user and the one representing the topic. For the weighting function a version of the *TF-IDF* model, well-known in Information Retrieval, has been employed. In particular, the equation for weighing the user is as follows:

$$u = \left\langle \left(e_1, \log\left(\frac{|D_u|}{|d : e_1 \in d|}\right) \cdot w_{e_1,t} \right), \dots, \left(e_n, \log\left(\frac{|D_u|}{|d : e_n \in d|}\right) \cdot w_{e_n,t} \right) \right\rangle \qquad (3)$$

while the equation for weighing the domain is as follows:

$$ka = \left\langle \left(e_1, \log\left(\frac{|D|}{|d : e_1 \in d|}\right) \cdot w_{e_1,t} \right), \dots, \left(e_n, \log\left(\frac{|D|}{|d : e_n \in d|}\right) \cdot w_{e_n,t} \right) \right\rangle \qquad (4)$$

The vectors so obtained are then compared using the cosine-similarity metric. The obtained results, comprised between 0 and 1, describe the user's expertise level in that specific knowledge area.

– *Entity Frequency.* This method, as the previous one, relies on the computation of the cosine-similarity between vectors, but differs from the previous one for the weighing of the vector. In this case, the vector describing the user's profile is constituted by elements which, for each entity belonging to the user's profile, have associated the number of user's documents that contain that entity.

$$u = \left\langle \left(e_1, \left(\frac{|d : e_1 \in d_u|}{|D_u|}\right) \right), \dots, \left(e_n, \left(\frac{|d : e_n \in d_u|}{|D_u|}\right) \right) \right\rangle \qquad (5)$$

The weighing of the vector related to the knowledge area takes place analogously and is described as follows:

$$ka = \left\langle \left(e_1, \left(\frac{|d : e_1 \in d|}{|D|}\right) \right), \dots, \left(e_n, \left(\frac{|d : e_n \in d|}{|D|}\right) \right) \right\rangle \qquad (6)$$

The two vectors are then compared through the cosine-similarity technique, which returns a score expressing the user's expertise in that specific subject.

Collaborative Approach. The system developed according to the collaborative approach analyzes information concerning co-citations among documents related to a particular topic. More specifically, a graph containing documents and their co-citations is built. Such a graph is then analyzed via the HITS algorithm, which for each entity p within the graph calculates the *authority score $A(p)$* and the *hub score $H(p)$*. Once the ranking of documents is obtained, sorted by their authority value, the ranking of the authors corresponding to those documents is generated. Assuming the possibility that several documents can be written by the same author, it was decided to assign the authority value to the user according to the Eq. 7, which allows us to modify how much weight to assign to the sum of all the authority values of the documents produced by the author or the maximum authority value among the user's documents:

$$Authority(u) = A \cdot \lambda + B \cdot (1 - \lambda) \tag{7}$$

The λ parameter identifies a value between 0 and 1. A and B are respectively the values given by the sum of authority values and the maximum authority value among documents written by the candidate user. In Fig. 3, the diagram of the overall collaborative approach is shown. In this approach, unlike the previous one, the edges of the graph database are only related to the co-citations among documents.

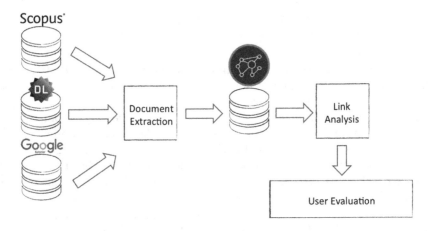

Fig. 3. Collaborative approach schema.

2.1 Experimental Evaluation

To evaluate the performance of our system, we carried out some experimental tests on six candidate users using both approaches. Those candidates were selected so that u_2, u_3, and u_5 were to be considered actually *experts* on the knowledge area of interest, while the other candidates were less experienced. As to the content-based approach, we obtained the results shown in Table 1. In particular, the first two columns show data when the candidates were evaluated through the co-occurrence of terms and those occurrences were subsequently multiplied by the weight that entity obtains related to the subject, based on the ontology extracted from Wikipedia. The third column shows the results by comparing by means of the cosine-similarity the vectors weighed through a weighing based on the Log-Entity. The vector is weighed by the occurrences of the entities within the user's production and the product with the relevance value that given entity obtains with respect to the topic under consideration. The last columns show the results obtained with the Entity Frequency method while varying the reference domain, that is, taking into account the first n elements of the list of entities in descending order of frequency within the graph.

Table 1. Experimental results of the content-based approach

User	Occurr.	Weighed occurr.	Log-Entity	Domain elements				
				Total	Top40	Top30	Top20	Top10
u_1	0.63	0.66	0.72	0.58	0.73	0.73	0.71	0.67
u_2	0.59	0.61	0.68	0.80	0.87	0.87	0.90	0.93
u_3	0.59	0.62	0.73	0.67	0.78	0.77	0.81	0.88
u_4	0.63	0.64	0.69	0.50	0.58	0.57	0.55	0.47
u_5	0.43	0.46	0.62	0.67	0.78	0.77	0.79	0.87
u_6	0.29	0.30	0.21	0.41	0.53	0.52	0.57	0.68

Table 2 shows the results obtained for the same candidate users through the collaborative approach. Notice the maximum authority value obtained by a document produced by the candidate user, the sum of the authority values related to each document of the graph associated with the candidate user u, and the value given by Eq. 7 with $\lambda = 2$.

Table 2. Experimental results of the collaborative approach

User	$\lambda = 0.2$	Maximum authority value	Sum of authority values
u_1	0	0	0
u_2	0.16	0.10	0.39
u_3	0.12	0.10	0.20
u_4	0.02	0.01	0.03
u_5	0.01	0.01	0.02
u_6	0.02	0.01	0.06

The obtained data allow us to make some interesting observations. It can be noted that the content-based method considering the occurrences, whether not weighed or weighed by the relevance of the entities within the context, does not seem to produce results as expected. The Entity Frequency method, especially in its filtered version (i.e., based on the extraction of the top-n entities belonging to the domain), instead shows satisfactory results. The candidate users, which were assessed based on their generated content, were evaluated on their experience so to obtain positive values but differentiated, and the score gap between the expert users known to us and the other candidates is a faithful picture of the supposed accuracy of this method. Especially in the version with $n = 10$, the results show reliable values. Finally, the scores obtained through the collaborative approach show that the algorithm built through the HITS implementation performs rather trustworthy evaluations of expert candidates, but only if within the dataset (i.e., the graph built on the co-citations among the different documents) the expert candidate u's documents were found. For instance, the collaborative approach was not able to assign a value to the candidate u_1's expertise, which is therefore set equal to 0.

3   Conclusions

In this article, we have described a system for the implicit assessment of a user's expertise in a specific knowledge area. The development of two main approaches allows us to choose between one or both of them, thus enabling the system to overcome their individual weaknesses. The experimental results show that in some situations the content-based approach can be better, in others the collaborative one is to be preferred. Hence, the best results may come from an integrated solution. The heterogeneous structure of the graph database chosen for the system implementation actually enables complex queries to be satisfied based on the different stored information.

Among the possible future developments, we would like to increase the number of knowledge bases (i.e., available documents) to enhance the reliability of the system output. As for the experimental evaluation, we plan to test our system on other domains and allow testers to provide explicit feedbacks on the received results.

References

1. Arru, G., Feltoni Gurini, D., Gasparetti, F., Micarelli, A., Sansonetti, G.: Signal-based user recommendation on Twitter. In: Proceedings of 22nd International Conference on World Wide Web, WWW 2013 Companion, pp. 941–944. ACM, New York (2013). http://doi.acm.org/10.1145/2487788.2488088
2. Balog, K., Fang, Y., de Rijke, M., Serdyukov, P., Si, L.: Expertise retrieval. Found. Trends Inf. Retr. **6**(2–3), 127–256 (2012). http://dx.doi.org/10.1561/1500000024
3. Biancalana, C., Gasparetti, F., Micarelli, A., Miola, A., Sansonetti, G.: Wavelet-based music recommendation. In: WEBIST 2012 - Proceedings of 8th International Conference on Web Information Systems and Technologies, pp. 399–402 (2012)

4. Biancalana, C., Flamini, A., Gasparetti, F., Micarelli, A., Millevolte, S., Sansonetti, G.: Enhancing traditional local search recommendations with context-awareness. In: Konstan, J.A., Conejo, R., Marzo, J.L., Oliver, N. (eds.) UMAP 2011. LNCS, vol. 6787, pp. 335–340. Springer, Heidelberg (2011). doi:10.1007/978-3-642-22362-4_29. http://dl.acm.org/citation.cfm?id=2021855.2021886

5. Biancalana, C., Gasparetti, F., Micarelli, A., Miola, A., Sansonetti, G.: Context-aware movie recommendation based on signal processing and machine learning. In: Proceedings of 2nd Challenge on Context-Aware Movie Recommendation, CAMRa 2011, pp. 5–10. ACM, New York (2011). http://doi.acm.org/10.1145/2096112.2096114

6. Biancalana, C., Gasparetti, F., Micarelli, A., Sansonetti, G.: An approach to social recommendation for context-aware mobile services. ACM Trans. Intell. Syst. Technol. 4(1), 10:1–10:31 (2013). http://doi.acm.org/10.1145/2414425.2414435

7. Biancalana, C., Gasparetti, F., Micarelli, A., Sansonetti, G.: Social semantic query expansion. ACM Trans. Intell. Syst. Technol. 4(4), 60:1–60:43 (2013). http://doi.acm.org/10.1145/2508037.2508041

8. Bologna, C., De Rosa, A., De Vivo, A., Gaeta, M., Sansonetti, G., Viserta, V.: Personality-based recommendation in e-commerce. In: CEUR Workshop Proceedings, vol. 997 (2013). Cited by 6

9. Caldarelli, S., Gurini, D., Micarelli, A., Sansonetti, G.: A signal-based approach to news recommendation. In: CEUR Workshop Proceedings, vol. 1618 (2016)

10. D'Agostino, D., Gasparetti, F., Micarelli, A., Sansonetti, G.: A social context-aware recommender of itineraries between relevant points of interest. In: Stephanidis, C. (ed.) HCI 2016. CCIS, vol. 618, pp. 354–359. Springer, Cham (2016). doi:10.1007/978-3-319-40542-1_58

11. Gurini, D.F., Gasparetti, F., Micarelli, A., Sansonetti, G.: iSCUR: interest and sentiment-based community detection for user recommendation on Twitter. In: Dimitrova, V., Kuflik, T., Chin, D., Ricci, F., Dolog, P., Houben, G.-J. (eds.) UMAP 2014. LNCS, vol. 8538, pp. 314–319. Springer, Cham (2014). doi:10.1007/978-3-319-08786-3_27

12. Gurini, D.F., Gasparetti, F., Micarelli, A., Sansonetti, G.: Temporal people-to-people recommendation on social networks with sentiment-based matrix factorization. Future Gener. Comput. Syst. (2017). http://www.sciencedirect.com/science/article/pii/S0167739X17304077

13. Gurini, D., Gasparetti, F., Micarelli, A., Sansonetti, G.: A sentiment-based approach to twitter user recommendation. In: CEUR Workshop Proceedings, vol. 1066 (2013)

14. Gurini, D., Gasparetti, F., Micarelli, A., Sansonetti, G.: Analysis of sentiment communities in online networks. In: CEUR Workshop Proceedings, vol. 1421, pp. 17–20 (2015)

15. Feltoni Gurini, D., Gasparetti, F., Micarelli, A., Sansonetti, G.: Enhancing social recommendation with sentiment communities. In: Wang, J., Cellary, W., Wang, D., Wang, H., Chen, S.-C., Li, T., Zhang, Y. (eds.) WISE 2015. LNCS (LNAI and LNBI), vol. 9419, pp. 308–315. Springer, Cham (2015). doi:10.1007/978-3-319-26187-4_28

16. Kleinberg, J.M.: Authoritative sources in a hyperlinked environment. J. ACM 46(5), 604–632 (1999). http://doi.acm.org/10.1145/324133.324140

17. Onori, M., Micarelli, A., Sansonetti, G.: A comparative analysis of personality-based music recommender systems. In: CEUR Workshop Proceedings, vol. 1680, pp. 55–59 (2016)

Breaking News Commentary: Users' Reactions to Terrorist Attacks in English-Speaking Twittersphere

Kaja J. Fietkiewicz$^{(\boxtimes)}$ and Aylin Ilhan

Heinrich Heine University, Universitätsstr. 1, 40225 Dusseldorf, Germany
{Kaja.Fietkiewicz,Aylin.Ilhan}@hhu.de

Abstract. The micro-blogging platform Twitter is increasingly applied for breaking news dissemination and commentary. The users become so-called citizen journalists, as in some cases they are the first ones to report on breaking events. This paper investigates the tweeting behavior of Twitter users in view of three terrorists' attacks that stroke Europe in 2015 and 2016, the attacks on Charlie Hebdo in January 2015, in Paris in November 2015, and in Brussels in March 2016. These attacks were triggering events for a wave of tweets showing support (#PrayForParis, #PrayForBelgium), solidarity (#JeSuisCharlie, #JeSuisBruxelles) or promotion of values like freedom of speech and press (#FreedomofSpeech). This study sheds light on the basic information behavior of English-speaking Twitter users participating in the information exchange on these three events.

Keywords: Twitter · Information behavior · Terrorist attacks · Tweeting

1 Introduction

Social media have become an important channel for people to share information [8]. Especially since 2006, when the social media platform Twitter got online [3] and the users started answering the question on Twitter's interface: "What are you doing right now?" [5]. With time, it became a "microphone"- platform, where millions of users constantly post their opinions, comments and thoughts. "Users literally post everything going through their minds in an almost unconscious manner, making the [social media] stream facts-reach but also feelings-intensive at the same time" [4]. Twitter users have exactly 140 characters to express what they feel, what they do and what they think about. They are not limited to posting the so-called "tweets," but due to Twitter's hybrid nature, can make use of the push and pull service. They can search for tweets, they are interested in by using hashtag (#) or user accounts, they can also follow other users and news channels [7]. Furthermore, they can include diverse multimedia (pictures, videos), links to external websites (outside the Twittersphere) and linkages to other Twitter accounts through the so-called "@"-mentions (hence, links within the Twittersphere) in their tweets [5]. Letierce et al. [9] categorized Twitter user into subcategories "from experts to amateurs by participants, media and so on" there are no limits – everyone can use Twitter.

© Springer International Publishing AG 2017
C. Stephanidis (Ed.): HCII Posters 2017, Part I, CCIS 713, pp. 428–434, 2017.
DOI: 10.1007/978-3-319-58750-9_59

People do not only want to consume content provided by others, but rather to produce own tweets. Java et al. [6] investigated reasons for which interactions on Twitter take place. They categorized these reasons into "daily chatter", "conversations", "sharing information/URLs" and "reporting news". According to Mano and Milton [10], the user-generated content on breaking news or events is a key factor of the so-called citizen journalism. Niekamp [11] defines the citizen journalism as "the involvement of non-journalists in gathering, writing and disseminating information." It could be understood as "an active role in the process of collecting reporting, analyzing and disseminating news and information" [2].

This was also the case during the Charlie Hebdo attacks. All over the world, people sorrowed for victims and their family members by using Twitter. After the first tweet with the hashtag #JeSuisCharlie, reports by news agencies, YouTube videos and, in general, global reactions of the community followed [5, 12]. In very short time, the introduced hashtag became a symbol for solidarity with the victims and unity against terror. Salovaara-Moring [12] explains the #JeSuisCharlie as follows: "These three words became a metaphor for organizing news flows, opinions, affects and participatory events in the digital media ecosystem. It became a global slogan adopted by supporters of the freedom of expression." According to An et al. [1], the "hashtags #CharlieHebdo and #JeSuisCharlie ('I am Charlie') became an explicit endorsement of freedom of expression and freedom of the press, and travelled fast and wide in Twitter." In this study, we will investigate the tweeting (or information) behavior of Twitter users in view of these terrorist attacks and two subsequent attacks that took place in Paris and Brussels.

The first triggering event chosen for the investigation is the already mentioned terrorist attack on the editorial office of Charlie Hebdo in Paris in January 2015. The second triggering event are the attacks in Paris in November 2015, and the third one are the attacks in Brussels in March 2016. We aim to investigate how the Twitter community tweeted about these events. Are there recognizable differences in user behavior between the three investigated attacks? And, are there changes in user behavior during the seven days after the attack? This investigation is based on the following research questions:

- RQ1: What is the dissemination and impact level (number of RTs and likes) of the tweets on the three triggering events and how does it change over the period of one week?
- RQ2: How often do the users include external links (normal links) and links within the Twittersphere (@) in the tweets on the three triggering events and how does this information behavior change over the period of one week?
- RQ3: Is there an association between embedding links (external and internal) and the dissemination and impact level (number of RTs and likes) of the tweets on the three triggering events and how does it change over the period of one week?
- RQ4: Is there an association between embedding external and internal links in the tweets on the three triggering events and how does it change over the period of one week?

2 Methods

With the help of the Python application Tweepy and partially manually via Twitter advanced search interface, we have collected 21,000 tweets from English-speaking Twittersphere. From all "top" tweets for each day of the week after the attack we randomly selected 1,000 tweets. We have chosen only the "top" tweets since they are the most popular ones with the potentially highest impact and dissemination level. We searched for the tweets by using the most trending hashtags. For the first terrorist attack in Paris we selected tweets posted from 7th to 13th of January 2015 which included the hashtags #JeSuisCharlie or #CharlieHebdo. For the second investigated attack, which also took place in Paris and involved suicide bombers and several mass shootings across the city, we selected tweets posted from 13th to 19th of November 2015, which included hashtags #PrayforParis, #PeaceforParis or #NousSommesParis. The last investigated terrorist attack was the one in Brussels that occurred at the Brussels airport and the Maalbeek metro station in the city center, here, the gathered tweets were posted from 22nd to 28th of March 2016 and included hashtags #PrayForBelgium, #JeSuisBruxelles, or #BrusselAttacks.

The gathered Twitter data was saved into a database and further processed with Excel and Python. All external links (starting with http://) and all internal links, mentions (marked with "@"), were automatically extracted with Python. After the data was prepared, we conducted statistical analysis with SPSS. Besides the descriptive statistics, we applied Pearson's point-biserial correlation to investigate potential correlations between embedding external or internal links and the number of retrieved likes and RTs. We also computed the chi-squared values for the association between embedding external and internal links in one tweet.

3 Results

The first research question concerns the dissemination and impact level (number of RTs and likes) of the tweets about the three triggering events and its change over a period of one week. As we can see in the Fig. 1 (left column), the tweets on triggering event got the most likes and RTs on the second day after the first triggering event (Charlie Hebdo). For the other two triggering events the tendency is different. The tweets got in average the most tweets on the 1st day, followed by an abrupt drop on the second day and low levels of dissemination throughout the whole week. The second research question concerned the embedding of external links ("link") and links within the Twittersphere ("@") in the tweets on the three triggering events. As we can see in Fig. 1 (right column), there were more internal links on the first two days considering the first triggering event. From the 3rd day, the tweets included more external links (34%–46% of the tweets) than internal ones (31%–33%). Looking at the second triggering event, only on the first day there were slightly more internal (7.4%) than external links (6.9%). On the remaining days, 31% to 45% of the tweets included external and 22.9% to 33.4% internal links. As for the last triggering event, there were more external (30.9%–52.1%) than internal links (18.6%–29.4%) included in the tweets on all seven days.

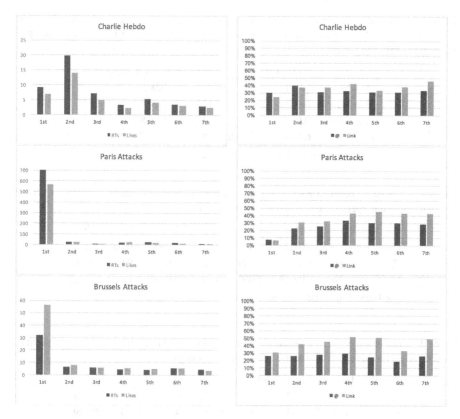

Fig. 1. The dissemination and impact level of tweets represented by the average number of likes and retweets per day (on the left) and percentage of tweets including external and internal links ("link" and "@" respectively) (on the right).

The third research question regards the association between embedding links (external and internal ones) and the dissemination and impact level (number of RTs and likes) of the tweets. Table 1 shows the overall correlation values between these variables for all three triggering events. The only significant correlations are given for the second triggering event, the Paris terrorist attacks. There appear to be weak and negative correlations between embedding internal and external links and the number of retrieved likes and retweets. This means that tweets with links are more likely to receive less likes or retweets. There were no significant correlations for the other two triggering events.

Table 2 presents the correlation values between embedding internal links ("@") and the number of retrieved likes for all three triggering events (TE1–TE3) and each of the seven days. When investigating the association for each day separately, the only significant correlations appear to be given for the third triggering event on the 5th (positive correlation) and 7th day (negative correlation). However, both are very weak.

Table 1. Overall correlation values between embedding external and internal links ("link" and "@"), and the level of impact and dissemination ("like" and "RT") of the tweet for the three investigated triggering events

	Charlie Hebdo	Paris attacks	Brussels attacks
@ x like	−0.011	−0.03*	−0.005
@ x RT	−0.011	−0.031**	−0.008
link x like	0.005	−0.032**	−0.015
link x RT	0.008	−0.035**	−0.014

*p < 0.05, **p < 0.01, ***p < 0.001

Table 2. Correlation between embedding internal links (@) and the number of retrieved "likes" for each triggering event ("TE") and each of the seven days.

@ x like	1st	2nd	3rd	4th	5th	6th	7th
TE1	0.003	−0.021	−0.04	−0.02	−0.035	−0.036	−0.017
TE2	−0.033	−0.022	−0.029	−0.037	−0.024	−0.027	0.037
TE3	−0.015	0.019	−0.007	−0.041	0.073*	−0.004	−0.07*

*p < 0.05, **p < 0.01, ***p < 0.001

Table 3. Correlation between embedding internal links (@) and the number of retrieved "RTs" for each triggering event ("TE") and each of the seven days.

@ x RT	1st	2nd	3rd	4th	5th	6th	7th
TE1	0.02	−0.021	−0.037	−0.022	−0.047	−0.032	−0.008
TE2	−0.034	−0.02	−0.043	−0.036	−0.024	−0.032	−0.009
TE3	−0.015	−0.01	−0.031	−0.049	0.039	−0.013	−0.069*

*p < 0.05, **p < 0.01, ***p < 0.001

When considering the association between internal links and the number of RTs (Table 3), the only significant correlation is given for the third triggering event on the 7th day. This correlation is negative and weak.

The correlations between embedding external links and the number of retrieved likes are shown in Table 4. Here, again, the only significant values are given for the third event on the 7th day. The correlation is negative and weak. There were no significant correlations between embedding external links and the number of RTs (Table 5) for any of the triggering events.

Table 4. Correlation between embedding external links and the number of retrieved "likes" for each triggering event ("TE") and each of the seven days.

Link x like	1st	2nd	3rd	4th	5th	6th	7th
TE1	−0.62	0.034	−0.042	−0.052	0.008	−0.032	−0.009
TE2	−0.01	−0.01	0.023	−0.034	−0.03	−0.034	−0.006
TE3	−0.022	−0.061	0.019	0.032	−0.06	−0.041	−0.078*

*p < 0.05, **p < 0.01, ***p < 0.001

Table 5. Correlation between embedding external links and the number of retrieved "RTs" for each triggering event ("TE") and each of the seven days.

Link x RT	1st	2nd	3rd	4th	5th	6th	7th
TE1	−0.038	0.037	−0.033	−0.046	0.015	0.009	0.033
TE2	−0.017	−0.017	0.055	−0.028	−0.031	−0.039	0.039
TE3	−0.018	−0.053	−0.003	0.043	−0.056	−0.043	−0.054

*p < 0.05, **p < 0.01, ***p < 0.001

Table 6. Chi-squared table for association between embedding external links and embedding internal links for all three triggering events (TE1-TE3).

Link x @	@ not included	@ included	Sig.
TE1	60.92%	39.10%	0.000
TE2	70.90%	29.10%	0.000
TE3	72.41%	27.59%	0.001

*p < 0.05, **p < 0.01, ***p < 0.001

The fourth research question concerned the association between embedding external and internal links simultaneously in the tweets. As we can see in Table 6, for all investigated triggering events the most tweets including external links did not include internal "mentions" at the same time (60.9%, 70.9% and 72.4% respectively).

4 Discussion

In this study, we investigated the tweeting behavior of users in English-speaking Twittersphere in view of three triggering events being terrorist attacks. The analysis of average number of RTs and likes that the analyzed tweets included showed a tendency of higher impact and dissemination on the day of the triggering events, followed by an abrupt drop on the following six days.

Regarding the embedding of links, the users include more external links than internal ones (links to other Twitter accounts). Also, there are more users who only include one type of link in the tweet. There were only few weak correlations between embedding links (either internal or external) and the number of received likes or RTs. This confirms our previous findings that including links in tweets in the context of such triggering events does not necessarily affect the number of received RTs or likes [5].

Interesting aspects to investigate in future research would be a content analysis of tweets, which is another possible factor influencing the number of likes and RTs. Furthermore, a more detailed characterization of the link types included in the tweets could explain the higher or lower dissemination levels. Finally, an analysis of hashtags and the context words included in the tweets could shed light on the attitudes and emotions of the users towards the breaking news.

Acknowledgments. We would like to thank Dr. Elmar Lins for his assistance during the data analysis and Prof. Wolfgang G. Stock for his supervisory support.

References

1. An, J., Kwak, H., Mejova, Y., De Oger, S.A.S., Fortes, B.G.: Are you Charlie or Ahmed? Cultural pluralism in Charlie Hebdo response on Twitter. In: Proceedings of the 10th International Conference on Web and Social Media, ICWSM 2016, pp. 2–11, Cologne, Germany (2016)
2. Bowman, B.S., Willis, C.: We media: how audiences are shaping the future of news and information. The Media Center at The American Press Institute, Reston (2003)
3. Farhi, P.: The Twitter explosion. Am. J. Rev. **31**(3), 26–31 (2009)
4. Herrera-Viedma, E., Bernabé-Moreno, J., Gallego, C.P., de los Ángeles Martínez Sánchez, M.: Solidarity in social media: when users abandon their comfort zone - the Charlie Hebdo case. Icono 14 **13**(2), 6–22 (2015)
5. Ilhan, A., Fietkiewicz, K.J.: User behavior in the Twittersphere: content analysis of tweets on Charlie Hebdo attacks. In: Proceedings of the iConference 2017: Effect, Expand, Evolve. 22–25 March 2017. Wuhan University: iSchools, IDEALS, Wuhan, China (2017)
6. Java, A., Song, X., Finin, T., Tseng, B.: Why we Twitter: understanding microblogging usage and communities. In: Proceedings of the 9th WebKDD and 1st SNA-KDD 2007 Workshop on Web Mining and Social Network Analysis, pp. 56–65. ACM (2007)
7. Kaplan, A.M., Haenlein, M.: The early bird catches the news: nine things you should know about micro-blogging. Bus. Horiz. **54**(2), 105–113 (2011)
8. Lerman, K., Ghosh, R.: Information contagion: an empirical study of the spread of news on Digg and Twitter social networks. In: Proceedings of the Fourth International AAAI Conference on Weblogs and Social Media, pp. 90–97 (2010)
9. Letierce, J., Passant, A., Decker, S., Breslin, J.G.: Understanding how Twitter is used to spread scientific messages. In: Web Science Conference, 26–27 April, pp. 1–8, Raleigh, NC, USA (2010)
10. Mano, W., Milton, V.C.: Citizen journalism and the BBC. In: B. Mutsvairo (ed.) Participatory Politics and Citizen Journalism in a Networked Africa, pp. 244–261. Palgrave Macmillan, UK (2016)
11. Niekamp, R.: Community correspondent: one broadcaster's attempt at citizen journalism. Southwest. Mass Commun. J. **24**(2), 45–53 (2009)
12. Salovaara-Moring, I.: #Je suis Charlie: networks, affects and distributed agency of media assemblage. Conjunctions **2**(1), 103–115 (2015)

Does Negative News Travel Fast? Exploring the Effect of News Sentiment on Interactive Spiral

Jie Gu[1(⊠)], Jing Tian[2], Xiaolun Wang[2], and Hong Ling[2]

[1] Shanghai Academy of Social Sciences,
Zhongshanxi Road 1610, Shanghai, China
gujie@sass.org.cn
[2] School of Management, Fudan University,
Guoshun Road 670, Shanghai, China

Abstract. The interactive essence of Web2.0 impacts news industry: users are extensively engaged in content creation and value contribution, yet a growing concern is that users' interaction may amplify the negativity bias, resulting in a worrying media environment such that negative news drive out positive news. Focusing on interactive spiral of online news, this study examined the relationship between title sentiment and users' different-stage reactions, including reading, commenting, like/dislike voting and forwarding. Against the traditional view that "negative news travels fast", this study harvests opposite influence of title sentiment in different stages: although attracting users to read, title negativity decreased both the number of forwards and forwarding ratio.

Keywords: Web 2.0 · Online news · Title sentiment · Interactive spiral

1 Introduction

Web2.0 has changed the way of human-computer interaction, switching users from passive audiences to active participants in information communication and broadcasting. The interactive essence of Web2.0 significantly impacts the news industry. According to a 2016 Pew Research report, over 38% of Americans were online news consumers [1]. In China, 61.9% Internet users check online news every day [2]. Compared to printed news, online news adopts interactive features, which allow users to express opinion, give feedbacks and easily share news to social media friends. Users' active behaviors have transformed the propagation of news from a linear line to an **interactive spiral** in which users' serial actions (reads, comments, likes, dislikes and forwards) combine to shape news diffusion process.

Despite of the prosperity of online news industry, a growing concern is that users' interaction may amplify the negativity bias, resulting in a worrying phenomenon that negative news drive out positive news in Web2.0-based news media space. Given the limited screen, news titles–which are the abstract of news content–give the first impression and influence users' decisions to whether click into the news. Under the pressure of information overload, users are more attracted to news with negative and

© Springer International Publishing AG 2017
C. Stephanidis (Ed.): HCII Posters 2017, Part I, CCIS 713, pp. 435–442, 2017.
DOI: 10.1007/978-3-319-58750-9_60

irritant titles. Recognizing this fact, journalists and editors are motivated to produce negative news titles, sometimes even inconsistent with news content.

However, whether negatively-titled news can travel fast is still an open question to be answered. From negativity bias perspective, negative-titled news does attract more attention and reaction. Yet from impression management perspective, users are reluctant to transmit negatively-titled news, especially when their behavior is visible by social media friends. Under this condition, the "travel path" of negatively-titled news is cutoff. Through the lens of interactive spiral, this study divided users' interactive response into three stages: attention (whether to click to read news), reaction (click like/dislike, leave comment) and sharing (forward news to social media friends). This study aimed to shed light on the above conflicting conjectures by answering the following questions:

1. Does negative-titled news dominate online news market, as we are worried about?
2. How does the sentiment of news titles influence users' different-stage behaviors?
3. Is users' feedback of news content consistent with title sentiment? (more likes for positively-titled news and more dislikes for negatively-titled news)
4. Does the interactive spiral of news vary across different news types?

The rest of this study proceeds as follows. We first reviewed literature on negativity bias and impression management theory, which guide the theoretical logic for this study. Then we described data preparation and analysis works. Preliminary results were reported. We finally listed future research plan.

2 Literature Review

Online news portals adopt interactive features to engage users into the diffusion of news [3]. Online news is read, voted, commented and shared to reach new audience, circulating into interactive spiral of news communication. Focusing on negatively-titled news, this study investigated the effect of title negativity on interactive spiral based on two streams of research: negativity bias and impression management theory.

2.1 Negativity Bias

Negativity bias refers to people's asymmetric response to negative and positive information [4]. In general, negative information is more potent and dominant than positive or neutral information. Negativity bias is evident in many domains, including public opinion [5], product review [6] and economic decisions [4]. It is notable that negative information catches more attention and executes greater impact in people's attitude and behaviors.

Negativity bias is also evident in online news. The limited reading time and small screen demand users' quick decision upon news titles to determine whether to click into the details. As predicted by negativity bias, users tend to be attracted to negatively-titled news which catches their eyes at the first place. Users are also more likely to react to negatively-titled news. For example, they click the like or dislike button, or comment to express their opinion or criticize the reported event. Noticing this trend, journalists and editors deliberately package news titles to appeal to their news consuming audience.

Enlightened by negativity bias, this study would like to empirically test the guess about title negativity. Three propositions were developed.

Proposition 1 (P1): Titles of online news are more likely to be negative than be positive or neutral.

Proposition 2 (P2): Compared to positively- or neutrally-titled news, negatively-titled news wins more reads.

Proposition 3 (P3): Compared to positively- or neutrally-titled news, negatively-titled news gets more user reactions. Specifically, negatively-titled news gets more comments and more votes. Due to its negative nature, negatively-titled news get more dislike votes and less like votes.

2.2   Impression Management Theory

Impression management theory describes the process whereby people attempt to manage the impression others form about them [7]. In particular, people tend to convey positive information to establish good self-image and avoid transmitting negative information in fear of negative evaluation perceived by audiences. The latter tendency is also noted as MUM effect, which depicts how people keep mum about negative events. Previous work found that negative information has a greater impact on impressions than positive information does [8]. Researchers found that MUM effect is more salient when the audiences are socially relevant [9].

Users' motivation to manage impression determines what news they share. Many online news portals adopt the interactive feature that allows users to share news to their social media friends. Although users may be interested in negatively-titled news by themselves, they prefer to keep this as private behavior. Therefore, negatively-titled news may not receive a lot of forwards as the sharing feature is designed for. Instead, title negativity is likely to cut off the travel path of news. Taking the impression management perspective, this study proposed that:

Proposition 4 (P4): Negatively-titled news received less forwards than positively- or neutrally-titled news.

Besides the four above propositions, this study also expected a type-varied effect of title negativity on interactive spiral of news. Specifically, the effect of title negativity may be less salient in some "cool" news type, such as technology. Also, when news are tagged as "hot", forwards may increase as users are less concerned about their impression given the thought that many others are interested in the news.

Figure 1 depicted the research framework of this study.

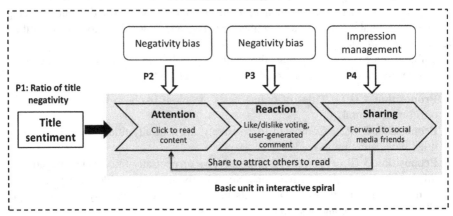

Fig. 1. Research framework

3   Data Preparation

This study tested propositions based on online Chinese news from Jinritoutiao.com, a popular daily news portal in China. We tracked news that were posted in March 2015, and sampled 10942 news distributed in three categories (technology, society and hot news with high popularity listed in a separate page). We snapshotted the number of users' reads, like/dislike votes, comments and forwards 24 h after the news were published, constituting dependent variables used in our analysis. These variables provide objective and accurate measurements of users' different-stage interactions.

We conducted sentiment analysis on news titles using Boson NLP. Boson NLP is a Chinese-based open-source content analysis tool (http://bosonnlp.com/) [10, 11]. Boson NLP is popular because it provides context-specified lexicons such as news, social media content and word-of-mouth reviews in different industries. Based on its news lexicon, we calculated the negative probability of each news title. A news title was categorized as negative or positive if the negative probability was above 0.6 or below 0.4. Otherwise the news title was categorized as neutral. Two dummy variables, title negativity and title positivity, were used to represent the three sentiment categories. The interaction between title sentiment and reads was included in our analysis as another key independent variable on user reaction and sharing behaviors. The interaction term measured how title sentiment expands or narrows the effect of users' reads on their following actions emerged later in the process of interactive spiral. We also controlled for another three variables: title length, the number of previewed images, and news type (hot, technology and society), as they may impose effect on the interactive spiral. Variable descriptions were showed in Table 1.

Table 1. Variable descriptions

Variables	Variable measurements	Mean (standard deviation)
Reads	Number of reads	105208.6 (334424.5)
Like	Number of "like" votes	317.7268 (1892.75)
Dislike	Number of "dislike" votes	295.6057 (1510.75)
Comment	Number of comments	924.6115 (4963.25)
Forwards	Number of forwards	412.607 (1522.13)
Title positivity	1-positive title, 0-negative or neutral	0.3358 (0.47)
Title negativity	1-negative title, 0-positive or neutral	0.4742 (0.49)
Number of Image	Number of previewed images	0.57 (1.17)
Title Length	Number of words in title	18.9341 (5.35)

4 Estimation and Preliminary Results

To investigate P1, we counted the number of news titled positively, neutrally and negatively. Among the total 10942 news, the number of negatively-titled news was 5189 (47%), which was larger than the number of positively- and neutrally titled ones, which are 3675 (34%) and 2078 (19%) respectively. We furthermore conducted t-test between title negativity and title positivity, and the t value was 21.0574, which significantly rejected the null hypothesis that title negativity had a smaller means compared to title positivity. Results consistently indicated that online news was more likely to be titled with negative sentiment. Therefore, P1 was supported (Fig. 2 and Table 2).

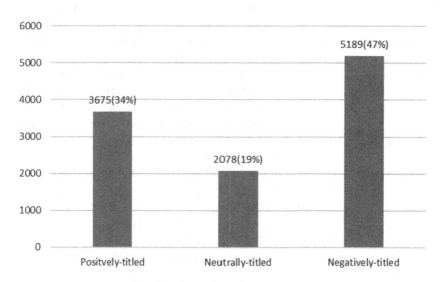

Fig. 2. Distribution of title sentiment

Table 2. T-test of title sentiment

Group	Obs	Mean	Std. err.	Std. dev.	[95% Conf.Interval]	
Negativity	10942	0.474228	0.004774	0.499358	0.46487	0.483585
Positivity	10942	0.335862	0.004515	0.472312	0.327011	0.344713
combined	21884	0.405045	0.003319	0.490912	0.39854	0.411549
diff		0.138366	0.006571		0.125487	0.151245

diff = mean(negativity) − mean(positivity) H0: diff < 0
t = 21.0574

Ordinary least squares (OLS) regression was used for data analysis. We ran regression on reads, like, dislike, comment and forwards respectively to investigate the impact of title sentiment on users' different-stage interactions. Table 3 showed the estimation result.

Table 3, Column 1. We first assessed the relationship between title negativity and user reads. The estimated coefficient of negatively-titled news (*Negativity*) on users' reads was positive and significant. This result suggested that negatively-titled news

Table 3. Impact of title sentiment on user interaction

	(1)	(2)	(3)	(4)	(5)
DV	Reads	Like	Dislike	Comment	Forwards
Reads		0.00325***	0.00297***	0.00569***	0.00356***
		$(4.60e - 05)$	$(3.21e - 05)$	(0.000136)	$(2.97e - 05)$
Positivity	−39,003***	195.1***	−93.26***	−272.3**	46.35*
	(8,842)	(41.79)	(29.20)	(123.8)	(27.05)
Negativity	14,898*	−84.14**	75.30***	200.9*	−70.34***
	(8,363)	(39.50)	(27.60)	(117.0)	(25.57)
Reads*negativity		−0.0015***	0.00128***	0.00162***	−0.00038***
		(0.000113)	$(7.87e - 05)$	(0.000334)	$(7.29e - 05)$
Reads*positivity		0.00267***	−0.0007***	0.00265***	0.00105***
		(0.000129)	$(9.00e - 05)$	(0.000381)	$(8.33e - 05)$
Number of image	11,775***	−17.75	−12.87	−33.70	29.57***
	(2,712)	(12.82)	(8.954)	(37.95)	(8.295)
Title length	2,522***	0.836	1.205	−19.12**	1.917
	(581.7)	(2.749)	(1.920)	(8.139)	(1.779)
Society	−220,170***	−96.62***	3.397	−1,645***	−51.00**
	(7,476)	(36.67)	(25.62)	(108.6)	(23.73)
Technology	−250,947***	−23.68	20.74	−1,363***	81.62***
	(9,746)	(47.46)	(33.16)	(140.6)	(30.72)
Constant	222,526***	23.61	−51.94	1,860***	24.83
	(14,380)	(68.66)	(47.97)	(203.3)	(44.44)
Observations	10,942	10,942	10,942	10,942	
R-squared	0.094	0.370	0.517	0.196	

***p < 0.01, **p < 0.05, *p < 0.1; Standard errors in parentheses

were more likely to capture users' attention and further translate into more reads, which supported P2.

Table 3, Column 2–4. With regard to user reactions, title negativity significantly decreased like votes (Column 2), increased dislike votes (Column 3) and number of comments (Column 4). Title positivity got the exactly opposite influence on users like/dislike votes, but increased comments, just like negatively-titled news. The results showed that (1) news with clear sentiment (either negative or positive) attract users to comment to express their opinions; (2) users' like/dislike feedbacks are consistent with title sentiment. Therefore, P3 was supported.

Table 3, Column 5. With regard to user forwards (Column 5), the coefficient of *Negativity* and *Reads*Negativity* were both significantly negative. Although more reads received, the negatively-titled news obtained less forwards and less forward ratio compared to positively- or neutrally-titled ones. The spiral from reads to forwards is notably shrunk for negative-titled news. Therefore, P4 is supported.

The result also indicated a type-varied trend in users' different-stage interactions. Society news (*Society*) were found to be less likely to receive reads, comment, and forwards. Technology news (*Technology*), received less reads compared to hot issue type while winning more forwards.

5 Additional Insights

It is notable that some control variables were significant in our results and provided additional insights. First, *Number of Image* had a significantly positive effect on user reads (Table 3, Column 1) and forwards (Table 3, Column 5). With regard to length of news title, its coefficient (*Title Length*) was significantly positive in the regression of reads (Table 3, Column 1), suggesting that a long news title may catch user attention.

6 Future Research Plan

We will extend this study in several aspects. Firstly, content analysis will be used to compare the consistence between title sentiment and content sentiment. Secondly, the type-varied effect will be the focus of our future research. A guess is that users have different expectation of news title and content style across news types. Thirdly, user experiment will be conducted to examine the under-covered decision-making mechanism. By doing these, we aim to develop a systematic framework for the interactive spiral of online news.

Acknowledgement. This work was supported by the China Ministry of Education-China Mobile research grant (#MCM20150402).

References

1. Center, Pew Research, How Americans get their news (2016). http://www.journalism.org/2016/07/07/pathways-to-news/

2. CNNIC, China Internet Network Information, 2016 China Internet News Market Research Report (2016). https://www.cnnic.net.cn/hlwfzyj/hlwxzbg/mtbg/201701/P020170112309068736023.pdf

3. Rasmussen, S.: News as a service: adoption of web 2.0 by online newspapers. In: D'Atri, A., De Marco, M., Braccini, A., Cabiddu, F. (eds.) Management of the Interconnected World. Springer, Heidelberg (2010)

4. Rozin, P., Royzman, E.B.: Negativity bias, negativity dominance, and contagion. Pers. Soc. Psychol. Rev. **5**(4), 296–320 (2001)

5. Soroka, S.N.: Good news and bad news: asymmetric responses to economic information. J. Polit. **68**(2), 372–385 (2006)

6. Berger, J., Sorensen, A.T., Rasmussen, S.J.: Positive effects of negative publicity: when negative reviews increase sales. Mark. Sci. **29**(5), 815–827 (2010)

7. Tedeschi, J.T.: Impression Management Theory and Social Psychological Research. Academic Press, Cambridge (2013)

8. Singh, R., Teoh, J.B.P.: Impression formation from intellectual and social traits: evidence for behavioural adaptation and cognitive processing. Br. J. Soc. Psychol. **39**(4), 537–554 (2000)

9. Tesser, A., Rosen, S., Batchelor, T.: Some message variables and the MUM effect. J. Commun. **22**(3), 239–256 (1972)

10. Qiu, X., Qian, P., Yin, L., Wu, S., Huang, X.: Overview of the NLPCC 2015 shared task: Chinese word segmentation and POS tagging for micro-blog texts. In: Li, J., Ji, H., Zhao, D., Feng, Y. (eds.) NLPCC 2015. LNCS (LNAI), vol. 9362, pp. 541–549. Springer, Cham (2015). doi:10.1007/978-3-319-25207-0_50

11. Min, K., Ma, C., Zhao, T., Li, H.: BosonNLP: an ensemble approach for word segmentation and POS tagging. In: Li, J., Ji, H., Zhao, D., Feng, Y. (eds.) NLPCC 2015. LNCS (LNAI), vol. 9362, pp. 520–526. Springer, Cham (2015). doi:10.1007/978-3-319-25207-0_48

Analyzing Users' Search Patterns to Explore Topic Knowledge from Aggregated Search Results

Yen-Chun Huang[1], Yu-Ping Ho[1], and I-Chin Wu[2(✉)]

[1] Department of Information Management,
Fu-Jen Catholic University, New Taipei City, Taiwan
[2] Graduate Institute of Library and Information Studies,
National Taiwan Normal University, Taipei, Taiwan
icwu@ntnu.edu.tw

Abstract. Combining and assembling different search results to achieve a clearer focus and better organization is a challenging research issue of aggregated search. The goal of this research is to assemble useful and relevant in-formation from one or multiple sources and then present it via one interface, rather than as a ranked list. That is, we propose a framework and then develop the *WikiMap^p* application based on the three main components of an aggregated search framework. In this research, we adopt the concept and principle of the program theory evaluation (PTE) and extended evaluation measure (EEM) to refine our application and use zero-order state transition (ZOST), and multiple lengths of maximal repeat patterns (m_MRPs) (i.e., a re-fined MRPs method) to observe and analyze users' search move behaviors with the interface, as well as the relationship between those moves and task accomplishment. In this way, we aim to identify the best sequences of search move patterns that lead to successful searches. Our preliminary evaluation results show that *WikiMap^p* actually helps users achieve better task performance by using the topic map tool in the interface.

Keywords: Aggregated search · Extended evaluation measures · Pattern analysis · Search moves

1 Introduction

Users who set certain queries find the search engine does not fulfill their information needs, especially when users cannot explain exactly what they are looking for. For instance: when the user submits the query "iPhone7", they may want to see a promotional video of the iPhone7, not just the pages related iPhone7. In addition, a user's information needs are quite often spread across several pages that are hyper-linked due to the distributed characteristics of web content. Thus, assembling search results from multiple sources has been an important research area for many years [1]. This is why there are aggregate searches.

Aggregated search is a general term for cross-vertical aggregated search (cvAS), whose aim is the retrieval of different types of useful information or topics from

© Springer International Publishing AG 2017
C. Stephanidis (Ed.): HCII Posters 2017, Part I, CCIS 713, pp. 443–449, 2017.
DOI: 10.1007/978-3-319-58750-9_61

multiple sources, which are then assembled into a unitary interface. A cvAS engine not only presents web pages, but other types of information as well (e.g., images, videos, and blogs). Basically, research on aggregated search has taken three main directions: source (vertical) selection, result aggregation and presentation, and interest and evaluation [2].

We design a series of user-oriented search tasks [4] based on the concepts of the program theory evaluation [5] and the extended evaluation measure [6]. In this research we focus on a proposed framework based on the concepts of the aggregated search and then conduct the evaluations. We also consider the outcomes provided by the tools of the system, or conceptualize differently, the benefits searchers derive from using the observed tools. The objectives of this research are listed below.

1. Interface implementation and improvement: Based on our previous research, we refine one of the information visualization (IV) tools of the *WikiMap^P*; i.e., topic network (TM). The TM is regarded as a useful IV tool for helping users find relationships among concepts for a subject. However, it still lacks flexibility, so we add features to the tool based on our previous observations.
2. In IR evaluation there are modest attempts to standardize search tasks. In this study, we conduct a user study to evaluate the aggregated search interface for a specific topic based on the program theory evaluation (PTE) and extended evaluation measures. We also propose m_MRPs based on ZOST and MRP concepts [3] to analyze sequences of search move patterns made by searchers.

We develop the presented *WikiMap^P* application based on the refined generic framework of the aggregated search. Through the objectives, we aim to find the best sequences of search move patterns that lead to successful searches.

2 The Framework

We propose a framework based on the three main components of an aggregated search system: query dispatching (QD), nuggets retrieval (NR), and result aggregation (RA) [2]. We introduce the concepts as below.

Query Dispatching: Query dispatching (QD) is the beginning of the query processing mode. It can choose to respond from the query source and then trigger a specific answer. In the proposed applications, the first article that a user finds interesting is defined as a seed article (query), and an article related to a seed query is called a link-related article of n degrees. The proposed framework retrieves all link-related articles within n degrees.

Nuggets Retrieval: Nuggets retrieval (NR) is the process between QD and result aggregation. It can retrieve entire or parts of documents; not just textual retrieval, but also a word, a document, a web page, an image, a video, or sentences [2]. In this work, we assemble the results from the search engine and Wikipedia. We adopt link strength (LS) measure and NGD algorithm to analyze the relationship between articles, and then construct the final topic network. For the information retrieved from the web pages we adopt the Google search API to retrieve pages related to the user query.

Result Aggregation: That is, the system can assemble the search results with more than a ranking action and the actions can be used alone or combined. We summarize the aggregate functions in Table 1.

Table 1. Aggregate actions of WikiMap^p

Actions	Tools or features in WikiMap^p
Sorting	Uses the search bar to search for keywords. When the user finishes entering a query they click the search button. The keyword is split and nuggets of useful information make a new merging result and then extracts the information the user needs; e.g., title and abstract
Grouping	Topic Map (TM) – we use Link Strength Measure (LSM) to build the initial network, and then Normalized Google Distance (NGD) analysis to determine the degree of association of two term concepts Topic Hierarchy Tree (HT) – We adopt k-clique based on social network analysis (SNA) to construct the topic hierarchy tree generated from the TM
Merging/Splitting/Extracting	Semantic Paths suggestions - in the proposed interface we first integrate the semantic path suggestions with TM. The semantic paths are based on our proposed "Hybrid Topic Based Semantic Path Inference" algorithm (HTSPI). The algorithm finds the most representative paths in the TM

3   Changes to the Application

In this study we adopt Program Theory (PT) as the evaluation framework, which evaluates systems and search behaviors. The main process in PT can be divided into four categories: inputs, activities, outputs, and outcomes. For instance, the input value sets a search query. When the user inputs a search action there are two or more independent variables that affect each other through call activity, caused by the interaction of actors and their behaviors, information items, collections, and context [5]. The result the user receives is called output, which is ultimate in the process of inquiry to generate understanding and knowledge (outcome).

As shown in Fig. 1, *WikiMap^p* provides three different visualization tools (Wikipedia (②), Topic Hierarchy Tree (TM) (⑨), and Topic Map (⑩)). (③) is the "Google search tool". When searchers type the key words in the search bar they click the search button (④) (⑤) and sixteen search results appear, including titles and abstracts. Term suggestions are given (⑥) based on the records of the web pages browsed by searchers. The TF-IDF calculates after sorting and chooses the top 12 words shown in (⑦), and the searcher can click the left button to automatically add these words to the search column.

As addressed earlier, searchers reflect that the TM could be useful, but the layout is not easy to operate. To help searchers improve task performance with the aid of the application, we refine the TM in this research. In the TM tool *WikiMap^p* (⑩), when the

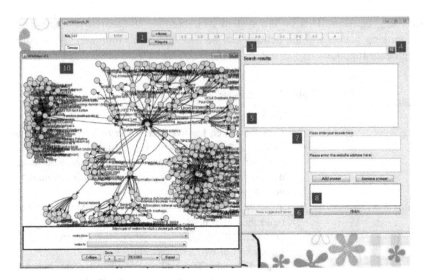

Fig. 1. A snapshot of the interface of WikiMap^P

searcher selects "picking" mode they can collapse and expand the nodes easily. When the searcher selects the "transforming" mode they can drag the subject map by using the left button of the mouse wheel, zoom in or zoom out the TM, and click the left button on the node to open the Webpage.

4   The Evaluation Design and Results

4.1   The Evaluation Design

A total of twenty participants at Fu-Jen Catholic University (Taipei) performed the search tasks during the evaluation. All participants had similar learning backgrounds and computer skills when the test was conducted. Students taking the Information Retrieval (IR) course were selected because they had at least a basic background knowledge of the IR subject. We designed four types of tasks: indirect relationship, direct relationship, topical knowledge, and an open question about topical knowledge. Due to page limitations, we did not report the rationale used to design the tasks. This is the same as in our previous work, which has proven that the tasks can reflect how the interface helps users search, explore, or gain knowledge [6].

In this research we analyze the users' task performance by using our proposed interface - i.e., *WikiMap^P* - compared to the basic Wikipedia.com. We mainly adopt gain function, as shown in Eq. (1), to verify if the user can accomplish the task correctly and efficiently.

$$\text{Gain} = \text{Score}/\text{Time Cost} \qquad (1)$$

4.2 The Task Performance

Herein, we show the results of task performance.

Observation 1 (Tasks 1 and 2): For Task 1, the users of the *WikiMap^P* interface performed significantly better than those using the basic interface (Wikipedia) for searching the indirect relationship task. For Task 2, the users' value gain in *WikiMap^P* is the highest, whereas their gain values in Wikipedia is the lowest. However, this did not pass the significance test. We found *WikiMap^P* provided IV tools that users used to take less time to finish the task, which helped users get better scores for the relationship-based tasks.

Observation 2 (Tasks 3 and 4): For Task 3, the users of the *WikiMap^P* interface performed significantly better than those using the basic interface (Wikipedia) for searching topical knowledge. Users became more familiar with IV tools and were willing to spend time on node collapse, expand functions, and viewing the pages. For Task 4, the users of both interfaces achieved similar results for an open question for the topic (Table 2).

Table 2. The t-test results of the gain value

	WikiMap^P		Wikipedia		Wikipedia compare with WikiMap^P	
	Avg.	Std.	Avg.	Std.	t-test	Sig.
Task 1	2.03	1.65	0.14	1.55	4.213	0.002***
Task 2	1.33	0.46	0.91	1.11	1.048	0.321
Task 3	1.42	1.01	0.30	0.98	2.362	0.042**
Task 4	0.55	0.23	0.45	0.45	1.588	0.1467

*Significant at $p < 0.1$, **Significant at $p < 0.05$, ***Significant at $p < 0.01$

4.3 The Search Move Analysis

In this section we mainly analyze the users' search behaviors by using the IV and search tools. We first conduct the correlation coefficient analysis to verify how the tools support the users to accomplish each task. We then present some of the search move results of the ZOST and MRP analysis [3].

Observation 1 (IV tools vs. Gain): Fig. 2 shows that all of the tasks are positively correlated with the topic map (TM), whereas some of tasks may have negative correlation with the tools, especially in Task 1. This indicates that our refined TM tool can help users successfully finish tasks. Of note is that Task 1 is the most difficult of the four tasks; however, it is highly correlated with the TM tool.

Herein, we present the results of Task 1 by using ZOST and m_MRP analysis.

Observation 2 (ZOST): Fig. 3 shows there are four search moves in the Google Search Tool, and five search moves in Topic Map (TM), initially. Moreover, there are

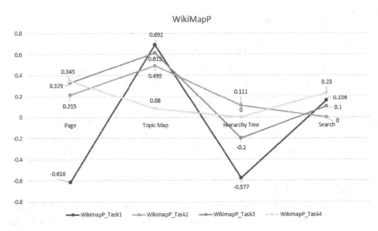

Fig. 2. The correlation analysis between IV tools and gain in *WikiMap^P*

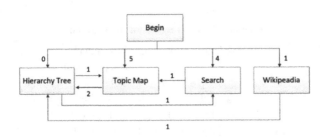

Fig. 3. The frequencies of the zero-order transition in Task 1

some moves between the Hierarchy Tree (HT) and TM. The video shows the users prefer using the TM tool to find the answers in Task 1. Thus, we confirm that our refinement of the TM tool can help users quickly understand the concepts of the task.

Observation 3 (MRP): According to Table 3, users always use [A+ (Topic Map) or C+ (Search)] as their primary tool to find the answers. This is because "A+" provides more functionality and interactive interface to satisfy the user's needs. "C+" is the tool they usually use in their daily lives. A+ and C+ can be used interchangeably for searches, which can help users increase their own knowledge. Users that search through IV tools can have a more enhanced answer rate. This can close the gap with users in the process of information searching.

Table 3. The MRPs in *WikiMap^P*

M_MRP	Task 1
1-Pattern	TM, Search, TM→HT, Search→TM, HT→TM
2-Pattern	TM TM, TM TM→HT, Search, Search
3-Pattern	TM TM, TM, Search, Search, Search

5   Conclusions

The main goal of this research is to explore users' search processes and task outcomes with each different IV tool and with the improvement application *WikiMap^P*. Based on an analysis of the results of the IV tools, we find that users of *WikiMap^P* can achieve the best task performance, as using the IV tools can help them get a higher gain value. In addition, our improvement of the Topic Map helped users achieve better search performance. Aligned with this research, we will conduct large scale evaluations and report on the results in detail in the future.

Acknowledgments. This research was supported by the National Science Council of Taiwan under Grant MOST 105-2410-H-003-153-MY3.

References

1. Kopliku, A., Pinel-Sauvagnat, K., Boughanem, M.: Aggregated search: a new information retrieval paradigm. ACM Comput. Surv. (CSUR) **46**(3), Article No. 41 (2014)
2. Kopliku, A.: Approaches to implement and evaluate aggregated search. Doctoral dissertation, Université de Toulouse, Université Toulouse III-Paul Sabatier (2011)
3. Wildemuth, B.M.: The effects of domain knowledge on search tactic formulation. J. Am. Soc. Inf. Sci. Technol. **55**(3), 246–258 (2004)
4. Borlund, P.: Experimental components for the evaluation of interactive information retrieval systems. J. Doc. **56**(1), 71–90 (2000)
5. Järvelin, K., Vakkari, P., Arvola, P., Baskaya, F., Järvelin, A., Kekäläinen, J., Keskustalo, H., Kumpulainen, S., Saastamoinen, M., Savolainen, R., Sormunen, E.: Task-based information interaction evaluation: the viewpoint of program theory. ACM Trans. Inf. Syst. (TOIS) **33**(1), Article No. 3 (2015)
6. Wu, I.C., Vakkari, P.: Supporting navigation in Wikipedia by information visualization: extended evaluation measures. J. Doc. **70**(3), 392–442 (2014)

Chat Support System to Recall Past Conversational Topics Using Tags

Junko Itou[1]([✉]), Rina Tanaka[2], and Jun Munemori[1]

[1] Faculty of Systems Engineering, Wakayama University,
930, Sakaedani, Wakayama 640-8510, Japan
{itou,munemori}@sys.wakayama-u.ac.jp
[2] Graduate School of Systems Engineering, Wakayama University,
930, Sakaedani, Wakayama 640-8510, Japan

Abstract. In this article, we propose a chat system that helps users remember and resume past conversations by using tags. In computer-mediated communication such as online chat, it is often difficult in communication to continue conversations regarding issues that have been discussed in the past because they may have forgotten the contents of the issue. We focus on the nouns as the information on the topic and we develop a chat system "tag chat" that helps users remember past conversations. Our system adds tags for each chat logs based on words that were used in the chat and displays the tags when users restart the interrupted chat. As a result of two experiments with the proposed system, it revealed that by showing tags the proposed system helps users to virtually effortlessly recall the topics of past conversation.

Keywords: Chat · Tag · Topic · Reminder · Morphological analysis

1 Introduction

In this paper, we propose a chat system that uses tags to help users recall and resume past conversations.

In mediated synchronous communications such as online chat, conversational contents are often mixed because users typically discuss several topics in the same session. Users are also apt to forget what they were talking about with their online interlocutors. Therefore, it is often difficult in such scenarios to resume conversations about issues that were being discussed in the past.

Several related systems focusing on online chat or memory recall have been proposed. However, the systems proposed to date do not have functions to help users recall past conversational topics [1–3], or assume that users do not reread past logs to recall the contents of past chats [4]. By contrast, our system shows words associated with an ongoing chat topic onscreen to the user at any given time. The words presented are nouns extracted from chat logs by morphological analysis. Users can select multiple words as tags to represent the topic, and which help to subsequently remind them of the content of the relevant conversation.

© Springer International Publishing AG 2017
C. Stephanidis (Ed.): HCII Posters 2017, Part I, CCIS 713, pp. 450–457, 2017.
DOI: 10.1007/978-3-319-58750-9_62

This paper is organized as follows: in Sect. 2, we describe the related work on chat communication focusing topics. In Sect. 3, we explain our proposed system, which supports recommencement of past chat topics by tagging chat logs. A validation test for our system will be given in Sect. 4. Finally, we discuss conclusions and future work in Sect. 5.

2   Related Work on Chat Communication Focusing on Conversational Topics

Opportunities of computer mediated synchronous communication are increasing and many remote communication systems have already been proposed. One of existing typical chat services are Skype[1] and LINE[2].

Skype allows users to register their icons, user names, and notifications indicating their statuses or moods. A chat history is shown once the user logs out. Users are also allowed to restart conversations with chat partners. LINE is a communication application that allows text and multimedia image communication. A message is shown in a balloon-shaped textbox, along with a timestamp and "message read" mark. New messages are inserted under old ones in the same window. In these services, it is possible to save each conversation as a text file. However, only the messages and their transmission times are recorded. Thus, users need all conversation logs while relying on their memory to determine where the relevant conversation was interrupted, or what they were talking about at the time.

Kawabata et al. proposed a system that extracts chat topics from a chat room using a history of messages [1]. This system presents suitable words for an ongoing conversation in a chat room in order to introduce other users, who have not yet joined the conversation, to the chat contents. In this system, a chat log saved every five minutes is divided into three parts - a "current conversation" (i.e., the conversation ongoing at the time), a last-minute conversation, and a past conversation. This system extracts nouns from each log using the Japanese morphological analyzer MeCab [5]. The log for a "current conversation" is used to obtain the characteristics of the conversation in the relevant chat room. Since last-minute topics tend to shift to a current topic, the last-minute log is analyzed to extract the characteristics of the current topic. For users who have conversed about specific subjects in the past, the system considers it likely that they will be chatting about similar issues at any given time. In order to incorporate the features of user participation in the conversation at this stage, the system extracts nouns from chat logs and gleans the conversational theme at the time. Users' intentions are not reflected in this classification since the results of analysis in this system are only used to classify conversations into broad topics such as food, hobbies, politics, and economic. Moreover, Kawabata et al.'s system does not help remind users of past chat topics.

---

[1] skype: https://www.skype.com/en/.
[2] LINE: https://line.me/en.

In all prevalent chat and instant messaging services, users can simultaneously pursue multiple topics in a conversation. At the same time, it is sometimes difficult to accurately grasp the flow of the conversation when multiple topics are being discussed, especially if several users are participating in the conversation. Collective Kairos Chat [4] is a chat support system where users can determine the degree of importance of each message. This system allows users to delete chat messages from the log at different speeds. The chat screen in the system has three columns, and messages are divided in accordance with their degree of importance as determined by all users. When chat participants have off-topic conversations, they assign the relevant messages to the column containing relatively less important messages. The log of the column containing highly important messages flows slowly, whereas the logs of the less important columns flow more quickly. As a result, important messages germane to a given theme are displayed for longer, and messages and conversations tangential to the theme are shown briefly in order for users to obtain chat logs as the collective memory of the discussion reflecting the preferences of all participants. The criterion for the importance of a message is whether it is associated with a given theme. Hence, Collective Kairos Chat does not cater to situations where multiple conversational topics are spanned in a short time.

The existing research on summarization of meeting focuses on automatic text summarization or extract of key sentences [6,7]. In these method, the key points are presented so that user can understand the contents, the structure and the purpose of the meeting in a short time. However, users' intentions or key phrases which users want to keep in memory are not reflected to the summarization as with Kawabata et al.'s system

In this paper, we propose a support system to facilitate checking the contents of the past issue and to restart chatting on the issue by tagging and registering topics switch timing.

3   System Framework

3.1   Design Method

Our goal is to implement a chat system that supports recommencement of past chat topics by tagging chat logs. The proposed system is designed as follows:

1. In order for users to continue discussion on a past chat topic, information regarding the topic is needed. However, because keeping track of all logs takes time and effort, our proposed system registers nouns from chat messages as tags.
2. The proposed system only presents candidate tags to users. Users can choose and freely register tags from the candidate tags presented by themselves.

3.2   System Overview

Our proposed chat system consists of a server and two clients connected to a network. Chat texts are sent to the server and the texts are stored with its sent

Chat log   Chat window   Tag extraction and registration window

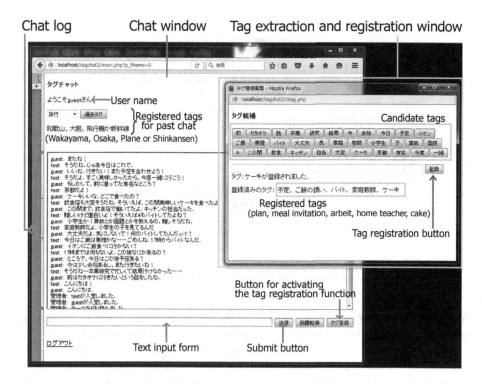

Fig. 1. Overview of a client screen.

time, the user name and the serial number in the database. In the client chat log field, only the user name and the sent texts are displayed. Each client has a candidate tag extraction function, a tag registration function, and a tag display function. Figure 1 gives an overview of the chat screen of a client.

3.3 Tag Registration Function

The tags registered by users for past chats are shown at the top of the chat window. Users click the button at the bottom of the screen to simultaneously activate the tag registration function and launch the tag extraction and registration window. The system then runs the tag extraction function and shows candidate tags to users as buttons. On clicking a candidate tag button, a message is presented indicating that the candidate has been recorded as a tag for the conversation. A list of already registered tags is also displayed on the window.

3.4 Tag Extraction Function

The tag extraction function analyzes the chat log of ongoing chats using MeCab [5], a Japanese language morphological analyzer. The log data are divided into parts of speech, and only nouns are used as candidate tags. The extracted nouns

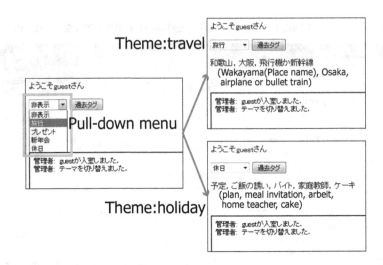

Fig. 2. A list of themes and tags registered with the selected theme.

include overlapping words or words that do not make sense, such as pronouns, suffixes, and emoticons. Thus, certain nouns are selected as candidate tags.

The extracted candidate tags are displayed as a button on the window. Additionally, a user can register free words other than candidate tags as a tag. A user enters free words in the manual input form and presses the tag registration button, then the words are registered a tag. Figure 1 shows that the tags "meal invitation" and "home teacher" correspond to free words tags.

3.5   Tag Display Function

The tag display function displays the tags registered by using the tag registration function in the past chat. The proposed system displays the registered tags respectively for each chat topic or theme. Figure 2 shows the screen for selecting a theme.

The themes are displayed in a list. When a theme is selected from the pull-down menu and a display button is pushed down, tags registered with the theme in the past chat are displayed. The screen after selecting the theme is shown in the right of Fig. 2. Users can freely switch the display of themes during chat.

4   Evaluation Experiments

4.1   Experimental Overview

We performed comparison experiments to investigate whether displaying tags in our system helps users to easily recall past conversational topics.

Sixteen college students participated in our experiments. These participants were divided into eight pairs. All participants were accustomed to handling keyboard input and were familiar with chat conversations. The participants were asked to chat while sitting in the separate room in order to prevent directly conversations.

Two experiments were conducted with an interval of six days. In the first experiment, all participants used a comparison system to collect data about the last topic for the second experiment. The comparison system is only removed the tag display function from the proposed system so tags on the last topic are not displayed during the experiment using the comparison system. As there had been no registered tags in the first experiment, the participants used the comparison system.

In the second experiment, four pairs of participants used the proposed system while the other four pairs used the comparison system. The former pairs read the registered tags in the first experiment before starting the second experiment, whereas the latter pairs read all of the chat logs.

The conversations of the participants were on the following two themes: "travel" and "New Year's party." In the theme "travel", the participants plan to go on a trip with several friends on a spring vacation. In the theme "New Year's party", the participants plan to hold a New Year's party with classmates. Each pair chatted for ten minutes using the systems for each theme in each experiment, and registered tags during the chat. At the conclusion of the each experiment, we asked the participants to answer a few questions.

4.2 Experimental Results

The results of participants' responses to our questionnaire are listed in Table 1. Each number signifies the total number of persons who selected that particular evaluation value.

Since the tag registration operation was identical in both systems and both themes, we conclude that differences between the systems did not affect the responses to item (ii) and the registration of tags was not troublesome for users.

From the results of item (i) and (iv), although the participants using the proposed system did not remember much of the content of the first experiment chat, they were able to chat about the theme concretely. In addition, considering the results of item (iii) and (vi), it is difficult to remember the chat content specifically in the method of remembering based on memory, it is clear that the participants were able to remember topics to a certain degree in the method of browsing the registered tags.

Comparing the results for item (v) to those for item (vi), it can be seen that the values for both systems were similar. However, it can also be seen from the results for item (vii) that participants felt that reading all of the previous chat logs was tiresome. Thus, it is possible that tags are less burdensome for users to recall previous chat contents. Additional answers optionally provided by participants also indicated that they tended to rely on the concreteness of tags.

Table 1. Questionnaire results obtained in the two experiments.

Questionnaire item	Theme	System	Value				
			1	2	3	4	5
(i) I remember the contents of the chat in the first experiment (Before participants read the registered tags or chat logs)	Travel	exp_p	0	4	0	2	2
		exp_c	0	1	1	5	1
	Party	exp_p	1	1	2	3	1
		exp_c	0	3	0	5	0
(ii) Tag registration was exasperating		exp_p	0	5	1	1	1
		exp_c	0	6	2	0	0
(iii) I was able to start chatting about the last topics smoothly		exp_p	0	1	3	2	2
		exp_c	0	0	1	7	0
(iv) I was able to chat about the theme concretely		exp_p	0	2	1	3	2
		exp_c	0	1	2	3	2
(v) I was able to recall the contents of the last topics by reading the registered tags		exp_p	0	0	0	4	4
(vi) I was able to recall the contents of the last topics by reading the chat logs		exp_c	0	0	0	2	6
(vii) Reading the chat logs was tiresome		exp_c	0	0	1	7	0

Evaluation value: 1: strongly disagree, 2: disagree, 3: neither, 4: agree, 5: strongly agree.

exp_p: The experiment was performed using the proposed system.

exp_c: The experiment was performed using the comparison system.

5   Conclusion

In this article, we proposed a chat support system that helps users continue conversational topics from past chats. This system checks the contents of past conversations by tagging them based on their contents. The system applies Japanese morphological analysis to chat logs and displays nouns used in the chat as candidate tags. Users can then select and register tags that they deem helpful in remembering chat contents. Tags registered in previous chats are displayed on the upper side of the chat screen.

We performed experiments to compare our proposed system, which displays tags associated with past topics, with the comparison system that did not display registered tags. The results of comparison experiments indicate that by showing tags the proposed system helps users to virtually effortlessly recall the topics of past conversation.

In future work, we plan the following: implementation of an experiment considering the influence of order effects and theme, improvement of the interface on tag registration function and implementation of the tag delete and sorting function.

Acknowledgements. This work was supported by JSPS KAKENHI Grant Number 16K00371.

References

1. Kawabata, T., Satou, T., Murayama, T., Tada, Y.: The construction of the topic extraction system base on statement history in the chat room. In: Proceedings of the 77th National Convention of Information Processing Society of Japan, vol. 72, no. 1, pp. 385–386 (2010). (in Japanese)
2. Adams, P., Martel, C.: Conversational thread extraction and topic detection in text-based chat. In: Sheu, P.C.Y., Yu, H., Ramamoorthy, C.V., Joshi, A.K., Zadeh, L.A. (eds.) Semantic Computing, pp. 87–113. Wiley-IEEE Press, Hoboken (2010)
3. Matsumoto, M., Matsuura, S., Mitsuhashi, K., Muarkami, H.: Supporting human recollection of the impressive events, using the number of photos. In: ICAART 2014 - Proceedings of the 6th International Conference on Agents and Artificial Intelligence, vol. 1, pp. 538–543 (2014)
4. Ogura, K., Matsumoto, Y., Yamauchi, Y., Nishimoto, K.: Kairos chat: a novel text-based chat system that has multiple streams of time. In: Proceedings of the CHI 2010 Extended Abstracts on Human Factors in Computing Systems, pp. 3721–3726 (2010)
5. MeCab: Yet Another Part-of-Speech and Morphological Analyzer. http://taku910.github.io/mecab/. Accessed 17 Mar 2017
6. Lee, J., Song, H., Park, S.: Two-step sentence extraction for summarization of meeting minutes. In: Proceedings of the 2011 Eighth International Conference on Information Technology: New Generations (ITNG 2011), pp. 614–619 (2011)
7. Nagao, K., Inoue, K., Morita, N., Matsubara, S.: Automatic extraction of task statements from structured meeting content. In: Proceedings of the 7th International Joint Conference on Knowledge Discovery, Knowledge Engineering and Knowledge Management (KDIR-2015), pp. 307–315 (2015)

Collection of Example Sentences for Non-task-Oriented Dialog Using a Spoken Dialog System and Comparison with Hand-Crafted DB

Yukiko Kageyama[(⊠)], Yuya Chiba, Takashi Nose, and Akinori Ito

Graduate School of Engineering, Tohoku University, Sendai, Japan
yukiko.kageyama.s2@dc.tohoku.ac.jp

Abstract. Designing a question-answer database is important to make natural conversation for an example-based dialog system. We focused on the method to collect the example sentences by actual conversations with the system. In this study, examples in the database were collected from the conversation logs, then we investigated the relationship between the response accuracy and the number of the interaction. In the experiment, the transcriptions of the user's utterances are added to the database at every end of the interaction. The responce sentences in the database were created manually. The result showed that the response accuracy appropriateness improved as increasing the number of the interactions and saturated at around 70%. In addition, we compared the collected database with the fully handcrafted database by the subjective evaluation. The score of the user satisfaction, dialog engagement, intelligence, and willingness to use were higher than the handcrafted database, and these results suggested that the proposed method can obtain more appropriate examples to the actual conversation from subjective point of view.

Keywords: Spoken dialog system · Non-task-oriented dialog · Dialog collection

1 Introduction

Recently, many research works on non-task-oriented spoken dialog systems have been carried out actively [1–3]. Most of the non-task-oriented dialog systems employ the example-based system. Developing a large-scale example-response database is necessary to make a natural dialog for such dialog systems. There are lots of method for constructing the database, such as manual development [4] or collecting from web resources [5, 6]. However, the hand-crafted examples does not always coincide a user's actual utterance, and the automatic collection method sometimes collects inappropriate responses or unusable examples.

Collecting the examples by actual conversations with the system seems to be one of the promising approaches. Several works employed this approach (i.e., [7]); however, these works lack attentive analyses, such as how much examples can be collected by iterating the interactions or how different the characteristics of the database from that developed by conventional approach.

© Springer International Publishing AG 2017
C. Stephanidis (Ed.): HCII Posters 2017, Part I, CCIS 713, pp. 458–464, 2017.
DOI: 10.1007/978-3-319-58750-9_63

In this study, we focus on the example collection by the conversation, and investigate the relationship between the response accuracy and the number of the interaction, and we compared the performance of the collected database with the fully hand-crafted database by the subjective evaluation.

2 Examples Collection by Conversation with Spoken Dialog System

We prepared initial databases and started the example collection. The transcriptions of the participants' utterances and the response sentences were added at every end of the dialog.

2.1 Initial Example-Response Database

The initial databases were composed topic by topic, which include example-response pairs corresponding to greetings, backchannels, and task-specific interactions. We assumed four topics of the dialog: cooking, movie, meal, and shopping. We also assumed the conversation style as chatting between friends (assuming that the participant and the dialog agent are friends). In the dialog, the participants were instructed to ask the dialog agent what she had done yesterday on the assumption that she (the dialog agent) had led a human-like life. The initial database was constructed with the questions about the daily events she supposed to do. Table 1 summarizes the number of pairs of each database.

Table 1. The number of the pairs of the topics

	Cooking	Movie	Meal	Shopping
Greeting	47	47	47	47
Backchannels	6	6	6	6
Topic	369	376	434	469
Total	422	429	487	522

2.2 Procedure of Example Collection

Table 2 shows the flow of the method for collecting example sentences for topic t. Let I be the total number of the interaction, D_i^t be i-th database of topic t, and D_{CSJ} be a document set of the Corpus of Spontaneous Japanese (CSJ). Here, each participant talks with the system only once and the index of the iteration corresponds to the speaker index.

For the automatic example collection, detecting examples out of the current database E_i and generating the response are required. However, the focus of this paper is investigating the response appropriateness relating to the number of the iteration, and both of them were conducted manually. The utterances were translated to add to the database.

Table 2. Procedure of example collection for topic t

Algorithm 1 Expansion of database D_i^t
Set initial database D_1^t
for $i = 1, \ldots, I$ do
$\quad$ i-th person talks with the system $S(D_i^t, M_i^t)$
$\quad$ Extract examples out of the database E_i^t
$\quad$ Update the database $D_{i+1}^t \leftarrow D_i^t \cup E_i^t$
$\quad$ Train language model M_{i+1}^t by $D_{csj} \cup D_{i+1}^t$
end for

3 Analysis of Response Appropriateness by Iterating Dialog

3.1 Experimental Conditions

The dialog experiments for the example collection were conducted in a sound-proof chamber. Twenty-five persons (15 males and 10 females) participated the experiment. When a participant made an utterance, the system calculated the similarity between the speech recognition result of the utterance and example sentences in the database, and selected the response corresponding to the most similar example as the system's utterance. The cosine similarity was used for the similarity calculation. The system was implemented based on MMDAgent [8]. MMDAgent is an open-source toolkit for building the speech interaction system. The language model was trained using the sentences in the CSJ and the examples of the initial databases to accommodate a task-specific utterance. The language model was re-trained every end of the dialog using the collected examples.

The experiments were separated into two sections. In the first section, the participants made 10 input utterances to investigate the appropriateness of each response of the database D_{i-1}. The participants evaluated each response as "appropriate" or "not appropriate". After that, as the second section, they engaged in the dialog for the example collection for three minutes without appropriateness evaluation. The participants asked the agent what she had done yesterday. The dialog was user initiative one, and the participants asked the agent and the agent responded them.

3.2 Measurement of Appropriateness

We defined the coverage as an index of appropriateness of the system's responses. The coverage C_i^t of topic t of i-th participant (equals to i-th dialog) is calculated as follows:

$$C_i^t = \frac{R_i^t}{N_i^t} \tag{1}$$

R_i^t is the number of the response evaluated as appropriate and N_i^t is the number of the interchanges ($N_i^t = 10$). In the following section, we investigated the appropriateness of the response based on the coverage.

3.3   Experimental Results

Figure 1 shows the trend of the coverage by the number of the interaction. Horizontal axis is the average coverage score of 5 interactions. The result of the speech recognition is denoted as RECOG and the transcription is as TRANS. The blue line shows the trend of RECOG. As shown in the figure, the coverage improves until 11–15-th interaction, and remains flat after that. Because RECOG contains recognition error, the appropriateness of the response was also analyzed based on the manual transcription. The responses of the transcription were selected based on the Eq. (1), and the appropriateness was judged by a majority-vote of three evaluators (male: 1, female: 2). The red line of the figure shows the trend of TRANS. The tendency of the TRANS is similar to RECOG, and the coverage is saturated at 11–15-th interaction around 75%. More interactions are required to improve the appropriateness, but the efficacy of the example collection seems to be decreased because the remaining examples are interchanges of deeper interaction.

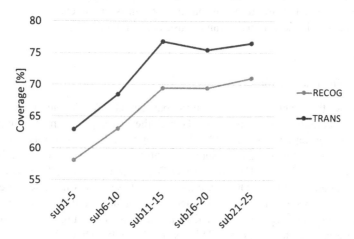

Fig. 1. Coverage of user's utterance with respect to number of interaction (Color figure online)

4   Comparison the Collected Databases with Hand-Crafted Databases by the Dialog Experiments

The collected databases were compared with the hand-crafted databases to investigate the efficacy of the example collection by the conversation. In this section, we denote the collected database as DIALOG and hand-crafted one as HANDCRAFTED.

4.1 Experimental Condition

The experiments were conducted by using DIALOG and HANDCRAFTED on the same conditions (except for three minutes interactions) with the previous Section. 10 subjects (male: 8, female: 2) participated the experiment. The DIALOG collected by 25 interactions is ranged from 550 to 600 sentences. The HANDCRAFTED database was created by 10 persons (male: 6, female: 4). One database creator made around 50 or 60 examples. The database creators were provided the initial database, and made the example sentences while assuming the possible interactions. The response sentences were developed by one person (the first author) for the consistency. Here, if the same example is included in DIALOG, we assigned the same response.

We constructed 8 systems preparing DIALOG and HANDCRAFTED database for each topic. The order of the topic presented to the participants was fixed, and HANDCRAFTED systems were presented first for randomly selected two topics out of the four topics. They made ten utterances for interaction with each system, and evaluated the response appropriateness at every end of the interaction. After the experiments, they answered the questionnaire for the subjective evaluation. The participants answered the following four questions using the five-grade Likert scale, one (not at all) to five (very much).

- Satisfaction: whether the user was satisfied with the dialog with the system.
- Engagement: whether the user felt that the dialog is engaged.
- Intelligence: whether the user felt that the system is intelligent.
- Willingness: whether the user want to use the system again.

4.2 Experimental Result

Table 3 shows the coverage averaged on the participants. We denoted the coverage of the speech recognition result as RECOG and the coverage of the transcription as TRANS. The appropriateness of TRANS was evaluated by the majority vote of three annotators (male: 1, female: 2). As shown in the table, the coverage of the DIALOG database was higher than the HANDCRAFTED database in both RECOG and TRANS cases. The coverage of DIALOG is around 70%. These results indicate the examples collected by the conversation is more suited to the actual use then handcrafting.

The results of the subjective evaluation are summarized in Fig. 2. The error-bar of the figure shows the standard error. This figure shows the DIALOG database outperformed the HANDCRAFTED database in all of the items. Using the unpaired t-test, we obtained the significant difference in satisfaction ($N = 40$, $t = -2.85$, $p = 0.006$), engagement ($N = 40$, $t = -3.42$, $p \leq 0.001$), intelligence ($N = 40$, $t = -3.34$, $p = 0.001$), and willingness ($N = 40$, $t = -2.18$, $p = 0.016$). Therefore, the example

Table 3. Coverage of databases

	Handcrafted	Dialog
RECOG	45.25%	66.50%
TRANS	50.75%	67.60%

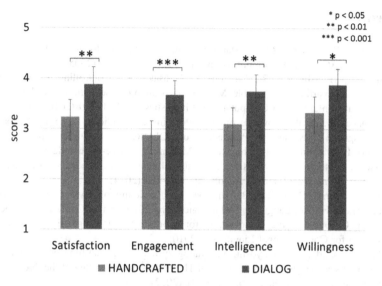

Fig. 2. Subjective evaluation results for system

collection by the conversation can construct the outstanding database in terms of not only the coverage but also the subjective evaluation. In particular, Engagement showed the largest difference among the evaluation items. It is suggested that the examples for the deeper interaction is especially important for the chat-style conversation. Many of the databases of the conventional systems are constructed by the developer while assuming the actual dialog, but it is not easy to cover the flows of possible conversation. Therefore, a framework to collect the examples by the interaction is important for the future dialog system to construct appropriate database at low-cost.

5 Conclusion

In this research, we examined the example collection method by the conversation for example-based dialog system and showed the efficacy of the method by several analyses. We found that the coverage of the example saturated at 75% by iterating the interaction 15 times. Then we compared the database collected by conversation with the fully hand-crafted database. The examined approach outperformed the hand-crafted method at Satisfaction, Engagement, Intelligence, and Willingness. In particular, the difference between Engagement scores was larger than the other scores, and the example collection by the conversation was efficient to obtain the more appropriate examples to the actual conversation than conventional approach.

In a future work, we will investigate the characteristic of the collected examples to clarify the difference from the hand-crafted examples. In addition, we are going to examine the methods to detect the out-of-database examples and generate the response automatically.

References

1. Bickmore, T.W., Picard, R.W.: Establishing and maintaining long-term human-computer relationships. ACM Trans. Comput.-Hum. Inter. **12**(2), 293–327 (2005)
2. Meguro, T., Higashinaka, R., Minami, Y. Dohsaka, K.: Controlling listening-oriented dialogue using partially observable Markov decision processes. In: Proceedings of 23rd International Conference on Computational Linguistics, pp. 761–769 (2010)
3. Higashinaka, R., et al.,: Towards an open-domain conversational system fully based on natural language processing. In: Proceedings of COLING, pp. 928–939 (2014)
4. Sugiyama, H., Meguro, T., Higashinaka, R., Minami, Y.: Large-scale collection and analysis of personal question-answer pairs for conventional agents. In: Proceedings of International Conference on Intelligent Virtual Agents, pp. 420–433 (2014)
5. Ritter, A., Cherry, C., Dolan, B.: Unsupervised modeling of Twitter conversations. In: Proceedings of Human Language Technologies: The 2010 Annual Conference of the North American Chapter of the Association for Computational Linguistics, pp. 172–180. Association for Computational Linguistics (2010)
6. Bessho, F., Harada, T., Kuniyoshi, Y.: Dialog system using real-time crowdsourcing and Twitter large-scale corus. In: Proceedings of The 13th Annual Meeting of the Special Internet Group on Discourse and Dialog, pp. 227–231 (2012)
7. Traum, D., et al.: Evaluating spoken dialogue processing for time-offset interaction. In: Proceedings of SIGDIAL, pp. 199–208 (2015)
8. Lee, A., Oura, K., Tokuda, K.: MMDAgent-a fully open-source toolkit for voice interaction systems. In: Proceedings of IEEE International Conference on Acoustics, Speech and Signal Processing, pp. 8382–8385 (2013)

Combining Sentimental and Content Analysis for Recognizing and Interpreting Human Affects

Stefanie Niklander[✉] and Gustavo Niklander

Universidad Autónoma de Chile, Santiago, Chile
{stefanie.niklander,gustavo.niklander}@uautonoma.cl

Abstract. During the last years, sentimental computing has gained special attention as the improvements achieved related to human affects, which are required abilities for many HCI applications. Particularly, sentimental analysis has successfully been used on social networks to extract useful information for different purposes. However the task remain difficult due to the several complex requirements that the correct human affect analysis implies. In this paper we propose a combination of sentimental and content analysis for the recognition and interpretation of human affects. We provide interesting results using as case study the #NiUnaMenos (Not One Less) social movement, which demands for an end to femicide and violence against women.

Keywords: Emotional computing · Affective computing · Content analysis · Social networks

1 Introduction

Sentimental analysis, emotional and affective computing have gained special attention during the last years as the improvements that have been achieved in the recognition, interpretation, processing, and simulation of human affects, which are required abilities for many HCI applications [2,3]. Particularly, sentimental analysis also known as opinion mining employs methods from natural language processing, text analysis and computational linguistics to interpret information from a given source. It has successfully been used on social networks to extract useful information specially for instance for customer services and marketing concerns.

In this paper, we present an hybrid sentimental-content analysis in order to improve the recognition and interpretation of human affects. Content analysis is a research technique that has extensively and fruitfully been used in the computational linguistic field for the objective, systematic and quantitative description of a given communication. We employ as case study the #NiUnaMenos (Not One Less) social movement, which demands for an end to femicide and violence against women. We select this case as several human affects are involved. This movement started on Argentine and was rapidly viralyzed to Latin America and

© Springer International Publishing AG 2017
C. Stephanidis (Ed.): HCII Posters 2017, Part I, CCIS 713, pp. 465–468, 2017.
DOI: 10.1007/978-3-319-58750-9_64

worldwide as a powerful sign of protest in order to stop misogyny. We gather a corpus composed of tweets using the #NiUnaMenos hashtag. This corpus is firstly analysed by state-of-the-art sentiment analysis algorithms, employing 10 different levels of human affects from fully negative to fully positive in order to improve the certainty of results. This output is then re-evaluated by content analysis so as to refine it and eliminate inconsistencies. Interesting results are obtained and discussed about the use of this hybrid in order to the correct recognition and interpretation of human affects specially for the emotional strength of the analyzed study case and in general for any communication context.

The remainder of this paper is organized as follows: Next section provides the analysis and results followed by conclusions and some directions of future work.

2   Analysis and Results

We have gathered a corpus of about 300 tweets that used the #NiUnaMenos hashtag from randomly selected accounts in order to avoid an unfair evaluation. We firstly employ the SentiStrength [4] tool to pre-process the data. SentiStrength performs automatic sentimental analysis on texts by estimating the strength of positive and negative sentiment in parallel as human being does [1]. It employs a range from -1 (not negative) to -5 (extremely negative) and from 1 (not positive) to 5 (extremely positive). Table 1 details the values encountered by SentiStrength for the analyzed tweets. After this pre-processing phase we analyze the data via content analysis.

Table 1. Strength of positive and negative sentiment

	number of tweets
-5 value	0
-4 value	23
-3 value	31
-2 value	49
-1 value	202

	number of tweets
1 value	232
2 value	42
3 value	20
4 value	6
5 value	5

Before starting the content analysis, we may observe that most of tweets fall into the "not negative" and "not positive" category. Moreover, the tool did not tagged any tweet with -5, situation which seems to be very positive. We may think that only using the information given by the pre-processing we can have a general opinion of the whole context. However, applying only sentimental analysis is not completely feasible this purpose and it is necessary to deeply analyze the content by a second technique.

When applying content analysis, we observed several tweets that caught our attention, we highlight some of them since our opinion is that its content is extremely negative, however no -5 value is encountered by the sentimental analysis pre-process.

– RT @elliberalweb: #NiUnaMenos. La asesinaron a golpes delante de su hija y quemaron la casa. (She was beaten to death in front of her daughter and her house was burned).

In our opinion this tweet should be tagged as "extremely negative" due to its hard content including words with clear negative strength such as "beaten", "burned" and "death". A similar situation occurs with the following two tweets.

– RT @ARGNoticiasok: Se arrojó de un taxi en movimiento para evitar abuso sexual #Inseguridad #Taxi #NiUnaMenos ... (He jumped from a moving taxi to avoid sexual abuse #Insecurity #Taxi #NiUnaMenos...).
– RT @LaAlamedaMor: #NiUnaMenos asesinada, violada, desaparecida, levantada, prostituida, golpeada, discriminada #Feminicidios #Morelos (#NiUnaMenos murdered, raped, disappeared, raised, prostituted, beaten, discriminated #Feminicides #Morelos).

Then, from another standpoint, the following tweet as well as previous ones have negative strength, however we may think that those tweets are positive since they support the #NiUnaMenos movement.

– RT @vervemediaes: No más pérdidas de identidad, no más miedo, humillaciones, insultos y palizas. #NiUnaMenos hay salida (No more loss of identity, no more fear, humiliation, insults and beatings. #NiUnaMenos there is an exit).

Finally, we can also detect ironies on some tweets, which are clearly teasing movement such as the tweets stated below. This is hard to detect for a sentimental analysis tool.

– RT @FeliLoGlobo: Me comera 8 medialunas, #NiUnaMenos (I would eat 8 croissants, #NiUnaMenos).
– RT @ElGallo_ar: @dzapatillas @inadi Las #NiUnaMenos jamas mencionan estas desigualdades, que se jubilen a los 65 como los hombres (The #NiUnaMenos never mention these inequalities, they must retire at 65 like men).

We have applied the complete content analysis by hand to most negative and positive tweets, for space reasons we do not include the whole analysis in this paper, but we can conclude that while the sentiment analysis gives us valuable data, it is still necessary to apply a manual technique in order to have access to the richness of those messages and correctly interpret the context where they are placed.

3 Conclusions and Future Work

In this paper we have studied the combination of sentimental and content analysis, sentimental analysis allows one to systematically study affective states by using natural processing techniques, while content analysis focuses on systematic and quantitative description of a given communication form. We have employed as case study the #NiUnaMenos (Not One Less) social movement due to its emotional strength. We have collected a set of tweets, which have firstly been pre-processed by using the SentiStrength sentimental analysis tool and then studied by content analysis. We may conclude that the automatic sentimental analysis is a powerful tool for alleviating the manually content analysis process. However, it is hard to have a full evaluation by only using this pre-process. Richer information is gathered when after the pre-processing, another content analysis technique is employed. As future work we aim at deeply analyzing this combination by exploring other similar thematics strongly involving human affects.

References

1. Berrios, R., Totterdell, P., Kellett, S.: Eliciting mixed emotions: a meta-analysis comparing models, types, and measures. Front. Psychol. **6**, 428 (2015)
2. Buimer, H.P., Bittner, M., Kostelijk, T., van der Geest, T.M., van Wezel, R.J.A., Zhao, Y.: Enhancing emotion recognition in VIPs with haptic feedback. In: Stephanidis, C. (ed.) HCI 2016. CCIS, vol. 618, pp. 157–163. Springer, Cham (2016). doi:10.1007/978-3-319-40542-1_25
3. Khan, A.M., Lawo, M.: Recognizing emotional states using physiological devices. In: Stephanidis, C. (ed.) HCI 2016. CCIS, vol. 618, pp. 164–171. Springer, Cham (2016). doi:10.1007/978-3-319-40542-1_26
4. Thelwall, M., Buckley, K., Paltoglou, G., Cai, D., Kappas, A.: Sentiment strength detection in short informal texts. J. Am. Soc. Inf. Sci. Technol. **61**, 2544–2558 (2010)

Emotional Computing and Discourse Analysis: A Case Study About Brexit in Twitter

Stefanie Niklander[(✉)]

Universidad Autónoma de Chile, Santiago, Chile
stefanie.niklander@uautonoma.cl

Abstract. During the last years, emotional computing has emerged as a field of Human Computer Interaction, where algorithms are able to recognize emotions in order to take better decisions in a given context. However correctly recognizing emotions is known to be a difficult task, specially in social networks which is plenty of stereotypes, metaphors, ironies and multi-word expressions that make the process hard to succeed. In this paper, we propose to pre-process the data by using emotional computing algorithms to then employ discourse analysis for the study of the information viralyzed through social networks. We provide interesting results using as case study the Brexit.

Keywords: Emotional computing · Affective computing · Discourse analysis · Social networks

1 Introduction

During the last years, emotional computing has emerged as a field of Human Computer Interaction, where algorithms are able to recognize emotions in order to take better decisions in a given context [2,3]. This approach is particularly useful for entities that need to carefully analyze the information that is viralyzed through Internet, particularly via social networks. For instance, from companies that want to receive feedback from customers about their recently launched products to governments that need to gather people opinions about a new law project or an important situation. However, the information reproduced via social networks is known to be hard to precisely analyze as people employs stereotypes, metaphors, different writing styles, multi-word expressions, and ironies expressed in an informal language that are hard to interpret and as a consequence to automatically analyze.

In this paper, we present how emotional computing can smartly be combined with discourse analysis to study the complex information viralyzed through social networks. Discourse analysis is a qualitative and interpretive methodology that has largely been employed to analyze different socio-cultural phenomena in an effective manner via different communication mechanisms. Particularly, we employ as case study the Brexit. We collect a corpus from a set of randomly chosen Twitter accounts. Such a corpus is firstly preprocessed by state-of-the-art

© Springer International Publishing AG 2017
C. Stephanidis (Ed.): HCII Posters 2017, Part I, CCIS 713, pp. 469–472, 2017.
DOI: 10.1007/978-3-319-58750-9_65

sentiment analysis (opinion mining) algorithms. We tag sentences by using different levels of negativeness and positiveness in order to improve the accuracy of evaluations. Then such evaluations are refined via discourse analysis. Interesting results are discussed about the use of this synergy in order to get helpful negative/positive feedback particularly for the analyzed study case and in general for any communication context.

The remainder of this paper is organized as follows: Next section provides the analysis and results followed by conclusions and some directions of future work.

2   Analysis and Results

Brexit is a portmanteau of "Britain" and "exit" referred to the prospective withdrawal of United Kingdom from the European Union. The Brexit is an interesting case study from which we have gathered a corpus of about 200 tweets that used the #Brexit hashtag from randomly selected accounts in order to avoid an unfair evaluation. The evaluation is done on two stages, in the first stage the data is analyzed via SentiStrength [4] which performs automatic sentimental analysis on texts, while in the second, discourse analysis is employed. Table 1 illustrates the evaluation given by SentiStrength for the analyzed tweets. Negative sentiment are valued from -1 (not negative) to -5 (extremely negative) and 1 (not positive) to 5 (extremely positive) is used to positive sentiments. Let us note that sentences have positive and negative evaluation at the same time, process based on the natural evaluation done by the human being [1].

Table 1. Strength of positive and negative sentiment

	number of tweets
-5 value	0
-4 value	0
-3 value	1
-2 value	24
-1 value	167

	number of tweets
1 value	179
2 value	12
3 value	1
4 value	0
5 value	0

Our purpose in applying sentiment analysis was to determine the opinion of people on the Internet about #brexit, trying to identify users who are against or in favor of the movement. The results obtained show that most users who used #brexit did so by posting messages that were rated "not negative" in 167 opportunities and as "not positive" 179. Only 24 times these were rated -2 and in 12 as $+2$, which leads us to determine that the comments are framed within a neutrality of opinions and have both positive and negative elements in their comments.

Let us note that sentiment analysis leaves out the stopwords because they are considered as lacking information to the message, however, in some cases these connectors can change the meaning of the sentence. After applying the automatic sentimental analysis, we study the data with content analysis to obtain a more detailed result of the posted messages.

From the set of analyzed tweets we may highlight the following ones:

– RT @UKIPNFKN: Free health cover for Britons in Europe is under threat via @theeconomist #Brexit #EHIC #Holidays https://t.co/FbImliHPod
– RT @HansOudijk1: The #English seem to have lost their mind. They want #brexit no matter what. Including breaking up their country. https://

We emphasize the previous messages, since we observed that a strategy very used in social networks in this subject is to emphasize the negative effects that this implementation would bring to the British. One of them could be the lack of free health insurance in Europe and the fact that Brexit is going to split its country in two. The first thing we observe is that they are based on assumptions, not on facts that are already proclaimed to determine the harm that this would cause in British citizens, therefore, they try to generate fear in the population without a certain base.

In the following tweets that we emphasize, we do not observe an open criticism, however, other strategies are used to deliver their position on this issue in the social network.

– RT @RCorbettMEP: Daily Express is forced to retract entire article claiming #Brexit has some benefits:
– RT @BonnleGreer: As I've said before: #Brexit is a Tory proxy war. A very old one. V.dangerous.
– RT @POLLiticss: Do you want more Mosques in your country or neighbourhood?? #brexit

The first tweet states that a mass media is being forced to publish positive information of this fact, generating doubt about the independence of the mass media. In the second tweet, it is affirmed that the Brexit would be producing a "conservative war", putting in alert that within this sector there are diverse opinions divided in relation to the subject.

The last message highlighted has a different tone, as it is openly xenophobic, asking if they want mosques in their neighborhood. This discrimination is directly addressed against Muslims and their way of life and religion.

In short, we can conclude that although messages were not openly published with a negative tone with #brexit, and that the tool of sentiment analysis is of great help for the analysis, the language is so complex and ambiguous that sometimes it is almost impossible that a computer tool analyzes the different nuances of grammar, slang, colloquial expressions, sarcasm, etc.

3   Conclusions and Future Work

In this paper we have studied the combination of sentimental and discourse analysis, sentimental analysis allows one to systematically study affective states by using natural processing techniques, while discourse analysis is a qualitative and interpretive methodology to analyze different socio-cultural phenomena. We have employed the #brexit as case study. We have collected a set of tweets, which have firstly been analyzed by using the SentiStrength sentimental analysis tool and then analyzed by discourse analysis. We may conclude that the sentiment analysis tool is of great help for such an study, however the language is so complex and ambiguous that sometimes it is hard to perform a deep study with automatic tools and as a consequence classic manual techniques are still required.

This is ongoing work and a straightforward line of research is to deeply analyze this combination by exploring other similar thematics using a large amount of input data.

References

1. Berrios, R., Totterdell, P., Kellett, S.: Eliciting mixed emotions: a meta-analysis comparing models, types, and measures. Frontiers Psychol. **6**, 428 (2015)
2. Buimer, H.P., Bittner, M., Kostelijk, T., van der Geest, T.M., van Wezel, R.J.A., Zhao, Y.: Enhancing emotion recognition in VIPs with haptic feedback. In: Stephanidis, C. (ed.) HCI 2016. Communications in Computer and Information Science, vol. 618, pp. 157–163. Springer International Publishing, Cham (2016)
3. Khan, A., Lawo, M.: Recognizing emotional states using physiological devices. In: Stephanidis, C. (ed.) HCII 2016, pp. 164–171. Springer International Publishing, Cham (2016)
4. Thelwall, M., Buckley, K., Paltoglou, G., Cai, D., Kappas, A.: Sentiment strength detection in short informal texts. J. Am. Soc. Inf. Sci. Technol. **61**, 2544–2558 (2010)

Automatic Quantification of the Veracity of Suicidal Ideation in Counseling Transcripts

Omar Oseguera[(⊠)], Alex Rinaldi, Joann Tuazon, and Albert C. Cruz

Computer Perception Lab, California State University,
Bakersfield, CA 93311, USA
ooseguera@csub.edu

Abstract. Crisis intervention and suicide prevention organizations have saved lives through the use of their phone, instant messaging, and text massaging intervention services. With the increased use of social media and internet-based chat, many people post about their suicidal ideation on websites like Twitter and Facebook. Our study aims to contribute to the literature of identifying suicidal ideation in text by using a corpus of publicly available counseling transcripts from Alexander Street categorized by symptom, applying sentiment analysis with the help of Linguistic Inquiry and Word Count (LIWC) Receptiviti Application Programming Interface, and performing experiments to predict if a transcript describes a suicidal patient based on sentiment analysis data. Our initial results appear promising, and we hope this research can be used in conjunction with those analyzing social media text to improve the efforts of technology-based suicide prevention.

Keywords: Suicide · Sentiment analysis · Machine learning

1 Introduction

According to *The American Foundation for Suicide Prevention* (ASFP), suicide is the 10th leading cause of death in the USA [1]. Many organizations, such as the *Trevor Project* and the *National Suicide Prevention Hotline* provide services over phone, chat, and text-message with hopes of deescalating someone's suicidal state or directing them to other available mental health and suicide prevention service providers [17]. According to *Internet World Statistics* there are over 320,000,000 internet users in the United States alone [7], and AFSP states 44,193 Americans die by suicide each year [1].

Sentiment Analysis is the field of study that analyzes opinions, emotions and attitudes, of a person toward some entity and its attributes in written text [10]. Sentiment Analysis tools such as Linguistic Inquiry and Word Count (LIWC) are able to perform analysis of text and return an analysis to identify the psychological state of that text [9]. The application of sentiment analysis for the detection of suicidal thoughts, otherwise known as suicidal ideation, has been carried out with publicly available social media data from Twitter, Facebook, Tumblr, etc. as well as in clinical studies [4, 13]. To the best of the authors' knowledge, we are the first study to predict the veracity of suicidal ideation from counseling transcripts.

© Springer International Publishing AG 2017
C. Stephanidis (Ed.): HCII Posters 2017, Part I, CCIS 713, pp. 473–479, 2017.
DOI: 10.1007/978-3-319-58750-9_66

Our study is a continuation in the use of sentiment analysis for suicidal ideation detection. The authors of [12] define suicide as the act of intentionally ending one's own life. Suicidal ideation refers to thoughts of engaging in behavior intended to end one's life. [12] also makes the distinction between suicide and self-injury, which the latter refers to a person who does not have the intent to die, such as one engaging in self-mutilation and self-harm. We perform sentiment analysis on a corpus of therapy transcripts from Alexander Street categorized by symptoms such as depression and suicidal ideation, use mutual information to select relevant sentiment analysis features from LIWC's Receptiviti Application Programming Interface (API), and train a machine learning classifier to automatically predict if a text sample belongs to one of Alexander street's suicide-related categories: suicidal ideation, self-harm, self-mutilation and suicidal behavior.

2 Motivation and Related Work

A number of suicide awareness and prevention organizations are in existence in an effort to reduce suicide rate [17], yet many people do not seek the appropriate help due to social stigmatization. This lack of reporting, along with geographical and juridical factors lead to unreliable statistics on suicide, and even more for nonfatal suicidal behavior (such as ideation) [5]. In [12], it states that people tend to underreport behavior related to sensitive or shameful topics such as drug use and suicidal behavior. When offering alternatives such as anonymous surveys, rates of reported suicidal behavior increase.

The increase in communication through the internet has created diverse online communities. In [4], there are references to multiple studies related to suicide and the world wide web. Some studies focus on websites dedicated to engagement in suicidal behavior, while in [8], there is a review of online resources for suicide intervention and prevention, resulting in a need for more evaluation of and development of such resources. The reality of communication about suicide on the Internet is evident by the existence of bulletin boards, chat rooms, web forums and newsgroups [4]. We hope that our research can provide a means of improvement to suicide prevention via the Internet.

The literature on Sentiment Analysis on suicide related text has made use of social media data. In Burnap et al. [4], a number of machine classification models were developed with the goal of classifying text on Twitter relating to communications around suicide. Their classifier distinguished between suicidal ideation, defined as having thoughts of suicide [12], reporting of a suicide, memorial (condolence), campaigning (such as petitions), and support (information on suicide). The researchers built a set of baseline classifiers using the following features extracted from Twitter posts: (1) lexical features such as frequency of Parts of Speech (POS) labels per tweet such as nouns and verbs, (2) structural features such as the use of negations in a sentence and the use of mention symbols in tweets (indicators of replies or reposts on Twitter), and (3) emotive and psychological features that could be found in statements expressing emotional distress [4]. This was achieved with the use of annotators, suicide researchers, and software tools like Linguistic Inquiry and Word Count (LIWC). By creating an ensemble classifier, a combination of base classifiers, they were able to achieve a 0.728 overall F1-measure for all of their classes, and a 0.69 F1-measure for the suicidal ideation class. For the F1 measure, higher is better.

Our research is novel in that we are not using social media text or annotators. Instead, we have acquired a corpus of therapy session transcripts from Alexander Street [2], which have already been categorized by their symptom, suicidal ideation, suicidal behavior, self-harm, etc. We then applied sentiment analysis with LIWC's Receptiviti API to those transcripts, performed feature selection to obtain the most relevant features, and trained a number of machine learning classifiers to predict whether one of our sample transcripts belongs to one of Alexander Street's suicidal categories.

3 Technical Approach

Our approach consisted of Data Collection and Text Processing, Sentiment Analysis, Feature Selection with Mutual Information, and Machine Learning (see Fig. 1).

Fig. 1. System overview.

3.1 Data Collection and Text Processing

We collected a total of 745 Transcripts from Alexander Street's *Counseling and Psychotherapy Transcripts Series* [2]. These transcripts were plain text and categorized by symptoms and topics such as Anxiety, Depression, Shame, Suicidal Ideation, Suicidal Behavior, Self Harm and Self Mutilation (see Fig. 2).

Class	Number of Transcripts	Percentage
Suicidal	83	11%
Not Suicidal	662	89%

Fig. 2. Overview of transcripts by suicidal and not suicidal.

The transcripts contained conversations between a therapist and their client in the following format:

CLIENT: Somehow it is your fault if you are not hearing back…It's not my fault.
THERAPIST: When I am responding it is naively right now because I don't go
home and see with you what you are doing.

These transcripts were not always in the therapist-client order as shown above, but they always had a therapist and client in the conversation. For our experiment we required the client conversation text only, which we achieved with a set of regular expression (RegEx) and pattern matching rules. RegEx is like a mini programming language, which allows one to describe and parse text. With RegEx we only grab the text following a 'CLIENT:' pattern and stopping when reaching a 'THERAPIST:' pattern. We performed this process on each of our transcripts categorized by their symptom.

3.2   Sentiment Analysis

Once we collected all of the transcripts and grabbed the client data only, we then used Linguistic Inquiry and Word Count's Receptiviti API to perform sentiment analysis [15]. Receptiviti generates all of LIWC's variables with an additional 50 validated measures of psychology, emotion, tone, sentiment, and more. For every transcript, each word is compared against a dictionary, and each dictionary identifies which words are associated with a certain psychology-related category [9]. Once an entire transcript has been processed, the percentage of total words that match each of the dictionary categories is calculated. These categories are the features used in our experiment. Complete transcripts were processed one at a time, and used the returned 124 features as our samples for each transcript.

3.3   Feature Selection

Receptiviti provides 124 features for each transcript submitted. These features range from parts of speech labels and word count, to sentiment oriented features such as depression, health-oriented, and extraversion (outgoing). In order to identify the most relevant features for our classification task, we performed Feature Selection with Mutual Information using the *scikit-learn* Python library.

Mutual Information is a non-negative value between two variables which measures the dependency between the variables. The result is zero only if two random variables are independent, and higher values mean higher dependency [16]. Mutual Information will allow us to select features that have a better effect on classifying our text as suicidal.

$$E(X; Y) = \sum_x \sum_y p(x, y) \log \frac{p(x, y)}{p(x)p(y)} \tag{1}$$

$$E(X; Y) \geq 0 \text{ iff } p(x, y) = p(x)p(y) \tag{2}$$

where X and Y are random variables, $p(x, y)$ is the joint distribution, and $p(x)p(y)$ is the factored distribution [11].

In our experiment we perform Feature Selection with Mutual information, then select the features that are in the top 30th percentile of the highest scores returned. This was implemented with the *scikit-learn* SelectPercentile function, which uses a specified function (Mutual Information) and a specified percentage N as its parameters in order to return the top N^{th} percentile from the specified function. After performing Mutual Information, we reduced our 124 features from Receptiviti to 37 features. Some of these features include depression, openness, extraversion, and agreeable. Some of the removed features include word count, positive emotion, and drives.

3.4 Machine Learning

Similar to the work in [4], we used Support Vector Machine (SVM), Decision Trees (C4.5), and Naïve Bayes. [4, 6] have both listed SVM classifier as yielding promising results when classifying depression. The following classifiers were used for our Machine Learning step from *scikit-learn*: logistic regression, linear discriminant analysis, K-NN, C4.5 [14], Naïve Bayes and a linear SVM.

4   Experimental Results

In order to test our data, we performed a 10-fold Cross Validation. Cross Validation is used to test our classifiers on the same data that we train them on. A fold represents how many partitions the data will be split to be trained and tested in every iteration. When randomly generating a fold, we ensured that the a-priori rate of both classes was even because of over-representation of the non-suicidal class (Fig. 2). The following figure shows our metrics for each classifier (Fig. 3).

For each classifier, Accuracy measures the percentage of inputs that were correctly labeled in the test set. Figure 3 shows our highest accuracy percentages around 89% for Logistic Regression, Linear Discriminant Analysis(LDA), K-Nearest Neighbors (K-NN) and Linear Support Vector Machine (Linear SVM). All of the classifiers have an Accuracy of more than 80%.

Precision is a measure of how many items we identified were relevant, and Recall is a measure of how many of the relevant items were identified. These metrics take into account the False Positives (FP) which are the irrelevant items incorrectly identified as

Classifier	Accuracy	Precision	Recall	F1-score
Logistic Regression	0.8960	0.74	0.86	0.79
LDA	0.8942	0.79	0.83	0.80
K-NN	0.8970	0.79	0.83	0.81
C4.5	0.8830	0.84	0.84	0.84
Naïve Bayes	0.8040	0.82	0.76	0.78
Linear SVM	0.8960	0.74	0.86	0.79

Fig. 3. Comparison of cross validation results for each classifier

relevant, False Negatives (FN) which are the relevant items incorrectly identified as irrelevant, and True Positives (TP) which are the relevant items correctly identified as relevant [3, 11].

Our classifiers show a Precision of 74% for Logistic Regression and Linear SVM, 79% for LDA and K-NN. For Recall our classifiers show 86% for Logistic Regression, 83% for LDA and K-NN, and 86% for Linear SVM.

The F1-score is a harmonic mean of Precision and Recall [3, 11]. Our classifiers show an F1-score of 79% for Logistic Regression and Linear SVM, 80% for LDA, and 81% for K-NN.

Our results can be improved by obtaining sentiment analysis features for every paragraph in each transcript, and by keeping our ratio of suicidal to non-suicidal samples from being skewed. With such modifications we hope to increase the performance of our classifiers.

5   Conclusion

Electronic means of suicide prevention can be improved with research on the detection of suicidal ideation in text. In this paper we collected a corpus of therapy transcripts from Alexander Street, performed Sentiment Analysis with help of LIWC's Receptiviti API, and trained machine learning classifiers to automatically predict if a text belongs to a suicide-related category. Our classifiers performed with accuracies ranging from 80–89%, showing promise of detecting suicidal ideation in therapy transcripts. We hope our work will advance the effectiveness of electronic suicide prevention strategies in today's society.

Acknowledgements. This work was supported by the NSF grant HRD-0331537 (CSU-LSAMP). The views and opinions of the authors expressed herein do not necessarily state or reflect those of the United States Government.

References

1. AFSP Suicide Statistics Page. https://afsp.org/about-suicide/suicide-statistics. Accessed 14 Mar 2017
2. Alexander Street Counseling and Psychotherapy Transcripts Series. http://alexanderstreet.com/products/counseling-and-psychotherapy-transcripts-series
3. Bird, S., Klein, E., Loper, E.: Natural Language Processing with Python. O'Reilly Media, Sebastopol (2009)
4. Burnap, P., Colombo, G., Scourfield, J.: Machine classification and analysis of suicide-related communication on Twitter. In: Proceedings of 26th ACM Conference on Hypertext and Social Media (2015)
5. Crosby, A.E., LaVonne, O., Melanson, C.: Self-directed violence surveillance: uniform definitions and recommended data elements. Division of Violence Prevention, Centers for Disease Control and Prevention, National Center for Injury Prevention and Control (2011)

6. De Choudhury, M., Gamon, M., Counts, S., Horvitz, E.: Predicting depression via social media. In: Proceedings of 7th International AAAI Conference on Weblogs and Social Media (2013)
7. Internet World Stats America Stats Page. www.internetworldstats.com/stats14.htm. Accessed 19 Mar 2017
8. Jacob, N., Scourfield, J., Rhiannon, E.: Suicide prevention via the internet: a descriptive review. Crisis **35**, 261–267 (2014)
9. Linguistic Inquiry and Word Count. https://liwc.wpengine.com
10. Liu, B.: Sentiment Analysis. Cambridge University Press, New York (2015)
11. Murphy, K.P.: Machine Learning: A Probabilistic Perspective. The MIT Press, Cambridge (2012)
12. Nock, M.K., Borges, G., Bromet, E.J., Cha, C.B., Lee, S.: Suicide and suicidal behavior. Epidemiol. Rev. **30**(1), 133–154 (2008)
13. Pestian, J.P., Matykiewicz, P., Linn-Gust, M., et al.: Sentiment analysis of suicide notes: a shared task. Biomed. Inform. Insights **5**(Suppl. 1), 3–16 (2012)
14. Quinlan, J.R.: Programs for Machine Learning. Morgan Kaufmann, Burlington (1993)
15. Receptiviti API Homepage. http://www.receptiviti.ai
16. Scikit-Learn Homepage. http://scikit-learn.org/stable/index.html
17. SPRC Organizations Page. http://www.sprc.org/organizations/%20national-federal. Accessed 18 Mar 2017

End-to-End Dialogue with Sentiment Analysis Features

Alex Rinaldi[(⊠)], Omar Oseguera, Joann Tuazon, and Albert C. Cruz

California State University, Bakersfield, CA, USA
arinaldi1@csub.edu

Abstract. Psychiatric assistance for suicide prevention does not have a wide enough reach to help the number of victims who commit suicide every year. To help people cope with suicidal thoughts when formal care is unavailable, we propose an artificial intelligence, text-based conversational agent that generates responses similar to those of a counselor. The application will offer a temporary channel for expression that serves as a transition to speaking with a professional psychiatrist. We expand upon existing approaches by utilizing sentiment analysis data, or scores that rank the emotional content of users' text input, when generating responses. We also train a response generation system based on a dataset of counseling and therapy transcripts. We posit that inclusion of sentiment analysis data provides marginally better responses based on quantitative metrics of quality. We hope our results will advance realistic conversation modeling and promote further research into its humanitarian applications.

Keywords: Sequence-to-sequence learning · Dialogue system · Conversational agent · Chatbot · Recurrent neural network · Sentiment analysis

1 Introduction

Psychiatric care and counseling is a vital deterrent to suicide, but not everyone is able or willing to seek these resources. A 2011 survey by the American College Counseling Association studies this problem in the college setting. According to the survey, 80% of students who died by suicide did not seek help from their school's counseling center [1]. A 2013 Journal of American College Health survey finds at risk college students do not report suicidal thoughts primarily because they believe they don't need professional treatment, lack time, or prefer to solve personal problems without help from others [2].

One solution that overcomes these barriers is providing channels for expression that do not require formal care. Social media provides one such channel, but it does not guarantee a safe environment. Suicide hotline services can help, but have limited resources and are generally reserved for emergencies. [3] suggests methods that are completely anonymous and do not require human contact have benefits when detecting suicidal thoughts and behavior. According to [3], 2–3 times more people reported suicidal behavior when using written or computerized anonymous surveys. One possible channel to express and counter suicidal ideation while remaining anonymous and without human contact is a mobile application where users can write down their thoughts. This provides the benefit of being constantly available, but it lacks the

C. Stephanidis (Ed.): HCII Posters 2017, Part I, CCIS 713, pp. 480–487, 2017.
DOI: 10.1007/978-3-319-58750-9_67

directed nature of a survey or the responsive nature of a counseling session. In addition, mobile journaling applications like *Day One* already exist. A better solution is a journaling app that provides responses to the user's input, helping guide the expression of his or her thoughts in the same way a counselor would. Our approach takes the form of a text-based conversational agent, or an artificial intelligence that produces responses to a user's text input. The agent would be explicitly advertised as an artificial intelligence, providing the benefit of anonymity described in [3]. It would provide a temporary channel for expression that could transition into more formal psychiatric care. The rest of this paper will describe initial experiments to make this application possible.

2 Related Work and Motivation

Our approach builds upon several current approaches to developing a conversational agent, while offering three main novelties:

1. Including sentiment analysis data as part of the problem domain
2. Enhancing sequence-to-sequence dialogue generation with feature-level fusion
3. Training on a dataset of therapy and counseling sessions.

2.1 Sentiment Analysis and LIWC

Psychotherapists are required to understand and react to the emotional state of their patients. For a text-based conversational agent serving a similar purpose, some measure of the emotional content of input text is necessary for producing an appropriate response.

Detecting and quantitatively representing emotion in text is an area of research known as Sentiment Analysis, which has recently been implemented in a software application known as Linguistic Inquiry and Word Count (LIWC) [4]. LIWC provides additional features to help process the semantic and emotional content of user input. It groups words into semantic categories, including those related to basic language functions like "personal pronoun" and "auxiliary verb," as well as psychological constructs including "cognition," "positive emotional tone," and "affect" [4]. Since LIWC categories are meant to help represent the meaning of text, we posit that an artificial intelligence system should utilize LIWC categories to provide more meaningful responses.

To the best of our knowledge, [5] is the first attempt to use LIWC features to generate responses in a conversational agent application. [5] attempts to take a specific conversational objective or goal (like recommending a restaurant), and generate a response that achieves the objective while generating a user-defined "personality" (such as extroverted or introverted). LIWC scores are used to train parameters that select and combine sentence structures from a handmade database to evoke the personality. This application of LIWC scores is too limited for our problem, however. Unlike in a commercial application, the conversational objective of a therapist is complex and always changing, making it difficult to model.

2.2   Retrieval and Generative Methods for Responses

[5] is an example of a retrieval-based method because it generates a response by selecting from a database of pre-defined responses (or "templates" for responses in this case). While retrieval-based methods are widely used because predefined responses are more grammatically correct and consistent, they are too limited for our application; in [5] a specific goal is required. Paper [6] attempts to produce more dynamic responses by selecting from a large dataset of responses in social media with a trained probability distribution over the possible responses, but constructing a dataset of every possible counselor response is impossible without responses sounding too contrived.

[7–10] use a more dynamic approach called sequence-to-sequence generation. Originally proposed in [11] as a method for translating between two languages, sequence-to-sequence approaches process input one word at a time and produce output one word at a time, resulting in the potential for unique responses for every input. The model is based on a combination of two recurrent neural networks (RNN). Sequence-to-sequence generation is data-driven; it is trained using a large corpus of text conversations, and attempts to learn common language patterns between all inputs and responses.

2.3   Fusion with Sentiment Analysis Features

One common problem among sequence-to-sequence implementations is that while the output follows common language patterns, it has little meaning in relation to the input. Sequence-to-sequence generators can converge to generate the most simple, frequent responses like "Yeah" as shown in Fig. 2. One solution may be to include additional semantic information to help direct the learning process.

[10] proposes inputting combining additional information along with the user input. It uses a set of features representing general qualities about the speaker (such as ethnicity) in combination with each input word to help the system generate more personalized responses. This is known as feature level fusion, and is meant to improve an artificial intelligence system's performance by providing multiple sources of information. Influenced by [5], we apply this concept to our problem by combining LIWC categories for each input word with the word itself. We predict that providing the model with semantic and sentiment information about each word will help detect semantic patterns between the input and output responses and generate output that is more meaningful and emotionally relevant.

[12, 13] provide frameworks for performing feature level fusion in RNNs for emotion recognition in video. We will use a similar approach for combining vector representations of words with LIWC category vectors as described in the technical approach. [7, 8] both use vector embedding of words to reduce dimensionality when working with a large vocabulary – each word in the vocabulary is assigned a lower-dimensional vector. We will therefore concatenate the LIWC categories with a vector embedding of each word.

2.4 Dialogue Corpus

While approaches [7, 9, 10] use datasets mined from social media sites, movie and television scripts, and IT help desk conversations to train their conversational models on general dialogue, our conversational agent has a more focused purpose on providing psychological help. Therefore, we have decided to train our model on a dataset of Counseling and Therapy transcripts provided by Alexander Street [14]. The dataset includes 725 typed, anonymous transcripts of recorded therapy sessions categorized by self-reported symptoms such as suicidal ideation and depression. In total, there are approximately 86,000 input-response pairs.

3 Technical Approach

In this section we detail the sequence-to-sequence model with LIWC feature level fusion and the training process. Figure 1 provides an overview of the approach.

First, all words in the dataset are replaced with an integer representing the word's position in the vocabulary for the top V_I and V_o most frequently occurring words in the client and therapist datasets, respectively. Words outside of the vocabulary are replaced with an "unknown" token, and the end of each turn in the conversation is marked with an "EOS" (end-of-sentence) token. Tokens are converted into their one-hot vector representation before being embedded and input to the encoder cell. The client token sequences are fed to the model, and the therapist token sequences become the target for evaluating output as described below.

The model for the sequence-to-sequence RNN follows Google's provided implementation of [11], with a feature fusion method based on [12]. The encoder cell receives a word belonging to a vocabulary of size V_I embedded to a vector representation of size E. Each input word embedding $e_n \in \mathbb{R}^E$ is concatenated with its corresponding LIWC categories (a vector $l \in \mathbb{R}^C$ where C is the number of categories - 1 indicates the word belongs in a category, 0 otherwise) to form the fused input vector $v_n \in \mathbb{R}^{C+E} = [e_n, l_n]$.

In each encoder step, the RNN cell updates its current hidden state $h_n \in \mathbb{R}^{C+E}$ as a function of the previous hidden state and the current fused vector:

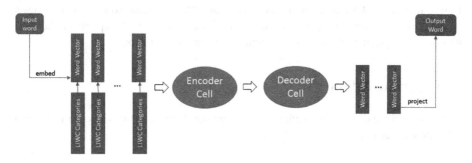

Fig. 1. Overview of proposed model.

$$h_n = f(\pmb{h_{n-1}}, [\pmb{e_n}, \pmb{l_n}]) = f(\pmb{h_{n-1}}, \pmb{v_n}) \tag{1}$$

And f is a linear combination of the hidden state and input subjected to hyperbolic tangent:

$$f(\pmb{h_{n-1}}, \pmb{v_n}) = \tanh(\pmb{W_{h,e}}\pmb{h_t} + \pmb{W_{v,e}}\pmb{v_n}) \tag{2}$$

Where $\pmb{W_{h,e}}, \pmb{W_{v,e}} \in \mathbb{R}^{(C+E)\times(C+E)}$. In the output decoder, Eqs. (1) and (2) are used to update the hidden state with different parameters $\pmb{W_{h,d}}, \pmb{W_{v,d}}$. The hidden state must be projected to the size of the output vocabulary V_o to achieve an output:

$$\hat{\pmb{o}}_n = g(\pmb{h_n}) = \pmb{O}\pmb{h_n} \tag{3}$$

Where $\pmb{O} \in \mathbb{R}^{V_o \times (C+E)}$. The output token is the index in the vocabulary as determined by the vector index with the highest value:

$$w_n = \underset{i}{\mathrm{argmax}}([\hat{o}_{n,i}]) \tag{4}$$

The parameters $\pmb{W_{h,e}}, \pmb{W_{v,e}}, \pmb{W_{h,d}}, \pmb{W_{v,d}}, \pmb{O}$ are optimized through gradient descent by minimizing the log perplexity of the softmax loss between the output logit $\hat{\pmb{o}}_n$ and the one-hot vector representation of the target word $\pmb{o}_n$ (from a therapist utterance) for all words in a given sequence of length N. Equation (5) uses the softmax function to convert the output logit into a probability distribution over the vocabulary, and (6) is the log perplexity over all probability distributions in the sequence.

$$\varsigma(\hat{\pmb{o}}_n) = \frac{e^{\hat{o}_{n,v}}}{\sum_{i=1}^{V_0} e^{\hat{o}_{n,i}}} \text{ for } v = 1 \dots V_o \tag{5}$$

$$loss(\hat{\pmb{o}}_n, \pmb{o}_n) = -\sum_{n=1}^{N} \pmb{o}_n \log(\varsigma(\hat{\pmb{o}}_n)) \text{ for } n = 1 \dots N \tag{6}$$

The equations above provide a basic implementation of the RNN sequence-to-sequence model. As noted in [11], it is possible to improve the performance of the model on long sequences of words by using Long Short Term Memory (LSTM) cells while still using feature fusion. An LSTM has an input, output, and "forget" gate, so Eq. (3) becomes a function of the output gate in this implementation. As we will explain in the next section, the type of RNN cell is a parameter in our experiments.

4   Experimentation

In this section we discuss the methods to prepare our dataset, test it with our model, and evaluate our results.

4.1   Preparation of Data

All transcripts are processed so that every session is a single-turn conversation (the patient speaks once, then the therapist speaks once). If a client or therapist speaks for multiple turns, the turns are concatenated together. Transcriber annotations like "inaudible" are removed. All pairs of client and therapist turns from all sessions are combined into input and response datasets (without altering the order of turns in the transcripts), resulting in 86,593 client-therapist pairs.

4.2   Selection of Parameters

The sizes of the input and output vocabularies V_I and V_o as well as the embedding size E are optimized through a grid search. Also, the type of RNN cell is a parameter (Basic and LSTM).

4.3   Training Specifics

Based on the implementation provided for [11], input and output sequences must have static length, so input-response pairs are categorized based on lengths of 10, 20, 30, 40, with our implementation adding 50, 60, and 70 to accommodate longer inputs. Inputs above this length are trimmed. In our dataset, 20.2% of inputs have length 70–100 and must be trimmed, resulting in 69,059 usable client-therapist pairs. Also, to help direct training target fused vectors are fed to the decoder RNN instead of generated fused vectors at each time step during training. During the test phase, output fused vectors are first projected into the vocabulary space, re-embedded, and the fused before being fed to the decoder at the next step. A variable learning rate is used, and gradient clipping is implemented to prevent exploding gradients.

4.4   Evaluation of Results

Unfortunately, there is no established metric for evaluating the quality of generated dialogue. Also, our output is subject to the constraint of being "emotionally relevant" to the user's input. [10] attempts to use human evaluation to compare models, but considering the unchecked ethical ramifications of evaluating our conversational agent and the incremental nature of advances dialogue generation (the Turing Test is far from solved), we use unsupervised methods to evaluate the quality of our responses in comparison to other models.

[8] and [7] agree on using perplexity between generated responses and the target dataset as a metric for measuring dialogue generation quality. Perplexity is obtained by taking the exponential of Eq. (6) and should be minimized. Our method divides the conversation dataset into training and test sets of sizes 70% and 20% respectively, and compares methods by summing the perplexities over all responses in the test set.

Influenced by [5], we also propose a simple metric to evaluate whether or not responses are emotionally relevant. Paper [5] uses LIWC scores to test whether generated sentences reflect the personality they are meant to evoke. We evaluate our model's responses against other models by root mean square difference between LIWC scores for the test set and generated responses.

Quantitative comparison of results as well as qualitative analysis will be provided for the proposed method, the baseline sequence-to-sequence implementation provided by Google for [11].

5   Discussion and Conclusion

Figure 2 demonstrates some of the shortcomings of the basic sequence-to-sequence approach implemented by Google for [11]. When trained on our Counseling and Therapy dataset, the generated responses is often "Yeah" or "Mm hm." This makes sense, as the therapist is often simply encouraging the client to continue speaking. When responding to emotional statements where the therapist needs to play a more supportive or responsive role, this kind of response may be inappropriate.

By including semantic and sentiment analysis in our model, we expect responses that are more meaningful in terms of the input. While qualitatively evaluating this is unfeasible in the short term, we expect our unsupervised metrics to yield marginally better results than the baseline and other state of the art methods. Future work will involve exploring methods to process longer responses and entire conversations when producing responses. We hope to encourage more research in using affective computing for humanitarian applications.

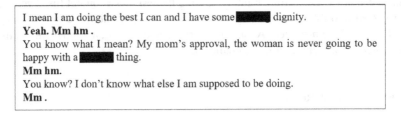

Fig. 2. Responses generated by the baseline sequence-to-sequence model are highlighted in bold. Inputs are trimmed examples from the client dataset (examples must be trimmed to accommodate the baseline sequence-to-sequence implementation). Expletives are redacted for this publication.

Acknowledgements. The authors (gratefully) acknowledge financial support from NSF under grant HRD-0331537 (CSU-LSAMP).

References

1. Gallagher, R.P.: National Survey of Counseling Center Directors 2011, vol. 26. American College Counseling Association (2011)

2. Author Manuscript: College Students at Elevated Risk for Suicide. vol. 61, pp. 398–406 (2014)

3. Nock, M.K., Borges, G., Bromet, E.J., Cha, C.B., Kessler, R.C., Lee, S.: Suicide and suicidal behavior. Epidemiol. Rev. **30**, 133–154 (2008)

4. Pennebaker, J.W., Boyd, R.L., Jordan, K., Blackburn, K.: The Development and Psychometric Properties of LIWC2015. University of Texas at Austin, Austin (2015)

5. Mairesse, F.: Learning to adapt in dialogue systems: data-driven models for personality recognition and generation. p. 285 (2008)

6. Ji, Z., Lu, Z., Li, H.: An information retrieval approach to short text conversation. Arxiv - Soc. Media Intell. 1–21 (2014)

7. Serban, I.V., Sordoni, A., Bengio, Y., Courville, A., Pineau, J.: Building End-To-End Dialogue Systems Using Generative Hierarchical Neural Network Models, vol. 8. AAAI (2016)

8. Yao, K., Zweig, G., Peng, B.: Attention with Intention for a Neural Network Conversation Model. In: NIPS Workshop on Machine Learning for Spoken Language Understanding and Interaction, pp. 1–7 (2015)

9. Vinyals, O., Le, Q.V.: A neural conversational model. In: ICML Deep Learning Workshop, p. 37 (2015)

10. Li, J., Galley, M., Brockett, C., Gao, J., Dolan, B.: A persona-based neural conversation model. **10** (2016). arXiv:1603.06155

11. Sutskever, I., Vinyals, O., Le, Q.V.: Sequence to sequence learning with neural networks. In: NIPS, pp. 3104–3112 (2014)

12. Chao, L., Tao, J., Yang, M., Li, Y., Wen, Z.: Long short term memory recurrent neural network based multimodal dimensional emotion recognition. In: Proceedings of 5th International Workshop on Audio/Visual Emotion Challenge, pp. 65–72 (2015)

13. Chao, L., Tao, J., Yang, M., Li, Y.: Multi task sequence learning for depression scale prediction from video. In: 2015 International Conference on Affective Computing and Intelligent Interaction, ACII 2015, pp. 526–531 (2015)

14. Counseling and Psychotherapy Transcripts Series. http://alexanderstreet.com/products/counseling

Avatar Life-Review: Seniors Reminiscing Through Virtual Bodies

Semi Ryu[1,2(✉)]

[1] Department of Kinetic Imaging, School of the Arts,
Virginia Commonwealth University, Richmond, VA, USA
sryu2@vcu.edu
[2] Doctoral Program in Information and Knowledge Society, Barcelona, Spain

Abstract. This paper will discuss experiences of older adult participants and the artist as a mediator and participant in ten avatar life-review sessions held at a senior living facility in Richmond, Virginia. The avatar system uses lip-synchronization, motion detection, and sentiment analysis to playfully engage the user's life-review process. The system offered female and male interactive avatars for four developmental stages: childhood, adolescence, young adulthood, and elderhood. Participants' experiences are studied anthropologically as a mode of personal and communal ritual and person-centered care in a common theatrical environment.

Keywords: Avatar · Virtual · Life review · Seniors · Reminiscence · Embodiment · Oral storytelling · Mixed reality · Interactive · Aging · Anthropology · Person-centered care

1 Introduction

This paper will present the participants' experience as a mode of personal and communal ritual and person-centered care in a common theatrical environment in ten life-review sessions held at a senior living facility in Richmond, Virginia, from March through June 2016. Therapeutic potential will be discussed in the user's personal engagement with the avatar, sense of anonymity, distancing effects, and emotional release. Each life-review session was followed by lengthy community talks, building strong empathetic bonds between the storyteller, the artist (mediator) and the audience (residents). Moreover, the avatar movie screening brought everyone together reflecting on all those stories told via avatar. Later, the avatar movie was distributed to the participant's family members and grandchildren enriching intergenerational relationships.

We observed striking patterns of interaction inflected by physical limitations of the older adults' bodies and technical limitations of the life-review system, which shaped the users' verbal and kinetic expression revealing surprising engagement during the storytelling process. The sentiment analysis and response features contributed to empathetic relationships among the storyteller, the artist, and audience.

Finally, this paper addresses the artist's experience as an active participant in this life-review event. Originally inspired by Korean shamanic ritual, the avatar life-review process generates cross-cultural dialogues among American seniors and Korean-born artists all seeking enriched communication.

© Springer International Publishing AG 2017
C. Stephanidis (Ed.): HCII Posters 2017, Part I, CCIS 713, pp. 488–496, 2017.
DOI: 10.1007/978-3-319-58750-9_68

2   Virtual and Augmented Body

In *Body without Organs* (BwO), Gilles Deleuze defines the virtual as a potentiality that becomes fulfilled in the actual. Though not yet material, it is real [1]. The virtual body facilitates the discovery of potential selves. Maurice Merleau-Ponty describes the body as neither subject nor object [2]. The body constructs its surroundings virtually, operating as a subject through movement, but doing so within objective space. A phantom limb persists vividly for the amputee—a phenomenon that cannot be explained in solely psychological or physiological terms [3]. In the same way, the phenomenal body can reveal the situation of the augmented body we encounter in mixed reality prompting meditation on embodiment, perception, and human experience. The distinct modulation of time and space provided by virtual reality technology facilitates a dynamic mode of phenomenological experience that can help us examine what it means to be human in the digital age. Phenomenological embodiment can be understood as a quantum state of paradox—neither here nor there; neither subject nor object [4]. It parallels the distancing effect used in drama therapy and therapeutic puppetry to promote healing by mediation between virtual and actual bodies.

Virtual and augmented reality have become part of our daily lives; our bodies are constantly mediated, represented, and multiplied via technology. In the flux of multiple bodies, spatiality and temporality, it is possible and necessary to discuss the role of human bodily experience in complex relationship with our digital reflections.

The avatar life-review was designed to facilitate this discussion. Its lip-synchronization and gesture-tracking features facilitate simultaneous speech between the virtual and physical body. In this embodied speech process, the human storyteller is augmented into a virtual storyteller, facing each other, simultaneously speaking, moving, and reflecting in a spiraling flow.

3   Person-Centered Care and Anthropology

Carl Rogers developed his non-directive form of talk therapy with the aim of supporting the patient's autonomy and self-exploration. He advocated for "unconditional positive regard," a practice of accepting and supporting a person regardless of what he or she says or does [5]. Unconditional positive regard supports deep empathetic relationships by promoting trust and free expression. The avatar life-review system was designed to support the user's autonomous storytelling, while providing digitally mediated reflective listening allowing the storyteller to see and hear the story as an actively listening other might. Through detection and analysis of the storyteller's voice, words, gestures, and reflection of those behaviors via avatar animation, background images, music, and ambient sound, the system functions as an empathetic listener, but crucially also allows the user to function as an empathetic listener to herself simultaneously without judgment remaining unconditionally positive. The audience, artist, and storyteller build strong empathetic relationships mediated by emotionally responsive background sound and visuals.

The participant's experience is the most critical element in avatar life-review, involving embodiment, self-perception, emotion, and phenomenological reality mediated by technology. All participants—storytellers, the artist/mediator, staff, family, etc., contribute to a shared experience.

In his book, *Where the Action Is: The Foundations of Embodied Interaction*, Paul Dourish problematizes the dichotomy between "user" and "designer," noting that the designer is always also a user [6]. Grudin (1993) argues that these terms influence our understanding of systems according to the way computer engineering faced initial design problems [7]. The term "user" is commonly understood as a general category of non-experts, denying dimensions of the participants' experience as genuine. But user experience is more than a pattern of behavior; it is phenomenological and subjective. We need to acknowledge their meaningful engagement with the system [8]. From an anthropological perspective, the designer (artist) is also considered an active participant with many dimensions of experience within system, including imaginary projections, expectations, interaction, etc. [9]. In our avatar life-review sessions, the artist actively participated as a designer, storyteller, mediator, observer and audience; meanwhile, the users actively contributed to the shaping of the emergent experience and to the ongoing development of the system.

4   Thematic Observation: Avatar Life Review

The technical design of the avatar life-review system was important, but planning for its use by older adults in the residential setting was crucial, requiring a careful anthropological approach [10]. Ten older adult participants volunteered to participate in avatar life-review sessions at a senior living facility in Richmond, Virginia. We gathered qualitative data via interviews, observations, video, field notes, and surveys. The following themes were discovered based on these data:

1. Personal Immersion 2. Social Engagement 3. Technology 4. Improvisation and Mediator

4.1   Personal Immersion

We had planned to test the project in private rooms to promote exposition of subjects' personal stories. To our surprise, the elder home gave us access to their common theater space for avatar life-review sessions, which supported a different dynamic. In this theater setting, participants were public storytellers with an audience of staff, residents, participants, and team members. It was challenging for the participants to tell a personal story in this context; however, very interesting personal engagement emerged in the follow-up sessions.

When Mrs. C entered the theater, she began, "I am going to tell a sad story today." It was surprising since previous stories told by residents had been positive. I knew telling a sad story would be even harder in this unexpectedly public environment. Mrs. C told her story about her father, from when she was 6 years old. He had scolded her badly when she surprised him in jest. She acted out a wonderful dramatic performance identifying strongly with the avatar, using broad physical gestures and an animated tone of voice. She concluded with a single sentence, repeated in different voices:

Fig. 1. An avatar tells her childhood story with sad and angry emotions (© Semi Ryu. Photo: Brianna Ondris.)

"please help me to forgive him." The first seemed to belong to the avatar, speaking forthrightly, but the second was different—Mrs. C's voice, weeping and trembling. Her tears surprised us. She confessed she rarely cries. She spoke of her experience as "such a good release," and described a sense of "anonymity" of being able to disclose something, not as herself, but as the avatar. This sense of anonymity is related to distancing effects in drama therapy, where participants feel safe relating hidden emotions and stories. The system allowed her to talk to herself, rather than talking to another such as psychiatrist in a potentially judgmental situation (Fig. 1).

Mr. W., a 90-year-old gentleman with a husky voice, also built a strong emotional relationship with his avatar. He started his life-review using a boy avatar to tell his story from elementary school. In the middle of storytelling, he began looking for his teacher. I changed the avatar from a boy to a young woman, upon which he started making his conversation with the avatar as if she were his teacher. He pleaded, "why didn't you love me?" "come close to me," "hug me."

We paused, as we judged he was too immersed into the avatar. Then he stood up slowly with his walker, walked to the screen and tried to touch the avatar image. His own shadow in the projector light erased her image. It was a heartbreaking moment for the viewers.

Participants developed new modes of expression involving unique patterns of gesture and speech while engaged with the avatars. In part, the forms of these gestures were inflected by the theatrical environment; we look forward to further experiments in more personal settings to compare the variant dynamics.

4.2   Social Engagement

The avatar life-review was conducted in a common theater space building an interesting tension between private and public. The presence of an audience made personal engagement more challenging, but lengthy discussions followed each life-review creating a strong empathetic community. Cross cultural discussions emerged involving traditional Korean culture, different modes of communication, etc., as the artist became a part of this community. We celebrated similarity through empathy; difference through conversation (Fig. 2).

Although the system was designed around the avatar, participants were conscious of the audience's presence and responses. Each story was followed by applause. We shared joy, grief, anger, and many feelings about fathers, husbands, mothers-in-law, children, and other relations. The avatar system's sentiment analysis and enhancement algorithms amplified these empathetic relationships as the screen and sound responded to the emotional quality of the storytelling, reflecting the empathy of listeners.

We tried various setups to experiment with the relationship of audience, storyteller, and avatar: audience located before or behind the storyteller, central or diagonal screen placement, etc. In a central setting with the audience located behind, some participants felt uncomfortable; they felt it was poor manners to turn their backs on the audience, although the avatar was facing them. Some participants wanted to watch the audience's response during their storytelling, to be engaged with audience more than the avatar.

The aspect of communal ritual was evident after each life-review session. Often, the audience surrounded the storyteller and dynamically expressed their impression, empathy, encouragements, and similar experiences, using warm body language such as hugs and hand-holding. This occurred consistently and involved everyone, including observers, mediator, residents and staff members. This social engagement was also

Fig. 2. Residents watch a participant's avatar life-review performance (© Semi Ryu. Photo: Brianna Ondris.)

highlighted on the screening day when we showed all of the recorded avatar video in the same theater.

The participants enjoyed watching their own avatar performance as well as others'. Often, they were surprised by witnessing their own stories as avatar performances. The distanced setting brought a fresh perspective on stories they told via avatar; some were surprised by their own words. Participants wanted DVD discs of their avatar video to watch again with friends and family members.

4.3   Technology

The system was adjusted based on the residents' feedback. Avatar's faces were updated to more cheerful expressions on the request of residents. They wanted to engaged with happier looking avatars and probably happier aspects of their memories. The avatar originally had head motion tracking and lip-sync only. But we observed the significant role of hand gestures in older adult's speech. The residents also wanted full upper body interaction. The final prototype incorporated full upper body interaction with hand-gestures, lip-sync, and sentimental response.

The technical setup was challenging, due to the physical limitations of older adult users. The Microsoft Kinect sensor requires straight body registration. However, the participants were usually sitting in the chair in a reclined posture which made body registration difficult and unstable. We tried to make the system work optimally, but realized the participants' comfort is more important for natural storytelling process. Wearing headsets created a connection between artist and participant, and built a sense of trust. It was like placing a crown or ceremonial headwear on each participant to guide them to an alternate world (Fig. 3).

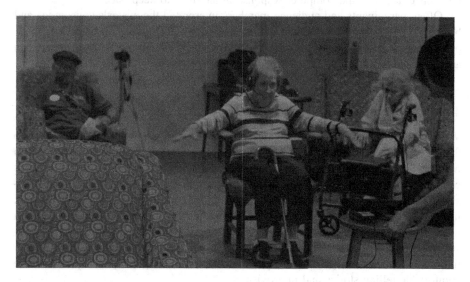

Fig. 3. A participant registering her body with the Kinect sensor (© Semi Ryu. Photo: Brianna Ondris.)

Some participants' jewelry conflicted with Kinect sensors due to reflections. But if jewelry was important to their identity, we couldn't ask them to remove it. We had anticipated a moderate number of technical conflicts but, as always, the particular challenges surprised us.

Technical limitations of the prototype system prompted unexpected negotiations with the technology by the older adult users. For example, one participant was speaking the words "in my heart," and trying to make her avatar touch her heart. Since finger detection had not been implemented yet, it was a challenging motion for the avatar—not quite detecting her hand on her chest. Suddenly, she stood up and repeated the phrase "in my heart," trying to elicit an appropriate response from the avatar. She also tried to create a hole with her fingers, but when the avatar's fingers did not follow, she spun her hands together, to express the notion of "hole." New gestural language emerged to suit what the technology can support. The older adult users continually challenged the system, discovering ways to express their emotions despite its limits.

We didn't expect older adults to be so kinetically animated in their storytelling. As noted above, their hands served as another speech organ, but with the avatar system, the entire upper body was engaged. I felt a strange sense of guilt when the avatar couldn't fully support the user's emotional expressions. They wanted to express emotions through gestures such as kissing, hugging, or touching the heart. There was something beautiful about their wishes, struggles, and humor in relationship with the avatar.

The sentiment analysis system can detect emotions in the user's speech. Background images and sounds were modified based on detection of 6 emotions, to support an empathetic connection between storyteller and audience. These changes were managed by both automatic and manual means, creating a semi-automatic solution. Emotions in their stories were complex and changed rapidly. The artist/mediator often intervened ahead of the computer response in an effort to keep pace.

Often, participants and audience members interpreted the avatar's appearance and behavior differently, even when it was unchanged. They seemed to base their interpretations on who is telling the story, and how she/he interacted with it, rather than according to an impartial, abstract analysis of its gestures.

4.4   Improvisation and Mediator

We demonstrated hand puppetry as a familiar analogy, to explain avatar interaction to the older adult participants. This 21st century puppet can be used to discover hidden memory and feelings through improvisational storytelling. However, most participants came with a prepared story. They seemed to have practiced the story before the sessions. But eventually they began to improvise, and volunteered to participate again, inspired by others' stories. We offered a weekly topic to help them to prepare, but often residents prepared stories they wanted to tell, regardless of topic. Participants usually said their story would be very short, but often turned out longer than anticipated. Over time, the line between private and public was blurred as participants became more comfortable telling stories and improvising.

For the artist, actively participating as a mediator, designer, audience, and story-teller, the avatar life-review was an amazing sharing experience. For over ten years, she has explored virtual puppetry inspired by Korean shamanic ritual. She has explored cultural factors in the emotional psyche—in particular the Korean notion of Han—in paradoxical relationships between virtual puppet and puppeteer [11]. She has recently begun to apply these to the study of, and therapeutic interventions in, the aging psyche of the senior population.

This cultural background is uniquely connected with the therapeutic potential of avatar life-review. Korean culture differs from Western culture in many aspects. As a society with a strong Confucian heritage, we value our elders highly and seek them out for guidance and connection. Direct eye contact is regarded as a challenge towards one's elders; averting one's eyes is more respectful. Life-review sessions became an opportunity to mediate these cultural differences. The residents were fascinated by Korean culture—food, clothing, traditional costumes, Confucianism—often leading to cross-cultural discussions after life-review sessions.

5   Gerotranscendence and Future Direction

Life expectancy in Western industrialized nations continues to rise. Today's retirees are likely to live another twenty-five healthy years or more. We must prepare for this emerging reality by adapting the culture to better integrate older adults into their communities [12].

Our work on the avatar life-review system was premised on the notion of gero-transcendence—a developmental stage that occurs when an individual who is living into very old age shifts perspective "from a materialistic and rational view of the world to a more cosmic and transcendent one, normally accompanied by an increase in life satisfaction" [13]. Older adults' storytelling performances, filled with emotion, positive energy, and humor, provide excellent material for younger generations to listen and learn from those perspectives—for their own sake as emerging adults who will have to negotiate that same difficult balance of matter and spirit and for the sake of communal integration with elders.

The first prototype of the avatar life-review system focused on the basic structure and has not yet been tried with a variety of experimental techniques. We see broad potential for evolution to enhance future users' experience. We value the opportunity this study afforded us to realize the importance of emotional expression in our stories. Even the systemic breakdowns brought about unforeseen returns: we realized how important it is to touch our own hearts, to hug and kiss our beloved others, real and virtual.

Further studies on avatar life-review will explore diverse challenges: early memory loss in older adult population, PTSD patients, and diversity in society, to increase awareness of, and adaptation to, racial, cultural, and gender difference through person-centered care and anthropological research.

Acknowledgments. This research was supported by VCU Arts and the VCU Presidential Research Quest Fund. I thank Dr. John Priestley for assistance with copy editing this paper.

I would also like to show my gratitude to Dr. Stefano Faralli and CoPuppet team members who have worked hard on the *VoicingElder* project.

References

1. Deleuze, G.: A Thousand Plateaus: Capitalism and Schizophrenia, pp. 96–100. Bloomsbury Publishing, London (1987). Print. https://doi.org/10.2307/203963
2. Merleau-Ponty, M.: Phenomenology of Perception, pp. 103–105. Routledge Classics, London (1945). https://doi.org/10.4324/9780203936108
3. Merleau-Ponty, M.: Phenomenology of Perception, pp. 88–90. Routledge Classics, London (1945). https://doi.org/10.4324/9780203936108
4. Capra, F.: The Tao of Physics. Shambhala Publications, Boulder (1975). https://doi.org/10.1017/s003693060002651x
5. Rogers, C.: Client-Centered Therapy: Its Current Practice, Implications and Theory. Constable, London (1951). https://doi.org/10.1037/h0053095
6. Dourish, P.: Where the Action Is: The Foundations of Embodied Interaction, p. 548. MIT Press, Cambridge (2001). https://doi.org/10.1162/leon.2003.36.5.412
7. Grudin, J.: Interface. ACM **36**(4), pp. 112–119 (1993). https://doi.org/10.7146/dpb.v19i319.6709
8. McCarthy, J., Wright, P.: Technology as Experience. The MIT Press, Cambridge (2004). https://doi.org/10.1145/1015530.1015549
9. Pink, S., Ardevol, E., Lanzeni, D.: Digital Materialities: Design and Anthropology, pp. 121–124. Bloomsbury Academic, London (2016). https://doi.org/10.5040/9781474295789.ch-001
10. Dourish, P.: Where the Action Is: The Foundations of Embodied Interaction, p. 96. MIT Press, Cambridge (2001). https://doi.org/10.1162/leon.2003.36.5.412
11. Ryu, S.: Sensing without Sensing. In: Kerckhove, D., Almeida, C. (eds.) The Point of Being, pp. 175–178. Cambridge Scholars, Bristol (2014)
12. Bianchi, E.: Living with elder wisdom. J. Gerontol. Soc. Work 45 (2005). The Haworth Press. https://doi.org/10.1300/j083v45n03_06
13. Tornstam, L.: Gerotranscendence: A Developmental Theory of Positive Aging. Springer Publishing Company, Berlin (2005). https://doi.org/10.1017/s0144686x06225261

HCI Research and History: Special Interests Groups on Facebook as Historical Sources

Mechtild Stock$^{(\boxtimes)}$

Kerpen, Germany
MechtildStock@gmail.com

Abstract. In this article, we discuss whether Social Network Services (SNSs), especially Facebook, are sources for microhistory or history from below. It can be shown that SNSs indeed form a valuable source for historical science. However, due to the huge amount of data in SNSs there is a problem not to be overwhelmed with unmanageable large data sets. Our proposal to structure the data sets is to apply informetrics and statistical methods as means of quantitative history. We work with a case study, i.e. *Kerpener und Ex-Kerpener*. This special interest group on Facebook addresses Kerpen (a small town in Germany) as well as its historical development. We are going to analyze about 2,000 wall posts of the group during 2014. For each post, we investigate its type (text, image, and video), category, topic, number of likes, shares and comments as well as the author's name. The article concludes with a list of decision criteria for historically relevant and credible Facebook wall posts as sources.

Keywords: HCI research · Microhistory · History from below · Facebook · Information science · Facebook metrics

1 Introduction: Facebook and History from Below

Human-computer interaction on social media is sometimes directed to local or regional cultural information. Prime examples for such interactions are microblogs on Twitter [3] or special interest communities on social networking services (SNSs) as Facebook which are related to contemporary and past local history [7]. In this article, we discuss whether SNSs are sources for history, especially for microhistory [2, 5]. "Microhistory" [1] or "history from below" [9] is history from the perspective of common people. Lay historians and average people act as citizen scholars. SNSs, with their well-documented dialog and content, appear to be excellent sources for constructing an account of history from below. It can be shown that SNSs with their processes of dialogs of "common" people indeed form a valuable source for historical science [8]. Here, historians and archivists are able to locate additional information, which cannot be found through any other sources. Due to the huge amount of data in SNSs, the greatest problem is being overwhelmed with very large datasets [6]. One aim of our study is to divide the amounts of posts and comments into two groups, namely, historically relevant items and less relevant or not credible items (Fig. 1).

We worked with a case study, namely *Kerpener und Ex-Kerpener*. This German Facebook group addresses Kerpen as well as its historical development. We analyzed

© Springer International Publishing AG 2017
C. Stephanidis (Ed.): HCII Posters 2017, Part I, CCIS 713, pp. 497–503, 2017.
DOI: 10.1007/978-3-319-58750-9_69

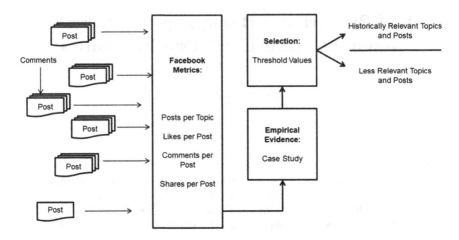

Fig. 1. Research model.

all wall posts of this special interest group during 2014. The article will have practical implications for cultural heritage institutions, e.g. archives [4]. This combination of HCI research, information science and history succeeded as a research approach that can be expanded to include other SNS groups which postings and observations may help produce a fuller historical record of both our time and place.

Facebook is an SNS, an important and popular kind of social media. On Facebook, people are able to create huge amounts of data. A crucial aspect is the credibility of the data. "This kind of system provides first-hand data, but one pressing problem is to distinguish true information from misinformation and rumors. In many cases, social media data is user generated and can be biased, inaccurate, and subjective" [6, p. 113]. Therefore, we need methods to separate historically relevant information from misinformation and rubbish.

To manipulate such "big data" in information services as Facebook, we apply quantitative methods borrowed from information science, more precisely from informetrics. Informetrics originates in scientific communication. It measures the dialog in science in terms of publications and citations. In SNSs, there is dialog as well. The wall posts act as articles; the likes, comments and shares are analogues to citations.

2   Methods

Our case study for history from below is the special interest group *Kerpener und Ex-Kerpener*. This Facebook group addresses Kerpen as well as its historical development. Kerpen is a town of 65,000 inhabitants (2012) located in the German Rhineland. The aim of this moderated group is to preserve historical images and videos and to make them accessible. The group *Kerpener und Ex-Kerpener* was founded in 2012 and was able to attract 5,455 members (by the end of 2014).

At the appointed date of January 19, 2015, we downloaded all wall posts of the group *Kerpener und Ex-Kerpener* from 2014 to an offline HTML file (about 42 MB).

We only gathered the visible comments in our offline file. We ignored all those posts lacking in content (e.g. posts without any text, image or video). Our file consists of 1,951 wall posts in total. In consequence of the huge amount of comments (26,319) we decided not to evaluate their content. We constructed a database with the following field scheme: date (month, day), day of the week, author, type of post (text, image, video, text and image, text and video – intellectually coded), shared post (post from external source), number of likes, number of shares, number of comments, kind of image and video (current image, old image, current placard, current video, old video – intellectually coded), content category (intellectually coded), content description (keywords – intellectually coded). First of all, we roughly screened the posts in order to summarize and to determine content categories. Nine categories are the result of our analysis: caution (warnings), curiosity ("what is happening there?"), current impression ("current" means only some months old), news, notice (announcements, tips), old impression, private (all posts of private nature, including recommendations and requests for help), report/criticism (complaints, experiences), request (questions of general interests).

3   Results

In 2014, 1,951 posts in *Kerpener und Ex-Kerpener* have been written by 582 different members; hence the share of active members is 10.67%. Only a small segment of members is really active in writing wall posts. The majority of members obviously does not trigger discussions, yet some people response to wall posts by liking, sharing and commenting. Others, indeed, are only "lurkers" and pure consumers. A wall post in the year 2014 has on average 13.17 likes, 0.85 shares and 13.49 comments (Table 1). Who are the active members, regularly contributing posts? We sorted the entire set of posts by authors. We can identify an extremely left-skewed distribution. This means that there are only few highly productive authors and a long tail of authors contributing two posts or one per year. 24 authors produce 50% of all posts. The most productive author alone is responsible for 15.27% of all posts.

We have ranked our wall posts according to numbers of likes, shares and comments. The rankings of posts by likes and shares are – similar to the authors' distribution – left-skewed distributions. Only few wall posts get many likes and shares. In most cases, the group members like current and old impressions. The top-liked post is an image of a wrong place-name sign at the new motorway A4 (Berg*dorf* instead of Berg*heim*) (Table 2). The interest in Michael Schumacher (a famous former Formula 1 driver) is understandable, since Michael once was a citizen of Kerpen. A moderate highly liked wall post is an impression of winter in Kerpen.

How does the distribution of shares look like (Table 3)? Most of the top wall posts by number of shares are private requests and requests for help; the others are warning notices. One post occupies a high position in the ranking. 722 members share the wall post searching for a hit-and-run driver. Two posts cover the issue of burglary and ask for attention. Six further posts are devoted to dogs and cats, e.g. dog found, dog poisoned, cat disappeared, and – most horrible – cat halved). We summarize that shares are used for current events. The more shares the more historically irrelevant the wall

Table 1. Kerpener *und Ex-Kerpener*: Basic figures (2014) (N = 1,951)

Basic figures	Kerpener und Ex-Kerpener
Number of posts	1,951
Number of members	5,455
Number of unique post authors	582
Share of active members	10.67%
Number of top post authors	24
Number of likes	25,686
Likes per post (average)	13.17
Number of shares	1,658
Shares per post (average)	0.85
Number of comments	26,319
Comments per post (average)	13.49
Number of images and videos	1,236
— Number of current images	*679*
— Number of old images	*427*
— Number of current placards	*111*
— Number of videos	*19*

Table 2. Top posts by number of likes (N = 1,951)

Rank	Likes	Kind of post	Description
1	640	Current impression	Wrong place-name sign (Berg*dorf* instead of Berg*heim*)
2	338	News	Michael Schumacher awake
3	275	Old impression	Winter in Kerpen (2010)

Table 3. Top posts by number of shares (N = 1,951)

Rank	Shares	Kind of post	Description
1	722	Request for help/private	Wanted: hit-and-run driver
2	175	Caution	Burglary/tramp's sign
3	161	Request for help/private	Found dog

posts seem to be. But there are exceptions: The posts about burglary are not necessarily historically irrelevant, however.

Shares and likes do not need much cognitive effort; they are just one click, a touch of a button. Contrariwise, to produce a comment (maybe including images and videos besides pure texts) requires elaborate cognitive work. The top posts by number of comments include requests, notices, news, current impressions and warnings (the mentioned post about burglary) (Table 4). A hot topic in Kerpen is an empty apartment tower which has been set on fire several times. Questions of general interest (e.g., What do you associate with Kerpen?) trigger high numbers of comments. The often commented post about the kiosk around the corner describes a shop with an upholstered

Table 4. Top posts by number of comments (N = 1,951)

Rank	Comments	Kind of post	Description
1	359	Notice	Fire: Apartment tower Maastrichterstraße
2	353	Request	What do you associate with Kerpen?
3	299	Current impression	Kiosk around the corner

sofa on the sidewalk in front of the house. Within the top commented posts you can identify historically relevant posts (such as the problematic apartment tower) as well as gossip and tittle-tattle (e.g. the kiosk around the corner).

Our results clearly exhibit highly significant differences between multimedia and text-only posts in terms of the average numbers of likes and comments, but no statistically noticeable difference with regard to the average number of shares. Multimedia posts received on average 17.77 likes per item in contrast to only 4.73 likes per textual post. This is nearly four times the amount in favor of multimedia posts. In contrast, text-only posts gain 19.13 comments on average, while multimedia posts only get 10.41 comments on average. This is just about twice as much, but now in favor of textual posts. Obviously, multimedia posts often provoke many likes (meaning "This image pleases me," and therewith everything has been said) and only few comments. Text-only posts lead to the opposite user behavior. Such posts are moderately high liked, but provoke a lot of comments.

Outstanding categories by the average number of likes are old und current impressions. Both categories receive more than 23 likes per post. Obviously, people do like old as well as new images of their hometown. In contrast to the high number of likes, both impressions' categories only get moderately high numbers of comments (about 11 and 12 comments per post) and actually no shares. Only very few likes per post go to the categories private and request, but both categories include large numbers of comments (private 15 and request 28 comments per post). Private posts and requests of general interests call for answers (comments) and not for likes. There is just one category getting lots of shares: caution. Wall posts in this category are devoted to current burglaries and to warnings concerning dangerous situations for cats and dogs. Here, fast information dissemination is important, which can be reached by immediate sharing of the caution-posts. Additionally, these posts have high numbers of comments (29 on average) and moderately numbers of likes (8 on average). All other categories contain only small numbers of shares or no shares at all.

Top topics are defined by the absolute number of wall posts, sorted by keywords. We identified three topics as "Top Topics." Do these posts provide historically relevant information in addition to news reported in local newspapers? The top topics show moderately high numbers of likes and comments as well as nearly no shares. 30 wall posts are on the topic thunderstorm. In the local press (*Kölner Stadtanzeiger*; June 10, 2014), we only find one article. In the wall posts, people report on subjective feelings, concrete impressions of vested interest, and offers of help. 25 wall posts are devoted to the topic Maastricht Street. This subject is frequently reported in the local press, too. The *Kölner Stadtanzeiger* covers, among others, arson attacks on the unoccupied building (June 2, 2014), actions by the city administration of Kerpen (June 6, 2014), and security problems of the residents (June 26, 2014). In contrast, the wall posts concentrate on offense, on personal experience and hints to handle the problem. One wall post on the topic Highway A4 reports the wrong place-name sign Bergdorf instead of Bergheim (our top-liked post). This post was even the source of an article in *Kölner Stadtanzeiger* (September 16, 2014).

4 Discussion

Decision criteria for historically relevant and credible Facebook posts as sources are:

- high number of posts per topic in a given time interval (e.g., a year) (but one has to know which topics are relevant – our approach was to index all posts through categories and keywords),
- there is a high probability of historical relevance for the categories old impression, current impression and news; additionally perhaps selected posts from the notice and report/criticism categories,
- historically relevant multimedia posts (images, videos) have a moderate high number of comments and a high number of likes,
- some wall posts of historical relevance exhibit a high number of comments,
- high numbers of shares seem to be indicators for rapid requests and warnings which are seldom historically relevant.

To sum up: Facebook is an important source which complements other historical sources. On Facebook you can find information you will hardly find elsewhere: first-hand impressions, images and comments of "common people." Since we only worked with one case study, it is necessary for further scientific investigations to analyze other Facebook groups which are interested in historical aspects of their environment. Additionally, the application of Facebook metrics should be broadened and calibrated. All in all, the new combination of HCI research, information science and historical science proved to be successful and is expandable.

References

1. Brewer, J.: Microhistory and the histories of everyday life. Cultural Soc. Hist.: J. Soc. Hist. Soc. **7**(1), 87–109 (2010)
2. Davalos, S., Merchant, A., Rose, G.M., Lessley, B.J., Teredesai, A.M.: 'The good old days': an examination of nostalgia in Facebook posts. Int. J. Hum. Comput. Stud. **83**, 83–93 (2015)
3. Malone, M.: Tweeting history. An inquiry into aspects of social media in the Egyptian revolution. In: Hall, B.L., Clovers, D.E., Crowther, J., Scandrett, E. (eds.) Learning and Education for a Better World, pp. 169–182. Sense, Rotterdam (2012)
4. McCown, F., Nelson, M.L.: What happens when Facebook is gone? In: Proceedings of the 9th ACM/IEEE-CS Joint Conference on Digital Libraries, pp. 251–254. ACM, New York (2009)

5. Nack, F.: Social media in history. In: Proceedings of the 2012 International Workshop on Socially-aware Multimedia, pp. 51–56. ACM, New York (2012)
6. Pinheiro, A., Cappelli, C., Maciel, C.: Providing tools to enable information audit in social networks. In: Stephanidis, C. (ed.) HCI 2015. CCIS, vol. 529, pp. 113–117. Springer, Cham (2015). doi:10.1007/978-3-319-21383-5_19
7. Silberman, N., Purser, M.: Collective memory as affirmation: people-centered cultural heritage in a digital age. In: Giaccardi, E. (ed.) Heritage and Social Media Understanding. Heritage in a Participatory Culture, pp. 13–29. Routledge, London (2012)
8. Stock, M.: Facebook: a source for microhistory? In: Knautz, K., Baran, K.S. (eds.) Facets of Facebook. Use and Users, pp. 210–240. De Gruyter Saur, Berlin (2016)
9. Thompson, E.P.: History from below. Times Literary Suppl. 7, 279–280 (1966)

Beyond Retail Therapy: Can the Relationship Between Affective Data & Consumer Behavior Be Utilized to Develop User-Directed E-Commerce Personalization?

Isabel Wellbery, Franziska Susanne Roth, and Thomas Fortmann[✉]

Zalando SE, Tamara-Danz- Straße 1, 10243 Berlin, Germany
iwellbery@gmail.com, thomas.fortmann@Zalando.de

Abstract. We present a first *in situ* attempt to explicate the relationship between consumer behavior and affective state. We adapt Bradley and Lang (1994)'s Self-Assessment Manikin as a feature on our e-commerce platform, tracking how self-reported affective state maps onto specific behavioral patterns. We discuss the potential for utilizing affective feedback as a means of user-directed personalization.

Keywords: E-commerce · Emotion · Consumer behavior

1 Introduction

Decades of academic research in the fields of psychology, behavioral economics, and philosophy have struggled to understand the often disruptive role that emotions play in our decision-making [1]. While classical philosophers such as Plato and Spinoza had already insisted that emotion is an obstacle to rational thought, more recent empirical work in psychology has demonstrated that even in the presence of persuasive factual information affect plays a key role in determining many of our choices (for a review, see Loewenstein [2]). The prioritization of affective information over strictly 'factual' counterarguments has been found to persist even when participants were instructed in models of rational choice or explicitly told to focus on statistical information to guide their decisions [3, 4]. As this literature makes evident, any comprehensive theory of (economic) decision-making must make an attempt to pin down the complex role of emotion. For example, several studies demonstrate that affective states easily transfer from one situation to the next (work frustration sublimating into not tipping a cab driver; see e.g., Excitation Transfer Theory, Zillmann [5]), altering participant risk-assessments, risk aversion, and resource allocation [6–8]). Experimental laboratory studies have also begun to untangle the relationship between affective state and economic decision-making. Priming subjects with a negative affect (e.g. disgust), for example, Samuelson and Zeckhauser [9] and later Eich et al. [10] found an increase in status quo bias, delaying decision-making altogether. In an experimental e-commerce in a laboratory setting, Park et al. [11] found that participants who were primed with a positive affect were more risk-prone and demonstrated greater purchase intent overall.

© Springer International Publishing AG 2017
C. Stephanidis (Ed.): HCII Posters 2017, Part I, CCIS 713, pp. 504–508, 2017.
DOI: 10.1007/978-3-319-58750-9_70

Despite the wealth of interdisciplinary literature on the relationship between affect and economic decision-making, few attempts have been made to explore these dynamics outside the laboratory and in the context of new internet-based mediums. To date, we are aware of no research that examines e-commerce retail behavior patterns and their relationship to a user's affect in situ. The goal of the here presented research therefore is two-fold: On the one hand, we represent an effort to fill the gap of field studies in this domain by attempting to explicate the relationship between self-reported affective states and consumer behavioral patterns on our e-commerce retail platform. On the other hand, we discuss how these insights can be utilized to develop a framework for a user-driven, dynamic approach to deepen user experience personalization. In doing so, we flip the traditional conception of the relationship between emotion and consumer behavior from a proactive model, inferring consumer feelings based on actions, to a reactive model, receiving consumer feedback on their affective state to generate moment-by-moment personalization.

1.1 Methodology

Developing a methodology for our research on an e-commerce platform faced a dual challenge: First, we needed to instrumentalize a measure of user affect that would offer sufficient psychometric validity for our purposes. Second, our measure needed to seamlessly integrate into our platform in terms of design while being intuitive in terms of usability. As a business, the stakes for us are high when integrating any new feature, and these high usability standards informed our methodology from the start.

Our affect-feature was derived from "the Affective Slider" by Betella and Verschure [12], a digital slider feature adaptation of the well-established psychometric measurement "the Self-Assessment Manikin (SAM)" by Bradley and Lang [13]. We decided to utilize this measure due to its decades of established validity and replicability [12] in social science research. Building a psychometric measure directly into the shopping platform, we argue, will allow for a less disruptive shopping experience than an external questionnaire (e.g. a pop-up or follow-up survey), thereby yielding more representative data.

While we based our basic design elements on Betella and Verschure (2016)'s slider [12], we also incorporated descriptive words from the semantic differential by Bradley and Lang [13] to make salient the purpose of the feature to users who may be surprised to encounter such a feature in e-commerce. Our feature measured two affective scales: (1) mood (scale ranging from unhappy to happy, with two emojis at the endpoints of the scale; see Fig. 1); (2) arousal (scale ranging from calm to excited, with two smileys at the endpoints of the scale, see Fig. 1). Users were able to indicate their mood by using the slider on the scale. A UI designer also ensured that the feature fit organically into our platform in terms of design (e.g. font, color) without disrupting the psychometric measurement's validity.

Fig. 1. A screenshotted image of our affect slider adapted from Betella and Verschure (2016).

1.2   Qualitative User Test

Before introducing our feature directly onto the platform, we conducted a qualitative user test (N = 4, 2 females) at our on-site laboratory. We conducted this initial user test, on the one hand, to establish how users would react to an affect feature on the platform (i.e., their willingness to disclose affective information, their intuitions about purpose, etc.) and to identify any usability problems with the feature (e.g., misunderstanding where to click), on the other. Using semi-structured interviews, a researcher guided each participant through our app and the feature, continuously asking them to articulate their expectations, intuitions, feedback, and likes and dislikes. After using the feature (which appeared immediately upon accessing the mobile app), each participant took some time freely to browse the shopping app in general. Each interview was observed via livestream in a second laboratory by the other researchers. Participant interviews lasted approximately 30–45 min, and were followed up by a 20-minute wrap-up session by a group of researchers. After all 4 users had been interviewed, researchers conducted a general revision, coding patterns of feedback among all participants.

1.3   Results and Discussion

Going into the user test, we had unclear expectations of user reactions to our affect feature, in particular we had worried that users might feel skeptical about providing feedback on their emotions with an e-commerce platform. Within the context of our small sample, this concern however was quickly dispelled as all users approached the new feature, to be sure, with some confusion, but also with an overwhelming sense of curiosity. In addition, none of our test persons expressed any worries about privacy issues even after being asked explicitly whether this could be an issue. Participants also held strong assumptions as to what the feature ought to do – most commonly suggesting that their affective feedback would trigger a change in terms of color and clothing item suggestions. Participants expressed some frustration, however, when there were no immediate, visible changes to the app based on their feedback.

Our second concern had been related to the design of the feature and its integration within the app. We encountered several issues in the area of usability. More specifically, the sliding functionality of the feature (and thereby the ways to express nuance in their affective states) was not immediately obvious to all participants. Several participants attempted to click directly on the emojis (scale endpoints).

The conclusions drawn from this initial qualitative test, both in terms user expectation management and design, will be invaluable for improving our methodology for our upcoming quantitative A/B test. Even with the limitations of a small sample size and the confines of a laboratory setting we were able to derive initial insights into how an affect feature could be integrated into our platform and improve shopping personalization.

2 Next Steps

At this stage in our research, we are developing our affect feature to go live on our e-commerce mobile application with an improved design. By tracking user's feedback on the app and their subsequent behavior on the platform (e.g. conversions, interests, inspiration susceptibility, etc.), we intend to establish behavioral patterns based on affective state. While our approach to the A/B test is exploratory at this stage, our expectations are informed by the rich literature on economic decision-making and affect. Following, Park et al. [11], we expect to replicate *in situ* that participants who indicate a positive affective state on our feature will demonstrate greater purchase intent than participants who indicate a negative affect. Our aim in detecting patterns of affect and behavior, however, is not purely scientific: We will discuss how this data may be utilized to improve user experience, for example, by allowing users more easily to find items that 'match' their mood on our platform. In the age of increasingly sophisticated algorithms inferring user affinities, we seek to make the case that meaningful personalization can benefit from a close alignment with academic literature on decision making generally and well-established psychometric approaches specifically.

Acknowledgments. We would like to thank all participants, Zalando SE, and the UX Research department for making this research possible. Special thanks go to Riccardo Buzzotta.

References

1. Greco, M., Stenner, P.: Emotions: A Social Science Reader. Routledge, London (2008)
2. Loewenstein, G.: Out of control: visceral influences on behavior. Organ. Behav. Hum. Decis. Process. **65**, 272–292 (1996)

3. Desteno, D., Li, Y., Dickens, L., Lerner, J.S.: Gratitude. Psychol. Sci. **25**, 1262–1267 (2014)
4. Lerner, J.S., Keltner, D.: Fear, anger, and risk. J. Pers. Soc. Psychol. **81**, 146–159 (2001)
5. Zillmann, D.: Excitation transfer in communication-mediated aggressive behavior. J. Exp. Soc. Psychol. **7**, 419–434 (1971)
6. Frijda, N.H.: Facial expression processing. In: Aspects of Face Processing, pp. 319–325 (1986)
7. Han, S., Lerner, J.S., Keltner, D.: Feelings and consumer decision making: the appraisal-tendency framework. J. Consum. Psychol. **17**, 158–168 (2007)
8. Ariely, D., Loewenstein, G.: The heat of the moment: the effect of sexual arousal on sexual decision making. J. Behav. Decis. Making **19**, 87–98 (2006)
9. Samuelson, W., Zeckhauser, R.: Status quo bias in decision making. J. Risk Uncertainty **1**, 7–59 (1988)
10. Eich, E., Forgas, J.P.: Mood, cognition, and memory. Handb. Psychol. (2003). doi:10.1002/0471264385.wei0403
11. Park, J., Lennon, S.J., Stoel, L.: On-line product presentation: effects on mood, perceived risk, and purchase intention. Psychol. Market. **22**, 695–719 (2005)
12. Betella, A., Verschure, P.F.M.J.: The affective slider: a digital self-assessment scale for the measurement of human emotions. PLoS ONE (2016). doi:10.1371/journal.pone.0148037
13. Bradley, M.M., Lang, P.J.: Measuring emotion: the self-assessment manikin and the semantic differential. J. Behav. Ther. Exp. Psychiatry **25**, 49–59 (1994)

Ergonomics and Models in Work and Training Support

Intuitive Real-Time Multidimensional Diagnostic Ultrasound Image Optimization Technology

Giampaolo Borreani[1], Carlo Biagini[2], Roberto Pesce[1],
Luca Bombino[1], and Leonardo Forzoni[1(✉)]

[1] Esaote S.p.A., Genoa, Italy
leonardo.forzoni@esaote.com
[2] Centro Diagnostico Pubblica Assistenza Signa, Florence, Italy

Abstract. Diagnostic Ultrasound (US) is an operator and patient dependent examination where anatomical and hemodynamic analysis settings have to be adjusted in real-time while scanning.

Several techniques were developed so far to perform the US acquisition and post processing adjustments quickly and to maximize their easiness.

A new Easy Adjustment Technology (E.A.T.) was recently prototyped in order to drastically simplify the operator system set up to only three macro-parameters related to the desired effect in terms of: contrast/smoothness, detail/speed, resolution/penetration.

A multidimensional algorithm varies simultaneously several internal system parameters to modify the image in the direction of the macro-parameter varied by the user. No prior knowledge of US physics or technology is required to adjust the macro-parameter, the effects of which are directly visible on the echo image in real-time (for instance, to optimize the level of smoothness with respect to US image contrast).

The aim of the E.A.T. is to increase productivity, reduce sonographer's work-related musculoskeletal disorders due to extensive use of the US system control panel and to increase diagnostic confidence based on the intuitive optimization of the sonographer's desired effect, instead of an engineering approach to real-time scanning optimization.

Keywords: Diagnostic Ultrasound · Image optimization · Easy Adjustment Technology · easyMode

1 Introduction

Diagnostic Ultrasound (US) is an operator and patient dependent examination where anatomical and hemodynamic analysis settings have to be adjusted in real-time while scanning (Fig. 1).

More and more US investigations are performed per day worldwide, with productivity being one of the main key drivers for users [1].

US systems are used for many clinical applications (Adult Cardiology, Pediatric Cardiology, Neonatology, Vascular, Adult Cephalic, Ophthalmic, Abdomen, Small

© Springer International Publishing AG 2017
C. Stephanidis (Ed.): HCII Posters 2017, Part I, CCIS 713, pp. 511–518, 2017.
DOI: 10.1007/978-3-319-58750-9_71

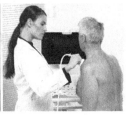

Fig. 1. Examples of US scanning in different clinical applications – Obstetrics (left); Cardiology (center); Musculoskeletal (right).

Parts, Thyroid, Urology, Musculoskeletal, Obstetrics, Gynecology, Breast, Lung ultrasound, Intraoperative, Neurosurgery, Fusion Imaging for traditional and non-traditional applications for both diagnostic and interventional purposes, Interventional Radiology, Critical Care, Emergency).

Furthermore, the patient population can be represented by Fetal, Neonatal, Pediatrics, Adult, while the user profile, intended to cover the full range from novices to expert users, is populated by Sonographers, Medical Doctors, Radiologists, Surgeons, Veterinary practitioners, Midwives, Paramedics. Due to their wide diffusion, US systems are used also by non-sonographers; therefore, a higher level of usability has been urgently requested in recent years.

These new paths in the use of US have completely changed the customers' approach to US technologies and devices, as well as the market perception of such diagnostic technology, which is the only one, in the field of complex diagnostic imaging, characterized by a real-time nature [2].

The UI ergonomics and workflow of the US systems is nowadays of primary importance due to the increased use of US systems in the everyday clinical practice even by "non-sonographers", as well as the increased attention to the problem of Work-related Musculoskeletal Disorders (WRMSD) for sonographers [3–6].

2   Methods

Several techniques were developed so far to perform the US acquisition and post processing adjustments quickly and to maximize their ease of use. Just to highlight the most important:

- Preset - Pre-defined image setting depending on the chosen body district;
- Auto Gain – Automatic Gain reset to a pre-defined level (which usually varies per application);
- Automatic Adjustment - Real time parameter adjustment to a pre-defined target type of image;
- Continuous Automatic Adjustment – Continuous real time parameter adjustment, which varies depending on the acquired echo image characteristics.

An easy adjustment technology was recently prototyped with the goal to simplify the operator system set up. Easy Adjustment Technology (E.A.T.) offers a real time parameter modification, which takes into account the final effect the operator wants to obtain on the image (resolution/penetration; frame rate/details; smoothing/contrast), instead of being based on the adjustment of the technical parameters of the US system (direct changes on Dynamic Range, Gray Map, Scanning Lines, Spatial Compound, etc....).

a. *Presets*

Most US systems have preset modes that provide better imaging better imaging of specific organs of the body [7].

Preset (to set the acquisition parameters to pre-defined values) is the basic technique to group and speed up the optimization of acquisition parameters.

The Preset activation and selection control is one of the most important ones in an US system. Selecting the right preset for the particular region of the body under examination makes scanning much easier. Built-in Software assists not only with dedicated labelling and measurements, but it enables better images and clips to be acquired. Moreover, also the physical parameters are optimized for the desired application [8].

The correct scanning preset has a large impact on the quality of the image. The US system optimizes the image for each particular scan type, for example abdominal preset vs. pelvic or gynecological preset. Any US study has to begin by selecting the correct probe and appropriate preset for the type of exam being performed [9].

In any case as ultrasound machines have developed, the amount of practitioner input required to achieve an acceptable image has diminished, possibly resulting in an increased reliance on presets and the ultrasound machine's optimization button. Whilst under average conditions presets provide an appropriate starting point, the practitioner is still expected to utilize the full range of ultrasound machine functions to make adjustments and manually optimize the image [10].

Additional manual adjustments may be necessary in most of the cases, which forces the operator to know and apply in real time changes related to physical and technical principles of US technology.

b. *Auto Gain*

Changing the Gain is analogous to amplifying or suppressing the volume of signal in an image. By adjusting the gain up and down, you may find it easier to visualize certain structures. Most of the US machines are equipped with an Auto Gain, which is the machine's interpretation of the optimal level of gain for the body part or structure being scanned. When first starting out with scanning, the use of Auto Gain is likely going to be a useful tool [11].

As the US beam travels deeper into the patient body, the returning echoes are attenuated, resulting in less resolution. A feature known as Time Gain Compensation (TGC) allows the sonographer to adjust the image brightness at specific depths. The top row of sliders controls near field gain, whereas the bottom row of buttons controls far field gain (Fig. 2). Most of the US systems have an Auto Gain control, which resets the machine back to standard gain presets for the type of scan (Preset selected) being performed [12].

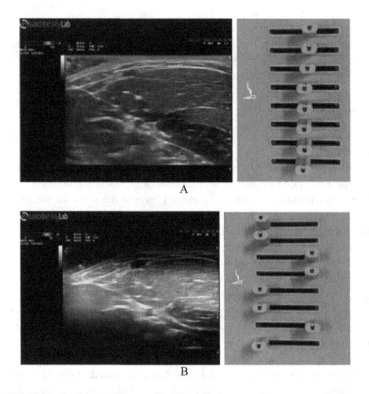

Fig. 2. TGC sliders position effect on the US echo image – homogenous TGC setting (A); inhomogeneous TGC of the near and distant fields (dark) with respect to the middle field (saturation).

c. Automatic Adjustment

Organ specific imaging (or tissue specific imaging) is an approach applying automatic adjustment of the scanner commands (gain, image optimization algorithms, TGC, etc....) depending on the organ that the operator has selected for viewing (through dedicated Preset selection). This results in shortening the investigation time and also in some degree of standardization of images [13].

Automatic adjustment has been introduced relatively recently in order to automatically optimize the echo image to a defined histogram obtained by the analysis of expected similar acquisitions.

This technology, even if recently improved, cannot consider specific patient and/or examination dependent characteristics, which anyway forces the image appearance to a predefined histogram representation (always related to US physics and technical knowledge).

d. Continuous Automatic Adjustment

It represents the latest update of the Automatic Adjustment, where it is the operator that recalls the Automatic Adjustment function once the image quality is not satisfactory, instead of having the US system automatically and virtually continuously re-apply the Automatic Adjustment function once the echo image characteristics change with respect to a pre-defined group of parameters.

e. Easy Adjustment Technology – E.A.T.

A new technology was recently implemented on a US system prototype with the goal to simplify the operator system set up to only three macro-parameters related to the desired effect in terms of: contrast/smoothness, detail/speed, resolution/penetration.

The goal of such Technology was to simplify the tuning process of the image by the operator considering the adjustment based on the desired effect to apply to the image, instead of forcing the US system user to understand and master the technical and physical US parameters and then to act on them for their optimization.

3   Results

In all the traditional techniques for image quality adjustment listed above (Preset; Auto Gain; Adjustment; Continuous Automatic Adjustment) some manual adjustments may be needed on the image obtained after the technique re-call (Preset; Auto Gain) or after the output of image processing (Automatic Adjustment; Continuous Automatic Adjustment). These adjustments have to be performed considering the usual technical and physical parameters of the US system, therefore forcing the US user to master the physics and implemented technology, which is behind the echo image acquisition and formation.

These approaches, therefore, assume a deep technical knowledge of the sonographer, therefore possibly limiting the US use to expert users and, in any case, possibly lengthening the US use learning curve, as it must include a large section related to physics, technology and the so-called "knobology" which considers how the technical theory has been implemented within the US system and how the operator has to deal with (usually such implementation is US system producer dependent and it may vary also between different systems of the same producer).

E.A.T. was developed in order to overcome the limits of traditional image set up and adjustment technologies, and it is currently in the implementation phase on a US prototype system. Tests are in place on phantoms and ex vivo with respect to the above listed technologies.

In order to develop E.A.T., the US operator approach to US system parameters adjustment was completely reconsidered: instead of starting from an engineering point of view and then declining it on how the clinicians have to approach and apply it, the focus of the technology development and implementation was the sonographer's point of view.

With E.A.T., the US system understands and reacts according to the user's needs, instead of forcing the sonographer to understand the technology and its internal processes.

In the traditional approach, the US technology and physics has to be understood to obtain the desired clinical outcome (in terms of echo image characteristics needed for a confident diagnosis), while in the E.A.T. environment it is the US system which has to re-organize itself in terms of acquisition, processing and visualization parameters to ensure the outcome desired by the US system user.

This outcome was obtained by re-thinking the US processing and its related controls in a multi-dimensional space, where the standard parameters are varied along one of the E.A.T. space dimensions, following a pre-defined curve with a particular path and slope depending on its content, variation and starting/ending levels.

Within the E.A.T. multidimensional space each single traditional parameter represents a line in a single dimension. While the E.A.T. space is adjusted, several single dimension parameters are changed according to a multi-dimensional matrix.

For a given E.A.T. multidimensional space direction (for instance, contrast/ smoothness) some single dimension space parameters can be involved (e.g. Dynamic Range, Dynamic Compression, Gray Map, Image quality enhancement algorithm parameters, etc....; see Fig. 3). To correlate the three points of the multidimensional space to the one-dimensional space of each single parameter, a correspondence matrix with single dimension parameters was defined (for instance, the two range extreme points: max contrast/max smoothness and the factory default setting as multidimensional intermediate point). A parametric curve for each single dimension parameter was computed as the best fit with respect to the above mentioned three points. Therefore, when the US system user adjusts the E.A.T. along one of the multidimensional lines, all the related US system acquisition and processing parameters change, each one following the computed curve simultaneously, modifying the image in real time from one extreme setting to the other. The parameters, which are changed within the E.A.T. multidimensional space, are available to the US system user within the traditional U.I., as well as some internal – not user-accessible – parameters of the US system.

The E.A.T. user interface is constituted by three virtual sliders on the touch screen, which are an integral part of the US system control panel (see Fig. 4).

In E.A.T. a multidimensional algorithm simultaneously varies several internal system parameters to modify the image in the direction of macro-parameter varied by the user (resolution/penetration; speed/detail; smooth/contrast). No prior knowledge of US physics or technology is required to adjust the macro-parameter, whose effect is directly visible on the echo image in real-time (for instance, to optimize the level of smoothness with respect to US image contrast).

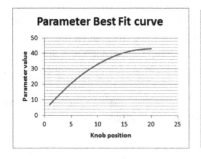 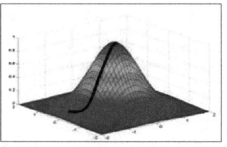

Fig. 3. Single dimension space parameter (left); E.A.T. multidimensional space (right).

Fig. 4. E.A.T. user interface virtual sliders.

The traditional system adjustment environment is separate with respect to the E.A. T. environment, due to the completely opposite approach to the US system set up and tuning process, and also because the E.A.T. result may have an outcome in a multi-dimensional space point which cannot be achieved with any multi-parameter adjustment obtained in the traditional technically/physically-focused approach).

4   Conclusion

The E.A.T. US system optimization approach was carried out by completely re-thinking the US system user approach to image optimization: from forcing the sonographer to deeply understand US physics and technology (the implementation of which varies from one US system producer to another), to an intuitive approach that enables the operator to concentrate only on the effects he/she wants to obtain on the final echo image in terms of optimization and balancing between resolution and penetration, smoothness and contrast, improved image details of increased frame rate in terms of acquisition and visualization.

E.A.T. was developed with the goal to:

- reduce the number of End User image controls;
- obtain faster changes in image settings also for US users with limited knowledge of the system workflow;
- reduce the possibility to obtain « bad tuning » configuration for not expert US users.

The aim of the E.A.T. is to increase productivity, reduce sonographer's work-related musculoskeletal disorders due to extensive use of US system control panel, and to increase diagnostic confidence based on the intuitive optimization of the sonographer's desired effect, instead of an engineering approach to real-time scanning optimization.

E.A.T. advanced optimization technique is suitable for drastically simplifying the sonographer approach to Ultrasound by freeing the operator from the deep knowledge needed to optimize image and hemodynamics acquisition parameters, especially in more complex clinical applications such as Radiology, Cardiology and OB-Gyn.

References

1. Forzoni, L., Guraschi, N., Fertino, C., Delpiano, M., Santambrogio, G., Baselli, G., Andreoni, G., Zambarbieri, D., Carniglia, E., Fusca, M., Mazzola, M.: Case study of integrated ergonomic assessment of a portable echograph. In: Proceedings of 4th International Conference on Applied Human Factors and Ergonomics (AHFE), San Francisco, CA-USA (2012)
2. Andreoni, G., Mazzola, M., Matteoli, S., D'Onofrio, S., Forzoni, L.: Ultrasound system typologies, user interfaces and probes design: a review. In: Proceedings of the 6th International Conference on Applied Human Factors and Ergonomics AHFE 2015, Las Vegas, USA (2015)
3. Vannetti, F., Atzori, T., Pasquini, G., Forzoni, L., Modi, L., Molino-Lova, R.: Superficial electromyography and motion analysis technologies applied to ultrasound system user interface and probe ergonomics evaluation. In: Proceedings of the 5th International Conference on Applied Human Factors and Ergonomics AHFE 2014, Kraków, Poland (2014)
4. Mazzola, M., Forzoni, L., D'Onofrio, S., Marler, T., Beck, S.: Using Santos DHM to design the working environment for sonographers in order to minimize the risks of musculoskeletal disorders and to satisfy the clinical recommendations. In: Proceedings of the 5th International Conference on Applied Human Factors and Ergonomics AHFE 2014, Kraków, Poland (2014)
5. Andreoni, G., Zambarbieri, D., Forzoni, L., Mazzola, M., D'Onofrio, S., Viotti, S., Santambrogio, G., Baselli, G.: Motion Analysis and eye tracking technologies applied to portable ultrasound systems user interfaces evaluation. In: Conference Proceedings of the IEEE ICCMA 2013 (2013)
6. Mazzola, M., Forzoni, L., D'Onofrio, S., Standoli, C.E., Andreoni, G.: Evaluation of professional ultrasound probes with santos DHM. Handling comfort map generation and ergonomics assessment of different grasps. In: Proceedings of the 5th International Conference on Applied Human Factors and Ergonomics AHFE 2014, Kraków, Poland (2014)
7. Bolliger, C.T., Herth, F.J.F., Mayo, P., Miyazawa, T., Beamis, J.: Clinical Chest Ultrasound: From the ICU to the Bronchoscopy Suite. S. Karger AG, Basel (2009)
8. Daniels, J.M., Hoppmann, R.A.: Practical Point-of-Care Medical Ultrasound. Springer International Publishing AG, Switzerland (2016)
9. Chui, D.S., Moi, M.: A Field Guide to Bedside Ultrasound. FriesenPress, Victoria (2016)
10. UK National Screening Committee (2012) NHS Fetal Anomaly Screening Programme (NHS FASP) - A guide to getting the most from the ultrasound equipment when measuring Nuchal Translucency
11. Daniels, J.M., Dexter, W.W.: Basics of Musculoskeletal Ultrasound. Springer, New York (2013)
12. Wu, T.S.: Ultrasound, An Issue of Critical Care Clinics, vol. 30(1). Elsevier Inc., Philadelphia (2014)
13. Tchacarski, V., Krasteva, R., Mincheva, E., Boueva, A., Iliev, I., Popov, D.: Atlas of Diagnostic Ultrasound: Ultrasonography. Valery Tchacarski, Sofia (2015)

An Analysis and Evaluation Procedure in Civil Aircraft Flight Deck Design

Dayong Dong[✉], Baofeng Li, Haiyan Liu, Wenjun Dong,
Hongtao Liu, and Zhefeng Jin

Shanghai Aircraft Design and Research Institute, Shanghai, China
dongdayong@comac.cc

Abstract. As we all know, flight crew error in system design and certification have great related to the flight safety. Human error is affected by a number of factors, including system design, training, operations, and pilots' previous experiences. Human error is difficult to predict, and it cannot be prevented entirely; even experienced, well-trained pilots using well-designed systems will commit errors. Understanding of the causes of pilot error can minimize the likelihood of these occurrences and be used to create more error-resistant and error-tolerant systems.

In this paper, an analysis and evaluation procedure based on human cognitive information processing model was introduced for civil aircraft flight deck interface design. In this procedure model, information including display, alerting, tactile etc. have been considered as input in the Perception stage. Controls including push button, switch, lever etc. have been considered as output in the Response Execution stage. Two kinds of subject evaluation method were introduced. One is paper-pencil evaluation using modified Cooper-Harper Rating scale based on flight deck interface and description, the other method is flight deck walk through evaluation based on the typical scenario tasks.

When the system interface or operation procedure, which have potential hazard of crew error have been identified, the error prevention or error tolerant features will be considered in detail in the flight deck interface design according to the error classification.

Error management concept has been introduced to the flight deck human factor requirements development. Effective error management means that the system design facilitates error detection and recovery and/or ensures that the effects of errors on how the system functions are obvious. Information to help the flight crew detect errors consists of indications provided during normal operations. Indications alerting to a specific error or system condition, or indications of external hazards or operational conditions.

These analysis and evaluation procedures have been used in single aisle civil aircraft flight deck design in China.

Keywords: Flight deck · Human error · Evaluation · HMI · Human factor

© Springer International Publishing AG 2017
C. Stephanidis (Ed.): HCII Posters 2017, Part I, CCIS 713, pp. 519–525, 2017.
DOI: 10.1007/978-3-319-58750-9_72

1 Introduction

Up to now the commercial aviation system is the safest transportation system in the world, and the accident rate is the lowest it has ever been. However, accident analyses have identified flight crew performance and error as significant factors in a majority of accidents involving transport category airplanes. Flight crews contribute positively to the safety of the air transportation system using their ability to assess complex situations and make reasoned decisions. However, even trained, qualified, checked, alert flight crew members can make errors. Human error is affected by a number of factors, including system design, training, operations, and pilots' previous experiences. Human error is difficult to predict, and it cannot be prevented. An understanding of the causes of pilot error can minimize the likelihood of these occurrences and be used to create more error-resistant and error-tolerant systems. Some errors may be influenced by the design of airplane systems and their flight crew interfaces. A system that is error resistant makes it difficult to commit an error, e.g., through clear and simple designs. A system that is error tolerant provides the ability to mitigate the errors that are committed, e.g., by allowing the automated system to monitor flight crew actions or through the use of electronic checklists that provide a reminder of tasks to be completed [1].

Accidents often result from a sequence, or combination, of flight crew errors and safety related events. The design of the flight deck and other systems can influence flight crew task performance and may also affect the rate of occurrence and effects of flight crew errors. Human error is generally characterized as a deviation from what is considered correct in some context. In the hindsight of analysis of accidents, incidents, or other events of interest, these deviations might include: an inappropriate action, a difference from what is expected in a procedure, a mistaken decision, a slip of the fingers in typing, an omission of some kind, and many other examples. The regulation CS25.1302/FAR25.1302 is focus on human errors. The rule text is:

§25.1302 Installed systems and equipment for use by the flightcrew.

This section applies to installed systems and equipment intended for flightcrew members' use in operating the airplane from their normally seated positions on the flight deck. The applicant must show that these systems and installed equipment, individually and in combination with other such systems and equipment, are designed so that qualified flightcrew members trained in their use can safely perform all of the tasks associated with the systems' and equipment's intended functions. Such installed equipment and systems must meet the following requirements:

(a) Flight deck controls must be installed to allow accomplishment of all the tasks required to safely perform the equipment's intended function, and information must be provided to the flightcrew that is necessary to accomplish the defined tasks.
(b) Flight deck controls and information intended for the flightcrew's use must:

(1) Be provided in a clear and unambiguous manner at a resolution and precision appropriate to the task;
(2) Be accessible and usable by the flightcrew in a manner consistent with the urgency, frequency, and duration of their tasks; and
(3) Enable flightcrew awareness, if awareness is required for safe operation, of the effects on the airplane or systems resulting from flightcrew actions.

(c) Operationally-relevant behavior of the installed equipment must be:

(1) Predictable and unambiguous; and
(2) Designed to enable the flightcrew to intervene in a manner appropriate to the task.

(d) To the extent practicable, installed equipment must incorporate means to enable the flightcrew to manage errors resulting from the kinds of flightcrew interactions with the equipment that can be reasonably expected in service. This paragraph does not apply to any of the following:

(1) Skill-related errors associated with manual control of the airplane;
(2) Errors that result from decisions, actions, or omissions committed with malicious intent;
(3) Errors arising from a crewmember's reckless decisions, actions, or omissions reflecting a substantial disregard for safety; and
(4) Errors resulting from acts or threats of violence, including actions taken under duress.

[Doc. No. FAA-2010-1175, 78 FR 25846, May 3, 2013]

The unique aspect of rule 25.1302 is that it considers the flight crew task as the guiding element for assuring safe operation of the aircraft. It is the task that defines what equipment needs to be used when, in what order, by whom and in what combination with other installed equipment. Note however that it is not the task that is being certificated, but the integrated combination of installed equipment that enables safe task execution in this particular flight deck design.

2 Pilot Information Processing Model

A model of pilot information processing stages provides a framework for analyzing the different psychological processes used in interacting with flight deck systems and for carrying out a task analysis (See Fig. 1). The model depicts a series of processing stages or mental operations that typically (but not always) characterizes the flow of

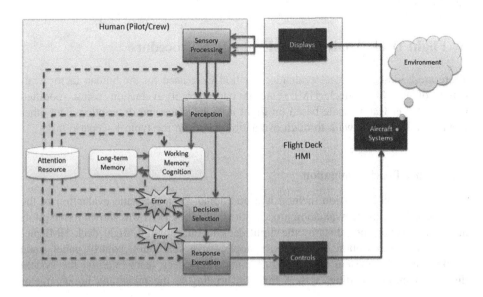

Fig. 1. Pilot information processing model [2]

information as a pilot performs tasks in flight deck. Consider as an example the task of the pilot control airplane by using flight mode control panel (FMCP). The first thing is to get information by pilot's senses. The information for the pilot may be speed and altitude indication on the (Primary Flight Display) PFD, or the order from the controller, or other information in the flight deck.

But sensation is not perception, and of this large array of sensory information only a smaller amount may be actually perceived by the pilot. Perception involves determining the meaning of the information, and such meaning is derived from past experience. This past experience is stored in pilot's long term memory for understanding the situation. After perception, information processing follows decision or selection based on the pilot cognition. Next step, the pilot will response to the information input manipulating the FMCP. The airplane then response the input of control, and the corresponding status information will represent through the PFD and navigation display (ND) as the feedback loop.

The attention is a vital tool for much of information processing. It plays two qualitatively different roles [3]. In its first role as a filter of information that is sensed and perceived, attention selects certain elements for further processing, but blocks others, as represented by the smaller output from perception than input to it. Thus, the pilot may focus attention fully on the flight control. In the second role attention acts as a "fuel" that provides mental resources to the various information processing stages, as indicated by the dashed lines as shown in Fig. 1. Some stages demand more resources in some tasks than others.

In this pilot information processing model, flight deck (Human Machine Interface) HMI is the evaluation objects. The displays mainly refer to the information on the PFD, ND and EICAS, alerting, tactile etc. and the controls mainly refer to the button, switch on the overhead panels and console, levers, etc. An analysis and evaluation procedure based on pilot information processing model was carried on the civil aircraft flight deck interface design.

3   Flight Deck Analysis and Evaluation Procedure

There are 2 kinds of subject evaluation method were used for the human factor evaluation of the flight deck HMI. One is paper-pencil evaluation using modified Cooper-Harper Rating scale based on flight deck interface and description. The other method is flight deck walk through evaluation based on the typical scenario tasks.

3.1   Paper-Pencil Evaluation

The paper-pencil evaluation method is a traditional mean for static evaluation of the flight deck HMI. In the evaluation process, the flight deck HMI was shown to the pilots and human factor specialists by the flight deck layout drawing, flight deck HMI pictures, system description documents, synoptic page snap shot, control panel static mockup, etc. The system design engineer and flight deck team interpret the system displays, controls, alerting, system function briefing to the pilots and human factor specialists. By understanding the system design philosophy and the detail information, the modified Cooper-Harper Rating scale was used to give the scale for the displays, controls, alerting based on the flight deck HMI evaluation criteria. The flight deck HMI evaluation criteria were developed by the flight deck team on the basis of 25.1302. Here is example a checklist for the display information elements organization [4].

ORGANIZATION AND MANAGEMENT OF INFORMATION ELEMENTS

Formatting/Layout

- *Arrangement of information on the display*
  Page format, structure and organization (e.g., "Basic T")
  Consistent positioning or relative positioning of information on the display
  Consistency with other flight deck displays
- *Consistency with user expectations and internal logic*
- *Indication of active regions (controls) and off-screen material*
- *Labels (e.g., for menus, scales, modes, and units)*
  Intuitiveness, location, orientation.

3.2   Walk Through Evaluation

The walk through evaluation is a task based dynamic evaluation on a specific platform with part or full flight deck system functions. Before evaluation test, the test scenarios were developed according to the system characteristic. Evaluate the flight deck systems as guided by the tasks required in the order as described by the mission time line/flight phase.

In accordance with the guidance found in AMC 25.1302/AC25.1032-1 the initial human factors evaluation of the flight deck will address the following aspects of each of the installed systems and its interface.

- The control interfaces
- Information Presentation
- Multifunction interfaces
- System behavior

For each system interface component, the degree of integration, complexity and novelty will also be assessed. Human performance issues and pilot's comments were recorded.

Different platform plays its role in the human in-the-loop evaluation. A physical mock-up of the flight deck or display system may be used early in the display design, e.g., to address anthropometric considerations such as the reach and visibility of the display. Part-task evaluations that emulate display capabilities for a single system or a group of systems can be used to identify usability issues, e.g., in an office setting. Note that the results of these part-task evaluations may be somewhat limited because tasks are being performed in isolation. Simulator evaluations offer the opportunity to collect feedback through a high-fidelity integrated emulation of the flight deck and operational environment, but the results may be limited by the extent to which the simulator is able to accurately capture the operating environment.

The flight deck evaluation will also be used to assess the operational behavior of the installed equipment and perform an initial analysis of the flight decks error management facilities. The major impetus for the rule 25.1302 (d) was to promote error tolerant design of flight deck equipment. The flight deck interfaces (both individually and in combination with respect to their associated flight crew tasks), will be subject to initial evaluation to establish if they support the prevention of error; trapping error, or the mitigation of its consequences. The initial information analysis for error detection will take three basic forms:

- Assessment of indications provided to the flight crew during normal monitoring tasks
- Evaluation of crew alerts that provide interruptive information of an error or resulting aircraft system condition
- Evaluation of 'global' alerts covering a multitude of possible errors by annunciating external hazards, aircraft envelope or other operational conditions.

When the system interface or operation procedure, which have potential hazard of crew error have been identified, the error prevention or error tolerant features will be considered in detail in the flight deck interface design, according to the error classification.

4 Conclusion

Flight crew error in system design and certification have great related to the flight safety. Human error is affected by a number of factors, including system design, training, operations, and pilots' previous experiences. Human error is difficult to predict, and it cannot be prevented entirely; even experienced, well-trained pilots using well-designed systems will commit errors. Understanding of the causes of pilot error can minimize the likelihood of these occurrences and be used to create more error-resistant and error-tolerant systems.

An analysis and evaluation procedure based on human cognitive information processing model was introduced for civil aircraft flight deck interface design. In this procedure model, information including visual display elements, alerting, tactile etc. have been considered as input in the perception stage. Controls including push button, switch, lever etc. have been considered as output in the Response Execution stage. Two kinds of subject evaluation method were introduced.

The analysis and evaluation procedures mentioned above have been used in single aisle civil aircraft flight deck design in China.

References

1. Ahlstrom, V., Longo, K.: Human Factors Design Standard (HFDS) for Acquisition of Commercial Off-The-Shelf Subsystems, Non-developmental Items, and Developmental Systems (DOT/FAA/CT-03/05 HF-STD-001). Atlantic City, NJ: US DOT Federal Aviation Administration William J. Hughes Technical Center (2003)

2. Wickens, C.D., Hollands, J.G.: Engineering Psychology and Human Performance, 4th edn. Psychology Press, Park Drive (2000)
3. Wickens, C.D., McCarley, J.M.: Applied Attention Theory. CRC Press, Boca Raton (2008)
4. Yeh, M., Jo, Y.J., Donovan, C., Gabree, S.:. Human factors considerations in the design and evaluation of flight deck displays and controls. Flight Decks (2013)

Investigation on Driving Habits of Chinese Truck Driver

Junmin Du[1,2], Hui Lu[1], Weiyu Sun[1], Xin Zhang[3(✉)], Huimin Hu[3],
and Yang Liu[4]

[1] School of Transportation Science and Engineering,
Beihang University, Beijing, China
[2] Airworthiness Technologies Research Center,
Beihang University, Beijing, China
[3] Ergonomics Laboratory, China National Institute of Standardization,
Beijing, China
zhangx@cnis.gov.cn
[4] Beijing Foton Daimler Automotive Co., Ltd., Beijing, China

Abstract. The understanding on driving habit is the essential foundation for human-machine interface design of truck cab. In order to obtain the truck driver's characteristics and driving habits, an investigation was made on Chinese truck driver. The methods of one to one discussion and driving behaviour record were used in the investigation. Through the study, the characteristics of Chinese truck driver user group, driving schedule and behaviour habits, and the main factors affecting the current driving comfort were obtained. It is conluded that the primary practitioners of truck driving in China were young males. The majority of truck driving tasks were carried out in the daytime with long hours driving. Turck drivers had certain behaviour habits, such as steering wheel gripping mode and the usage of foot pedal. The improvement on devices ergonomics were expected, including seat size and back shape, steering wheel grip size, seat belt fixed position, mirrors adjustment, foot pedal, etc. The results were helpful for understanding Chinese truck driver group features and needs, as well as providing references for design of the truck cab.

Keywords: Truck driver · Driving habit · Investigation · Human-machine interface

1 Introduction

Driving comfort of the truck makes great contribute to road safety and driver's health. As the essential foundation for human-machine interface design of truck cab, driving habit is expected to be understood in the design period. However, in the current domestic design process, the consideration on driving habits is insufficient, which results in inconveniences and safety risks on road. For instance, because of the lack of survey on driver's habit of driving posture, as well as unsuitable seat design, a large amount of truck drivers felt tired and back uncomfortable very soon on road [1]. If it is a long distance driving, the driver's control on the vehicle is impaired strongly [2]. The solution is to take full account of the driver's characteristics and driving habits in the

© Springer International Publishing AG 2017
C. Stephanidis (Ed.): HCII Posters 2017, Part I, CCIS 713, pp. 526–531, 2017.
DOI: 10.1007/978-3-319-58750-9_73

design process of truck cab. This paper aims to obtain the truck driver's population characteristics and driving habits.

Based on the above considerations, the characteristics of Chinese truck driver user group, driving schedule and behaviour habits, and the main factors affecting the current driving comfort were obtained by the investigation. The results were helpful for understanding Chinese truck driver group features and needs, as well as providing references for human machine interface design of the truck cab.

2   Research Contents and Methods

2.1   Research Contents

The methods of one to one discussion and driving behaviour record were used in the investigation. The primary topics in this investigation were as follows.

- Truck driver group characteristics, including gender, age, anthropometry and occupational distribution.
- Driving schedule habits, including driving frequency, driving time, rest time, driving duration, tolerance to fatigue.
- Driving behaviour habits, including steering wheel gripping mode and adjustment, sitting posture and seat adjustment, pedal and brake using frequency and habit on different type of road, mirror using habit and adjustment, dashboard and switch buttons using habit and adjustment, etc.

2.2   Research Methods and Implementation

(1) One to one investigation

According to the research content, the truck driving habits investigation questionnaire was developed. The investigation was carried out in the form of one to one discussion, which was prior to the driving behaviour record.

(2) Driving behaviour record

Driving behaviours of the truck drivers were recorded by two sets of traffic recorder. The first set of the recorder was placed on the lower left side for recording the driver's foot operation. The second set of the recorder was placed on the right side window of the cab for recording the driver's arm action, body posture, seat postion and driving scenes. The driving tasks were basic road operation, including straight drives, turns, brakes and stops. Two types of road conditions, urban roads and highways, were considered. The actural driving habits were find out by the analysis of driving behaviours records.

The one to one investigation and driving behaviour record was conducted in Daxing and Changping District, Beijing, China. Seven truck drivers participated in the study. All of them had the valid driver license and more than one year truck driving experience. Drivers who had completed the investigation and driving tasks were given cash as rewards.

3 Results

3.1 Truck Driver Group Characteristics

Participants' age were between 26 to 45 years old (35.43 ± 7.21). Their heights were 174.00 ± 1.41 cm, weight 77.14 ± 7.65 kg. It can be seen that the truck drivers were all young males, whose physical function were at the best level of human being life, such as reaction speed, strength and endurance.

According to Chinese National Standard, GB10000-88 Human dimensions of Chinese adults, the P50 height of males from 18 to 60 is 167.8 cm, the P90 height is 175.4 cm, the P95 weight is 75 kg, the P99 weight is 83 kg [3]. Taking account of the tendency of Chinese adults' body dimension and weight keeping increasing in recent years, it could be classified that the overall height level of the participants was medium-high, the weight was medium-heavy.

All participants were self-employed, no one employed by delivery company.

3.2 Driving Schedule Habits

The investigation of driving schedule is related with driving frequency, driving time, rest time, driving duration, tolerance to fatigue.

Participants reported that all of them did driving tasks on each day. In the past one year, the least mileage drived by participants was 25,000 km; the majority of drivers drove from 30,000 to 60,000 km; the largest mileage was 130,000 km. The majority of drivers drove in the daytime, the minority drove at night. Within 24 h, the total driving duration (excluding rest time) of most drivers was from 3 h to 5 h; the minority drove from 2 h to 6 h.

For most of the drivers, the significant feeling of fatigue appeared after driving continuously 3 h to 4 h. A small number of drivers felt the fatigue after 3 h to 6 h. One of the participants reported that the fatigue was dull until driving continuously 12 h to 13 h. The total driving duration overall was 4 h to 6 h mostly, very few was up to 11 h.

3.3 Driving Behaviour Habits and Related Driving Experience

(1) Steering wheel gripping mode

The most common steering wheel gripping mode (driving straight) was gripping by two hands with the right hand on higher position (see Fig. 1); or gripping by left hand with the right hand hanging or resting on the gear lever (see Fig. 2); or gripping by right hand with left hand hanging or resting on the door frame (see Fig. 3). The minority of dirvers gripped the steering wheel by two hands with the same height, or with the left hand on higher position. None of the participants gripped the steering wheel by two hands with reverse gesture.

The majority of participants were satisfied with the steering wheel diameter. But they complained that the grip size was small. The steering wheel sleeve had to be used to fix this problem. The adjustment range of steering wheel height and angle was

Fig. 1. Gripping by two hands

Fig. 2. Gripping by left hand

Fig. 3. Gripping   by
right hand

appropriate for all participants. The participants evaluated the feedback force of the steering wheel was comfortable and easy to operate, except one of the participants evaluated the steering wheel was heavy and difficult to operate.

(2) Sitting posture and seat adjustment

The participants reported that the adjustment on seat was same regardless of the road conditions (highway, urban or rural roads). Whether driving in daytime or at night, the adjustment on seat, steering wheel, rearview and driving posture was same.

The air cushion seat was used on all of the participants' truck. Its adjustable height range was about 10 cm. The majority of participants felt the seat height was suitable; two participants felt the seat height was too high even after adjustment; one participant felt the seat waved during driving. The adjustable front-rear range was suitable for the participants except one participant complained uncomfortable.

The position of the seat height adjustment device was good for most of the participants. The minority of participants were unsatisfied with it because they had to get off the truck to do the adjustment. The position of the seat front-rear adjustment device was suitable for all of the participants.

Participants were satisfied with the seat depth and seat hardness. Some complains and suggestions related with the seat were given by participants as follows.

- The seat back was uncomfortable. The improvement of headrest, back cushion and waist support were expected.
- The seat surface was small. A wider seat was expected.
- The distance between the steering wheel and the seat was small. It should be wider.
- The shock absorption capability of seat should be improved.
- The seat belt could not across the shoulder properly for a few participants. The imporvement of the seat belt positon was expected.

(3) The usage of foot pedal

The using frequency of the foot pedal, from high to low, was the accelerator pedal, the clutch pedal and the brake pedal.

The using frequency of foot pedal was affected by road condition. On the highway, the accelerator pedal was used the most frequently; on the urban road, the three types of foot pedal were used as equivalent frequency; on the rural road, the acceleration and clutch were used more than brake pedal.

All of the participants felt the operation force needed by the accelerator pedal was suitable. Most of the praticipants felt the operation force needed by the clutch pedal and the brake pedal was suitable. A few participants complained the operation force needed by the clutch pedal and the brake pedal was large. The distance between the accelerator pedal and the brake pedal was appropriate. Participants reported that the feeling of foot fatigue was strong after one day's driving work, especially the right feet.

The operating force of pulling the handbrake was suitable for all of the participants. The operating force of shifting gears was suitable for most of the participants except one participant complained the force was large. Most of the participants thought the size of the gear lever handle was appropriate, a few participants felt the handle size was small.

(4) Mirror adjustment

Most of the participants did not adjust the rearview mirror during driving. One participant reported he adjusted the left rear view mirror sometimes during driving.

The participants reported that the adjustment of the left rearview mirror was easy. But the vast majority of participants reported that the right rearview mirror was difficult to be adjusted. In order to adjust the right rearview mirror, the driver had to get off the truck or assisted by another person.

The biggest outside blind areas were near the the right front wheel and the rear of the truck. The participants reported it was inconvenient to check these areas.

(5) The usage of truck electronic system

The usage frequency of truck electronic system is shown in Table 1. Driving condition and non-driving condition were considered. The numbers in the table represented the amount of participants.

The frequently used controllers of electronic system were expected to be located at easy touched area. The participants reported that the manual adujstment of swithes/

Table 1. The usage frequency of truck electronic system

Controller	Driving condition			Non-driving condition		
	Frequently used	Occasionally used	Rarely used	Frequently used	Occasionally used	Rarely used
Entertainment system (such as radio) switch/adjustment button	$\sqrt{}$(2)	$\sqrt{}$(2)	$\sqrt{}$(3)	$\sqrt{}$(1)	$\sqrt{}$(2)	$\sqrt{}$(4)
Air condition system switch/adjustment button	$\sqrt{}$(2)		▪ $\sqrt{}$(3) ▪ $\sqrt{}$(2) no air conditioner		$\sqrt{}$(1)	▪ $\sqrt{}$(4) ▪ $\sqrt{}$(2) no air conditioner
The switch of inside lights	$\sqrt{}$(1)	$\sqrt{}$(2)		$\sqrt{}$(2) usually used at night	$\sqrt{}$(3)	$\sqrt{}$(2)
Other switches		$\sqrt{}$(2) Fog lamp switch (if foggy)			$\sqrt{}$(1) Electric heating tubing switch (in winter)	

buttons on the console was convenient, no matter it was in driving condition or non-driving condition. On most of the trucks, the controllers of entertainment system, air condition system and some other electronic system were laid on the console. However, on some of the trucks, the controllers of entertainment system were laid overhead of the driver. The involved participants said it was hard to operate in driving condition because of its requirement to eyes. All of the participants were satisfied with the postion of inside lights' switches, which were located at the roof. Some of the participants complained the glove box was a little bit far from driver.

4 Conclusion

According to the investigation, the following conclusions could be obtained related with the characteristics of Chinese truck driver user group, driving schedule and behaviour habits.

(1) The primary practitioners of truck driving in China were young males.
(2) The majority of truck driving tasks were carried out in the daytime with long hours driving.
(3) Turck drivers had certain behaviour habits, such as steering wheel gripping mode and the usage of foot pedal.
(4) The improvement on devices ergonomics were expected, including seat size and back shape, steering wheel grip size, seat belt fixed position, mirrors adjustment, foot pedal, etc.

The results were helpful for understanding Chinese truck driver group features and needs, as well as providing references for design of the truck cab. More efforts should be done on improving truck drivers' safety and health.

Acknowledgement. This research was supported by National Natural Science Foundation of China under project: driver distraction strategies research based on in-vehicle technologies using (project number 71601007). This research was also supported by the National Key Technology R&D Program under project: control devices ergonomics design technology and standards research (project number 2014BAK01B02).

References

1. Yin, M.: Research on human machine interface design for automobile cab. Xihua University (2014)
2. Wang, H.: The parametric design of the automotive seat and the arrangement of seat and panel in the automotive cab. Nanjing University of Aeronautics and Astronautics (2008)
3. GB10000-88. Human dimensions of Chinese adults (1988)

Formulation of Diagnostic Expertise in Oral Health Care and Its Application to Clinical Education

Kyoko Ito[1(✉)], Haruki Sao[2], Takashi Nagamatsu[2], Junko Nagata[3],
and Kenji Takada[4]

[1] Office of Management and Planning, Osaka University, Suita, Japan
ito.kyoco@gmail.com
[2] Graduate School of Maritime Sciences, Kobe University, Kobe, Japan
1407085w@stu.kobe-u.ac.jp, nagamatu@kobe-u.ac.jp
[3] Faculty of Medicine, University of Miyazaki, Miyazaki, Japan
knjunko@gmail.com
[4] Faculty of Dentistry, National University of Singapore, Singapore, Singapore
kenji_takada@nuhs.edu.sg

Abstract. Visual inspection of a patient's physical condition is an important step in the diagnostic process. This preliminary check is indispensable for dental/medical practitioners to properly assess, in a clinical environment, the presence or absence of abnormalities as well as the pathologic status of the patient. A highly skilled visual inspection results in effective treatment planning, whereas a crude, low-skilled inspection may likely result in diagnostic errors and subsequent prolongation of the treatment period. For students and inexperienced residents to acquire the highly sophisticated skill of visual inspection, it would be crucial to master skills and techniques performed by expert practitioners in the process of visual inspection. In this study, we focus on eye motion as a parameter that describes gaze behavior. This metric should reflect the expertise utilized by proficient dental practitioners during a visual inspection of a patient's face and oral cavity. We select the orofacial region as the site for diagnosis. This region manifests an intricate three- dimensional configuration and is strongly relevant to food intake, respiration, verbal communication, and aesthetics. It is an important part of the body that requires proficient visual judgment for proper diagnostics. We have conducted an experiment. The participants were two highly experienced dental doctors. The results of the experiment show that there would be the patterns of eye movements for diagnosis and it would be categorized in some patterns.

Keywords: Formulation · Expertise · Eye-tracking · Diagnosis and health care

1 Introduction

The pursuit of upgrading the quality of medical care and, more specifically, dental care and its associated technology, would lead to affluent and emotionally satisfied societies; people could spend life with high self-esteem and respect of the communities they belong.

© Springer International Publishing AG 2017
C. Stephanidis (Ed.): HCII Posters 2017, Part I, CCIS 713, pp. 532–539, 2017.
DOI: 10.1007/978-3-319-58750-9_74

Visual inspection of a patient's physical condition is an important step in the diagnostic process. This preliminary check is indispensable for dental/medical practitioners to properly assess, in a clinical environment, the presence or absence of abnormalities as well as the pathologic status of the patient. A highly skilled visual inspection results in effective treatment planning, whereas a crude, low-skilled inspection may likely result in diagnostic errors and subsequent prolongation of the treatment period. For students and inexperienced residents to acquire the highly sophisticated skill of visual inspection, it would be crucial to master skills and techniques performed by expert practitioners in the process of visual inspection.

Efforts to formulate and utilize the expert knowledge are not new in engineering fields [1]. Also, a previous study documented how physicians examine radiographs, with observation time and sites used as parameters [2]. In addition, there are development of an automatic dento-facial anatomy recognition system using head radiographs [3] and a clinical decision-making system for judging whether to or not to extract teeth, with both systems using a template-matching technique [4]. This study is the first one that investigates the experimental formulation of the professional expertise that is employed in the visual inspection of dental patients. Two-dimensional images of clinical pictures are used to obtain the judging process of the dental experts.

2 Method

In this study, we will focus on eye motion as a parameter that describes gaze behavior. This metric should reflect the expertise utilized by proficient dental practitioners during a visual inspection of a patient's face and oral cavity. A previous study [5] has documented that the eye movements while gazing at an object vary significantly depending on the observer's concern about the targeted object, or the intention of the gaze. Another study [6] examined how the 'bonsai' is appreciated in space by tracing the movement patterns of the eyes, and found there to be a significant difference between novice and experienced individuals.

In this study, we select the orofacial region as the site for diagnosis. This region manifests an intricate three-dimensional configuration and is strongly relevant to food intake, respiration, verbal communication, and aesthetics. It is an important part of the body that requires proficient visual judgment for proper diagnostics. We aim at formulating patterns of eye movements that are assumed to be characteristics to proficient dental practitioners during the visual inspection. As a means to measure the eye movements, an eye tracking system is employed to investigate the sites and times of the visual inspection (Fig. 1). The flow of this study is provided as follows:

1. Develop a set of fiducial images for inspection
2. Design an experiment, and
3. Analyze the data.

As for 1., three kinds of images are prepared as fiducial images. (1) Facial images with different profile convexity and lip posture/competency. Likewise, (2) tumor photos with different severity (CT photos). And, (3) intraoral images of leukemia with different severity of gingival bleeding and/or leukoplakia. As for 2., it is designed to

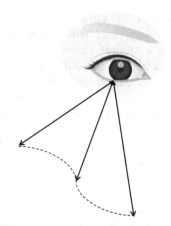

Fig. 1. How do highly skilled expert practitioners' eyes behave in an inspection?

investigate precise experimental conditions and procedures. As for 3., dental expertise that is used during the visual inspection by and characteristic to proficient practitioners is considered qualitatively and quantatively. With the basis of these points, an experiment is conducted [7].

3   Experiment

3.1   Purpose

In order to formulate the professional expertise, the purpose of this experiment is as follows:

- Is there any pattern in visual inspection of the orofacial region, which is characteristic of a proficient dental practitioner?
- Is so, how does it differ by each practitioner?

3.2   Method

Four kinds of fiducial images are employed as stimuli to induce eye motions. The target diseases are mandibular protrusion, maxillary protraction, tumor (CT) and leukoplakia. The participants of the experiment are the experienced dental practitioners with much experience of diagnosis for the diseases. So, the participants are two experienced dental doctors. They exposed to the images in order to record the eye movements while they are observing the target images. As for the procedure of the experiment, the interview for the participants is conducted for the reflection after the recording. With the basis of the consideration, the method is as follows:

Table 1. Contents of the images.

Disease	Number of patients	Number of diagnostic image
Mandibular protrusion	3	12
Maxillary protraction;	8	8
Tumor (CT)	2	4
Leukoplakia	1	8

- Participants: two dental doctors (X (with experience for over 40 years) and Y (with experience for over 20 years)
- Exposed images: 32 (refer to Table 1)
- Measuring equipment: Tobii Pro X2-30 (Tobii Technology AB)

The procedure of the experiment is as follows:

1. Have an instruction by the experimenter
2. Take lessons for viewing some images (measure eye movements) after the calibration
3. View an image and diagnose it one by one for measuring the eye movement (32 images)
4. Explain the contents for the diagnosis one by one while viewing the results of the eye measurement (32 images)

All the experiment is recorded by two video recorders. The utilization of the images has been approved by the ethics committee of School of Medicine, University of Miyazaki.

3.3   Results

The apparatuses in the view of an image and the reflection are shown respectively in Figs. 2 and 3.

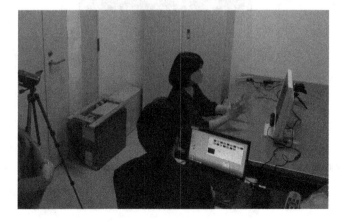

Fig. 2. Participant Y looks at an image.

Fig. 3. Participant Y explains how she looked at the image.

The average times for viewing an image are 7.9 (X) and 26.1 (Y) seconds. Before and after displaying an image, a black display is inserted. When a participant finishes the diagnosis for an image, the participant says "I finished it" etc. as the cue, and the next image is displayed. The time for viewing an image is between a black display and the next black display.

The results for measuring eye movements are shown in Figs. 4, 5, 6, 7, 8 and 9. Figures 4 and 5 show for "mandibular protraction" (front) by X and Figs. 6 and 7 do by Y. Figures 8 and 9 show for "mandibular protraction" (side) respectively by X and Y.

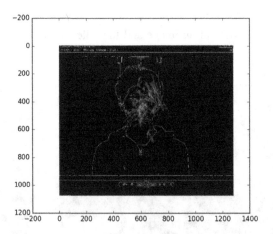

Fig. 4. Eye movement in the inspection for "mandibular protraction" (front) (i) by participant X.

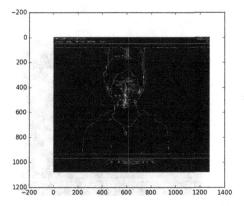

Fig. 5. Eye movement in the inspection for "mandibular protraction" (front) (ii) by participant X.

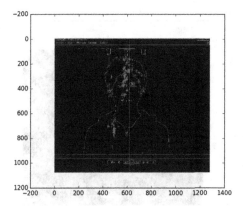

Fig. 6. Eye movement in the inspection for "mandibular protraction" (front) (i) by participant Y.

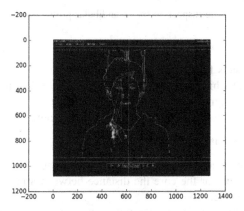

Fig. 7. Eye movement in the inspection for "mandibular protraction" (front) (ii) by participant Y.

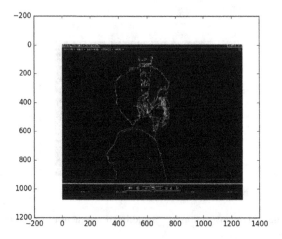

Fig. 8. Eye movement in the inspection for "mandibular protraction" (side) by participant X.

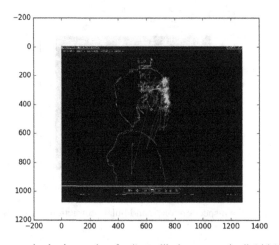

Fig. 9. Eye movement in the inspection for "mandibular protraction" (side) by participant Y.

The reflection of X was included as follows:

- It took a few seconds for the diagnosis of an image.
- The eye movement which I did not do was shown, but it was the part that I thought it is the noise for diagnosis and perhaps I did look at.
- As a whole, my eye movement was from top to bottom.

The reflection of Y was included as follows:

- I thought what cure each disease needed for each image.
- Some images needed for the cure the distance between a point and another point, and I saw the distance.
- The results of my movement sometimes were not corresponded with what I expected.

The results show there would be a pattern of eye movement and each experienced practitioner would have each pattern.

4 Conclusion

To formulate the diagnostic expertise applied during visual inspection for dento-maxillo-facial diagnosis, we have conducted an experiment for measuring the eye movement. Though proficient dentists based on their abundant knowledge and experiences have acquired the expertise, we aim to transform the knowledge into a form that is transmittable and feasible for use in clinical education. In order to utilize the knowledge and observational skills cultivated by the oral health experts themselves for the purpose of improving the diagnostic skills of inexperienced dentists. And, we aim to elucidate whether there is any difference n the patterns of performance between the proficient practitioners. The results of the experiment showed that there would be some patterns of the eye movement and might be some difference between the practitioners. In the near future, we would like to analyze the results in more detail, for example, the common points and different ones. And, when the number of the participants increases, we will find the some category of the pattern and the main points.

References

1. Darlington, K.: The Essence of Expert System. Pearson Education, Upper Saddle River (2000)
2. Kundel, H.L., Nodine, C.F., Lawrence, T.: Searching for lung nodules: the guidance of visual scanning. Invest. Radiol. **26**, 777–781 (1991)
3. Tanikawa, C., Yagi, M., Takada, K.: Automated cephalometry: system performance reliability using the landmark-dependent criteria. 'Angle Orthod. **79**(6), 1037–1046 (2009)
4. Takada, K., Yagi, M., Tanikawa, C.: Computational formulation of orthodontic tooth-extraction decisions, part 1: to extract or not to extract. Angle Orthod. **79**(5), 885–891 (2009)
5. Yarbus, A.L.: Eye Movements and Vision. Plenum Press, New York (1967)
6. Miura, T.: Eye movements in apprehension of bonsais: the effect of knowledge and experience. In: Proceedings 16th Congress of the International Association of Empirical Aesthetics, pp. 95–96 (2000)
7. Ito, K., Sao, H., Nagamatsu, T., Nagata, J., Takada, K.: A fundamental study on formulation of diagnostic expertise in oral health care. Corresp. Hum. Interface **18**(10), 1–6 (2016). (in Japanese)

Assessment of the Working Chair Using Affects the Whole Service Process in B Ultrasonic Examination

Xinxiong Liu[✉], Daojun Qian, Lei Wu, and Jie Xu

Department of Industrial Design,
Huazhong University of Science and Technology, Wuhan, China
xxliu@mail.hust.edu.cn

Abstract. This study based on service design methods to probe the practical problems of sonographer working motional status during B ultrasonic examination, which includes the upper arm muscle fatigue because of repetitive scanning motion in the status of suspending whole arm without any supporting and the strain of lumbar muscles and shoulder pain after working status that body moving forward or backward without proper multi-points supporting to relieve whole upper body weight. Combined the service design method with whole B ultrasonic examination to consider errand specific wrist motions, hand grips pressures, scanning positions, and maintained posture during a procedure. The results shows: (1) Sitting experience: compare with the old chair in sitting and controlling, because of Saddle shape Cushion fit the thigh muscle, sonographer's lower body can control the chair easily and smoothly, especially random change the seated position for different part scanning; (2) Scanning experience: sonographer's whole arm muscles feel definitely comfortable than before during the scanning procedure, the adjustable arm supporting device offer a fulcrum that in case of whole arm muscle strain, and lower lumbar and back feel better because of the after daily working as well. (3) Product emotional feeling: the whole chair uses the dark black and grey, of 85% sonographer considering the dark color means professional skills and attitude.

Keywords: Service design · B ultrasonic examination · Sonographer's health · Dynamic supporting

1 Introduction

With the rapid pace of economic development in China, service industry as the tertiary industry to occupy the whole national economy. One of the large area in service industry is a medical domain, China has tremendous population in the world so that healthcare faced even more difficult and specific problems than other countries. Based on the literature review, Liang et al. [1] described the doctor-patient relationship plays an important role in patient satisfaction with healthcare service. Obviously, the number of the doctor group is less than the patient group, it means the doctor as the service provider is confronted with enormous working intensity per working day and the mental health problem. There is a relevant connection between the doctor's working

© Springer International Publishing AG 2017
C. Stephanidis (Ed.): HCII Posters 2017, Part I, CCIS 713, pp. 540–547, 2017.
DOI: 10.1007/978-3-319-58750-9_75

strength level and the patient's satisfaction. There is less research to focus on it, However, based on the literature, [2] Ciloglu et al. identified the passenger seat conform factor during the air traveling, [3] Hiemstra-van Mastrigt et al. proposed the active seating for the car passenger conform based on the physical inactivity of workers in many occupations is becoming an increasing problem (Straker and Mathiassen). According to survey, [4] Muir et al. reported that 22% of workers scan less than five hours per day, 67% scan between five and seven hours, and 11% scan more than seven hours per day. Only 45% of workers take more than three breaks of ten minutes or longer during the workday, and 55% of workers take two or fewer breaks per day. It conduct the sort of health problems especially lack of to adjust the work-rest time cycle during working status.

This study uses the service design methods to observe the B-ultrasound sonographer's examination process and identify the problems in the real environment, collecting the qualitative data to dig work-related injuries that include the B-ultrasound sonographer's neck and interscapular pain, upper arm muscle injury, lumbar muscle strain and shoulder pain, elbow pain, hand/wrist pain. The main reason of these problems is the heavy workload and body abduction in working status. These two factors refer to the user action reorganizing and the physical evidence from the perspective of service design thinking. Service blueprint and task analysis grid help us to refine the problems that we explored, it turns out that the working chair refer to the healthcare service physical evidence that needs redesign necessarily. Accompany with the evidence be redesign, the original user action will be changed and optimized as well. So that we designed a new ergonomic chair with an adjustable elbow support device to serve the sonographer's body could release elbow muscle straining and bringing the comfort feeling. Furthermore, it will advance the efficiency based on the service provider's action that from the touch-point between the doctor and seat to the whole interaction among the different stakeholders in the service processes.

2 Methods

This study uses the service design method to conduct the research and design in the holistic perspective. We used the Shadowing, Questionnaire, Behavioral Mapping and Ethnography as the observing research tool, in addition, the service blueprint and task analysis grid as the design tool. As the part of service design sectors, we examined the key problem of whole the physical evidence through sonographer task analysis grid, the ergonomic chair conduct the important role of the whole examining process in the diagnostic room. [5] Moggridge argued that the evidencing means taking the ideas and animate them as tangible evidence of the future. This kind of "archeology of the future" enables the designers to make early qualitative judgments about the implication of the design solution they're conceiving. In this study, we analyzed and proved the effect of chair using situation, that situation concluded the physical evidence redesign could improve the whole service process from the sonographer's body comfortable level and mental feeling degree of satisfaction to the efficiency of the entire examination.

3 Problem of the Sonographer's Working Status

3.1 Problem in Service Processes

Each medical practitioner provides much more time and energy service than patient, it result in doctor have working hours and intensity problems during the each daily examination. We evaluated the correlation between injuries sustained in the workstation and factors such as age, gender, workload and intensity, scanning techniques, previous medical problems, and physical activity.

According to the survey, shoulder and neck pain were the most frequently reported for various age sonographer groups in Wuhan union hospital, as illustrated in Table 1, most sonographers experience discomfort in the shoulder, neck, wrist, lumbar muscles.

Table 1. Medical diagnostic results of sonographer's sick part in Wuhan union hospital

Medical diagnostic results	Total number	Percentage
Periarthritis of shoulder	121	51.3%
Strain of lumbar muscles	104	44.1%
Neck muscle tissue injury	77	32.6%
Tenosynovitis	71	30.1%
Lumbar disc herniation	56	23.7%
Carpal tunnel syndrome	24	10.2%
Arthritis	22	9.3%
Cubital tunnel syndrome	15	8%

In addition, sonographers are postponing injuries treatment and forgetting the proper rest because of tremendous patient during daily working status, as time goes by, sonographers frequently forget even neglect the body fatigue and muscle strain.

3.2 Problem in Field Observation

Roughly 90% of the sonographers have significant musculoskeletal discomfort with their routine work in Medical imaging department. Meanwhile, sonographers demonstrate common physical disorders that include postural deficits, muscular imbalances, and poor dynamic stabilization of the upper body during the interview. We found the series of problems other than the problems they illustrated. Figure 1 depicts the service process working process by image that include different age and gender variables record.

Male sonographer put his arm suspend in the air without any supporting in the examination, which in order to avoid touching patient's belly that result in discomfort to patient, on the contrary, female sonographer put her arm on patient's body during the subconscious status. These two micro-behaviors originated from the sonographer's cognition that they consider the definition of touching patient's body. However, the male sonographer strain his arm muscle for long time bring fatigue and pain.

FIELD IMAGE	AGE	GENDER	MUSCLE PROBLEMS	CHAIR PROBLEMS
	59	Female	1.The arm muscle be in the state of tension without supporting 2.The lumber muscle be in an incorrect state when the body turning	Without any arm supporting and lack of the lumbar supporting
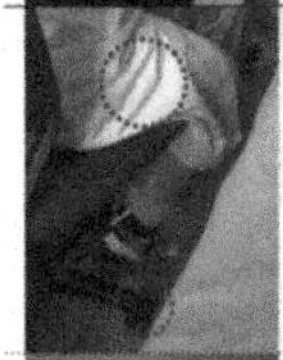	45	Male	1. The femoral muscle tension 2. The Ankle joint fatigue	1. Without the foot pedal
	31	Male	1.Chronic lumbar muscle strain 2. Low waist pain 3.lumbar disc herniation	1.Without the fitting cushion and back 2.Without the dynamic supporting structure

Fig. 1. Investigation of workstation

he description and frequency pattern of pain were similar across all age groups with slight variations. [8] Evans et al. reported Pain continues to be related to pressure applied to the transducer, abduction of the arm, and twisting of the neck and trunk (Evans, Roll and Baker).

4   Observation Results

4.1   Problem Matrix and Defining

There are serious problems during the checking period than other process such as preparing steps and connecting assistant steps, and the doctor will adjust their own posture frequently along with checking as well. Simultaneously, the changeable behaviors bring the irrational working posture on doctor's body muscle, which can result in the muscle fatigue complication over time. Figure 2 describes the service blueprint of the B-ultrasound doctor in the examination, the orange blocks refer to the steps that can be optimized, and the key physical evidence in these processes is the ergonomic chair that makes interaction between the service provider and the customer. B-ultrasound examination requires the sonographer to hold the transducer in a proper plane of scanning. Conversely, it's complex and dynamic posture during the exami-nation, dynamic and repetitive movements of specific regions of the scanner's body are then needed to manipulate the transducers and to adjust the monitor Armstrong et al. (1984).

Service Blueprint (Sonographer's profile)

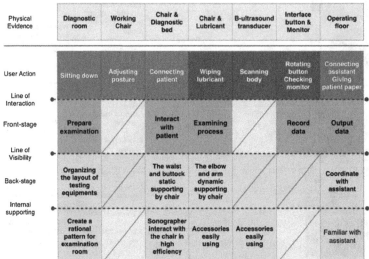

Fig. 2. Service blueprint of B-ultrasound during examination

4.2 The Pattern of Body Dynamic Supporting

The main requirements include the elbow dynamic supporting and the body forward dynamic supporting. The elbow dynamic supporting pattern could make sure the sonographer's arm have a rational fulcrum to avoid the repetitive muscle stress during examination. Sonographer holds the ultrasound transducer in the right hand and to adjust the arm, elbow, hand wrist randomly within the body regions constantly changed in the examination. In addition, there is a necessary to equip a rational fulcrum for upper arm muscle when sonographers adjust their motion along with different body part especially as the important part of the body scanning procedure. Beside, sonographers interact with the interface of B ultrasonic examination instrument accompany with the body regions changed and checking the monitor, in the meantime, sonographer's body parts are changing with the working states conversion. To analyze the basic motions consist of the body forward and backward, the body spinning around in the status of shifting between examining body and checking monitor. Therefore, the rational supporting pattern needs to satisfy the whole body forward, backward and turning motion.

5 Design

5.1 The Subjects

The upper arm pain and the shoulder blade fatigue that we can improve. Sonographer manipulates the interface button and watching monitor by left hand and holds the B-ultrasound transducer to scan different body parts by right hand, there are two types of motion include body lean forward and backward without supporting, it will bring the whole arm muscle strain and lumber muscle pain after long time working. Consequently, the adjustable elbow dynamic supporting device and the forward motion structure that under the ergonomic cushion to satisfy the dynamic body supporting when sonographer move forward or backward as the examination body part changing.

5.2 Ergonomic Design Concept

Considering the whole dynamic body motion, the new chair adds the four evolutional patterns consist of the adjustable upper arm dynamic supporting device, dynamic forward tilting structure, sliding pedal, saddle shape cushion. Figure 3 shows the functional construction of each part of the ergonomic chair.

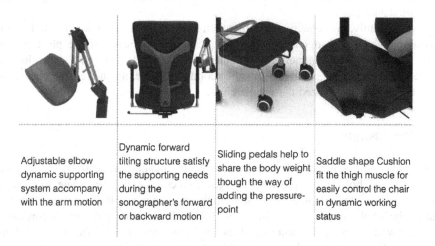

| Adjustable elbow dynamic supporting system accompany with the arm motion | Dynamic forward tilting structure satisfy the supporting needs during the sonographer's forward or backward motion | Sliding pedals help to share the body weight though the way of adding the pressure-point | Saddle shape Cushion fit the thigh muscle for easily control the chair in dynamic working status |

Fig. 3. Functional design for working behaviors

6 Estimation Results

The survey is aimed at the estimation of the chair using experience during the working process, which indicated examination of different body part and interaction between sonographer and patient. We using a 5-point scale, with 1 indicating strongly uncomfortable, 3 indicating neutral comfortable, and 5 indicating strongly comfortable.

Through the Fig. 4 shows the new chair brings the data generally increasing, in particular, the upper arm muscle and lumber muscle had significant improvement because of the elbow dynamic supporting pattern and the dynamic forward tilting structure that all offered by the adjustable elbow supporting device and the forward and backward. The crucial part of touch-points in the examination processes have had more optimized effectiveness partly than ever. Using the new working chair we can find the scanning process and the preparing process had been advance in certain extent.

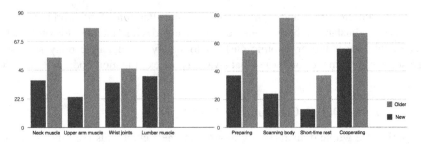

Fig. 4. Sonographer's muscle comfort assessment and touch-point evaluation

Besides, after some training recommendations the sonographers even experienced staff reinforce the self-awareness of the short-time rest such as moving the fatigue upper body or standing.

Consequently, the effectiveness of touch-points is advanced in Fig. 4. For the measuring variable comprehensively, the questionnaire consist of the physical and mental satisfaction. Eventually, we counted the data and analyzed the results, the consequence shows the positive results like comfortable feeling and resilient mentation after the prototype replaced the former chair.

7   Conclusions

This study validate that redefine and discovery the connection between the physical evidence and whole service processes is significant correlative. Meanwhile, to examine the physical evidence optimization during the will improve the working efficiency during the whole service process in the field of medical service industry. According to the discovering the real B-ultrasound examination, defining the frequent problems within the body muscle in the whole service process, designing the chair prototype on the basis of the frequent problems, depending on the service blueprint to matrix and solve the key testing muscle problems of doctor such as wiping lubricant, holding the probe to examining body and rotating button to check monitor. Consequently, it can be assumed that the working chair can cover more body motion and that body subconscious behavior will bring mistake posture without good design chair.

Although the physical evidence get better, the working onsite management and job process coaching should be a consideration by hospital administrator, such as flexible scheduling and working body motion cognitive training such as short-time regular exercise. Increasing the physical fitness will promote sonographer's mindset and positive lifestyle. The sonographer's working process includes the physical and mental activity, so that make these two factors seamless connect could optimize the touch-point effectiveness.

References

1. Liang, C., Gu, D., Tao, F., et al.: Influence of mechanism of patient-accessible hospital information system implementation on doctor-patient relationships: a service fairness perspective. Inf. Manag. **54**, 57–72 (2016)
2. Ciloglu, H., Alziadeh, M., Mohany, A., et al.: Assessment of the whole body vibration exposure and the dynamic seat comfort in passenger aircraft. Int. J. Ind. Ergon. **45**, 116–123 (2015)
3. Hiemstra-van Mastrigt, S., Kamp, I., van Veen, S.A.T., et al.: The influence of active seating on car passengers' perceived comfort and activity levels. Appl. Ergon. **47**, 211–219 (2015)
4. Muir, M., Hrynkow, P., Chase, R., et al.: The nature, cause, and extent of occupational musculoskeletal injuries among sonographers recommendations for treatment and prevention. J. Diagn. Med. Sonogr. **20**(5), 317–325 (2004)
5. Moggridge, B.: Designing Interactions. The MIT Press, Cambridge (2007)
6. Wihlidal, L.M., Kumar, S.: An injury profile of practicing diagnostic medical sonographers in Alberta. Int. J. Ind. Ergon. **19**(3), 205–216 (1997)
7. Lahlou, S. (ed.): Designing User Friendly Augmented Work Environments. Springer, London (2009)
8. Evans, K., Roll, S., Baker, J.: Work-related musculoskeletal disorders (WRMSD) among registered diagnostic medical sonographers and vascular technologists: a representative sample. J. Diagn. Med. Sonogr. **25**, 287–299 (2009)
9. Guo, L.X., Dong, R.C., Zhang, M.: Effect of lumbar support on seating comfort predicted by a whole human body-seat model. Int. J. Ind. Ergon. **53**, 319–327 (2016)

Finding 3D CAD Data Production Methods that Work for People with Visual Impairments

Kazunori Minatani[✉]

National Center for University Entrance Examinations, Komaba 2-19-23,
Meguro-ku, Tokyo 153-8501, Japan
minatani@rd.dnc.ac.jp

Abstract. This study presents available 3D CAD data production methods that work for people with visual impairments. Standard CAD programs rely heavily on GUI, making it impossible for them. The best way for them to produce 3D CAD data would be to describe the 3D data file itself. As one of such methods, SCAD direct source input method is introduced. It then presents objects produced using that method to illustrate the effectiveness of such methods.

Keywords: CAD · 3D printer · OpenSCAD · People with visual impairments · Blind persons

1 Introduction

The main barrier to the use of 3D printers among the visually impaired is that almost every task in the 3D printing process requires visual recognition of 3D objects shown on a computer screen. At present, there is no way to express to visually impaired persons in the necessary detail the manipulations of a 3D object when it is represented as a graphic image on a computer screen. A commercially available tactile graphic display, for example, is limited to binary expressions of 48×64 dots. [1] An experimental dynamic multilevel tactile touch display is developed and planned to make into product. [2] However its resolution is limited to 40×60 dots. Therefore, to find 3D CAD data production methods that work for people with visual impairments non-standard methods must be examined.

Tests were done under the following conditions. Two potential platforms (operating systems) for running the software used to manipulate the 3D objects were examined: Microsoft Windows 10 and Linux (Debian 8.0). Microsoft Windows was ultimately selected, as the software it uses to handle 3D objects currently has the most extensive features. In this examination on Windows platform, JAWS for Windows [3] was used as a standard reference screen reader with NVDA [4] used for weighted comparison. For Linux, the author went with a command-line interface (CLI) program, as it was thought to offer the most features. Because CLI programs do not serve as an intermediary for operating target graphics, they can ensure usability by persons with visual disabilities, and the majority can be used with screen readers.

© Springer International Publishing AG 2017
C. Stephanidis (Ed.): HCII Posters 2017, Part I, CCIS 713, pp. 548–554, 2017.
DOI: 10.1007/978-3-319-58750-9_76

2 Practical Testing to Produce 3D CAD Data

2.1 SCAD Direct Source Input Method

The best way for people with visual impairments to produce 3D data would be to describe the 3D data file itself. As mentioned earlier, both CAD and CG software rely heavily on graphical user interfaces, making it impossible for those with visual impairments to use them to create 3D data. On the other hand, if the 3D data files output by these types of software are in a text-based format, it means that they can be written and edited using standard document editing software—and people with visual impairments have no UI-related obstacles when it comes to this task. Fortunately, most 3D data files can be written in text format, making this approach an incredibly promising one.

Although a text-based approach can theoretically be used with STL data, however, practically speaking it is incredibly difficult. STL [5] descriptions can be recognized as text data and edited using a standard text-editing program. Furthermore, STL is a widely-used file format for both CAD and CG programs, so as long as it can be used, a variety of data can be created.

However, because it is a general-purpose data format, it demands low-level descriptions. STL must represent objects by arranging triangular mesh data within a three-dimensional space. It is not practical for a human operator to directly write this information for the following reasons. First, representing objects as a combination of all of their triangular surfaces requires massive computing. For example, even a basic form like a six-sided cube must be described as a combination of twelve right triangle surfaces. Second, STL represents object surfaces, and must describe a closed object in order to express a three-dimensional form. There is no tolerance for corrupted or inconsistent data, as strict computational operations are required.

OpenSCAD data is a form of CAD data that is more abstract that STL. It is also possible for human operators to write OpenSCAD data directly. OpenSCAD is a type of CAD software designed to create a programmable CAD environment. [6] Users can write 3D data by using values to specify the size of basic geometrical forms (rectangular solids, cylinders, spheres, and so on) as well as their configuration coordinates. The Fig. 1 is a screenshot of OpenSCAD 3D data in the process of being created.

The object being described is shown on the screen as a graphic, and the user uses the display to check the appropriateness of their description and make corrections if necessary. The data is saved as character strings input by the user. The software can also display the object as the sum, product, or difference of multiple geometrical forms. Because the program is designed to automatically generate the objects, it can be used to describe conditional jumps, loops, variable substitution, and arithmetic operations. If it were possible to eliminate object confirmation via the GUI while producing OpenSCAD data that maintained its practical efficiency, it would be a promising method of 3D data production for users with visual impairments. This method of 3D data production is referred to as the **SCAD direct source input method** below.

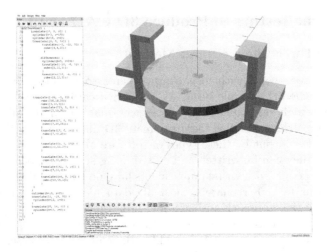

Fig. 1. A screenshot of OpenSCAD

2.2 Overview of Testing

The author ran tests to see whether having people with visual impairments use OpenSCAD to produce 3D data that satisfied certain conditions was a practical solution. At this stage of research, the purpose was to identify a production method that could serve a practical purpose. For this reason, the author used the practical strategy of having the author himself, who is completely blind, as the visually impaired subject attempting to create 3D data.

The conditions for the 3D data to be produced was to create a practical three-dimensional object of minimum complexity. People with visual impairments who cannot create 3D data on their own must ask sighted persons to create it for them, describing what they want in words. For this reason, the author tried to create 3D data that had sufficient complexity that it would be difficult to explain in words. More specifically, this study's minimum requirement was that the object be a combination of multiple geometric solids. OpenSCAD is a type of CAD software, and CAD is mainly used to design and manufacture practical components. For this reason, the author attempted to create a three-dimensional object that had a practical purpose.

2.3 Test Examples

The author's test examples are shown below. Note that it was not able to use screen reader softwares to operate the OpenSCAD GUI. The author therefore used a general-purpose editing program to create SCAD data and then convert it into STL format using a Linux CLI to run OpenSCAD.

The author created a headphone cable reel. The Fig. 2 shows the object he printed out as well as how it looks when it is in use.

Fig. 2. The headphone cable reel

The shape was described to combine a cylinder plus rectangular solids, with a space cut out to store the cable. The listing 1 is its SCAD source code.

Listing 1.1. "SCAD source code of the headphone cable reel"

```
difference () {
  translate ([0, 0, 0]) {
    cylinder (h=3, r=18);
    cylinder (h=10, r=4);
    translate ([0, 0, 10]) {
      translate ([-2, -21, 0]) { cube ([4,4,3]); }
      difference () {
        cylinder (h=3, r=18);
        translate ([-18, -6, 0]) { cube ([2,12,3]); }
        translate ([16, -6, 0]) { cube ([2,12,3]); }
      }
    }
    translate ([-28, -5, 0]) {
      cube ([56,10,3]);
      cube ([3,10,3]);
      translate ([53, 0, 0]) { cube ([3,10,3]); }
      translate ([7, 0, 0]) { cube ([3,10,26]); }
      translate ([7, 0, 24]) { cube ([6,10,2]); }
      translate ([0, 0, 10]) { cube ([10,10,3]); }
      translate ([46, 0, 0]) { cube ([3,10,26]); }
      translate ([43, 0, 24]) { cube ([6,10,2]); }
      translate ([46, 0, 10]) { cube ([10,10,3]); }
    }
  }
  cylinder (h=13, r=2);
  translate ([0, -10, 0]) { cylinder (h=13, r=2); }
  translate ([0, 10, 0]) { cylinder (h=13, r=2); }
}
```

Next, the author created an adapter that allowed users to simultaneously use a braille display and a laptop computer. A braille display is a device that shows computer screen outputs in braille to assist persons with visual impairments. It uses a piezoelectric element to move the points that make up braille characters up and down. [7] A standard display can show about forty characters per line. Braille displays designed for mobile operation have a set of keys above the screen, which can be used to input information into a smartphone or similar device. There is no need to use this set of keys when the display is used with a laptop computer, since the computer already has a keyboard. The author created an adapter that would allow the use of the laptop and the braille display without the keys above screen getting in the way. The objects are shown in the Fig. 3 along with how they look when assembled and when in use.

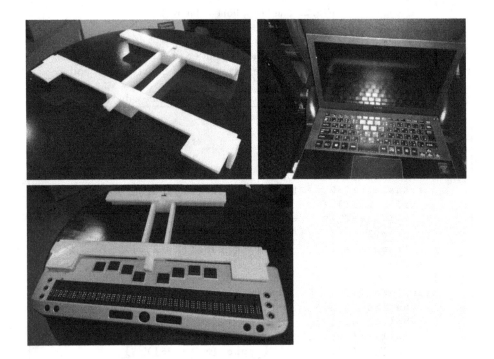

Fig. 3. The mobile braille display frame: assembled and in use

Because the adapter is meant to be portable, the author broke it into five pieces for easy storage. The central piece was described as a large rectangular solid with five small rectangular solid pieces missing. The objects are shown in the Fig. 4 along with how they look when disassembled and when stored. The other four pieces of the adapter fit together with the central piece for use and storage. In order to achieve this configuration, the 3D data had to be designed with detailed clearance specifications along the sides where the pieces fit together. It was difficult to fully explain how to set this clearance using words alone.

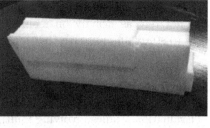

Fig. 4. The mobile braille display frame: disassembled and stored

3 Conclusions and Future Challenges

3.1 Conclusions

Producing 3D CAD data allows people with visually impairments to define the size and positioning of geometrical solids with numerical values and then arrange these solids to create basic forms—SCAD direct source input method. For this paper's test examples, the author confirmed availability of creation of practical three-dimensional shapes with minimum complexity. The production of 3D data is the heart of the 3D printing process, and it is highly significant that the author was able to review certain methods for doing this.

3.2 Future Challenges

By using the SCAD direct source input method with CAD software, the author confirmed a way of producing 3D data. That method, however, was met with following two challenges.

The first is developing assistive features to improve the readability of SCAD source data. The SCAD direct source input method allows users to review the 3D data forms they produced by memory and rereading the source code. It requires a tremendous amount of mental work. Particularly in the case of input errors or other situations where the desired input results are not achieved, the work needed to correct them is equivalent to debugging the entire source code. A feature capable of converting source code by replacing numbers with variable substitution or arithmetic operation results should significantly improve the efficiency of the above tasks. Another helpful feature would be one that told the user the range within which the 3D data existed in three-dimensional space. It would be possible to add this to OpenSCAD as an optional feature. Finally, we could expect similar results by an enhanced interpreter feature for OpenSCAD— assuming that the restrictions making it impossible to operate the OpenSCAD GUI via a screen reader were lifted.

The second challenge is developing a SCAD direct source input method that does not rely as heavily on memory and computation. For example, there is room to study an approach that makes combined use of something like building blocks. If 3D data only consists of rectangular solids, counting the number of units would be a technique that could be utilized to identify from the 3D data the size of the object as well as its distribution coordinates. A technique like this could be expected to simplify 3D data production.

Evaluation studies involving multiple participants would be an effective way of testing possible solutions to each of the two challenges facing CAD-based data production described above.

Acknowledgment. This work was partly supported by the Health Labour Sciences Research Grant.

References

1. DV-2. http://www.kgs-jpn.co.jp/index.php?%E8%A3%BD%E5%93%81%E8%A9 %B3%E7%B4%B0#s46a1117 (in Japanese)
2. APH - Graphiti Graphics Display. http://www.aph.org/graphiti/
3. JAWS Screen Reader - Best in Class. http://www.freedomscientific.com/Products/ Blindness/JAWS
4. NV Access. https://www.nvaccess.org/
5. Burns, M.: Automated Fabrication: Improving Productivity in Manufacturing. PTR Prentice Hall, Upper Saddle River (1993)
6. OpenSCAD - The Programmers Solid 3D CAD Modeller. http://www.openscad. org/
7. Cook, A.M., Polgar, J.M.: Essentials of Assistive Technologies. Mosby, Maryland Heights (2012)

Evaluating 360-Virtual Reality for Mining Industry's Safety Training

Shiva Pedram[1(✉)], Pascal Perez[1], Stephen Palmisano[1],
and Matthew Farrelly[2]

[1] University of Wollongong, Wollongong, Australia
spedram@uow.edu.au
[2] Mines Rescue, Woonona, Australia

Abstract. Virtual Reality (VR) is the most recent technology used to train workers for extreme event scenarios. VR training occurs in a safe and controlled environment which allows the replicable testing of scenarios. Like any other training method, VR based training must be evaluated. This paper reports the trainees' (mines rescue brigades men) state of mind prior attending 360-VR training and experiences of trainees in 360-VR training. Their perceptions of the realism, success and usefulness of this 360-VR training are discussed, and limitations and implications for future research are identified.

Keywords: Virtual Reality · Evaluation · Safety · Training · High risk industry · Mining industry

1 Introduction

Current vocational training systems often fail to fulfil high risk industry's training requirements [1]. Even when organizations invest heavily in their training, they still may not achieve their training objectives (despite the expenditure, time and resources devoted). The need for effective workplace learning has encouraged industries to incorporate various technologies in their training [1]. Virtual Reality (VR) is the most recent technology used to train employees for extreme event scenarios. VR training occurs in a safe and controlled environment which allows the replicable testing of extreme scenarios.

Implementing virtual reality as a training environment initiated form military and has become popular between various industries such as medicine, pilot training, surgical skills, driving, train driving, rehabilitation, educating children and others [2]. VR gained its popularity since:

- It is not feasible and in most cases impossible to duplicate the extreme scenarios in physical world. Therefore, time and cost creates limitations to use real life training.
- There are an endless number of scenarios to train workers for, and it is not feasible to create one off training such as putting a building on fire for fire fighters to train them. Also, there is no guarantee to have a successful training in one session and there might be a need to repeat the session.

© Springer International Publishing AG 2017
C. Stephanidis (Ed.): HCII Posters 2017, Part I, CCIS 713, pp. 555–561, 2017.
DOI: 10.1007/978-3-319-58750-9_77

- There is serious risk involved when conducting training in physical world. Such as training miners for situation where the sealing collapse.
- In virtual world trainees can experience and repeat all scenarios as much as they need to become master in it and always there is a room to make mistakes.

However, like any other training method, VR based training must be evaluated. Unlike operational training, it is not possible to evaluate the success or usefulness of the safety training sessions solely based on the outcome of the training session (since we have to wait for accidents to happen and afterwards, we might be able to conclude how much training transfer from VR to real world has had happened). Although systematic frameworks for evaluating VR-based training are well documented in aeronautics, they need to be adapted for more socially complex situations like underground mining where workers need to perform collective tasks in a confined and hazardous environment (natural risks and dangerous machinery). To date, research on VR-based safety training (as opposed to operational training) for the mining industry is scarce; The paper first introduces the case study; then, it describes the methodology before presenting evaluation results. Finally, we draw conclusions regarding the effectiveness of VR-based safety training in the context of our study.

2 Participants and Study Context

2.1 Technology-in-Use

The research was conducted in collaboration with Mines Rescue Pty Ltd, a training provider for the coal mining industry in Australia that operates four training stations in New South Wales (Woonona, Lithgow, Newcastle, Singleton and Woonona). Each centre delivers classroom, onsite and VR-based training programs ranging from induction courses for new recruits to highly specialised courses for more experienced miners.

Our study focussed on training programs developed for the mine rescue brigades. These brigades are made of five to seven highly specialized volunteers who act as primary responders in case of major mining incidents or accidents. Each volunteer is an already experienced underground miner. The methodological framework was designed and tested at Woonona station, located only a few kilometres from the University of Wollongong.

Although Mines Rescue Pty Ltd has invested in a variety of VR technologies (individual domes, 360° immersive theatre, GEN4 desktop immersive simulation and, more recently, Oculus Rift), this paper focuses exclusively on the training programs developed for the 360° immersive theatre (360-VR). The 360-VR is a 10 m diameter, 4 m high cylindrical screen that displays a 3D stereo, 360° virtual environment, providing a fully immersive experience to participants equipped with 3D glasses (Fig. 1).

2.2 Participants

Between March and July 2015, 94 trainees interviewed for this study and all of the participants in the study were male, aged between 24 and 64 years, with their time

Fig. 1. 360-VR training (Coal Services Pty. Ltd.)

spent in mining and mines rescue ranging from between 5 and 40 years. The participants in this study were 94 experienced underground miners who had volunteered to join the rescue brigade.

3 Methodology

In users' opinion technique users are asked to give their opinions on the conducted training, the method of the training and the features affecting the process. This technique is only useful if it is not possible to measure performance and training outcome. However, this technique does not reflect on knowledge creation and training transfer [3].

The researcher attended all the 360-VR training sessions to observe trainees experiences. She also distributed the questionnaires directly before and after these training sessions. The pre-training questionnaire was distributed to participants prior to them attending the 360-VR training. The aim of this questionnaire is to measure the trainees' state of mind and experience with technology prior the training. After the VR training, the post-training questionnaire was distributed to measure the participants' learning and experiences as a user. Other key questions asked about the participants' perception of the perceived level of realism, the success and the usefulness of the VR training.

Primary data was obtained using Likert Scale based Questionnaires. Our pre- and post-training questionnaires were based on items taken from established questionnaires such as GEM [4], ITQ, PQ [5], SSQ [6], DSSQ [7], IMI [8], UIQ [4] and GEQ [9]. Due to limits on our testing time (which prevented use of the full questionnaires) key items taken from standard questionnaires to measure each factor of interest. These factors had been identified by previous studies as being important for the success of VR training. In order to check that each group of items was still measuring the same factor (i.e. as the original full questionnaires), ensured that the Cronbach's Alpha value for each factor was above 0.7.

4 Results and Discussion

Tables 1 and 2 summarise the mean values for each of the pre-training and post-training factors where Likert scales ranging from highly disagree (0) to highly agree (5).

Table 1. Mean value for pre-training factors

Type	Factor	Lower	Mean	Upper
Pre training	Gaming experience	1.3137	1.4185	1.5179
Pre training	Sense of alert and presence	3.8348	3.9427	4.0505
Pre training	Sense of stress	2.5461	2.7312	2.9162
Pre training	Sense of motivation	4.1142	4.2007	4.2873
Pre training	Sense of confidence and competency	3.8454	3.9355	4.0256
Pre training	Sense of worry	2.6344	2.828	3.0215
Pre training	Sense of competition	3.021	3.2151	3.4091
Pre training	Sickness	1.3285	1.359	1.3895

Even though trainees had limited gaming experience ($M = 1.4$) but they have been motivated ($M = 4.2$) to attend the training. Moreover, they reported better than average scores for "ease of use" ($M = 3.6$), "enjoyment" (M = 3.8), "presence" ($M = 3.3$), "usefulness" ($M = 4.09$) and perceived learning ($M = 3.5$) (scores out of 5).

To better understand the success of 360-VR as a training tool Cross-tabulations has been performed. Cross-tabulations between "perceived realism" and "perceived success" (Table 3) and between "perceived realism" and "perceived usefulness" (Table 4) showed that while trainees typically found the training sessions useful and perceived them to be successful, many felt that it was not really consistent with their real life experience. It would appear that perceived usefulness plays important role in forming the perception of success with high correlation ($r = .609$, $P < .05$) and that the level of realism is not necessarily a deciding factor ($r = .356$, $P < .05$).

Table 2. Mean value for post-training factors

Type	Factor	Lower	Mean	Upper
Post training	Sense of engagement and interaction	3.3292	3.4663	3.6034
Post training	Sense of ease of use	3.5325	3.6957	3.8588
Post training	Sense of fatigue	2.1646	2.3258	2.4871
Post training	Sense of enjoyment	3.803	3.8966	3.9902
Post training	Sense of stress, pressure and tension	2.1497	2.2317	2.3138
Post training	Sense of presence	3.1904	3.3015	3.4126
Post training	Sense of realism	2.8941	3.1989	3.5036
Post training	Sense of usefulness	3.9517	4.092	4.2322
Post training	Success	3.201	3.401	4.102
Post training	Sickness	1.3237	1.3931	1.4626
Post training	Perceived learning	3.3467	3.5301	3.7136

Table 3. Perceived success * perceived realism cross-tabulation

			Perceived realism					Total
			Highly disagree	Disagree	Neither agree or disagree	Agree	Highly agree	
Perceived success	0–25%	Count	0	1	0	0	0	1
		% within realism	0.0%	5.6%	0.0%	0.0%	0.0%	1.2%
	25–50%	Count	4	3	3	0	0	10
		% within realism	40.0%	16.7%	8.1%	0.0%	0.0%	11.9%
	50–75%	Count	6	9	18	7	1	41
		% within realism	60.0%	50.0%	48.6%	38.9%	100.0%	48.8%
	75–100%	Count	0	5	16	11	0	32
		% within realism	0.0%	27.8%	43.2%	61.1%	0.0%	38.1%
Total		Count	10	18	37	18	1	84
		% within realism	100.0%	100.0%	100.0%	100.0%	100.0%	100.0%

Table 4. Perceived usefulness * perceived realism cross-tabulation

			Perceived realism					Total
			Highly disagree	Disagree	Neither agree or disagree	Agree	Highly agree	
Perceived usefulness	Not very useful	Count	0	1	0	0	0	1
		% within realism	0.0%	5.6%	0.0%	0.0%	0.0%	1.2%
	Not useful	Count	0	0	1	0	0	1
		% within realism	0.0%	0.0%	2.7%	0.0%	0.0%	1.2%
	Neutral	Count	2	1	1	2	0	6
		% within realism	18.2%	5.6%	2.7%	11.1%	0.0%	7.1%
	Useful	Count	9	13	28	7	1	58
		% within realism	81.8%	72.2%	75.7%	38.9%	100.0%	68.2%
	Very useful	Count	0	3	7	9	0	19
		% within realism	0.0%	16.7%	18.9%	50.0%	0.0%	22.4%
Total		Count	11	18	37	18	1	85
		% within realism	100.0%	100.0%	100.0%	100.0%	100.0%	100.0%

Additionally, Table 5 indicates 59 out of 85 trainees found the 360-VR session to be useful and 32/85 stated 75–100% it was successful as a training environment to deliver content.

Table 5. Perceived success * perceived usefulness cross-tabulation

			Perceived usefulness					Total
			Not very useful	Not useful	Neutral	Useful	Very useful	
Perceived success	0–25%	Count	1	0	0	0	0	1
		%within usefulness	100.0%	0.0%	0.0%	0.0%	0.0%	1.2%
	25–50%	Count	0	1	3	6	0	10
		%within usefulness	0.0%	100.0%	50.0%	10.2%	0.0%	11.6%
	50–75%	Count	0	0	2	40	1	43
		% within usefulness	0.0%	0.0%	33.3%	67.8%	5.3%	50.0%
	75-100%	Count	0	0	1	13	18	32
		%within usefulness	0.0%	0.0%	16.7%	22.0%	94.7%	37.2%
Total		Count	1	1	6	59	19	86
		%within usefulness	100.0%	100.0%	100.0%	100.0%	100.0%	100.0%

5   Conclusion and Future Research

It is concluded that mine rescue brigadesmen typically had positive learning experiences in 360-VR. Even though VR training is not common practice in the mining industry it appears to have been well received.

However, there is a need for further research as:

1. The current sample size was only 94 participants and only 85 has responded to all the questions. Thus, to be able to generalise our findings about VR as an industry training tool, larger sample size is needed.
2. While the current study focussed on the importance of the VR's technological features and the users' training experience, other factors were observed by the researcher to be important, such as (i) the trainees' attitude toward the technology prior attending the training; (ii) the fit of the technology for the particular training scenario; and (iii) the industry's culture are important factors. To the best of our knowledge these three factors have received little empirical attention.
3. Since 360-VR is being used as "safety training" tool it is almost impossible to be able to measure its success or transfer of training immediately as oppose to "operational training" where trainees performance can be measure straight after they are back to the mine. For safety training accidents must happen first and if it happened then brigades men performance might be measured. Therefore an alternative assessment strategy has been considered for future research.

References

1. Pithers, R.T.: Improving Learning Through Effective Training. Social Science Press, Katoomba (1998)
2. Tichon, J., Burgess-Limerick, R.: A review of virtual reality as a medium for safety related training in mining. J. Health Saf. Res. Pract. 3(1), 33–40 (2011)
3. Nutakor, D.: Design and Evaluation of a Virtual Reality Training System for New Underground Rockbolters. ProQuest, Ann Arbor (2008)
4. Taylor, G.S., Barnett, J.S.: Training capabilities of wearable and desktop simulator interfaces. DTIC Document (2011)
5. Witmer, B.G., Singer, M.J.: Measuring presence in virtual environments: a presence questionnaire. Presence: Teleoper. Virtual Environ. 7(3), 225–240 (1998)
6. Kennedy, R.S., Lane, N.E., Berbaum, K.S., Lilienthal, M.G.: Simulator sickness questionnaire: an enhanced method for quantifying simulator sickness. Int. J. Aviat. Psychol. 3(3), 203–220 (1993)
7. Matthews, G., Joyner, L., Gilliland, K., Campbell, S., Falconer, S., Huggins, J.: Validation of a comprehensive stress state questionnaire: towards a state big three. Pers. Psychol. Europe 7, 335–350 (1999)
8. McAuley, E., Duncan, T., Tammen, V.V.: Psychometric properties of the intrinsic motivation inventory in a competitive sport setting: a confirmatory factor analysis. Res. Q. Exerc. Sport 60(1), 48–58 (1989)
9. Taylor, H.L., Lintern, G., Hulin, C.L., Talleur, D.A., Emanuel Jr., T.W., Phillips, S.I.: Transfer of training effectiveness of a personal computer aviation training device. Int. J. Aviat. Psychol. 9(4), 319–335 (1999)

Hearing Finds and Posture in Workers of the Improvement of the Manioc in Sergipe State, Brazil

Tereza Raquel Ribeiro de Sena[1], Maria Goretti Fernandes[2],
Marcos André Santos Guedes[3(⌂)], and Ângelo Roberto Antoniolli[4]

[1] Audiology Department, Federal University of Sergipe, São Cristóvão, Brazil
tr@trsena.com.br
[2] Physiotherapy Department, Federal University of Sergipe, São Cristóvão, Brazil
[3] Federal University of Sergipe, São Cristóvão, Brazil
marcosguedes@hotmail.com
[4] Health Sciences Post-Graduation Program, Federal University of Sergipe,
São Cristóvão, Brazil

Abstract. The cassava's processing is developed from artisanal way in Flour's House in Brazil. In most cases, the workers are of the female gender and with low schooling. Working conditions are poor, the journey is exhaustive, the mental load of work favors the occurrence of accidents, excessive fatigue and premature wear being responsible for the illness of the worker. The aim of this study was to identify the complaints related to the ergonomics, with emphasis on acoustic comfort and postural aspects of workers during the process of Flour processing of cassava root. Were evaluated 99 female workers, aged between 18 and 81 years, that develop activities of scraping the bark of the cassava root, in the job of scraper. The data were analyzed and the results revealed exhaustive work, risk of accidents at work by cutting instrument, static work with inadequate body postures, continuous noise uncomfortable, lack of personal protective equipment, body fatigue, tinnitus, insomnia, neck pain and difficulty breathing. This study may highlight that the work of cassava scraper is uncomfortable. The intense noise measured and the corporal postures at work can be related to complaints of insomnia, cervical pain, fatigue, tinnitus and can lead to lack of attention, stress, accidents at work. We believed that the adoption of hygiene measures at work can contribute to intense noise reduction and overload in musculature, favoring the health of cassava processing worker.

Keywords: Occupational health · Human engineering · Sound contamination

1 Introduction

Brazil is the fourth largest producer of cassava [1] and the cassava flour your is present in everyday life of the Brazilian people. The Northeast stands one of the main consumers and second national producer, in which the production process is mostly manual and familiar, and corresponds to 24% of the national production [2]. Manioc flour is handmade produced in the flour houses in the labour activity of scraperer.

© Springer International Publishing AG 2017
C. Stephanidis (Ed.): HCII Posters 2017, Part I, CCIS 713, pp. 562–565, 2017.
DOI: 10.1007/978-3-319-58750-9_78

In most cases, the function of scraper is developed by women. The workplace is collective, the workers are seated in a shed in which manioc roots are deposited in piles to be peeled. Security conditions are very poor. The work is performed in the position, squatting next to the unpaved ground, unpaved, with support in solid wood pieces of approximately 1 ft.

In this context, it is believed that the ergonomics has as a basis the interdisciplinary knowledge, in order to adapt the work to the characteristics of the trabalhadores [3]. Under this point of view, complaints submitted by scrapers of cassava may favour the work process analysis with aims to your adaptation.

This study aimed to identify complaints related to hearing and corporal posture of scrapers in the production chain of manioc.

2 Material and Method

This is a cross-sectional study conducted with Flour House's workers located in rural villages in the State of Sergipe, brazilian northeastern, in the year 2016.

Female workers aged between 18 and 81 years that developed work activities scraping cassava roots been evaluated and responded to the questionnaire with questions about, schooling, working conditions, hearing and musculoskeletal complaints.

The sound level meter used was Instrutherm model DEC 490, IEC type II, with a range of 30 to 130 dB, with balancing of circuit "A", slow integration time, 0.1 dB resolution and coupled a wind shield, and, according to brazilian labor law, the microfone of the sound meter was held next to the driver's ear [4]. The intermittent noise measured was 77,2 dBA.

Data were analyzed by descriptive statistics and Chi-square Tests of Pearson and Fisher exact.

3 Results and Discussion

Foram avaliadas 99 trabalhadoras com média de idade de 39 anos (DP = 14) e o grau de escolaridade de ensino fundamental incompleto foi observado em 46,5% (46) da amostra.

Were evaluated 99 female workers with an average age of 39 years (SD = 14) with the educational level of primary education incomplete in 46.5% (46) in the sample.

The work environment can cause physical and mental demands, therefore, it is important the analysis of workers' fatigue [5, 6].

The workdays for more than 8 h was reported by 37.4% (37) of the workers and the complaints related to corporal posture more prevalent were: neck pain at 60.6% (60), fatigue in the arms 52.5% (52) and tiredness in the legs 46.5% (46).

In addition, the average age of the start work early of 12 years (SD = 5) can be related to health impacts that can be enhanced by early exposure to agents of occupational hazards [7]. Among the workers who reported neck pain, 60.6% (60), the early age of onset of labour activities, on average to 12 years (SD = 5), was crucial to the emergence of the complaint (p = 0.041). The account of fatigue in the arms also occurred in 45.4% (45) of the scrapers with complaint of neck pain (p < 0.0001).

In rural areas, workers of the agriculture family, plant, crop and process the cassava roots. Occupational risk factors to which the worker is exposed are associated mainly to musculoskeletal injuries [8, 9]. Agents were identified risk of accident by cutting tool (blade of the knife used to scrape the bark of the cassava), vegetable dust dispersion, ergonomic factors (poor posture, sitting in massive wood trunk in cube format of approximately 1 ft next to the ground, legs inflected, lack of support of the forearm during the scraping) and continuous noise of 77,2 dBA (value not suitable for activities requiring attention and may lead to accidents at work) [10].

As for the self reporting of hearing health, 27.3% (27) reported perception of hearing loss and 82.8% (82) of the workers never held hearing exams. The most prevalent health complaints reported were headache that occurred in 51.5% (51), Insomnia in 21.2% (21), and one of the complaints directly related to noise-induced hearing loss [11], the most frequently encountered were: tinnitus in 51.5% (51), dizziness in 33.3% (33), ear fullness in 28.3% (28) and discomfort to intense sounds 22.2% (22). The self perception of hearing loss occurred in 37.4% (37) of those who reported neck pain (p = 0.053), thus it is believed that exposure to noise associated with postures can trigger a greater discomfort in these workers.

4 Final Considerations

This study may highlight that the working conditions in the homes of flour are uncomfortable to workers who perform the scraping of cassava peels. The presence of intense noise exceeds the value set for activity that require more attention on the part of the worker, 65 dBA, may be related to hearing complaints submitted. In the same way that the absence of appropriate furnishings, early age of initiation of work and postural found complaints have increased even more the picture of discomfort reported by the workers.

In this context, actions related to health and safety at work should be developed in interdisciplinary team with the proposal to improve the health conditions of rural worker.

References

1. FAO: Food and Agriculture Organization of the United Nations. Main results and Metadata by Country (2010)
2. IBGE: Instituto Brasileiro de Geografia e Estatística. Indicadores IBGE Estatística da Produção Agrícola (2016)
3. Crandall, B., Klein, G., Hoffman, R.: Working Minds: A Practicioner's Guide to cognitive Task Analysis. The MIT Press, Cambridge (2006)
4. Brasil. Ministério do Trabalho. Limite de tolerância. Portaria 3214 de 08 de junho de 1978 – NR 15 Anexos 1 e 2 [Norma regulamentadora na internet], June 1978. http://portal.mte.gov.br/legislacao/norma-regulamentadora-n-15.htm. Accessed 30 Nov 2016

5. Van Dijk, F.J.H., Swaen, G.M.H.: Fatigue at work. Occup. Environ. Med. **60**(1), 1–2 (2003)
6. Moriguchi, C.S., Alem, M.E.B., Van Veldhoven, M., Coury, H.J.C.G.: Cultural adaptation and psychometric properties of Braziliam Need for Recovery Scale. Revista de Saúde Pública **44**(1), 131–139 (2010)
7. Fassa, A.G., Facchini, L.A., Dall'Agnol, M.M., Christiani, D.C.: Child labor and musculoskeletal disorders: the Pelotas (Brazil) epidemiological survey. Publ. Health Rep. **120**(6), 665–673 (2005)
8. Fathallah, F.A.: Musculoskeletal disorders in labor-intensive agriculture. Appl. Ergon. **41**, 738–743 (2010)
9. United States Department of Labor. OSHA Technical Manual (OTM) Section VII: Chapter 1 (1999)
10. WHO: World Health Organization. Guidelines for Community Noise. Noise sources and their measurement (1999)
11. Le Prell, C.G., Henderson, D., Fay, R.R., Popper, A.N. (eds.): Noise-Induced Hearing Loss: Scientific Advances, pp. 223–254. Springer, New York (2011)

Single Trial Analysis of Body Sway Caused by Several Matrix-Shaped Tactile Stimuli on Body Trunk

Masaki Terada and Masafumi Uchida[✉]

The University of Electro-Communications, 1-5-1, Chofugaoka,
Chofu, Tokyo, Japan
uchidamasafumi@uec.ac.jp

Abstract. Postural control is an essential function of the human body. Basically, postural control uses several senses and information from the body as input. After processing the input, the body provides output to the muscles for control. In this report, we examine a method wherein the body is caused to sway in a specific direction using several matrix-shaped tactile stimuli (MSTS) that are located on the skin of the trunk. To clarify the relationship between body sway and the MSTS, we measure the sway caused by the MSTS using a high-speed camera, a stabilometer, and two acceleration sensors. However, each subject's data exhibits individual differences, and therefore, each trial data exhibits a different feature. We discuss the effects of each MSTS on body sway and evaluate the dynamics of body sway. We then propose a single trial analysis method based on the clustering method and a mixtures of Gaussian.

Keywords: Tactile stimulation · Body sway · Body trunk

1 Introduction

Postural control is an essential function of the human body in daily life [1], [2]. A decline in postural control function leads to accidents and injuries [3]. Elderly people are correspondingly lower weaker in sensory, cognitive, and motor function as compared with younger people. Anyone will experience a decline in postural control function. Several studies on the relation between external stimulus and center of gravity fluctuation have been reported in research on human control functions. Taguchi investigated the relationship between visual motility stimulation and center of gravity fluctuation [4]. Fujita *et al.* reported the association between electrical stimulation and center of gravity fluctuation [5]. Ochi *et al.* reported on the oscillation of the center of gravity due to the vibration stimulus to the neck muscle [6], and Sakuma *et al.* reported the center of gravity fluctuation caused by vibration stimulation to the body trunk and lower limb muscle [7].

Support for postural control function is always required. Visual and auditory senses are occupied with information collected at the attention and consciousness

© Springer International Publishing AG 2017
C. Stephanidis (Ed.): HCII Posters 2017, Part I, CCIS 713, pp. 566–574, 2017.
DOI: 10.1007/978-3-319-58750-9_79

levels. However, tactile sense does not require attention and consciousness and does not hinder daily life [8]. Tactile sense is considered appropriate as an information input site for posture control function. In previous studies, body sway using tactile stimuli was caused in the specific experimental environments [9].

In this paper, we examine a method wherein the body is caused to sway in a specific direction using several matrix-shaped tactile stimuli (MSTS) that are located on the skin of the human trunk. We create four tactile stimuli devices by arranging a vibrator in a 4×3 matrix, as shown in Fig. 1. Two tactile stimuli devices are placed on the front and back sides of a subject's body, as shown in Fig. 2. T, the vibration time of the vibrator, and τ, the time difference between vibrators, are called tactile stimuli parameters (T, τ). If the relationship between the tactile stimuli parameters and body sway is clarified, there is a possibility of controlling body sway. In this report, we measure the body sway using a high-speed camera, a stabilometer, and two acceleration sensors. We then investigate the relationship between tactile stimuli parameters and body sway.

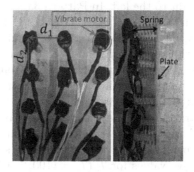

Fig. 1. MSTS device

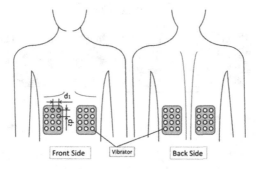

Fig. 2. Mounting positions of MSTS device

2 Generating the Method for the Obtaining MSTS Pattern

In this experiment, Fig. 1 shows the MSTS device by arranging the vibrators (Tokyo Parts Corp., P/N: FM34F) in a 4×3 matrix. The distances d_1 and d_2 between the vibrators in a group were $d_1 = d_2 = 3$ cm. MSTS devices were placed on the front and back sides of the body as shown in Fig. 2. In this experiment, MSTS patterns as shown in the Fig. 3 were applied. In Pattern 1, the vibrators on the front and back sides vibrated in the order of A- B- C. Vibration start time differences between the vibrators were provided at symmetrical positions across the trunk. We expected the body sway from front to back based on a pyramid image penetrating the body from front to the back. In Pattern 2a, vibrators on the front and back sides vibrated in the order of A- B- C- D- E- F. We expected the body sway from left to right based on a flat plate image passing from the left to the right. Pattern 2b was symmetrical to the MSTS pattern described Pattern 2a. We expected the body sway from right to left based on a flat plate image passed from the right to the left. In Pattern 3a, the vibrators on the front and back sides vibrated in the order of A- B- C- D- E- F. Differences in vibration start times were provided between the vibrators at symmetrical positions across the trunk. We expected the body sway from front to back and from left to right based on a prism image penetrating the body from front to back. Pattern 3b was symmetrical to the MSTS pattern described in Pattern 3a.

We expected the body sway from front to back and from left to right based on a prism image penetrating the body from front to back. We introduce two parameters, in detail, T and τ, where T is the duration for applying the stimulation, and τ is the time difference of the vibration start time between the vibrators. We obtained five values for T ($T = \{100, 200, 300, 400, 500\}$) ms and

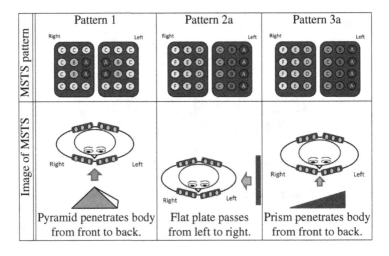

Fig. 3. MSTS pattern

seven values for τ ($\tau = \{0, 100, 200, 300, 400, 500, 600\}$) ms for Patterns 1, 3a, and 3b. We obtained five values for T ($T = \{100, 200, 300, 400, 500\}$) ms, and six values for τ ($\tau = \{100, 200, 300, 400, 500, 600\}$) ms for Patterns 2a and 2b. By combining these values, we were able to provide 30 or 35 combinations of (T, τ) for each MSTS pattern.

3 Experimental Method

Figure 4 shows the experimental system, which includes three personal computers (i.e., PC1, PC2, and PC3). PC1 was responsible for applying stimulation signals to the vibrators and recording mouse-click tasks and acceleration data measured by two single-axis acceleration sensors (PCB Piezotronics Corp., P/N: 393B31) and a three-axis acceleration sensor (Hitachi Metals Ltd., P/N: HB203). PC2 recorded high-speed video that traced markers using a high-speed camera (Ditect Corp., P/N: HAS-L2). Figure 5 shows the traced marker mounting positions. PC3 recorded the center of gravity using a stabilometer (Nitta Corp., BPMS). The sampling frequencies of the high-speed camera and stabilometer were 1000 and 80 fps, respectively. One single axis acceleration sensor was placed on the subject's head while the other sensor was set on the ground. A three-axis acceleration sensor was placed on the subject's right wrist. The acceleration data was recorded using a sampling frequency of 1 kHz. Each subject stood on the center of the stabilometer and maintained their left arm close to their body and aligned with their shoulders. Additionally the subjects raised their right hand up to shoulder level toward a mouse.

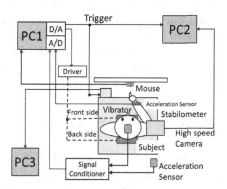

Fig. 4. Experimental system

This experiment began with the audio stimulus, which was a single tone of 1 kHz. Stationary stimulus was applied 500 ms after the initiation of the audio stimulus. Stationary stimulus was based on the MSTS having a time difference between the vibrators on the front and the vibrators on the back. For the stationary stimulus, the vibrators on the front and the vibrators on the back

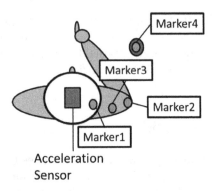

Fig. 5. Marker mounting positions

vibrated at the same time. In this experiment, (T, τ) of the stationary stimulus was (300, 200) ms. After repeating the combination of audio stimulus and stationary stimulus nine times, the subject clicked a mouse with the finger of their right hand when they heard the tenth audio stimulus. Next, the subject returned their right hand to the previous position. The motion of the right arm was measured by a three-axis acceleration sensor. The MSTS pattern was applied when the acceleration value reached the threshold value. A time interval of 30 s from the first audio stimulus was considered as one cycle. Five cycles were conducted consecutively, which was considered as one set. The high-speed camera and the stabilometer recorded data for a period of 8 and 10 s from each MSTS pattern. The two single-axis acceleration sensors measured data during the experiment from the beginning to end. Our experiments were conducted until all (T, τ) combinations were applied once for each MSTS pattern. The (T, τ) combination was randomly determined each time. Our experiments were also conducted when stationary stimulus and no stimulus were applied for each MSTS pattern. According to this experiment, we provided 32 or 37 experimental data points for each MSTS pattern.

4   Single Trial Analysis of Body Sway

First, we set $t = 1$ as the time when applying the MSTS pattern finished in the time series recorded as sampling frequency 1 kHz from the high-speed camera, stabilometer, and single-axis acceleration sensor. The time series from $t = 1$ to N was then removed. The data of the stabilometer was resampled to 1 kHz data by cubic spline interpolation. If the subject's left-right direction was the x direction and the front-back direction was the y direction, the removed two-dimensional data $\boldsymbol{X}_{T\tau} = [\boldsymbol{x}_{T\tau} \; \boldsymbol{y}_{T\tau}]^{\mathrm{tr}}$ was shown as Eq. (1), where $-^{\mathrm{tr}}$ indicated a transposition, and $x_{T\tau}[1] = y_{T\tau}[1] = 0$.

$$\boldsymbol{X}_{T\tau} = \begin{bmatrix} \boldsymbol{x}_{T\tau} \\ \boldsymbol{y}_{T\tau} \end{bmatrix} = \begin{bmatrix} x_{T\tau}[1] \; x_{T\tau}[2] \; \cdots \; x_{T\tau}[t] \; \cdots \; x_{T\tau}[N] \\ y_{T\tau}[1] \; y_{T\tau}[2] \; \cdots \; y_{T\tau}[t] \; \cdots \; y_{T\tau}[N] \end{bmatrix} \quad (1)$$

When $^{(i)}\boldsymbol{X}_{T\tau}$ was divided by n point width, it was divided into $I = \frac{N}{n}$ time divisions. $^{(i)}\boldsymbol{X}_{T\tau} = \left[^{(i)}\boldsymbol{x}_{T\tau}\ ^{(i)}\boldsymbol{y}_{T\tau}\right]^{\mathrm{tr}}$ in time division i $(i = 1, 2, \ldots, I)$ is shown as Eq. (2).

$$^{(i)}\boldsymbol{X}_{T\tau} = \begin{bmatrix} ^{(i)}\boldsymbol{x}_{T\tau} \\ ^{(i)}\boldsymbol{y}_{T\tau} \end{bmatrix} = \begin{bmatrix} ^{(i)}x_{T\tau}[(i-1)n+1]\ ^{(i)}x_{T\tau}[(i-1)n+2] \cdots\ ^{(i)}x_{T\tau}[in] \\ ^{(i)}y_{T\tau}[(i-1)n+1]\ ^{(i)}y_{T\tau}[(i-1)n+2] \cdots\ ^{(i)}y_{T\tau}[in] \end{bmatrix}$$

(2)

There were 32 or 37 combinations of (T, τ) in each MSTS pattern, and one time series $^{(i)}\boldsymbol{X}_{T\tau}$ was obtained. We applied clustering based on a mixtures of Gaussian of 32 or 37 $^{(i)}\boldsymbol{X}_{T\tau}$. The EM algorithm was used for parameter estimation of the probability distribution, $^{(i)}k$ and $^{(i)}l$, which were the effective cluster numbers of $^{(i)}\boldsymbol{x}_{T\tau}$ and $^{(i)}\boldsymbol{y}_{T\tau}$ for time division i and were respectively provided from 1 to 32 or 37. k $(k = 1, 2, \ldots, {}^{(i)}k)$ and l $(l = 1, 2, \ldots, {}^{(i)}l)$ were set as cluster identification numbers. We set $^{(i)}_{k}\boldsymbol{x}_{T\tau}$ and $^{(i)}_{l}\boldsymbol{y}_{T\tau}$ as the mean vector of the probability distributions of each cluster. The trajectory $^{(i)}_{kl}\boldsymbol{X}_{T\tau} = \left[^{(i)}_{k}\boldsymbol{x}_{T\tau}\ ^{(i)}_{l}\boldsymbol{y}_{T\tau}\right]^{\mathrm{tr}}$, which is represented by k and l, $^{(i)}_{k}\boldsymbol{x}_{T\tau}$ and $^{(i)}_{l}\boldsymbol{y}_{T\tau}$ to which the two-dimensional data $^{(i)}\boldsymbol{X}_{T\tau} = \left[^{(i)}\boldsymbol{x}_{T\tau}\ ^{(i)}\boldsymbol{y}_{T\tau}\right]^{\mathrm{tr}}$ in time division i of tactile stimuli parameter (T, τ) is allocated. This represented the characteristic behavior of i in (T, τ) as relatively determined through a series of clustering. $\overline{^{(i)}_{kl}\boldsymbol{X}_{T\tau}}$ in time division i is shown as Eq. (3).

$$\overline{^{(i)}_{kl}\boldsymbol{X}_{T\tau}} = \begin{bmatrix} \overline{^{(i)}_{k}\boldsymbol{x}_{T\tau}} \\ \overline{^{(i)}_{l}\boldsymbol{y}_{T\tau}} \end{bmatrix} = \begin{bmatrix} \overline{^{(i)}_{k}x_{T\tau}}[(i-1)n+1]\ \overline{^{(i)}_{k}x_{T\tau}}[(i-1)n+2] \cdots\ \overline{^{(i)}_{k}x_{T\tau}}[in] \\ \overline{^{(i)}_{l}y_{T\tau}}[(i-1)n+1]\ \overline{^{(i)}_{l}y_{T\tau}}[(i-1)n+2] \cdots\ \overline{^{(i)}_{l}y_{T\tau}}[in] \end{bmatrix}$$

(3)

$\overline{^{(i)}_{kl}\boldsymbol{X}_{T\tau}}$ is expressed as the trajectory. The length $^{(i)}_{kl}L_{T\tau}$ of trajectory $\overline{^{(i)}_{kl}\boldsymbol{X}_{T\tau}}$ is defined. Then, $^{(i)}k$ and $^{(i)}l$ were decided to by Eq. (4).

$$\left(^{(i)}k, {}^{(i)}l\right) = \arg\max_{(k,\,l)} \left(\max_{T,\,\tau}\left(^{(i)}_{kl}L_{T\tau}\right) - \min_{T,\,\tau}\left(^{(i)}_{kl}L_{T\tau}\right)\right)$$

(4)

In this report, we set $N = 3000, n = 500, I = \frac{N}{n} = 6$. Figure 6 shows an example of the raw trajectories $\left(^{(1)}\boldsymbol{X}_{T\tau}, {}^{(2)}\boldsymbol{X}_{T\tau}, \ldots, {}^{(i)}\boldsymbol{X}_{T\tau}, \ldots, {}^{(I)}\boldsymbol{X}_{T\tau}\right)$ before analysis. Figure 7 shows an example of estimated trajectories $\left(\overline{^{(1)}_{kl}\boldsymbol{X}_{T\tau}}, \overline{^{(2)}_{kl}\boldsymbol{X}_{T\tau}}, \ldots, \overline{^{(i)}_{kl}\boldsymbol{X}_{T\tau}}, \ldots, \overline{^{(I)}_{kl}\boldsymbol{X}_{T\tau}}\right)$ after analysis. In Figs. 6 and 7, the red lines indicate the trajectories of time division $i = 1$, the orange lines indicate $i = 2$, the yellow green lines indicate $i = 3$, the green lines indicate $i = 4$, the blue green lines indicate $i = 5$, the blue lines indicate $i = 4$. Starting points of $^{(i)}\boldsymbol{X}_{T\tau}$ and $\overline{^{(i)}_{kl}\boldsymbol{X}_{T\tau}}$ were corrected as $(x, y) = (0, 0)$.

Second, $^{(i)}\boldsymbol{X}_{T\tau}$ and $\overline{^{(i)}_{kl}\boldsymbol{X}_{T\tau}}$ were corrected to $n + n = 2n$ dimensional vectors $^{(i)}\boldsymbol{X}_{T\tau}^{\mathrm{vec}} = \left(^{(i)}\boldsymbol{x}_{T\tau}, {}^{(i)}\boldsymbol{y}_{T\tau}\right)$ and $\overline{^{(i)}_{kl}\boldsymbol{X}_{T\tau}^{\mathrm{vec}}} = \left(^{(i)}_{k}\boldsymbol{x}_{T\tau}, {}^{(i)}_{l}\boldsymbol{y}_{T\tau}\right)$. We applied

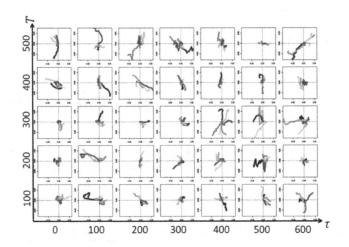

Fig. 6. Raw trajectories before analysis (Pattern 1) (Color figure online)

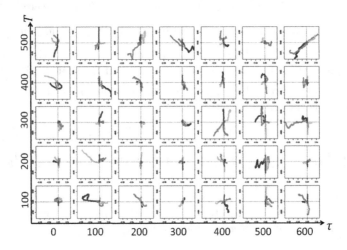

Fig. 7. Estimated trajectories after analysis (Pattern 1) (Color figure online)

clustering based on contaminated normal distribution to $32+1$ or $37+1$ vectors composed of 32 or 37 kinds of $^{(i)}X^{vec}_{T\tau}$ and $\overline{^{(i)}_{kl}X^{vec}_{T\tau}}$ of a combination of (T,τ). To classify each vector as vectors having the same characteristics as $\overline{^{(i)}_{kl}X^{vec}_{T\tau}}$ of no stimulus, we set the number of clusters to two. We analyzed $^{(i)}X^{vec}_{T\tau}$ for all (T,τ) by the above process, and then, binarized the condition shown as Eq. (5).

$$\delta\left(\boldsymbol{X}^{vec}\right) = \begin{cases} 0, \ \boldsymbol{X}^{vec} \in (\texttt{Cluster include no stimulus case}) \\ 1, \qquad\qquad\qquad \texttt{otherwise} \end{cases} \tag{5}$$

5 Result

We experimented with ten subjects and indicate the result for one subject. Figure 8 shows the result of $\delta \left({}^{(i)} X_{T\tau}^{\text{vec}} \right)$ in each division of each MSTS pattern. Figure 8 is shown as white when $\delta \left({}^{(i)} X_{T\tau}^{\text{vec}} \right) = 0$ and red when $\delta \left({}^{(i)} X_{T\tau}^{\text{vec}} \right) = 1$. In Pattern 1, it was confirmed that the number of (T, τ) allocated to clusters different from the no stimulus case was large in time divisions $i = 1$ and 3. In Patterns 2a and 3b, it was confirmed that the number of (T, τ) allocated to clusters different from the no stimulus case was large in time divisions $i = 1$, 2, and 3. In Pattern 2b, it was confirmed that the number of (T, τ) allocated to clusters different from the no stimulus case was large in time divisions $i = 1$ and 2. In Pattern 3a, we confirmed that the number of (T, τ) allocated to clusters different from the no stimulus case was large except time division $i = 2$. Moreover, we confirmed that the number of (T, τ) allocated to clusters different from the no stimulus case was large between time division $i = 1$ to 3 except for Pattern 3a. Consequently, there is a possibility that body sway caused by the effect of tactile stimuli was delayed between 1 and 150 ms after applying the tactile stimuli.

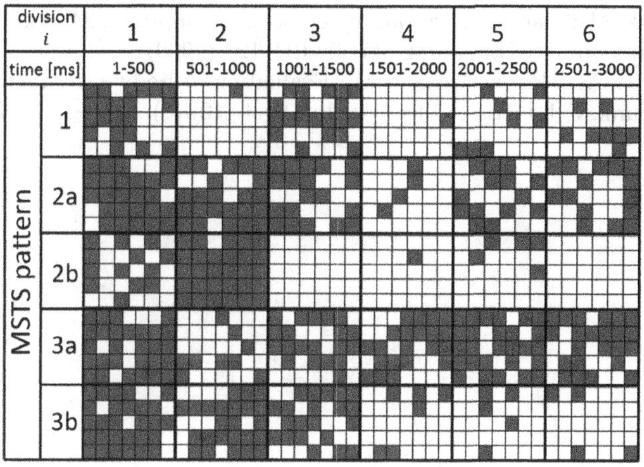

Fig. 8. Result of $\delta \left({}^{(i)} X_{T\tau}^{\text{vec}} \right)$ (Color figure online)

6 Conclusion

In this report, we measured body sway through the effect of tactile stimuli and derived the estimated trajectory using clustering based on a mixtures of Gaussian. We suggested that body sway through the effect of tactile stimuli was delayed between 1 and 1500 ms after applying the tactile stimuli. However, the relationship between tactile stimuli parameters and body sway was not clarified and is a problem for future studies.

This work was supported by JSPS KAKENHI Grant-in-Aid for Scientific Research (C) Number 25330406.

References

1. Hase, K.: Postural control for quiet standing. Jan. J. Rehabil. Med. **43**(8), 542–553 (2006)
2. Ishizaki, H., Pyykko, I.: Postural control in elderly persons - effect of vision on accidental falls. Equilib. Res **54**(5), 409–415 (1995)
3. Ogaya, S., Ikezoe, T., Tateuchi, H., Soda, N., Tsuboyama, T., Ichihashi, N.: The relationship of fear of falling and daily activity to postural control in the elderly. J. Jan. Phys. Ther. Assoc. **37**(2), 78–84 (2010)
4. Taguchi, K.: The effects of the optokinetic stimulation on the center of gravity - the results of normal subjects, **26**(Suppl.1), pp. 182–191 (1980). Copyright
5. Fujita, K., Noguchi, T., Minamitani, H., Tomatsu, T.: Feedback control method for paraplegic standing by functional electrical stimulation. Inst. Electron. Inf. Commun. Eng. **J75-D2**(4), 791–798 (1992)
6. Ochi, A., Banno, Y., Kanai, A., Morioka, S.: Influence of residual effects following neck vibration stimuli on displacement of center of gravity during standing movement. Soc. Phys. Ther. Sci. **21**(4), 427–432 (2006)
7. Sakuma, A., Aihara, Y.: Influence of proprioceptive input from leg, thigh, trunk and neck muscles on the equiribrium of standing. Nihon Jibiinkoka Gakkai Kaiho **102**(5), 643–649 (1999)
8. Fukumoto, M.: Human interface out of box : can you input on 24-hours!? - Wearable interfaces. Inf. Process. Soc. Mag. **41**(2), 123–126 (2000)
9. Hasegawa, R., Maleki, A., Uchida, M.: Evaluation of body sway tactile stimuli on the body trunk. IEEJ Trans. Electron. Inf. Syst. **136**(8), 1135–1141 (2016)

Formalization Modeling of Maintenance Based on Agent

Shu-jie Tian[1,2], Bo Wang[1(✉)], Li Wang[1], and Dan Xu[2]

[1] National Laboratory of Human Factors Engineering,
China Astronaut Research and Training Center, Beijing 100094, China
wowbob@139.com
[2] Department of Industrial Design, Xi'an Jiaotong University,
Xi'an 710049, China

Abstract. Petri network is a conventional method of maintenance modeling. However it cannot characterize the hierarchical structure and time sequence characteristics of maintenance activities, and it is more difficult to model maintenance therblig, which is the atomic unit in maintenance activities. Based on the extension theory and Agent, the formalization representation of the therblig is defined in this paper, and the definition of maintenance activity is transformed into a description of multiple variables. The validity of the method is verified by examples.

Keywords: Human-machine interaction · Maintenance therblig · Formalization action representation · Agent · Extension theory

1 Introduction

Maintenance tasks are an important way to ensure the normal operation of the product. Essentially, maintenance is also a kind of typical human-computer interaction activity, which is changed by the interaction between human and machine. In order to analyze the relationship of human and machine in maintenance activities, the modeling of maintenance activities is the first step in the study of maintenance. The whole process of the maintenance task and the object properties involved are analyzed.

As a conventional method of maintenance modeling, Petri net is used to construct the relationship of human and object in the interaction activity [1–3]. In fact, in order to more systematically research on the complex activities, it is important to bring a multi-hierarchy and multi-granularity analysis method [4]. Moreover, maintenance activities have hierarchical structure. In the research of maintenance activities, maintenance activities are usually divided with bottom-up approach into several levels [5]. therbligs are the lowest level of maintenance activities [6].

The interaction between human and machine in maintenance activities shows up as the sequential and timing relationship among therbligs. Petri net is better to describe the discrete event system which is multistage, concurrent and asynchronous, but it is difficult to characterize the hierarchical structure and time sequence characteristics of

© Springer International Publishing AG 2017
C. Stephanidis (Ed.): HCII Posters 2017, Part I, CCIS 713, pp. 575–582, 2017.
DOI: 10.1007/978-3-319-58750-9_80

system. In addition, "human" activities change state of "machine" in the maintenance activities, In other words, that change the relationship of human-computer interaction.

However, model based on Petri network is so poor in reusability that a new model of maintenance activities is constructed. Therefore, it is very necessary to propose a flexible and multi-granularity method to describe the interaction between human and machine in the maintenance activities.

Formalization description is a method to describe the properties of the system by the mathematical theory and form [7]. As a standard language describing the characteristics of system, it is standard that can describe the time characteristics, the internal structure, behavior characteristics of the system by the strict rules and definitions. As an effective method to establish the system model, it is integrated that provides a complete and unified framework to describe, establish and validate system [8]. Formalization description can not only describe the characteristics and structure of maintenance activities more accurately, but also make up for the deficiency of Petri Network.

According to the hierarchical structure of the maintenance activities, as the lowest level of maintenance activities, therbligs can model all hierarchy of maintenance activities from the bottom to the top. In this paper, Based on the extension theory of the description of the relationship between things, as the bottom of maintenance task, maintenance therbligs are redefined. Based on Agent theory of the concepts of state, action, activity and behavior [9], the formalization representation of the therblig is defined, and the definition of maintenance activity is transformed into a description of multiple variables. The validity of the method is verified by examples.

2 Decomposition and Definitions of Maintenance Activities

The decomposition of maintenance is to decompose the complex task to the basic task, so as to show the man-machine relationship and the "human" property in the maintenance task. Based on the analytic hierarchy process, this paper establishes the decomposition rule of the maintenance task, which is defined according to the external constraints such as the maintenance target and the environment. Specific rules are as follows.

(1) the top level includes the maintenance objectives, environmental conditions, and the associated objects and operations.
(2) for maintenance, first of all, it is necessary to maintain the target and the environment and other external constraints to the first level. The complex tasks are divided into the basic tasks according to the sub objectives and constraints.
(3) The sub objective is composed of several functional points, according to which the next level is divided.
(4) the lowest level is the smallest human-computer interaction system.

The maintenance is divided into four levels, which are maintenance work, Maintenance activity, elementary maintenance and therblig.

Agent is a behavioral entity that has the characteristics of autonomy, interactivity, responsiveness and initiative [10]. According to the Agent theory of the concepts of state, action, activity and behavior, not only the four hierarchies of maintenance activities are defined and described, but also the interactive relationship between human and machine is explained [11, 12]. Specific definitions are as follows.

Definition 1. Therblig is the smallest operation unit in the maintenance activities.

Definition 2. Elementary Maintenance Activity consists of a series of therbigs by sequence and time. The relationship of therbligs is the "order", "and" and "or".

Definition 3. Maintenance activity consists of a series of elementary maintenance activities on the condition.

Definition 4. Maintenance work consists of a series of maintenance activities on the condition.

3   Formalization Modeling of Maintenance

3.1   Description of Therbligs

Essentially, the execution of the therbligs is a process that changes not only themselves but also the relationship of human and machine in maintenance activities. The change is the process where one state transforms into another. In order to describe this process, this paper introduces basic element of extension theory to describe maintenance therbligs as agent.

In the extension theory, basic element is to describe the world of an atomic element, can be expressed as

$$B = (O, c, v)$$

Where O denotes the object; c is feature; V is representation attribute value When an object has n characteristic attributes, the basic element is represented by an n-dimensional. According to the different objects, the basic element can be divided into matter element, Affair element and relation element. Matter element, Affair element and relation element can further describe the problem comprehensively.

Thus, the maintenance therbligs can be composed of "human" matter element and "machine" matter element and "interactive action" affair element. Expressed as:

$$Act = [H, I, M]$$
$$H = \{c_{h1}, c_{h2}, \ldots, c_{hn}\}$$
$$I = TR(c_{i1}, c_{i2}, \ldots, c_{in})$$
$$M = \{c_{m1}, c_{m2}, \ldots, c_{mn}\}$$

Where Act is the maintenance therbligs; H is "human" as matter element; M is "machine" as matter element; I is "interactive action" as affair element; c_H, c_i and c_m represent feature attributes.

Attribute values are static and dynamic. Dynamic attribute values can change themselves over time, while static attribute values are fixed. The attribute values of H and M are static attribute values. The attribute values of I is a dynamic attribute value. In order to definite the complete and independent concepts of all therbligs, our static properties of the H and M values are put forward.

$$H = \{HA, HS, HM, HD, HP, HT\}$$

Where HA is Human actuator; HS is Human actuator shape; HM is Human force method; HD is Human force direction; HP is Human posture; HT is Human tool;

$$M = \{MS, MM, MP, MG, MR\}$$

Where MS is Machine size; MM is Machine modeling; MP is Machine position; MG is Machine operation guide; MR is Machine operating restriction.

All the maintenance therbligs can be represented by this method, and the formal description of each maintenance therblig is unique.

3.2   Description of Elementary Maintenance Activity

Elementary Maintenance Activity consists of a series of therbigs by sequence and time. The relationship of therbligs is the "order", "and" and "or". These relations can be represented by a relation element. Elementary Maintenance Activity (acts) can be expressed as:

$$Acts = [A, R]$$
$$R = (T, L)$$

Where: A- the collection of therbligs; R- the timing and logical formula of therbligs, indicating the timing relationship "T" is the "before" and "after". Logical relationship "L" between the therbligs is the "order", "and" and "or".

3.3   Description of Maintenance Activity

Maintenance activity consists of a series of elementary maintenance activities on the condition. Maintenance Activity (Atv) can be expressed as:

$$Atv = <I, C, Acts >$$

Where: I - the purpose and intent of the maintenance operation; C - the collection of conditions or environmental factors, representing the condition or environment to stimulate the maintenance operations. the impact of stimulation divides into three kinds. The first one is its own factors, such as the difficulty of operation, operation time, complexity and so on. The second kind of individual factors is the impact of individual's operation ability and cognitive level. The third kind of environmental factors is the spatial size of the working environment, lighting, noise, and climate and so on. The first two belong to their own influence, the latter one is outside the impact; Acts - elementary maintenance activities, Acts $\in$ As, As - the collection of all elementary maintenance activities.

For example, Maintenance activity (Atv) can be showed as:

$$Atv1 = <I1, \quad C1, \quad Acts1>$$
$$I1 = \{Intention\ Description\}$$
$$C1 = <c1: \quad Condition\ Description>$$
$$Acts1 = <A1, \quad R1>$$
$$A1 = <Act1, \quad Act2, \quad Act3, \quad Act4, \quad Act5, \quad Act6>$$
$$R1 = (T1, \quad L1, \quad L3)$$
$$T1 = Act1 \rightarrow Act3 \rightarrow Act4 \rightarrow Act5$$
$$L1 = Act2 \lor Act3 \lor Act7$$
$$L2 = Act5 \lor Act6$$

3.4 Description of Maintenance Work

Maintenance work consists of a series of maintenance activities on the condition. Maintenance work (W) can be expressed as:

$$W = <G, C, A, Atvs>$$

Where G is the set of all the purposes in the maintenance; C is the set of all factors that affect the maintenance activities; A is the set of all motivations in the maintenance. Atvs is the set of all Maintenance activities. Maintenance work represents the process of human-machine interaction by the triple in this formula.

4 Verification

In order to verify the validity of the formalization modeling method based on agent, we take an activity (W0), which is adapted from the literature [11, 12]. This method and Petri net are respectively used to model W0.

First of all, using this method, it can be formalized as follows:

W0 = <G,C,A, Atvs>
  G = <g1,g2 g3>
  C = <c1,c2>
  A = <Act1,Act2,Act3,Act4, Act5, Act6, Act7, Act8, Act9 >
  Atvs=< Atv1, Acv2>
      Atv1 = <I1, C1, Acts1>
        I1 = < g1,g2>
        C1 = <c1>
        Acts1 = <A1, (T1,T2;L1)>
            A1 = <Act1, Act2, Act3, Act4, Act5>
            T1 = Act3→Act4
            L1 = Act2∧Act4∨Act5
            T2 = Act1→Act5
      Acv2 = <I2, C2, Acts2>
        I2 = <g3 >
        C2 = <c2>
        Acts2 = <A2, (T1,T2,T3;L1,L2)>
            A2 = <Act6, Act7, Act8,Act9 >
            T1 = Act8→Act9
            L1 = Act7∨Act9
            T2 = Act6→Act9

Similarly, the active W0 can be modeled based on Petri net, as shown in Fig. 1.

$$P = \{p_1, p_2, p_3, p_4, \ldots, p_{11}, p_{12}\}$$
$$T = \{t_1, t_2, t_3, t_4, \ldots, t_9\}$$

Where: P is a set of finite places based on Petri nets; T is a set of finite transitions based on Petri nets.

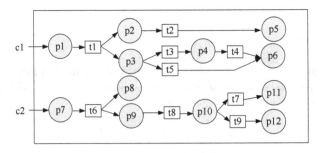

Fig. 1. Petri's expression of W0

It can be seen that the Petri net model is consistent with the method of this paper in dealing with the distribution and concurrency. The validity of the method is verified by examples.

5 Conclusion

In the future, on-orbit maintenance activities are complex and varied, and the operating procedures are diverse [13]. Therefore, it is necessary to study on-orbit maintenance activities in a more systematic way.

In order to study and analyze the maintenance activities more systematically, according to Agent theory and the formal definition of therbligs, this paper defines and describes elementary maintenance activities, maintenance activities and maintenance works. The effectiveness of the method is verified by practical application. The method of multi-granularity formalization solves the problems of the expression of complex hierarchical and sequential-timing relationship in the modeling process of maintenance activities. This paper will further study the method of automated modeling process of maintenance activities.

Acknowledgments. This work was supported by the foundation of National Key Laboratory of Human Factors Engineering, Grant No. HF 2012-Z-B-05, SYFD130061813, SYFD18061610.

References

1. Chew, S.P., Dunnett, S.J., Andrews, J.D.: Phased mission modelling of systems with maintenance-free operating periods using simulated Petri nets. Reliab. Eng. Syst. Saf. **93**(7), 980–994 (2008)
2. Yang, Y.: Modeling and analysis of collaborative maintenance process based on synthesis of Petri net. J. Beijing Univ. Aeronaut. Astronaut. **37**(6), 711–716 (2011)
3. Jiang, S., Liu, P., Zhang, X.: Method of process-modeling in virtual maintenance based on petri net. J. Syst. Simul. **11**, 025 (2007)
4. Zhang, Y.P., Zhang, L., Wu, T.: The representation of different granular worlds: a quotient space. Chin. J. Comput. **27**(3), 328–333 (2004). Chinese Edition
5. Vujosevic, R., Ianni, J.: A Taxonomy of Motion Models for Simulation and Analysis of Maintenance Tasks. Iowa Univ Iowa City Center for Computer Aided Design (1997)
6. Li, X., Hao, J., Liu, H.: Design and realization of maintenance therblig model in virtual maintenance simulation. China Mech. Eng. **16**(2), 156–160 (2005)
7. Li, H.C., Shi, M.L.: Workflow models and their formal descriptions. Chin. J. Comput. **26** (11), 1456–1463 (2003). Chinese Edition
8. Yan, H., Guo, R.: Research on formal description model of directional relationships. Acta Geodaetica Cartogr. Sin. **32**(1), 42–46 (2003)
9. Ferber, J.: Multi-agent systems an introduction to distributed artificial intelligence. Addison-Wesley, Reading (1999)
10. Wooldridge, M.J., Jennings, N.R., Kinny, D.: The Gaia methodology for agent-oriented analysis and design. Autonomous Agents and Multi-Agent Systems, vol. 3. Kluwer Academic Publishers, Netherlands, pp. 285–312 (2000)

11. Junhai, C.: Agent-based discrete event simulation modelling framework and its application study in system RMS modeling and simulation. A Doctor Dissertation of Armour Force Engineering Institute (2002)
12. Cao, J., Zhang, H., Xiong, G.: Formalization description method of agent behaviors for multi-agent simulation. Acta Simulata Systematica Sinica **11**, 008 (2004)
13. Huang, W., Tian, Z., Wang, C., et al.: Research and practice of ergonomic requirements and evaluation technology in manually controlled rendezvous and docking of spacecraft. Manned Spaceflight **21**(6), 535–544 (2015)

Outside the Virtual Screen: A Tangible Character for Computer Break

Sy-Chyi Wang[1], Jin-Yuan Chern[2(✉)], Chung-Ping Young[3],
Wei-Hsin Teng[4], and Xiao-Yi Xiong[5]

[1] Department of E-learning Design and Management,
National Chiayi University, Chiayi, Taiwan
kiky@mail.ncyu.edu.tw
[2] Department of Health Care Administration,
Chang Jung Christian University, Tainan, Taiwan
chern@mail.cjcu.edu.tw
[3] Department of CS and Information Engineering,
National Cheng Kung University, Tainan, Taiwan
dryncku@gmail.com
[4] Department of Visual Communication Design,
Kun Shan University, Tainan, Taiwan
jeffteng3d@yahoo.com.tw
[5] Department of Information and Communication,
Kun Shan University, Tainan, Taiwan
orzorzooo@gmail.com

Abstract. Prolonged-sitting computer use has contributed to certain unhealthy symptoms such as visual impairment and musculoskeletal disorders. To help reduce the health risk and promote healthier computer use, researchers have devoted a lot of time and effort developing user-friendly computer stretch/ massage programs for prolonged-sitting computer users. However, computer users also expressed their concern on long-term adoption of the programs. Therefore, this study aimed to develop and bring a proposed 3D character from the virtual world (in computer break software) to the real world. This study designed, developed and actually produced a "tangible" 3D character with 3D printing technology, which could be touched, held, and interacted with real time. A microcontroller, consisting a central processing unit (CPU), was pre-programmed to adjust for the ON duration of red, yellow and green LEDs light color to sense computer users' working status via ultrasonic sensor. A quantitative questionnaire survey was used to collect users' evaluation along with a face-to-face interview to solicit in-depth feedback of user experience. The prototypes were tested with 10 volunteer undergraduate students followed by a series of modifications. The overall satisfaction reached a high score of 4.68 (based on a 5-point Likert scale). Generally they thought the Daniel was useful to alert user's sitting duration in front of computer and they would be willing to recommend it to friends. Currently a more robust evaluation with more participants is under way. The next issue will be the impact of the created interactive device on users' working efficiency and task performance.

Keywords: Prolong sitting · Computer user · Interactive device · Computer break · 3D character

© Springer International Publishing AG 2017
C. Stephanidis (Ed.): HCII Posters 2017, Part I, CCIS 713, pp. 583–587, 2017.
DOI: 10.1007/978-3-319-58750-9_81

1 Introduction

Extended computer use has drawn the public's attention to its potential health risk in recent years due to its possible contributions to symptoms of visual impairment, musculoskeletal injuries, skin problems, and even emotional disorders [1]. It is claimed that among the many possible causes of injuries, not taking regular breaks from computer work is an important factor [2, 3].

In response to the concern about extended computer use, a lot of research effort has been devoted to developing preventive programs such as computer software packages or hardware devices. Optimistic and prospective results have been observed. For example, van den Heuvel et al. [4] reported a positive effect on recovery from complaints of work-related disorders through the use of software programs stimulating regular breaks and exercise. Marangoni [5] proposed an intermittent stretching exercises program and found that the interventions contributed to a significant reduction in musculoskeletal pain associated with working at a computer workstation. Wang and Chern [6] found that the computer break/stretch/massage program significantly affected the participants' computer-related health behaviors during the experiment period.

While most people have been aware of the potential benefits of the programs alike to their health, it caused our attention that they might still hesitate on the adoption of the interventions. Part of the reason is that they think the frequent breaks may diminish their attention level and work performance as well. In response to the concern, we came up with an interactive "tangible Daniel" for the purpose of informing prolonged-sitting computer users of the time and intensity of screen focusing activities.

2 Methods

The key concept of the proposed "tangible Daniel" is to keep computer users staying on the 3003-rule track (taking 3 min break away from computer screen after 30 min sitting). Therefore, after a user has been sitting in front of the screen for more than 30 min, the ultrasonic sensor, controlled by an embedded IC chip, would send a signal to the "tangible Daniel" (with LED light bulbs installed inside) to make the color of his outside look turn red (see Fig. 1). To the contrary, as long as the user moved away from the computer screen, Daniel would resume normal color.

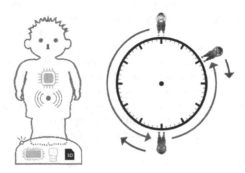

Fig. 1. Concept of Daniel and operational timing (Color figure online)

Three different level settings were built for the users to set up for their preferences—3003 and 5005 (3 min break after 30 min work and 5 min break after 50 min work); 3006 (6 min break after 30 min work, and so on); and 3010 (10 min break).

The production of Daniel is the core task for the project (Fig. 2). First, the designers worked on reshaping the proposed 3D design model "Daniel" for the shape, style, color, ergonomics, etc., to make the model suitable for the body movement and interactive devices installation. The most difficult challenge was to make sure there was enough space inside "Daniel" to allow the programmer to install and wire some chips, buttons, lights and sensors as well as batteries for the interactive functions.

Fig. 2. The production process of 3D printing and completed Daniel

Second, the designers worked on tackling the mechanism issues such as how to actually install and fix the devices (chip, battery, LED light bulbs...) inside Daniel's belly (Fig. 3); and how to open up Daniel's body for battery replacement, etc. The concern arising here is to how to make an optimized trade-off between shape design (user's perspective) and functioning demands (producer's challenge).

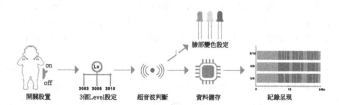

Fig. 3. Installation of embedded components into the Daniel

Next, after the figure and shape was settled, an IC chip was embedded inside Daniel's body to control for the LED color changing and motor driving mechanism. In fact, the IC chip is the core technology of the proposed Daniel.

Figure 4 shows the block diagram of the embedded computing system, which is programmed to sense the computer user's working status with the aid of user monitoring program via ultrasonic sensor, and subsequently responds with the appropriate stage of LEDs. The transition among the control stages is designed as a state diagram and is programmed in the flash memory. A microcontroller, consisting of a central

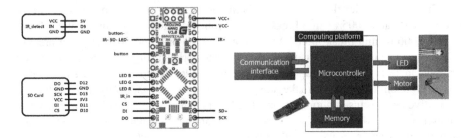

Fig. 4. A block diagram of the embedded computing system and electric circuit diagram (Color figure online)

processing unit (CPU), executes the program to adjust the ON duration of red, green and blue LEDs to mix up the specified light color.

3   Conclusions and Suggestions

After the completion of the prototype Daniel, a series of testing and modifications followed through the participation of 10 volunteer undergraduate students. A quantitative questionnaire survey was used to collect users' evaluation along with a face-to-face interview to solicit in-depth feedback of user experience.

Overall, the satisfaction of the product reached a high score of 4.68 (based on a 5-point Likert scale). Generally they thought the tangible Daniel looked cute and was useful to alert user's sitting duration in front of computer. Based on their own experience and perception, they would be willing to recommend it to their friends in the future. Meanwhile, they raised some concerns about the design of the prototype. For example, they thought the figure size was kind of big, which might make it inconvenient to be carried around; the changing color of LED light seemed too dim to attract the user's attention; and, the figure was relatively tall, which would make it look unsteady.

In summary, this study followed previous research attention on the negative effects of extended computer use and designed a prototype Daniel aiming to alert extended computer users to "stand up" and even "stay away" from the computer from time to time. It is expected that a healthy computer behavior would be pursued for prolonged computer users, especially for the tech-savvy generation.

Currently a more robust evaluation with more participants is under way. After a positive evidence is observed, the impact of the created interactive device on users' working efficiency and task performance will serve as the next research issue in the near future.

References

1. Hayes, J.R., Sheedy, J.E., Stelmack, J.A., et al.: Computer use, symptoms, and quality of life. Optom. Vis. Sci. **84**(8), E738–E755 (2007). doi:10.1097/OPX.0b013e31812f7546

2. Broughton, A.: Eurofound: place of work and working condition (2008). http://www.eurofound.europa.eu/ewco/studies/tn0701029s/tn0701029s_4.htm

3. Elsevier Health Sciences: Prolonged daily sitting linked to 3.8 percent of all-cause deaths: investigators estimate limiting sitting to less than 3 hours per day could increase life expectancy. ScienceDaily, 23 March 2016. www.sciencedaily.com/releases/2016/03/160323142345.htm. Accessed 14 Mar 2017

4. Van den Heuvel, S.G., Looze, M.P., Hildebrandt, V.H., et al.: Effects of software programs stimulating regular breaks and exercises on work-related neck and upper limb disorders. Scand. J. Work Environ. **29**(2), 106–116 (2003)

5. Marangoni, A.H.: Effects of intermittent stretching exercises at work on musculoskeletal pain associated with the use of a personal computer and the influence of media on outcomes. Work **36**(1), 27–37 (2010)

6. Wang, S.C., Chern, J.Y.: Time-scheduled delivery of computer health animations: "Installing" healthy habits of computer use. Health Inform. J. **19**(2), 116–126 (2013). doi:10.1177/1460458212461492

Ambidexterity in Mobile Collaboration: Balancing Task- and Socialization-Oriented Communication in Team Member Interaction

Xiaolun Wang[1], Jie Gu[2(✉)], Jing Tian[1], and Yunjie Xu[1]

[1] School of Management, Fudan University,
Guoshun Road 670, Shanghai, China
[2] Shanghai Academy of Social Sciences,
Zhongshanxi Road 1610, Shanghai, China
gujie@sass.org.cn

Abstract. Due to the affordance to synchronous information exchange and anytime-and-anyplace communication, mobile instant messaging system (MIMS) becomes increasingly important in project collaboration. Compared to traditional team-collaboration information systems, MIMS better supports both task- and socialization-oriented communication in project member interaction, yet whether this feature improves project performance is still a question to be answered. Analyzing 120 responses from team members in different projects, this study got two interesting findings: (1) Project performance is directly affected by offline team relationship, including work interdependence and social strength. (2) Online communication in MIMS (total number of task- and socialization-oriented communications and the percentage of social communications) interacts with offline team relationship and task type, thus impact project performance under certain conditions. Overall, this study provides a better theoretical understanding of mobile collaboration, and also offers practical implications for how and when to use MIMS in teamwork.

Keywords: Project collaboration · Project performance · MIMS · Task interdependence · Social communication

1 Introduction

Mobile Technology has profoundly changed the way of human-computer interaction. Over 20 years ago, Short Message Service (SMS) has revolutionized the way people communicate. Synchronous information exchange at anytime in anyplace without meeting with each other comes true. Recently, with the evolution of smartphones, a new wave of mobile instant messaging system (MIMS) has gained considerable attention. Applications such as WhatsApp, Line and WeChat allow mobile users to send real-time text, photo or even video messages to individuals or groups of friends at no cost. Compared to traditional SMS, except for more technical functions, MIMS provides a convenient way of connecting with small communities, where people can communicate and share information to a specific group of people. Besides, fluid and natural social communication is also one of the main reasons for users' migration to

© Springer International Publishing AG 2017
C. Stephanidis (Ed.): HCII Posters 2017, Part I, CCIS 713, pp. 588–595, 2017.
DOI: 10.1007/978-3-319-58750-9_82

MIMS [1]. People can talk about their personal life freely in MIMS's conversations, with no limitation of characters, format, cost or just a sense of formality.

Owing to the above characteristics, MIMS can support both task-and socialization-oriented communication in project member collaboration, and has been widely used in team-based projects nowadays. However, whether MIMS improves project performance is still a question to be answered. On one hand, synchronous, convenient and informal interactions within a group stimulate more information exchange in teamwork, accelerate the speed of response and action, and promote a sense of cohesion between team members. On the other hand, the chat-alike communication style in MIMS leads to the problem of information overload and attention distraction, as well as weaken the boundary of superior-subordinate relationship [2]. Overall, although information sharing is critical in effective teamwork, we cannot simply argue that MIMS is suitable for project collaboration due to the coexistence of both task-and socialization-oriented interactions.

Therefore, we attempt to tackle the following two research questions in this paper: (1) Whether the technology of MIMS can improve project performance? (2) How can we better use MIMS to facilitate teamwork? To answer the above two questions, this study examined the effect of MIMS communication (balance between task- and socialization-oriented interaction) on project performance under certain context (task type, work interdependence, social relationship). Based on communication performance theory [3], we propose the interactive mechanism between offline relationship, online communication, and objective offline project performance. 120 responses from members in consulting and IT projects were collected, and support most of our hypotheses. Our analysis results provide a better theoretical understanding of mobile collaboration, and offer practical implications for how and when to use MIMS in teamwork.

The rest of this study proceeds as follows. We first reviewed literature on communication performance theory and factors influencing project performance. Then we propose our research model and hypotheses. Research methods and data analysis results were reported next. Finally, we discuss the implications of this study.

2 Literature Review

2.1 Communication Performance Theory

Communication performance theory is widely used to examine the application and value of human-computer interaction technology at work. The main logic is that "appropriate use of HCI tools can promote workplace communications and thus improve work performance". So we naturally link online communications to offline project performance.

However, with the development of MIMS, these tools can not only stimulate task-oriented interactions, but also generate socialization-oriented ones, merging both work and interpersonal relationships [3]. Undoubtedly, effective information sharing and social relationship maintenance are of equal importance in teamwork [4]. But when we merge work and life together, authority of leaders and efficiency of work will be undermined. Therefore, the relationship between communications and work perfor-mance become complicated and is worth our attention.

2.2 Team Input, Team Process and Team Performance

Stewart and Barrick (2000) proposed IPO Theory (Input-Process-Output) in teamwork research, and emphasized that both team inputs and team processes influence team performance [5]. Team inputs can be regarded as the original state of the team member and characteristics. Team process means how people communicate, cooperate, and execute before fulfilling the project. Jointly, the two parts determine team performance and work outcome.

Specifically, we summarize the main factors influencing team performance from the IPO perspective. On one hand, the most important team input is the relationship between team members. Bock et al. (2005) proposed that formal and rigid organizational structure is not always good for teamwork [6]. Contrarily, informal interactions under close social relationship are helpful for tacit knowledge sharing, thus lead to greater cooperation outcome. On the other hand, team process can be captured through team member interactions. Difficulties in knowledge sharing and integration have been identified as key factors hindering project process [7]. So, both explicit and tacit knowledge sharing can contribute to better member satisfaction and teamwork performance.

3   Research Model and Hypotheses

Figure 1 depicted the research model of this study. Based on Communication Per-formance Theory [3], we propose that technology of MIMS can enhance project per-formance through increasing both task- and socialization-oriented communications.

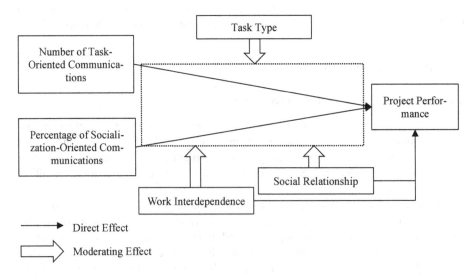

Fig. 1. Research model

Correspondingly, offline formal relationship (work interdependence) and informal relationship (social strength) will interact with the online interactions, thus jointly impact project performance. Besides, effectiveness of MIMS will also be affected by different task types.

3.1 Effect of Online Task- and Socialization-Oriented Communications on Project Performance

Based on communication performance theory, team communications is positively associated with project performance. In other words, effective information sharing is critical in successful projects. MIMS help users react instantly in an online group, and the multi-lateral, near-synchronous form of communication can even match the openness and transparency under face-to-face interactions [3]. Therefore, with the help of MIMS, information, knowledge, and other resources can be quickly exchanged for accomplishing teamwork. Team members can negotiate both task and socialization-oriented topics online at anytime in anywhere. Such knowledge sharing reduces uncertainties in work and maintains social connections in a virtual team, thus contributes to better project performance including team satisfaction and outcome quality. Therefore, we propose H1, and argue that more communications in MIMS can improve project performance. Conversely, previous research found that, when a work team turns into a social team, team performance will decrease significantly. The reason is obvious, if team members take too much time in chatting, precious working time will be occupied, just as H2 hypothesized:

H1: Number of total communications in the workgroup of MIMS is positively associated with project performance.

H2: Percentage of socialization-oriented communications in the workgroup of MIMS is negatively associated with project performance.

3.2 Effect of Offline Task- and Socialization-Oriented Relationship on Project Performance

As the fundamental part of team input, offline team relationship between members determines their working enthusiasm, tacit cooperation, and eventually team performance. On one hand, when they cooperate and work interactively to complete tasks, they depend on each other for reciprocal work inputs and form a close cooperative relationship in work. This intimacy in project collaboration forms an atmosphere of mutual assistance, which leads to higher project performance. On the other hand, when team members are both colleagues and friends, the rigid superior-subordinate relationship will be mitigated. Under such close interpersonal relationship in a work team, everyone will communicate, share, and help each other like a harmonious family, which is good for project collaboration. Therefore, we propose H3 and H4:

H3:   Offline formal relationship (work interdependence) in the team is positively associated with project performance.

H4:   Offline informal relationship (social strength) in the team is negatively associated with project performance.

3.3   Moderating Effect of Offline Relationship and Task Type in MIMS Usage

We further argue that online communication and offline relationship should have an interacting effect, and jointly impact project performance. First of all, when team members rely on each other in work, instant and frequent communications become more vital in project cooperation. The delay of one member will negatively impact all members in the team, thus slow down the project process, leading to a worse team performance. We propose H5, and denote the moderating effect of work interdependence. Secondly, when the social relationship between team members is close, they will naturally have more communications in the workgroup of MIMS. This intimate information exchange will further reinforce their relationship, thus form a virtuous circle and result in more tacit cooperation and better project performance. Therefore, we propose that social strength in the team will also moderate the relationship between online communications and team outcome, as H6 argues:

H5:   Offline formal relationship (work interdependence) between team members positively moderates the relationship between online communications (number of total communications and percentage of socialization-oriented communications) and project performance.

H6:   Offline informal relationship (social strength) between team members positively moderates the relationship between online communications (number of total communications and percentage of socialization-oriented communications) and project performance.

Another important factor in team collaboration is task type. For conceptual tasks where negotiations and communications play an important role in project fulfillment (i.e., consulting) [8], MIMS is a great technological advance and can improve project performance significantly. Synchronous information exchange function realizes anytime-and-anyplace communication for group members. On the contrary, behavioral tasks focus on executing and completing projects (i.e., software development). Because leaders only need to assign tasks to group members without too many negotiations, MIMS seems unnecessary for this type of group. In a word, task type determines the importance for spontaneous communications, thus play a moderating role during the project process. We propose H7:

H7:   Task type (behavioral task vs. conceptual task) positively moderates the relationship between online communications (number of total communications and percentage of socialization-oriented communications) and project performance.

4 Methodology and Results

4.1 Instrument Development

We developed an instrument (e.g., questionnaire) to measure each latent constructs in the model. Subjects were required to answer all the questions based on the last project they have just fulfilled. For subjective constructs, that is, work interdependence, social strength, and project performance, we used three to four question items recognized in previous literatures [9–11]. For instance, to measure project performance, we inquired the efficiency, speed, internal and external effectiveness in the project collaboration. A seven-point scale measurement was used. For objective constructs such as number of communications, in order to mitigate memory bias, we asked subjects to report their impression about the maximum, minimum, and average time of communications in the workgroup of MIMS each day. The final number was calculated by the widely used formula: (maximum number + 4 * average number + minimum number)/6. In the measurement of task type, we referred to McGrath (1984), and asked subjects about their time allocation for four kinds of work (plan, decide, negotiate, and execute) in their project. When most of the team's effort is put on making plans, decisions and negotiations, we classify it as a conceptual task. On the contrary, a behavioral task focuses on executing and completing the project [8].

4.2 Data Collection

To analyze the impact of MIMS in project collaboration, we have to choose subjects whose job is project or team-based. So, our questionnaires were sent to employees in only consulting and software development companies. A pilot test with 20 subjects was conducted to collect both qualitative and quantitative feedback. Minor revisions were made based on subjects' feedbacks. In our main test, we sent out our questionnaires to 200 subjects, and received 154 ones back. Excluding invalid questionnaires with missing data, 120 effective questionnaires were left. Altogether, there were 57 males (47.5%) and 63 females (52.5%), the mean age was 28.1.

4.3 Data Analysis Result

Although the sample size was relatively small, an exploratory factor analysis indicated that the instrument had satisfactory convergent and discriminant validity. Then, we proceed to validate our structural model. Partial Least Squares (PLS) analysis was used because it allows for the incorporation of both reflective and formative constructs, i.e., project performance, present in our model. The results of structural model analysis are shown in Table 1.

We test the direct effect of both team input (member relationship) and team process (communications) at first. The result shows that neither type of online communications has a significant impact on project performance, failing to support H1 and H2. A possible explanation is that, although more interactions contribute to prompt information sharing, it might also cause information overload problem, thus do not benefit

Table 1. Results of structural model analysis

Direct effect	DV: project performance	Moderating effect	DV: project performance
Total communications	0.055 (0.073)	Work interdependence* Total communications	0.100* (0.052)
Percentage of social communications	−0.116 (0.081)	Work interdependence* Percentage of social communications	−0.140 (0.098)
Work interdependence	0.436*** (0.070)	Social strength* Total communications	−0.007 (0.129)
Social strength	0.429*** (0.094)	Social strength* Percentage of social communications	−0.028* (0.015)
		Task type* Total communications	−0.085 (0.109)
		Task type* Percentage of social communications	−0.153*** (0.048)
R-Square		0.31	

Notes: ***$p < 0.01$, **$p < 0.05$, *$p < 0.1$; Numbers in parentheses are standard errors.

project collaboration. The reason for percentage of social communications is similar, more interactions unrelated to work might distract people's attention and waste their time. Therefore, communications in MIMS is not always good for project performance. However, original team relationship impact team performance directly. When members in a team have a higher work interdependence and stronger social strength, their project outcome will be significantly improved. This finding is consistent with H3 and H4, validating the importance of team input.

For the moderating effects, we have several interesting findings. First of all, when team members have to rely on each other to complete their task, more communications in MIMS will show a significantly positive effect, but more social interactions do not help much. Secondly, when team members are very close friends, project performance will decrease with a higher percentage of social communications. In this circumstance, people actually do not need more social interactions in their work, the redundant information become a pure waste of time. However, more number of communications does not show a significant effect. In summary, more communications in workgroup of MIMS will be better under closer task-oriented relationship, but more social communications in MIMS will be worse under closer social-oriented relationship. Finally, we show that for behavioral tasks which do not need a lot of negotiations, when team members have social interactions more frequently, the project performance will decrease significantly. Thus, H5, H6, and H7 were all partially supported.

5   Discussion and Implications

This paper analyzes the interactive relationship between online communication, offline relationship, and final project performance. We have several important theoretical implications. First of all, we extend communication performance theory and prove the double-edged effect of communications in MIMS, which do not always promote project performance due to more social interactions in worktime. Secondly, we combine offline team relationship and online communications together, and find their influence on team performance, which provides a new respective for O2O (Online to Offline) research. Our practical implications are also profound. MIMS is not always a good tool in teamwork, managers should be careful about how and when to use it. For instance, when work interdependence is high, synchronous information exchange in MIMS should be encouraged. However, when social strength between team members is close, they shall not talk too much about personal life in MIMS. Besides, MIMS is more suitable for conceptual tasks rather than behavioral tasks.

Acknowledgement. This work was supported by National Science Foundation of China (grant #71471044 and 71531006), and the China Ministry of Education-China Mobile research grant (#MCM20150402).

References

1. Church, K., Oliveira, R.D.: What's up with WhatsApp?: comparing mobile instant messaging behaviors with traditional SMS. In: International Conference on Human-Computer Interaction with Mobile Devices and Services, pp. 352–361 (2013)
2. Ou, C.X.J., Davison, R.M., Zhong, X., Liang, Y.: Empowering employees through instant messaging. Inf. Technol. People **23**(2), 193–211 (2010)
3. Dennis, A.R., Fuller, R.M., Valacich, J.S.: Media, tasks, and communication processes: a theory of media synchronicity. MIS Q. **32**(3), 575–600 (2008)
4. Li, D., Chau, P.Y.K., Lou, H.: Understanding individual adoption of instant messaging: an empirical investigation. J. Assoc. Inf. Syst. **6**(4), 102–129 (2005)
5. Stewart, G.L., Barrick, M.R.: Team structure and performance: assessing the mediating role of intrateam process and the moderating role of task type. Acad. Manag. J. **43**(2), 135–148 (2000)
6. Bock, G.W., Zmud, R.W., Kim, Y.G.: Behavioural intention formation in knowledge sharing: examining the roles of extrinsic motivators, social-psychological forces, and organizational climate. MIS Q. **29**(1), 87–111 (2005)
7. Walz, D.B., Elam, J.J., Curtis, B.: Inside a software design team: knowledge acquisition, sharing, and integration. Commun. ACM **36**(10), 63–77 (1993)
8. McGrath, J.E.: Groups: Interaction and Performance, vol. 14. Prentice-Hall, Englewood Cliffs (1984)
9. Campion, M.A., Medsker, G.J., Higgs, A.C.: Relations between work group characteristics and effectiveness: implications for designing effective work groups. Person. Psychol. **46**, 823–850 (1993)
10. Faraj, S., Sproull, L.: Coordinating expertise in software development teams. Manag. Sci. **46**(12), 1554–1568 (2000)
11. Henderson, J.C., Lee, S.: Managing I/S design teams: a control theories perspective. Manag. Sci. **38**(6), 757–777 (1992)

Author Index

Printed in the United States
By Bookmasters